ALSO BY HELEN SHEEHY

Margo: The Life and Theatre of Margo Jones

All About Theatre

Eva Le Gallienne

Eva Le Gallienne

A BIOGRAPHY

HELEN SHEEHY

Alfred A. Knopf   New York   1996

THIS IS A BORZOI BOOK
PUBLISHED BY ALFRED A. KNOPF, INC.

http://www.randomhouse.com/

Library of Congress Cataloging-in-Publication Data
Sheehy, Helen, [date]
Eva Le Gallienne / Helen Sheehy. — 1st ed.
p.   cm.
ISBN 0-679-41117-8
1. Le Gallienne, Eva, 1899– .   2. Actors—United States—Biography.
I. Title.
PN2287.L2896S54   1996
792′.028′092—dc20   96-13778
[B]   CIP

Manufactured in the United States of America
First Edition

FRONTISPIECE:
Eva Le Gallienne as the Duke of Reichstadt, Napoleon's exiled son, in L'Aiglon, *1934*

For Eloise Armen

Je le ferai quand-même!

SARAH BERNHARDT

The soul's joy lies in doing.

ELEONORA DUSE

Contents

Eva Le Gallienne

PART ONE

1899 - 1915

Eva Le Gallienne and her mother, Julie Nørregaard
Le Gallienne, c. 1902

I would peer into those magic shadows
and see the stage.

T HE THÉÂTRE SARAH BERNHARDT on the place du Châtelet in Paris
was one of the most beautiful theatres in the world. Owned and managed
by Sarah Bernhardt, who starred there from 1899 until 1923, the theatre
reflected her taste as well as her practical mind. It seated seventeen hundred and
had an enormous stage, with enough backstage space to store the sets for five productions. Huge chandeliers cast their radiance on the walls and seats, both covered in yellow velvet. The stage curtain was red silk velvet and emblazoned in gold
lettering with Bernhardt's initials and her motto: "S. B. Quand-Même."

In December 1906, as a special Christmas treat for her seven-year-old daughter, Eva, Julie Nørregaard Le Gallienne secured two tickets to *La Belle au bois
dormant* (The Sleeping Beauty). In the play, the sixty-two-year-old Sarah would
act the part of the young Prince Charming. Over the years, Julie had seen Bernhardt perform in *Fédora, Froufrou, Hamlet, L'Aiglon,* and *La Dame aux camélias,*
and she considered Bernhardt a great actress; but she worried that Eva, an extremely precocious and perceptive child, might see only an old woman foolishly
trying to act like a boy.

Eva had looked forward to the play for weeks. She had learned to read and
write at five, and she knew the story of the Sleeping Beauty as well as the fairy
tales of Andersen and Grimm. She imagined herself as all the different characters
in the books she read—a wicked witch, an ugly duckling, Hansel or Gretel,
sometimes Sleeping Beauty and sometimes the Prince.

Before the matinee, Julie and Eva dined at Boulant's on the boulevard des Ital-
iens at a table by the window, where they could watch the people strolling along
outside. After lunch, they walked to the theatre, bought a souvenir program,
admired the portraits by Mucha, Clairin, and Abbéma of Sarah in her different
roles, and finally they took their seats in the first row of the first balcony.

The house lights dimmed, the footlights flickered, and the curtain rose on a
dark wood inhabited by birds, animals, and frogs, who all spoke in rhyming
verse. The scene changed to the hall of a castle, where an old woman sat at a

spinning wheel. Suddenly, Eva heard the sound of a voice—"high, clear, vibrant, electric, unforgettable."

An upstage door opened, and a young boy leapt onto the stage. "His hair was reddish gold; his eyes, which dominated the pale face, shone with a youthful gaiety," Eva recalled; "he wore the classic doublet and hose and his arms were full of great sprays of lilac which he flung at the old woman's feet, calling her his beloved grandmother and holding her in a long embrace until the waves of applause that greeted his entrance had subsided."

Eva remembered thinking "in a confused kind of way that this Prince was more radiantly alive than anyone I'd ever seen; as though he lived more intensely, more joyously, more richly than other people."

When the curtain fell at the end of the performance, the child Eva sat in a trancelike silence, staring at the red velvet curtain, hoping that it would rise again. Her mother coaxed her from her seat and led her out of the theatre. They walked home to their apartment on the rue de Regard.

Sarah Bernhardt had opened a door and beckoned Eva into a place filled with beauty and endless possibility, a place ruled by the imagination, where a woman, even an old woman, could become whatever she wished.

WHEN SHE WAS THREE, Eva had seen a stage production of Kingsley's *The Water-Babies* at London's Drury Lane Theatre and had been possessed by a wish to *be* a water baby. But her reaction to *The Sleeping Beauty* was different. Instinctively understanding the dual nature of acting, she wanted to be Sarah Bernhardt *and* Prince Charming.

Years later, Le Gallienne considered writing a book about the self-education of an actor, using her own life as an example. By the age of seven, Eva knew London, Copenhagen, and Paris, and she could speak, read, and write English, Danish, and French. She had an appreciation of art, theatre, and literature. Most important, Eva had the unconditional love of two strong women, her Danish mother and her British nanny. Since her mother was separated from Eva's father, the English poet and writer Richard Le Gallienne, Eva grew up in a home filled with women's voices and devoted to women's work, with no father at the center to be indulged or catered to. Eva learned that her absent father was a weak, unfaithful alcoholic, a man who didn't pay his debts, an untrustworthy, even dangerous man. Still, Richard was a constant presence. His books, his photograph, and a framed poster of his best-selling novel *The Quest of the Golden Girl* were always on prominent display in their home, underscoring Julie's teaching that while Eva should despise her father's character, she must honor his art.

Eva had only one clear memory of her father from childhood. The year was 1903, and she was four years old. She was a strong, healthy girl, tall for her age,

*Sarah Bernhardt as the Prince
in* The Sleeping Beauty, *c. 1906,
one of fifteen male parts she
acted during her career*

with vivid blue eyes and long honey-brown hair streaked with gold, and possessed, her parents believed, "remarkably alert brains." She was sitting in a tiny wicker armchair in the day nursery on the ground floor of the Le Galliennes' four-story home in the St. John's Wood area of London. Through open French doors, she watched and listened as Richard and Julie Le Gallienne walked up and down along the sanded garden path. Eva thought that her parents were beautiful: later she would characterize her father as the image of a romantic poet and describe her mother as looking like a princess. Richard was lean and of medium height, with a Grecian-coin profile, wavy black hair, pale skin, and blue eyes. Julie was tall and slim-hipped, with translucent ivory skin, luxuriant ash-blond hair, Nordic blue eyes, and the proud bearing of a Viking. Eva recalled that the fragrance of Richard's pipe tobacco drifted into her nursery, followed by the sound of voices. She could not catch the sense of her parents' conversation, but, extraordinarily sensitive to the slightest variation in pitch and timbre and inflection, she would always remember her father's well-modulated, "low & very agreeable" tones interspersed with the "angry or excited" sounds of her mother's Danish-accented English. Eva's memory of the scene ended abruptly when Susan Stenning, her nanny, caustically remarked, "You'd think *she* was the man, she talks so loud."

It was not surprising that Susan Stenning would disapprove of Julie Le Gallienne raising her voice to her husband. In her black dress with snowy, well-starched collar and cuffs, Stenning was the picture of a Victorian nanny. Although she was just a few years younger than the prematurely gray Susan Stenning, Julie was a woman who smoked cigarettes, made her own money and her own decisions, and had no qualms about challenging male authority or social conventions. These two radically different women, as different as Victorian melodrama and Ibsen's realism, raised Eva Le Gallienne. While Susan Stenning nurtured Eva and instructed her with well-worn aphorisms like "Strike while the iron is hot," "Where there's a will there's a way," and "Count your blessings," it was Julie Le Gallienne who gave Eva an aesthetic education, and it was Julie who taught Eva that she must find out who she was and then try and become that person. It was a lesson Julie had learned from Henrik Ibsen.

JULIE NØRREGAARD was born on March 16, 1863, in the town of Flensborg in southern Denmark, but she grew up in Copenhagen, where her father worked as a government official. Called "the Athens of the North," Copenhagen had fine theatres, art museums, and an upper-class culture devoted to literature and philosophy. The city was home to an intelligentsia led by philosopher Søren Kierkegaard, who was eight years younger than another Copenhagen resident, Hans Christian Andersen.

Eva never tired of hearing her mother's stories of her childhood in Denmark. She would often ask to hear the story of how Julie had sat on Hans Christian Andersen's bony knee while he read her a fairy tale. Julie felt as if she had been born under a lucky star, and she remembered her childhood as a golden time, filled with laughter, traditional celebrations, and loving uncles and aunts and cousins. She lived in a gracious home, surrounded by books, bouquets of flowers in Chinese jars, lovely petit-point hangings and delicate lacework crafted by her mother. She was devoted to her blond-bearded, handsome bear of a father, who traveled to London and Paris and brought back books and magazines for her. She especially treasured one gift from her father, a hand-carved, camel-backed pencil box, which she gave to her daughter. Eva liked to open the box and trace her fingers across her mother's name, written in large, bold letters.

Julie Nørregaard had the honor one season of opening Copenhagen's Troll Ball. Sophisticated and self-assured, with a quick wit, and, some said, a too-sharp tongue, Julie received her first proposal of marriage at fifteen and attracted a parade of distinguished suitors, including generals, counts, barons, and ambassadors. Julie might have drifted into an early marriage and settled for a placid domestic life; but, inspired by the ideas of two remarkable men, she did not.

Le Gallienne's Danish maternal grandparents, Johan Peter Nørregaard and Bet Nørregaard

Georg Brandes, the Danish scholar and the first literary critic of truly international stature, often lectured in Copenhagen, and his talks were popular with young people. Since her parents thought their teenage daughter too young to attend Brandes's lectures, Julie sought the aid of a very old great-aunt, who arranged that her grand-niece's twice-weekly visits should coincide with the Brandes lectures.

Julie described the experience of listening to Brandes as the moment when her life literally opened up, like a window thrown wide. She and dozens of others would crowd into the corridor outside room number 7 at the University of Copenhagen. If the porter was late opening the room, they would hammer impatiently on the door. Inside, they would press closely together, and except for a gray head here and there, it was "youth and youth everywhere." When Brandes's tall, lithe figure appeared on the platform, the crowd burst into a frenzy of clapping for the man the older generation called a "free-thinker, a destroyer of the young, a blasphemous scoundrel." Julie thought he looked like a "blue-black raven." Brandes spoke of Goethe and Zola and Nietzsche, and Julie realized how ignorant she was of books, people, and events. Brandes talked, too, of a new type of woman, a self-possessed, skeptical young girl who "does not throw herself at the first man who asks her," a young woman with a "man's seriousness, power of decision, and will." Never in her life, Julie wrote, had she "felt herself so wide awake, so intently alive."

This new kind of woman captured the imagination of the Norwegian playwright Henrik Ibsen. On December 4, 1879, Ibsen's play *A Doll's House* was published in Copenhagen. All eight thousand copies of the first edition sold out in one month. On December 21, 1879, Julie Nørregaard, then sixteen, attended the world premiere of *A Doll's House* at Copenhagen's Royal Theatre. Carved above the proscenium arch of the theatre are the words "Ej Blot til Lyst"—Not Only for Amusement. Many were not amused by Ibsen's play. Some excoriated it; others likened it to a bomb exploding. To Julie Nørregaard it was a revelation. It's difficult now to imagine the extraordinary impact that *A Doll's House* had on its first audience. Watching and listening to Nora Helmer tell her husband "I believe that before all else I am a human being" was to experience the death of an old order and the birth of a new world.

The influence of Brandes and Ibsen on Julie Nørregaard cannot be underestimated. It was as if she had been reborn. Stimulated by Ibsen's challenge to social conventions, not only in *A Doll's House* but in *Ghosts* and his other plays, and inspired by his belief that the primary purpose of every human being was to find out who she was and then become that person, Julie decided to create a life that she wanted to live. She found a job working as a journalist for the newspaper *Politiken*. There she was formally introduced to Brandes, who contributed to the newspaper, and the two became friends. The revolutionary Brandes turned out to be a womanizer, a man who declared that no woman had ever refused him. From his letters to her, it's clear that Brandes admired Julie's beauty as well as her mind, and while she was flattered by his attentions, she avoided intimacy with him. Julie kept her other suitors dangling and attentive, but she refused to marry. Filled with her own sense of purpose and destiny, Julie planned to escape the fate of Ibsen's Hedda Gabler. But like Hedda, Julie loathed boredom. "The world is full of wonderful surprises," she wrote, "and I want my share of them, if I am ever to be happy."

In the early 1890s, accompanied by her sister, Ellen, Julie left Copenhagen to live in London. At first, she supported herself by working at the Danish Art School, introducing and selling Danish handcrafts. From her London base, with frequent trips to Paris, she wrote *Politiken*'s first fashion column, under the pen name "Eva." She also contributed fashion articles to various London newspapers and wrote a "Silhouette" of Georg Brandes for *The Yellow Book*. Years later, Julie's great nephew Peter Thornton observed that "Julie and Ellie were Scandinavian women of the nineties—far in advance of most of the women of their day."

During the 1890s and early 1900s, in fashion and decorating columns for *Politiken* and English newspapers, Julie wove social and literary commentary and her own personal philosophy into her articles. "The real secret of the modern woman's charm," she said, "lies in the fact that she has a personality and is not afraid of expressing it. No longer hampered by the narrow lines of old-fashioned conventions . . . she can allow herself to feel and think, as she, in accordance with her nature, was meant to feel and think."

Julie had definite opinions about fashion and about life. She had impeccable taste, an eye for detail, and an abhorrence of anything "dull" or "common." She insisted that to be well dressed had little to do with money or position. She held Sarah Bernhardt up as an example of "chic modernity," but she also believed that a shop girl outfitting herself on twenty pounds a year could achieve the same distinction if she revealed in her clothes her own unique personality.

In her columns, titled "Woman's Ways," Julie encouraged women to think for themselves on everything from making coffee to the color of mourning dress, and she urged them not to become "abject slaves of all those little commonplaces which commonplace minds have raised as idols of the day."

In 1896 Julie wrote about *A Doll's House,* using literary terms, but the article was really a deliciously erotic appeal for women's sexuality. It was perfectly acceptable, she argued, for Nora to show Dr. Rank her silk stockings. Nora was only following the customs of Scandinavia, where it was not considered vulgar for a woman to "remind a friend of her pretty feet, ankles, and knees, by showing him the dainty silent tissues with which they are to be covered. . . . The English poet sings sonnets to his mistress's eyebrow, but never does he dream of writing the fairy tale of her feet." By this time, Julie had a thorough knowledge of English poets. In fact, her column "Woman's Ways" often appeared nestled side by side with the "Books and Bookmen" column of the English poet Richard Le Gallienne.

ON DECEMBER 9, 1894, when Julie Nørregaard first saw Richard Le Gallienne standing on the stage of the Playgoers Club in London preparing to give a lecture, she decided, "That is the man I shall marry!"

Julie listened to his lecture, titled "The World, the Flesh, and the—Puritans," and laughed along with the rest of the audience at Richard's humorous attack on marriage. After the talk, Julie shook hands with Richard. She was mesmerized by his charm and undeterred by Richard's radical views on marriage—after all, she was a rebel herself. Now thirty-one (almost three years older than Richard), Julie had rejected some of the most eligible young men of Copenhagen, and she was determined to settle for nothing less than marriage to a rising star of English letters. He was a lean and muscular man who could easily bike seventy miles a day. When he wasn't on his bicycle, Richard dashed about London in a black cape lined in red silk, and he let his thick, dark hair grow to his shoulders. Ever aware of his image, Richard's first act in becoming a poet was to add "Le" to his stolid Gallic name, an effect, Oscar Wilde observed dryly, which made his whole name sound ungrammatical.

It was Wilde, lecturing in Le Gallienne's hometown of Liverpool in December 1883, who first inspired Richard to become a writer. By 1891 he had written four books and dozens of critical reviews and miscellaneous essays. In his regular "Logroller" newspaper column, he promoted the books of his friends. His poetry had brought him a limited fame, but his lectures and talks in London and in Liverpool brought him widespread attention. People who never opened a book of poetry recognized the name Le Gallienne.

Julie appreciated Richard's fame, but his views on the "woman question" also appealed to her. He championed the right of women to smoke cigarettes, wear divided skirts, ride bicycles, and earn their own living. But despite his modern views, Julie's friends warned her that Richard Le Gallienne was *not* the sort of man one married. His various indulgences—romances, drinking, and spending—were well known in the London literary world, but, as Eva wrote later, her mother "would have her poet, and marry him she did, though two human beings less suited to one another would be hard to imagine."

Just a few months after their first meeting, they were lovers. In a letter to Julie written a few weeks after their affair began, Richard sounded dazzled and breathless. "What new spell has my witch woven for me," he wrote, "spells of the dear white magic of her wonderful love & her wonderful mind! to think that . . . you have given me the key of the garden, where grows these magic flow-

Julie Nørregaard in London in the early 1890s

Eva's father, Richard Le Gallienne, strikes a pose for a publicity postcard in the late 1890s.

ers." In another letter, he could hardly contain himself: "I love you, love you, love you—my darling Julie." The only dark cloud in the letter was a lament about "poor, poor Oscar! It seems wrong to be happy in the thought of thee when I turn to the thought of him." In April 1895 "poor Oscar" had endured the terrible exposure of a public trial. Eventually Wilde's liaison with Lord Alfred Douglas would be fully revealed, resulting in Wilde's public humiliation, financial ruin, and imprisonment. In October 1895, when Richard purchased a small bundle of Oscar's manuscripts (sold to pay Wilde's debts), he told Julie: "It certainly could not have fallen into more reverent hands than yours or mine."

Obviously Richard had compassion for his friend, but he also could not resist purchasing valuable manuscripts even if he had to do so on credit. Women and books were Richard's passion and his downfall. "Few young men of twenty-one would devote a good third of their first published volume of poetry to poems in praise of books," Eva observed, suspecting her father had "a touch of smug satisfaction at his own erudition."

Actually, Richard, who lacked a university education, felt inferior to his London literary contemporaries who had attended Oxford or Cambridge. His family background, too, was unprepossessing, although Richard's father, John Gallienne, handsome and white-haired in his old age, looked more like a distinguished Gallic gentleman than the brewery manager that he was. The son of an adventuring sea captain, John Gallienne steered another course, into the safe middle-class harbor of Liverpool. Austere and high-minded, he never smoked and rarely drank alcohol. He kept a daily diary written in a beautiful hand, and every Sunday he shut himself in his study to read sermons. At least once, though, John Gallienne had strayed from his narrow path. When he married Jane Smith, the daughter of a Lancashire weaver and five years his senior, "there was already a baby five months on the way."

That baby, named Richard Thomas Gallienne, was born in Liverpool on January 20, 1866. Richard was the eldest son, spoiled by four sisters, a baby brother, and his mother, who mediated between Richard and his father. Despite John Gallienne's stern example and the intensely religious atmosphere of his solidly middle-class home, Richard would later bow down "to no code but the rootless, shifting morality of the artist."

At twenty-one, Richard left his father's house, and that same year his first book, *My Ladies' Sonnets,* was published privately. He moved to London, where he lived with his close friend the actor Jimmy Welch, who was in love with (and later married) Sissie Gallienne, Richard's favorite sister. With the help of the Bodley Head publisher John Lane, who employed him as a book reader, Le Gallienne embarked on a career in journalism, writing reviews, often "logrolling" promotional pieces for Bodley Head books, and he continued to publish his own poetry.

*Richard Le Gallienne
with his sisters, 1891,
before he left Liverpool
for London. Left to right:
Sissie (his favorite sister),
Margaret, standing,
and Chattie*

In 1891 he married Eliza Mildred Lee, a sometime waitress with Spanish and Gypsy blood. Mildred claimed to be clairvoyant, and since Richard often left her alone in their seedy home outside London while he pursued his career in the city, she brooded and had nightmares of impending evil. In London, Richard indulged his twin addictions, drinking liquor and buying books, and ran up debts in taverns and shops. Once a month he attended meetings of the Rhymers' Club. Richard (not known for the depth of his thought) had the distinction of being the best-looking poet in a group which included the not-yet-famous W. B. Yeats and other, lesser poets of the 1890s. While Mildred waited patiently and morbidly at home, Richard philandered with actresses, married women, and whoever caught his wandering eye. In fact, Richard's sexual exploits were so excessive that his biographers called him an "erotomaniac."

Somehow he found time to write. In addition to his poetry and essays, Richard was a respected and well-known book critic for the London *Star*. Despite all his efforts, lack of money was a constant worry. On December 6, 1893, Richard's responsibilities increased when he became a father. Christened Hesper, the baby girl had dark hair and violet eyes and the classic Gallienne nose.

For immediate cash, Richard turned to a lecture tour. When he returned home in May, he found the roses in bloom and six-month-old Hesper growing "fatter and bonnier every day, a pathetic contrast to her worn little mother." Stricken with typhoid fever and needing the care of a full-time nurse, Mildred gradually grew weaker and weaker. On May 20, 1894, Richard wrote his father pleading for money. The next day Mildred Le Gallienne died.

Stricken with guilt, Richard Le Gallienne carried Mildred's ashes with him for almost thirty years. Richard's biographers wrote that in a sense Richard died, too, when his wife died. They accepted his tragic pose that Mildred's death caused him to look back "incessantly, to youth, to spring, to the Mildred of the golden years. Back to the time before . . . desire failed."

LESS THAN A YEAR after Mildred's death, though, when Richard Le Gallienne took Julie Nørregaard's hand, he found himself in the presence of a woman quite different from the shy, lower-middle-class Mildred. His desire, rather than failing, ignited. He still drank excessively, fell into black moods, and thought he was "on the way to madness," yet he consoled himself with "soft lights, vermouth," and his "naughty Julie's . . . white limbs."

Julie Nørregaard rekindled his passion and inspired his most successful book, an 1897 novel titled *The Quest of the Golden Girl.* Sometimes she joined him at a country inn and they stayed together, registering as brother and sister. When they were apart, he wrote to her almost daily, signing his letters "Asra" and addressing Julie, with some awe, as "Dear Sphinx."

While he worked, he kept her picture on his writing desk. "I have had that *panther* portrait of you on my desk all day," he wrote, "—that one in which you are crouching to spring, with your teeth gleaming with your own devilish sweetness through the sweet chink of your dear devouring mouth, & your left paw stealing stealthily over the chair back—my own panther you shall tear the big lion to pieces tomorrow if you will, & have his heart—(Coeur de Lion!) for Thursday's breakfast."

Soon this literary lion and predatory panther would marry, and in time they would produce an offspring—a daughter named Eva, whom they would call "Cat"—a creature who thrills at its own natural superiority, instinctive fierceness, and cunning, and who absorbs its world with both deep attention and distant cold detachment.

Eva met her father through his letters, written mostly on blue paper in tiny, cramped handwriting, and through his words came to understand the man she had never really known. She knew his poetry well, though, and didn't consider it first-rate. She concluded that Richard would "have been happier if he hadn't felt he had to be a poet & something out of the ordinary."

Richard and Julie newly wed at their first home at Kingswood Chase,
Waggoners Wells, 1897

But her parents were not ordinary. Richard even took vicarious enjoyment in Julie's flirtations, which might or might not have been innocent. Writing to Julie in Denmark when she was there to interview Brandes, Richard said, "My dear one, I do so love you to be admired by men like Brandes." For her part, Julie took an understanding, sophisticated view of Richard's various flirtations. She stalked her literary lion with compassion, charm, and ready cash. In addition to making her own living, she read proofs of *The Quest of the Golden Girl*, decorated his Chancery Lanc flat, and lent him money. She bought Hesper expensive presents and even took the child with her on visits to Denmark. Julie overwhelmed Richard with her steadfast attachment, prompting him to tell her, "I pay you two of the greatest compliments I know: I love, & fear you! (the very worship we pay to God!)."

In her campaign to win Richard, Julie even befriended her rival, American artist Ethel Reed, who was Richard's lover. The two women formed a close attachment and struck an arrangement—since Julie planned to marry Richard, Ethel promised to give him up. Richard proposed a ménage à trois, but apparently the two women wouldn't comply, and in January 1897 Richard wrote to

Julie to say that he had the marriage license and had paid two shillings for it. Their wedding was set for February 12.

The wedding day was a disaster. On their way to the Marylebone Town Hall their hansom cab got stuck in a traffic jam. Annoyed by the delay, Richard walked ahead, leaving Julie to pay the fare. At the town hall, already irritated and out of sorts, the luckless bridegroom discovered that he had managed to lose the ring. A witness was sent off to buy a replacement, and then finally Richard and Julie were pronounced man and wife. Coincidentally, that same day *The Quest of the Golden Girl* was published. It had been an arduous, emotionally exhausting courtship, but Richard had his novel and his golden girl, and Julie had her literary lion.

"POOR THING!" Eva exclaimed as she read her father's letters, filled "*ad nauseam* with money worries." Burdened already with Richard's outstanding debts, plus the heavy expense of keeping up a flat in London and a home in Kingswood Chase, the couple soon found themselves drowning in a flood of bills. Richard begged a loan from his father, and he and Julie decided to try their luck in America. On January 26, 1898, leaving Hesper with her Gallienne grandparents, Richard and Julie boarded the R.M.S. *Teutonic*. Unfortunately, almost immediately, as if the weather itself were commenting on their rocky marriage, a hurricane battered their ship. The gale finally subsided, and on February 3, 1898, encrusted with ice from stem to stern, the *Teutonic* steamed into New York harbor.

They stayed at the elegant Waldorf-Astoria on Fifth Avenue but soon moved into the less fashionable and less expensive Hotel Grenoble on Seventh Avenue. Reporters sought out Richard and bombarded him with questions, which he answered with studied courtesy. "He is rather tall and very slender," one reporter noted, ". . . and his head of hair is enormous." Richard submitted to endless questions about the length of his hair. "They say it isn't manly," he answered. "I'm glad I'm not manly if manliness consists in having one's hair trimmed with the lawn mower and taking an attitude of arrogant superiority to woman."

Billed as the "leader of the English decadents," Richard made his New York debut at the Lyceum Theatre on February 18. Dressed all in black—after nearly four years and a second marriage he was still mourning for Mildred, he explained—but black also particularly suited his aureole of dark hair, his fair skin, and his seductive blue eyes. He read five of his "prose fancies," reverently, "as one reading the Bible—and there is no doubt that he considers them just as inspired and important," one critic sniped.

The newspapers gave him a great deal of attention; he read and lectured several more times at the Lyceum and at women's clubs in and around New York.

But Richard's act was largely watered-down Wilde, and New York had already seen the real thing. After a lecture trip to Chicago, Richard found that the cost of living was too great for them both to stay in America. So, on May 25 Julie sailed for England and then to Denmark, leaving Richard to the heat of a New York summer.

In letter after letter, he pined for Julie and complained of the scorching heat, his asthma, his loneliness, and his poverty. He wrote, too, of visiting Seymour, Connecticut, one weekend in June and playing "Sven-Gallienne" to blond, blue-eyed Therissa Worster, a wealthy socialite who dreamed of becoming a singer. Artists needed patrons, and Richard was not above using his charm and reputation to gain a weekend in the country, the attentions of a lovely young woman, and important contacts. Richard called Julie his strength, his confidante, and his partner; "side by side we shall conquer," he said. He was elated when Julie wrote him that they were to have a child. The thought of a child, the longed-for son— a son conceived in New York, perhaps the only legacy of their ill-fated trip— restored Richard. He wrote to Julie, asking about their little "Michon," the name they wanted to give their son.

Unable to tolerate the heat of New York any longer, Richard borrowed his passage money, and on July 16 sailed for London and on to Copenhagen, where he joined Julie and four-year-old Hesper in a lake house outside Copenhagen. For the next few months, Julie turned out articles and columns while Richard worked feverishly on his novel *Young Lives*. With Julie's income, another stipend from John Gallienne, and the expected sale of Richard's novel, they managed to secure enough money to take them back to England to prepare for Julie's January confinement.

The Le Galliennes returned to London in November and moved into lodgings on Albion Street, Hyde Park. Almost immediately, even though she was heavily pregnant, Julie separated from Richard and moved into rented rooms on Doughty Street near her brother and sister-in-law Jimmy and Sissie Welch. With their support and the help of her sister, Ellen, she waited for the birth of her child. Richard, as usual, wrote letters. "When is that naughty little son of ours going to shine out from his clouds?" he asked, and then nattered on about "Eros and Aphrodite."

Julie was not amused. She was furious with Richard and deeply hurt. In *Mavi,* an autobiographical *roman à clef* she wrote some years later, Julie explained her move to Doughty Street and described the event that soured her relationship with Richard and marked forever the relationship she would have with her only child. She had returned to their flat unexpectedly and had caught Richard in bed with one of her close friends. Devastated by Richard's betrayal, Julie vowed to her unborn child that "you and I belong completely to each other, nothing must ever come between us . . . we will have to forget him. You are going to be my great adorable secret, in which he shall never have part. You are going to be mine—mine now and always—just mine."

At seven in the morning on January 11, 1899, at 42 Doughty Street, after a long and agonizing labor, Julie delivered, not Richard's hoped-for son, but an "exceptionally healthy, exceptionally large" baby girl. In an act which marked the girl-child as hers, Julie named the baby Eva, her own pen name. The next day, acting more like a fan than a father, Richard sent the baby a bouquet and enclosed his card: "To Eva from her loving father." When he was allowed to see the child, he thought that she was "a little mirror of her mother."

In the months following Eva's birth, Julie and Richard reconciled for a time, but Julie told Richard that things were looking "pretty black." In December 1899 Julie arranged a traditional Danish celebration for Eva's first Christmas. Eva was too young to remember the holiday, which the family spent at Chiddingfold, a Georgian manor house that Richard had found on a bicycling tour through Surrey. Her half-sister, Hesper, who was five years older than Eva, remembered, however, and told Eva that a drunken Richard had struck Julie and threatened her with a carving knife, and that when he had gone after his daughters, Nanny locked the sisters in the nursery. Afterward, ashamed and afraid to face Julie in person, Richard wrote a note blaming his behavior on his alcoholism and begging Julie to forgive him.

Julie did forgive him, but they spent most of the next few years apart. Julie and the children would often summer in Copenhagen, and Richard would travel throughout England gathering material for a new book or live for months at a time in New York City, returning to England only for brief visits. Julie enjoyed this arrangement, telling Richard, "I am happy. I have an ideal home, the children, my work, & your love there far away, which means peace."

Julie's peace was shattered when Richard returned to his family in August 1903 after a long visit to New York. Julie knew of and accepted Richard's various love affairs; in fact, she herself was involved in a relationship, with a younger man, Dr. Folmer Hansen, a Danish doctor-diplomat with curling blond hair and blue eyes. She was not upset by Richard's infidelity. But some time between August and October of 1903, Richard did something that Julie could not pardon. Again, Richard attempted to explain his behavior. "It was the old filth & poison of my mind coming again to the surface for no reason at all," he wrote, "except the reason I haven't the courage to write." He was "terrified" of himself, he said, and begged over and over that Julie believe that he was truly sorry and forgive him.

This time Julie could not. She told Richard that she wanted a divorce, and then she took Hesper and Eva with her to Copenhagen, where they stayed with Julie's mother. Writing to Julie on October 17, 1903, on a ship bound for America (where he would live for the next twenty-seven years), Richard said goodbye and wished that "Asra could have made you happier—but you see he was only Richard."

Julie on holiday with her stepdaughter, Hesper Le Gallienne, and Eva,
then about sixteen months old, 1900

Years later, when Hesper talked "about old family gossip" and hinted at dark family secrets, Eva found the stories grim and depressing. Whatever Richard's crime was, it seems not to have been discussed openly by Eva or her sister. Eva sensed, though, that her father was a "strange man in many ways."

Perhaps an answer can be found in Richard's own words. After his separation from Julie, Richard published a prose fancy titled "Eva, the Woodland and I," in which he wrote of three-year-old Eva, with seduction in her heart, offering him the "wild apple of idleness and sunshine," tempting him away from his work into the woods. Once they are in the woods, he shows Eva an adder that he has caught, a "sinuous, sinister beauty." Richard forces open the snake's "cruel mouth," so that Eva can see his "evil forked tongue." "O, isn't he pretty?" says Eva. "Let me take hold of him." Richard "had to deny her that indulgence; one of the few I ever denied her, for I know of few with which she is not strong enough to be intrusted." Father and daughter are caught by Eva's mother, who says, "Aren't you ashamed of yourselves?" They free the snake, and Eva's mother takes the child away, "into captivity."

According to the story, Julie was able to rescue three-year-old Eva, but it's not clear what abuse eight-year-old Hesper might have suffered. What is clear is that after Richard and Julie separated, Julie took both of Richard's daughters "into captivity." A few months later, realizing that she could not afford to raise two children, Julie arranged that Sissie and Jimmy Welch, who had no children, act as Hesper's guardians. Although Richard continued to write to Julie and would occasionally send Eva a note, he did not communicate with Hesper until her eighteenth birthday, when he wrote her an odd, jaunty letter in which he blamed her for failing to keep in touch with him. Hesper and Eva did not see their father again until they were adults. Without a mother and cut off from her father, Hesper suffered through a miserable, unhappy childhood, shuttled from one Gallienne relative to another. Her only happy days, she said later, were spent with Julie and Eva in Paris or with Nanny and her sisters at the Stenning family home in Farncombe.

After weeks of healing with the Nørregaard family in Copenhagen in late 1903, Julie set about fashioning a life for herself and Eva that didn't include Richard. "I have had a hell of a time," Julie wrote Sissie Welch. "I am in the midst of it all yet, but a quiet strength has grown out of it. . . . You know I have always had an absurd faith in my own star . . . so with a tiny bit of luck I still believe things will come right."

WHILE SHE MADE arrangements to settle in Paris, where she planned to support herself and Eva with translation work and her journalism, Julie sent Eva and Hesper to spend Christmas of 1903 with Nanny at the Stennings' Elizabethan cottage in Farncombe. Eva, always sensitive to her surroundings, loved the ancient house, especially its "old, old garden filled with apple-trees and flanked by a hedge of hop-vines . . . a garden full of mystery and wonder."

In early 1904, Hesper went to live with Jimmy and Sissie Welch in London, and Nanny and Eva crossed the English Channel to join Julie in Paris. Julie had found a fifth-floor apartment in an old house at 60, rue de Vaugirard, the longest street in Paris. The drawing room was eclectically elegant, with Art Nouveau wallpaper, contemporary paintings on the walls, an Empire sofa and sideboard, a daybed piled with pillows, an Oriental rug on a terra-cotta floor, a glass-front bookcase crammed with books, and a mantel still life of flowers in crystal vases, framed photographs, assorted bibelots, and a peacock plume. Living in such a comfortable atmosphere, Eva did not discover until much later "the true heroism of both my Mother and Nanny." With no help from Richard, Julie managed to scrape out a frugal living. During 1904, Nanny worked without wages, "worked in a way that she would previously have considered beneath her," said Eva. "She scrubbed, cleaned, did the washing, cooked, and looked after us entirely."

It was a hand-to-mouth existence, and the apartment was often cold. When tears threatened, her own or Eva's, Julie would tell the story of Ibsen seeing the

Julie and Eva toasting their first Paris apartment in 1904

Eva with her British nanny, Susan Stenning, in Paris, 1905

first performance of *Brand*. The play had moved him to tears. "Ikke tude!" (Don't blubber!), he had admonished himself.

"Ikke tude," "trofast og glad" (loyal and happy), "Do try to be sweet, Nutie" were all repeated again and again by Julie to her headstrong "Cat." Nanny's method of discipline was more dramatic and more cruel. When Eva had been especially naughty, Nanny packed a bag, put on her straw bonnet with blue ribbons, threw her nurse's cloak over her shoulders, and pretended to leave the house, never to return. Eva screamed, yelled, cried, searched for her in all the rooms, working herself into a frenzy. Finally, when Nanny reappeared from her hiding place, Eva shouted "I will never do it again!" and begged her to stay until Nanny finally relented. Exhausted and overwrought, Eva would cry herself to sleep, vowing repentance. Plagued, or blessed, she liked to say, with the vitality of fifty devils, Eva was naughty again, of course, and this melodramatic scene was repeated again and again.

High-spirited and devilish as Eva was, Susan Stenning doted on her "pet lamb." She gave Eva her first doll, a Victorian beauty with a painted china face. Baby Eva, not yet two, took one look at the doll and flung it away. The fragile porcelain head shattered, leaving just the stuffed calico body and black stockings. Instead of punishing Eva, Stenning made the doll a new head of rugged cotton and painted on new features. Eva accepted the doll, named her Bessie, and whenever she grew tired of Bessie's face or whenever it got dirty, it was a simple matter to draw on a new face. "To me she was a real person," Eva said, "and was the only doll I ever have loved."

When she wanted to take Bessie with her to a children's party, though, Nanny insisted that six-year-old Eva leave the doll behind, warning that "little ladies don't behave like that." Already uncomfortable in a starched party dress, in a rage of frustration, Eva screamed, "I don't want to be a little lady. I won't be a little lady. I don't want to go without my Bessie!" Eva went to the party sans Bessie, but she refused to act like a lady and sulked in a corner. In years to come, Eva dated her "distaste for parties" from this incident.

While Nanny was Eva's disciplinarian, Julie was her teacher. Julie—"Mam," Eva called her—surrounded her daughter with books, read aloud to her from Andersen and Grimm; and when Eva learned to read at five, Julie placed no restrictions upon her reading choices. The first book Eva read by herself was *Robinson Crusoe;* then she "developed a veritable passion for Dumas," followed by "an orgy of Dickens and Thackeray." To encourage Eva's intellectual development, Julie gave her a desk "with little drawers and pigeon-holes" and her own bookcase.

Julie opened doors for her into the world of culture and passed on to Eva her own exquisite taste. She treated Eva as a companion and took her on Sunday expeditions to see Blériot fly at Orly, "to the Bois de Boulogne; to Versailles . . .

Bessie, Eva's first doll,
which she kept
for the rest of her life

Eva (left) and Hesper (right) on summer holiday in 1906 at the Stenning cottage in
Farncombe, Surrey, with the Stenning sisters, Julia, Anne, and Susan, Eva's nanny

and best of all," Eva recalled, "to Ville d'Avray where, beside the pond immortalized in [George] Du Maurier's *Peter Ibbetson,* we would take our *déjeuner* at the Hotel Cabassud, and walk back to Neuilly through the woods, returning home by way of the little river steamer on the Seine."

Paris was a "wonderful place to grow up in," Eva wrote later. "All around one is harmony of line and a richness of life and beauty." The city was filled with abundant life—the smell of roasting chestnuts, women's perfumes, strong garlic breaths; the "sharp tooting of taxi horns," and the "clop-clop of hooves on cobblestones." Every afternoon Nanny took her to the Luxembourg Gardens, where Eva bought "flavored soda-waters, sugar-sticks, chocolate-creams, and long strips of licorice" with her fifty-centimes-a-week allowance. She took mandolin lessons once a week at the music store on the corner and attended a neighborhood kindergarten. Julie believed in developing Eva's body as well as her mind and enrolled her at the Gymnase George, where she studied gymnastics and advanced ring and trapeze work. When Julie watched six-year-old Eva at the gym, she thought her "quite wonderful. The man uses her as a model for the others . . . it seems also when you watch the child as if her little soul flew out in the room with the movements, so intense is she on doing it well."

In childhood photographs, Eva looks older than her years; her wide, penetrating blue eyes stare at the camera. Dressed elegantly and simply, usually in blue, she topped her long, curling hair with a child's version of one of Julie's fashionable hats. A bravado and toughness are evident in the photographs of Julie and her daughter. They both gaze steadily and unsmilingly at the camera, yet there's a delight in creating a scene.

By 1907, when Eva was eight, as Julie had hoped, things began to "come right." She wrote Sissie Welch about an "unnecessarily hard and unkind letter" she had received from John Gallienne. "It made me set my teeth hard, and I realized that only in the strength of my own nature lies salvation for Eva and me in the future." With her usual resourcefulness Julie had apprenticed with one of the large Parisian milliners. Since John Gallienne had refused her request for a loan, she borrowed capital from friends, sold some furniture and a few of her gowns, and launched her own hat shop under the name Madame Fédora (in honor of one of Sarah Bernhardt's most popular plays), since she did not want to use Richard's name. During the day, the drawing room of their new, larger apartment at 1, rue de Fleurus, served as the salon. Next door was the workroom, where Julie made the hats with the help of an assistant. The shop, patronized mostly by Americans, theatre people, and Julie's writer friends, became quite successful.

Thoroughly British Susan Stenning had never gotten used to Paris, and in 1909, when Eva was ten, she returned to England. Julie gave Eva a kitten to soften the loss, but the departure of Nanny, who had taken care of Eva from the time she was six weeks old, was devastating. Eva later wrote that it was "my first real grief."

With the success of her hat shop, Julie could afford to send ten-year-old Eva to the Collège Sévigné, a highly regarded secular school for girls. Madame Curie enrolled her daughters, Irène and Eve, there a few years later, and Eve Curie would write that "permanently imprinted upon us" was "the taste for work . . . a certain indifference toward money, and an instinct of independence which convinced us both that in any combination of circumstances we should know how to get along without help."

On her way to school, Eva walked through the Luxembourg Gardens to the gate opposite the Théâtre de l'Odéon. Sometimes the scene dock door would be open and she would "peer into those magic shadows and see the stage." Classes at the Collège Sévigné were held in large rooms with "immensely high ceilings and tall narrow French windows, beautiful *boiseries,* parquet floors and wonderful carved mantelpieces." In an atmosphere redolent with the pungent smell of French ink, the girls sat at black old-fashioned desks and took notes as lectures were given by "distinguished professors, all specialists in their own fields." Classes met only from eight to twelve, but "they made you use your own brains," Eva said. "I think it is the best form of education imaginable."

After school, Eva would lunch with her mother and then go off on her own when Julie went back to the hat shop. Eva struck up a friendship with Jo Mielziner, the son of American artist Leo Mielziner. Jo, "a pink-faced little rogue of a boy," who was two years younger than Eva, would later become a leading American theatre designer. Her best friend, though, was Ellen Koopman, an American girl who also attended the Collège Sévigné. Ellen and her brother, Bernard, the children of the painter Augustus Koopman, lived in the same building as Eva and her mother. Eva and Ellen's favorite game, Eva wrote, was going to the Luxembourg Gardens and "doing what was forbidden. If there were signs 'Do not walk on the grass,' we would roll on it. . . . We climbed the statues, we waded in the fountains, we made fortresses out of the iron chairs for hire; in other words we were a terrible nuisance and had a marvelous and unforgettable amount of fun."

Eva also made enemies—especially among proper French girls. Louise Berton, her classmate at the Collège Sévigné, recalled how she disliked Eva. She was "often dressed in blue," Berton remembered, and was a "very independent little girl. The teachers and classmates did not like her very much because she was too proud of herself wanting always to be admired!" Plus, Berton continued, Eva's personality was "strong" and her wild behavior was "strange."

Eva had a strong ego, self-assurance, and natural authority. But she could be hurt and didn't hesitate to strike back in retaliation. Wounded by a classmate named Marcelle, who had been critical of her behavior and her family background, Eva wrote her a furious letter. Eva demanded that Marcelle not treat her "like a dog as you did before I've had enough of that and if you continue I will do something you won't like. I am from as good a family as you are and maybe better. I have better manners than you do because if you had them you would treat me properly." Marcelle's mother gave the letter to Eva's teacher, who said that she had always "had a good opinion of Eva" and was surprised at the letter, but noted that Marcelle "may have been unkind to Eva." The teacher forwarded the letter to Julie Le Gallienne. Perhaps Julie smiled at the proud signature on the letter—Eva Nørregaard Le Gallienne—as she carefully stored it away with the rest of her daughter's archive.

AS HER HAT SHOP flourished, Julie could afford more theatre tickets and more trips abroad. Eva saw Sarah Bernhardt in *La Dame aux camélias* and *La Reine Elisabeth* and soon would have the opportunity to meet her in person. On a trip to England, she saw Forbes-Robertson's Hamlet. "As Mam knows the Robertsons very well, we were asked to their boxe, & afterwards we went behind the scenes on to the stage & into the dressing room," Eva wrote. "It is extraordinary how different it looks from behind!" Maurice Maeterlinck's symbolist play *The Bluebird* had a profound effect on her, especially the children's search for the bluebird of happiness and their realization that "real happiness is found at home." She marveled at Nijinsky and Karsavina in the first season of Diaghilev's Ballet Russe, adored the great actors Coquelin and Lucien Guitry, but found the comic actress Réjane "fat and ugly." She saw Max Reinhardt's production of *Sumurun*. She went to the Comédie-Française, France's great national theatre, to the Louvre, the Musée de Cluny, and the Tuileries. On the stage of her Danish toy theatre, she recreated many of the productions, and she fashioned scenery and special effects from her own imagination, beginning her lifelong interest in stage design as well as invention.

Eva often spent long Christmas holidays and summer vacations in Copenhagen, where her grandmother Bet Nørregaard taught her Danish by reading Hans Christian Andersen in the original and by teaching her the songs and nursery rhymes of Scandinavia. Julie's brother, Kai Nørregaard, took Eva to Denmark's national theatre, the state subsidized Royal Theatre in Copenhagen, founded in 1819. The theatre's motto, "Ej Blot til Lyst" (Not Only for Amusement), would be an inspiration for Le Gallienne's own vision of a national theatre for America. Kai's son, Mogens, became her close friend. The two cousins would confide in one another and love one another until they were both octogenarians. Mogens was such a devoted Le Gallienne fan and archivist that he collected, annotated, and filed every note, letter, clipping, and photograph she sent him.

Eva forged closed ties with the Nørregaards, but her contacts with her Gallienne relatives were infrequent. In August 1911 she visited Grandfather Gallienne

Eva in Copenhagen with her
grandmother Bet Nørregaard
and her favorite cousin,
Møgens Nørregaard, c. 1909

in Birkenhead and also saw Hesper, who was spending her summer vacation there. Grandmother Gallienne had died the year before, but John Gallienne made the girls feel welcome. Eva was fond of her grandfather. He admired her voice and told her she should make something of it—plus, he didn't scold her too much when her pet mouse, "Mou-mou," ate his stamp collection. "I think dear old Granddad is sweet," Eva wrote her mother. Well tutored by Julie's highly developed aesthetic sense and already something of a snob, Eva appraised the Gallienne home and noted, "The furniture is not tasteful but very comfortable."

A tearful John Gallienne sent her back to Julie and asked Eva to convey a conciliatory message to her mother. "He said I was to tell you this," Eva wrote. "That he could weep over us when he thinks how Daddie has neglected us when he thinks how well he cared for him and all the others and then he *ought* to have cared for us." Richard always had a ready excuse for his failure to support his daughters. "Really, I shouldn't be half a bad Daddy," he told Julie, "& indeed quite a charming person if only I had more money."

Richard was too preoccupied with his new love, Irma Hinton Perry, to consider the welfare of either of his daughters. In 1906 Hesper and Sissie (who was divorced from Jimmy Welch) had moved in with Julie and Eva in Paris. During that time, Hesper enjoyed a happy family life. The two half-sisters played together, even created their own magazine; but perhaps because of their age difference or because Eva was jealous of Hesper's intrusion, they never became close. They would maintain contact all their lives, and Hesper was devoted to and in awe of her little sister, but Eva remained somewhat aloof with Hesper. When they were both middle-aged, Eva told her diary that "Hep bores me just as much as she always had—ever since we were children!"

When Sissie died in July 1907, Hesper was sent to live with Jimmy Welch and his new wife, who soon sent her off to her Gallienne grandparents, who packed her off to an English boarding school. Hesper wrote plaintive letters to Julie and Eva, often asking if they knew where her father was.

Meanwhile, Julie continued to press Richard for a divorce, since she wanted to marry Folmer Hansen. Finally, when Richard himself wanted to remarry, the divorce judgment was signed in New York on July 3, 1911. Although in the official divorce document Richard agreed to pay five hundred dollars a year for Eva, he never contributed to her support. Richard's failure to meet his obligations had a profound effect on Eva. "A debtor who won't even try to pay his debts," she said later, "nothing seems to me more contemptible than that."

A few months later, on October 27, 1911, Richard, his now gray hair cut conventionally short, married Irma Hinton Perry in Darien, Connecticut. He became stepfather to her thirteen-year-old daughter, Gwen, who took the name Le Gallienne, and afterward always referred to herself as Eva and Hesper's sister, a practice that infuriated them both. During the wedding ceremony, when asked "Do you take this woman . . . ?" a drunken Richard burbled, "You bet I do," and then toppled over backwards. Despite this inauspicious beginning, the marriage would last for thirty-six years.

Julie was free to marry Folmer Hansen, but Hansen disappeared from her life—perhaps he had returned to Copenhagen or taken a diplomatic post in South Africa, where he had been assigned earlier. In later years, Julie told her daughter that it was for Eva's sake that she hadn't married Hansen. "I don't know why I should have been an obstacle," Eva wrote, "except that I didn't like him very much because once he picked me up very violently and lifted me high in the air and banged my head hard on the ceiling!" Another obstacle might have been Julie's age. In 1911, when she was finally free to marry, she was forty-eight years old, and by the standard of the day she was already an old woman.

JULIE'S CLOSE FRIENDS William Faversham and his wife, Julie Opp, and their two sons had taken over Richard Le Gallienne's Chiddingfold lease years earlier, and Julie and Eva spent long summer vacations with the Favershams.

William Faversham, "Uncle Will" to Eva, stood in as her surrogate father during her summer vacations in England; she would always remember him with "tenderness, warmth, and everlasting gratitude." Faversham contrasted quite dramatically with Richard, who only remembered her once or twice a year, with a gift of a book or a dollar bill.

Handsome Will Faversham and Julie, who had a voice "like a haunted frog pond," were matinee idols in New York, but in the summer they played country squire and lady, opening Chiddingfold to all their actor and writer friends, including Suzanne Ainley, Forbes-Robertson, Maxine Elliott, Constance Collier, Arnold Bennett, and Ben Webster, his wife, May Whitty, and their daughter, Margaret Webster.

"Uncle Will & Aunt Julie made of hospitality a fragrant joyous thing," Eva remembered, but she was still just a guest in a house that had once belonged to her father, a man who had failed to provide a home for his family. The Favershams created a home and a way of life paid for by working actors, a lesson not lost on Eva. Years later, in her own home in Connecticut, she would attempt to recapture some of the beauty of Chiddingfold, especially the garden with its "herbaceous borders glowing with a thousand flowers . . . above all the roses—tree-roses—rambling roses—rose-bushes . . . old fashioned English tea roses, covering the sun-dial, crowding across narrow moss-grown paths."

At Chiddingfold she met her mentor and first acting teacher, Constance Collier, Herbert Beerbohm Tree's leading lady at His Majesty's Theatre in London. "I thought I had never seen anyone more lovely to look at," Eva remembered. "She was very dark, with a vivid, glowing face; her dress was a curiously exciting color, a kind of Pompeian red, and seemed a perfect frame for her rather violent beauty." Introduced to Eva, Collier took her hand and said, "I'm told you want to be an actress?" Eva answered affirmatively and was thrilled when Collier added, "You have a good voice for the Theatre. I have a feeling you'll be all right."

"This was the beginning of a great friendship between us," Eva wrote. "I was her slave from then on and hero-worshipped her with all the intensity of my twelve years." Collier coached her in Shakespeare, trying "to make me see the values in the beautiful speeches, to bring out the music without losing sight of the meaning. . . . She was a very severe critic, a ruthlessly honest teacher."

When Collier first met Eva Le Gallienne, she found her

an amazing child, with all the indications of the greatness of her character. . . . I have a vision of her now starting off for camp. . . . She was mounted on an old white horse . . . and there was a tremendous look of earnestness and determination in . . . those eyes of hers, that are so wide and penetrating! They are the most characteristic thing about her; brilliant

At Chiddingfold in June 1913. Left to right: Mrs. Opp; William Faversham; Julie Opp
Faversham; Hugo Rumbolt; Constance Collier; Eva; Julie Le Gallienne; Ben Webster; his
wife, May Whitty; and Suzanne Sheldon. In front are William and Philip Faversham.

and star-like. . . . She flipped the old horse to start. . . . She looked like Don
Quixote starting out on his adventures. . . . The next day a bedraggled but
undaunted Eva arrived for equipment. It seems that in the night her tent
had blown down and she had been pinned underneath it. She was only a
child in the darkness and the cold. . . . I asked her if she had cried out for
help. And her answer was so characteristic. She said, "No, of course not. I
built it up again." And that, I think, is typically her attitude toward life.

Eva said later that she didn't pay much attention to another guest that summer, Margaret Webster, but with her precise eye for detail she did remember a
"very small, rather plump child, her brown hair worn in two tight little plaits,
her big blue eyes made rounder by large round-lensed glasses." Margaret Webster
recalled that "having the advantage of some five years over . . . me, [Eva] pursued her own solitary purposes with silent concentration. She climbed to the top
of the cedar tree in order to read in peace. She had her own bicycle. She was a
Girl Guide and wore a uniform . . . most dazzling to my eyes."

The crowning event of Eva's visit to Chiddingfold during the summer of 1913 was winning the donkey race at the village fair. She won a twelve-day clock and a barometer. She treasured her special possessions in the same way she cherished special friends. She kept the clock ("It has a good honest face," she would say) and the barometer in good working order for the rest of her life.

The summer of 1913 was her last summer as a child. In addition to her weeks at Chiddingfold, Eva visited Nanny and her sisters in Farncombe, confiding to her mother that while she was there, she got her period for the first time. "I am quite alright. Dear old Nan was luckily here." She spent several weeks at a Girl Guide camp, earning her naturalist badge by collecting more than seventy varieties of wildflowers and grasses. Constance Collier invited her for a week's stay in Kent, where she worked on Shakespeare monologues and played tennis. While she was enjoying herself in England she thought of her mother in Paris, "who has to slave & work as no other woman ever has worked to keep a lazy kid like me!" She told her mother that

> Uncle Will goes to New York Wednesday. Oh! if only I were going with him to act. . . . If you only knew how awful it is to me to sit here, comfortable, enjoying myself, having everything payed for me & to know that the one who is paying for all this, is my own darling Muk. . . . Miss Collier has told me that when she was 14 she kept her father & mother in comfort. Why shouldn't I try to help you! As I suppose I can't go to America, I am in any case studying two or three Shakespearean parts. . . . I have bought a complete Shakespeare's works in 4 volumes for 6 shillings. . . . I know that it will take a long time of hard work and many disappointments before I could earn much money, but I should always feel that I was doing something worth doing.

Later, Margaret Webster would see that happy summer of 1913 as the end of the Edwardian Age and the beginning of a new era. "The gracious living, the ordered pattern, the solid present, the secure and predictable future never came again," she said.

WILL FAVERSHAM wanted Eva to join his company and go to America, where he planned to present *Julius Caesar* with Constance Collier as Portia. To Eva's "dismal and bitter disappointment," Julie Le Gallienne thought her fourteen-year-old daughter was "too young to start work." She decided that Eva needed the finish of an English boarding-school education and enrolled her in Court-field, "one of many thousand of the 'better schools' in England," Eva said, "to which little girls are packed off at the age of eight, to be released at the age of sev-

enteen or eighteen, perfect young English ladies." After a visit to London, where
Hesper helped her buy the clothes required by Courtfield, Eva, feeling hideous
in her new dark blue serge long-skirted suit, green high-collared shirt, green,
blue, and red tie, and stiff sailor hat, took the train to the seaside town of
Bognor, where she entered her "dreary prison."

The Collège Sévigné had prepared her well, and after taking placement
exams, she was enrolled as a senior, with girls of sixteen and seventeen. Assigned
a cubicle of her own, she decorated it with pictures of Sarah Bernhardt, Constance Collier, and Henry Irving and tucked her Shakespeare volumes under her
pillow. Eva wrote later that as one used to the "free and responsible life . . . surrounded by an interesting and stimulating atmosphere, accustomed to thinking
for myself . . . to being treated, not as a child (and therefore inferior) but as a
human being whose opinions were worth consideration, to me who had proudly
been entrusted with a latch-key of my own at the age of eight, and had even
crossed the Channel alone on two occasions," she now had to acclimate herself
to a school that was "smug, straitlaced and in every way conventional." "Boring!" she exclaimed in letter after letter to her mother. "The girls here
are . . . very petit bourgeois! They are so different from French girls. In some
ways nicer, for they aren't so sneaky but oh! so slow to grasp anything!" She
found the ugliness of her surroundings, the stultifying atmosphere, and the lack
of freedom singularly depressing.

"Sunday in a select English Academie for Young Ladies!" she wrote Mam.
"What could be more awful!" The punishment for saying "ripping" or "rotten"
was twenty-four hours in bed with bread and water. "So I shall have to look out,"
Eva said. She thought the dancing was "a waste of money," just polkas and barn
dances, nothing useful in a modern ballroom. In her free time after supper,
though, Eva taught the other girls the tango, "under the name of the Victorian
dance for if Miss Wall heard the name she would have forty fits!"

Her teachers, however, had quite a good opinion of Eva. Just weeks after her
arrival, on September 17, 1913, the headmistress wrote Julie that "[Eva] is already
a favourite not only with the girls but with the teachers. She has personality and
what an attractive singing voice! Miss Wall and I both notice, too, how frank and
open she is in her nature." The teachers were "delighted with her intelligence,"
but noted that she seemed "restless."

After a few months at Courtfield, Eva's natural good spirits and leadership
qualities asserted themselves. "I was too much of an egomaniac," she wrote later,
"and had too great a sense of my own importance, to consent to being an 'outsider' very long." She excelled at riding and played left wing on the hockey team.
She debated the French teacher on the merits of "the tango versus the waltz,"
and while the French teacher argued for the waltz in fast French, Eva countered
with arguments in equally fast French and won the debate for the tango. With

the help of the sheet music and magazines Julie supplied, Eva knew twelve versions of the tango, could play ragtimes on the piano, and at impromptu concerts sang "Egypt" (a "coon song") and "Alexander's Ragtime Band" in her contralto, which was the deepest voice in the school.

If the school forbade something—in fact, if *anything* was forbidden—"that only made it the more exciting," Eva thought. She and several other girls would sneak out of their cubicles to have midnight feasts or run along the beach in the moonlight or go to the cinema. "The element of danger . . . was invigorating," she said. When she and several of her friends were caught for visiting out of their cubicles after lights out, they were given, Eva said, a "killing punishment"—they were confined to their beds for twenty-four hours and took meals in the dining room wearing their dressing gowns. To curb their youthful exuberance, strict silence was enforced at breakfast, in the passages, on walks, and at tea.

At Courtfield, the girls were forbidden to kiss one another. Forbidden kisses only made them more exciting for Eva, and apparently for most of the other girls as well. Eva told Hesper that when Miss Wall "asked us all who had kissed during the term, every hand except two went up. The punishment was bed & we all have to pay a 1 shilling fine. That is beastly as you know *je ne suis pas riche!* Anyway my consolation is that I have had my shilling's worth!"

She continued to pour out her dreams to her Danish cousin Mogens in long letters. She missed Paris and Mam terribly. "All the people here seem so dull & so uninteresting," she wrote. "I feel that living abroad as I have done, I have quite different feelings & ideas from most of these girls & I am sure they sometimes think I am a bit mad. Before, when I lived in Paris, Mother always said she could never stand living in England & I never quite understood what she meant. But now that I live here myself, I know just exactly what she means. . . . The whole atmosphere is so depressing. You have sometimes to make an effort to be cheerful, while in Paris you are always cheerful." By the end of the letter, she had written herself out of her depression, declaring, "I think it is much better to take things smiling & to put a grin on everything. If you moped at every little petty bother, you could never get on in the world."

IN NOVEMBER 1913, Eva wrote her mother to console her over the death of her pet cat, but assured her that soon Julie would "have her real Cat who loves you more." Julie had written of lunching with Sarah Bernhardt, and Eva begged her mother to get her anything, "a pin, a flower, a bit of waste paper, it doesn't matter what, from her house & send it to me. I know it seems silly, but you can't know what it would mean to me. . . . She is for me a religion almost, I worship her & anything that had been near to her, would, to me, be of more value than a pearl. . . . I am sure you understand."

Julie understood her Cat very well, and when Eva joined her in Paris for a holiday, Mam announced she had tickets to the December 16 opening of Bernhardt's new play, *Jeanne Doré*. It was Bernhardt's last appearance in a full-length play and one of her few realistic roles. "It was . . . a thrilling evening," Le Gallienne wrote later. "The great theatre was packed with all the most interesting personalities in Paris." Julie pointed out "Cécile Sorel, Anatole France, Tristan Bernard who wrote the play, Edmond Rostand, and particularly Ida Rubinstein, who sat in the left-hand stage box, tall and regal, wearing a huge ermine wrap with a stand-up collar and seven Bird-of-Paradise plumes in her elaborate coiffure."

When Sarah appeared, the audience applauded "for at least five minutes." Noted for her other, more glamorous roles, in *Jeanne Doré* Sarah played an old woman who tries to save her son from the guillotine. "Her performance was a miracle of realism, so touching, so unerringly well-observed, so bewildered and crushed by sheer human sorrow, that the public was moved to tears of tender compassion," Le Gallienne recalled.

Julie took Eva backstage after the performance, and soon the girl found herself looking in "speechless wonder at that extra-ordinary face." When Bernhardt smiled at her, Eva noted her "strange grey-green eyes . . . heavily framed in blue," her pale face, and her bright scarlet mouth with "small flecks of the scarlet paint" stuck to her teeth. Eva kissed her hand, and when Sarah smiled at her and kissed her on both cheeks, Eva was overcome with "such intense joy that it was almost agony." She had been unable to express a word to her idol and could not speak on the way home in the cab. As a child, whenever she was "profoundly moved by either gratitude, joy, anger or sorrow," Eva said, "I was equally solemn, equally inarticulate." She didn't wash her face for days, not wanting "to rub away the kisses of *La Grande Sarah*."

JULIE AND EVA spent the 1913 Christmas holidays in Copenhagen. Christmas was Eva's favorite time in Copenhagen, and she would continue all her life the traditions of *jule aften,* Christmas Eve, celebrated by the Nørregaard family. Dinner started with a rice porridge with an almond hidden inside. The lucky one who found it won a candy prize, and Eva said, "I can never remember a Christmas dinner without the joy of winning the coveted marzipan." Roast goose, "stuffed with prunes and apples and decorated with little Danish flags," came next. After dinner the drawing-room doors were opened to reveal the tree, laden with flickering candles, candies, and toys and stacked round with presents. The family joined hands and everyone danced around the tree singing a Christmas carol. "Dear, sweet, warm people!" Le Gallienne wrote. "How strange it is that Scandinavians are usually thought cold and a little dreary. They are so gay, so generous, so human."

With the assistance of her brother, Kai, that January Julie arranged a ball in Eva's honor to celebrate her fifteenth birthday. "I felt completely grown up," Eva wrote later. Partnered by her tall, blond cousin Mogens, Eva wore a white ball gown with long gloves, and since she was "the guest of honor, and . . . a foreigner who had lived in Paris and London, who spoke several languages, who was to be an actress and who had even met Sarah Bernhardt (Mogens had given me good publicity!)," she said, "I soon had my card filled up, and I was never off my feet." She danced until four in the morning.

"How you gained everyone that evening!" Mogens wrote his cousin. "You are one of the persons who are making everybody nice and glad oh!—how a gift! I must thank you for giving me the big, wide, open horizon into the world. . . . You will never be able to understand that fully because you are giving the light and I am receiving."

"After this exciting and glamorous holiday Bognor seemed a dull place indeed!" sighed Eva. Schoolgirl intrigues and doing what was forbidden offered some excitement, though. Her special friend, thirteen-year-old Bea Harrison, was being "perfectly beastly," Eva complained to Mogens. When the girls met in Eva's cubicle, "I kissed her," Eva reported, "& then she said: 'I have no kisses for you, I must keep all my kisses for another person!' meaning Violet, of course. I did think it mean of her."

As a senior Eva was sent to town to run errands and found opportunities to buy her favorite marzipan. "It is against the rule," she said, "but then—one can't always obey rules, can one?" Eva had no intention of becoming a "perfect young English lady" who obeyed every rule, and she convinced Julie to allow her to leave Courtfield early in the term. Julie agreed that she could come home to Paris and help her with some translation work. Hesper had a secretarial job in Paris and would be staying with them at Julie's new, larger apartment and salon at 8, rue Tronchet.

Miss Wall kissed Eva goodbye and asked her to remember the talks they had had. "The only thing is that sometimes in her little lectures," Eva told her mother, "she introduces God or religion and then I always feel such a heathen because I can't believe in God. I have tried, because I think it good to have some faith, but rather than be a Christian in an outer form only, as so many people are, I prefer to give it up altogether."

At fifteen, Eva Le Gallienne's religion was the theatre and her idol was Sarah Bernhardt. Her life had purpose: "I *do* wish I could become a great actress," she told Mogens, "you don't *know* how I wish it!" In the spring of 1914, Julie Opp Faversham, who knew Bernhardt well, arranged for Eva to deliver a note to Sarah after a performance of *Phèdre*. Eva sat in the "peanut gallery," at the Théâtre Sarah Bernhardt, and while she later wrote that she had "no very clear recollection of the performance of *Phèdre*," she remembered Sarah clearly and described Bernhardt's voice in detail: "I remember the astonishing use of the Alexandrines—the incredible rapidity; the clarity of each syllable; the extraordinary range of the voice—at times muted and caressing—at others savage, almost raucous, the searing passionate words tearing at the throat."

When the performance ended, Eva ran "down the seven flights of stairs from the top gallery, and arrived breathless at the pass door." Sarah's secretary, a man with a dyed black moustache, nicknamed "Coco Rouge" by Sarah, at first closed the door on Eva, but he relented when she waved Julie Opp's message. "He took the telegram, read it . . . and told me to come in and wait: Madame would see me in her dressing room when the other visitors had departed." Eva was taken into a brilliantly lighted room filled with mirrors. Sarah, still in her heavy theatre makeup, sat at an enormous dressing table "littered with jars, bottles, brushes, powder puffs."

"Madame Le Gallienne, the friend of Madame Faversham!" announced Coco Rouge, with feigned dignity.

"Mais, mon Dieu, c'est un bébé!" Sarah cried.

Eva was mortified when Sarah laughed and the rest of Sarah's retinue joined in her laughter. Then, Eva remembered, "with an imperious gesture she stopped the laughter, her smile was full of tenderness as she put her arms round me and gave me an understanding hug. She soon put me at my ease, asking me many questions, gradually drawing me out until, to my surprise, I found myself talking to her quite easily. She kept my hand in hers and I looked with wonder at the sensitive nervous fingers, heavy with rings, the tips painted scarlet to the middle knuckle."

Sarah was horrified when she discovered that the girl had arrived unaccompanied by either maid or governess. When Eva told Sarah that she had her own latchkey from the age of eight, Sarah "cast her eyes to heaven in despair at the insane behavior of these foreigners." Finally, she let Eva go, "with many injunctions about care in crossing the streets and not talking to strangers. She kissed me again and filled my arms with flowers."

While many saw only the "siren charm" of Sarah Bernhardt, it was that plus the intelligence in her work that attracted Le Gallienne. In an essay she wrote years later, she said that "much of Sarah's work might have been described as intellectual. . . . She was a tireless worker; her productions were based on meticulous research, on careful attention to the minutest detail; her plays were clearly and logically presented, but with an unerring eye for theatrical effect. . . . Both as actress and director, her work had a tidy, organized brilliance that was somehow very French."

Later that year, after Eva had searched futilely for a copy of Sarah's memoirs, *Ma Double Vie,* which were out of print, R. H. Philipson, a wealthy Englishman who was a close friend of her mother's, loaned her his copy. Over an eight-

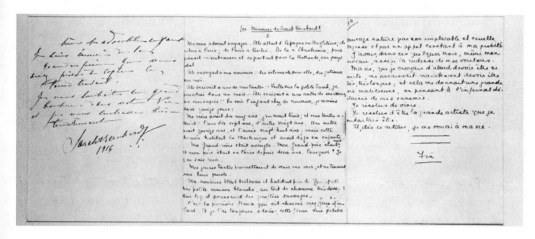

The first and last pages from Eva's handwritten copy of Bernhardt's memoirs
with Sarah's inscription

month period, Eva copied the book by hand and returned it to an amazed
Philipson, who took her eight hundred pages of cheap tablet paper and had
them bound into two "splendid volumes of blue and gold." A few years later,
when Le Gallienne and Bernhardt met again in New York, Sarah inscribed the
book to her: "Chère et adorable enfant, je suis émue de la grande peine que vous
avez prise à copier ce grand travail. Je vous souhaite un grand bonheur dans votre
vie et je vous embrasse tendrement!"

Le Gallienne placed the volumes (a "monument to what has sometimes been
called my incorrigible stick-to-itiveness!") on her bookshelf, but she carried with
her always the intangible qualities of Sarah's spirit reflected in her memoirs. The
book revealed Bernhardt's courage in the face of gossip and a sometimes hostile
press, her extraordinary vitality, and her inability to compromise, and showed
her to be a successful businesswoman who ran her own theatre, an artist who was
in control of her own life and destiny, and a woman who lived life on her own
terms outside the boundaries of conventional society. Eleonora Duse, who in a
few years would replace Bernhardt as Le Gallienne's role model, found Sarah
Bernhardt's example an "emancipation."

DURING THE SPRING OF 1914, Eva spent two weeks in the American Hospital at Neuilly recovering from an appendicitis operation. To while away the
time, she read *Anna Karenina* in French, followed the progress of Sarah Bernhardt's tour, and wrote and received letters, including one from Constance Collier, who had returned to England. Collier was planning a production of

Maeterlinck's antiwar drama, *Monna Vanna,* at the Queen's Theatre in London and asked Eva if she would be interested in playing her handmaiden. Coincidentally, R. H. Philipson had invited Eva and Julie to visit him in London for several weeks that summer, so Eva wrote back "a glowing letter of acceptance."

"[Philipson] is most frightfully rich & we are living the life of millionaires, which is really rather nice," Eva wrote Mogens after they had settled in Philipson's "huge apartment on Portland Place" in London. Philipson's young American-born wife had recently died, and, Eva wrote later, "he was bitterly unhappy. His friends flocked to him."

Before her rehearsals started on July 10, Philipson took her to Clarkson's, "the most famous wig-maker and make-up vendor in London," and bought her a complete makeup box, containing enough makeup to last her "many years, covering the widest range, from a 'fair young girl' to a 'robust old man!' " Clarkson also included a new hare's foot for applying and blending the makeup and, of course, for good luck.

Eva practiced applying her makeup at two eight-hour dress rehearsals. Her nonspeaking part had been changed from a handmaiden to a pageboy who would carry Monna Vanna's train. Her first professional role would not be the usual ingenue part given to beginning actresses; instead she would play a character part, wearing a fifteenth-century pageboy's clothes and tucking her long hair under a square-cut Florentine wig. Her sagging tights worried her until "one of the young men took pity on me and showed me how to use pennies—the large old-fashioned English kind—placed inside the tights near the top and tied in position with string, drawing the material up around them."

On the afternoon of July 21, the Queen's Theatre was filled with pink roses, the favorite flowers of England's Queen Alexandra (the daughter of Christian IX of Denmark), who attended the opening with her sister, the dowager empress of Russia. The queen had received a special invitation from Constance Collier. "I thought, if so great a queen conferred her patronage on the play, it would silence every criticism and gain for Maeterlinck the honour he deserved," Collier said. Hundreds of people were turned away at the door and the theatre was full, with people crowding onto the steps between the seats.

"It was most frightfully exciting," Eva wrote Mogens. "People gave me lovely presents: Mr. Philipson: a lovely piece of Japanese jade on a platinum chain. Mother: a silver ring with a big amethyst, one which Father gave her, & Hep a book of poetry (French). Then when I got to the theatre I found two beautiful bouquets one from Gabrielle Dorziot, the French actress & the other from Mr. Philipson. Also a letter from Uncle Jim [Welch] & one from Harry Ainley & 8 wires! Was'nt it ripping?" Eva gave Constance Collier a "big basket of growing Lilies of the Valley" and was "very pleased" when she saw that Collier put all her other flowers outside her room, keeping only the lilies inside. Five minutes before the overture began, Le Gallienne, in an act she would later see as utterly thought-less and selfish, "rushed down to Constance Collier's room . . . with the most per-fect disregard of her nerves . . . and proceeded to put a few last touches to my wig. . . . Instead of throwing me out, she helped me with the utmost patience."

During the performance, Eva "was'nt a bit frightened & felt quite at home & not a bit selfconscious on the stage." "If one tries," she wrote Mogens, "one can see the audience very clearly, but I did'nt want to, so I tried to forget everything & live in the play & I succeeded. Mother was awfully pleased with me & I think I have gone a little bit further in convincing her that I may be able to act."

Monna Vanna was a popular and critical hit, and the run was extended to evening performances at the Lyric Theatre. Julie returned to her Paris hat shop and, accompanied by Hesper, who was staying with Jimmy Welch, Eva saw al-most every play in town. By July 31 she had seen *Pygmalion* with Sir Herbert Beerbohm Tree and Mrs. Patrick Campbell, *My Lady's Dress* starring Gladys Cooper, Chaliapin in Russian opera and Karsavina in *Schéhérazade,* Oscar Asche and Lily Brayton in *Kismet, The Great Adventure* with Harry Ainley, *When Knights Were Bold* starring Jimmy Welch, and the American entertainer Elsie Janis in *The Passing Show* at the Palace Theatre.

Eva "was most frantically 'smut' " on Elsie Janis, saw her show several times, and was particularly fond of Elsie's imitation of Sarah Bernhardt. One afternoon Eva waited for Elsie to appear at the stage door after her matinee. When Elsie walked out speaking French to her maid, Eva seized the opportunity. Elsie heard "a rather husky Barrymorean voice say: 'Bon jour, Mlle. Janis. Vous étiez plus épatante—épatante que jamais cet après-midi.'

"The French was perfect," Elsie recalled. "The voice was arresting. . . . I stopped. We conversed in rapid French. . . . No matter what role she may play . . . I always see the light of that slim, dauntless little girl standing in the slush and mud of a London street."

AT THE END OF JULY, Eva wrote to Julie in Paris: "Aren't the threats of a Eu-ropean war too terrible? . . . America would be the only safe place!" On August 3, Germany declared war against France, and the next day England declared war on Germany. "It'll be over in three weeks, everyone confidently remarked," Le Gallienne wrote later. "No one was really worried; people were surprised and rather excited; it was a new sensation." When Julie appeared unexpectedly in London, Eva knew it was serious. Her mother reported of hysteria in Paris: "the banks were besieged, the stations jammed with people." Julie had fled with nothing but her handbag and was "ill with exhaustion and worry."

Philipson invited them to stay on with him in Portland Place as long as they liked. Julie set up a small millinery salon on the premises of a London dressmaker, and since *Monna Vanna* had closed, Eva began making the rounds of theatrical producers. Harley Granville-Barker promised Eva a job in the next play he produced, but the war had already brought changes in the theatre. Streetlights dimmed, some theatres closed, and there was a paper-money scare. Granville-Barker couldn't give Eva a job, but he did give her a piece of advice which she said was the most important thing anyone ever told her, explaining, in part, her lifelong addiction to learning and study. "Know everything," he said, "and use it."

With the assistance of Philipson, who helped with the tuition, Eva auditioned and was accepted at the Academy of Dramatic Art (later the Royal Academy of Dramatic Art), commonly called Tree's Academy after its founder, Sir Herbert, who established the training school in 1904. At the academy she studied ballet dancing, fencing, voice production, elocution, Delsarte (gesture training), and took two acting classes, modern drama and comedy and classic drama and comedy. She also signed up for the class in French plays, and she knew it was greedy, but since "my French was exceptionally good, I had the opportunity to play all the best parts in the performances!"

An actor's stature in the English theatre was equated with versatility, and during her nine-month stay at the Academy of Dramatic Art, Eva played a wide range of roles. One cold, foggy London morning, in a small rehearsal room smelling of soot, she played Juliet for the first time and spoke Juliet's lines to Romeo "Wilt thou be gone? It is not yet near day . . ." and for a brief time she felt transported outside herself into another realm, a state of grace that she would attempt to recapture throughout her artistic life.

Transcendent experiences were rare, however; and at Tree's Academy, she studied the practical techniques of the stage. She learned to make a graceful "long arm"—gesturing from the shoulder instead of the elbow. She learned to transform herself quickly with makeup, costume, and body line from a bearded old peasant in one scene to Blanchette, a young French girl, in another. The rush of rehearsals, performances, wig and costume fittings, she found "dreadful and lovely at the same time. I love a real good rush with not a minute to waste."

At the end of November, the academy students were examined by professional actors to determine who would receive scholarships—a "perfectly awful day," Eva said. "We had to go in, onto the stage, recite for elocution about 10 lines of Shakespeare & then do 2 stage falls & facial expression for Delsarte. . . . I thought I should faint or do something silly, but once on the stage, all fear left me."

The three judges—one of them was actor Ben Webster, Margaret's father—awarded twenty-one-year-old Dulcima Glasby and fifteen-year-old Eva Le Gallienne special honorable mentions. In the somewhat Olympian tone that was beginning to creep into her writing, Eva told Mogens that she found it "a great

*Laurette Taylor,
one of Eva's first
American friends,
in Arthur Hopkins's
1925 production of*
In a Garden

defect in Miss Glasby, that she can only speak one language. I have scarcely any, in fact no real friends who cannot speak a little French. So many of my associations & interests are French that I am always alluding to them & putting without thinking French words & expressions into my speech."

Even though Constance Collier didn't speak a word of French, Eva remained devoted to her, visited her in the country on weekends, and helped her learn "Carillon," a French poem which Collier planned to recite on behalf of the war effort. In turn, Constance, whose crib had been a theatre makeup table, passed on theatre lore to Eva, describing the legend of Harlequin, that ancient, masked figure who holds a transforming wand—a stick of grease paint.

In the spring of 1915, Constance invited Eva to join an exclusive theatrical dancing club which Collier and American actress Laurette Taylor had started. "They have accepted me as a member which is a great honor as only people who dance very well are allowed," Eva said. The club met several afternoons a week, from four to six. "It is splendid for me as I meet all the stage people there & get to know them well," Eva wrote. "You bet I shall be there every time." At the club, she danced with Elsie Janis, with Constance, with actress Marie Löhr, and with Laurette Taylor ("a genius," Eva thought), who was in London playing in *Peg o' My Heart.* It's not clear if men were allowed in the dancing club, but in Eva's letters to Mogens, she listed only women partners, although she told him that she had gone out often in the evenings with her old friend from Paris John Bodington, the son of her mother's lawyer.

Going out with a male friend did not mean, however, that she was ready to put up her hair. "No!!!" she said emphatically. "I have *not* my hair up, thank God!" Eva's honey-colored hair streamed down to the middle of her back. She knew that once she set aside her ribbons and piled her hair into coils on top of her head, by conventional society standards she was no longer a girl. She would be labeled a marriageable woman, condemned not only to endless hours of hair-dressing but to conventional expectations as well.

During their Easter vacation, Julie and Eva visited Hindhead, Surrey, where Julie showed Eva the first home she had shared with Richard. The weather was dreary, but they took long walks, rested, read, and grated on one another's nerves. Later, Le Gallienne looked back and could "imagine nothing worse than being in the constant company of a young, willful, selfish, highly intelligent, but completely ignorant girl of 16! Poor Mam!" Sometimes poor Mam resorted to shouting "Selfish pig!" when Eva defied her. After being exclusively in each other's company for days, both mother and daughter, who had a low tolerance for boredom, longed to return to the excitement of London.

In addition to her work at the academy, Eva performed in several benefits in the spring of 1915, including playing Pierrot in one performance of *Le Baiser* for two thousand Belgian refugees and acting with Constance Collier in a scene from *Julius Caesar* for Shakespeare's birthday matinee at His Majesty's Theatre. For several months, she also worked evenings in one of the auxiliary war kitchens, run by the Girl Guides, that supplied hospitals with food for the returning wounded. "They were all Cockneys there," she wrote. "It was wonderful training for me."

She put the training to good use. Her first speaking part on the professional stage was Elizabeth, a Cockney maid, in a play called *The Laughter of Fools.* Lyall Swete, who had directed her in scenes at Tree's Academy, chose her after an audition that Eva found embarrassing and exciting at the same time. She stood on a bright stage, "being looked over" from the dark auditorium by Swete and Frank Curzon, the play's manager. They talked about her height. She was five foot four. Was she too tall or too short? They asked her to remove her shoes. She

For her role as Pierrot in Le Baiser *in 1915, Eva copied Sarah Bernhardt's
makeup in the part.*

did, revealing her big toe poking out of a hole in her black stocking. They laughed. They asked her to read a scene in a Cockney dialect. She dropped her *h*'s obediently. They asked her to whistle "Snooky Ookums." She "produced a rather breathy and faltering version." The men laughed again. Were they laughing at her or with her? She thought that was "the end of all my chances, and that I would be told to go away and never, never return." She fumbled for her shoes and walked to the stage door. Swete called out to her as she was leaving, "Where are you off to? I haven't told you about the rehearsal call."

She withdrew from Tree's Academy. Since the goal of the school was to train and place actors in the professional theatre, she had graduated with honors. She reported to the Prince of Wales Theatre for rehearsal and met the rest of the company. The rehearsals ran from ten until six over a period of five weeks, and her salary was three pounds a week. Frank Curzon was pleased with her progress and told her that her work "could not be better" and that she "was a born actress." To demonstrate his pleasure, he gave Eva her own dressing room "with a telephone and everything jolly!" Constance Collier showed up at a dress rehearsal to give "encouragement and some useful hints." Eva felt happy, she said, because "I had worked with the greatest conscientiousness." On opening night, she ate a large dinner and did not feel nervous. She went to the theatre early to spend time alone in her dressing room, looking at her flowers and messages of good luck and preparing herself mentally and physically for the job ahead.

Elizabeth was a character part, but "all my faults suited the part perfectly," she wrote later, "my awkwardness, my clumsy movements, my rather deep, monotonous voice, my solemnity." She played the role in "deadly earnest" and on opening night was rewarded with roars of laughter from her first "Yes'm" and "No'm." She used her academy training in stage falls to score comic points. On her second entrance, dressed in her maid's uniform with starched white apron, she carried a large tray of soup plates into the dining room, tripped and fell flat, sending the dishes flying. More laughter. On her last exit in the third act, she received her first exit applause, and at the end of the play she was given a solo call. She took her bow and saw in "the dark house . . . something white fluttering in the first balcony. It was darling Nanny, who, bursting with pride, found clapping insufficient and was waving her handkerchief madly." It was the only time Susan Stenning ever saw Eva act. She died a few years later. Always on opening nights, Le Gallienne said, "I look for that waving handkerchief and somehow feel that in spirit she is there."

Julie, so nervous that she had been unable to eat, was elated and proud. The newspapers announced the arrival of a "brilliant new comedienne." The Le Gallienne name, already familiar to London ears, along with the support of Eva and Julie's friends in the theatre community, helped create interest in Eva. "It is funny," she wrote Mogens, "as soon as one becomes a public character & a professional, as I am now, one begins to get letters from photographers asking for sittings, & from papers asking for interviews."

All the press attention was flattering, but there was one kind of attention that she didn't want. In many ways Eva was a remarkably sophisticated sixteen-year-old, far beyond other girls her own age, but in other ways she was an innocent, much more naive than her mother was at the same age. A week before the opening of *The Laughter of Fools,* Jack Hobbes, a young actor in the company, grabbed her as she walked through a dark passage in the theatre. "He took hold of me & wouldn't let me pass," Eva confided to Mogens, "& then he took me in his arms & kissed me twice on the mouth. It is the first time I have been kissed by a man & I *did'nt* like it, especially as I am *not* in love with him. He says he is with me, but I don't believe him, & I am sure he does the same to every girl he can get hold of. . . . He is so strong. Of course I did'nt respond! By the way, I need'nt tell you to keep this to yourself & if possible burn this page."

ZEPPELIN RAIDS forced *The Laughter of Fools* to close after a three-week run. "You can't imagine what it was like," Eva said. "The streets all dark, and those huge birds of prey hovering over us—and laughter only in the theatres; terror everywhere else."

Eva received seven offers for parts, but there were no guarantees that any of the plays would run for more than a week. "Why don't you go to America?" Constance Collier suggested to Julie. "It would be much better for Eva as the theatres have not suffered as much over there, & she would have every chance with the Favershams to back her, & with her wonderful notices, she should be able to do very well over there." Julie wrote to the Favershams, who cabled back, "Think plan good. Excellent chances. Try sail 24th!"

On July 23, the day before they sailed on the *St. Louis* to America, Eva appeared with an all-star cast in *Peter Ibbetson,* a performance arranged by and starring Constance Collier at His Majesty's Theatre. Once again Queen Alexandra was in the audience. Eva played the tiny part of a maid, all in French, but it was, one critic noted, "a very bright little bit of French."

In her brief professional career, Eva had played twice before the Queen and had appeared in an entire royal family of theatres, including His Majesty's, the Queen's, and the Prince of Wales. She had acted only character roles, transforming herself into four different people: Pierrot, a Florentine pageboy, a Cockney slavey, and a French maid. Two palm readers had told her that she would "have a very great success on the stage" and also "that when about 25 she would start to write as well as act & would have a great success." Eva felt sure that "fame and fortune" awaited her in America. The Favershams and Constance Collier and her old friends the Koopmans had talked to her of America as a "vast free country of inexhaustible possibilities, where the opportunities for work would be greater and more varied." America was a safe place, but she hated to leave Hesper and all her friends, and "loathed leaving . . . dear England & France especially at this terrible time."

Eva packed her new crocodile-skin dressing case engraved with the initials *ELeG,* which Mr. Philipson had given her, stowed her makeup kit and Sarah's memoirs in her trunk, and didn't forget to include Bessie, her doll of many faces. She hugged a miserable, sobbing Hesper goodbye. Who knew when they might meet again? She said au revoir to Constance, knowing that she would soon see her in America, where Collier planned to present *Peter Ibbetson.* "We started in misery," Eva said, "and left a group of forlorn people . . . but I think it was quite worse for them. . . . After all, I was up & doing, going to new & interesting things."

Seventeen years earlier, Julie Le Gallienne had crossed the Atlantic with Richard Le Gallienne in the middle of a hurricane in a futile search for fame and fortune in America. Now, she faced the journey again with their daughter. The summer sea was calm, but German submarines lurked, as well as other dangers yet unknown. Julie stood on the deck of the *St. Louis* and looked down at her "little Cat." How incredibly fast the years had gone, Julie often told her daughter. At fifty-two, she was still an elegant, striking woman, tall and straight, but she was tired. She was ready to place some of the burden she had carried on the slim shoulders of her daughter.

It was a burden, a heavy one, but it was also an entitlement, and the sixteen-year-old girl accepted willingly, eagerly. It was natural that she follow the example set by her mother and Nanny, by Sarah Bernhardt and Constance Collier—strong, working women who made their own way in the world. The responsibility for herself and for Julie, the "question of making our living," Eva Le Gallienne said, "now rested with me." She was well equipped. She had her mother's Viking blood, the health and high spirits of a young animal ready to pounce, and the intelligence and determination to conquer where Richard Le Gallienne had failed.

PART TWO

1915 - 1923

Eva, then seventeen, posing for publicity photographs
with her Chihuahua, Picot

How I do enjoy being on my own hook.

THE CROSSING on the *St. Louis* took eight days. Rough seas sent most of the passengers to their cabins, which was fine with Eva, since she had "never seen such a bevy of hideous & stupid & bromide people." She conquered her queasiness, she claimed, with willpower. Fortunately, Elsie Janis, who happened to be on board, was a good sailor, and Eva and Elsie prowled "round and round the promenade deck, and each time round we would talk in a different language or in English with a different accent."

The entrance of the *St. Louis* into New York harbor on a hot and hazy August afternoon impressed her so much that she "couldn't speak." Later, in a letter to Mogens, she described the experience: "We came in to New York in a slight fog which I thought a rather wonderful effect. First the Statue of Liberty which, tho' very fine, I could live without. But then, these amazing sky scrapers slowly emerging out of the mist, like some huge monsters, were weird & marvellous. So many people call them hideous. I don't agree there. They have their own beauty, just as impressionist pictures have theirs—to the people that understand that kind of beauty."

After the ordeal of customs, she put on a "starched grin" and talked to the press. Although the reporters primarily directed their questions to the well-known Elsie Janis (later called "the Sweetheart of the AEF" for her work entertaining the troops), they asked Le Gallienne about her acting ambitions. "I always want to do character work," the sixteen-year-old replied. "I won't play an ingenue." Motoring over the "endless" Fifty-ninth Street Bridge made her giddy, but soon she and Julie were relaxing at the Favershams' summer house in Mattituck, Long Island. The sprawling house set on sixty acres and complete with fishing pond, sandy beach, and boats was further proof for Eva that a life in the theatre could be fine indeed.

Before taking up the burden of making money, for two weeks she swam, fished, sailed, and fascinated the two Faversham boys and their friends. Fascinating the adults proved more difficult. One evening, she "had to recite 'Carillon' . . . & various other silly ass things," she wrote Hesper. "Anyway I won Auntie Julie over to my side & she now believes in me as an actress. Uncle Will always has believed in me, he & Connie always have & they were the only ones."

Using the Favershams' house on East Seventeenth Street as a base and escorted by William Faversham, Eva met most of New York's theatrical managers. In the evening, she went to the theatre. "Broadway at night is wonderful," she wrote. "You come out of a theatre & think it is sunlight. It is crammed with light & electric signs & advertisements . . . amazing after the darkness of London." What struck her about American acting was that "every actor tried to help the other. There was no feeling of selfishness as there so often is in London, when one man or woman seems to say 'I am the only one on this stage, all the others can go hang.' "

At times, she suffered "fits of homesickness & depression" and longed for her friends in London and Paris. Except for Laurette Taylor, whom she found "dear, so sweet & unaffected," she didn't like what she had seen of American girls. "They all seem to me 'henroosty,' " she wrote Hesper. "If you and Connie were over here I should be so very happy!"

Meanwhile, she worked on the three-room apartment that she and Julie had found opposite the Favershams' house at 210 East Seventeenth Street. They called it the bird's nest. They saved money by scavenging furniture from William Faversham's theatrical warehouse, and they painted and papered, using a rich, warm yellow paper for the walls, set off by black painted trim. Eva crafted bookshelves out of wooden grocery boxes for her favorite "chef d'oeuvres" of literature and for her cherished photographs: "chef d'oeuvres of nature: beautiful women."

A MONTH AND A HALF after Eva's arrival in the United States, Harrison Grey Fiske offered her a small part and several understudies in a play called *Mrs. Boltay's Daughters.* At the first rehearsal, she discovered that her small bit was Rose, a black maid. Tree's Academy, however, had not prepared her to speak black dialect. Desperate to save the job and the fifty-dollars-a-week salary, Le Gallienne explained her dilemma to Merle Maddern, a young actress who played one of the daughters. Maddern taught her the dialect, and Eva repeated the words "parrot-fashion."

On October 24, 1915, Eva Le Gallienne made her American debut at the Comedy Theatre, presenting, she wrote later, an "astonishing portrait of a colored maid with very bright blue eyes shining out of a smeary chocolate-colored face and speaking a grotesquely bewildering dialect: part British, part cockney, with here and there a dash of Irish."

When she heard that Richard Le Gallienne had seen the play, the thought of her "Daddy coming in to see his long lost daughter & finding a merlotter" made her "roar with laughter." Apparently, Richard did not attempt to contact her, since Julie had made it clear that she and Eva would have nothing to do with him. In fact, many of Richard's old friends "have chucked him," Eva confided to Hesper.

When Hesper wrote in November 1915 that she planned to come to America and live with Richard and Irma, Eva reported that the news "knocked me flat." Julie feared for Hesper and strongly objected, but Hesper was now nearly twenty-two and old enough to make her own decisions. Eva longed to see Hesper, but she laid down her conditions in a letter to her half-sister: "Only one thing must be understood . . . I don't wish to see R. LeG at all. . . . Otherwise— between you & me everything will be as always." Eva wrote to Mogens that she was amazed at Hesper's decision, since "RLeG is a very feeble staff to lean on." Her only connection with Richard Le Gallienne was the linking of their names in newspaper articles. Although she was curious about her father, for the time being Eva would remain estranged from him.

In December 1915, after just a few weeks of unemployment, she was cast as Jennie, a comic Cockney servant in Austin Strong's play *Bunny.* Strong, whom she had met at the Favershams', suggested her for the part and insisted that she be hired after the manager turned her down because he thought her authentic Cockney dialect was not believable. "No one will know over here," the manager shrugged. "Inartistic!" said Le Gallienne.

Again, on opening night, Eva didn't feel nervous. Fellow cast member Marie Tempest warned, "Just you wait till you know a little more about it; the nervousness will come, and instead of getting better as the years go on it will grow worse and worse!" *The New York Times* announced that Eva Le Gallienne "arrives on the stage with a flourish, acting . . . with high spirits and no little skill." Despite a strong, experienced cast, *Bunny* closed after a two-week New York run.

Determined to occupy her idle hours and add to her growing library, Eva had plucked five volumes of Gibbon's *The History of the Decline and Fall of the Roman Empire* from the set of *Bunny* and had begun reading during her waits between scenes. An ardent book lover—"just like your father," Mam would say—she was in the "midst of a veritable orgy of reading." Between her visits to theatrical managers, she frequented the New York Public Library, where she discovered Walt Whitman. She also read Ibsen's plays, "particularly . . . *The Master Builder,*" and listed the parts she wanted to play by the time she was thirty-five: Hilda in *The Master Builder,* Hedda Gabler, Peter Pan, Marguerite Gautier in *La Dame aux camélias,* Juliet, and the Duke of Reichstadt in *L'Aiglon.*

While Eva focused on developing her inner experience, Julie, who knew the importance of individual style, worked on her daughter's outer appearance. Dresses, skirts, and coats in Eva's favorite blues, violets, and purples were chosen for their long, lean, monochromatic lines, without fussy details or frills, making her appear taller. At five-four, three inches shorter than Julie, Eva was sensitive about her height and usually added two inches when anyone asked how tall she was. She depended on and deferred to her mother's taste, and on her theatrical rounds she was elegantly dressed, hatted, and gloved. Intensely professional, solemn and serious, with impeccable European manners, a resonant, flexible voice, and the energy and vitality of youth, Eva made a distinct impression on managers, who were more used to giggling girls. Her father's name and her sponsor Will Faversham were also assets in the small world of New York theatre.

Producer George C. Tyler, who had introduced Mrs. Patrick Campbell and Eleonora Duse to the American stage and who had produced Faversham's hit *The Squaw Man,* auditioned Eva for a new play called *The Melody of Youth,* by Brandon Tynan. Could she talk with a brogue? he asked. "Yes," she fibbed. Tyler assigned her the part of Mary Powers, an Irish ingenue. "Not very thrilling," said Eva. "I have to make myself look as pretty as possible, & be as sweet as can be." The brogue didn't present a problem—Laurette Taylor coached her, and since Eva had seen *Peg o' My Heart* a dozen times in London, she merely imitated Taylor's speech and pitched her voice into a higher register.

The laughter that she had to produce on cue in the middle of the second act presented an entirely different problem. "The solution of merely seeing something funny and laughing at it never occurred to me," she wrote later. "I was not sufficiently relaxed for that." She would pursue the art of relaxation for years to come, battling with tenseness "until it is eliminated in everything but your hands; you succeed in chasing it out of them, and find it turns up in your toes! If you banish it from your throat it will lodge in your solar-plexus, effectively killing all true flow of emotion!" Other cast members gave her advice and kidded her about "that dreaded laugh" and tried to help her. They also teased her about her constant reading and study. When one of the actors saw her reading *Romeo and Juliet* and made fun of her, Eva decided to "keep my dreams and ambitions strictly to myself." Sensitive and easily hurt by even good-humored criticism, she learned to disguise her studious nature except with those who shared similar passions.

The Melody of Youth had a four-month run, and on the seventy-five dollars a week that Eva earned, she and Mam lived quite comfortably and "were able to start a savings account and felt quite prosperous." She felt quite popular, too. She was the new girl in town, and *Town and Country* featured her, looking winsome and girlish, wearing a ruffled, beribboned costume and broad-brimmed hat pulled fashionably low over her right eye, in part to disguise the fact that her right eyebrow drooped lower than her left. As she grew older, the droop of her right eyebrow grew more pronounced, but Le Gallienne became adept at disguising that fact. She also exploited the difference, often to comic effect, by raising or lowering her eyebrows independently of one another.

HER SUCCESS in *The Melody of Youth* led to her first leading role, Patricia Molloy in *Mr. Lazarus,* a light comedy which allowed her to play a boardinghouse servant transformed into a Cinderella-like beauty through the kindness of a stranger who may be her lost father. *Mr. Lazarus* played New Haven, Washington, D.C., and a short season in Chicago before finally opening in New York for a brief run. In his review of the play, John Corbin of *The New York Times* noted that "Miss Le Gallienne plays with a delicacy of which she has hitherto remained unsuspected. In her first two appearances here last season she bounced and whooped it up scandalously, but this is all gone. Perhaps she is mending her ways."

In a letter to Mogens, written August 16, 1916, on the train between Chicago and Atlantic City, just over a year since her arrival in America, Eva poured out her news and her impressions:

My dear Mogie—

I feel very much ashamed of myself for not having written to you for such an age—but I just simply hav'nt had the energy. The 9 weeks season we had in Chicago was very tiring owing to the immense heat & then the terrible Western custom of playing Sunday nights, which means that you never have a night off. . . . And this part is especially tiring. You see, not being a master of technique & the tricks of my trade, I simply have to throw myself heart & soul into the part & really *become* Patricia Molloy, in order to create the illusion. I don't think I've been so terrified in my life as I was the first night when we opened in New Haven which is fortunately a small town—for I played badly—. I was so nervous that I couldn't feel or think of what I was doing—I just walked through the part as in a dream, & felt sort of dazed & bewildered & profoundly depressed. I had indigestion for a week from nerves—& altogether I was most absurd. By the time we reached Chicago I was quite at home in my part & at ease, & gave a good performance the first night & got wonderful notices much to my delight. For tho' I had received good notices at the other towns I knew I had'nt deserved them. I think if you're honest with yourself you can always tell wether you're good or not. Now we are on our way to Atlantic City where we play till Saturday—then two days at a little town near New York called Stamford—& then! several weeks holiday! Hurra! I'm simply dying for a rest. . . . You ask me what I think of Chicago? I will tell you—: It is more American than any other city I have yet been in. New York is very cosmopolitan & is not so very different from London or Paris in atmosphere. But Chicago has all the materialism, crudeness & brute strength of the young animal. It is full of energy & vigor. Absolutely commercial.

From what I could make out, art means rather little to them. There are a great many young men all trying to become great men in the artistic world. Impressionist painters of the maddest style. Young poets who lose money madly by publishing their books of "free verse" & peculiar eccentric magazines of the most radical types. These represent Chicago art. Very interesting & new & struggling.

Influenced by the steady presence of Julie Le Gallienne, who traveled with her daughter, Eva showed unusual intelligence and maturity. In letter after letter to Mogens and Hesper, sometimes using the Olympian tone that had marked her writing even as a child, she examined her life with the same penetrating insights she brought to the exploration of a new part.

On Americans: "It is to me amazing to see the ignorance [of] old art or literature or anything that is old in fact. They seem to be essentially a race for the present & the future. The past seems to matter little. I suppose that is natural. It is like a child & they are a race of children."

On acting: "When I get a new part, I always read it thro' & then imagine it— see it before me, walking, talking, living—all quite away from myself. I examine it in this way & make friends with it, & when I play I am two different people, myself & at the same time the character I happen to be playing. . . . I never 'study' a part, as so many actresses do. They sit with the lines in their hand & learn it by heart & walk through it. I do it all in my head, in my imagination. When I'm preparing to create a new part, I think of nothing else. All day long, whatever I may be doing, or whoever I may be with, I live with the character, going over scenes with it, learning to know and care for it, till it becomes another self."

On her career: "As you progress in the profession, first nights become more & more terrible—that is because you realize that you have a certain reputation to uphold. When you're quite a beginner & have never done anything at all, it doesn't matter so very much if you make a hit or not, but just now, it would be fatal for me to make a failure & therefore nerves grow on you more & more, & I nearly go mad before the first performance. . . . New York has now been able to see me as a mulatto, as a cockney slavey, as a cockney coquette & as an Irish ingenue. I've really had the most amazing luck."

On one subject, however, her tone changed from Olympian certainty to adolescent confusion as she struggled to define and articulate feelings that puzzled her. Mogens again became her confidant. In December 1915 she wrote: "[Merle Maddern] is the only person to whom I have felt at all attracted since I have been over here. . . . You know what I'm like. . . . I want just one or two people I really love—& the rest can go hang. It is strange too, that boys or young men don't interest or attract me in the least, so I have no 'amours' to tell you about. Mother is always saying how peculiar I am about it! She says she used to be a 'divil' at my

age, flirting & liking men to make love to her. I have no such wishes, however. . . . You know, they say one can never be a great artist till one has known 'la
divine amour.' I should love to hear what you think on the subject."

In another letter written to Mogens, in February 1916, she took up the subject
again. "It is curious, young men don't attract me at all! I've never been in love
nor thought of it. I have one or two very good boyfriends of whom I am very
fond, but we are 'comrades' & it ends there. You will say I am very young to
think of anything else but it seems to me most girls think of nothing but flirting
from the age of 14 & up. There must be something peculiar with me for I never
give it a thought."

From her mother, Eva had learned that she should be true to her own nature,
and clearly she knew that she was attracted romantically to women. While she
believed "that a great many girls are fools, that doesn't prevent them from being
attractive," especially beautiful women like Merle Maddern, whose picture she
added to her bookshelf gallery of beauties, which included Bernhardt, Constance Collier, and various artistic female nudes. Except for Mogens all her close
relationships were with other females. Her first kiss from a boy had been forced
and unpleasant. Still, while she was not attracted to boys, she enjoyed teasing
them. She flirted with and tried to fascinate young men, such as her co-star, Tom
Powers, in *Mr. Lazarus,* who had fallen in love with her. She encouraged his attentions and the company of other young men who escorted her to the theatre
and to parties. She delighted in playing the role of femme fatale with many
admirers—a role she had observed Julie play often.

Eva denied it emphatically, but she loved being adored. "No!" she told Mogens, who had sent her an admiring letter. "You mustn't think I am so wonderful. I'm not at all! No! No! I've just been fortunate enough to have had an
exceptionally interesting existence & therefore I probably have broader & ma-
turer ideas than most girls of my age." Eva did have "broader" ideas. Her hori-
zons were not circumscribed by traditional expectations, and she simply did not
recognize any boundaries in her development as a person. At an early age, she
possessed a strong, intact self. Her soul was that of a searching artist; her vitality
and her appetite for experience were enormous. And she had the good fortune
to grow up in an atmosphere free of stifling bourgeois conventions. Her mother
had taught her "to become a thinking being, free in one's soul," and her father
had obeyed no code "but the . . . shifting morality of the artist." Like her parents, Eva Le Gallienne followed her own desires—even if she knew those desires
were different or even strange.

In February 1916, Eva had claimed that she wasn't giving love a thought,
but by the fall of 1916, the seventeen-year-old was thinking about *amour* a great

deal. From a Danish cousin, she had learned of Mogens's new friend, a young man. With subtle delicacy, she wrote Mogens: "I understand so well what you feel for him & I wish I could talk with you about him. It is impossible to write those things. You understand." Mogens did understand, and Eva soon told him about her feelings for her special friend. "I have a wonderful friend," she confided, "Margaret Mower . . . she is like a Princess." Later, she wrote Mogens that while Margaret was "not a very good actress," she had "the sort of beauty that makes you want to fall down on your knees and worship it. She has without doubt the most perfect mouth I ever saw on any human being. Full of wonderful curves, very red & passionate. She has auburn hair and blue eyes. I think you would love her. I do." In Margaret Mower, Eva had met someone like herself, someone to share all the joys of first love—it was an exhilarating, affirming experience for Eva, made even more exciting because Margaret, who spoke impeccable French, was appearing with Sarah Bernhardt during Bernhardt's American tour.

At Bernhardt's opening at the Empire Theatre in December 1916, Le Gallienne sat in a front-row seat in the balcony, and she leapt to her feet with the rest of the audience to applaud Bernhardt's art and her gallantry in continuing to act even after the amputation of her leg. Neither age nor a wooden leg could dim Bernhardt's radiance. Eva had saved petals from the flowers Bernhardt had given her in Paris, and she kept them in a gold locket which she wore for good luck when she performed. She also collected Bernhardt anecdotes. Fifteen minutes before the operation to remove her leg, Sarah, who had tied her hair up with little white ribbons, looked in the mirror and exclaimed, "Oh! I look like a girl at her first communion!" When Sarah's American manager wired her and asked if she would exhibit her leg, Sarah immediately wired back, "Which one?"

During Bernhardt's New York tour, Eva attended every performance. She visited Bernhardt backstage, where Sarah signed the memoirs that Eva had so painstakingly copied. Bernhardt allowed her to stand backstage near the stage entrance, and Eva watched as Sarah, "talking, talking, talking—a constant flow of words, sometimes punctuated by a scream, 'Crétin!' or 'Sal boche!,' " was carried in a sedan chair from her dressing room to the stage. She never forgot Bernhardt's portrayal of Jeanne d'Arc, and later described "that amazing moment when this woman of seventy-six, wearing an artificial leg which caused her untold misery, stood facing the judges and in answer to the question, 'Jeanne, quel âge as-tu?' unhesitatingly replied, 'J'ai dix-huit ans!' Everyone in that audience believed her, and rightly—for at that moment it was true."

ON JANUARY 11, 1917, Eva turned eighteen and marked the occasion by beginning a diary—a practice she would continue sporadically for the next sixty-

*In her first leading role, as
Patricia Molloy in* Mr. Lazarus,
*Eva transformed from a servant
girl (above) into an engaged
young woman (below).*

six years. "I am 18 and getting nervous," she wrote. "And yet 18 is a much better age than 16—one begins to feel one's power—the power of youth & a fair amount of decent looks, & a certain glamour that goes with the stage."

Julie and Eva had recently moved to a new, larger apartment, enabling Julie to give afternoon parties. To celebrate Eva's birthday, Julie invited Hesper (who had moved from Richard's house in Rowayton, Connecticut, to her own apartment in the city); an assortment of titled ladies; writer and lecturer Lewis Hind; theatre people William and Julie Faversham, Maxine Elliott, Lyall Swete, and Estelle Winwood; and various newspaper reporters. One of the reporters scrutinized the Le Gallienne girls and observed that they "make a curious and interesting study, for Eva is very like her Norse mother, while Hesper, the child of Le Gallienne's early days, is exactly like her father." Although he was not invited to the party, Richard Le Gallienne sent three books to Eva and flowers to her and Julie. "I felt rather strange—decidedly so," wrote Eva. "It seemed so funny getting flowers from him."

Tom Powers, her *Mr. Lazarus* co-star and frequent escort to dances and the theatre, called in the afternoon and "stayed ages," she wrote. "Poor devil I felt he was on the verge of saying things & kept hindering him & finally got him to the door & rang for the lift & then he took me in his arms & told me in French how much he cared. Poor old Tom. The lift interrupted him. I told him I'd write. It's the first time anyone has acted so with me. I'm sorry I can't make him happy." After enacting this mock-romantic scene, Eva attended a supper party at the Favershams', where she was made to recite "Tipperary Days"—an anticlimax to a heady, exciting day. The fact remained that she was "getting nervous" because she was responsible for herself and her mother and didn't have a job.

When *Mr. Lazarus* closed in the fall of 1916, she had had several offers, and accepted the ingenue lead in *Mile-a-Minute Kendall,* an Oliver Morosco production. At the final dress rehearsal, producer Morosco saw the play and "was disgusted" with the performances and the approach taken by the director. He took over the rehearsals, and Le Gallienne remembered, "Every point . . . every nuance, every note of tender sincerity, every pause, the whole musical fabric . . . was discarded and shattered. In its place were substituted speed, noise, pep, punch and the other ingredients . . . considered essential to the success of a Broadway production." She tried, but she couldn't satisfy Morosco's ideal of an ingenue, and he fired her.

"What a salutary blow it was to me, after all!" Le Gallienne wrote in her first autobiography, *At 33.* "Every bit of conceit was knocked clean out of me and as I sat licking my wounds . . . I realized what a silly fool I had been . . . and saw the immensity of all I would have to learn if I was ever to be allowed one day, many years from then, to serve the Theatre with some degree of competence."

High-sounding words, but evidently Le Gallienne at thirty-three had forgotten what she had written in her diary in 1917. Eighteen-year-old Eva didn't creep into a corner and "lick her wounds." Far from losing faith in her, when they discovered she was available, managers sought her out. She replaced an actress in a play called *In for the Night* by James Savery, which had opened on January 11. "I couldn't play the part as it is, but my idea is to get them to completely rewrite it," Le Gallienne said, "make it French & young & attractive & . . . plus chic!" The other cast members resented the changes and extra rehearsals (at that time actors were not paid for rehearsals, only for performances), but Le Gallienne convinced the playwright to rewrite her part, and even had a role written in for her new little Chihuahua, Picot.

The play closed after twenty-eight performances, and once again she was out of work. In between her rounds of managers' offices, she visited and lunched with Constance Collier, had a film test ("but the man wanted a vampire and I looked—alas—too innocent"), rode horses in Central Park, saw plays, went out to dinner, danced almost every night, and sat for her portrait for the handsome painter and set designer Ben Ali Haggin.

At a party at Ben Ali Haggin's, William Faversham introduced her to Eleonora Sears. Eighteen years older than Le Gallienne, who looked at her with awe, Sears became another of Eva's role models, a guide for the young woman, who actively sought out female mentors. The friendship of "Eleo" (as everyone called her) and Eva would endure until Sears's death in 1968. Eleo was the great-great-granddaughter of Thomas Jefferson, an heiress to a real estate and shipping fortune, and a society leader in her hometown of Boston and in Newport and New York as well. One of the most fascinating personalities of her time, Eleo Sears pioneered and popularized women's sports. An outstanding tennis player and four-time women's doubles champion, she excited the tennis world by rolling up her sleeves and exposing her bare arms when she played. For decades she was America's finest horsewoman. Before World War I she played polo with men's teams, wore pants, and rode astride. Sermons were preached against her, gossip circulated about her sexual preference, but with her money and power she laughed off the criticism and continued to do exactly as she pleased. Although Sears was briefly engaged to Harold S. Vanderbilt, she never married, preferring the company of women. Her good friend the Prince of Wales, later King Edward VIII, said that she was his "favorite dance, squash, and tennis partner."

She became Eva Le Gallienne's favorite tennis partner as well. Eleo Sears called Eva "Le Gal," and while the two women were not intimate friends, they shared their different lives with one another. They played tennis, went to sporting events, and whenever Le Gallienne appeared in a play in Boston, she visited Eleo and gave her theatre tickets. To know and be influenced by this remarkable woman was fortunate for Le Gallienne, who had always been lucky in her choice

Eleonora Sears, America's first woman super-athlete, c. 1917.
She won more than 240 trophies, battled for women's equality in sports,
and was inducted into both the Horsemen's Hall of Fame
and the Tennis Hall of Fame.

of mentors. Years later, she reflected on "the value of hero worship—now become suspect. It has merely gone underground, for it is a basic property." The late nineteenth century produced many women like Eleo—"a company of Amazons," Katherine Anne Porter called them. "Freedom to them meant precisely freedom from men and their stuffy rules for women."

LE GALLIENNE MOVED both in select society circles and among the theatre elite. On February 4, 1917, she attended a dance at New York's Coterie Club with Lynn Fontanne, Laurette Taylor, and Taylor's husband, J. Hartley Manners, author of *Peg o' My Heart*. There she danced with John Barrymore. She found him different from what she had expected, "very serious and intense & I should imagine very ironical & cynical. I have the feeling he's laughing at everyone all the time." Later, they all went to Douglas Fairbanks's party for Mary Pickford at the Algonquin, where Le Gallienne saw Elsie Janis and other theatre friends, danced with Barrymore, Fairbanks, and some "new men," and met an attractive Miss Fernandez and made a date with her, only to snub her later when she learned that Miss Fernandez was not nearly so attractive in the daytime—"the Spanish senorita evidently only an evening product."

Caught up in her mother's social whirl, which involved the Favershams' theatre and society circle as well as Eva's own widening group of friends and acquaintances, she was often torn between Julie's scheduled lunches, teas, and fittings, and her own full calendar. Her late nights (she often stayed out until 4:30 a.m. dancing) began to strain her relationship with her mother as well. It must have been difficult for Julie to see her "Cat" growing up and away from her. Thus, the atmosphere in their flat was often stormy, sometimes escalating into *drames*, Eva said, between the two strong women.

Still, Julie and Eva lunched and shopped together, often joined by Hesper or Margaret Mower. On the rare evenings Eva spent at home, she read or played with a Ouija board, trying to puzzle out the future. She continued to study in the main reading room of the public library. "There is so much to read & everything interests me so much," she enthused. "I want to read everything & I don't know where to begin. One should have 100 brains & 100 eyes to be able to read all one would like to."

Whenever she could, she saw Margaret Mower. "It was wonderful to see her again," Eva wrote on January 13, 1917. "I made her some food & altogether took great care of her. I realized afterwards that love can make even the most selfish of people forget themselves for I found that I had myself eaten nothing, nor thought of food, tho I afterwards felt myself to be very hungry."

She went again to see Bernhardt, who was playing in Brooklyn in *La Reine Hécube* and appeared like "a shell of her old self . . . not even trying to act."

Afterwards, Le Gallienne stood in the doorway of Bernhardt's dressing room and watched a "completely absorbed" Sarah, a roll of bills in one hand, "counting out sums of money." Sarah looked up. "Suddenly it was as though a light had been turned on," Le Gallienne remembered.

> The entrancing smile, the graciousness, the charm—sheer magic. . . . She put the money down on the make-up shelf and beckoned me to come to her. . . . She had mistaken me for someone else, for she thanked me effusively for "ces beaux mouchoirs," and I knew I hadn't sent her any handkerchiefs. I went over and knelt beside her chair. For the last time I looked up into that extraordinary face; the make-up was heavier than ever, and carelessly put on. She looked a thousand years old, yet somehow ageless. . . . I asked her if there was nothing I could do for her; she thanked me but said her maid had gone out to fetch something and would be back directly. I kissed her hand and started towards the door. Suddenly, in a voice like a girl's, she cried out, "La semaine prochaine je rentre en France!" She looked entirely different—young and radiant. She's a magician—a witch, I thought. I smiled back at her and waved goodbye.

At about the same time that Le Gallienne said goodbye to Sarah, she became infatuated with another artist whom she would idolize and study—Russian-born Alla Nazimova, who was starring in *Ception Shoals* in New York. When Eva saw the thirty-eight-year-old Nazimova act for the first time, she was overcome. "It was too marvellous. Nazimova, I mean, the play not so. I think Nazimova is the only actress over here who has a touch of Sarah's greatness. It's because she isn't afraid. She doesn't try to please the public. She tries to make them think & live." Under the management of the Shuberts ten years earlier, Nazimova had played in Ibsen's *Hedda Gabler, A Doll's House,* and *The Master Builder* in New York. In 1915 she played the Keith vaudeville circuit and vamped on the silent screen. With her pale skin, dark blue eyes with thick-fringed lashes, and her sinuous body that struck improbable poses, Nazimova seemed the embodiment of the female vampire, a characterization that she loathed. She aspired to art, not caricature, and she wanted something to do, she wrote her sister in 1914, to regain her self-respect. In the play *Ception Shoals,* she played Eve, the daughter of a lighthouse keeper, and exploited her exotic dark-haired beauty by appearing in a bathing suit, her body glistening with mineral oil to appear wet.

Eva became almost a daily visitor to *Ception Shoals.* Walter Wanger, Nazimova's manager, befriended her and told her she could have seats whenever she liked. While she and Margaret Mower had "a great strong feeling" for one another, Eva was beginning to feel a growing "*culte* for the marvellous creature" Nazimova. When Nazimova heard about the young actress who attended her performances so faithfully, she sent a note to Eva and asked her to come back to her dressing room. The older woman welcomed the adulation of such an attractive young admirer, and if she did not see Eva at a performance, she would ask, "Isn't Miss Le Gallienne here? Where is Miss Le Gallienne?" Nazimova invited Eva to join her company and go on tour with her, but Le Gallienne had already committed herself to a West Coast tour of *Mr. Lazarus.*

Nazimova being Russian, Eva explained to Mogens, "she has quite a strong & fascinating accent, full of rolling 'rrrr's' and other weird & russian sounds. She is not beautiful, but elf-like—she has tremendous magnetism—not the sort of attractive, charming magnetism Laurette has, but a strong, compelling, passionate magnetism that just seizes you & carries you right off your mental feet, till you don't know what you're doing or saying or thinking."

Magnetism, charisma, sexual allure—whatever the name, it's the force shared by all great actors who can enthrall and hold an audience: a force that unites mind, body, and voice until all are one and inseparable, flowing into one another with a kind of inevitable power. Infatuated with Nazimova the woman, Eva studied her magnetism just as she had studied Bernhardt's. Before she left on her tour, Eva visited Nazimova for "a marvellous hour" and took away a picture of her to add to her collection.

A FEW DAYS LATER, on March 8, 1917, Julie and Eva boarded the train for the long trip to San Francisco. Eva took along *The Daisy,* a play by Ferenc Molnár which had been translated from Hungarian into English and the setting transplanted to Cockney London. Aware of Eva's other Cockney roles, director Alexander Leftvich wanted her to play the leading role of Julie. The part "cast a spell" over her, and she perceived that the play was superior to anything she had worked on before. Her other travel reading, mostly French, included Baudelaire's *Les Fleurs du mal, Les Poésies nouvelles* by Alfred de Musset, *Les Misérables, La Dame aux camélias,* Whitman's *Leaves of Grass,* and the lyric poetry of Sappho.

Undoubtedly still under the influence of Nazimova, at the first rehearsal of *Mr. Lazarus* (renamed *The Happy Stranger*), Eva "fairly vamped" her co-star Raymond Van Sickle "off his feet" and took him to lunch with her. Then she "hawled him back to the theatre & rehearsed him stiff for an hour." The boy responded appropriately. He "hangs round me all the time & keeps paying me compliments," Eva wrote. "I'm afraid I don't snub him—why should I deprive myself of an adorer? It all adds to the fun of life."

She didn't limit her vamping to her fellow actors, but during the tour she practiced her skills on anyone attractive who happened to be around. Picot's veterinarian had a "wonderful son of 16" and Eva "fell in love with him at once, and determined to vamp him violently. I finally got him to say he wished he didn't have to work so he could come to the theatre. Then of course I got him to give up his work & asked him to come and stand in the wings & watch the play. He is most attractive. I got him quite devoted. I gave him a picture. I had a strange feeling of possession."

The Happy Stranger played a two-week run in San Francisco, followed by a series of one-night stands in Arizona. Audiences liked the play and found the seventy-two-year-old star, W. H. Crane, especially appealing and enjoyed watching blue-eyed Eva, her long golden-brown hair streaming down her back, transform herself from a grubby maid to a lovely maiden. Crane's reliance on Le Gallienne to remember his lines as well as her own kept her occupied onstage. "It was certainly splendid training," she recalled. "There was scarcely a performance when the darling old man did not forget some lines, and always in different scenes! I was kept busy keeping my mind and emotions on my own mood, and at the same time holding myself in readiness . . . when I saw that S.O.S. look in his eye!"

Most of the time, though, despite the novelty of new sights, she was "bored to death." She missed Hesper, Margaret Mower, and New York and moaned that there was "no one at all thrilling within 500 miles!" She wrote letter after letter to Margaret Mower and when she never received a reply, she decided that Margaret had forgotten about her or had found someone else. Eva stopped writing and vowed to become a "hardened cynic." If she didn't have something to occupy her mind entirely, Eva told her mother, she got "restless and dissatisfied and grumpy." This was hardly news to Julie. The strain of traveling with her exceedingly vital daughter finally became too much for her—and even for tiny Picot, who was ailing and nervous as well. Julie and the dog stayed in Pasadena and took a ten-day holiday while Eva traveled with the *Happy Stranger* company to Arizona.

"Arizona is the most marvelous place I ever saw," Eva wrote Mogens. "Nothing but desert—the sun baking down on red rocks and sand and the sky *couleur de lapis lazuli.* The only plants cactus of many kinds & weird shapes." In Bisbee, she put on overalls and a hard hat and crawled on all fours through the Copper Queen mine, exhorting every workman she met to "be sure and attend the play!"

Reunited with Julie in Pasadena, she found that her mother looked "splendid—at least 10 years younger." Julie urged her daughter to rest, but Eva declared that "the boredom of this life seems terrific after the excitement of one-nighters." To allay her boredom, she studied Russian, speaking with Nazimova's accent to help her get into the spirit. She persuaded a member of the company to teach her to drive and learned easily—in "five minutes," she boasted. Her lifelong romance with cars and driving stemmed from the "marvelous feeling" it gave her, "a sensation of power—possession," she explained.

When she learned that the *Happy Stranger* tour would end prematurely, leaving her unemployed until the *Daisy* rehearsals began in New York, she took a summer-stock job with the Alcazar Theatre in San Francisco. For the first time, eighteen-year-old Eva handled the business negotiations without Julie's help or presence. "I feigned absolute indifference," she said. "[The manager] offered 100—and I beat him up to 160 and fares . . . including sleepers. That was pretty good . . . I think I shall always handle all my own business myself."

During her three-month stay in San Francisco, she performed in *The Cinderella Man, The Rio Grande,* and *Pierre of the Plains,* a silly melodrama with silent-screen cowboy William Boyd. She played twelve performances a week while rehearsing at the same time. Richard Bennett, the star of the company, who also directed *The Cinderella Man,* "was a splendid actor," Le Gallienne wrote, "abominably rude . . . but invariably right." He pointed out and ridiculed her annoying mannerisms, such as nodding her head on particular lines or making unmotivated staccato movements with her right hand.

The work was exhausting, the plays mediocre, but it was excellent training; and the more work Le Gallienne had, the better she liked it. "How I pity those people that have no work in which to center all their thoughts and activities and ambitions," Eva told Mogens. "It's so wonderful to work and make one's own living."

Leaving the orbit of New York theatre to tour was invaluable in her development. For the rest of her life Le Gallienne would tell young actors that the best education they could have would be to get out of New York and tour, preferably in repertory. Keeping a role fresh on a long tour, handling diverse audiences, coping with boredom, building stamina and character, dealing with different directors, actors, and managers, plus managing the petty details of daily life on the road were all welcome challenges. She was experiencing the freedom of creating a life for herself. "How I do enjoy being on my own hook," she wrote. It didn't matter what others did; she would choose her own path. A mystic friend once told Le Gallienne that she was "born to be always alone & yet surrounded by people." She agreed. "I feel that so strongly."

Her introduction to the wide-open expanses of the West (plus the time she had to think and dream) broadened her outlook, sparking grandiose visions, charming in their unabashed youthful joy. "I'm not going to let the lazy spirit of America ruin my enthusiasm & determination," she crowed. "I'm going to rise to the very top of my art & I'm going to rouse the people of this somnolent country someday!"

EUROPE CALLED and America roused itself enough that summer of 1917 to send the first of its troops to France. American theatre, too, was rousing itself.

Again, the wake-up call came from Europe—culturally decades ahead of America. The Swiss designer Adolphe Appia and the English designer Gordon Craig had published revolutionary ideas which advocated freeing the stage from the tyranny of literalism. In Germany, producer-director Max Reinhardt experimented with theatrical spectacle, and in Russia, Konstantin Stanislavsky's Moscow Art Theatre brought acting to a higher level of art. Already rich in the tradition of established institutional theatres, Berlin, Paris, and London blossomed with small art theatres presenting provocative new dramas. Americans traveling on the Continent paid attention to this theatrical ferment and envied Europe's cultural riches. Immigrants, especially on New York's Lower East Side, yearned for the culture they had left behind and packed the Irving Place Theatre to see foreign stars play Gorky, Ibsen, Shaw, and Molnár.

In New York and in cities around the country art theatres sprang up. Many of these, like the Provincetown Players, founded in 1915 by George Cram Cook, hoped to establish permanent repertory companies along the lines of the great European theatres. As the century progressed, the American theatre would follow two distinct paths: art and show business. Sometimes the paths would intersect, but for the most part the contrast was clear. In a few years, Eva Le Gallienne would choose which path she would follow. Later, she would champion her choice, but at the moment she and her mother depended on her paycheck, so the luxury of making this choice was not possible.

Upon her return to New York in the fall of 1917, Le Gallienne found that the production of *The Daisy* had been cancelled. Since she had felt sure of playing Julie, she had not kept in touch with managers, and once again she returned to the business of making rounds and selling herself to producers. Almost immediately she was cast in a small part in *Saturday to Monday*, a new comedy by William J. Hurlbut, which had an interesting premise: a husband and his suffragist wife agree on a marriage contract binding them to spend only weekends together (hence the title). By the final curtain the suffragist has decided to become a seven-day-a-week wife, and the play degenerates into "incredible burlesque," said one reviewer. The *New York Times* critic noted the "rather astonishing vitality" that Eva Le Gallienne brought to her small part. The play soon closed—deservedly, Le Gallienne felt—after only sixteen performances.

"The average plays here in New York are awful," Eva wrote Mogens. "There have been innumerable failures—& the business in the theatres is very poor." The great artistic and financial success of the season was *Peter Ibbetson*. Starring Constance Collier and both John and Lionel Barrymore, the play garnered wonderful reviews and lines at the box office. "I was so happy for Constance Collier's sake," Eva continued to Mogens. "She worked so hard to get it put on—& for two years she went round trying to get the managers interested in it. But they were such fools—they could neither see the beauty or the commercial value of it. So then she collected the money herself & produced it."

When *Saturday to Monday* closed, William Faversham came to Eva's rescue and gave her a small role in his all-star revival of *Lord and Lady Algy.* Wearing a clinging satin gown and wafting a "huge emerald green ostrich feather fan," eighteen-year-old Eva played a primarily ornamental role, which left her time for more intellectual pursuits such as observing an earlier generation of personality actors. The only possible reason for the production of such a weak play, one critic conjectured, was for the pleasure of viewing Maxine Elliott from every possible angle as she crossed with metronomelike precision from right to left to center and back right again.

Later, Le Gallienne described the impact of Maxine Elliott:

> She sometimes took me to lunch at Child's, then on Broadway not far from the Broadhurst Theatre where we were rehearsing. The entire restaurant ceased to function for a moment as she entered. Her beauty was so incredible it took people's breath away. Very simply dressed in . . . violet corduroy that matched the violet of her eyes which were set in her head with what the Irish used to call "a smutty finger"—no make-up needed or used. A cream-like complexion. . . . Black hair and eyelashes so long & black that, had they been false, they would have seemed excessive! No wonder all heads turned. . . . And this was when she must have been close to fifty. . . . She used to say to me sometimes: "Eva! Never be a great beauty!" I assured her that this was an impossibility. "You suffer two deaths," she continued, "and the first is by far the worse."

One night during the run of *Lord and Lady Algy,* Eva waited backstage with Maxine Elliott. "Something had gone wrong with the performance," she remembered. "The house was packed. Miss Elliott turned to me. 'Never mind,' she said. 'We have their money.' "

Ethel Barrymore, who had met Eva at the Favershams', was sorry to see Eva playing such a foolish role in *Lord and Lady Algy.* "Come with me and I'll give you a better part," she said. The part was that of her daughter, the ingenue lead in Barrymore's new production, *The Off Chance,* at the Empire Theatre—a drawing-room comedy which opened in February 1918.

The two seasons Le Gallienne spent playing and touring with Ethel Barrymore in 1918 and 1919 "were of immense importance," she believed, in the development of her work. She appeared in two plays with Ethel, *The Off Chance* and *Belinda.* The plays were simple vehicles for Ethel Barrymore to display her polished skill. In both plays Eva was cast as Barrymore's daughter, and in voice and presence their likeness was considerable. Eva's work was sound art, said the critics, "skillful and charming" and "girlishly fresh." Le Gallienne gave the credit to Ethel Barrymore. "It is impossible to overestimate the advantage to young players working at the side of the great ones of their profession," she said. "Unconsciously rather than consciously you absorb the best elements in acting. The whole theatre is imbued with the psychic force of a great actor, and the atmosphere becomes curiously charged with a compelling vitality. Nothing can be careless, uninteresting, or humdrum in such surroundings."

It was a great honor to be invited to play in Barrymore's company, a group noted for high-quality acting. Ethel detested bad acting and could not bring herself even to speak to an incompetent actor. (The story goes that when asked what were the three most dreadful words in the English language, Barrymore replied, "Cornelia Otis Skinner.") It was Ethel Barrymore's impeccable timing, though, that had the most influence on Le Gallienne. Ethel could take an "absolutely banal" line, Le Gallienne remembered, like "Are we ready? Why don't we go?" and with her delivery evoke a roar of applause from the audience. From Ethel she also inherited the *look,* which Eva called "number eight" and made into her own, but whenever she used it onstage, she thought of Miss Barrymore. The look—head tilted, left eyebrow raised over a glaring, unblinking eye, right eyebrow lowered over a slightly closed eye—could shrink a latecomer into cowering submission or stop a cougher in mid-cough.

Sometimes Ethel was difficult, didn't show up for rehearsals, was in a vile temper, or forgot her lines and Le Gallienne had to prompt her. "Ethel was like a thundercloud," Eva wrote one day on tour. "I hate her sometimes." Playing daughter to such a tempestuous mother cannot have been easy, but it was also a privilege, and Le Gallienne had the sense to know it. "Underneath any moodiness or occasional temperamental fireworks," Eva said, "[Ethel] has a warmth and a generosity of spirit which compel undying devotion in anyone who has ever known her."

ON NEW YEAR'S DAY, 1918, Eva wondered what 1918 would be like: "It should be interesting. But then nearly all my years are interesting—& that's a great deal." As the year progressed, Eva felt that she had been blessed by a lucky star. She had interesting work with Ethel Barrymore; and she had fallen in love, had found "her wonderful one," the divine *amour* that she had yearned for—a prerequisite, she believed, in the development of her artistic self.

Her "wonderful one" was Mary Duggett, a pretty extra in the *Lord and Lady Algy* company. Although she was ten years older than Eva, Mary Duggett looked quite young. Mary—or "Mimsey," Eva called her—was tall and willowy, with long legs, a sweet, dimpled face, and a beguiling smile. Time after time, when

Ethel Barrymore and Eva in The Off Chance, *1918. When Barrymore missed
rehearsals, Eva would play Ethel's part as well as her own, "just for fun."*

Eva argued with her mother or was out of sorts and "in search of comfort," she ran to Mimsey and "found it there." For months, from December 1917 until spring 1918, they spent every day together. When Julie left town for several days to visit the Favershams in the country, Eva moved in with Mary. In February, Eva was "so full of the joy of life," she told her diary, "I could have yelled & danced all up & down the avenue. Mimsey is perfectly wonderful to me. I'm very happy."

Although worried that Mary might fall in love with Alla Nazimova, Eva took her backstage to meet the Russian actress. Nazimova "was marvellous as ever," Eva said, "& we were both thrilled." On March 1, 1918, Eva, dressed as a prince, Mimsey, attired as a slave girl, and a male friend, costumed as a eunuch, attended the Chu Chin Chow Ball, a theatrical masquerade to raise money for the war effort. "The Pageant was a great success. M. looked lovely," Eva wrote. "I felt some opera glasses on me all the time & after the show I was walking round in the crowd—when a man came & told me Nazimova wanted me at her table." Eva couldn't resist Nazimova's charm and thoughtlessly deserted Mimsey to be with her. Nazimova was "wonderful—just like old times," Eva wrote. "I was happy—so happy! Stayed with her all evening and b'fast too."

When Nazimova played a short season of Ibsen that spring, Eva watched her performances from the front row. While Julie Le Gallienne believed that Nazimova's Nora in *A Doll's House* had been definitive, she infuriated Eva by laughing at Alla's portrayal of Hedda Gabler and Hilda Wangel. Julie's critical judgment was shared by John Corbin of *The New York Times,* who called Nazimova's Hedda a "Continental lounge-lizard, a pasty-faced exotic," and her Hilda a "vulgar little flirt making eyes at the Master Builder." Nazimova was clever, had a strong personality, Corbin allowed, but he found her mannerisms repellent and her diction ridiculous: in Nazimova's tortured accent, "this house" became "the souse" and "vine leaves" came out "wine lees."

Infatuated and obsessed, Eva didn't care what anyone else said. She continued her hero worship. She kept up her Russian studies and practiced by sending Nazimova letters in Russian.

While Mimsey had the glamorous Nazimova to contend with, Eva's rivals were more threatening. Mary had a number of male friends; the most ardent was a young man named Harry. When one of Mimsey's admirers joined them for dinner, Eva often refused to eat or pleaded an upset stomach, or when all else failed, she simply "had hysterics." Harry's presence prompted the worst reaction; he literally made her sick. The reward for Eva's behavior was tender care by solicitous, gentle Mimsey.

Still, Mary's attitude disturbed Eva. Although astrologer Evangeline Adams had advised the two women to use Harry as a "dupe," Eva did not understand Mimsey's tolerance of his presence. Of course, Eva had her own male friends.

There was Donald—a "little mutt," she called him, but she couldn't help being interested in him. "C'est plus fort que moi," she shrugged. "He's the only boy who's ever in the least degree moved me." And there was Tony, whom, she announced with great delight, she "teased to death." She reported in her diary that "Tony came to see us. . . . He clutched me madly to him for a couple of times. I laughed & said I thought all that was over. I think he has a series of people he gets thrills from. He's just like a young animal." A few days later, Tony reappeared and "tried to make love to me again," Eva wrote. "But he looked dirty & had been eating onions so I really couldn't have it."

Although Eva enjoyed flirting with men and testing her powers of attraction, she had fallen in love with a woman, and she decided, quite rationally, in a world arranged for male and female pairs, it would have been so much simpler if she had been born a boy. Sometimes she tried out the idea by putting on a boy's cap, pants, and boots, and when she "felt up to mischief" she dressed in her boy's things and went out. "Awfully exciting," she said. Doing what was forbidden would always carry a powerful charge for her.

When she appeared in a full-page spread in *Town and Country*'s June 1918 issue wearing Abercrombie & Fitch sports clothes, including an English riding habit, a St. Albans golf outfit, and a Scotch tweed Banff mountain climbing suit, with the jacket slung boyishly over the belt and her long hair tucked under a wide-brimmed silk hat, she thought she looked dashing and wicked in her male attire. She hoped that Nazimova would see the pictures. Eva did look wonderful, but instead of projecting dangerous allure, she looked elegantly adorable, wide-eyed and healthy.

As Eva's relationship with Mary Duggett developed, her relationship with her mother began to change. Julie had devoted herself to Eva, had concentrated all her energy and intelligence to taking care of her daughter and promoting her career. Eva longed to break free of Julie, to strike out on her own and live with Mimsey, but she feared hurting her mother. On April 8, 1918, when long talks and arguments had failed to settle the issue, Eva wrote Julie a letter: "I wish I could make you feel as I do—that a little separation would strengthen & deepen the love & understanding that must be between us—that is between us—but that has been fogged over & distorted by many months of nervous worry & restlessness on both sides. *There is nothing I want less in the world than a 'break' between us.*" Eva told Julie of her plan: "That we should let the flat at once (and we could easily. I know of two people already who would take it) & that you should go & take a room in the country." Eva would take "a small room next door to Mary—with a communicating door for seven dollars a week. . . . Mam darling, remember how well you felt in Pasadena, how happy you were.

IT ADDS A LOT TO THE FUN TO BE RIGHTLY DONE UP

MISS EVA LE GALLIENNE

This Abercrombie & Fitch advertisement was an unusual commercial endorsement for Eva, 1918.

It'll do you good to get away from my often irritating & at all times nervous personality. . . . You wanted to be totally free too, sometimes, when you were 19. . . . So won't you feel a little softer in your heart towards me—& consider my plan?"

Eva spent the night with Mimsey, and the next day went to hear Julie's reaction to her proposal. "She had quite misunderstood my letter," Eva said, "& told me in a sharp voice to fetch my things & take the room. . . . Now I feel that I really belong to Mimsey and she to me." Julie must have felt a mixture of pain and pride at raising such a daughter—one who could be so lovingly articulate and so infuriatingly patronizing at the same time. Perhaps Julie became fully aware of her daughter's sexuality at this time. There is no evidence in Eva's writings about her mother, in their letters, or in Julie's diary or papers that Julie ever disapproved of Eva's homosexuality. Too, Julie was a sophisticated, cultured woman who moved in literary and artistic circles where homosexuality was accepted. Their rift didn't last a week. When Eva arrived at the flat to get her desk, she and Julie fell into each other's arms and wept. "It was a hateful situation," Eva said, "& I was just as miserable as she." Their separation, as Eva had predicted, did deepen their love and friendship. It also helped that Julie liked and approved of Mary Duggett.

Through Eva's intervention with Ethel Barrymore, Mary was hired as an understudy and extra in *The Off Chance* and went along on the tour. Not only was Mary a loving companion, especially when Ethel was in a rotten temper ("Thank God I have my Mimsey," Eva would sigh), but she made sure that Eva took her vitamins and castor oil, packed her bags for her, and generally looked after her welfare. While Julie continued to be Eva's most trusted critic and confidant, the one person who would tell her the brutal truth about her acting, her character, or her clothes, Mary Duggett became the emotional center of Eva's life.

Around the time that Eva was negotiating her separation from her mother, she decided to go see her father. She visited Richard at his studio in Washington Square. Richard was in his early fifties, but Eva thought that he was "the handsomest man I'd ever seen." Their first visit lasted six hours. Later, Eva wrote that "we had a grand time 'discovering' each other. . . . There was nothing he didn't know about poetry and literature, and he had the kind of student's mind I've always envied." After reuniting with his daughter, Richard wrote to Julie asking for a reconciliation: "Our romance is still to me one of the most precious things in my life . . . the mention of 'Denmark' makes my heart beat like a boy's. . . . I have wondered if it would be possible to have a 'little Dinner with the Sphinx' together."

"Dear I should love it, & I love you suggesting it," Julie responded, "yet don't let us think of it."

Julie's reply was an opening for Richard, who could never resist a romantic opportunity.

Dearest Julie . . .

To see your handwriting awaiting me made my heart give a little gasp. . . . It was strange & wonderful to see Eva the other night. She was lovely, a really young princess—and how astonishingly you in so much & nothing that I could notice of her wicked Daddy! How strange it must be for you to see your dream . . . come true, so romantically & so brilliantly. . . . I congratulate you, dear, on your achievement. . . . It is good to think we are even in this city together. There is Romance, isn't there, dearest Julie, even in that—

Richard (whose secret name is still "Asra")

ACTUALLY EVA DID SHARE some of her "wicked Daddy's" traits, including Richard's addiction to romance. Like Richard, who was married to faithful Irma but longed for Julie, his golden girl, Eva loved Mimsey and usually "went to sleep in Mimsey's arms," but Nazimova "haunts me day & night," Eva confided to her diary. "I can't help it."

During the *Off Chance* tour, she had "dreadful obsessions" about Nazimova, but Mimsey's steady companionship was a comfort. In December 1918, however, a beau of Mimsey's, "the exquisite Harry," showed up in Boston, lunched with Mimsey and motored with her. Eva feared that Mimsey was growing tired of her. "I hope not," she wrote. "I'm so intensely devoted to her, to feel her love going is very hard. I wonder."

Months of touring, playing one-night stands, and sleeping on trains exhausted Le Gallienne, who suffered from tonsillitis and dental problems (brought on by her addiction to marzipan). Plus, she was thoroughly bored with playing the part of the Duchess. Financially, though, the tour was a success. In June 1919, when Eva and Mimsey returned to New York, they rented a new, larger apartment together on West Fifty-second Street and were able to have some idle weeks. Aided by a small stipend from her parents, Mary began a serious study of music while Eva looked for work and continued her study of Russian.

"I finally found a play," she wrote, "in which I was interested and in which my services were required—a difficult combination!" The play was *Lusmore* by Grace Heyer, and Eva played the part of Eithne, a blind girl. The opening of the play, however, was delayed by the actors' strike. The actors' union, Actors' Equity, founded in 1913, lacked real clout and bargaining power; but now the stagehands' and the musicians' unions had joined with Equity to demand fairness and simple decency from the managers. Actors from the lower echelons of the profession were often required to rehearse week after week without pay and could be dismissed without prior notice; they often had to furnish their own costumes; and actors were sometimes left without transportation when a show suddenly closed out of town. By 1919, Equity had grown to more than four thousand members, public opinion was on their side, and Ethel Barrymore, who was surprised to discover that she was a life member of Equity, threw her considerable influence behind the strike. The managers soon capitulated.

While Le Gallienne, too, was a member of Actors' Equity, she did not support the strike. She believed that acting was a fine art, not a common trade. Even though the actors in *Lusmore* were playing under an Equity contract, "owing to the strike our rehearsals were stopped last Thursday," she told Mogens. "We could get no men to move our scenery or work our lights and stage effects. . . . It seems almost incredible, that a beautiful artistic production, wonderfully put on, with the most charming scenery you ever saw, should be stopped by carpenters and moving men. Such is democracy! As for me, I'm beginning to think a well governed *autocracy* is the only form of government worth having."

Unfortunately, *Lusmore* was a slight play and closed after a month. Eva's old friend Elsie Janis had just returned from Europe, though, and was putting together a show called *Elsie Janis and Her Gang,* performed with ex-servicemen. One day Eva stopped by Elsie's rehearsals at the George M. Cohan Theatre to say

*In her first vaudeville appearance, in December 1919, Eva danced with
Elsie Janis, who played a soldier to Eva's French cocotte.*

hello. "Come with me and the gang," Elsie said. "I want to do a scene between a doughboy and a French girl." Eva, who had nothing better to do, thought, Why not? She wore a bobbed, jet-black wig, smudged her eyes with feline green shadow, painted on a beauty mark, stuffed her rather large feet into high French heels, and, partnered by Elsie costumed as a soldier, danced a tango, a waltz, and a finale Castle walk. "It was great fun," Eva said, "so different from anything I had been accustomed to." It was also good experience, since Elsie Janis was considered by many to be the greatest music-hall artist of her time.

LE GALLIENNE WAS RELEASED from the production to take the lead in a London success, *Tilly of Bloomsbury* by Ian Hay. The play opened in Washington on January 24, 1920, but Eva, stricken with influenza, played only two performances. The influenza turned into pneumonia, and Hay took her back to New York on the train.

Now that her daughter was twenty-one and fully grown-up and had Mary Duggett to look after her, Julie Le Gallienne, as Eva had initially suggested, lived quietly in the country, devoting herself to re-establishing her writing career and contemplating a return to Europe. During the weeks that Eva was recovering, Richard Le Gallienne invited her and Mary to have supper with him and met Mary for the first time. "I was so happy with you & Mary the other night," he wrote. "Give her my love, please—I liked her so much—no wonder you are fond of her."

Eva regained her health, and the Shubert office insisted that she read a script they proposed for her. The play, *Not So Long Ago* by Arthur Richman, was a "delightful, whimsical comedy," she discovered. Her part of Elsie Dover was "one of the best character-comedy roles" she had ever read. Set in the 1870s in New York City, the fairy-tale plot revolves around Elsie, the daughter of an inventor, who supports herself by sewing for the Ballards, an aristocratic old family. While spurning the attentions of a salesman suitor, Elsie invents a romance with the Ballards' handsome son, and, in true fairy-tale tradition, despite parental obstacles and misunderstandings, the imaginary love affair becomes real, and in the end, Cinderella marries her prince.

After almost five years of steady work in the American theatre, Eva had played fifteen roles in a variety of plays. While most of her notices had been good, she had not appeared in a hit. To ascend to the next level in the theatre, she needed a role to take her there. Fortunately for Eva, *Not So Long Ago* was produced by Lee Shubert, who paid particular attention to the production. Tryouts in New Haven and Washington, D.C., led to rewrites, cast changes, and new costumes. By the time the play arrived in Boston for a few weeks' run, it was ready for the important Boston critics.

*Eva (center) with Margaret Mosier and Leatta Miller in her first
Broadway hit,* Not So Long Ago, *1920*

On opening day in Boston, Eva was not well, probably from nerves, and spent the day in bed with a hot-water bottle "& some gin that a kind soul brought me—& which saved my life." At the opening performance, however, her illness was forgotten because "the audience was so wonderful!" Her costumes were "a great success," she wrote Julie. "Especially my white one in the last act which causes gasps of delight from the public (always easily vanquished by white organdy!)."

The company continued to rehearse to ready themselves for the New York opening, but Eva managed to get away one day to watch Helen Hayes, who was also playing Boston. "I think she's adorable," Eva wrote Julie. "And full of talent—I was most pleasantly surprised in her—think she's very clever. I went back afterwards to tell her so, and she seemed very pleased. She seems a nice little thing." A few days later Eva and Helen Hayes were guests of honor at a luncheon sponsored by the Boston Professional Women's Club. Eva's reaction to the luncheon illuminates her early aversion to large social gatherings which required a measure of public relations and self-promotion. She described the event:

We were all stood in a line before lunch—& then 100's of women walked down the line "meeting" us! I never thought such a thing possible! I almost had hysterics it was so funny & so utterly idiotic—a funny dried up—typically *Boston* woman—would come up & say: "I am Mrs. Smith how do you do!—I hope you will have a charming afternoon with us—we're so glad to welcome you!" And that repeated hundreds of times with comic variations was too absurd. Then—the lunch. All the guests of honour were seated at a long table raised on a platform—& all the others sat at smaller tables in front of the platform—& glared at you—between bites. I was so nervous & shy—I couldn't eat a damn thing—& then the President, a funny bird like little woman, made a speech in which she introduced each guest—& you had to get up & make a bow & be applauded. And then some men got up and made boring speeches & a lady got up & sang "Lo Hear the Gentle Lark" several notes *flat* & another lady got up & shrieked out a recitation about "Oh! to be Alive in Such an Age!"

As they matured, Hayes and Le Gallienne would follow different paths in the American theatre and as a result would develop decidedly different careers. The distinguished critic of the *Boston Transcript,* H. T. Parker, known by his initials H.T.P. (which his assistant Brooks Atkinson quipped stood for "Hell to pay"), who observed both actresses over several years, pinpointed out the difference between the two women. Miss Hayes, he wrote, had "instinctive facility at her calling, acting at high nervous tension and dowered besides with infectious high spirits, but she was always the same." Eva Le Gallienne, he continued, is "a youthful actress, who is already resourceful and apt with way and mean—voice, gesture, play of face and all the rest; who can define, disclose and differentiate character, who has plentiful charm, personality and high spirits, yet who keeps them steadily in service of the play and to the part. Miss Hayes . . . pleasantly displays [herself]; Miss Le Gallienne works as artist in her medium."

To be called an artist by an important critic was high praise indeed. Because of this early approval and acceptance not only by the critics but also by members of Boston society led by Eleo Sears, Le Gallienne would always be particularly fond of Boston. Boston was still out of town, though. The real test was New York, and thinking of the New York opening made her "dreadfully nervous."

Not So Long Ago opened at the Booth Theatre on May 4, 1920. It was a "great event in my life," Le Gallienne recalled. She and her co-star Sidney Blackmer received call after call. *The New York Times* lauded the play as "one of the most gracefully written and charming plays of the year . . . beautifully played, in particular by Eva Le Gallienne [who] is appealingly beautiful."

Lee Shubert had taken a chance on a new play and a young playwright, had cast good actors instead of star names, and had supported the production tech-

*Lee Shubert, the oldest
of the Shubert brothers.
Le Gallienne complained
that during her long career
she repaired every toilet
in every Shubert theatre
from coast to coast.*

nically and financially. His courage paid off, and following the second New York performance of *Not So Long Ago,* he signed Le Gallienne and Sidney Blackmer to three-year contracts.

With Eva's career under the guidance of Lee Shubert and her emotional life steady and serene with Mary Duggett, now was the time, Julie Le Gallienne felt, to return to Europe. She missed her family and friends and her work for *Politiken.* The vow she had made twenty-one years earlier to baby Eva had been fulfilled. There was nothing more for her to do. In September 1920, five years after she first arrived in America, Julie Le Gallienne, then fifty-seven, set sail alone.

EVA BASKED in her success and prosperity, but she "gradually grew restless." Lee Shubert wanted to keep her happy and occupied and gave her scripts to review. Although pleased with her enthusiasm and interest in all aspects of theatre, he warned her against versatility and advised her that the sure road to success with a capital *S* was to "choose a type and stick to it." Le Gallienne conceded that he was right, but she had no intention of following his advice. "What a bore!" she groaned.

With Mary Kennedy, a young actress in *Not So Long Ago,* Le Gallienne devised a plan for a Young People's Theatre to "get together all the successful young players who felt as we did the stultifying influence of the long-run system . . . and work on some of the great plays of the world, simply for the joy of the work itself, without any thought of performing them publicly." Among those they enlisted were Margalo Gillmore, Henry Hull, Katharine Cornell, and Tom Powers. Eva wrote to Minnie Maddern Fiske, Nazimova, and other leading actors, asking them to serve on an advisory committee. Mrs. Fiske and Nazimova lent their support, and the group planned to present workshop performances for an invited audience. Soon, several people in the group saw the commercial possibilities of presenting performances, and Eva's initial workshop plan was pushed aside. "I washed my hands of the whole business," she wrote. "I was bitterly disappointed and hurt."

Not So Long Ago closed on Broadway on August 28, 1920, and Le Gallienne had a month's respite before embarking on a national tour of the play. She and Mimsey stayed in town and weekended with friends in the country. Eva renewed her relationship with Nazimova, but perhaps because of Le Gallienne's new stature as an up-and-coming star, her earlier passionate hero worship of Alla changed to a more equal friendship. She and Mimsey visited Nazimova and her husband, Charles Bryant, at Nazimova's Port Chester, New York, home. "I think she was pleased with the way I have changed & developed since she last saw me," Le Gallienne wrote. "We stayed up till 2—reading Russian, French and English poetry—and talking about everything under the sun and moon. She was really immensely impressed and pleased with my Russian—and that made it all seem so tremendously worth while." In turn, Eva and Mimsey invited Nazimova to dinner in New York. "It was really lovely—and she was very pleased with the way we live," Eva said.

Eva wanted Mimsey to accompany her on the long tour, but Mary decided to stay in New York and continue her music and voice lessons and join Eva for Christmas in Chicago. Le Gallienne packed a trunk with books and a number of German and Russian plays that Nazimova had suggested and left on her cross-country trek.

The tour was a financial success, and she and Sidney Blackmer were given the star treatment and the best dressing rooms, but from time to time they had to confront Lee Shubert about the filthy conditions or poor management in some of his theatres. Le Gallienne was sought out by society people in the various towns. On her two-year tour with Ethel Barrymore, who was a darling of the social set, she had met many prominent people in cities across the country and formed lasting friendships with those who sent flowers, invited her to lunches, dinners, and teas, and came backstage to welcome her to Boston or Pittsburgh or St. Louis. Edgar Scott and his wife, Hope, who would later be the model for

Tracy Lord in Philip Barry's *The Philadelphia Story,* visited her backstage whenever she played Philadelphia. Edgar Scott shared Le Gallienne's birthday, and for
over sixty years her "twin" sent cards and flowers. Another admirer, Al Lehman
of Pittsburgh, a wealthy steel man and arts patron, became a cherished friend
(later they shared an affinity for low Paris night spots). The generous Lehman
showered Eva with the typical gifts from a fan to a star, including flowers and
furs—and when he knew Eva better, an all-steel garage.

During the *Not So Long Ago* tour, Eva enjoyed all the attention and accolades
garnered by her star billing. With star billing, however, came certain responsibilities. It's an unwritten rule of the theatre that in return for their largesse,
wealthy theatre patrons expect personal contact with the artists they support.
Eva took a superior, somewhat contemptuous attitude to the often fawning
attentions of her public, and, unlike Ethel Barrymore, she would not become
society's pet. "How I hate the Middle West," she wrote,

> it's even worse than ever. So many extraordinary people have come up
> since the war—and made fortunes—and insist on taking their place in the
> Sun—only they don't know how to do it. . . . I went to a big party given
> by Mrs. Joseph Fish . . . and she invited all the prominent theatrical peo-
> ple now playing in Chicago—using such names as Ethel Barrymore &
> Jane Cowl to induce the nicer "Society" people of Chicago to go to her
> party. We none of us knew Mrs. Fish—and were all awfully interested to
> see what it would be like. Ethel was there looking lovely and very *dis-
> traire*—I think she thought the whole thing killing—and one couldn't help
> that. The house was very nouveau riche—and everything was obviously
> "decorated" by one of Chicago's wildest and most expensive Decorating
> Firms:—Mrs. Fish was very nervous and more than a trifle intoxicated—
> so we had a wonderful time!

It was difficult for Le Gallienne to find intellectual equals among her own age
group. At twenty-one she felt old—as if she had "lived at least 10 lives already."
Her aristocratic manner, natural authority, and formidable intellect could be intimidating. One writer later described Le Gallienne's large blue eyes as having
"so startling and penetrating an intelligence that they affected one like an electric shock." Later, she would be able to act a facsimile of folksiness, but she simply did not have the common touch, that trait so endearing to the American
public.

On tour Le Gallienne continued to study actors she admired. When she
learned that Mrs. Fiske was playing a special Sunday matinee in New York, Eva
took the train from Baltimore just for the day to see her work. As usual, she sat
in the first row of the theatre so that she could observe Mrs. Fiske closely. "She

seems to me the embodiment of everything mental," Eva wrote. "You can almost hear her brain click . . . she fascinates one's mind—for one's heart or soul never enter into it. She's like a kind of intellectual caviar—And she never makes a mistake—perhaps that's what's so baffling about her. Her readings are perfect—her phrasings inspiredly brilliant—She is flawless.—I wonder whether she is so from age—or whether that has always been so—Often, I think, older people resort to flawlessness—in their effort to make up for other qualities of which they are no longer masters. I should like to have seen Mrs. Fiske 20 years ago."

DESPITE THE perennial discomforts of touring—bad food, dirty hotel rooms, crowded trains, and poorly equipped theatres—Le Gallienne glowed with happiness, vitality, and satisfaction with her life. Of course, she was playing an effervescent, multifaceted character in a soap bubble of a play. Throughout her life, except when she played repertory, Le Gallienne's own mood would be determined in large part by the character she was playing. While she was Elsie, Eva grew loving and forgiving of her father, and Richard Le Gallienne wrote her occasionally, calling her his "faraway lover." He commiserated with her about the "awful human desert" of the Middle West and shared her joy in having Mimsey in her life. Like Julie, Richard accepted his daughter's choice of lovers. "I am glad you love each other so," he wrote Eva. "Certainly [Mimsey] is a darling."

Not long after the tour returned to the New York area in late January 1921, Eva's happy bubble burst. In a letter to her mother, written in large, angry scrawls, Eva blurted out the reason for her unhappiness: "Mimsey was married last Tuesday to a man called Stuart Benson." Apparently, Mimsey did not want to break the news of her impending marriage while Eva was on tour, so she had waited until Eva returned to New York. Later, Mimsey bitterly regretted her decision to marry, but at the time it had seemed her only choice. She was lonely without Eva in New York, and since she was not a dedicated artist like Le Gallienne, she did not have a consuming interest or any means of earning a living. Her parents expected her to marry, and Mimsey wanted the financial security and the social life that marriage offered. Le Gallienne was devastated, "quite exhausted nervously," and felt like "running away from everything and taking a rest." Nazimova had asked her to visit her in California for a month after the play closed, and now, with nothing to keep her in New York, Eva planned to go.

A week later, she wrote again to Julie from the apartment that she once had shared with Mimsey. Generously or guiltily, Mary Duggett had left all her furniture behind. "I'm still alive you see—I'm leaving for California on Tuesday. . . . I'm simply dying to be off. . . . *Nichevo!*—as the Russians say—that seems best to express Life—as well as Death. . . . I shall write to you on the

Mary "Mimsey"
Duggett Benson

train—and I hope to send you from California—some nice cheerful letters—full of sunshine—This one is full of something different I'm afraid." Julie had bred toughness into Eva, but she knew all too well the sound of a heart breaking.

In entry after entry in her diary, Eva had written of her love for Mimsey. The two women had lived together, had shared their lives for more than three years, and Eva believed that they belonged together. Whatever bitterness and anger and pain Le Gallienne felt, though, she would not indulge her feelings; instead she hardened herself into a kind of stoic acceptance. "Ikke tude," her mother had taught—don't blubber. Don't feel sorry for yourself and wallow in misery.

Now, left devastated and grieving by Mimsey's marriage, she was quite alone. Hesper had married Robert Hutchinson of Philadelphia in May 1918 and was not available to comfort her. At such a moment, Eva longed for "Mamkin," but they were separated by an ocean and circumstances. Now, in addition to sending her mother a regular monthly check of one hundred dollars, Eva ordered an additional two-hundred-dollar draft on a Paris bank, so that while she was in California, Julie, too, could "go South for a while. . . . We'll both be basking in a maternal Sun at least—that is always something," Eva wrote bitterly.

GETTING OUT OF TOWN, travel and change, new sights—rather standard antidotes to depression and despair—had their salutary effect on Le Gallienne, especially her first view of the Grand Canyon. But her stay at Alla Nazimova's estate at 8080 Sunset Boulevard brought more disillusion. Nazimova's lush, sundrenched estate, called the Garden of Alla, with its Spanish colonial house surrounded by flowers and tropical plants and featuring a swimming pool with underwater lights in the sinuous shape of the Black Sea, would seem an ideal place to heal her wounds and perhaps begin a new love affair. But despite the bright California sun, dark cynicism permeated Le Gallienne's letters. "You don't sound very happy Mamkin darling—but then who is happy in this chaotic and uncomfortable World?—I know of no-one—least of all myself. So you see— we're all in the same boat."

Eva had traveled to Hollywood at Alla's invitation, and she had expected that she would be exclusively with Nazimova. But if Eva had an affair with Nazimova at this time, it was brief. Alla worked all day at MGM filming *Camille,* and Le Gallienne quickly discovered that her intelligent idol, the great Ibsen interpreter, was acting like a self-absorbed prima donna. Eva also wanted to explore the possibility of working in the movies, but after visiting the set of *Camille* she wrote her mother: "I can't see how anyone can stand pictures except as a convenience from a financial point-of-view—And ye Gods! how they spoil one—It hurts to see an artist like Nazimova in such an environment—and under such impossible and harmful influences—And she is not proving herself strong enough to withstand them.—I'm sorry: I think artistically she is done for. Of course she's at a dangerous age—42—and I suppose more susceptible than at any other time— but she is behaving very foolishly in every way—and has quite lost her sense of values."

Hollywood columnist Sheilah Graham later observed that "Hollywood in the early twenties, with Alla installed as a popular hostess in her mansion, was bursting with . . . excitement and vitality." Attending Nazimova's lavish dinner parties with guests from the *Camille* company, who included Rudolph Valentino, writer June Mathis, designer Natacha Rambova, starlets, and various other celebrities, did not appeal to Le Gallienne, who spent long hours at the Krotona Institute for Theosophy discussing the essence of God and the spiritual nature of the universe. There she met the poet and social critic Max Eastman, whom she liked very much. Although she had planned to stay for a month, Eva concluded that Nazimova and her friend Rambova (whose real name was Winifred Shaughnessy) were simply "insane," and she asked a friend in New York to concoct an urgent wire demanding her return.

WHILE EVA MEDITATED in Hollywood feeling lost and forgotten, actor Joseph Schildkraut in New York was thinking lovingly about the young actress with the ice-blue eyes, the caressing voice, and the strange French name that he had seen months earlier in *Not So Long Ago.* "Pepi" Schildkraut had been so impressed by her beauty and the "great sensitivity and the honesty of her acting" that he had run backstage to meet her, almost knocking her down with his ardor. Eva Le Gallienne must play Julie in Molnár's *Liliom,* he told the Theatre Guild. He would accept no one else. The problem was that no one knew where she was. Like Cinderella, Eva had simply disappeared, leaving no forwarding address, not even with her manager, Lee Shubert.

The twenty-five-year-old Schildkraut, dashing and handsome, with Old World charm coupled with an electrifying sexuality, was the son of the great German and Yiddish actor Rudolph Schildkraut. Joseph had studied at the American Academy of Dramatic Art and had performed with Max Reinhardt's company in Berlin and at New York's Irving Place Theatre. Schildkraut had sold the Theatre Guild on *Liliom* primarily because he wanted to play the title role. The Theatre Guild knew that other American producers had rejected the script in its previous British incarnation as *The Daisy* because of its risky subject matter and loose dramatic form of a prologue and seven scenes. Even Schildkraut's father scoffed at the idea that the plot would appeal to a Broadway audience— "a Hungarian barker of a merry-go-round who kills himself in the middle of the play and then goes to an imaginary police station in heaven and returns to earth again."

Committed to producing quality plays and introducing American audiences to European dramatic literature, the Theatre Guild committee, headed by Lawrence Langner and Theresa Helburn, decided to take the risk and do the play "as a kind of personal indulgence." They were making lots of money with the long-running *Mr. Pim Passes By,* and they reminded themselves that the best way to spend the money would be to put it back into the theatre. They signed Schildkraut to a long-term contract and engaged Benjamin Glazer to translate the play into English while keeping the Hungarian locale. Frank Reicher, a Hollywood director of German extraction who could communicate effectively with Schildkraut, was hired to direct. Lee Simonson would design the sets. Everyone was ready to rehearse, but they still didn't have their Julie. The Theatre Guild wanted to approach other actresses. Schildkraut demanded Eva Le Gallienne.

After her flight from the Garden of Alla in early March 1921, Eva returned to New York eager to immerse herself in work, only to find that Lee Shubert had nothing but a bedroom farce. So when she learned that the Theatre Guild wanted to see her about a new play, Le Gallienne rushed to their offices. Schild-kraut insisted that she take the part immediately. Eva asked to read the play first and took the manuscript home. When she opened the script, she realized happily that "the play was *The Daisy* and Julie was my Julie." After getting Lee Shubert's permission, Le Gallienne signed a contract with the Theatre Guild. In doing so, she aligned herself with the most prestigious producing organization in New York. At a time when the most commercially successful plays in New York were *The Bat* by Mary Roberts Rinehart and the musical review *Biff! Bing! Bang!,* the Theatre Guild presented quality plays and attracted the best actors in New York.

Before Eva began rehearsals, she reassured her mother: "Don't worry about me now Mam darling, I was a bit low for a while—but I've never felt better than I do now—and I'm simply dying to get to work." Long hours of meditation in California and solitude on the train had given Eva time to heal from the pain of her break-up with Mimsey. Also, she was emotionally resilient, with a strong sense of self, and even though Mimsey's sudden marriage had been devastating, a love affair, any love affair, would never be as important to Le Gallienne as her work.

From her many New York friends, whom she relied on to send her news of Eva, Julie knew that Eva was living alone, and she also knew that Eva craved and needed companionship. Julie Le Gallienne probably suggested to Julie Lentilhoss, a European friend who lived in New York, to renew her friendship with Eva. Suddenly, a new companion appeared in Eva's life. You were right about her, Eva wrote to her mother: Julie Lentilhoss "is a thoroughbred, and a marvellous friend—I'm really devoted to her—she's been wonderful to me."

"NEVER WERE THERE two such contrasting personalities as [Joseph Schild-kraut] and Eva Le Gallienne," said Theresa Helburn. "All they had in common was a love of the theater and a European tradition of acting." It was Helburn's job to discipline the unruly Schildkraut. "[He] was young, electric, naughty, and exciting. [Pepi] spoke German to Frank Reicher and Hungarian to the orchestra leader. To all women he spoke nonsense."

Women usually found Pepi's shaggy good looks and bounding enthusiasm irresistible, but Eva arched her back and resisted. When Pepi came too close, Eva swiped at him with sharp words or a stinging slap. Once, while they rehearsed Liliom's death scene, with Schildkraut stretched out and Eva bending over him, Pepi slyly reached up and fondled her breast. Eva picked up Schildkraut's offending hand and held it first to her cheek and then to her lips. Suddenly, she lashed out, biting Schildkraut's hand. Helburn recalled that during rehearsals "it got to the point where Eva, in a rage, decided to leave the theater altogether, but I persuaded her to hang on, a decision for which all theater-lovers are profoundly grateful." By the end of rehearsals, Eva had made it clear that she adored his talent but loathed his advances. Schildkraut never got over his fascination with Eva, even asking her to marry him. He called her "Evale" and she called him "Pepkin," treating him firmly and maternally, as if he were an adorable but unruly child.

Years later, after many acting partnerships, Eva said, "Pepi, it's so wonderful; when we work on the stage, magic occurs." Schildkraut agreed. "We are a wonderful team," he said, "but our approaches are diametrically opposite. I start with all the tricks, props and technical things and then discard the props, discard this, discard that, more essence, more essence, more extract, until I have it. In the first rehearsal [Eva] would mumble something or other and little by little . . . she opens up like a blossom."

To portray the servant girl Julie, a young woman who chooses to live openly with a coarse roughneck who beats her—a tender, courageous woman who submerges her own personality in Liliom's—she first had to create Julie in her mind. Le Gallienne rehearsed Julie during the day, and in the evenings she continued to work. She did her best work, she said, at concerts. For example, after attending a concert of the National Symphony Orchestra at Carnegie Hall with Willem Mengelberg conducting a program of Mozart, Strauss, and Wagner with soloist Sergei Rachmaninoff, she wrote that "the music seems to bring especially vivid and comprehensive pictures." Le Gallienne composed a part, thinking of her role as a continuous piece of music, orchestrating the silence of thoughts, so that each moment, each word, each gesture flowed inevitably and spontaneously forward. The intricacy and subtlety of this kind of work require discipline, imagination, and dedication, as well as a responsive, flexible voice and a face and body tuned to reveal the slightest nuance or embody the grandest gesture.

Le Gallienne did not neglect the outer form of Julie. She searched for days in secondhand stores to find just the right pair of worn, battered boots that would become the keynote to the servant girl's character. After initially insisting that director Frank Reicher leave her entirely alone, she observed that his work with the other actors was unusually fine and sensitive. "I felt I had been an idiot, decided to make peace overtures," she said. "He helped me greatly with my performance, showing me how to build up and project clearly a point . . . or the value of a longer pause here or the danger of too long a one somewhere else."

At one of the dress rehearsals of *Liliom,* Eva added her own directorial touch to the play. In his dying breath, Liliom wonders if he will see God. Le Gallienne noticed that Julie's Bible had fallen open at the Beatitudes, and her eye fell on the line "Blessed are the pure in heart: for they shall see God," which echoed Liliom's dying words. Frank Reicher agreed that Julie's reading of the Beatitudes should close scene five. The moment, which does not appear in the published version of *Liliom,* became one of the most memorable and moving in the play.

Beatrice Terry (Mrs. Muskat), Joseph Schildkraut (Liliom), and Eva (Julie)
in Molnar's Liliom *(1921), the source of the 1945 musical* Carousel.
Eva grounded her characterization in Julie's scuffed and ill-fitting men's shoes.

As the April 20 opening loomed, Le Gallienne, as usual, became increasingly anxious. The day before the opening she was "nervous to the point of hysteria," and a few hours before the performance she lost her voice. But after the curtain rose at the Garrick Theatre on Lee Simonson's set, which evoked Molnár's Budapest poetically and imaginatively rather than literally, the audience watched a "weary, white-faced, stoop-shouldered little waif" enter the stage, look over her shoulder, and say in a quiet, lyrical voice that everyone could hear quite clearly, "Did you ever hear of such a thing? What's the matter with the woman anyway?" Critic John Mason Brown attended the opening of *Liliom* and would never forget the entrance of Julie, and later he would praise Eva Le Gallienne as a "figure who knows no parallel in our contemporary theatre." What he and the rest of the audience did not know was that between scenes, Le Gallienne ran to her dressing room to "suck lemons in order to be able to croak at all." At the final curtain, the audience roared their approval, cheering, standing on their seats, shouting with joy.

The Theatre Guild had considered *Liliom* a huge risk; instead it was a great commercial and artistic success, playing for more than a year on Broadway and a year on tour. With the success of *Liliom* and its free-form construction, other playwrights began experimenting with the traditional three-act and four-act formats.

After the opening performance, deaf to the applause and possessed of a firm belief that she had been a dismal failure, Le Gallienne was so miserable that she shut herself in her dressing room with only her framed photograph of Ethel Barrymore for company. She cried in despair while Schildkraut crowed outside, "They loved me! They loved me!" Like Mrs. Fiske, who loathed opening nights and insisted that no critic had ever seen her act, Le Gallienne, too, never felt she played well at openings.

But the critics raved, and several mentioned that Le Gallienne reminded them of Duse. (Eva didn't like to dwell on that comparison, saying, "It frightens me.") And John Blair was one of many audience members who added their voices to the general praise. In a letter to *The New York Times* he wrote that "her acting moved me as can only music. . . . One was not arrested by detail—it was all spirit—spirit on its way heavenward."

Overnight, Le Gallienne and Schildkraut were stars. The production soon moved to the larger Fulton Theatre to accommodate the crowds. Le Gallienne was pleased with the better acoustics at the Fulton and her new, more elegant dressing room, though she felt "so strange in it" since it was the scene of her first meeting with Nazimova during *Ception Shoals,* when she had been an aspiring young actor. Now, like Nazimova, she was a star. Later that year, Nazimova saw *Liliom.* The events of that February at the Garden of Alla seemed ages away, and Le Gallienne warmed herself on Alla's praise. "She was very marvellous to me," said Eva. "It meant so much more than I could ever express."

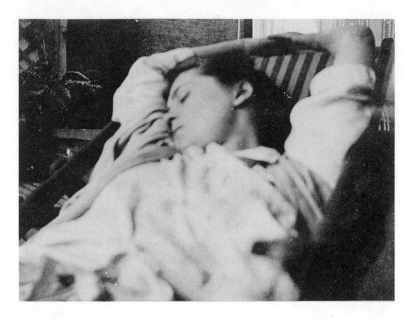

Eva on the rooftop terrace of her downtown Fifth Avenue apartment, 1922

MONTH AFTER MONTH, even in the heat of summer, audiences stood in line in front of the Fulton Theatre for tickets. The Sold Out sign seemed to be a permanent fixture at the box office. Le Gallienne's percentages piled up in her savings account, and she bought a ten-thousand-dollar life insurance policy and named her mother beneficiary.

Soon, though, the attention, the flattery, the requests for interviews, the invitations, all became too much. "I'm getting sick of hearing about it," Eva told her mother, "so much so that I shut myself up like a hermit and never go out." In July she moved downtown to a rooftop apartment at 10 Fifth Avenue. She decorated her rooms like an English cottage, painted the walls a soft green, hung bright chintz curtains, and filled her small study with a desk and books. On Sunday, her day off, Julie Lentilhoss visited, and they spent most of their time on the roof, puttering with plants or just stretched out in deck chairs. On hot summer nights, they lay on the roof, smoked cigarettes, and looked at the stars, not yet dimmed by the bright lights of New York City.

When she did go out, Eva spent most of her time with the older people of the theatre, like Ethel Barrymore and playwright Zoë Akins. She was an honored guest at a Drama League luncheon and found the experience "tiresome and hateful." But she enjoyed playing a benefit performance with Ethel Barrymore. "It was divine," she said, "and so sweet when she forgot her lines and I had to prompt her—just as I always used to." Le Gallienne found the young theatre people "simply impossible—dreadfully dull and silly and such awful gossips—and so frivolous . . . as well as being so self-satisfied with their own work." Her studious nature set her apart; her sexuality stirred gossip and curiosity; and her high-mindedness stimulated teasing and pranks. She had been furious when her *Not So Long Ago* co-star Sidney Blackmer suddenly burst into her dressing room stark naked.

Eva made time, though, for old friends like Al Lehman of Pittsburgh, who saw the play as he passed through town on his way to Europe. It's not clear who made the first move, but Eva reconciled with Mimsey (now Mrs. Stuart Benson), who was discovering that married life could be exceedingly difficult. Hesper Le Gallienne (who had retained her own name) and her new husband returned from an extended European trip that summer, and Eva grew fond of Robert Hutchinson—an acquired taste, she said, but Hesper loved him and that was what mattered. Elsie Janis came into town, saw the play, and didn't like it, but pleased Eva by admiring her performance.

True pleasure for Le Gallienne, though, would always be found in her work. Julie was an exhausting, consuming part, but it was in a minor key. She longed to stretch herself, "to strike a major note." In preparation for the parts that lay ahead of her, she read and studied, and began taking piano lessons in anticipation of playing Hedda Gabler. She struck up a friendship with the Russian actor Jacob Ben-Ami, who had seen *Liliom* and come backstage to introduce himself. After analyzing his work in *Samson and Delilah,* Eva felt that he was the greatest natural artist she had yet seen, a master of conveying thought and silences on the stage. Eva and Ben-Ami discussed working together and began planning matinee performances of *The Seagull* and *The Master Builder.* In a Scandinavian bookshop on Third Avenue, she discovered copies of Ibsen plays in the original and began a serious study of Hilda Wangel as Ibsen had conceived her, an exuberant, vital, utterly ruthless young woman. "It's amazing how much of her character and quirkyness is lost in the translation," she said. She continued her language studies with Russian-born Irina Skariatina. In her apartment, books in five languages overflowed the shelves and spilled onto tables. Her summer reading included Shaw's *Back to Methuselah,* Knut Hamsun's *Growth of the Soil,* and stacks of plays—mostly bad, she said—that managers and playwrights sent her daily.

LE GALLIENNE'S WELL-ORGANIZED schedule of work and study was violently disrupted during the third week of October 1921. After an evening performance of *Liliom,* a man she knew, an actor, entered her dressing room. They were alone. The man knocked her to the floor and raped her. Perhaps Eva had arranged a date with him; it's possible that she had led him on and he had been

days. After that, she said, she never admitted that she was either a boy or a girl. She called herself one of the "half-tone people."

There was nothing half-tone about Mercedes's appearance. Her features were all sharp contrasts: a sleek helmet of ebony hair; black eyes; pale, powdered white skin; a slash of red lips; a prominent chin. Some described her as looking like a vampire or a snake. Actually, Mercedes's strong features, with beaklike nose and sharp eyes, were more reminiscent of a hawk's. When Mercedes smiled, though, the bird of prey disappeared into deep dimples and gleaming white teeth. Mercedes wore sweeping black cloaks and (before she took up wearing pants) long, dramatic skirts, and black high heels with silver buckles.

In 1920, Mercedes, then twenty-seven, married Abram Poole, a sculptor and painter, who was ten years older. She occupied herself with the usual pursuits of a New York socialite—gossip, good works, the arts. A member of the Lucy Stone League, Mercedes kept her own name and dreamed of becoming a great poet or a saint. She would not realize either ambition.

Her pursuit of Le Gallienne was well timed. Mercedes knew that Eva had missed several performances, and it's likely that she also heard the whispered reports that Eva had been raped. Mercedes's impact on Eva was considerable and immediate. Mercedes, six years older than Eva, thought of herself as an artist and an intellectual. She claimed that she had read all of Shakespeare and Cervantes and seventeen volumes of history by the time she was nine. Mercedes courted Eva with expensive presents and flattery, but she conquered her with a powerful eroticism that aroused, perhaps for the first time, an intense, adult carnality in Le Gallienne. Just a few weeks after meeting Mercedes, Eva was in sexual thrall to the older woman. Julie Lentilhoss returned to Europe, and by February 1922, when Eva was on tour with *Liliom,* Mercedes dominated Eva's life. They exchanged letters almost daily. Eva wrote that she had an "agonizing aching" that never stopped, except, of course, during Mercedes's brief visits.

Separation from Mercedes inspired Eva to poetic heights. Playing Julie night after night on tour, with no other outlet for her enormous vitality, she poured her energies into her letters to Mercedes. When they were together, there were often arguments, usually brought on by jealousy. After one scene, Eva apologized to Mercedes for behaving "very foolishly this afternoon. My love contains elements of possession & intolerance." There are devils in her, Eva said, and she was jealous of anyone else's sleeping with Mercedes and "evoking that Christ-like feeling which is spiritually so akin to passion." When they were apart, there were expressions of love and adoration. Like Julie in *Liliom,* Eva professed that she would love Mercedes until the end, no matter what. And in the same way that Julie submerges her personality into Liliom's, Eva began to sink her own self into that of Mercedes.

To feel closer to Mercedes, Le Gallienne dabbled at Spanish, using Spanish phrases in her love letters. She replaced her engraved "ELeG" stationery with new stationery emblazoned with a tiny silver shield and the motto "Force et Confiance." She cut her hair to shoulder length and pulled it back tightly and severely into a knot, the way Mercedes liked it. Her writing style changed, too, becoming more like Mercedes's overwrought, purple prose, filled with images of Spanish mysticism. Her love for Mercedes was like a "light before an altar," Eva wrote in April 1922. "I love you—I love you so insanely." Images of madness and lunacy permeate Eva's letters over and over again in a consistent refrain.

Writing daily letters to Mercedes impinged on her writing time to her mother and Mogens. When Julie scolded her for not writing more often and for neglecting Mogens, who was recently married, Eva replied, "Ah—you will say I am just like Daddy!—and you are probably right—why is it one must always inherit faults & fight for virtues?! . . . I know I am a rotter—but try & bear with me please—and know that I have a hard fight to be even as decent as I am."

At times, in her letters to Mercedes, Eva sounded as if she was improvising a great dramatic role borrowed from some overblown romantic melodrama. Perhaps she was. Or perhaps she was acting just like a young woman crazy in love. She played the coquette, teasing Mercedes with tales of being "hurled from one man's arm to another" at a Boston dance. She played the analytical philosopher, advising Mercedes to give her up "until a happy time when our spiritual and psychic bonds could once more become part of the expression and transmutation of our physical longing." She played the romantic lover: "You came to me with the scent of acacia blossoms—and it is to you I say I love you!—and it your child I carry under my heart." The "child" Eva carried was de Acosta's play *Jehanne d'Arc,* which she had begun to write for Le Gallienne. After meeting Eva, Mercedes turned her writing efforts from poetry to playwriting, and Eva began contacting producers about investing in *Jehanne d'Arc.*

On tour, in town after town, people who had known Le Gallienne wondered at her transformation. She seemed a different person. Eva agreed, feeling that she had changed "so completely & so fundamentally" since meeting Mercedes. Or was it the role that had changed—the buoyant Elsie replaced by the repressed, abused Julie of *Liliom?*

During the spring of 1922, Eva and Mercedes planned a European summer vacation. Although she was committed to the *Liliom* tour, Eva renewed her passport, wrote to her mother that she was coming for a visit, and warned that Julie would find her "very changed." At the end of May, just days before she sailed on the *Mauretania,* she fainted at the theatre, doctors were called, and it was discovered that she was having a "nervous breakdown." Hesper and Mimsey took care of her, packed her bags, and delivered her to the boat.

Mercedes was already in Paris, and Eva, miraculously recovered from her nervous breakdown, wrote her daily, supplementing her letters with radio cables, containing the message "I love you insanely" in both English and French. When she wasn't scribbling endearments to Mercedes, she paced the deck like a caged cat.

Before she could join Mercedes in Paris, Eva had to endure a stay with her mother in London. Julie Le Gallienne took one look at her daughter and pronounced that Eva looked terrible. She particularly loathed Eva's severe new hairstyle. After spending a few days with her overwrought daughter, Julie concluded that Eva was quite insane. "I think you will simply have to marry me—in order to keep me alive!" Eva wrote to Mercedes in Paris. "My longing for you is like a madness."

Eva went through the motions of going to the theatre with her mother, visiting old friends, and shopping, but after a week she fled to Paris. Al Lehman was in town, and she took him to a "dump in Montmartre" where a "couple of cocottes came over & sat at our table." Le Gallienne danced with one of them and got Lehman to give the women a couple hundred francs, but she yearned for Mercedes. Her longing was "like a fever burning me up," she said, "and if you only were my husband, I should feel I had the answer to life." Of course, Mercedes already had a husband. After instructing her mother to tell friends that she was traveling with Mercedes and her husband, Eva joined Mercedes at the Hôtel Foyot. Abram Poole made himself scarce, and Mercedes and Eva went to the opera, dined, and danced, and visited Rouen to see where Joan of Arc was buried.

A few weeks later, after a short trip to Venice, Eva and Mercedes traveled to Budapest, where Eva was the guest of Ferenc Molnár. A luncheon in her honor turned into an all-day party culminating in a guided tour of the amusement park that was *Liliom*'s real-life background. While Eva took her first plane ride back to Paris, Mercedes journeyed to Constantinople, where, she later claimed, she first glimpsed the haunting beauty of the Swedish actress Greta Garbo.

In England again, Eva sent Mercedes letters almost daily, her vocabulary shrunken to little more than "insane": "I love you insanely," or the variation "I want you insanely." She reported that she rushed about insanely. Not satisfied with two or sometimes three letters a day from her lover, Eva said that she would go insane if she didn't hear from Mercedes more often. She was also having a ghastly time with her mother, who (perhaps understandably) continued to insist that Eva had gone insane.

As a respite from her mother, before Eva sailed for America she visited the Stenning home in Farncombe. Susan Stenning—Nanny—had been dead for several years, and Eva visited her grave. She played dominoes with Nanny's sisters and showed them Mercedes's photograph. "They wouldn't believe the picture of you was a lady at all," Eva told Mercedes. "They were quite sure it was a gentleman! I was tempted to tell them it was my husband."

In September 1922 Eva boarded the *Mauretania* for home. "A trip of this kind shows one definitely that there are only two things which save human beings from being cabbages: Love and Work," she said. Obsessive love and obsessive work possessed Le Gallienne at this time. Later, she would never be able to comprehend why she, who had always thought of herself as independent and self-sufficient, would sublimate her own ambition in a fierce attempt to find producers for Mercedes's work; or why when they were separated she had barely enough energy to drag herself out of bed. I believe in you, she told Mercedes, who was insecure not only about her writing but about Eva's faith and commitment to her. In the love drama she was playing out, Eva transformed Mercedes into an object of worship, writing of "the hope of someday being able to kiss your feet & crouch there—with your wonderful hands on my head—in a benediction. . . ." Le Gallienne wore a gold band on her little finger that Mercedes had given her and dreamed of being married to de Acosta and shouting their love "to the stars."

When Eva returned to New York in September 1922 to prepare for further touring with *Liliom,* she heard gossip about the relationship. She faced "the old nastiness," she wrote to Mercedes. "I must tell you that Nazimova has apparently behaved like a thorough cad." Le Gallienne's reference is unclear; but in an earlier letter to Eva, Nazimova had wondered if Mercedes's *Jehanne d'Arc* would be worthy of Eva's talents. Undoubtedly, there was considerable gossip about Eva's obsession with de Acosta, much of it generated by Mercedes herself, an incessant talker, who spoke to Eva's theatre friends and her own society circle about their plans together. In her letters, Eva encouraged Mercedes to work and stay away from meaningless people. "We *will* do *Jehanne,*" she promised.

Finally, 1922 ended and the close of the long *Liliom* tour was in sight. Springfield, Providence, Columbus, Richmond, Washington—the tour was a gray blur of towns and hotel rooms with few bright spots. In Washington, D.C., Eva met Alice Paul, the leader of the National Woman's Party. They discovered that they not only were kindred spirits but also shared the same birthday. Eva described Paul as such "a quiet, retiring, unobtrusive little woman to have done such amazing things." Le Gallienne joined the Woman's Party and agreed to speak out if she was needed.

Sixteen-year-old Rose Hobart, who played Liliom and Julie's daughter, was close to Eva at this time. Hobart became a noted character actor in both theatre and film, and Le Gallienne was her first teacher. "I thought she was incredible," Hobart remembered. "She taught me everything. She gave me copies of all the plays of Shakespeare, Walt Whitman, poetry, books of all kinds. She was my instructor on all kinds of important things, like what kind of a human being you should be." Hobart hero-worshipped Le Gallienne and said, "She was my first really big love. I would try to see her after the theatre, but Eva would never let

Mercedes de Acosta and Eva on holiday in Europe, 1922

me stay in her room after midnight. I didn't really understand anything about it at the time."

In Washington, D.C., though, after the close of the Saturday-night perfor-mance, Le Gallienne allowed Rose to wait in her drawing room on the train while she attended a party. The train was not scheduled to leave until three a.m. "I remember I was sitting in there," Hobart said, "and she walked in the door and started pacing the floor like a lioness and I thought, Oh no, I better get out of here. She's upset and maybe I'm not supposed to be here. She finally turned around and saw me and said, 'What are you doing here?' I said, 'I just came in to say good night.' Suddenly, she dropped to her knees in front of me, put her head in my lap, and started crying like no woman I had ever seen cry before. I was demolished. I didn't know what was happening. And finally what came out was that she had been at some diplomat's party and a lady said that if Eva re-mained at the party she would have to leave. She made a big fuss about it. And this tore Eva apart."

A few years later, when Hobart was in another play, an actress told her that Le Gallienne was a lesbian, "in a way that was just awful," Rose recalled. The woman also told her that people thought she and Eva had been lovers. Rose spent the next few days trying to sort out her feelings. "I had to admit to myself that Eva had tried to protect me through the tour," Hobart said. "I also realized that the way I had idolized her had made it difficult for her to explain the situation to me." Rose called Le Gallienne and asked to see her. "When I got to her door," Hobart remembered, "Eva took one look at me and said, 'You've heard.' Eva invited me in and began to talk. 'You can only judge people by how they treat you, right?' she said. I said right. 'Have I ever done anything to hurt you?' I said no, of course not. And she said, 'Well, I'm looking for beauty in my way, and it's not everybody's way.' " Le Gallienne's friendship with Rose, whom she called "funny little thing," endured. Later, Hobart played Julie in the film version of *Liliom* and gave a performance based on her immersion in Eva's interpretation of the role.

When Le Gallienne had toured Washington, D.C., in *Not So Long Ago* a few years earlier, she had attended many parties without incident, but her involvement with Mercedes de Acosta had become widely known in both theatre and society circles, making her the target of malicious gossip. While Mercedes had the refuge of a husband and marriage, Le Gallienne had no such protection and no desire to conform to any standards other than her own. Despite the pain she sometimes endured, Le Gallienne never wavered in her belief in the rightness of her sexual nature or of her artistic ideals. "What I always abhor," she said, "is 'middle' in anything, wether it be 'west' or 'class' or anything else that falls between two stools."

In a letter to her mother, in an unadorned style quite different from the ornate prose she used in her letters to Mercedes, Eva sketched her stark surroundings (Allentown, Pennsylvania) and described her defense, her protection, against a sometimes harsh reality: "This is one of the worst towns we are to play. The hotel is gloomy & down-at-heel. I have a room with a window off in a corner—& one dirty electric light high up in the centre of the grey ceiling. There is a table—an uninviting bed—two chairs—an old dresser—a wooden clothes tree. The window looks out on a fire escape. But all this is unreal—non-existent & unimportant. Inside me there are stars & the blue sky—& the great infinite Ocean. Tomorrow is my birthday. I shall be alone. It was not possible for Mercedes to come. I am glad she is not to come to this hideous & depressing place. Better that we should be together in our thoughts, for they are always beautiful and radiant."

KNOWING THAT Eva would soon be available, New York managers began to contact her and send her plays. Lee Shubert discovered that her contract expired in June 1923 and wooed her with an expensive leather case filled with perfume. Mercedes had other plans for Le Gallienne. Just as *Liliom* closed at the beginning of February, de Acosta finished her latest play, *Sandro Botticelli*. When commercial managers turned down the play, Eva and Mercedes raised the money to produce it in a three-week special engagement at the Provincetown Theatre.

While she rehearsed *Sandro Botticelli,* Eva took the opportunity to see as much theatre as possible. The Moscow Art Theatre was playing New York for the first time, and Le Gallienne saw many performances from her usual front-row seat. While she and other theatre people had read of the inspired playing of Stanislavsky's company, the actual experience was a revelation. Le Gallienne introduced herself to Stanislavsky; she became friendly with members of his company and was welcomed backstage. She particularly loved the Moscow Art Theatre productions of Chekhov's *The Three Sisters* and *The Cherry Orchard.* She studied the Russian acting technique, which seemed "not like acting at all," she wrote, "it is all so absolutely life-like." Stanislavsky, then sixty, had moved away from his earlier concern with external realism in the creation of character to concentrate on an inner, imaginative reality. Le Gallienne observed that Stanislavsky's method placed great importance on ensemble playing, which created an environment for the characters. In contrast, some of the Broadway plays she saw, like Jane Cowl's production of *Romeo and Juliet,* were showcases for stars. She was particularly critical of Nazimova's performance in the melodramatic *Dagmar.* "It really is unbelievable," she wrote, "that a woman of her intelligence could bring herself to do such a thing. . . . She really is such a fine artist—& I think she could really have been very great. But commercialism caught hold of her."

Something had caught hold of Le Gallienne as well, and for the moment she chose to believe that it was art. As she rehearsed *Sandro Botticelli* and created the character of Simonetta, she discovered that the play was actually a scenario, a thin outline that refused to come alive. Mercedes had based her play on the story of the painter's love for Simonetta Vespucci, the most beautiful woman in Florence. Simonetta visits the artist in his studio. She is naked under a flame-colored cloak. In a dramatic gesture, she removes the cloak, revealing her beauty, and instead of making love to her, Botticelli paints her. When she protests, he shouts, "My God, don't talk! I can't paint when you talk." Simonetta runs off naked into the cold night, catches pneumonia, and dies.

Populated by fifteen famous Italian characters, with elaborate sets, the play strained the resources of the tiny Provincetown Theatre. The house seated just 190 people, but on opening night it overflowed with those eager to see the new play and glimpse Le Gallienne in the nude. All they saw when Eva/Simonetta dropped her cloak was a brief view of her bare back, which excited gasps in the audience. When she turned to face Botticelli, her long blond wig covered her breasts and a strategically placed high-backed chair hid everything else. "It was curious," Eva wrote her mother, "just as I lay on Simonetta's bed, ready for the death scene on the opening night, Merle [Maddern] said very quickly and casually 'do you know that Sarah [Bernhardt] is dead'—then I closed my eyes—the curtain went up—and I died myself."

While the actors were praised, the reviews were scathing for Mercedes. She was called a "yearning society amateur." Her writing was so florid that it reminded critic Percy Hammond of a seed catalog. Others were more blunt—the play was not worth doing. Eva wrote later that playing Simonetta made her so miserable that during the death scene she would hold her breath until she fainted.

AFTER THE FAILURE of her play, Mercedes threatened to stop writing altogether. Le Gallienne begged her to learn from her mistakes and keep working. To cheer her up, Eva sublet her apartment and moved into Mercedes's house during May 1923. Abram Poole was traveling, working on painting commissions, and they had the house to themselves.

In May, Le Gallienne was back on stage in an Actors' Equity benefit production of *The Rivals,* getting good training, she said, playing with "wonderful old comedians." She sent *Jehanne d'Arc* to various managements, who stalled with offers of their own for Le Gallienne. She met Max Reinhardt, who wanted her to play Strindberg's *Dream Play,* but not until the end of the year. The Theatre Guild asked her to join their organization; she put them off. Gilbert Miller of the Frohman Company cabled from Europe offering her the title role in the American premiere of Ferenc Molnár's new play, *The Swan.* Delighted with Eva's performance in *Liliom,* Molnár wanted her to play his "swan," the Princess Alexandra. The contract was lucrative, and the elegant Alexandra quite a contrast from the stoop-shouldered Julie. Le Gallienne accepted happily.

With Eva's work ensured for the fall, Eva and Mercedes sailed once again for Europe and a six-week summer holiday. They stayed in Paris, where Eva saw Hesper and Robert Hutchinson and Mogens, who were visiting there as well. She shopped in Paris for Princess Alexandra's clothes, buying earrings, a tiara, and fans, and had the gowns designed by Molyneux. While Mercedes stayed in Paris, Eva went to London and visited her mother. She wrote almost daily to Mercedes, and while the letters still contained messages of "wanting you insanely," another tone, demanding and aristocratic, crept in. She reminded Mercedes, for example, to fill in the number on her trunk, to send for the lamps, and to pick up the sample of blue lace at Molyneux.

"One of the most important events in my life took place during this European visit," Le Gallienne recalled. As a girl, she had worshipped Sarah Bernhardt. When Sarah died, it amounted, she wrote, to "the burial of my religion." Art to Eva was akin to religion, and the deepest religion, she felt, was that of hero worship. In London that summer of 1923, when she saw Eleonora Duse perform in *Così sia* at the Oxford Theatre, she sat transfixed on the floor of the first-row aisle.

Her description of the experience in an account that she wrote at the time reads like a religious awakening, and in many ways it was. Duse's photograph and words had helped her in a time of great need, when she had been physically and spiritually violated. The words "Force et Confiance" had become her prayer, so it was not surprising that the presence of the flesh-and-blood woman would have a tremendous effect. "I felt that for the first time I saw and understood the meaning of true Beauty," she wrote. "She seemed the Essence of Beauty—radiant with a white light that shone from her face & through the tips of her fingers. She seemed to me the embodiment of Pity—Compassion—Understanding—like Christ. I felt that as Peter & John followed Him—so would I follow Her. After the performance—I was in an ecstasy—unconscious of surroundings of people of so-called reality."

Later, in her biography of Duse, *The Mystic in the Theatre,* an older Le Gallienne took out the ecstatic language of her earlier account and spoke of Duse in terms of her impact as an artist. "Suddenly, I saw it happen," she wrote, "this thing that I had always dreamed of. I saw the stage take on an added dimension; I felt the vast audience grow still and sit as though mesmerized in the presence of a frail, worn woman, who, with no apparent effort, through the sheer beauty of the truth within her, through the sheer power of her spirit, reached out to each one of us and held us all enthralled. I saw the 'impossible' come true." After the performance of *Così sia,* Eva sent Duse flowers and a note saying, "You have given me strength and faith to live."

On the boat trip home, Le Gallienne befriended the impresario Morris Gest. A visionary showman, Gest had brought Max Reinhardt's productions and the Moscow Art Theatre to America. With the financial backing of Otto Kahn, he planned to present Duse in a series of New York appearances. Through Gest, Eva obtained free front-row seats for Duse's Tuesday and Friday matinee performances, which had been scheduled for the convenience of working actors.

The *Swan* company, directed by David Burton, began rehearsals at the Empire Theatre. Eva sublet her apartment to Hesper and Robert Hutchinson and stayed with Mercedes in her house at 134 East Forty-seventh Street. Since Abram Poole was in Chicago on business, she could be alone with Mercedes, and she enjoyed the comforts of meals, laundry service, and a location convenient to the theatre.

Eva liked the director and the company, especially handsome Basil Rathbone, who with his dark hair, slim, elegant figure, and chiseled features bore an uncanny resemblance to young Richard Le Gallienne. At first reading, *The Swan* seemed a simple romantic comedy to Eva. Set in a mythical European kingdom,

LEFT:

Eva as Princess Alexandra in The Swan. *The silver gown was designed for her by Molyneux.*

BELOW:

Basil Rathbone tutoring the young princes

the play revolves around the efforts of Princess Beatrice to marry her daughter, Princess Alexandra, to Prince Albert. To excite the prince's ardor and his jealousy, the princess flirts with the royal tutor. The tutor (played by Rathbone) falls in love with Princess Alexandra and fights a duel of words with the prince. In the end, Princess Alexandra rejects the tutor, chooses her royal duty, and marries the prince. As she rehearsed the play, Eva found that it was "developing into something more interesting and more subtle than I had thought—and more & more I doubt that it will prove popular . . . the point of view is so essentially European—and not proletarian in the slightest degree. . . . For although it satirizes the aristocratic life—& the pomp & ceremony of small courts—it in a way justifies them and makes their behaviour seem inevitable & rather beautiful in its cold & often self-sacrificing discipline."

The play opened in Detroit to excellent notices. In Montreal, however, Eva caught a bad cold, which she admitted was brought on by nerves. She was plagued by the insinuation that "if our little Swan is all right, the play will be a hit." She asked Mercedes to join her and take care of her. Mercedes replied that she couldn't get away, since Abram was in town, her friend Sheila was visiting, and anyway she was ill. Feeling neglected and jealous, Eva wrote to Mercedes: "It seems so ridiculous to me—so unfair & stupid, that he should be there, legally and by right—and in the face of the world and everyone in it—and that I should be always away from you—and in no way belonging to you in the eyes of the world—I sometimes want so insanely to proclaim loudly from the housetops that I am yours—and belong to you wholly and utterly. Will there ever be an answer to it all? I wonder." Fortunately for Eva, Mary Benson, still her devoted Mimsey, took the train to Montreal, stayed for a week, and nursed Eva back to health.

ON OCTOBER 23, 1923, the day of the New York opening of *The Swan,* Eva tried to calm her nerves, walking from Eighth Street to Central Park and then to the Majestic Hotel at Central Park West and Seventy-second Street, where Duse was staying. She bought a bunch of pansies, which she had heard were Duse's favorite flowers, wrote a note, and took them in to the hotel. In the lobby she met Désirée von Wertheimstein, Duse's companion and assistant, who took the flowers and said, "Madame Duse has read in the papers of your opening tonight. She has been thinking of you, and I know she wishes you success."

Eva went home to rest. Désirée soon appeared at her door. "Madame was very cross with me for not taking you up to see her," she said. "Will you come back with me now, at once? She wants to talk to you, but in case you can't come, she sent this letter." Eva opened the letter and read Duse's words, written in French: "Dear, beautiful child, Dear Artist who is suffering for her Art! I would so like to console you—tell you to be SURE of yourself. I scold myself for not coming to find you—and I dare not leave this room! Forgive—and be happy. You are in the light. Eleonora Duse."

Eva returned to the Majestic Hotel with Désirée. When she entered Duse's sitting room, Le Gallienne saw a frail woman with white hair brushed back from her forehead and a "strangely crooked face, as though one side had suffered more deeply than the other." Duse greeted her with outstretched arms. "Her eyes looked straight into mine," Eva said, "as though searching for something in me. I couldn't speak."

Duse seated Eva beside her on the sofa and continued to examine her. She took off Eva's hat and stroked her face and hair. They conversed in French, their shared language. Duse smiled and said, "You look like a young Venetian girl with that black shawl. And now, tell me: Where did you find those words 'Strength and Faith'?"

"But it was you who gave them to me, madame," Eva said, and told her of seeing the words on her photograph.

"How strange," Duse said. "And you give them back to me, just at the moment when I have such need of them."

When it was time for Eva to leave, Duse gave her some tiny roses and walked with her to the elevator. When Eva stepped in, she raised her arm in a farewell salute and said, "Strength and Faith! You will play well tonight—I know it."

That night a pouring rain soaked the first-night audience of *The Swan.* The translator sent a telegram saying, "Remember what is good weather for ducks is good weather for 'Swans.' " Latecomers straggled in wet and bedraggled all during the first act. For the first time in her acting experience, though, Le Gallienne "was able to play . . . without the paralyzing fear of failure, the self-centred longing for personal success, that had so often made my opening-night performances disastrous." She was nervous, she admitted, but "too grateful, too excited, too penetrated by the power of that extraordinary being, to give any thought to self; and this gave me a freedom I had never before experienced on the stage."

When the final curtain rang down at 11:20, the audience leapt to their feet in a standing ovation, calling the company back again and again. Basil Rathbone saw a man in the fourth row throw his hat in the air and learned later that it was Alexander Woollcott. The play was a tremendous hit, breaking the records of the Cort Theatre for advance sales, beating even the popular *Peg o' My Heart.* Lines a block long appeared outside the box office. The play made Basil Rathbone a star and confirmed Eva Le Gallienne's reputation as one of the theatre's finest artists.

John Corbin in *The New York Times* praised her performance as "admirable for its artistic restraint, its renunciation of all easy and obvious effects, and for the potency of its inward fires." The *Vogue* critic wrote that "Eva Le Gallienne has done nothing finer, and few of our younger actresses have ever done anything half so good. The portrait is complete, from the first cold moments to the last bitter ones, and in all the moments, passionate and resigned, that come between and after. Her strange beauty, her stranger repression, have never been so well matched by a part, and an inner flame of something strangest of all finds a chance to play across the poetry of *The Swan*." *Theatre* magazine praised her performance, but noted in passing that like Mrs. Fiske she was not softly feminine, while admitting at the same time that the part did not require it—that the princess kisses the tutor out of sympathy, not love.

Critic George Jean Nathan believed that the chief requirement for acting was a lack of intelligence. While he championed the career of Eugene O'Neill, who wanted to be an artist or nothing, Nathan resented actors, particularly women, who studied and took a serious approach to their work. He railed against what he considered the cold and intellectual acting of Mrs. Fiske and leveled the same charge against Eva Le Gallienne. Clare Eames, who was considered by Le Gallienne and other theatre artists to be brilliant, would hear the same criticism until her untimely death. Tellingly, Mrs. Fiske, Eva Le Gallienne, and Clare Eames all aspired to play the great roles in Shakespeare, Chekhov, and Ibsen. They were women who did not hide either their ambition or their intelligence.

In striking contrast to Nathan's view of actresses, female reporters, usually in monthly magazines or feature articles, often presented their view of "femininity" or "intelligence" in women artists. For example, after seeing Eva's Julie in *Liliom*, Elsa Gidlow pointed out in *Pearson's Magazine* in February 1922 the dangers of Eva's approach to acting: "It is not so easy to give the public interpretations . . . of women of flesh and blood when it wants, or think it wants, dolls and idols." In the December 1923 *Theatre*, Richard Willis anointed Le Gallienne as one of the up-and-coming geniuses of the theatre, sure to achieve lasting fame, but he could not resist chiding her for taking herself "too seriously." In contrast, almost in answer, two months later in the same magazine Ada Patterson described Le Gallienne this way: "The sign of the jutting brow . . . that hangs craglike above the clear, gray lakes of her calm eyes, is the outstanding feature of Eva Le Gallienne's face. It is curiously high, remarkably broad, extraordinarily full. It is crammed with brains, which she uses."

And what did Eva Le Gallienne think about her reviews for *The Swan?* "The next morning, when I read the notices," she said, "I was happy because they were all splendid, but somehow they didn't seem to matter quite as much as usual." What mattered most to her was the phone call she received from Eleonora Duse that afternoon. "You see! I was right—you played well!" Duse exclaimed.

After meeting Duse, she "began to realize . . . that in playing, as in any other art, one should abolish the personal and try to place one's instrument at the service of a higher, disembodied force." Ahead of her lay years of work and, she said, "particularly the necessity of a wide range of experience embracing to the greatest possible degree the finest dramatic material."

But where would she work? Broadway stardom meant playing the same character in a long run. Duse, who played only repertory, was appalled when Le Gallienne told her that she played *The Swan* eight times a week. "It's barbaric! You should refuse," she said.

"I should like to see dear Gilbert Miller's face if I attempted such a thing," Eva answered.

"Oh, those slave drivers!" said Duse. "Dear little Le Gallienne, you will kill your soul! Look! Go and join the Russians! That's it! Leave everything and join the Russians. They are the only true ones!"

Le Gallienne laughed and said that she didn't think she could—her mother would not approve.

"I am mad—don't listen to me! Ah! I am the enemy of mamas!" said Duse.

Le Gallienne would soon be twenty-five. She didn't want to leave New York, believing it to be "the future centre of art and indeed any kind of matured activity. The seeds and development still come from the old world—but they seem to come here for their final blooming." In May 1924 she took out her first papers as an American citizen—"so that in two years I will be a full-grown American," she told her mother. "I feel more and more that this is the New World—the Future—and I want to belong to it."

Where could she play Hilda and Juliet and Hedda and Peter Pan and Marguerite Gautier—all the classic roles that she had listed when she was sixteen? In a repertory theatre, of course, in Moscow or Paris or Berlin or Copenhagen. But where were the great repertory theatres of America?

"There are none," she realized.

PART THREE

1923 - 1931

Eva's favorite portrait of Eleonora Duse

It would be disappointing if great things were too easy.

DURING HER LAST TOUR to America in 1923, Eleonora Duse played a repertory of five plays. At her New York premiere, thousands of people were turned away, scalpers sold tickets for two hundred dollars a seat, and the opening night receipts totaled thirty thousand dollars. Afterward, Duse would receive no one in her dressing room—not even Gloria Swanson, Hollywood's biggest star.

Because of her work in *The Swan,* Le Gallienne did not attend the gala opening, but from a seat in the front row of the theatre she saw every Tuesday and Friday matinee performance of *The Lady from the Sea, Ghosts, Così sia, La porta chiusa,* and *La città morta.* She studied Duse, who acted without makeup, without wigs. Later, in her biography of Duse, Le Gallienne noted that Duse's voice was not an actor's voice. "Like everything else about Duse it was completely natural," she wrote. And Duse seemed oblivious of the audience. But after watching her again and again, Le Gallienne realized that Duse perfectly concealed her technical virtuosity. Duse's repose astonished her. "Sometimes she would sit in a chair for a long period completely motionless, holding us all spell-bound by sheer intensity of thought," Le Gallienne wrote. "She did not need physical motion . . . to convey her thoughts; she conveyed them because she *really* thought them. . . . She did not pretend to listen—she *really* listened. . . . There was never any sense of 'repetition'; everything she did, everything she said—or heard, or thought—seemed never to have happened until that instant. This was what made her seem so extraordinarily real." Le Gallienne observed, too, that there "was no hiatus between the thoughts and feelings of the characters Duse played, and herself as their interpreter. It was *one* process. In most actors, this process is divided; first there is the awareness of the thought, then the technical means used to convey it. Once Duse had built the architectural structure of a scene . . . she could forget it, and give herself wholly to the emotions it contained."

Duse's acting was an artistic revelation, but the personal relationship Eva had with the older woman was a spiritual awakening. Duse singled out Eva Le Gallienne as the only actor she would see privately in New York. In Duse's hotel room, "stripped of everything extraneous; no pictures, no flowers, very few books . . . and no mirrors anywhere," the two women talked frequently. "She treated me as an equal," Le Gallienne remembered. "She spoke of 'our work,' as though we were two colleagues who should understand and help each other."

During one of their conversations, Duse asked Le Gallienne what plays she wanted to do. *The Master Builder,* Eva replied. "Yes, yes! That is for you," Duse said. "Play it. . . . You must. Hilda Wangel is for you." Of Ibsen's other women that Le Gallienne wanted to play, Duse called Rebekka West in *Rosmersholm* "the most difficult . . . the most mysterious of all," and of Hedda Gabler she said, "Which is the demon? Which is the angel? . . . For both are there." Duse's subtle art was ideally suited to Ibsen's complex, multifaceted women. In characters like Rebekka West Ibsen explored the unconscious mind, and his dialogue is often oblique, the meaning submerged in the subtext. Actors must say the lines but act the undermeaning. To communicate fully, Duse aspired to a "total harmony" of "speech, mime, and gesture." Le Gallienne found it impossible to break down Duse's technique into separate parts, since she felt that Duse had achieved this "total harmony." "Her entire body, like that of an animal," Le Gallienne recalled, "was instantly obedient to the impulse of the brain." Also, Duse seemed unconfined by her body. She radiated an inner vitality that was almost tangible. Words seemed inadequate to convey Duse's ephemeral art.

Duse's art was different from Bernhardt's, Le Gallienne observed. Bernhardt's truth "was always that of a great actress," Le Gallienne felt. "Both on and off the stage [Sarah] was aware of the effect of every word and gesture. But this did not mean that she was false . . . paradoxical as this may seem, it is still entirely possible."

Like Bernhardt, Duse also possessed enormous charisma on and off the stage. "When she listened her eyes never left your face," Eva recalled. "The undivided attention she gave you was part of her extraordinary charm. There was something childlike about it . . . also something immensely flattering . . . dangerously so, perhaps; for it made you feel you really mattered to her."

When Duse apologized for not seeing Le Gallienne play in *The Swan,* Eva demurred that Duse's presence would have made her too nervous. "Ah! That abominable fear! One must conquer it," Duse said. "One must forget self . . . forget self . . . it's the only way!" She opened a small paperbound book to page seventy-five and indicated the last paragraph, which had been marked "by a vigorous thumbnail." " 'Most generous rewarder! Endow my body also with splendid clarity, with prompt agility, with penetrating subtlety, with strong impassibility,' " Eva read aloud. Titled *Prières de Saint-Thomas d'Aquin,* the well-worn book was marked throughout with penciled underlinings, creased pages, and a torn margin at one particular prayer.

As Eva said goodbye that day, Duse "went over to the window sill where a pot of four-leaf clovers was standing; she plucked three of them and pressed them between the pages of the little book, then held it out to me with one of those rare smiles of hers which seemed to illumine not only her own face but the whole room, the whole universe." Le Gallienne took the book home with her and studied the prayers and passages that Duse had marked. It seemed strange to Eva that a great actress would value prayers of praise to God and strive to emulate the selfless lives of the saints. Art, however, was Duse's religion; and to be a true artist, she believed, the ego had to be destroyed. It was only after years of work, and after she had written Duse's biography, that Le Gallienne understood Duse's mystical path.

In their conversations, Duse and Le Gallienne shared an intimacy so precious to Eva that she revealed her secret to only a chosen few. "I have never seen anyone who seemed as innately well-bred—a distinction of the spirit—a gentleness of manner that is simply divine," she wrote.

IN EARLY 1924, Eva moved from her downtown Fifth Avenue apartment to a ninth-floor, one-bedroom apartment at 212 East Forty-eighth Street. Her view of the East River and the Fifty-ninth Street Bridge was spectacular, but she took the apartment for another view—her bedroom window looked out on Mimsey Benson's bedroom window, directly opposite. Since their reconciliation several years earlier, Eva and Mimsey once again had become intimate friends. Le Gallienne clung tightly to her few but devoted friends. Often on weekends, sometimes accompanied by Mercedes, she drove her recently purchased Studebaker Special Six Roadster to Mary and Stuart Benson's Folding Key Farm in Weston, Connecticut. When he was home, editor/artist Stuart Benson worked in his book-filled study. Benson was a gifted artist, and he sculpted a bronze head of Eva, which he later gave to her. Mimsey was Eva's closest friend, and perhaps still her lover. "There is always a room in this house for Eva Le Gallienne," Mimsey vowed.

By this time, Eva's artistic ambition, inspired by her spiritual intimacy with Duse, had intruded on her decidedly carnal relationship with Mercedes de Acosta. For companionship, she had Tosca, a Cairn terrier puppy, who accompanied her everywhere; and ruthlessly, firmly, she began to eliminate, she wrote, her "personal life and relationships." The earlier fevered prose of her letters to Mercedes was replaced with repeated apologies for selfish, thoughtless behavior. While Mercedes pressed Eva to find a producer for her play *Jehanne d'Arc,* Le Gallienne turned to other projects, promising Mercedes that they would do the play, but not just yet.

While she played eight performances of *The Swan* each week, after securing the financial backing of arts patron Mrs. C. C. Rumsey, Eva produced and played the title role in three matinee performances of Gerhart Hauptmann's play *The Assumption of Hannele* at the Cort Theatre. She recruited actors from *The Swan* and friends from various other Broadway companies to fill out the large cast. When the director failed to appear, she took over the staging chores. For the dual role of the Schoolmaster and the Christlike Stranger, Eva chose her *Swan* co-star Basil Rathbone. She liked Rathbone "better than any man I have ever played with. He is entirely charming—very gentle and nice to me—and wonderful to play with (he is the first leading man I have ever had who is earnest and deeply sincere about his work—who never cheats or in any way shirks his end of things). He likes me too—and we both hope we may do many things together in the future."

Hauptmann's play tells the poetic tale of Hannele, a beaten and abused little girl who in a dying vision sees Christ and is rewarded with heavenly happiness. Thinking she looked too robust to play a starving child, and without considering the effect on her *Swan* princess, Eva dieted on black coffee, grapefruit, and For-mil-lac, achieving the gauntness of Hannele but also a new, emaciated look for Alexandra. When the pressures of the production and performances grew too much, she drew energy from a telegram Duse sent her from New Orleans. Don't ever doubt yourself, Duse told her. You will find strength in the new work. *Tout sera bien*—all will be well.

Stark Young in *The New Republic* called Le Gallienne's acting the best he had seen all season; other critics admired the company's willingness to forsake commercialism for art. The experience awakened Le Gallienne's interest in direction; and tutored by the stagehands at the Cort Theatre, she learned about scenery, lighting, and the technical problems of staging a large, complex show.

Under the influence of Duse and the martyred Hannele, the face Le Gallienne presented to the world in a long interview in *Theatre* in February 1924 was serenely intellectual. A few years earlier, after reading a biography of Michelangelo, she wrote: "What a marvellous life those artists led, how gloriously impersonal their lives—in some mysterious way detached . . . like some divine third sex—filled with inspiration above earthly human relationships." She liked to think of herself in the same way, imagining herself above the sexual fray, breathing the rarefied air of art. Of course, this was also an acceptable way of avoiding uncomfortable questions about her private life and loves. In the *Theatre* article, writer Ada Patterson described a cerebral Eva, with fine light-brown hair falling to her shoulders, robed in a gray brocade dressing gown, sitting in a straight-backed chair at a large desk in her book-lined study, holding a Bible.

Although Eva was familiar with the writings of Schopenhauer and Kierkegaard as well as the Bible, her personal philosophy was pure Viking. She told Patterson that she never expected anything from others: "Then if we receive nothing we are not disappointed. If we receive, it is a delightful surprise. . . .

*Although she was often described as beautiful in the roles she played,
Eva's beauty, which cannot be conveyed by still photographs like this snapshot
taken in 1924, was not in her features but rather in the mobility of
her expressions and the grace of her movements.*

Events drive us in upon ourselves again and again, and we grow stronger for the experience." She answered some of her critics who thought her conceited and cold. "The truth is my emotions are strong, and I wish they knew how humble I am. It is my shyness, and my self-consciousness, that cause me to seem cold. Acting seems to me like driving a horse. The horse is the emotional nature. One must always keep her hands on the reins. Sometimes we keep a tight hold upon the reins. Sometimes we slacken them. In ten years, or twenty, I may drive with slacker rein. I may permit my emotions fuller sway while on the stage. But as a beginner, one who has all to learn about the theatre, I hold my reins in a tight hand. Better control, for a time, even though some may call it coldness."

Would Ada Patterson have been astonished to discover that Le Gallienne occasionally drank gin, smoked cigarettes, delighted in the tricks of shimmy dancers, and loved passionately—or was she willingly contributing to Le Gallienne's creation of a public persona?

"When I left her," Patterson reported, "she stood beside the big, flat-topped desk, her fingers on the book with the faded cover."

"It has helped me," Eva said. "It brings gentleness to the world. The world needs more kindness"—words that "may have sprung from the sovereign mind," wrote Patterson, "or from the heart which she insists she possesses."

For her fervid outpourings about the soul, her admission of Bible reading, and her resemblance to a sin-free medieval maid, Eva was ridiculed by some of her peers, who at the height of the hedonistic 1920s pursued pleasure and partied with reckless abandon. But even before the *Theatre* interview, it was clear to uptown Broadway folk, especially younger theatre people, that Eva Le Gallienne set herself apart—a pious prig who affected devotion to art and looked down on ordinary actors in commercial plays who just wanted to make money and have fun.

General critical admiration of her achievements didn't help matters. Even Alexander Woollcott (who had charged her with coldness) grudgingly proclaimed that he had more respect for Eva Le Gallienne than any other actress. "It is not merely that she has played so excellently all season in *The Swan*," he wrote, "nor that, almost unaided, she produced *Hannele* with . . . one hand tied behind her back. Nor that, after so exhausting an adventure, she was able to spring, fresh, competent and well equipped, to the aid of the somewhat sorely beset Mme. Simone, now ensconced at the Gaiety for a brief season of French matinees. . . . She is that solitary and interesting phenomenon, a young person in the American theatre who actually works at her job."

A twenty-five-year-old Broadway star who played special matinees in faultless French as well as in English, who was devoted to Duse and read books in five languages, who was not married and was rumored to be either a lesbian or a virgin, was a strange phenomenon on Broadway. Her industriousness, her very na-

ture, seemed both a challenge and a rebuke. She appeared overly serious and humorless. What was she trying to prove? Why was she working so hard? What was
wrong with her?

"I seem to have an unquenchable thirst for work," Eva explained. "Nothing
else seems to matter. I have never felt so intensely about it before." Working,
playing different roles, directing and producing, used more facets of her multifaceted being. "The soul's joy lies in doing," proclaimed Duse, and Le Gallienne
shared that belief. The physical outlet provided by a lover was necessary and
healthy, but some aspects of personal involvement, such as listening to a lover's
problems, might be time consuming and distracting from her own ambition.
From 1924 on, all of Le Gallienne's lovers would be connected in some way to
her goal—creating art and becoming Eva Le Gallienne, artist.

ON APRIL 12, 1924, Eva received a telegram from Duse, who was staying at
the Hotel Schenley in Pittsburgh. Knowing of Le Gallienne's work in the French
matinees in addition to her *Swan* performances, Duse wrote: "Très heureuse
vous retrouver en pleine bataille. Tout sera bien. Tous souhaits. Tendrement" (I
am happy to find you in full battle. All will be well. All hopes. Tenderly). "It
seemed as though she were handing me on a torch of Courage," said Le Gallienne. The fact that it was the last telegram Duse sent to anyone would always
hold great significance to Le Gallienne. On the evening of April 5, Duse had
walked in an icy rain from the Schenley to the nearby Syria Mosque, where she
was to play *La porta chiusa*—The Closed Door. By the time Duse found the
stage door, she was soaked through and shivering. Pneumonia set in, and on
April 21 she died.

Le Gallienne met the train carrying Duse's body to New York City. While
three thousand people stood in silent tribute, Duse was carried into the Church
of Saint Vincent Ferrer. The priest had kindly given Eva a key to the church, and
for four days after her *Swan* performances she joined Désirée and a few members
of Duse's company. The church was quiet and dark, lit only by the soft colors of
votive candles that flickered under the statue of the Madonna and by the candles
placed around Duse's bier. After a Requiem Mass, Duse was returned to Italy
and buried in a small country cemetery in Asolo. A plain white marble stone inscribed "Eleonora Duse, 1858–1924" marks her grave.

In letters to Mogens, Nazimova, and Julie, Le Gallienne expressed her grief.
There was certainly a histrionic quality to Le Gallienne's suffering, but at its base
was the fact that Eva believed Duse had saved her life. Two and a half years ear-
lier in Mackie's Sanitarium, she had clung to Duse's photograph and her words
"I wish you strength and faith to live." "Force et Confiance" became Eva's prayer.
Duse had ceased to be a woman and had become a god. Eva told Mogens that

she often dreamed of Duse. In one recurring dream Eva walked down a long corridor, a door opened, and Duse beckoned her to come in. "So few here know what Madame Duse meant to me," she wrote Julie Le Gallienne, "so I have to try and conceal carefully my true feelings—otherwise I would be accused of affectation and pose—& many other charming things. How happy people are to try and destroy the things that we reverence—the things that feed our spirit— the things that give us joy and strength. It is something that becomes increasingly hard for me to understand—the joy of tearing down—it is like some awful sadism of the spirit."

IN MAY 1924, when the Actors' Equity strike closed *The Swan* and other Broadway shows, it was Le Gallienne's Olympian view that "the managers & actors have been behaving like a lot of stupid children—fighting & squabbling about a lot of nonsense." The strike may have been nonsense to Le Gallienne, who had a fat savings account and earned the percentages and salary of a Broadway star, but to many struggling actors it was important to fight for the requirement that managers post bonds with Equity insuring that actors would be paid for their work.

Still, the strike gave her a much-needed vacation and a rest for her eyes, which had been damaged by exposure, month after month, to bright, harsh spotlights. Wearing rose-colored protective goggles, she relaxed for two weeks at Mimsey's farm. She walked in the woods and worked on *The Master Builder,* which she had arranged to present that summer at Jasper Deeter's Hedgerow Theatre outside of Philadelphia. Founded by Deeter the year before, the theatre was conceived as a real repertory company, with the bill changing nightly.

After playing less than two weeks of *The Master Builder* to sold-out houses drawn by her stardom, Le Gallienne abruptly decided to leave. Used to the smooth-functioning, union-run theatres of Broadway, and to the treatment accorded a Broadway star, she displayed a star's temperament and complained about having to set her own stage before performances, about not having anyone to run the lights, about "disrespect and lack of courtesy" backstage, about being surrounded by "a very dirty atmosphere, deceit & lying." Le Gallienne had also allowed Mercedes de Acosta, then thirty-one, to play the young, naive Kaja in the play, which was a ludicrous mistake. On Friday, July 11, Le Gallienne announced that she was leaving the following Sunday. "Of course then, general consternation and the realisation that they had bitten off their own nose to spite their face!" she wrote angrily. She blamed Deeter for the situation and wondered about the future of such a poorly run theatre. A pioneer in institutional theatres outside New York, the tiny Hedgerow would endure, accumulating a repertoire

Eva as Hilda Wangel in The Master Builder. *Note the cigarette in her right hand. Eva, often asked to put out her cigarette in restaurants and other public places, took every opportunity to smoke onstage.*

of some two hundred plays, and boasting in promotional material that the distinguished Eva Le Gallienne had played there.

Working on Hilda in *The Master Builder,* however, had been a "mental tonic" for Le Gallienne. She had made a quick sketch of Hilda which would be the basis for the full portrait of the character which she hoped to create later. The real reason she chose to leave the Hedgerow so suddenly was that she wanted to get on to other things—like a restful vacation before returning to New York and *The Swan.*

AFTER PLAYING a few weeks in New York at the Empire Theatre, *The Swan* company moved to Chicago for a ten-week run and then embarked on a short tour of major cities. Le Gallienne found the experience delightful. She enjoyed everything—playing tennis, the beautiful fall weather, the receptive audiences, even various social engagements. In contrast, Mercedes, living in New York with Abram Poole, was depressed, demoralized, and jealous. With Eva's encouragement, Mercedes continued to submit her plays to other producers, but no one was interested in her work without the Le Gallienne connection.

While Mercedes longed for the old intensity of their relationship, Eva's passion had cooled, and she saw Mercedes's character and their involvement in a new light. "More and more it seems to me that one's personal life is unimportant," Eva told Mercedes. In the tone of a teacher speaking to a backward student, she lectured de Acosta: "You speak with such certainty of the glamorous joys of acting—the inspiration that must come from the public—the glow—the exultation—But these things only come on those impossible rare occasions when for a brief instant one feels oneself in intimate touch with the divine. . . . These sensations do *not* come from the public. And most often one's feeling is one of despair at the terrible distance that remains between oneself and the mountain top." Echoing her friend Eleonora Sears, Eva also advised Mercedes that "the glow of a body in action is a great healer for the mind that is torturing itself."

Why was Le Gallienne so buoyantly happy? Taking her own advice and playing up to five sets of tennis a day was one reason, but Basil Rathbone was another. They became lovers. Much of their attraction was undoubtedly propinquity. It was rare for a man to excite Le Gallienne's ardor, but she was attracted to Rathbone on every level—sexually, artistically, and spiritually. She adored his "long aristocratic legs," his gentle nature, and they shared artistic aspirations, planning to work together in the future in Ibsen's *Rosmersholm,* playing the doomed lovers Rebekka and Rosmer. At one point, Eva contemplated marrying Basil and having his child. Their relationship ended, according to Le Gallienne, when she overheard Rathbone telling other members of the company that he was sleeping with her. Later, she always referred to Rathbone as "my Basil" and would say that he was the only man that she could have married.

A furious Mercedes accused Le Gallienne of love affairs with both Rathbone and a Russian actress and, somewhat illogically, of being a "cold hard-hearted creature" ruled by her head. Time after time, she reminded Eva of her promise to do *Jehanne d'Arc*. Eva replied that she planned to see the French director Firmin Gémier in New York and talk to him about presenting Mercedes's play in France. "Since you have no faith—I must have Faith & *quiet*," she told Mercedes.

Le Gallienne had grown stronger and more self reliant since December 1921, when, vulnerable, emotionally scarred by rape, and playing the masochistic role of Julie in *Liliom,* she had first met Mercedes. In a letter that resounded with confidence, she wrote the older woman a personal declaration of independence: "And then this thing in me that hurts you so much—this not wanting to share every happening or every thought—I have tried to analyse that and I think it is perhaps the most masculine trait about me. A sort of terror of losing myself, my individual personal life—an insane desire for freedom. . . . It's a kind of ferocious, wild thing in me. I can't explain it further."

When Mercedes's visit to Chicago was cancelled because Julie Le Gallienne planned to vacation there for several weeks in October, Eva wrote melodramatically to Mercedes: "The thought of Mother's impending visit strikes terror to my heart." As she had feared, the highly critical Julie didn't particularly care for *The Swan* or her daughter's performance and advised Eva not to touch Mercedes's play *The Mother of Christ* for at least ten years. Eva wouldn't allow Julie to read *Jehanne d'Arc,* claiming that Mercedes was still working on it.

Much had changed since their last disastrous meeting in London; Eva reported that Julie was "more gentle with me." She delighted in indulging Julie with luxuries, and after all the hardships she and her mother had endured, Eva appreciated the comfort of ordering "anything you wanted to eat and to have it served in state in a comfortable sitting-room . . . to have a car . . . not to have to count every nickel before spending it. Yes, it was fun to be a successful young star; life was good indeed!"

When Julie returned to New York before sailing to London, she spent some time with Mercedes. Perhaps because she sensed that the danger was past, she told Eva that she had grown to love de Acosta. By November, after months of "hell," Eva and Mercedes had reached a new understanding—at least in their correspondence. Le Gallienne responded to a "beautiful letter" from Mercedes. Eva denied that she loved or wanted anyone else: "I have found you my dearest—and could never find I know anything that would be greater or more fulfilling." Mercedes had belittled Eva's "pathetic remarks about men" and her wish to have children, but Le Gallienne did not deny her maternal urge. "Well, they were perhaps fragments of the human *woman* in me (and you know well that I am very feminine)," she wrote, "perhaps I am not as far evolved as you and the great cosmic surge towards pro-creation perhaps occasionally strikes me—when you are immune to it. Who knows? Who can explain or judge the inner workings of one's spirit. I do not pretend to understand myself. I only vaguely feel, but with a growing clearness, that I have some work of service to do here—and in that you are inextricably bound up. I feel more & more that what happens to me personally is of little matter."

"WHAT NOW? Is this all? What next?" Le Gallienne had asked herself again and again during the enormously successful and financially lucrative run of *The Swan*. By the time the tour closed in the spring of 1925, she had translated *Jehanne d'Arc* and *The Mother of Christ* into French, convinced Norman Bel Geddes to direct and design both plays, and raised half the money to produce them. Not wanting a replay of the *Sandro Botticelli* humiliation in full view of all the Broadway devils, she arranged for the plays to be presented in Paris under the sponsorship of Firmin Gémier at the Théâtre de l'Odéon. As a girl she had walked past the Odéon and dreamed of playing there.

The fact that neither Bel Geddes nor de Acosta could speak French was considered unimportant. "I had great faith in Eva," Bel Geddes said, "and a great desire to spend the Spring in Paris." Eva thought Bel Geddes a "mad excitable creature (but with great talent and strength of vision)." He had little faith in the play. It's "episodic and undramatic," he told Mercedes. "The first order of business for you is to get your play in shape. The maid of Orleans is a big challenge to any author, but there is a good strong play in her story." George Bernard Shaw had proven that fact with his 1923 masterpiece, *Saint Joan*.

When Bel Geddes discussed his concerns with Eva, she assured him that Mercedes was completely rewriting the script. Bel Geddes had already received acclaim for designing *The Miracle* for Reinhardt. Since *Jehanne d'Arc* was a scenario, barely forty minutes of short scenes with cryptic dialogue interspersed with blackouts for scene changes, he saw an opportunity to test some of his ideas. Le Gallienne knew that the play was weak. She delayed showing the final version to Bel Geddes and refused to send her mother a copy. Mercedes sensed what Eva was feeling, and said at one point that she thought Le Gallienne was ashamed of her. But Eva had promised Mercedes that she would do the play, and she repressed any misgivings she had about the script.

At the first rehearsal in Paris, Eva read the play and Bel Geddes's opening address to the company in French. "The theatre is to me, always, only and above all the theatre," said Bel Geddes. "The stage is always the stage . . . so in this production the story of Jeanne d'Arc is handled purely as a thing of the theatre."

The multiple-level unit set of huge, deep blue cubes, looking like the skyline of a futuristic city, rested on horizontal platforms. A cyclorama wrapped around the back of the set. Specific locale would be created by the mob of extras (banners would become a gold wall at Rheims Cathedral, for example) and by the elaborate lighting system, which they had brought at a cost of eight thousand dollars from America.

At the final dress rehearsal, the whole enterprise almost collapsed because of Bel Geddes's faulty French pronunciation. When he asked the Frenchwoman who had executed his designs to adjust the costume of Cauchon, the chief inquisitor, she didn't hear him. Bel Geddes rapped her with his megaphone and shouted, "Cauchon! Cauchon!" The costumer was outraged. Not only had the crazy American director struck her with his megaphone, but even worse, he had called her a *cochon*—a pig. "The company was like a hornet's nest," Le Gallienne remembered. "We were all *des sauvages, des barbares Americains*." When the costumer's husband came at him with fists raised, Bel Geddes escaped, leaving Eva to move among the company explaining his mistake in perfectly accented French.

The opening of *Jehanne d'Arc* was reviewed by New York, London, Copenhagen, Berlin, and Paris newspapers. The fashionable audience included Ambassador Myron Timothy Herrick, Elsie de Wolfe, Arthur Rubinstein, Mrs. Vincent Astor, Mrs. Oliver Harriman, Condé Nast, the Cole Porters, Dorothy Parker, Zoë Akins, Constance Collier, various French officials, and a liberal sprinkling of titles. Several observers commented on Le Gallienne's striking resemblance to the traditional Jeanne d'Arc envisioned by sculptors and artists. Among the churning mob of extras, her slim, straight figure and pale cameo face lit by large, wide-set blue eyes stood out through stillness and simplicity of gesture and movement. Onstage for almost the full two hours of the play, enclosed constantly in a moving shaft of light, she found the opening evening an excruciating nightmare. She was "so nervous and exhausted I simply couldn't play," she said. But there were comic moments. "One of my knights, a huge Russian boy," she recalled, "became so interested in the fight that he simply would not give in, and being almost a giant he found it quite easy to . . . prevent them from capturing me. . . . Finally summoning up my slight knowledge of Russian, I yelled at him through the din: 'Please die, won't you! I implore you to die!' He looked at me in amazement and then, roaring with laughter, lay down and died—to the great relief of the enemy."

Later, Eva wrote that all her notices were bad—which meant that she did not read them, for, while the play was unanimously panned, her acting was praised. Many critics shared the opinion of the London *Daily Mail* reviewer: "Miss Eva Le Gallienne is an ideal Joan of Arc, supple, with extreme mobility of expression, and an ecstatic gaze that imparted mystic beauty to the coronation ceremony

Eva as Jehanne d'Arc

and intense pathos to the trial scene and the march to the stake. . . . She was enthusiastically applauded and recalled before the curtain a great number of times."

The real star of the production, though, was Norman Bel Geddes. Critics called his set and lighting designs and direction a miracle. Bel Geddes used light like a painter and scored the play like a composer, using sound to suggest psychological states. Two dozen little brass bells pealed out Joan of Arc's theme. In the stake scene, kettledrums rolled like thunder as the crowd gathered to burn the Maid. The drums increased in tempo as the mob filled the stage. As the flames leapt around Joan, she spoke "Jesu" softly, and suddenly the mob hushed and the drums stopped. "It was as though the bottom had dropped out of everything," Bel Geddes explained. "Silence had become more silent."

The moment was less exciting for Le Gallienne. "To be hurled in full armour, from 20 foot height down to stage level, tossed from the arms of one callous French super to the other . . . then to be put in heavy chains, on wrists and feet, clad only in a chemise of sack cloth, jostled by a crowd of supers, hurled to the ground, spat on and reviled, it was with some relief that I reached my comfortable stake."

Le Gallienne always asserted that more could be learned from failure than from success, and *Jehanne d'Arc* taught her much. In composing her own parts, she worked musically—marking her scripts for emphasis and pauses, using rhythms and tonal contrasts to modulate and build emotions. Le Gallienne learned from Bel Geddes that it was possible to use this technique on a production as a whole—weaving sound and light, simultaneous action, silences and rests, actors' voices and movements, shifting from key to key, and fusing all into a seamless work of art.

The French public and the critics detested the script. They couldn't be won with thrilling, pageantlike spectacle, no matter how well it was orchestrated. Mercedes was devastated. Not only was *Jehanne d'Arc* a failure, but the production of *The Mother of Christ* was cancelled. She blamed Le Gallienne. "She continues to make me feel a brute & a heartless inhuman wretch," Eva wrote. "However I have tried to ignore this—feeling deeply justified in my soul—& knowing that I have right too on my side." After three and a half years with Mercedes, Le Gallienne was no longer blinded by sexual passion. Twice she had faced public humiliation in de Acosta's plays; endangering her reputation a third time with *The Mother of Christ* was out of the question. Mercedes cared only about fame and celebrity, but worst of all, she simply did not have any talent—an inexcusable failing in Le Gallienne's eyes. Her long, tortured intimacy with de Acosta was nearing an end. Later, Eva claimed that she did not know why she became involved with Mercedes; "nothing in my life has ever been more baffling to me," she wrote, "more difficult to grasp." The reason is not mysterious. She had lost her self-control and submitted her will to another, because of their sexual relationship.

AS DE ACOSTA WAS fading from Le Gallienne's life, Alice De Lamar, an heiress, was arriving. Eva had charmed her into investing in *Jehanne d'Arc,* and Alice, who had an apartment in Paris, saw the performances. Attracted by Eva's beauty and her artistry, she had given Le Gallienne money for the production, but she went on to give her friendship and her love. Perhaps she would have liked a more intimate relationship, but she was painfully shy, and Eva was not interested in Alice as a lover. De Lamar would protect, support, and encourage Le Gallienne. Blessed with wealth but lacking artistic talent, she lived vicariously through the artists she helped. Le Gallienne was secure in the belief that the quality of her art would be sufficient gratification for Alice's patronage.

Alice De Lamar was a striking woman. In 1921, Mary Berenson described her as a "queer girl with lots of character, but all angles and resentments and revolts," adding later that "we got to like Alice De Lamar very much, but I do not see a happy life for her. Her early upbringing is against her." Dogged throughout her life by fortune hunters, who, according to Mary Berenson, hung about her like "a bad smell," Alice successfully avoided marriage and devoted herself to travel, philanthropy, and building various houses and gardens.

Alice had inherited a ten-million-dollar fortune in 1918 from her Dutch immigrant father, Joseph De Lamar, who had struck it rich in gold and copper mining. Alice's parents had divorced when she was quite young, and she was raised in Paris and New York City. She suffered through much of her lonely childhood in the large, gloomy Beaux-Arts De Lamar mansion on Madison Avenue. When her father died, Alice sold the mansion and all its contents. The house she later built for herself on the highest sand dune hill in Palm Beach reflected her personal taste for the art and architecture of Italy. As one of the earliest settlers in Palm Beach, when Ocean Beach Boulevard was just two grassy ruts, Alice helped found an arts community there and used her money to support her special interests—artists, architects, and aviators. Her close friends included architect Addison Mizner, conductor Leopold Stokowski, and designer Hubert de Givenchy. Alice's intimate companion was Russian emigré Lucia Davidova, a singer and dancer who had moved to New York before the Revolution. Alice probably met Davidova through Mercedes or Eva, who had studied Russian with her. Like her father, Alice was an extremely private person, and she did not want her philanthropy known.

When *Jehanne d'Arc* closed, Alice invited Eva to recuperate from the experience at her villa in Italy. Used to the constant chatter of Mercedes, Eva found

*Alice De Lamar, c. 1925. She was Le Gallienne's
patron for almost sixty years.*

De Lamar a refreshing change. "For the first time in so long I was consciously happy," Eva wrote. "Because I saw so much beauty—so much incredible beauty—without any interference of the *personal element*. . . . It was all free and quiet. . . . I found [Alice] to the highest degree a sensitive person—who allows other individuals their entire freedom—who makes no personal demands upon them—with whom one can remain for hours at a time *silent*—without misunderstanding. And when personally called upon, a creature of great strength & gentleness—& a kind of serenity of wisdom, naive & childlike. I am deeply grateful to her for all that."

BEFORE SHE SAILED for home, Le Gallienne went to Asolo and stood beside Duse's grave, "sad, but *good*," she said. She also wrote and asked for an appointment with Gordon Craig at his villa surrounded by orange trees outside Genoa. "Of course I know who you are," Craig wrote, "not the least being that (I believe) you are a remarkable actress." He said that he would be happy to see her and delighted to hear about America, "if you can say some thing anything honest to save the theatrical America for me in my heart. The place seems to me hideously false."

Tall and imposing with the grace and good looks of his actress mother, Ellen Terry, Craig captivated Eva with his magnetic presence and with his magnificent library. They spent hours together looking at old copies of *The Mask,* the theatre journal he had founded and edited, and rare theatre books. Eva shared some of her dreams about creating a new American theatre and sought Craig's advice. Touched by her interest, Craig recognized in Le Gallienne his own youthful fervor and offered a warning: "I am always happy to be a friend of yours . . . though I have for many years known that one can only be a useful friend to our brothers & sisters in this very fine affair of theatres, if one is rich in monies as well as big hopes & endurance."

After more than four months in Europe, in August 1925 Le Gallienne sailed home on the S.S. *Majestic,* possessed "by a strange *nostalgie* for America." Mercedes traveled with her. Also on the boat were a number of theatre people traveling to New York for the opening of the new season, including Leslie Howard, who would play opposite Katharine Cornell in *The Green Hat;* the Theatre Guild's Theresa Helburn; and Noël Coward, who would make his Broadway debut that fall as both playwright and actor in *The Vortex.* Coward recalled that Eva and Mercedes wore black and alternated "between intellectual gloom and feverish gaiety." Le Gallienne found Coward "perfectly charming—very amusing & sincere at the same time—and utterly unspoiled. We get on very well."

Eva got on especially well, too, with Coward's friend Gladys Calthrop, who was traveling to New York with him to design sets and costumes for *The Vortex.*

Calthrop was married to a military man, but she had been devoted to Noël
Coward since their first meeting in 1921. After just a few days' acquaintance, Le
Gallienne found Gladys "a brilliantly clever and a fascinatingly beautiful person—a really rare being." Gladys was an original. She moved easily in the English country-house set, and she was equally at home in the art world. Portraits of
Gladys reveal a woman with large, gray eyes, dark, smooth hair, pale skin, and a
serene expression. She designed her own smart look, accessorizing her clothes
with unusual jewelry. Like Eva, Gladys tended to talk about Art and Truth and
Beauty in capital letters, but she also had a quick wit that was a match for Coward's razor-sharp mind. According to Coward's biographer Cole Lesley, Gladys
"seems never to have questioned Noël's belief in his shining future, the future in
which she was to play so large a part; instead she encouraged and helped to plan
it with him." Le Gallienne noted Coward's dependence on his talented friend
and designer. "Noël owes much to her," Eva observed, thinking that Calthrop
would also be useful to her own theatre plans.

IN THE 1925–26 SEASON, 42 musicals and 170 plays opened on Broadway;
33 of the plays ran for 100 or more performances, qualifying as hits. American
theatre in the 1920s was so fertile, so deep with talent in all areas—playwriting,
directing, design, and acting—that the decade became known as a golden age.
Nurtured by the Provincetown Players, Eugene O'Neill found success on Broadway as well as in Berlin, London, Paris, Moscow, and Dublin. Producing organizations flourished, mounting so many plays in succession that the odds were good
that at least some would be successful. Times were good, and producers had
money. Playwrights like George S. Kaufman, S. N. Behrman, Philip Barry, Sidney
Howard, Ben Hecht, Charles MacArthur, and Elmer Rice wrote prolifically. With
few exceptions, the playwrights, directors, and designers were men, but the acting
profession was dominated by an extraordinary group of women—Eva Le Gallienne, Katharine Cornell, Helen Hayes, Laurette Taylor, Ethel Barrymore, Tallulah Bankhead, Margalo Gillmore, Clare Eames, Jeanne Eagels, Lynn Fontanne.

Was all this theatrical activity art? No, said critic George Jean Nathan. He
called 1925's two hit plays "flapdoodle." Le Gallienne thought Coward's *The Vortex* a fine play, but she shared her old enemy's opinion of *The Green Hat*. Based
on the melodramatic novel of the same name by Michael Arlen, the play bristled
with lines like "You have a white body that beats at my mind like a whip." Playing the decadent, promiscuous Iris March, Katharine Cornell wrapped her
tongue around sentence after silly sentence, sported a bright green felt hat, and
died dramatically at the end of the play by smashing her yellow sports car into a
large tree. The play, however, proved so popular that two hundred thousand
American women rushed out to buy copies of Cornell's green hat.

Le Gallienne attended the opening of *The Green Hat* and afterwards wrote: "All the Broadway devils present in full swing of low-cut dresses, jewels and much puffed and beffrizzled hair. A strange crowd. The play: extremely bad . . . like a mediocre Pinero play that one feels is 25 years old—& will never be young again. Katharine Cornell—striking, fascinating—but disastrously theatrical in a part that could only be interesting if treated with an honesty & a directness. . . . I suppose the play will be a great success—in a cheap sense for it is cheap—just that."

After a brief run in Schnitzler's *The Call of Life* for the Actors' Company, Le Gallienne decided to go into management for herself when the Actors' Company wouldn't produce *The Master Builder* for her. She had heard that Ann Harding planned to do the play, and Eva decided to present it first, to "make it mine." To produce, direct, and star in *The Master Builder,* even for matinee performances, was an enormous undertaking. She asked Gladys Calthrop to design the sets and costumes. Since Noël Coward had settled in to a run of *The Vortex,* which would be followed by a tour, Gladys was free to take the job. It's not clear whether their personal relationship preceded their professional association, but the women moved in together. Le Gallienne had a strong, competitive nature, and it must have pleased her that she had been able to woo away Coward's best friend and designer. Throughout her life, Le Gallienne coordinated her love relationships with her career—often beginning a new stage of her professional life with a new personal partner.

In her first autobiography, *At 33,* Eva tossed off her decision to go into management as a spur-of-the-moment choice based on her simple wish to play Hilda Wangel. But her decision to strike out on her own involved a deeper, more basic motivation. Writing years later in *With a Quiet Heart,* her second autobiography, she described a meeting with David Belasco. Called "the Bishop of Broadway," Belasco was considered the grand master of all producers, and he had a notorious reputation as a seducer of actresses. When Eva first met him in his private quarters at the Belasco Theatre, she was a teenager, not yet a star. From Eva's account of their meeting, Belasco offered her a contract, and his manner made her uncomfortable:

He fixed me with his black, piercing eyes as though he were about to hypnotize me. . . . My brain kept telling me that this was my great chance and that this suave, civilized gentleman was doing me a great honor by his faith in me and would help make me the fine actress I dreamed of becoming someday. . . . Yet somehow my whole inner being rebelled. I felt as though I were being swamped, suffocated, trapped in some strange way. My instinct told me that if I succumbed to this man's influence I would have to abandon my precious freedom of spirit . . . imprisoning me in a world over which I would have no control, where I would be a slave to the rules and regulations, both of thought and conduct, imposed by a powerful and relentless master.

When the interview ended, Eva walked out of the Belasco Theatre fighting "the feeling of panic rising in me." Not wanting to go home and explain to her mother that she had refused Belasco's offer, she walked from midtown up to Central Park, and then all the way down Fifth Avenue to Washington Square to the home of Fola La Follette, the wife of playwright George Middleton. Fola comforted her with a cup of hot tea as Eva explained that she would "abandon all my hopes of success, rather than submit to his powerful authority."

Since Le Gallienne possessed attributes traditionally assigned to men—intellectual arrogance, confidence, a powerful ego, and a sense of entitlement—it was not surprising that she would want, as her mother had before her, to seize control of her own life. Sometimes, though, she yearned for the road not taken. When Eva was playing in *The Call of Life,* she heard that Basil Rathbone had married Ouida Bergere. In a letter to her mother she said, "I still call him 'my' Basil, because I know that he really *is.* I miss him—but most particularly in Work I miss him (because after all that must be most vital to me). It is so hard to play with just a lot of ordinary actors, after playing with him."

JULIE LE GALLIENNE loved all the "band wagon" aspects of the theatre that Eva loathed, and when they were together the two women often argued about Eva's career, her clothes, even her eating habits. Both women were strong, with controlling personalities; but to Julie's credit, she did not intrude on Eva's life in America. Julie criticized but didn't judge, and was rewarded with a rare intimacy. In her correspondence with her mother, which reads like an intimate ongoing conversation, Eva knew that Julie was interested in every aspect of her day-to-day activities—her work, health, apartment, clothes and costumes, the books she was reading, her companions, as well as her ambitions, doubts, and fears. Using violet ink on blue parchment paper emblazoned with a silver shield and the motto "Force et Confiance," Eva wrote vivid, literate letters to her mother, but from time to time she worried that her letters might not be amusing enough, since she knew that a "dull dog" was Julie's bête noire. Most of the letters run at least four pages and many are eight to ten pages long. Unfortunately, few of Julie's letters to her daughter have survived; but she wrote lively, interesting letters to Mogens and her sister, Ellen, letters filled with descriptions of personalities, places, and books, and family gossip. The Le Galliennes were all accomplished writers with the ability to see themselves from the outside. A favorite family joke was Richard Le Gallienne's phrase "My Mefisto [*sic*] is always laughing at my Faust."

During her twenties, Le Gallienne kept only a sketchy diary, but at times her letters to her mother were as intimate as a private journal. From Julie, Eva received stringent criticism and unconditional love—both might have proved too oppressive without an ocean between them. During *Liliom,* Eva wrote Julie: "It must be wonderful to be able to create away from crowds—out of sight of one's public—it is a source of endless wonder to me, why the medium that has been thrust on me should be the most terribly exposed—so glaringly illuminated to all eyes. With my nature it is a curious paradox—& somewhat of a burden. This is not grumbling—I know it cannot be, & I wouldn't have it be otherwise—but it is sometimes very strange to me."

Eva was not writing just of her sexual nature or of a desire for privacy. She was exploring the difficulty of realizing her artistic ambitions in a show-business theatre world devoted, she believed, to self-promotion, greed, and shallow values. For over ten years Le Gallienne had worked as an actress in the theatre, learning her craft, and she had matured into a conscious artist. It was time, she felt, to strike out on her own. Le Gallienne's decision to produce *The Master Builder* was motivated not just by her desire to play Hilda Wangel; it was also an idealistic attempt to transcend personal ambition, to build something larger than herself, to find a place where art could be created, where work could be accomplished, as Hilda says, "free and high up."

Later, in the preface to her translation of *The Master Builder,* Le Gallienne wrote: "The play is a great poem. . . . To youth it is 'wonderfully thrilling,' and evokes a mood of fanatical idealism. To a mature artist it serves as a kind of warning and has elements of terror and bitter disillusionment. . . . Like many great works of art *The Master Builder* obstinately refuses to be pigeon-holed. It is a living entity and must be accepted on its own terms."

Like Hilda Wangel, Le Gallienne saw life as "a thrilling play in which, in her imagination, she acted a wide variety of thrilling parts." Eva refused to be typecast in any part, in the theatre or in her private life. Just as her name joined the masculine "Le" with the feminine "Gallienne," her nature, too, was a fusion of contradictions and sometimes warring opposites. Even the signature fragrance that she wore all her life, Eau de Verveine, created by Pierre Guerlain at the end of the nineteenth century, a light citrus *eau fraîche,* was made for both men and women. She was equally adept with right or left hand, and she also joked that her sexuality was "ambidextrous" as well. She craved solitude yet couldn't bear to be without a companion or an audience. She loved passionately and impulsively yet longed to be free of purely personal demands. Sensitive, easily hurt, and shy, she could be cold, arrogant, and aggressive. She was a natural, charismatic, independent leader and a devoted, hero-worshipping acolyte.

Her decision to produce, direct, and star in *The Master Builder* was a purely selfish act, and at the same time it was an act of altruism, since the production became the cornerstone of Le Gallienne's nonprofit Civic Repertory Theatre, perhaps the most altruistic institution in American theatre history—a theatre that formed the philosophical bedrock for off-Broadway and nonprofit institutional theatres, united a young American theatre tradition with a rich European heritage, left a legacy of artistic achievement and vision, and flung out a challenge yet to be answered. And, another irony, in creating this theatre, she would be "glaringly illuminated," "terribly exposed" to all eyes, both in her personal life and in her work, exposure which she professed to loathe; yet she coveted the spotlight and delighted in shocking conventional standards, in doing the forbidden.

"But why worry, what difference does it make what other people say and think?" Le Gallienne told a reporter for the *Woman Citizen* magazine. "You can learn and grow infinitely from a failure, as you can from a great sorrow, for life is only a progression in which we continually learn. You should not let yourself be greatly influenced by what other people say, good or bad. You must preserve a tiny place in you that's immune; and keep concentrated thought on your ideal. For the only thing that really matters is whether you have done good work to the best of your ability."

These words might have been spoken by Ibsen's twenty-three-year-old Hilda Wangel, who comes down from the mountains to inspire the master builder Halvard Solness to do the impossible. It's doubtful that Eva, who was always so possessed by the parts she played, could have launched her theatre if she had been acting a character other than Hilda Wangel. Hilda's qualities—her fanatical idealism, her ruthlessness, her fearless optimism, her confidence, her independence, her frank disregard for the opinions of others, her arrogance, her bravado, her radiant health, and especially her youth—were needed to build a new theatre for America.

LE GALLIENNE RECRUITED the *Master Builder* company from actors she knew and had worked with before. For Solness, Le Gallienne chose the versatile and distinguished Egon Brecher, who had played with her in *Liliom* and *The Call of Life*. Before settling in America, Brecher had played twenty years of repertory in Vienna and Berlin, acting some five hundred parts in twenty years. Other cast members included Sydney Machat, a young actor from the Hedgerow Theatre; dancer/actor Ruth Wilton; Eva's cousin Beatrice de Neergaard, who was a few years younger than she and who had, Eva believed, "the true instinct for the theatre"; and character actor Alice John. As she had for *Hannele,* Mrs. C. C. Rumsey provided the start-up money. Le Gallienne secured the Maxine Elliott Theatre and announced four matinee performances. After studying the play for several years, in the original and in William Archer's British translation, she flung herself "into it with all the confidence and assurance of youth and never stopped to question or analyse. If anyone had asked me at that time whether I understood what the part and the play were about, I would have laughed and said what Hilda says to Solness in the first act: 'To me it all seems so simple.' "

Initially, she used the Archer translations of Ibsen's plays, even though she thought they were "clumsy, old-fashioned and quite frequently misleading." In later productions, she evolved her own versions, with no thought to having them published. She directed her company using Stanislavsky's rehearsal technique. At the first rehearsals, they sat around a table, reading the play aloud, discussing various interpretations, agreeing on tempo, becoming accustomed to one another's voices and presences and to their characters before putting the play on its feet.

The Master Builder had not been seen in New York since Nazimova played it over eighteen years earlier, and Nazimova was in the audience at the opening matinee. Brooks Atkinson called Le Gallienne's performance transcendent: "To vary the *Punch* joke, she looks so much like a boy that one knows instinctively she must be a girl. From this less than neutral costuming her beauty shines with extraordinary, healthy radiance. Her acting, likewise, is extremely severe; she does not soften it with a gentle flow of gestures, oozing gradually from mood to mood. On the contrary, the different elements are kept distinct; and she flies from one to the next with an evanescent precision."

The matinees proved so successful that the Le Gallienne company moved to the Princess Theatre and settled in for a long run. Elated by the success of *The Master Builder,* she began rehearsing Ibsen's *John Gabriel Borkman,* with Egon Brecher playing the title role. Eva took the part of the middle-aged Ella Rentheim, which allowed her to display her versatility. To her core company of actors, she added her *Liliom* daughter, Rose Hobart, and the silver-haired British character actor J. Sayre Crawley, who with his fine, handsome features reminded Eva of her father.

Surrounded by a company of actor-friends, with Gladys Calthrop now in the dual role of live-in lover and art director, and with plans to have her own theatre close to fruition, Le Gallienne described her feelings at this time as "unspeakably happy." She defined happiness as "the fact of not being wasted; the knowledge that one's energies and talents are being used to the full." Her love affair with Gladys was fresh and new and exciting; their collaboration was satisfying and challenging; and, most important, their work was a public success. Although later it would seem incredible to Eva, for the next five years her life would go right and she would be "unspeakably happy."

During this time, Eva saw an unhappy Mercedes de Acosta occasionally for dinner and talks. Mercedes had been spending long weekends with the actress

*Gladys Calthrop was a pioneer
in the male-dominated field
of set design.*

Jeanne Eagels at Eagels's home in Ossining-on-the-Hudson, helping the actress control her drinking and drug habits. Since she claimed that she had not had time to work on anything new, Mercedes had hoped that Eva might arrange an American production of *Jehanne d'Arc*. Le Gallienne refused to do so. "Having to make you suffer has been anything but the easy thing you imagine it to be," Eva told de Acosta. In letters to Mercedes written in late 1925 and early 1926, as if to avoid any evidence of their connection, Le Gallienne did not sign her name—instead she drew a line where her signature should have been. By mid-1926, the letters and their contact stopped altogether.

With the creation of her theatre in mind, Eva began to assert herself socially. Accompanied by Gladys Calthrop and Noël Coward, she overcame her shyness and felt able to "face all those devils" at the 1925 Equity Ball. She costumed herself appropriately in a new black lace evening gown with a décolleté back.

She accepted an invitation from George Pierce Baker to speak at Yale University and then immediately regretted her decision. The thought of speaking to an audience filled with students and scholars was daunting. She attempted a written lecture, but gave up and jotted down a few notes on a sheet of paper. On Sunday, December 13, 1925, she spoke at Sprague Hall, and the event marked the first time an actress had formally addressed a Yale audience. Her lecture was a sell-out—more than seven hundred people jammed the recital hall, and dozens more were turned away at the door. The first ten minutes were "agony," but the audience, she said, was "tremendously enthusiastic and quick to take up every point." "America represents the world hope of the attainment of lofty ideals in dramatic arts," she said:

> One of America's greatest needs is to build up the theatre. In central Europe, it is a real part of the life of the people [but] Europe is tired. England and France are hopeless as a center of the development of dramatic art. Germany and Russia seem now occupied with the exterior of things, like lighting. . . . In London you see the aristocracy making signals to the actresses and the actresses signalling back. The success of the Washington Square Players, the Theatre Guild, the Actors' Theatre, the Provincetown Players has given hope of improvement, but the present need is for courage. Eugene O'Neill and Susan Glaspell have no superiors. The myth of European supremacy in the arts is fast fading. . . . Let us make the theatre of America stand free and high up, with no world peers.

WHEN *John Gabriel Borkman* opened in late January 1926, Le Gallienne played the worn-out Ella Rentheim in matinees at the Booth Theatre and in the evenings she acted Hilda Wangel at the Princess. Le Gallienne's portrayal of the two characters was helped by Gladys Calthrop's costuming. For the boyish Hilda, Eva wore snug corduroy pants stuffed into thick, muddy boots but also, true to Hilda's contradictory spirit, jeweled cufflinks and emerald earrings. As Ella Rentheim, she used makeup sparingly, relying instead on body line and her dark dress, cape, and muff to convey the melancholy middle-aged woman. *Borkman* was even more of a critical success than *The Master Builder*—Le Gallienne's portrayal was called a tour de force, and again she was compared to Duse. What was most astonishing to the critics and the public, who were not used to seeing actors work in repertory, was Le Gallienne's transformation into two different characters. Her direction and the ensemble playing of her company were also praised. The productions and Le Gallienne's management received excellent publicity and were accorded the stature of other Broadway offerings.

For February, Eva planned a tour of the major cities in the two Ibsen plays. Before she left, she announced a few special 10:30 a.m. matinees of *Borkman* and *The Master Builder* at a scale of fifty cents to $1.50 top. Every performance was sold out as soon as the advertisement appeared.

Confident that he had found the rebel actor he had been looking for, Otto Kahn, the banker and arts patron, gave Eva a loan of five thousand dollars to act as a "small backlog for the tour in case of need," a loan she was able to pay back in April 1926 before the end of the tour. On a quick trip back to New York to present her theatre plan to him, she put crisp, new thousand-dollar bills into an

Drawing on her vast wardrobe of wigs, Eva transformed herself into the gray-haired, delicately feminine Ella Rentheim in John Gabriel Borkman.

envelope and wrote, "To Mr. Kahn from Mr. Ibsen with many thanks." The gesture made a great impression on Otto Kahn. "The loans I make are seldom repaid," he said, "and this is the very first time I've been repaid in cash." Kahn backed up his enthusiasm with an additional twenty thousand dollars.

In Cincinnati she introduced her company to the plan, presenting them with a detailed rehearsal schedule and a list of plays. Three older actors experienced in European repertory, Egon Brecher, Beatrice Terry (niece of Ellen Terry), and J. Sayre Crawley, plus four young actors without any such experience, Harold Moulton, Sydney Machat, Ruth Wilton, and Beatrice de Neergaard, joined Le Gallienne and formed the nucleus of the Civic Repertory Theatre.

Mimsey traveled to Detroit and agreed to serve as Le Gallienne's personal representative and principal fund-raiser. "There is no one better fitted for that task—no one who knows & understands *me* better—no one who handles people as well," Eva felt. The theatre plan, Le Gallienne told her mother, was simple: "To have a People's Repertory Theatre, presenting the best plays—with fine acting & productions—at the *lowest possible prices—that* is the important part of the scheme. There will be no seat in the house at any performance over $1.50— and the popular matinee *top price* will be a dollar & lowest price *35 cents.* . . . Don't speak of this to anyone. It is I *know* a plan that can lead to very important results if correctly handled."

THE TOUR PLAYED to a profit in Washington, D.C., Baltimore, Pittsburgh, Hartford, Philadelphia, Cincinnati, St. Louis, Chicago, and Detroit. Audiences turned out to see Ibsen and Eva Le Gallienne, proving that New York wasn't the only city interested in good theatre. Later, Le Gallienne would champion nonprofit, subsidized theatres around the country, but first she had to prove that such a theatre could exist in New York City. The fact that she had won her "spurs in an individual way in the . . . commercial theatre" gave her the freedom to choose a path other than the well-traveled show-business thoroughfare. She did not think of her "people's theatre" as tucked away on some narrow sidetrack; her nonprofit, repertory theatre would be located in the theatre capital and would match the scale of commercial Broadway theatres.

When the news of her projected repertory theatre was announced in late May, newspapers all over the country picked up the story. The New York press and particularly the foreign-language press treated the announcement as front-page news. Her press agents flooded newspapers around the country with releases and photographs of Le Gallienne and her company of actors. A deluge of mail came to Mimsey's apartment office—requests for interviews, letters of support, and small donations, including $214.50 from Le Gallienne fans in a Denver bridge club.

In their articles, reporters highlighted the repertory aspect, the low prices, the idea of subsidy, and the fact that the theatre was created as a protest against commercialism. Unlike the Theatre Guild, which despite its art-theatre reputation was completely commercial, Le Gallienne's theatre would follow the pattern of the subsidized theatres of Europe: "I could not see why America should not have a repertory theatre subsidized by private capital in the same way that its opera companies and symphony orchestras are. Why should the drama be the only neglected art? . . . Millions were spent on libraries, museums, and music, but the Theatre was an outcast."

Previous attempts at a true repertory theatre in New York had failed, unable to compete with the star system devoted to long-run plays. As an actor, Le Gallienne loathed the boredom of long runs, saying it was like "using one set of muscles exclusively while the rest atrophy." A repertory theatre's value was that it kept plays alive, year after year, while constantly producing new ones, providing stability and tradition in an American theatre that lacked both. A repertory theatre also provided a home for a resident company of actors and technicians, whose primary responsibility, Le Gallienne believed, was not the glorification of personality but the interpretation of the play.

The Theatre Guild and other organizations had talked about creating a repertory theatre, but there were many unanswered questions. Would American audiences go to the trouble of looking up a repertory schedule? Would skilled, versatile actors play for lower salaries? Would playwrights give their new plays to a theatre that would insert them into the repertory instead of giving them a long, lucrative run? Would the expense of keeping a number of productions alive from year to year, with the constant scenery changes, prove prohibitive? Was there an audience for classic plays? In America wasn't the success of a venture determined by profit? Shouldn't the theatre pay its own way? Yes, these were all problems, Le Gallienne agreed, but not insurmountable. Libraries, museums, opera and dance companies all seemed to function just fine without making a profit. The only way to find out if a subsidized, nonprofit repertory theatre was possible in America, she said, was to start one.

"IT MUST BE REMEMBERED," Le Gallienne wrote later, "that in 1926 there was no cultural explosion. There were no foundations, great or small, set up to help the arts. . . . Before the great Depression, rich people were immensely rich and could do what they liked with their money—even keep it. No high taxes limited their fortunes. There was, therefore, no such bait as tax-deductible donations with which to tempt prospective backers. One had to wheedle, bully, or cajole—and I did all three quite shamelessly." She had "no qualms about asking rich people for their money," since the money was for a cause, not for her personally. Her most effective technique was to point out to a prospective donor "that whereas he had millions, I had nothing but my earning capacity; and if I was willing and eager to donate nine-tenths of that earning capacity to this venture, the least he could do was to contribute $10,000." Her wealthy and influential friends, such as Alice De Lamar, Al Lehman, Edgar Davis, John D. Rockefeller, Adolph Lewisohn, Jules S. Bache, Ralph Pulitzer, Otto Kahn, and Mrs. C. C. Rumsey, donated thousands of dollars and helped to raise even more.

Mary Curtis Bok (later Zimbalist), a soft-spoken, gentle woman with a fierce passion for the arts, became the Civic's biggest benefactor, simply writing checks of twenty-five or fifty thousand dollars with no strings attached whenever funds were needed. A resident of Philadelphia, Mary Bok had inherited the great Curtis Publishing fortune and founded Philadelphia's Curtis Institute of Music in 1924 with a donation of $12.5 million. "She loved Le Gallienne and she had this deep admiration and understanding of what Eva was trying to do and what she needed," recalled her stepson, Efrem Zimbalist Jr. One anonymous donor (probably Eleonora Sears) gave $24,965 to the Civic Repertory. Sears's name does not appear on any published list of contributors to the theatre, but because of her friendship with Eva, it's likely that she was the Civic's anonymous angel. Another angel was Le Gallienne herself, donating thousands of dollars from her own savings.

In her dealings with the wealthy, Le Gallienne capitalized on her youth, sincerity, and star status. Her "fanatic singleness of purpose often amused them," she wrote; "they thought it highly original of me to wish to abandon the delights of an assured Broadway career to devote myself to what they considered a strenuous and thankless job." She was "solemn and intolerant as only a young person possessed by a clear and all-absorbing dream can be." When she was refused, she often lost her temper, and sweet-natured Mary Benson would be called in to play diplomat.

But Eva also knew how to charm. Like her father she could become "Sven-Gallienne," using what she called her "magic," which she turned on and off at will. Her technique was particularly effective in one-on-one situations with reporters. Never taking her wide blue eyes off the writer, she answered questions in her warm cello voice, disarming them with her direct, unaffected manner.

When reporters wondered about her private life, she answered that she didn't have much of one. Why wasn't she married? "Certainly I am not thinking of marriage," Eva told them. "I still find Mrs. Calthrop, the young Londoner who shares my apartment with me, a most satisfactory chum." Although Eva didn't volunteer any information about her personal life, when she was asked she told the truth, or as much of the truth as she thought was necessary. Julie Le Gal-

*Mary Curtis Bok in 1930.
Eva called Mrs. Bok her
"fairy godmother."*

lienne took a different approach when she was asked if her daughter had any marriage plans. She would say that Eva was too great an artist and much too busy to marry.

Leaving Mimsey in charge of fund-raising and securing a theatre lease, Eva left for Europe in early June 1926 on a working vacation with Gladys. On the boat, they worked out the technical requirements of the six new plays—Gladys sketched out costume and set designs and Eva worked on staging and casting. In addition to *The Master Builder* and *John Gabriel Borkman,* her play choices represented a sort of United Nations of the theatre: Benavente's *Saturday Night* and Martínez Sierra's *Cradle Song,* Chekhov's *Three Sisters* (which had never been performed in English in America), Goldoni's comedy *La Locandiera* (also never seen in English), Shakespeare's *Twelfth Night,* and Susan Glaspell's *Inheritors* would alternate in the repertory.

After visiting their mothers in London, Eva and Gladys went to Paris, where Eva ordered wigs for her various roles. They drove the Studebaker roadster, which Eva had brought over on the boat, from Paris to Italy. Avoiding the larger towns, they stayed in tiny Italian villages, where they were welcomed by startled villagers who, Eva said, were "terribly excited to think we had come all the way from Paris—two women alone—it seemed to them extraordinary." In Florence they bought fabric for costumes and rummaged through secondhand stores for furniture and stage properties, including jewelry, copper and brass accessories, glass, and china. They shipped everything back to New York, at a savings, Eva claimed, of thousands of dollars. While Gladys stayed on in London for a month to design a Coward play, Le Gallienne sailed alone for home, feeling "like a shorn lamb in an icy wind," miserable without her companion. She cheered up when Mimsey cabled that she had been able to lease the Fourteenth Street Theatre for forty weeks at nine hundred dollars per week.

FINDING A THEATRE had been the most difficult problem. None of the Broadway theatre owners wanted to lease their buildings to a company playing at a box-office scale of $1.50 top, feeling that it would establish a dangerous precedent and hurt the prestige of their theatres. Before she left for Europe, Le Gallienne explored further downtown and found the Fourteenth Street Theatre on the north side of Fourteenth Street just west of Sixth Avenue. Warned that the theatre was too far downtown for Broadway audiences, Le Gallienne didn't care. After ten years of playing Broadway, she no longer had the neophyte's view of Broadway as the be-all and end-all of American theatre. She wanted to create another kind of theatre and hoped to attract a different kind of audience from all five boroughs and even from New Jersey—an audience who would ride the IRT, the BMT, the Hudson Tubes, or the Sixth Avenue Elevated—all converging at Fourteenth Street and Sixth Avenue, just a few steps from the theatre.

Built in 1866, the theatre was originally called Théâtre Français and described as "the most elegant theatre in New York." It had a distinguished history. Adelaide Ristori acted Lady Macbeth there before an audience that included President Ulysses S. Grant. In 1870, the theatre changed hands and became the Fourteenth Street Theatre. Edwin Forrest, America's first great tragedian, played King Lear there. One of the first American woman actor-managers, the imposing Laura Keene, took over the management in 1871, and it was in her company that little Minnie Maddern, later Mrs. Fiske, made her debut. Edwin Booth brought his Shakespearean repertory to the Fourteenth Street Theatre in 1876.

After the turn of the century, as the life of New York moved uptown and theatres clustered around the Times Square area, the Fourteenth Street Theatre began a slow decline. Distinguished artists playing the classics in repertory gave way to second-class companies playing melodramas, vaudeville, and burlesque. It remained mostly unoccupied from 1911 until 1926, when a third-rate Italian company, which recruited some of its actors from nearby speakeasies, performed there on Sundays. Le Gallienne learned that "the chief performer on these occasions was the prompter."

In June 1926, before she sailed for Europe, Le Gallienne stood on the sidewalk and looked up at peeling paint and fire escapes that cluttered the once-elegant neoclassical façade of the old theatre. Across the street was the Salvation Army, headed by Evangeline Booth, considered the world's foremost woman orator. Nearby were a Child's restaurant, secondhand clothing stores, and a warehouse. Inside the theatre, Eva found a filthy, neglected interior, uncarpeted floors, discolored walls, uncomfortable seats, and a powerful stench. But she also saw that "the stage was magnificent and there was a scene-dock running all the way back to 15th Street" (a feature that was used to great effect years earlier in the old melodrama *The Still Alarm,* when the horse-drawn fire engine thundered in from the scene-dock entrance and onto the stage). The horseshoe-shaped auditorium, with its extremely high ceiling and center dome, was "perfect to play in," she said, "and the floor was steeply raked. The lines of the high proscenium arch rose pure and elegant. The sight-lines were excellent and the acoustics marvellous. The seating capacity was eleven hundred, including a large gallery [with] a nice lot of 50-cent seats." The combination of oversized stage with a somewhat intimate auditorium was unusual. "On Broadway, where real estate values and the exigencies of show-business were the controlling factors," Le Gallienne noted, "the relative size of auditorium and stage was of necessity reversed." There was enough storage area to house many productions, essential for a repertory theatre, eliminating the cost of hiring Teamsters Union members to haul scenery from a warehouse. There was also space for adequate dressing rooms and scene and costume shops.

"A sense of tradition, of ancient glories, of an aura of greatness (long forgotten and almost buried under the layers of neglect and filth)," drew her to the shabby theatre. But there were other attractions important to her mystic sense. As she walked from the pass door onto the stage, her feet scuffled against discarded papers. Looking down, she saw a photograph of Duse staring up at her from an old Italian newspaper. She picked it up and imagined that it was a telegram Duse had sent saying "Tout sera bien!"—All will be well! Eva climbed the iron ladder up one hundred and ten feet above the stage and stood balancing on the oak girders of the grid, surrounded by a network of ropes. The sun streamed through the dingy skylight and she felt immediately "that this was where I wanted to work."

WHEN SHE RETURNED from Europe in August, a banner with "Welcome Le Gallienne" on one side and "Civic Repertory Theatre" on the other stretched across Fourteenth Street. Reporters and photographers descended upon her. Hating publicity, resenting the time it took, she tried to be charming, and she took on her publicity chores with such zeal that she inspired Alexander Woollcott to write an amusing article about her, titled "The Great Camera Mysteries." Noting the flood of Le Gallienne photographs, Woollcott wondered why there were so many more pictures of Eva Le Gallienne published than of countless

The Civic Repertory Theatre on Fourteenth Street in New York, c. 1927

other, lovelier actresses. "I have found it difficult to have my tooth pulled or my hair cut or my blood pressure taken without encountering in the ante-room some fresh portrait of Eva Le Gallienne," he mock-whined. A photographer informed him that Le Gallienne "has only to hear that a camera is receptive to slide down the brass rod and race to poise herself in front of it." According to the photographer, to angle a photograph of Mrs. Fiske, you needed two years; for Ethel Barrymore, one year; for Lillian Gish, seven months; for H. L. Mencken, two days; but Eva Le Gallienne could be ready in fourteen minutes flat. Photographers particularly liked her profile, focusing on the long, lovely line from the tip of her ear to her chin. She generated publicity because she constantly made news—opening more plays, acting in more plays, directing and producing more plays than anyone else in New York. To her mother, however, Eva admitted: "You would laugh if you could see your Cat. People seem to think she's quite important—and underneath it all, she is such a very small child."

She had a childlike faith in her theatre vision, but a grownup's understanding of the work and sacrifice required. More than forty thousand dollars in donations had been received by the end of June 1926, and Otto Kahn guaranteed twenty thousand dollars to pay the first season's rent. The old theatre got a

Nina Saemundssen, who was a noted sculptor of film stars,
works on a figure of Eva, c. 1927.

much-needed face lift. Painters and plasterers refurbished the façade, electricians hung lights spelling out "Civic Repertory Theatre" against a bright blue background, and at each pilaster a frame held the title of the plays to be presented. Cleaning women disinfected the interior and polished all the old brass. A new curtain, drapes, borders, and velours, new lines, new lighting instruments and switchboards, a cyclorama, floorcloths—all the basic theatre equipment was purchased.

To her core group of actors from the Ibsen tour, she added six versatile actors, including Danish-born Paul Leyssac (an old friend of her mother's) and character woman and superb mimic Leona Roberts. Additional actors and extras would be engaged on a show-by-show basis, but about twenty actors would be guaranteed twenty weeks of work at salaries ranging from sixty to two hundred dollars a week. Feeling that a theatre was not complete without live music, she hired Theodore Zarkevitch's five-member Russian orchestra. Since she would direct and act in all the plays, leaving her with little time for anything else, she gave Mimsey power of attorney to handle all business negotiations and her personal finances. She wrote her mother assuring her that she would not fail to send her one hundred dollars each month: "You can *always* feel secure my Sweet—you know that. On that point I haven't inherited daddy's nonchalance!"

AT THE END OF AUGUST, Le Gallienne took a small group of actors out to Weston, Connecticut, to work on *The Three Sisters*. Since Chekhov's plays had not been performed in English in America, the only performance of the play that Le Gallienne had seen was Stanislavsky's Moscow Art Theatre production. Later, she would make her own translation of the play, but for this first production the Civic used Constance Garnett's. "Groups that have just come together to do a play like *The Three Sisters* should know each other well," she said. She and Gladys stayed at Mimsey's farm, and the others lodged nearby at the rustic Three Bears Inn. "The weather was perfect," Le Gallienne remembered, "and we sat out in meadows filled with wildflowers, talking of Tchekov [*sic*] and establishing a sense of familiarity with his play, and with one another." Eva believed that "one cannot act in Tchekov's plays, one can only be." The actors improvised scenes, speaking and behaving as the characters would have behaved, and then actual dialogue was introduced. Eva recalled: "We would continue talking through the scene, with no feeling of heightened stress, no contrived inflections or artificial tricks of voice." Le Gallienne reminded the company of Chekhov's humor and marked all the laugh lines in her script. Chekhov's plays, Le Gallienne wrote, "seemingly so formless, are actually controlled by a rhythm as precise as that of a piece of music, the tempi of speech and movement must be meticulously established, while appearing to be utterly spontaneous." Their first performance was for Mimsey, who had read the play several times but had not understood it. "I felt as though I were looking through a keyhole—eavesdropping on real people," she said.

In late September, the company moved back to New York and began rehearsals on the stage for both *The Three Sisters* and Benavente's *Saturday Night*. At the same time, Eva and Gladys moved from the Forty-eighth Street apartment to a smaller apartment at 261 West Eleventh Street, just a few blocks from the theatre, where they spent almost all their time.

Fearing that the public expected their productions to be "dingy and arty . . . and gloomy," Eva chose the colorful, action-packed *Saturday Night* as her opening show. "I can't imagine how I could have been idiot enough to choose it," she wrote later. Set in a resort on the Riviera, the complicated play focuses on the fortunes of the court of the kingdom of Suavia. Le Gallienne cast herself as Imperia, an artist's model who sets out to rule through the force of her ideals. All the resources of the theatre were strained. Structured in five tableaus, the play required sets ranging from a music hall to a cabaret to a boudoir to a garden; costumes were needed for forty-three actors playing the speaking parts and extras playing gentlemen, circus performers, and Gypsies. At the first technical rehearsals, Le Gallienne discovered that her stage crew, some of them inherited from the Italian company, had neither the experience nor the competence required to manage such a technically complex show. To change Gladys Calthrop's sets between the tableaus took up to fifteen minutes—a long time for an audience to wait.

Le Gallienne staged the play in a week, using her numbered, color-coded blocking system—red for men, blue for women. She mapped out the groupings, movements, and actions in her script, then gave numbers and diagrams to the actors, showing them where to stand and move. Using the techniques she had observed Bel Geddes employ so brilliantly in *Jehanne d'Arc,* she orchestrated the sounds of the play to great dramatic effect. In the climactic scene in Cecco's tavern, to cover up the death scream of the murdered prince, the inhabitants of the sleazy tavern erupt into riotous excitement, a girl dances a wild tarantella, tambourines clash, an accordion plays, the girl collapses, and Imperia cries out, "How horrible!" In the script the scene ends, but Le Gallienne extended it: the stage is cleared, the people exit, the accordion goes on playing, Cecco closes and locks the door. Then "he finally goes up to the accordion player and with a brutal gesture stops him playing. The silence is sudden and intense. Then . . . CURTAIN."

In her mind, Le Gallienne could see the play as a complete vision, imagining its dramatic sweep and overall music, but she did not neglect subtle psychological details and character-revealing business, such as the moment revealed in this director's note from the *Saturday Night* prompt book: "During these few speeches Michael takes a cigarette from a case, carefully rolls it, prepares it with a drop of perfume & places it carefully in a long cigarette holder. He gives it to Imperia who takes it without noticing—without thinking—mechanically—wrapped in her own thoughts—like a cat. Tremendously aloof and impersonal. She moves very little. One should feel deep inside her a sanctuary to which she can completely withdraw, even in the midst of crowds." At the end of the scene, when Imperia exits, Le Gallienne directed that "Michael stands looking after her a moment, her cigarette holder with the cigarette still burning in his hand. He looks down at the cigarette & goes down to the table . . . where he carefully takes the cigarette from the holder & puts it out. Their whole life should be in this gesture."

On Monday night, October 25, 1926, limousines and taxis parked in front of the freshly painted entrance and dropped off what Le Gallienne called "the usual Broadway crowd of opening nighters." The curtain didn't go up until almost nine, and for the rest of the evening Le Gallienne suffered after every tableau and waited along with the audience as the inept stage crew struggled to change the sets, which upset her so much that she fumbled some of her lines. Noël Coward attended the opening and wrote that "it was more frightful than anything in the world, [Eva] was terrible, the production awful, and the play lousy! Two of Gladys's sets were very good."

Le Gallienne's only consolation was that *The Three Sisters* opened the next evening. "That is one of the joys of real repertory," she said, "one opening night is not the be-all and the end-all of a season." Using a directing technique quite different from her work on *Saturday Night,* Le Gallienne had rehearsed *The Three Sisters* onstage with the curtain down (to give the feeling of being in a room). The cast created their own choreography, moving and editing and changing until "we all felt right and as though we were truly living in those rooms," Eva said. During the last days of rehearsal, she stepped out of her role as Masha, raised the curtain, and shaped the performance from the front. The acoustics of the old theatre, she said, "were so marvellous that every word, even a whisper, carried to all parts of the auditorium, with no feeling of strain or effort." *The Three Sisters* opened to a packed house, and the audience loved it, except for a few who found the repetition of " 'Oh! to go to Moscow!' " "inordinately funny." When the curtain fell and after Le Gallienne had made her curtain speech, the audience continued to applaud the production, and the birth of a new acting company.

A few days later, the critic of the *Christian Science Monitor* wrote: "There is no evidence of 'stardom.' All are working for the good of the play, as a whole rather than for personal advantage—which is as it should be, but seldom is seen on Broadway—and the result is a performance rare in its unity."

The writer May Sarton, who first saw the Civic Repertory productions when she was just fifteen, watched *The Three Sisters* many times. She considered Le

*Egon Brecher as Vershinin
and Eva as Masha in
Chekhov's* Three Sisters,
1926

Gallienne a rare genius, able to "communicate a vision of life" through her artistry. Sarton never forgot Eva's performance of Masha. "Masha is sitting on the porch steps weeping unashamedly while the band plays, and the Captain she loves is marching off forever. Her foolish loving husband brings her a glass of water, and . . . Masha takes it in her two hands like a child. In extreme grief we become like little children, totally vulnerable, and in extreme grief we are thankful for tenderness. All of this Miss Le Gallienne conveyed with a gesture and showed us again in what moving ways acting may become a criticism of life." After years of conscious work and study, Le Gallienne was applying the lessons she had learned from her masters. From Sarah Bernhardt, she had learned that gesture is the expression of thought, and Duse had taught her that thought could be revealed through silence.

"WELL—THE WORST IS OVER," Eva wrote to her mother. "Now we are rehearsing *La Locandiera* which opens 3 weeks from Monday. Of course the work is simply *colossal*—but if we can only put the thing over it will be worth it. I wish so that you could have been with us—especially for *Three Sisters* which really goes awfully well. . . . Gladys' sets made a great hit—they all got hands & good notices—I'm so glad. . . . We are taking care of ourselves—even taking a tonic! We really *need* it! She sends much love."

Perhaps it was the strain of the work that proved too much for the young actor Sydney Machat, who had come from the Hedgerow Theatre in Pennsylvania to work with Le Gallienne in New York. "He was . . . a tall, raw-boned boy . . . who seemed consumed by an inner fire," Le Gallienne wrote. In early November, after a performance of *The Three Sisters,* his friends could not persuade the frenzied, babbling Machat to leave the theatre. At 4:30 a.m., Eva and Gladys were awakened by two young men from the company, who told them that Machat had gone temporarily insane. He was admitted to Bellevue Hospital, where the doctors advised him that the life of the theatre was too much for him. After a few months away from the Civic, he begged to return. Le Gallienne took him back, and for over a month he worked well in his old roles and also prepared for an important part in Susan Glaspell's upcoming *Inheritors.* Just before *Inheritors* opened, Machat killed himself. Since he had seemed fully recovered from his mental breakdown, the company was shocked. "All afternoon we hung about the stage in miserable little groups," Le Gallienne wrote later. "But the inexorable discipline of the theatre demanded action." They played that evening, though "our thoughts and hearts were with our lost comrade who had rebelled against life and broken with it."

Working in a repertory theatre, playing and rehearsing constantly, was a grueling life, and Le Gallienne's standards of dedication and discipline were high. Beatrice de Neergaard said, "It was as if we must always be fit, do our best, make the best of everything, because Eva was doing so much." Rose Hobart recalled that when she left for a few days to visit her husband in Rochester, New York, she didn't bother telling Le Gallienne because she would not miss any performances; but "Eva was really furious with me. I asked, 'When do you want me to leave?' She said, 'A week,' and I left the company." Scene painter Horace Armistead remembered a rehearsal that was delayed by a lighting designer who hadn't set the lights on time. "Setting a scene isn't easy, you know," he explained. "Easy!" said Le Gallienne. "Do you think anything in the theatre is easy?"

During the week of December 6, while directing *Twelfth Night* and rehearsing her role of Viola, Eva played Mirandolina in Goldoni's *La Locandiera,* Masha in *The Three Sisters,* Hilda in *The Master Builder,* and Ella Rentheim in *John Gabriel Borkman.* The role of Mirandolina, the mistress of the inn, who tames a woman-hating cavalier and finally marries a kitchen potboy, was an acting stretch for Le Gallienne and revealed one of the disadvantages of repertory. "Looking at the play with a director's eye," Le Gallienne wrote, "I felt I lacked the unction, the 'juice', for this robust, entrancing Italian peasant woman. It was like using a light

*Eva padded her bust
and hips and wore
Duse's earrings to
play Mirandolina
in* La Locandiera,
*the first Goldoni
play to be presented
professionally in
New York.*

white wine instead of good rich Burgundy." Although unsuited for the part, she was the only woman in the company with the technique to play the quicksilver Mirandolina. As usual, she transformed herself physically in body line, gesture, and movement as well as costume and makeup. The Civic's play reader, Helen Lohmann, who had been Duse's photographer and assistant and owned a collection of Duse memorabilia, presented Eva with the filigree hair ornaments that Duse had worn as Mirandolina. In an ongoing ritual, Lohmann would give Le Gallienne an item from her Duse collection on every opening night at the Civic. In a black fringed wig, antique drop earrings, bright red lipstick, and eighteenth-century Venetian brocaded silkwaist and tan-and-red peasant skirt with hip pads, Eva looked nothing like the androgynous Hilda or the despairing Masha or the middle-aged Ella.

Le Gallienne's day began with a fencing lesson from Giorgio Santelli, a former Olympic fencing champion, who taught fencing to the rest of the company and staged all the Civic's fight scenes. His fencing style was of "the Italian school, very flamboyant and dependent upon fast legwork and breadth of movement," Le Gallienne said. She thought fencing was the best form of exercise for the actor because "one's mind is kept just as busy as one's body. . . . It develops that precise coordination between thought and action that is such a necessary part of playing. . . . The movement is a direct result of a specific intention; the execution of this intention demands complete concentration, and complete concentration eliminates self-consciousness."

After fencing, she dressed in her working clothes, which, like Hilda Wangel's, were selected for practicality and comfort. Many of her clothes were designed and made to her specifications, including her loose-fitting white silk step-ins, embroidered with her initials, which served as combination slip and panty. She did not wear a bra. Under her softly tailored suits, she wore silk shirts with French cuffs in "her colors"—deep, strong shades of blue, violet, or purple, never pastels. She wore comfortable, flat-heeled shoes. She completed her ensemble with a pair of antique earrings from her large collection. The deep pockets of her suits held everything she needed—cigarettes, matches, notebook, pencils, and glasses—and eliminated the need for a purse. To accommodate various wigs, she wore her hair short. Except for a touch of lipstick, her face was scrubbed clean of makeup. In the mornings, she attended to theatre business with Mary Benson, including fund-raising, box-office reports, making up the monthly repertory schedule, drawing up the ad for the Sunday papers, which announced the schedule for the next two weeks, and giving interviews. From noon to five-thirty rehearsals were held on the stage. Afterwards, Eva walked home, ate dinner, slept for half an hour, and then returned to the theatre for the performance. Following the performance, she had appointments with actors or playwrights, finally getting into bed around two. In the most efficient arrangement of all, if Eva hadn't had time to meet with her scenic director during the day, Gladys was available to talk over dinner or late into the night.

SINCE SHE DIDN'T have time to attend any theatre herself, Eva depended on others to scout talent for her. It was Gladys who discovered the gifted Josephine Hutchinson and told Eva that she would make an ideal replacement for Rose Hobart, whom Eva had fired. Since Josephine's mother, Leona Roberts, was a company member, Josephine had seen a production of *Saturday Night* and had met Le Gallienne briefly. "Come on, it'll be fun," Leona told her. "Think how it will broaden you." Jo had learned everything she knew about acting from her mother, performing for three years with Robert Bell's Ram's Head Players in

Washington, D.C. Bell, the theatre-obsessed nephew of Alexander Graham Bell, had started the Ram's Head Players in Dupont Circle primarily for Josephine Hutchinson. During her time in Washington, the Bells treated Jo like a member of their own family. Jo grew close to them, and when Robert Bell proposed to her, she said yes. In 1925, they moved to New York, where he opened an acting school, and Jo had her first hit, playing Edie Tuttle in *A Man's Man* at the Princess Theatre, where Gladys Calthrop first saw her. Hutchinson was an ambitious actor, and leaving "a nice little play" on Broadway to play major roles in Shakespeare, Ibsen, and Chekhov in repertory downtown at a guaranteed salary in an important, well-publicized company was an irresistible opportunity.

"Hello, how are you?" asked Le Gallienne when she interviewed Jo Hutchinson at the Civic. "You'll have to get up in three things at once." Eva was a bit more effusive about Josephine in a letter to her mother. "This girl is really splendid," she wrote, "and such a darling. . . . She is wonderful as Irina. . . . It is marvellous to play with Hutchinson—she gives so much." Twenty-three years old, slim and long-legged, five feet five inches tall, with amber eyes in a heart-shaped face and a cloud of reddish-gold hair, Jo Hutchinson brought youthful freshness and innocence to the company. She had the experience, talent, and stage presence to carry a play alone, relieving some of Eva's burden.

Like Jo Hutchinson and many young actors in the 1920s, Katharine Hepburn wanted to act in repertory and to learn her craft. And the only place where she or anyone else could study acting in New York in the 1920s, Lee Strasberg pointed out later, was with Eva Le Gallienne at the Civic Repertory Theatre. "I asked her for a job, and she wouldn't give me one," Hepburn recalled. Le Gallienne had already hired the more experienced Hutchinson, and there was no place in her company for another young woman. "I loved to go see Le Gallienne in the plays she did," Hepburn said. "Le Gallienne was very similar to me in many ways—strong—you expected her to be the way she was."

With only two company rehearsals, Jo went on as Irina in *The Three Sisters*. "It was quite tough, but they were all wonderful to me," Jo recalled. "I would have made more money on Broadway, but I don't think I would have learned as much. The whole company did what she did. If she took high colonics, everyone did. She was like a guru. If she ate raw eggs, everybody ate raw eggs." Jo liked the calm, disciplined way Le Gallienne worked as a director. "Eva had a rare charisma," said Jo. "She was irresistible—she was fascinating. Her brain was so interesting. I learned so much just from listening to her talk."

Le Gallienne knew that "some actors must be cajoled, some bullied, some made love to, some goaded to anger, but all must be treated differently." A director needed "endless patience [since] actors look upon temperamental fits as their own special prerogative . . . [a director] must be firm . . . must never vacillate." It was "easy to know these things," she wrote, more difficult to put them into practice.

Le Gallienne needed a great deal of patience and firmness in her preparation of *Twelfth Night,* which was the Civic's 1926 Christmas offering. She had never directed or acted professionally in a Shakespearean play. "God save me from Shakespeare," she said about most productions she had seen. "I can't help being bored to death with him! (What sacrilege!)" She and Gladys decided to do away with all the traditional comic business associated with the play, which her older actors were particularly fond of, and decided to play "what is indicated by Shakespeare [which] makes the performance swift and simple—and . . . less dull than usual."

Twelfth Night proved popular, and as the other plays continued to build, the theatre for the first time showed a profit. The critics were enthusiastic: "Miss Le Gallienne Presents the New Modernity," headlined the critic for the *New York Sun.* "[She] presented last evening a highly stylistic and for the most part beautifully finished *Twelfth Night* modern to its rouged fingertips and sophisticated beyond anything that Shakespeare would have thought quite likely. It is a modernity which swings, oddly enough, back almost to Shakespeare's day. . . ."

The Civic Repertory company celebrated their first Christmas together with a party arranged by Mimsey, complete with a large Maine spruce, presents costing no more than fifty cents each, a buffet supper, and dancing onstage into the early morning. Mimsey, who was suffering from bronchitis, left with Alice De Lamar for a much-needed vacation in Palm Beach. A Civic Repertory press release bragged that the Civic was the only theatrical institution that could send its executive to Palm Beach for a month.

Eva and Gladys spent a quiet Christmas Eve opening their presents in bed. On January 9, 1927, a few days before her birthday, Eva wrote Julie: "On Tuesday I shall be 28 years old. So strange how the years fly by. . . . On February 7th I have to give a lecture at the Town Hall, for which I am to receive $300—It is a nightmare hanging over my head—but I could not refuse very well. I am to speak for an hour (just as I did at Yale)—on the Theatre. God help me! Send me good thoughts. I speak always extempore from notes. . . . I have never felt stronger than I do this year. . . . It seems that the work agrees with me miraculously. It is so largely a question of *habit.* . . . Blessings I send you always for the strength & energy of mind & body which you have given me. . . . Gladys sends you her love always."

ON JANUARY 24, 1927, the Civic Repertory opened *The Cradle Song* by Martínez Sierra. Le Gallienne's two old manager friends Sam Harris and Al Woods warned her not to do the play, calling it "dreary and mawkish." She disagreed. Set in a convent of Dominican nuns in Spain, *The Cradle Song* has a slight plot. A baby mysteriously appears at the convent door. The convent physi-

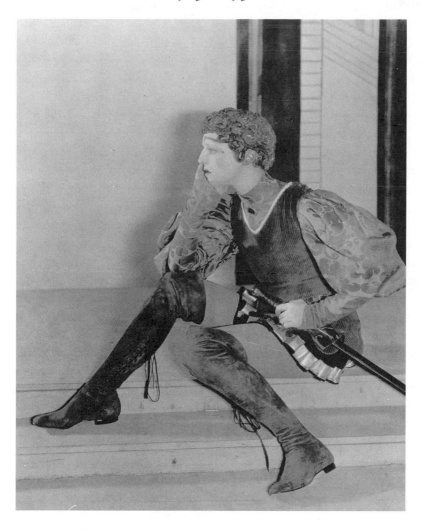

In her stylized production of Twelfth Night, *Eva (Viola disguised as Caesario) wore a yellow rope wig and a circle of red rouge.*

cian adopts the child and the nuns care for the foundling. The baby grows into Teresa, a lovely young woman. At the end of the play, Teresa plans to marry and move to America. "*The Cradle Song* is every bit as funny as it is touching," Le Gallienne believed. "The convent . . . is a microcosm of the world at large; we meet, in little, all the human foibles. . . . And nuns are far from being gloomy people; their very faith inspires a cheerfulness of mind."

The play was easily cast from her permanent company. Egon Brecher acted the physician; Beatrice Terry played the gentle prioress; Leona Roberts was the crotchety, humorous vicaress; Beatrice de Neergaard acted mischievous Sister Marcelle; and Eva cast herself as Sister Joanna, the protector of Teresa, played by Jo Hutchinson. Wearing Sister Joanna's outfit of woollen underwear, chemise, two petticoats, white scapular, veil, and headpiece induced her to write, "if ever I had thought of becoming a nun, any such idea has quite vanished! The discomfort of the clothes is simply colossal. Their bodies seem non-existent. What a strange life."

The Cradle Song was an instant smash hit, selling out at every performance. The critics raved about the charm of the play and the brilliance of the ensemble acting. The success of the play, however, led to an ugly battle with John Underhill, its translator, who wanted Eva to recast the play at the Civic and move the current production uptown to reap the financial rewards of Broadway. "How could I conceivably give away the strongest card in my repertory pack?" Le Gallienne asked him. It's a fragile play, she argued; how could he be certain it would survive "in the harsh climate of Broadway?" She argued further that in repertory at the Civic, the play would be kept alive for years, and his income, in the long view, might be as much as he would earn from a Broadway run.

Underhill looked upon her, Le Gallienne wrote later, "as an unreasonable, obstinate young woman, who stood between him and his rights." His attitude goaded her into telling him that without her the play would never have been produced at all. Feeling that she should give him something, she promised to send out a touring company the following season to the major cities. The tour played twenty weeks to excellent reviews, but suffered a financial loss because it was too delicate to compete in the commercial theatre.

The other reason why she refused to move the play to Broadway was more personal. She knew that if she played only the unhappy Sister Joanna, she would quickly go "into a Liliom-like decline. . . . But this afternoon having been heartbroken as Sister Joanna—I can turn tonight to the joyous Mirandolina."

PLEASED WITH the popular success of *The Cradle Song,* the Civic backers promised their continued support. In many reviews and articles, the critics mentioned again and again the diverse audience at the Civic Repertory. One reporter observed: "Amused young couples. Students with books under their arms. Young men, with eager eyes, huddled into shabby brown overcoats. Elderly gentlemen with thin, intelligent faces. Gray haired ladies who wear high net collars and black shoes and stockings and have read Chekhov. Servant girls who haven't read Chekhov, or heard of him, but like him just the same. People who haunt the reading rooms of the public library, and stand up at concerts . . . all the unspectacular New York people who love the theatre, who want to laugh and cry and be moved by it, and who can afford to come to this theatre where they pay only from 50 cents to $1.65 a ticket."

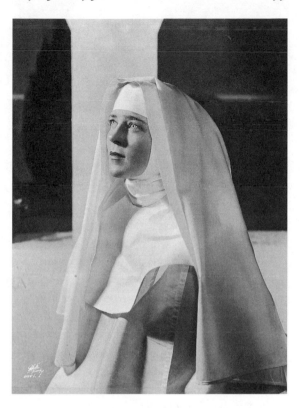

Sister Joanna of the Cross in
The Cradle Song, *1927*

The Civic advertised heavily in foreign newspapers, and Germans, Russians, and Eastern Europeans living on the Lower East Side felt at home in the old theatre with its wheezing noisy radiators and warped wooden floors. When Eva spoke at a Jewish women's club to sell one-dollar memberships, so that they too could feel they owned "a couple of bricks in the Civic," the enthusiasm and response was tremendous. Waving dollar bills, the women surrounded her, hanging on to her and hugging her. "I could hardly get out of the place," Eva said.

At Town Hall on February 7, before an audience of fifteen hundred people, one of Le Gallienne's topics was censorship, which threatened, she said, to narrow the scope of the theatre to the view of one small mind. But her main theme was national and municipal subsidy of the theatre. "The public is ready to receive the theatre as an integral part of national life," she declared, "as it is today in most parts of Europe. The whole fault lies with the system, which aims only to get instead of to give." She announced the Civic's membership drive and invited people to sign up on the spot. "It ended in a great scramble of excited ladies hurling dollars through the air at me," she wrote Julie. "Gladys says I ought to sell quack medicines."

Everyone seemed to be singing the Civic's praises. In a nationally syndicated article Alexander Woollcott described the Civic's achievements: "It is always off Broadway—usually in the most unexpected corners of the town—that the new life in the theater can be heard stirring." William Lyon Phelps, distinguished professor of English literature at Yale, proclaimed: "I regard the establishment of the Civic Repertory Theatre in New York by Eva Le Gallienne as one of the most significant events not only in the history of the American stage, but in the history of America, as the drama and civilization are inseparable. . . . It is this system which enables the inhabitants of any town where there is a repertory theater to hear the best of ancient and modern, of foreign and native plays." Editorials and feature articles were written; photographs of Le Gallienne, of Jo Hutchinson, of the company seemed to be everywhere, in New York newspapers and around the country. Was there anyone who didn't love the Civic Repertory?

George Jean Nathan didn't. Nathan established his reputation by writing abusive criticism. He wrote like a "low comedian with a slapstick and frightwig," said Brooks Atkinson. His prose was vicious, but his suits were beautifully tailored, and he looked like an elegant gentleman. He was so sensitive about his diminutive size that he refused to be seen with any woman taller than he. Writing in his usual blunt fashion in the January 1, 1927, issue of *American Mercury*, he said that Le Gallienne "has, in her entire previous playing career, given just one decent performance, and that was when another director used the whip hand over her [in *The Swan*]. As a directress, she has, in her previous career of direction, been somewhat less than negligible."

"George, George," chided Colgate Baker, in answer to Nathan's diatribe, "[you're terribly peeved that yours is] the only voice among the critics, and in fact among thousands who have seen gallant Miss Le Gallienne and her fine company this season, raised in dissent." She has accomplished, Baker wrote, what no one else has been able to achieve: "she has established a repertory company of the first class in New York City." As an actress she is never wrong "mentally or emotionally," Baker continued. "Indeed her power of mental suggestion is so marvellous that I can only think of one actress who had more of this uncanny effect and that was Eleonora Duse. I never thought that the ordinary ingenue role of the conventional Broadway play was suited to Miss Le Gallienne."

Nathan preferred the acting of Helen Hayes, who was currently in the popular Barrie play *What Every Woman Knows*. While Le Gallienne was producing, directing, and playing Hilda, Ella, Mirandolina, Masha, Sister Joanna, and Viola, Hayes was playing 268 performances of the long-suffering, devoted wife Maggie Wylie. But during the 1926–27 season the most sought-after ticket on Broadway was to Edouard Bourdet's new French play, *The Captive,* a subtle and complex script about a love affair between two women, starring Basil Rathbone and Helen Mencken. A young woman, Irene, is in love with the mysterious Madame D'Aiguines, a woman worshipped and feared by her husband, a woman so dangerous and fascinating that no woman is safe from her devastating charm. Since such a woman was a creation of the playwright's fantasy, to heighten the suspense, he cleverly arranged that Madame D'Aiguines never actually appear onstage. She lurks in the audience's imagination as a shadowy figure. An actress would have destroyed the fantasy and the fear, proving that a lesbian looked just like an attractive flesh-and-blood woman. Although one account places Le Gallienne at the opening of *The Captive* (it premiered when she was rehearsing *The Three Sisters* in Weston), she did not mention seeing the play in her personal papers. But *The Captive* had some odd connections to her own life. Basil Rathbone, her former lover, played the lover of Irene, who was in love with the mysterious Madame D'Aiguines, called a "shadow." And during her love affair with Basil, Eva had been involved with her own Madame D'Aiguines—Mercedes de Acosta.

THROUGHOUT THE 1920S, The National Woman's Party gained power and was supported by women like Le Gallienne (who headed the New York theatre chapter), Georgia O'Keeffe, and Ruth Hale, who, at dinners and special events, celebrated women's progress. Le Gallienne's achievements were the Woman's Party's achievements, and they proclaimed their pride in the fact that she was a "living example of the fact that women can succeed as well, if not better than, men in fields which are competitive." Other voices, though, resented the achievements of women. The Amazons have taken over the theatre and the ladies get all the chances, complained J. C. Furnas in the *New York Herald Tribune,* but he admitted that if women were barred from the theatre, it would be the ruin of the business. Percy Hammond in *Harper's* ran through a list of prominent actresses, named Le Gallienne the high priestess of the New York theatre, and plaintively asked, "Where are the men?" In roles that included long-suffering wives, defiant women-loving women, Shakespeare's heroines, and gentle nuns, women seemed to be standing astride American theatre. "The ladies have not only stolen the trousers of the other sex, but the spotlight," said one reporter.

For her final production of the season, Le Gallienne chose the work of a woman playwright, Susan Glaspell's *Inheritors*. The play, Eva said, "is a burning challenge to America, full of indignation against the results of a too rapid, too greedy prosperity in which the material has become the ultimate goal in complete disregard of spiritual and ethical values." Le Gallienne felt that Glaspell was "the greatest of our American dramatists. Her work is brave and strong and true." The person who sat in on the Civic's rehearsals of *Inheritors,* though, was "a quiet, very shy woman—one can't imagine her writing plays of such force," Le Gallienne said.

The audience, "young, keen, and responsive," observed the *New York Herald Tribune* critic, "listened with intelligence, and occasionally was so moved . . . that it interrupted the action with little bursts of applause." After the curtain calls, the audience shouted for Glaspell. Le Gallienne returned to the stage and asked for her. "Here I am," a timid voice said from the audience. The house lights were turned on; four men hoisted a frightened Glaspell to their shoulders and carried her onto the stage. She clung to Eva's hand as the cries of "Author! Author!" grew more insistent.

"You have to say something," Le Gallienne whispered.

"I can't! I can't!" Glaspell said frantically.

Le Gallienne recalled that she "firmly pushed her forward and left her alone in the center of the stage." The audience quieted. "I'm so glad you liked my little play," Glaspell said, and ran off the stage.

While the production, Glaspell's fine ideals, nobility of purpose, and ringing defense of individual freedom were praised, most critics agreed that her subject matter was dated and her play was loosely crafted. In the commercial theatre, after such dismissive reviews the play would have quickly closed. At the Civic, *Inheritors* became a permanent part of the repertory and found its audience.

WITH ALL SEVEN productions up and running and no new ones to rehearse, the company had time to relax. Then, in April, Eva had the mumps and, instead of remaining quarantined from the rest of the company, insisted on performing. While she could put in a replacement for her small role in *Inheritors,* using an understudy for her own leading roles would have had a disastrous effect at the box office as well as disrupt the other roles in the company. Sister Joanna's habit covered her swollen glands in *Cradle Song,* and in *La Locandiera* she tied a peasant kerchief around her head and face. Still, Le Gallienne said, "it is all very taxing . . . and extremely trying to one of my vanity." Fortunately, none of the other actors caught the mumps.

As usual, when she was ill, Le Gallienne wanted Mimsey to take care of her—and as always, Mimsey was there. In addition to her duties as the Civic's business manager, Mimsey nursed Eva "day & night." And where was Gladys? Perhaps the intensity of the work (designing costumes and sets for eight plays in one season) had begun to wear on her. Gladys is well, Eva told Julie, "but anxious I think for a change; well—so am I, but the actor's life is surely one of *discipline*—that is *good*—I like it." Tellingly, even in her letters, Le Gallienne exerted a director's control, shaping the way her lines would be read—underlining for emphasis and using dashes to indicate pauses. Eva would wait until her next letter to tell Julie that she and Gladys had separated, and in a rare lapse of logic she insisted: "*You must understand that nothing has happened between us*—but we both felt that we needed more freedom to work—more room—and you know we are both violent personalities & not particularly unselfish or gentle—so it will be better so—though I shall be lonely without her." Le Gallienne moved alone to a new apartment belonging to the Church of Saint John the Divine at 224 West Eleventh Street. It was large and comfortable and overlooked "lovely gardens with pigeons & squirrels & trees and flowers and heavenly sun pouring in all day."

Something, of course, *had* happened between the two women. Gladys had found someone else, and in mid-April, before the end of the season, she sailed to England with her new companion. Gladys had acquired an enormous amount of design experience at the Civic Repertory, but she missed England, and she particularly missed Noël Coward, who had been upset that she had stayed so long in America. Coward had teased her about her work with the "Civic Raspberry Company" and urged her to return to England. Le Gallienne had been dumped, losing both a lover and a scenic designer.

At the season's final performance, on April 30, the company played *The Three Sisters*. "The house was *packed*—70 people standing," Eva wrote Julie, "—and at the end they shouted and yelled & screamed—& Brecher made a speech to me on the stage on behalf of the actors—and then they went on shouting till I spoke myself, which was not easy as I felt like bursting with floods of tears. . . . I have been so lonely for Gladys—but it can't be helped. I wonder if you have seen her yet."

Le Gallienne did not tell Julie that Gladys's departure from the Civic was prompted in part by another reason—Eva's growing attraction to Jo Hutchinson. When Jo joined the company, one of the women had taken her to dinner and, perhaps thinking to warn Jo, hinted at Le Gallienne's lesbianism. The news had little effect on Jo. She was a twenty-three-year-old married woman who had spent almost her entire theatre career working with her mother, and she had lived a protected, sheltered life. At the time, Jo didn't really understand what a lesbian was. She did know that Eva Le Gallienne was "the strongest, most charismatic person she had ever met," a person who was much more attractive than her husband, Robert Bell. While she was fond of Robert, Jo realized that she had married him primarily because she had fallen in love with his family. Because of Jo's full schedule of rehearsals and performances, she spent very little time with him, and they lived separate lives. She spent most of her time with Le Gallienne at the Civic Repertory.

Actors often fall in love while working together. The rest of the world doesn't exist. First, they fall in love with the play and with their ability to feel it. Then,

With Jo Hutchinson, 1927

the work becomes all-consuming, and they are able to put the pain and joy of their own lives into the characters. At the Civic, not only were actors bonded by the work, but they were united by a belief in the importance of their low-priced people's repertory theatre. Attracted first by Le Gallienne's "elegant theatre mind," after weeks and months of working closely with Eva and exploring the most intimate nuances of character in long hours of rehearsal, sharing heartbreak, joy, and embraces onstage in play after play at the Civic and on tour, Jo Hutchinson believed it was inevitable and "natural" that they fall in love.

AT THE BEGINNING of the season, Le Gallienne had guaranteed her company a twenty-week contract; but with the addition of an end-of-season tour to Washington, D.C., Philadelphia, and Boston, they had almost thirty weeks of steady work. The tour made new friends for the Civic Repertory, gained some additional backers and members, played a benefit for Mississippi flood victims, and everywhere generated enormous publicity.

Alice Paul and the National Woman's Party reserved four boxes at Washington's National Theatre, decorated them in the party's colors of purple, white, and gold, and sent a delegation backstage to present a bouquet of spring flowers to Le Gallienne. In fact, a delegation from the National Woman's Party became a fixture at every Civic Repertory opening in Philadelphia and Boston as well as Washington. In each city, Le Gallienne spoke to student groups and civic organizations. Her presentation varied, but her theme never changed—each city should have a subsidized repertory theatre. And always there was a spiritual message. She told several hundred people at Boston's Public Library: "We recall the old Indian traditions, where the healer, blessed with a marvelous curative sense, lost his power when he commercialized it. We must not try to make a lot of money out of the theatre. We should think of it as an instrument for giving life, and quickening life; a means of making life worthwhile."

The tour closed in June 1927, with a profit of nineteen thousand dollars, but before she could take a working vacation to Europe, Le Gallienne had to decide on the repertoire for the second season. Script reader Helen Lohmann weeded out the new plays that were submitted, many from European as well as American playwrights. "I have no way of knowing how many—if any—good scripts were kept from me," Le Gallienne wrote later, "but I do know that I accepted some pretty bad ones that second season."

To her current repertoire of seven plays from around the world, she added the powerful Dutch drama *The Good Hope* by Herman Heijermans; a Danish satirical comedy called $2 \times 2 = 5$ by Gustav Wied; the German hit *Improvisations in June* by Max Mohr; a new American play, *The First Stone,* by Walter Ferris; and *Hedda Gabler.* After the season had been announced, Eva sailed to London and Paris, accompanied by the loyal Mimsey, who handled all the travel details.

In London, she managed to extricate herself from an invitation to stay at the home of one of her mother's friends. "You know I *loathe* accepting people's hospitality—wherever I am I like to feel the master of the place—another form of ego mania I suppose!" After a brief visit with Julie, she visited Alice De Lamar in Paris. During her Paris stay, she called on Isadora Duncan, who was preparing a recital. Isadora told her that because of lack of funds, she would not be able to include much of her new material in the recital. "How monstrous it seemed that an artist of her importance should be hampered in such ways!" exclaimed Le Gallienne. Duncan's recital at the Théâtre Mogador was her last performance anywhere, and Eva recalled, "I doubt if she ever had danced so marvelously as she did that day. She seemed to me to give to the dance the quality Duse gave to acting: a sort of cosmic understanding of all life, transmuted into sheer Beauty." During her time in Paris, Le Gallienne had several talks with Duncan. They spoke of Duse. "I remember Isadora saying: 'Never walk with your legs—follow your mind!' and this is what Duse did." There was a "haunting wistfulness" in Isadora's eyes when she spoke of Duse, Eva recalled. "[Duse] was strong," Isadora said. "She was the strongest creature I have ever known." Observing and talking with other artists was a way of "filling herself up again," and by the time Eva sailed for home in late July, her mind was clear and she was ready to return to work.

NO LONGER forced to share the Civic on Sundays with the Italian theatre company (whose lease had expired), Le Gallienne was able to hand-pick her own stage crew, including three department heads: John Ward, carpenter; Joe Roig, property man; and Henry "Henny" Linck, electrician. She acted as her own lighting designer, relying on Henny Linck to provide the technical expertise to implement her ideas. While many of the lighting designs and set conceptions were her own, she hired Cleon Throckmorton to design, build, and paint the sets in his studio. The distinguished Helene Pons created many of the costumes. The first year, the fact that the Civic was a novel, daring, and controversial organization generated news, but that would not be true the second season. Eva realized that "the steepest part of the road still lay ahead."

With the success of the first season and the guarantee of thirty weeks' work, many actors clamored to join the Civic. Le Gallienne hired the experienced Donald Cameron, whose work she had seen in Detroit at Jessie Bonstelle's theatre; Charles McCarthy, a young Carnegie Tech student; and J. Edward Bromberg, whom Egon Brecher had discovered. The short, round Bromberg had not been able to find work in the commercial theatre uptown, but Le Gallienne saw in him "one of those rare creatures, a young character actor."

Meetings with her loyal backers—Otto Kahn, Mary Curtis Bok, Alice De Lamar, and others—produced over fifty thousand dollars in subsidies for the Civic. De Lamar also donated antique furniture and properties to the theatre because, Jo Hutchinson recalled, "Eva wanted audiences to get used to the line of beautiful things." De Lamar was useful, too, in delicate personal negotiations. Through Julie, who moved in some of the same London social circles as Mercedes de Acosta, Eva learned that Mercedes had been spreading gossip that Alla Nazimova and Eva were feuding, which was not true. Alice De Lamar crossed on the same boat with Nazimova, Eva told Julie, and she "was able to get in a little good work in that direction. Mercedes got back a couple of weeks ago, but hasn't called me up or tried to see me. Thank God. I think Paris finished her— poor dear. I'm so sorry for her—She is an unfortunate soul."

EVA WROTE her mother long, newsy letters, but in the fall of 1927, as she waited for Julie, who was coming to New York to spend several months with her, she avoided mentioning a crucial bit of news. "When Mam arrived in this country she got the shock of her life when she found we were living together," recalled Jo Hutchinson. Josephine had separated from Robert Bell, and she had moved into Eva's apartment on Eleventh Street. Actually, Julie had been receiving letters and photographs from Eva describing "adorable" Jo for months, so she must not have been too surprised. Jo, then twenty-four, four years younger than Eva, had never been involved with a woman, but she did not question her love for Eva. "It was good and normal and healthy," she said later. "There was never any shame connected with our relationship." In dealing with a relationship that society considered abnormal, Jo followed Le Gallienne's lead. "Eva knew who she was and she was proud of who she was," Jo said. "She always said, 'one day the light will shine on this.' "

The apartment they shared was large. The spacious living room, with high ceilings, deep blue walls, and dark-oiled floors, had an old-world air. French doors overlooked the garden below. The room was sparsely furnished with a grand piano (Jo loved to play), a long Normandy table, and high windows curtained in deep blue French rep. The study and bedroom were lined with bookshelves and painted a deep blue.

There were several other rooms that Eva had used as storage, but they were now cleared to accommodate Julie. Eva had suggested that it might be best if she put Julie up at a nearby hotel, but Mam insisted on staying with her daughter. The arrangement was probably most trying for Jo, who was not used to Julie's rather imperial manner and emphatic opinions. Julie's waist had thickened and her blond hair had faded, but she was a vital and intensely feminine sixty-four-year-old. She dressed beautifully, usually in suits and hats with a veil, and she still wore an old-fashioned corset. Often with corset strings flying, she would sweep through the apartment, harangue Eva about some slight or some defect in housekeeping, denounce someone or other as a "dull dog," and then turn a critical eye on Jo. "I tell you straight out, Josie," she would say, scrutinizing Jo's new costume or dress, "you should *never* wear white." Eva would tease and mimic her mother's Danish accent and malapropisms ("Keep a stiff neck," Julie would say, or "I'll put a spook in her veal"), and tempers would flare, but there was much love and real affection.

Eva feared her mother's criticism of her performances, especially in the Ibsen plays. Julie Le Gallienne rarely missed a London opening and had seen most of Ibsen's plays when they premiered in Copenhagen. But Julie considered Eva's performance as Hilda by far "the most sensitive, the most lively performance of that role I have seen, and I have seen them all."

"I can't tell you how captivating it was to see all that Eva accomplishes," Julie wrote to Mogens after her visit. "She is a born general the way she conducts all the many different elements without any fuss, without any hesitation or quiver even in the most difficult moments. You will have to see it to believe it. Her tact, patience, and understanding of people is absolutely astounding." Julie particularly enjoyed sharing the honors and awards that Eva received at this time. *The Nation* chose Le Gallienne along with Lindbergh for its honor roll of 1927; and sponsored by the National Woman's Party, Le Gallienne won the 1926 *Pictorial Review* prize and a cash award of five thousand dollars, given for the most outstanding achievement by an American woman in arts, letters, science, industry, or social science—the first actress to receive the award. "In my speech of thanks I tried to make clear the fact that I had been completely and utterly selfish," Le Gallienne wrote later. "I had done what I wanted to do, the way I wanted to do it." The National Woman's Party sent her a congratulatory telegram conveying their delight "that this fine honor has gone to a woman who is a Feminist as well as an artist."

To keep her mother occupied during her stay, Eva set her to work with Paul Leyssac on a new translation of *Hedda Gabler.* When Julie returned to London in late January 1928, Eva sent flowers to the boat, a message that "I really do love you—appreciate you & am proud of you," apologized for any "nervous & unpleasant moments," and couldn't resist ordering Julie not to "scrub her berth with ammonia."

THE CIVIC REPERTORY'S second season opened with the sea drama *The Good Hope,* written by Herman Heijermans as a protest against Dutch shipping companies which, to collect the insurance, knowingly sent out rotten ships. The production featured new company members Alma Kruger and Donald Cameron, with Le Gallienne in a supporting role as a young woman whose husband is lost at sea. The new actors and the production were a hit, and Le Gallienne felt that it was her best work in direction to date. Her detailed prompt script reveals an intricate weaving of sounds (howling wind, crashing waves, melancholy violin), and her naturalistic stage groupings suggested old Dutch paintings. While the critics applauded the production, many complained about the bitter gloom of the subject matter and wondered why Le Gallienne couldn't allow herself to have some fun. Her answer was that the Civic, like Denmark's national theatre, was "Not Only for Amusement," and she had found an audience that shared that philosophy.

Amelia Earhart, whom Le Gallienne had introduced at a National Woman's Party dinner, attended *The Good Hope* with her flight crew a few days before their transatlantic takeoff. "She admired it greatly," Le Gallienne wrote later, but "she told me, giving me that engaging smile of hers, that half-way across the ocean at a particularly grim moment, one of the men had turned to her and muttered, 'The fish are dearly paid for!'—a line which recurs several times, like a refrain during the vigil of the women in the third act."

The next three plays introduced into the repertoire were all flops. "When anything was bad at the Civic it was entirely due to me," said Le Gallienne, "and it was also due to me when anything was good. . . . In that lay its weakness—but also, to a very great extent, its strength." With three flops in a row, she called again on "Ibsen—my saviour," and began rehearsing *Hedda Gabler.* Actually, the Civic was saved by the system of repertory: the strong plays—*The Three Sisters, The Master Builder, The Cradle Song,* and *The Good Hope,* which all played at 80 to 100 percent capacity—carried the weaker ones. The Civic's record of success was considerably better than Broadway's. During the 1927–28 season on Broadway, 233 dramas were premiered; 80 percent of them failed.

On March 9, 1928, at a Drama Study Luncheon at the Hotel Astor, Le Gallienne "crossed rapiers" in a debate with George Abbott, the writer and director later known as "Mr. Broadway." The greatest need today in the American theatre, Le Gallienne proclaimed to the audience of seven hundred, was "a series of national subsidized theatres" similar to the Civic Repertory. "I have no quarrel with Broadway," she said. "Broadway has been very good to me, but prices are too high there." The idea of a people's repertory theatre, like the Civic, she said, "can't possibly fail because it is based on a fundamental need of the great mass of the people. We may fail, but others will try, and if they fail, some one else will succeed." Abbott replied that if the "art type of theatre is so far above us, it shouldn't be here." He believed that "good plays cost a great deal of money and our commercial plays, the finest ever written, are worth the prices charged for them." Abbott defended the status quo, saying, "I don't think that any altruistic theatre, no matter how good the intentions of its directors, can compete with the present day American stage."

Their debate, in various forms, would be an ongoing argument in the American theatre, defined by the motto emblazoned in the Civic Repertory playbills: "The theatre should be an instrument for giving, not a machinery for getting." The irony, of course, which did not escape Le Gallienne, was that the reason her theatre received the enormous national publicity it did, and the reason that she had credibility as a spokesperson, was that she had proven herself in show business and abandoned her stardom for what some considered the martyrdom of "Saint Eva."

THE ABANDONING of a husband, though, was the story sought by some newspaper reporters in late February 1928 as they hovered around the Civic, "being very obnoxious," Jo Hutchinson recalled. Rumors flew that Jo and Robert Bell were separated. Robert Bell confirmed the story. "We are living apart and have been since last summer," he said. "Her work was at night and mine in the daytime and so we had no life together. My wife's work with Miss Eva Le

Gallienne in the Civic Repertory Theatre has taken all her time. Perhaps if she had not gone with Miss Le Gallienne this would not have happened. There wasn't even time for us to lunch together." Pestered by reporters who hung about until she consented to talk to them, Jo spoke angrily: "I have worked hard all my life and I have a right to live it as I choose, without having to tell anyone about it."

"Now, looking back," Jo Hutchinson said, "I did foolhardy things. We stayed in hotels together. But I didn't feel the world was watching." Protected by the enclosed theatre world at the Civic Repertory (the company called Eva and Jo the "Botticelli twins"), where their relationship was accepted by everyone, including Jo's mother, as normal and right, Jo did not concern herself with the outside world. According to Jo, Eva was oblivious to gossip—"I don't think she knew she was talked about." Le Gallienne, of course, *did* know; what Jo termed obliviousness was actually a hard-won Olympian detachment.

Tabloids made much of the separation, and papers around the country picked up the story, slyly noting that Hutchinson was Le Gallienne's favorite actress. *The New York Times* buried the separation story in two paragraphs on an inside page, but *Vanity Fair* later published a caricature of an embracing heroine and hero who bear a striking resemblance to Jo and Eva. "You are wrong in thinking that the young man in the sweater is Eva Le Gallienne," says the caption. The cartoon, titled "Clean Drama," can be read as either an exposé of their relationship or a knowing celebration of their romance. The publicity office at the Civic pasted all the articles and cartoons in the press scrapbook, and life went on as usual at the theatre.

Le Gallienne's sexuality was widely known to her wealthy society friends, to the press, and to her theatre peers ("I knew she was queer," said Katharine Hepburn, "but I didn't think it queer that she was"), and it became part of her mystique and part of her enormous appeal to both men and women.

Le Gallienne was powerful and charismatic, and "there were a lot of people trying to get close to her then," Jo recalled. "Streams of men and women came back to see her, and sometimes she succumbed to temptation." Once, when Jo attended a large party with Robert Bell, Eva turned up in disguise. "She wore an extremely short black dress, a short black wig, and danced and carried on. I was frantic that Bobbie would find out," Jo recalled. Eva was a "great flirt," said Jo. "One night Eva had been out with someone having a dinner meeting, and she brought him back to the apartment. It was very late, and they had been drinking. She was teasing him terribly." Jo got out of bed, went into the living room, and asked the man to leave. "With all of this Eva had great purity of soul," said Jo. "She was always searching, for religion, reading her Bible, studying."

The impact that Le Gallienne made on young people, particularly on young girls, was enormous. When Ruth Mendell and fourteen of her classmates from the Jamaica Normal School in Long Island saw *The Cradle Song*, they waited backstage to see Le Gallienne. The girls were shocked, titillated, and immediately infatuated when Eva appeared without her nun's headdress and smoking a cigarette. Le Gallienne graciously answered all the girls' questions. To experience such warmth, openness, and honesty was a revelation, Mendell told Le Gallienne fifty-three years later.

"JUST A WORD to let you know I am still living [the day] after Ibsen's Birthday!" Eva wrote Julie on March 21, 1928. To honor the "old Troll's" centennial and to show off its triumph as a repertory theatre, the Civic played *Hedda Gabler* at 10:30 a.m., a matinee of *The Master Builder*, and *John Gabriel Borkman* in the evening.

Somehow Le Gallienne also found time to write a long, thoughtful article for *The New York Times* titled "Grim Ibsen Triumphs at His Centenary." She had studied Ibsen for years and had heard her parents' accounts of meeting the playwright. Richard remembered Ibsen's sitting "stiffly and somewhat pompously at his very particular table in the cafe at Christiania; top hat with the mirror concealed in the crown, frock coat tightly buttoned," and Julie recalled a grumpy old man irritated by an actress's description of all the great "parts" he had written. "It's strange how easily I seem to fall in with Ibsen's women, just as you said, I seem to be really at home with them," Eva told her mother. "There seems to be no end to the subtleties and infinite variety of Ibsen's women," she believed.

In playing Hedda, Eva was guided by Ibsen's notes on the role, describing a refined, autocratic Hedda with gray eyes and an ice-cold repose. Since the last three plays had flopped, she rushed *Hedda Gabler* into production, planning to "take the leap and then work through playing." She invited Civic Repertory members to a few dress rehearsals on a first-come, first-seated basis and was amazed to find crowds of people showing up at 8:30 a.m. to get the best seats for the 10:30 a.m. curtain. The practice proved so successful she incorporated the preview performances into the regular schedule.

At one of the early out-of-town performances, when Hedda handed Lovborg the pistol, the audience laughed. Le Gallienne was furious. Constance Collier came backstage and listened to Eva damn the audience. "It was your fault," Collier told her. Le Gallienne then turned her fury on Constance. "It was your fault," Collier repeated. "You were too staccato. It must be legato, and it must be suggested, not done as a command, but an insidious suggestion: 'Take it, use it now.'" Le Gallienne admitted that Collier was right—Hedda was not a forthright person. "It never happened again. Ever," Eva said later.

Using Julie Le Gallienne and Paul Leyssac's translation, which had contemporary idioms and an easy conversational flow, Le Gallienne played Hedda in modern dress. Preceded by a puff of smoke from her cigarette, Hedda made her

Berenice Abbott's study of Eva as Hedda Gabler, 1927

first appearance onstage wearing a "clinging gown of dull yellow silk" with huge black pearls dangling from her ears, exciting "oohs and ahs" from the audience. "She has a strange, graceful beauty," said one observer, "like a lean, aristocratic and intangibly evil cat."

The Civic's production and the performances of Jo Hutchinson as Thea and Paul Leyssac as Tesman were generally praised, but Le Gallienne's modern interpretation of Hedda stimulated considerable controversy. The critics were divided—some preferred the more exotic interpretations of Alla Nazimova and Emily Stevens, while others called Le Gallienne's portrayal a subtle masterpiece of deception. Eva thought Stevens had played Hedda like a neurotic, "ill-bred dope fiend," without "a trace of the ice-cold control" that Ibsen described. About her own characterization, she agreed with critic Burns Mantle, who felt that Eva's portrayal was not consistently sustained. "It took me a long time to learn to play Hedda really well," she said later. "In these initial performances I think I was too harsh, too obviously unpleasant. Hedda's ruthlessness and cruelty should be more devious, and hence more dangerous." She also felt later that it was a mistake to wear modern dress, since Hedda's "perverse romanticism" seems only "valid against the background of the nineties," while the psychological truth is timeless.

A key to her interpretation was Hedda's pregnancy. When Thea and Lovborg discuss Lovborg's manuscript, their "child," Hedda/Eva felt the movement of her own unwanted and dreaded child. Later, alone in the room with Lovborg's manuscript, Hedda at first "rocks the manuscript to her breast as though it were the real child of the man she might have loved. She has reached the armchair by the fireplace and sinks down on it. She looks at the manuscript, sees Thea's careful writing; she fingers the first few pages, almost caressingly at first, then with increasing violence until they begin to crumple and tear under her hands that have become like claws, and the sense of destructive power grows in her, overpowering, at last uncontrollable; she snatches a few pages and with a sudden impulse holds them to the flame; they catch fire and she watches them burn in a kind of dazed ecstasy."

Robert Lewis, who saw Le Gallienne play *Hedda Gabler* many times, said, "When she said 'bored, bored, bored,' it shook the walls of the theatre." Le Gallienne believed that Hedda Gabler should be played with "truth, pace, humour, and excitement." In the preface to her translation of *Hedda Gabler,* Le Gallienne wrote: "Try to imagine the impact of Hedda Gabler on an audience that knew nothing about it; an audience that had not been told for fifty years by innumerable learned critics what to expect, what to think, what to feel. . . . The suspense must have been unbearable. . . . The play is short, but when the curtain falls we are intimately acquainted with every one of the characters involved; this is typical of Ibsen's genius. With all his economy of language and action, he makes us keenly aware of every facet of these people's natures."

A measure of the respect the first-line critics gave the Civic Repertory was the fact that when faced with the choice of attending *Hedda Gabler* or the Broadway opening of *Divorce à la Carte,* they chose to appear at the Civic's off-Broadway opening. Le Gallienne shrugged off the controversy. Innovators are always controversial, she believed, and she understood the nature of American dramatic criticism. The "harassed and hurried" critics reminded her of actors in a stock company, forced to play a new play every week with only five rehearsals and "no time for thought, analysis or study." Like a stock actor, the critic "naturally resorts to tricks, to externals, to short-cuts, it is his only hope of making the public believe he knows what he's about. He too must rush to make the deadline."

Publicity, even controversial, was good for the theatre and for the Civic's membership drive. Although the cost of running the drive had eaten up much of their profit, it had netted (with the help of Laurette Taylor and Walter Hampden, who donated their services as speakers) almost one hundred thousand card-carrying members, all part-owners of the Civic.

With her half sister, Hesper Le Gallienne, in the green room at the Civic Repertory Theatre under a photograph of their father, c. 1928

"MISS LE GALLIENNE seems above all a happy person," wrote Rena Gardner of the *Boston Herald,* who interviewed Eva during the Civic's end-of-season tour to Boston and Philadelphia. "Her poise is more than a social manner, it comes from within. She is busy doing the thing she loves best to do. Her life [is] filled with an absorbing interest." And what would she do when the Civic stood sturdily on its own feet? the reporter asked. Eva, stretched out languorously on her bed in a bright blue dressing gown, replied, "Oh, just live . . . you know, just live my life the way I want to live."

Her words inspired the smitten reporter into a poetic outburst: "She evokes another age, far removed from our restless today, a time when Leonardo lay for hours watching one tiny flower unfold, when living itself was a fine art. It is quite possible to picture Miss Le Gallienne, five years from now, bending her slender neck over a book in some quiet garden. She will have heavy earrings of turquoise or carved gold in her ears, and her own strange beauty like a pale little Russian princess, and she will sit very quietly in her garden."

The "Sven-Gallienne" role that Eva played for reporters was one of her finest, most mesmerizing performances. Like a cat who doesn't attempt to please, only to fascinate and beguile, she toyed with writers, seducing them with the idea that they would be the ones to penetrate her inscrutable appeal, her mysterious self-possession. Not surprisingly, in describing Le Gallienne writers returned again and again to the word "strange." Her beauty was unconventional, her mind extraordinary, her sexuality ambiguous; and too, perhaps to some of them she was simply a stranger—despite her American citizenship, still a foreigner, a cultured European.

But the *Boston Herald* reporter was right: Eva *was* happy. There were several reasons. First, she was deeply in love with Jo Hutchinson. Second, the Civic Repertory had played at over 75 percent capacity, and a third season was assured—a season that seemed particularly promising because Alla Nazimova had contacted her and asked to join the company. Other prominent actors had approached Le Gallienne about starring in a particular play, but Nazimova said she wanted to become a regular member of the company. Alla had separated from Charles Bryant, sold the Garden of Alla, auctioned off many of her possessions, and was practically bankrupt. She earned several thousand dollars a week in vaudeville, but she told Eva that she couldn't bear the circuit any longer. After seeing *Cradle Song* and *The Good Hope,* she said, she believed Eva's direction to be the finest in New York, and the Civic reminded her of the old days of the Moscow Art Theatre. Knowing that Eva doubted her ability to submerge her star persona into an ensemble company, Alla begged Eva not to be afraid of her. After seven years of unhappiness in her work, she wanted to feel needed. If Eva didn't want her, Alla dramatically announced, she would give up acting altogether. "I want to work at the Civic Repertory," she said.

"But we could never afford you," Eva replied.

Nazimova agreed to play for $250 a week.

"I am thrilled to death, everyone is," Eva told her.

Before the contract was signed, however, Alla stated certain conditions, which she detailed in long letters to Le Gallienne. She agreed not to be starred, but in return Eva must present *Katerina* by Andreyev, a play that Nazimova had tried in vain to get Broadway managements to produce for years. The title role was a stellar part for Nazimova, an acting vehicle to showcase her talents, not really suitable for an ensemble company. Even though she loathed the play, Le Gallienne optioned it and agreed to direct it. The opportunity of having Nazimova in the company, an artist whom she truly admired, would ease her burden of being the only box-office draw. She could concentrate on directing and cut back on her own appearances. Also, as she told Alla: "I have missed so terribly your brain these last years . . . it was awful to feel so definitely cut-off from a mind that has always seemed to me one of the most fascinating & stimulating in the world."

Eva arranged for Nazimova to have a dressing room with her own private toilet (which Eva did not have), and when Alla requested to live near her and the theatre, Eva found an apartment across the courtyard from her and Jo. She filled her letters to Alla with loving affection, ego-bolstering praise, and advice. Should she marry her lover, Paul Ivano? Nazimova wondered. "I don't know about marriage—is it necessary?" Eva asked. "I don't think it matters in the least what people say."

In April 1928, Nazimova signed her contract, the announcement was made, and the news stimulated the membership drive. The cynical side of Eva doubted Alla's motives—after all, Nazimova was a great star, whose idea of cutting out extravagance was trading her Rolls-Royce for a Cadillac. Would she be satisfied with $250 a week and no star billing? But the idealistic Eva was "thrilled about Alla, I really feel she is quite sincere in her desire to work once more in a simple genuine way." You must spread the news quite casually in London, Eva wrote Julie, so that word would get to Mercedes, who had told everyone that Alla "thought my work awful & had completely washed her hands of me." She also asked Julie to find out if Gladys Calthrop had really gone off to Italy with Mercedes; "surely [Gladys] couldn't be such a fool," she said. Later, Eva heard that the rumor was true and felt sorry for Gladys. "I simply feel that it is a question of time before she sees the light," she told Julie. "Don't worry about letters, darling. I haven't written a line to M. for 2 years—& to G. I scarcely ever write. . . . I wish they would all go & live in East India—in some far jungle!" Don't worry

about me, she assured her mother; "they can't hurt me anymore—I am well &
very happy & peaceful." In Jo Hutchinson, Eva believed that she had found an
ideal companion. For the first time she was the older woman in a relationship,
and at times she acted as Jo's teacher, in love and in work, but their union was a
true marriage. Seeing their happiness was difficult for Mimsey Benson. "Once,
we came home," Jo recalled, "and found Mimsey crying on the stairs. She was
terribly upset that she had left Eva and married. But it was too late."

THE FOUR WEEK Civic tour to Philadelphia and Boston had been a great
success, critically and financially. On June 4 and 5, 1928, the company inaugu-
rated the Berkshire Playhouse, a new theatre founded by Civic member Alexander Kirkland, with performances of *The Cradle Song,* which had been named one
of the year's best plays.

Tired of acting, Le Gallienne was happy to see the end of the season. She and
Jo packed up a menagerie of creatures, including Eva's Cairn terrier, Tosca; Jo's
Cairn puppy, Whisper; Tinker Bell, the kitten; several parakeets; the doves from
The Good Hope; and a canary that had appeared in *Cradle Song.* They drove to
Weston to spend the summer in Eva's tiny 1775 "shack" on four acres of rocky
land that she had purchased in 1927 for thirty-five hundred dollars.

For years, Eva had dreamed of having a home of her own, a "little place that
would *really* be *mine.*" Le Gallienne was "one of the venturesome souls who were
the very first outsiders to move to Weston before it was either convenient or
fashionable," says the town's history. Connecticut towns more convenient for
New York commuters, like Greenwich and Stamford, were growing rapidly, but
Weston's population in the 1920s was fewer than a thousand. The isolation and
beauty of the town attracted artists, writers, musicians, and theatre people.

"There can't be a house up there," Eva had said when Mimsey first showed her
the property. The tiny house sat isolated and alone on a natural rock promon-
tory surrounded by meadows, rocky ledges, and fields blooming with wild blue
iris. From the front door, Eva had a view over farmlands to the west branch of
the Saugatuck River. Standing on the huge boulders that jutted out from the
hilly meadows, she could gaze southeast over the treetops to Long Island Sound.

Legend held that the house was once occupied by "three old sisters—all
witches," whose ghosts from time to time returned. Local children, who liked to
sneak up to the old house in the hope of seeing a ghost, were disappointed when
the "lady from New York City" moved in and began fixing the place up. During
the fall and spring, at every opportunity Eva and Jo had stolen away from the
theatre and planted daffodil bulbs, snowdrops, and bluebells around the house.
They walked in the woods, and Eva soon learned to identify the wild woodland

flowers: bloodroot, named for the juice that runs like blood from its stem; lady's-slippers; Dutchman's-breeches; foxgloves; and the rare rattlesnake plantain. They furnished the few rooms, which had large back-to-back fireplaces, with antiques from Alice De Lamar's collection. During June 1928 Eva played two weeks of vaudeville (the balcony scene from *Romeo and Juliet* and a one-act play with Donald Cameron) and cleared twenty-eight hundred dollars a week. After cabling five hundred dollars to her mother, she paid off the mortgage, added a bathroom and hot-water heater, running water and a propane gas stove in the kitchen, and expanded the attic with a dormer and six-foot window. She hired a couple to work a few days a week putting in a garden and fixing up the house. Al Lehman donated a new steel garage from his steel works, and Le Gallienne turned in her Studebaker for a blue French Amilcar. "We are so happy here it is really a sort of heaven," she wrote.

In her attic workroom, she planned out the season's productions, using her model of the Civic equipped with a lighting switchboard, curtains, drops, and miniature furniture and props. Since she planned to introduce seven new plays into the current repertory, she designed a flexible unit set to minimize set changes, cut down on expenses, and save storage space. "I think I shall have to join the scenic artists' union," she said.

Eva and Jo took a day away from their heaven when Eva received an honorary M.A. degree at Tufts College. Wearing a cap and gown and seated among "the most lovely collection of old gray-beards," Eva looked like a child. Later, she laughed about the occasion and her ridiculous Latin diploma: "omnibus" was the only word she recognized. A natural aristocrat, Le Gallienne always felt that the winning of prizes and awards was bourgeois. Later, after she had accumulated hundreds of honors, whenever someone she did not admire won an award, she would mockingly repeat the lines of the White Queen in *Alice in Wonderland:* "Everybody has won and everybody must have prizes."

During the summer, she and Jo swam every day in a "heavenly deserted pool," took nude sunbaths on sun-warmed rocks, walked, read, played guitar and piano, and worked on the house and in the garden. The country is "*marvellous,*" Eva wrote. "I can't think why more people don't leave the cities." She felt "very grateful, & most undeserving of it all."

"SUCH A TIME since I've had a second to put pen to paper! And even now I am doing it between two breaths," Eva wrote her mother in October 1928. Her country idyll had ended in August, when she returned to New York to spend the *Pictorial Review* prize money on refurbishing the theatre—painting the interior green, gold, and black, carpeting the aisles and landings, and installing steel platforms and racks for scenery plus new footlights and a sunken trough for cyclo-

In 1927, Le Gallienne exchanged her American Studebaker roadster for a French
Amilcar CGS3 (pictured above with her Cairn terrier, Tosca). Alice De Lamar owned
three and preferred the "incredibly chic" Amilcars to her three seater Bugatti.
The bartender of the Ritz Bar in Paris named a cocktail—the Side Car—in honor
of the distinctive, tiny automobile.

rama lights backstage. The permanent company was expanded to thirty actors, and she interviewed and auditioned hundreds of applicants for a new apprentice program. "My idea," she wrote, "was to take some thirty or forty young boys and girls . . . accept them as apprentices to the work of the theatre. . . . They would be in intimate touch with a repertory theatre working at full speed." In the auditions, she tried to "sense their inner quality . . . some trace of sensibility or imagination, humor, or aspiration." Her free school, underwritten in part by Mary Bok, offered classes in fencing, dancing, speech, and makeup, and the students occasionally worked as extras in Civic productions. They also staged their own productions, and Le Gallienne and other company members critiqued their work. "If they had talent," she said, "they would know instinctively how to make use of the chances put before them."

She hired Aline Bernstein, who had designed sets and costumes for the Lewisohn sisters at the Neighborhood Playhouse, as the Civic's resident designer. Bernstein was living on Eleventh Street with Thomas Wolfe, who was

*Aline Bernstein, late 1930s.
In 1926, she became the
first woman to join the
scenic artists' union.*

struggling with *Look Homeward, Angel.* Wolfe called his section of the apartment a "stinking lair," but Bernstein's half was, like her personality, "trim, spare, certain, alert and orderly and ready instantly for work." In the middle-aged, motherly Bernstein, Eva found an artist "only concerned with the validity of the play, and serving the author." Using Le Gallienne's basic unit set idea, Aline designed sets that could be varied quickly and economically merely by rearranging door and window units, changing platform and stair levels, and switching draperies and set properties.

Irene Sharaff, a talented young art student, had submitted her design portfolio to the Civic Repertory. Le Gallienne liked her work and suggested that Aline look at the portfolio. Bernstein hired Sharaff, first as an unsalaried apprentice and then as her assistant. She assigned her to prepare costume and property lists for the first three plays—Molière's *The Would-Be Gentleman,* Jean-Jacques Bernard's *L'Invitation au voyage,* and Chekhov's *The Cherry Orchard.* Bernstein was fortunate to find such a gifted assistant. She often found herself tired—emotionally wrung out from her chaotic relationship with Wolfe. "She'd be standing there telling the seamstress what I should wear," recalled Jo Hutchinson. "While she was doing that and talking, the tears would just be rolling down her face . . . and all of us . . . just pretended not to see it—we'd go on talking and she would talk to us, and all the time there were those tears."

LE GALLIENNE AND JO did not play in *The Would-Be Gentleman,* the season opener, which gave them a night off together. The Molière comedy was a hit; and the first week played at $8,780—$3,000 ahead of the year before. (They needed about $7,500 a week to break even.) The next opening, the American premiere of Jean-Jacques Bernard's new symbolist play, *L'Invitation au voyage,* had a lovely set, with three high-arched French doors opening onto a terrace. Le Gallienne in the principal role of Marie-Louise looked alluring in a brown bobbed wig and "some of the prettiest dresses ever worn in Fourteenth Street." Bernard's play dealt in silences and moods and very little action. It was one of the "really outstanding failures of the Civic Repertory," but it was one of Le Gallienne's favorites. "We play it for our own delight," she said, "and the very real pleasure of a tiny, faithful audience, people who watch for it . . . and come back to it time and again."

Only Le Gallienne's meticulous organization and careful preparation during the summer could have enabled her to direct three plays in a row and play important roles in two of them. Rehearsals of *The Cherry Orchard* had begun in August with informal readings of the play with Nazimova. Alla was a cat, recalled Jo Hutchinson, and she required careful handling. "Alla was an entirely different actor than the Civic Rep actor," said Jo. "Our method was much more modern, and she was very theatrical. Alla was intelligent, and she sensed the quality in the company and fell into it." Le Gallienne's technique was to appeal to the artist in Nazimova, to include her and make her feel an integral part of the company and allow her to create her own interpretation of Madame Ranevsky (Le Gallienne's spelling of the name). Le Gallienne discovered that Nazimova was a tireless worker, "indefatigable in her search for just the right touch, the right nuance . . . never satisfied, never pleased with herself." Nazimova was not a director and had never played Ranevsky before, but Le Gallienne deferred to her many years of experience and did not hesitate to incorporate Alla's suggestions. Because both women set aside egos, theirs was a fruitful collaboration.

After three years of playing together, the Civic actors knew each other well. Remarkably, for such a controlling personality, Le Gallienne treated each actor with dignity and respect and never sought to impose her will on the individual creation of character. Jo Hutchinson could not recall one time when Le Gallienne ever raised her voice to an actor in anger. She never criticized an actor in front of another, and if she ever lost her temper, she carefully concealed it. She came to rehearsals prepared and did not make actors wait around or waste their time. A sign of her respect for her company was the use of last names during working hours—Mr. Brecher, Miss Hutchinson, Miss Roberts.

Le Gallienne blocked the overall movement and would make specific suggestions as to business and gesture, but the process of making the character live was left to the individual actor. While she used many of Stanislavsky's techniques in rehearsals, such as character analysis and discussions of motivation, Le Gallienne believed that the creation of character was a delicate, private art, and did not inflict her interpretation upon that creation. Leona Roberts, who developed her own following at the Civic, had a purely instinctive talent, "and woe to the director who tampered with it and tried to clutter it up with elaborate analyses and motivations," Eva said.

The Cherry Orchard, like all of Chekhov's plays, depended on "what goes on beneath the lines," Le Gallienne felt, "on the almost casual interplay between the various characters, on a truth and simplicity so thoroughly understood and digested that it becomes effective in a subtle unobtrusive way in no sense dependent on the usual theatrical externals." An example of this interplay was revealed in a tiny, subtle bit of business during the first act of the play. Madame Ranevsky suddenly speaks more softly, since, Chekhov says, she remembers that Anya is asleep. In Le Gallienne's direction in her script, Varya silently closes the door to Anya's room, which prompts Ranevsky's whispers. The business reveals the solicitude of Varya for her sister and points out that while Madame Ranevsky may be thoughtless, she is not uncaring.

Robert Lewis, who saw *The Cherry Orchard* many times, believed that Nazimova's Madame Ranevsky was "the most beautiful woman you ever saw in your life," but Le Gallienne's Varya "was unforgettable." He recalled that when Varya throws Trofimov's galoshes, "her whole frustration, her anger, everything was in that one gesture. She was incredible."

At the Civic, the actors had the use of the stage and furniture, properties, and costume pieces from almost the first day of rehearsals—a condition practically unknown in the commercial theatre, where actors often didn't see these items until the final dress rehearsals. The character of Gaev in *The Cherry Orchard,* for example, reclines in a chaise longue for most of the first act. Le Gallienne knew the importance of furniture and properties in revealing and delineating character. "That chaise-longue has become molded to his body," she wrote; "he is familiar with every threadbare spot in its upholstery, with every detail of its carving."

In preparing the production, Le Gallienne used as her model the Moscow Art Theatre's *Cherry Orchard* that she had seen in 1923, which had been successful because of the seamless ensemble playing of the company. "Whenever I read a set of notices praising to the skies the acting, the scenery, the costumes, and the direction, and dismissing Chekhov as a depressing, ineffectual dreamer whose play, like a museum piece, has no relation to life as we know it," Le Gallienne wrote later, "I know that once again he has been betrayed. . . . The stars of the stage may shine in all their box-office glory, but the true, modest, enduring star of Chekhov will have suffered a temporary eclipse."

Eva (Varya), Sayre Crawley (Firs), and Alla Nazimova (Madame Ranevsky)
in The Cherry Orchard, *1928*

To recreate Madame Ranevsky's faded country house with its orchard in the background, Le Gallienne used the whole expanse of the stage, extending the playing area all the way back to the scene dock on Fifteenth Street. The characters made their entrances from the side wings, and the visual effect was breathtaking. Ever alert to a comic opportunity, Leona Roberts, playing Charlotta, made her entrance riding in a baby carriage.

The opening attracted a sell-out crowd, many of them eager to see Nazimova, while others welcomed the chance to watch Chekhov's modern classic. Later, Irene Sharaff wrote that no other production ever had the magic created by the Civic Repertory's *The Cherry Orchard*. Aline Bernstein found original Worth dresses for Nazimova in shades of black and cream, and "although her features were large and rather coarse," Sharaff recalled, Alla applied makeup so skillfully that she gave the appearance of a "strikingly handsome woman . . . who looked like a Boldini portrait come to life."

Jo Hutchinson played Anya, and she felt that the production was the highest achievement of the Civic Repertory. "For actors to play Chekhov is like having a ticket to heaven," she said. "The people get so close and the feelings are so strong in each character. In an ensemble company each person is like an instrument, and if each actor plays truly then you're carried along with such force."

"It was a thrilling opening," Le Gallienne wrote her mother. "The ovation at the end lasted 8 minutes (Tupper [the stage manager] timed it!) & this in spite of the fact that I kept having the house lights turned on—so that they had an excuse for stopping applause if they wanted to. They wouldn't leave off until both Alla and I said a few words. She seems very happy about it all—& so far has behaved like an angel."

To Eva's delight, her direction and the entire ensemble received high praise from the critics. Brooks Atkinson in *The New York Times* called *The Cherry Orchard* perfection. "In a limpid, modulated performance Miss Le Gallienne's troupe conjures up the serenity of Chekhov's personality; and the impending doom of the central theme. . . . Nazimova . . . plays her part with a flowing rhythm that catches every evanescent mood and intonation in this character," he wrote, and he praised the acting of Le Gallienne, Paul Leyssac, and Jo Hutchinson as "pure light."

"NOW WE ARE OFF on *Peter Pan*," wrote Le Gallienne. "I am *mad* about it— I think it will give me a lot to play it—a little of what Hilda Wangel gives me."

Shortly before he died, her old friend R. H. Philipson, who had given Eva her first makeup kit and bound her copies of Bernhardt's memoirs, had interceded with James Barrie, and Le Gallienne acquired the rights to *Peter Pan* that spring. She also asked for the blessing of Maude Adams, who had created *Peter Pan* with enormous success on the American stage. "She was very polite, very kind, and I thought . . . very dull," said Le Gallienne. When she studied Adams's version of *Peter Pan,* she discovered that the part of Wendy had been curtailed and many of her lines given to Peter, even some of her "typical little-English-girl Victorianisms." Le Gallienne cast Jo Hutchinson as Wendy and restored all her original lines.

The difference between Le Gallienne's Peter and Maude Adams's can be clearly seen in their costume choices. Adams's feminine Peter wore russet-colored tights with garters. Le Gallienne's choices were more androgynous and more daring. After studying the F. D. Bedford drawings of Peter, Aline Bernstein designed a short tunic (just covering the flying harness) in faded delphinium blue with a few leaves clinging to it and a cap in the shape of a bluebell. Le Gallienne shed the traditional tights and kept her shapely legs and feet bare, covered only by a dark, tanned makeup.

Le Gallienne worked on the part of Peter during the summer in Weston, practicing her "crowing" on a large boulder, which she named the Peter Pan Rock. "I'm sweet, I'm sweet, oh! I'm sweet! Cock-a-doodle-do!" cries Peter. His ecstatic cry is "not coy or cute," Le Gallienne said, "he quite simply means it." She would play Peter as James Barrie wrote him, not in the "girlie-girlie" tradition that had sugar-coated the character. After practicing with the Schultz flying masters (who had rigged the flights in Adams's *Peter Pan*), Le Gallienne asked them to rig an audience fly. The high-domed ceiling of the Civic and its 110-foot grid were ideal, and she became the first Peter Pan to soar out over the audience, to the very edge of the balcony.

The Civic's production of *Peter Pan* was one of its most enduring successes, financially and critically, and a perennial holiday favorite of children and parents. In a view shared by many who saw the production, Robert Lewis said, "No actress since has come close, in my opinion, to the wild excitement of her Peter Pan." Actor Norman Lloyd recalled that *Peter Pan* "was real fairy-tale time. . . . She was sheer heaven when she flew. She had the guts of a lion. She would fly out from the stage to the first balcony, and if one kid had ever touched her and destroyed the swing of that wire she could have crashed into the stage coming back."

When he was a boy, Stewart Stern (who wrote the screenplays to *Rebel Without a Cause, The Ugly American,* and *Rachel, Rachel*) saw Le Gallienne's *Peter Pan,* and later he worked briefly with her. Over the years they shared letters, dinners, and gifts of thimbles. Stern wrote later that Le Gallienne's production of *Peter Pan* "never talked down. It never spared the lashes. It was about an utterly lost boy, a boy full of dash, braggadocio, jealousy, rage—a thief in the night who was heartbreakingly deprived, but never asked for pittance nor mourned over himself. . . . Le Gallienne's Peter was un-posey—a boy, not a girl trying to seem

Peter Pan, *1928. In Le Gallienne's production, the pirates wore boots with twelve-inch soles and towered over Peter and the children.*

like one by standing straddle-legged. He had a very dark face out of which the teeth and the whites of the eyes sparkled strangely and he rarely smiled."

Stern also praised Le Gallienne's flights: "The flying seemed to originate with the actor, not the man on the ropes, and it was easy and reckless. Le Gallienne made flying seem to that generation's children as glorious, dangerous, and forbidden, as Marlon [Brando] made motorcycles seem to his." Stern never forgot "that breath-catching curtain call: the unsmiling figure [of Peter] walking onto the stage, giving a rigid little bow, cap in hand—then allowing the cheers of the children to bring on Peter's smile, bigger and bigger, bigger than it had ever been in the play, and then soaring out over the audience, almost touching my hand as I leaned from the balcony, in goodbye."

That Christmas, Le Gallienne started a holiday tradition of giving a free matinee of *Peter Pan* for orphans and poor children from settlements around the city. Klein's department store contributed red balloons and sacks of candy. "None of us will ever forget the first of these matinees," Le Gallienne wrote. "The children did not know ordinary applause, and they simply yelled their approval. . . .

when Peter finally jumped on the barrel and with a mighty blow felled
Hook . . . the cheers that went up stopped the show for three minutes. I have
never heard such a noise inside a theatre."

THE 1928–29 THEATRE SEASON was commercially the worst in Broadway
memory. At the Civic Repertory, though, "business at the theatre is amazing,"
Le Gallienne said. The terrible season was blamed variously on the vicious national election campaign, which pitted Herbert Hoover against Catholic gover-
nor Al Smith; talking pictures; dirty, tasteless, or simply bad plays; incompetent
producers; or the high cost of theatregoing. Plays like *Nice Women, Chippies,
Marry the Man,* and *Tired Business Man* opened and closed almost simultaneously. Among the few successes were Hecht and MacArthur's *The Front Page,* the
Theatre Guild's production of O'Neill's *Strange Interlude,* and George S. Kaufman's *Animal Crackers,* starring the Marx Brothers.

In November, at the annual Equity Ball at the Hotel Astor, Le Gallienne appeared as the Spirit of Equity—an honor given in the past to Ethel Barrymore
and Laurette Taylor. With the success of the Civic, Le Gallienne became a
sought-after speaker. The Old South Meeting House Forum Series in Boston invited her to lecture on November 18, 1928, the first actor to speak there. "Those
grand old gentlemen who must have preached here, how they would turn in
their graves if they could see me here today," said Le Gallienne. "And if I had said
to one of those grand old gentlemen that after all, it was not so very extraordinary that a person of the theatre should speak from the pulpit of a church, because the theatre in its origin sprang from religion, he would surely have accused
me of blasphemy."

In her talk, which she would deliver in various forms for the rest of her life,
she defined the difference between her theatre and Broadway. "By the theatre,"
she said, "I mean true art of drama. . . . There is the art of drama and there is the
theatrical show business, just the same as in a museum of paintings you do not
hang up an advertisement for Lucky Strike cigarettes. You would not think of
comparing such pictures with the work of Rembrandt. . . . The theatre is just as
distinctly divided. In order for the theatre to be important once more to the people, commercialism must be banished from it."

She spoke about the value of repertory. "In the theatre there are plays which
you can not possibly understand or get full benefit from seeing them played just
once. . . . If I would say to you, just skim through the pages of a book and in half
an hour tell me what it is about, you would laugh at me. You go to a play like
The Master Builder or *The Cherry Orchard* or *Hedda Gabler,* you see it once and
you say I have seen *The Master Builder* and I don't understand it, therefore there

must be nothing in it. Go back. Think about it. . . . After all the fruit of a man's life such as Henrik Ibsen certainly cannot be devoid of everything. If you fail to get anything from it, it is your fault and not Henrik Ibsen's."

She closed her speech with a vision for the future. "Mind you, when I speak of the Civic Repertory Theatre, I do not mean just my theatre. I mean the idea that is behind it, because it does not matter a bit if I fail. That is not important, but what is important is that the idea should succeed and the idea will succeed because the idea is right and inevitable. . . . I believe everywhere in this country there will be eventually a People's Repertory Theatre, a theatre created by the people . . . so that . . . into the lives of their children may flow some of the beauty that springs from knowledge."

These words enraged George Jean Nathan, who resorted to name-calling. He ridiculed Eva's offering good drama at low prices to the masses, as if "any sailor's, delicatessen dealer's or pants presser's soul is to be effectually elevated by Ibsen's *The Master Builder.*" He told Le Gallienne to give up her *idée fixe* that "she is a reincarnated combination of Rachel, Joan of Arc, and Nat Goodwin, with faint but unmistakable overtones of Jesus," and urged her to "put on at bargain prices a few rowdy low French farces or exciting horse race melodramas."

As 1928 came to a close, there was no question of the Civic's failing. The company played ten performances the last week of the year, adding two holiday matinees of *Peter Pan,* and receipts totaled more than eleven thousand dollars—their best week to date.

By a stroke of scheduling good fortune, *The Would-Be Gentleman* played on Monday, December 31, and Le Gallienne and Jo were able to have two days' rest in Weston. "It is a cold clear night after a day of the most *brilliant* sunshine," Eva wrote her mother, who was spending the holidays with Hesper and her husband, Robert Hutchinson, in Kent, England. "We both feel like new people—we slept last night over 12 hours!" Writing her letter to Julie in her own home before a blazing fire, surrounded by a menagerie of creatures, with her "lamb" Jo reading close by, Le Gallienne had a full heart: "1928 has been for me a beautiful year. Good work and peace and happiness and *dignity.* I am grateful for it."

IN HER SPEECH at Old South Church, Le Gallienne's pointed reference to Lucky Strike cigarettes may have been prompted by Nazimova's using her connection with the Civic Repertory Theatre to sell cigarettes. Identified as a "Brilliant Dramatic Star now appearing with Civic Repertory Theatre" in full-page newspaper ads carrying her photograph, Nazimova announced, "I know an easy way to keep from getting fat . . . Light a Lucky instead of eating sweets." Although there is no evidence that she rebuked Alla for the advertisement, Le Gallienne, who did not believe in using her image to sell anything other than theatre, must have been annoyed. On the other hand, in article after article Nazimova read that her triumphant return to the stage was not her own achievement but that of the remarkable Eva Le Gallienne, who had brought her back. Gossip columnists sniped that Alla was playing second fiddle to Eva. Still, Nazimova had regained her artistry at the Civic and found a new companion in the young actress Glesca Marshall. Her work had been seen by a new, younger audience and by commercial producers. In a note to Eva in February, Alla thanked her for giving her life and happiness.

During the 1928–29 season the Civic Repertory would play to 94 percent capacity, and Le Gallienne was grateful for the boost that Nazimova had given to the box office. But as she directed Alla in the title role in *Katerina*, Eva's irritation with the play mounted. She found the melodramatic story ridiculous: Katerina, a woman falsely accused by her husband of adultery, defies him by making his suspicions real. Eva complained: "I hate *Katerina*—God knows how it will come out—it is so hard for me to work on something that is unsympathetic to me!"

Although some audience members giggled on opening night at the first entrance of Nazimova as Katerina—who, wearing a nightgown, runs from her husband, who wildly fires shots at her, misses, and shatters a plate—Le Gallienne felt that Alla gave a "magnificent performance." For the most part the critics agreed, and the production was successful enough to be included on the Civic's spring tour, along with *Peter Pan* and *The Cherry Orchard*.

In March 1929 Le Gallienne announced that Nazimova would return the next season to play in *The Seagull*, along with the great Yiddish actor Jacob Ben-Ami, who wanted to join them. The handsome Ben-Ami would add glamour and importance to the company. He also was a good director who "could produce a play for me now & then," said Le Gallienne. "Alla is very excited at the idea of having him with us—she likes him very much & admires his work. . . . Eventually we will have a *marvellous* company."

Unfortunately, it would be a company that did not include Nazimova. In Philadelphia and Boston, audiences preferred *Peter Pan* and *The Cherry Orchard* to *Katerina*. Glesca Marshall wrote later that Nazimova decided to quit the Civic Repertory when the tour closed in Boston and Le Gallienne failed to invite her to come onstage with the rest of the company to accept her thanks for the season. Jo Hutchinson recalled that the problems with Alla began in Philadelphia when her trunks were delivered to her room with labels saying "Eva Le Gallienne's Civic Repertory." According to Eva, the trouble started on tour when Nazimova "kept accusing me of 'starring myself'. . . . Mimsey pointed out to her that unfortunately that 'idea' was so tied up with my name that the papers in spite of all one could do to prevent them would come out with headlines: . . . 'Le Gallienne company presents' or 'Le Gallienne saves season' or things of that sort, over which of course we have no possible control."

It was naive of Le Gallienne to insist that she was not starring herself and disingenuous of both her and Alla to pretend that it could have been otherwise. Le Gallienne did not star in every production, but as the founder and moving spirit of the company, she was clearly the star of the Civic Repertory. There was also no reason to feel sorry for Nazimova. Not only had Alla succeeded in presenting *Katerina* (an ambition of many years), but she had also reestablished herself as a theatre artist, one who was now in demand in the commercial theatre. The following season she signed on with the Theatre Guild. Le Gallienne invited her old friend Merle Maddern to replace Nazimova in *The Cherry Orchard* and *The Seagull* and happily dropped *Katerina* out of the repertory.

AGAIN, EVA AND JO spent the summer in Weston. In the spring, they had planted a dozen rosebushes, and "they are simply *marvellous!*" she wrote, ". . . the most lovely yellow one Claude Pernet's and other more golden ones— & then a wonderful deep crimson bush—& several lovely pinks & reds." For weeks Eva did nothing but work in the garden, swim, and sunbathe, play with Tosca and Whisper's new puppies, read, and observe life around her.

Eva and Jo returned to town the first week in August to move out of their Eleventh Street apartment into a large apartment on the top floor of a building next to the theatre, where they could live more cheaply and efficiently. They would not have to dress in street clothes before going to rehearsals or performances, and a direct telephone line linked the apartment with backstage and the box office. Also, they could take their dogs up to the roof instead of down to the street.

During the same week, Le Gallienne auditioned two hundred applicants for the apprentice group and chose thirty. Among those selected were May Sarton, Burgess Meredith, Arnold Moss, Stella Moss, John Garfield, and Howard da Silva. Robert Lewis managed to slip into the apprentice company without an audition. Sometimes Le Gallienne and the rest of the company wished "the students far, far away! They are an undisciplined, selfish, arrogant lot as a rule," she wrote, "but they are so young; and if . . . you find someone who really has something, it's worth while putting up with the rest of them!"

When fifteen-year-old May Sarton, the solemn, plain-faced daughter of a Harvard professor, saw the Civic Repertory's production of *The Cradle Song* in February 1928, at the Hollis Theatre in Boston, it changed her life. Through a friend she was able to meet Le Gallienne in her dressing room. Overcome by the glamour of her surroundings, May poured out her hopes of becoming an actor and playing Hedda Gabler. Le Gallienne laughed at the girl's earnest fervor, but she thought May "seemed so alive with a very definite enthusiasm and ideal-

May Sarton, seventeen,
during her first year at the
Civic Repertory, 1929

ism . . . highly intelligent and of a pleasing personality." She advised May that college would be a waste of time if she planned to work in the theatre.

Although she had been accepted at Vassar, on August 31, 1929, Sarton was on her way to New York to join the apprentice group at the Civic Repertory. "For what I had felt streaming out from the stage at the Hollis was not the glamor of one personality (however powerful)," May wrote, "so much as something even rarer—and exceedingly rare in the theatre—the tangible proof of what serving an art rather than using it for one's own ends can mean to those involved. My first great love was, in fact, the Civic Repertory Theatre, that kind of falling in love which frees the deep creative stream and forces one to grow."

Burgess Meredith recalled that he met with Le Gallienne at a low point in his young life. Amherst College had kicked him out, and he had moved to New York and from one menial job to another. His piano teacher told him about the Civic's apprentice group. When he auditioned, Le Gallienne didn't allow him to finish. She stopped him and said, "Yes, you come along. I'm sure you'll be fine."

"It salvaged my life," he said.

"With us there may have been a little of the feeling that we were art and that everything else was junk," said Howard da Silva, "but it was supported by the fact that we had a real repertory going, we had our own life, our own season. . . . the few times I went uptown to Broadway, I ran away from that place as if it were the plague."

At the Civic, the apprentices took fencing lessons with Santelli, watched rehearsals and analyzed the acting, performed in their own work directed by each other or one of the professional company, and acted small parts in the productions. "The bits I acted in the various plays at the Civic were not as important to my development as the fact that I had a theatrical home," said Robert Lewis.

May Sarton never forgot her first opening at the Civic. "Now the theatre where we had sat so many hours in the dark was alive and alight with attentive human faces. What wonderful audiences they were!" When the curtain rose on *The Seagull,* the eleven-hundred-seat theatre was packed with three rows of standees. "We knew for the first time," said May Sarton, "what the Civic meant to the community."

Le Gallienne played Masha in *The Seagull,* another of Chekhov's women in black. "Just as in painting there is a note of black somewhere on the canvas, so Tchekov in his plays has nearly always that note of black in one of his female characters. . . . I think *The Seagull* is perhaps the most difficult of all his plays. In it, even more than in the others, it is a matter of catching a mood, particularly in the first act," she wrote. When the curtain fell, the audience applauded for five minutes, but the actors were miserable. It was an "evening of torture and agony. We were all horribly nervous & the performances seemed bad to us," Le Gallienne told her diary.

The notices, though, were some of the best the company had ever received. In *The Commonweal,* Richard Dana Skinner sensed "at last the full purpose behind her long arduous work in developing a company in which no one is a star, and in which each contributes to a perfected ensemble. . . . The new members of the company, Jacob Ben-Ami and Merle Maddern, finding themselves at once in this atmosphere, drop naturally into the parts assigned to them as two or three new players might be added to an orchestra." In *The New York Times,* Brooks Atkinson struggled to explain the spell the performances had cast over him. "When the curtain rises on this brooding Chekhov masterpiece, you may suspect that the pace of the performance is too deliberate and the silences too overwhelming. But presently you realize that all the beauty of the theatrical crafts and all the sincerity of histrionic feeling are evoking before your eyes a strange, sombre, infinitely sympathetic sweep of truth . . . acting it is almost the antithesis of acting the ordinary realist play. To be precise, it is an exercise in the overtones of acting. . . . but it is futile to describe individually the elements in this glowing performance."

In a long, analytical article, Atkinson wrote that the Civic Repertory was the most interesting theatre in New York. To be complete, he said, it needed only to

Eva as Masha in The Seagull, *1929*

do more new American plays, but Atkinson admitted that it was a difficult task, since popular playwrights preferred the royalties of Broadway based on long runs and high prices. It was for that reason that the Theatre Guild had abandoned the repertory idea. While he believed that Le Gallienne had developed as an artist, Atkinson feared that she was not giving herself good enough parts and was spending too much time on directing and producing, and was "likely to spoil a good actress in a versatile manager."

Even with all her duties at the Civic, Le Gallienne found time to study the work of artists she admired. When the Chinese actor Mei Lan-fang played New York, she attended several of his performances, sitting as usual in the front row of the theatre so that she could study his work closely. "I haven't been so excited about *anything* in the theatre for years," she wrote. "He is a great artist. He plays only women's parts, & his perfection & grace & subtlety are beyond words. The whole mise-en-scene incredibly interesting. There is so much to learn there. . . . He is *really* beautiful."

In countless reviews, articles, and essays, writers trumpeted the achievements of Le Gallienne and the Civic. On a trip to New York in September, Mrs. Herbert Hoover saw a performance of *The Cradle Song* and went backstage to shake Le Gallienne's hand. With the seal of approval of the First Lady, *Time* magazine selected Le Gallienne for its November 25, 1929, cover and chose a strange portrait of her in red lipstick, a bright blue silk blouse, her short light brown hair feathered back over her earringless ears, and an impassive, expressionless face. She looked like a determined young feminist. In the flattering but slightly patronizing article, titled "Civic Virtue," *Time* called her a "galvanic founder-directrix," and the Civic a place where "the plays change nightly, the standard does not." At a time when the popular attitude was hard-boiled cynicism, Le Gallienne dared to be idealistic. To the jaded, her words sounded like the pious pronouncements of a highbrow.

The press attention and what Brooks Atkinson called the "idolatry" of her associates surpassed any accolades she might have received on Broadway for a purely personal success. Her ego and her ambitions were enormous—she was called Top Sergeant, Little General, Joan of Arc, and the Napoleon of the Civic. In the spring of 1930, she added Shakespeare's Juliet to the list.

DURING THE SUMMER OF 1929, Le Gallienne and Aline Bernstein designed a production scheme for *Romeo and Juliet,* working out the plan on the model stage. "I wanted our production to give a sense of the Italy of that period," Eva said. "It should be colorful, violent, and above all *swift*. There should be no scene-waits, the whole story should flow without interruption and increasing in tempo and suspense till the final curtain. For it is after all, an awfully exciting story; it is not just a lyrical 'love fest.' To my mind the play is too often treated as a star vehicle, which robs it of its broader canvas, like looking at a detail in a painting and missing the meaning and drama of the *whole*."

The flexible stage and sets Bernstein and Le Gallienne designed anticipated the thrust stages of the mid-twentieth-century theatre and looked back to the open stage of Shakespeare's time. The orchestra was moved into a stage box, and the pit was covered with a platform, allowing entrances and exits from below and above. The stage itself looked like a town square, with flights of stairs against a deep blue background. A revolving triangular set piece became Juliet's chamber and balcony and the friar's cell. Only in the final tomb scene was the full expanse of the stage used, to reveal the shadowy churchyard and the skeletal ribs of an open tomb.

Le Gallienne had wanted Jacob Ben-Ami to play Romeo to her Juliet, had even planned to send him to Margaret Carrington, the speech teacher who had helped John Barrymore; but Ben-Ami, accomplished actor that he was, could not eliminate the Yiddish accents in his speech, accents more acceptable in the prose of Ibsen and Chekhov than in the poetry of Shakespeare. Instead, he played Prince Escalus of Verona. (His line "Rebellious subjects, enemies to peace" came out, Robert Lewis recalled, as "Ribalious sobjects, animies to piss.") Le Gallienne selected the less exciting but solid actor Donald Cameron as her Romeo. "Poor sweet, he is dancing & fencing & having violent massages & watching his food—and really his figure has become ten years younger already," she said. J. Edward Bromberg, short, plump, enormously talented, was cast as Mercutio. Leona Roberts played the bawdy Nurse. Howard da Silva, Burgess Meredith, and May Sarton all had small roles.

With the Civic Repertory well stocked with plays, Le Gallienne devoted ten weeks to rehearsing *Romeo and Juliet*. There was immense interest in the production—it would be her first major role that season and only her second attempt at Shakespeare. "Not that any of our individual performances will be inspiring," she wrote Julie, "but as a production scheme it is really quite thrilling & is turning out so far just as I saw it in my head. People seemed surprised at how quickly it was put together, but after all if you see a thing *clearly* in your mind it's not so difficult to execute it in actual line." Whatever its faults, she added, "the production will not be *boring*."

Tell the tale and tell it swiftly and truly was her concept. She cut the prologue, and the play opened with the pounding of drums and a savage street brawl. The fencing master, Santelli, staged the fight scenes and the duels. After fencing every day for several years, the company was well equipped to present realistic, thrilling fights. Juliet's first scene with the Nurse was eliminated, and she appeared first during the ball scene, discovered through Romeo's eyes.

By the end of the rehearsal period, "the most damnable stage when everything looks frightful," Le Gallienne was too close to the process to see it anymore and could only trust blind faith. On opening night, she "went round in the wings crying—& yet when I began to play I was happy. The music & sweep of the thing carrying you away on magical wings—it is so beautiful—& a great joy to be allowed to speak such lines."

The next day the critics united in praising the production, her Juliet, and the playing of the other principals, particularly Bromberg's Mercutio and Leona Roberts's Nurse. "No such chorus of praise has arisen from critics over a Shakespearean production in recent memory," said one reporter.

At this time, Eva's personal life was tranquil and satisfying. She and Jo were devoted to one another, and they had not been separated for three years. And after years of playing in repertory, learning her craft by doing, Le Gallienne was at the height of her powers. She had finally loosened the reins on her emotions, and the critics sensed it and were moved. "Miss Le Gallienne seems to have passed through a stage of coldness and critical introspection, only to emerge once more into the full flame of vital and intense artistry governed by forces that have been molded within," wrote Richard Dana Skinner. "The finest and most elastic performance of her career," said Brooks Atkinson in the *Times.*

Stella Moss, one of the dancers in the play, recalled that Le Gallienne's "concentration was so great. But she also had an awareness of the audience. She came off after doing a simply gorgeous performance of Juliet, and as she passed me, she stretched out her hand and cupped it and said, 'That audience—I had them in the palm of my hand.' "

"Now everyone wants me to be the great Shakespearean actress!" Eva wrote her mother. "It's really funny—but I don't care for *most* of his women's parts— Rosalind and Lady Macbeth perhaps—but I wish I were a man so that I could play Hamlet—the greatest play of them all."

BY THE END OF MAY, what Le Gallienne really wanted was rest. Before she could retreat to the country, she auditioned six hundred applicants for the apprentice program, opened her stage manager Tupper Jones's summer theatre, played scenes from *Hamlet* on the radio, and, feeling like George Tesman in *Hedda Gabler,* accepted honorary degrees and gave speeches at Russell Sage College and Smith College.

Finally, she and Jo retired to the country in a "sort of coma." The caretakers, who had moved into a small three-room house which Le Gallienne had built up the lane from the old house, had tended the garden, which now bloomed with roses, irises, and peonies. For days, Le Gallienne did nothing but absorb the "colours & the fragrance & the *peace.*" In a small barn next to the new house,

Playing Juliet to Morgan Farley's Romeo, 1930. To act Juliet's long onstage death sleep with no telltale rise and fall of her chest, Eva learned "to breathe with my back."

they arranged a workshop for Jo's loom and Eva's set model and tools. It was difficult at first for Le Gallienne to settle down to any work, because Jo had to be away. "I am afraid my Lamb will have to go to Reno for a week about her divorce," she wrote Julie. "I'm dreading it terribly. But it will be so good to get it *really over with*. She is well & lovely & sends you much love."

During Jo's ten-day absence, Le Gallienne spent the time in town, where she could be near a phone. She also went to the dentist—"might as well be thoroughly miserable," she groaned. She couldn't bear to think of Jo's making the trip alone. "You know we haven't been separated in three years," she wrote Julie. "Perhaps it's silly to feel that way, but I don't think so—on the contrary I think it's remarkable & lovely in this day when people think of nothing but how to get rid of each other!"

Jo had a good relationship with her husband, Robert Bell, and over the past few months they had worked out an amicable arrangement. To spare Jo a three-month stay in Reno, Bell, accompanied by his mother, established residency there. Their divorce was granted on the grounds of "extreme cruelty"—a necessary fiction concocted to gain the divorce. Jo would remain friendly with Bell and with Bell's second wife for many years. While rumors would persist that their divorce had been granted in a secret closed-door session because Eva Le Gallienne had been named as corespondent, actually, the divorce was granted in open court, and Le Gallienne was not named.

The press attention was considerably less than for the 1928 separation story, and with the theatre closed for the summer, reporters did not descend on the Civic as they had earlier. Le Gallienne sent the newspaper clippings to her mother. Most of the papers announced the divorce in a few matter-of-fact paragraphs. The *Daily News,* however, used a photograph of Le Gallienne and the headline "Bell Divorces Actress, Eva Le Gallienne's Shadow" (a reference to lesbianism that would have been clear to anyone who had seen or heard about *The Captive*). Without access to either Bell or Jo, the story merely repeated the quotes from the 1928 separation article. According to Robert Lewis, there was no particular furor stirred up by the divorce. "I don't remember anybody thinking anything about it."

In fact, because of her brave choice to live her life as she pleased, Le Gallienne enjoyed a freedom that some lesbians, living hypocritical, closeted lives in mock marriages, did not have. In her public life, Le Gallienne remained in a closet, but it was a closet with transparent walls. Later, she would disappoint her friend May Sarton that she did not define herself as a lesbian, as May had. There was no need for Le Gallienne to come out—she had been "out" all her life and had never disguised the fact that she lived with and loved women. While Le Gallienne fully accepted her sexuality, she was a theatre artist, and in the Dionysian world of theatre, all categories, divisions, groupings, and titles—including, she believed, those of sexual preference, gender, class, and race—were antithetical to art.

Born in 1899, Le Gallienne liked to say that she was a step ahead of the century, and her views, like her mother's before her, were ahead of her time. Lillian Faderman points out in her history of lesbian life in America that there were others like Le Gallienne, who "simply loved a particular female, or they preferred to make their life with another woman because it was a more viable arrangement if one were going to pursue a career, or they did not think about it at all—they lived as they pleased and saw themselves as uncategorizable individuals."

"If you hear any gossip," Eva told Julie, "you'll know it wasn't very serious. There wasn't much they could say because *she* divorced *him.*"

To celebrate the fact that Eva and Jo were together and committed to one another, Julie sent them a gift of "lovely silver" flatware. "Time flies too fast when one is *happy!*" Le Gallienne wrote. "It's all arranged the wrong way round!" She and Jo spent summer mornings riding their recently purchased horses through the woods and lanes of Weston. During the afternoon, while Jo wove on her loom in the barn, Eva read plays aloud to her. The Greek tragedies are "so magnificent, really more beautiful than *anything* for the theatre," Eva wrote, "but they require great acting! Sophocles' *Oedipus King of Thebes* is a miracle—but what men are there in our modern theatre to play it?"

Le Gallienne selected the plays for the coming season and worked out the productions on her model theatre. She planned to add seven plays to the repertory, including Schnitzler's long one-act play *The Green Cockatoo;* Jean Giraudoux's new play, *Siegfried;* a holiday production of *Alice in Wonderland* (using her own adaptation and featuring Jo as Alice and J. Edward Bromberg as the Duchess); Hjalmar Bergman's *The Nobel Prize;* Gordon Bottomley's *Gruach;* Ibsen's *Rosmersholm;* and Susan Glaspell's new play, *Alison's House.* The theatre would reopen with last season's hit, *Romeo and Juliet,* which had sold out at every performance.

At the end of August, after suffering an attack of tonsillitis, Le Gallienne entered the hospital to have her tonsils taken out—"the beastliest rottenest operation imaginable!" Her doctor admired her throat, telling her that she "had better control of it than anyone he had treated, even opera singers."

In September, Eva wrote her mother from her dressing room: "Just imagine, on the opening Day—which fortunately was *Romeo & Juliet* (there must be some star watching over me) Jo had an acute attack of appendicitis & had to be hawled off to the hospital at once. She was operated on at 6 p.m. & poor Mommy [Leona Roberts] & I had to leave the hospital to come down here just as they were bringing her out of the operating room. . . . Altogether this has been a year of 'getting rid' of things—appendixes, tonsils and husbands!"

By November, many of Le Gallienne's ambitious plans for the season had to be changed drastically. "Bad days—tiring *wearing days*," she wrote. The effects of the stock-market crash and the worsening depression were beginning to be felt in the theatre. On Broadway, except for musical comedies, shows were closing rapidly. "The number of people looking for jobs is simply *appalling*," she said. "The whole situation seems to me drastic & serious to a degree!" Because of Jo's weakened health and Aline Bernstein's "vague state," she decided to postpone the expensive new production of *Alice in Wonderland. The Nobel Prize, Gruach,* and *Rosmersholm* were also cancelled. She released Jacob Ben-Ami from his contract after his twenty-week guarantee. "He really isn't any good to me—though he's such a darling—I hated to have to tell him. He was sweet about it. I just couldn't face playing *Rosmersholm* with him (he would bore me so!) so I've given that up—and he is really not playing enough to warrant paying him that salary." What she needed, as the critics kept reminding her, was a young leading man who would be a match for her own talents. But where was such a person to be found?

To make matters worse, in November, just two months into the season, J. Edward Bromberg told her that he wanted to leave, since he had a "flattering offer" from uptown. Le Gallienne was too proud to beg him to stay and too considerate to hold him to his contract. She hired young, handsome Morgan Farley to play Romeo, put Donald Cameron in as Mercutio, and covered all of Bromberg's other character parts. "It was a damn nuisance," she said angrily, "however, I've never expected any loyalty from Bromberg. . . . I picked him out of *nothing* & built him up—& God knows nobody else in the theatre would have let him play Mercutio—but that's the way it goes." Bromberg's uptown offer was a supporting role in *The Inspector General* at the Hudson Theatre, which closed after seven performances. After working continuously at the Civic, he was out of theatre work for almost a year, finally joining the fledgling Group Theatre in September 1931.

The response to the Civic's American premiere of Giraudoux's *Siegfried,* the first time the French writer's work had been seen in America, was disappointing. The reviews were respectful, but the public found the play "talky and dull." The modern French theatre, "with its growing tendency towards difficult and sometimes obscure psychological subjects," was too abstract and "extremely hard to translate" for Americans. "Also, the Civic lacked a really strong leading man, especially in plays like *Siegfried* which needed a glamorous man and woman," said Jo Hutchinson. Schnitzler's *Green Cockatoo* also did poorly at the box office. Glaspell's *Alison's House,* a Chekovian drama set on New Year's Eve of 1899 and loosely based on the life of Emily Dickinson, with its highbrow theme of the sheer human cost of creating great art, appealed to only a limited audience. The Civic desperately needed a popular hit.

Le Gallienne decided to produce *Camille:* although, she said, "it is very strenuous for me as an actress—it is easier for me to carry a play myself than to show others how to carry it." She wanted to "play it with all the range" she had. "I've learned a lot through playing Juliet," she wrote. "I think it needs a big stroke— and I'm going to use music (*Traviata*) whenever I can—& really give it every help the theatre can think up. It *must have glamour!*"

As an artist, Le Gallienne detested the star system, but as a shrewd manager, she knew that the public would pay to see her in a great, bravura part, a part that Bernhardt and Duse and Ethel Barrymore had all played. When Le Gallienne "looked at you with those crystalline blue eyes," said Norman Lloyd, "she was imperious. She fashioned herself, considered herself, in the great line. She would never have considered herself a Bernhardt or a Duse, but she was in the line. She fashioned her life that way, and she aspired to that."

During the rehearsals of *Camille,* Eva suffered from bronchitis but continued to play, acting one performance of *Peter Pan* with a 103-degree temperature. She completed the audience fly and collapsed—a stagehand caught her limp body as she fell. The cast stood around in terrified silence until finally her eyes opened. "Put me down," she said. "They'll want to come backstage to see Peter—and they must see him!"

Le Gallienne had "astonishing vitality," May Sarton recalled, "but it is no wonder that she seemed to grow slighter and her eyes more enormous as the years of this strain went on."

Finally, in January 1931, Le Gallienne succumbed to bronchitis. Her old teacher Constance Collier took over rehearsals of *Camille.* Le Gallienne worked on her part while lying in bed, attending only three final dress rehearsals. The most difficult scene of the play for Le Gallienne was the scene in "which Marguerite is left alone to write the letter dismissing Armand in cruel terms. . . . [It] must be played with an emotion that dominates the silence and makes it eloquent." The death scene, which she played as a "happy death," was not difficult for her. It is "written with such a sense of simple human values," she said, "that if you open your heart to them, let their truth carry you, you cannot go far wrong; that is to say if your technique is equal to your emotion." At her death Marguerite is filled with joy at Armand's return, and Le Gallienne believed that "it is this very joy that kills her by its suddenness."

At the opening, she was still weak and having difficulty breathing, and a doctor gave her treatments in the wings between scenes. In black-and-white gowns designed by Helene Pons, a dark, curled, upswept wig, and dangling jeweled earrings, she had "a majestic radiance and beauty." Le Gallienne held nothing back and was rewarded at the opening with ten curtain calls, cheering, and wild shouts of joy. "It was her own Lady of the Camellias," said one critic, "which did not try to mimic the traditions of Bernhardt, Duse. . . . It was Eva Le Gallienne

in the greatest performance of her career, and the audience at the Civic Repertory Theatre, which stood three deep in the rear of the orchestra, applauded
without stopping to remove tear stains from cheeks and nose."

"If you see a mob pressing impetuously about the pock-marked portals of the
Civic Repertory Theatre these Winter evenings," wrote Brooks Atkinson, "you
probably will find that the bill is *Camille*. . . . With Miss Le Gallienne expiring
into sweet and silken limbo at the end of act four, it is a major hit that turns 'em
away at the box office."

The production was the biggest hit the Civic had ever had, and gave Le Gallienne the courage to make a drastic decision. "I have decided not to work next
year," she wrote Julie. "I simply *must* have a year off and get a chance to *think* &
study & fill myself up again with fresh *ideas* for the future." She and Jo planned
to spend the summer in the country and then make a study tour of the subsidized theatres of Europe. The decision was "splendid psychology," she felt, since
Camille was such a success. "They can't say I'm taking a year off because I've had
a failure!"

To end the season, the Civic played a gala week of only their successes—*Peter
Pan, Romeo and Juliet, Camille,* and two performances of *The Cherry Orchard*
with Nazimova. The closing performance was *Camille.* It was "something never
to be forgotten," wrote Le Gallienne. "I have never in this country seen anything
like it . . . a *rain* of flowers from all over the house—of applause & shouts—of
immense fatigue and of *hundreds* of people." From all over the theatre, people
cried out, "Come back! Be sure to come back. Don't go away!" At one a.m. her
fans still crowded around the stage door and refused to leave. Throwing a dressing gown over her Camille nightgown, Eva went down to talk to them and say
goodbye. "It seemed to prove," she wrote, "that even in *this* country the *glamour*
of the theatre is not dead."

In May, Glaspell's *Alison's House* won the Pulitzer Prize. Le Gallienne felt that
it would be cowardly to do nothing about it, so she accepted the Shuberts' offer
to produce the play on Broadway. To give the play a boost, after the Civic closed,
she and Jo played a week on Broadway before their replacements stepped in. "It
has really been *awful* playing on Broadway—the whole vibration is so foreign . . . strange and uncomfortable beyond belief," she said. The production
and later tour of *Alison's House* gave employment to many of her company; plus
she gave a fifty-dollar-a-week retaining fee to members of the company that she
wanted to keep when the Civic reopened in 1932.

In five years at the Civic Repertory, Le Gallienne had created a repertory theatre and an artistic home. She had produced thirty-two plays, played in most of
them, and directed all but two. In the repertory of drama from around the
world, the Civic had presented the classics of Shakespeare, Molière, Goldoni,
and Ibsen, and introduced American audiences to the work of Chekhov and

Marguerite Gautier in Camille, *1931*

The Civic Repertory was noted for its subtle and evocative lighting, such as this "cross" lighting effect on Marguerite's bed curtains.

Marguerite's death scene. Jo Hutchinson (Nichette), Alma Kruger (standing, Nanine), and Morgan Farley (Armand)

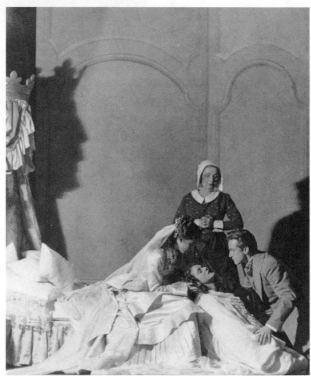

modern European dramatists like Giraudoux, Wied, and Bernard. She had made it possible for Susan Glaspell's plays to be seen and honored. The apprentice program had uncovered the talents of Burgess Meredith, Robert Lewis, Howard da Silva, Arnold Moss, J. Edward Bromberg, and May Sarton.

At the Civic, Le Gallienne's acting had been nurtured and developed along with that of Alla Nazimova, Josephine Hutchinson, Leona Roberts, Jacob Ben-Ami, Paul Leyssac, and Egon Brecher. Through the sheer force of her artistry and hard work, she won audiences and the critics and demonstrated a range and versatility beyond the reach of any of her contemporaries. She was thirty-two years old and at the peak of her powers. She had no rivals. Katharine Cornell, who was six years older, and Helen Hayes, who was one year younger, would reach their peak simultaneously four years later, in 1935, when Cornell played Saint Joan and Hayes acted Queen Victoria. Later, the press would invent an absurd contest, asking who should wear the title "First Lady of the American Theatre." When it came to a vote, Ethel Barrymore won.

Le Gallienne had no desire to be a lady. She was an artist and a pioneer. She had proven that a subsidized, nonprofit repertory theatre playing at low prices could flourish off-Broadway and attract a diverse audience, one that had increased in attendance from a low of 46 percent to 91 percent in five years. She had set a new course for the American theatre.

AT THE END OF MAY, Le Gallienne and Jo retreated to their house in Weston. Eva had replaced the caretaker couple with two congenial Frenchwomen, Sidonie and Marinette, who moved into the small, new house, and she engaged an Italian named Tony Gerace to come in daily and take care of the garden. There had been rumors that she was deserting the theatre for Hollywood, but the final gala week convinced the skeptics. The press were lavish in their praise of the Civic and accepted her promise to reopen in the fall of 1932.

Le Gallienne had already planned part of the 1932–33 season's schedule. She had convinced the Theatre Guild to give her the rights to *Liliom,* and she and Jo would have a year to work on the production of *Alice in Wonderland.* Also, publishers had expressed interest in her autobiography, which she thought she might call *From 1 to 31.* She looked forward with smug satisfaction to a year of rest and study made possible by her efficient, orderly management of her theatre and her life.

Since she was still recovering from bronchitis, for several days Le Gallienne did nothing but sleep, eat, and read. On Friday, June 12, she felt well enough to work in the garden. Even though the day was quite warm, since she was working in the prickly rosebeds she wore a long-sleeved flannel shirt and workman's overalls. Marinette called from the new house that she wanted to give the dogs a bath, but she couldn't get the propane hot-water heater to light. Le Gallienne replied that she would be up to help when she was finished with her work.

Since Weston was a rural area, there were no gas lines, and Le Gallienne, like many people who owned summer cottages or yachts, depended on bottled propane, which was inexpensive and easily transported but volatile and odorless. Jo followed Le Gallienne to the cellar door but stayed at the top of the stairs while Eva went down the steep cellar steps to light the heater. On her way down the steps, she struck a match to the wall. There was a "deafening explosion," and "the whole cellar became a mass of liquid fire." Instinctively, when she saw the blinding flash, Eva covered her face with her hands. She rushed up the steps and into the kitchen. Her hair was on fire, and she put her head under the sink faucet in the kitchen. Realizing that her shirt and overalls were ablaze, she ran outside, "tearing her clothes off as she ran," said Jo, and then she rolled over and over to put out the flames.

"I remember the shrill cries of the two Frenchwomen," Le Gallienne wrote later. "They sounded like agitated birds." Despite burns to her face, arms, and hands, Jo had the presence of mind to call the fire department. Neighbors who had heard the explosion also phoned for help. Jo found a sheet to cover Eva, and the gardener drove them to the hospital. The attendants at Norwalk Hospital were horrified when they saw Le Gallienne. She was semiconscious and in shock. Her body was covered with soot, her hair was singed from her scalp, her face was black and blistered, her arms and legs were a mass of inflamed blisters, and her hands hung in "long bloody strips."

"I regained consciousness for a few moments in the emergency ward," Le Gallienne recalled. "I could see nothing. . . . I felt an excruciating agony in my hands . . . the pain was so great that I felt as though my hands had been separated from the rest of my body. . . . I mercifully blacked out."

The hospital wanted to treat Le Gallienne immediately, "as if she were an ordinary person," recalled Jo. "I told them they couldn't touch her face. I called Mimsey, who called in her own doctor and a plastic surgeon. When anything went wrong, we always called Mimsey."

The next day, before Mimsey Benson and the Civic's press representative, Carolyn Darling, could shape the reports, newspaper headlines in cities around the country and around the world, in London, Glasgow, Paris, Copenhagen, and Berlin, announced that Le Gallienne might not survive, and that if she did live she would be scarred and disfigured. Mimsey sent a cable to Julie Le Gallienne with the news, but before it could reach her, a neighbor brought a newspaper with the headline "Famous Actress Burned in Explosion; May Live" next to a photograph of Eva in *The Swan.* Julie stared at the cruel headline and collapsed in shock. She was admitted to London's Royal Waterloo Hospital.

Little was known about the treatment for burns at that time. "Three things saved my life," Le Gallienne wrote later, "the heavy clothes I wore, the fact that I lit the match while still some way from the heater, and the fact that, temperamentally, I am not a screamer. Had I opened my mouth and drawn a breath to scream, my lungs would have been fatally injured." Also, her quick action in putting out the flames on her hair and her clothes contributed to her survival. With third-degree burns on her hands and wrists; second-degree burns on her face, arms, and legs; suffering from shock and dehydration and medical care that was virtually worthless as treatment, she was lucky to be alive.

Le Gallienne would come to believe that the explosion had cut her life in two. In one moment, her life changed irrevocably and her Olympian logic and efficient management were no match for life's nightmare illogic and grisly randomness. As she lay in the hospital, she felt as if she were starting over again; as though she were standing "on the threshold of a *new* life."

PART FOUR

1931 - 1942

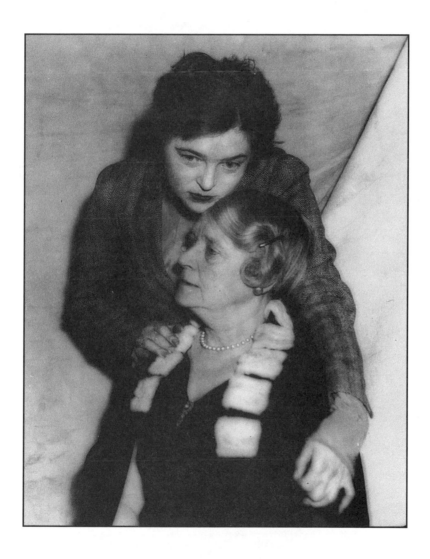

Eva and her mother during Julie's 1932–33 visit to New York.
Note Eva's left hand, which was scarred from the fire.
She disguised the missing tip on the little finger of her right
hand with makeup and nail polish.

Actors should be free, rebellious spirits. . . .
This insensitive and rapacious curiosity which has nothing
to do with the true love of the theatre has done much
to making creatures who should be artists mere peacocks
without brains and without souls.

L E GALLIENNE REGAINED consciousness and discovered that she was as helpless as an infant. Her first horrified thought was that she was blind. Because of her puffy, shapeless mouth, she couldn't move her lips to speak. Mimsey Benson, who had rushed to the hospital, sensed her panic. "It's all right, darling," she said. "You're not blind. It's just that your face is so swollen that your eyes can't open."

Six state highway patrolmen had put out the fire in the cellar, and her house was safe. Mimsey assured her that she had cabled Julie Le Gallienne, and Mary Bok called to tell Eva "not to worry about the financial end of things." Jo lay in a nearby hospital room suffering from less severe burns on her face, arms, and hands.

Le Gallienne hovered between life and death for more than a week. Her pain was excruciating, since painkillers of any kind were considered dangerous. Nurse Green, a heavyset Canadian woman who had served in the World War, helped her through sleepless nights by telling her of "all the agonies she had seen the men endure," and her own suffering, Eva wrote later, seemed "trivial by comparison."

Still, "it has all been painful beyond words," she told her mother in a letter that she dictated to Mimsey three weeks after the accident. Her face, she said, was "looking more and more like a baby's behind as the new skin comes through the blisters." Jo's superficial burns on her face, she reported, had somewhat the effect of a chemical peel; her new skin was "so clear . . . like a child's." Eva spared Julie knowledge of the full extent of her injuries. Lying in her hospital bed, her hands swathed in bandages, her body blistered, her swollen face pocked with thick brown scabs, Eva looked in a mirror and the only features that seemed in the least familiar were her blue eyes. She thought she resembled "a very ugly Chinese Buddha." When the bandages were unwrapped, she saw that her hands with long, tapering fingers were now "two masses of tumefied flesh, utterly shapeless, and with no trace of fingers or bone-structure of any kind."

Reconstructive surgery would not be possible for months. Initial treatment consisted of saline soaks; then the doctor slowly picked away the dead, burned flesh, "whittling down to the healthy cells that would build my hands again." Le Gallienne had always been vain about her good looks and proud of her well-tuned, responsive body—the instrument of her acting art—and to have that instrument mutilated and scarred was a devastating experience, both physically and emotionally. The accident also affected her public image. Overnight, she had changed from the beautiful, heroic Eva Le Gallienne at the height of her career to a pathetic, grotesque victim.

Six weeks later, at the end of July, to counter the headlines and sensational rumors that she would never work again, Eva held a press conference at the hospital. The second-degree burns on her face, arms, and legs had begun to heal, and she covered her singed hair with a hat and protected her hands in shapeless cotton gloves. She answered questions about her upcoming trip to Europe, but spoke primarily about the dangers of gas explosions. A distinguishing odor should be added to tank gas, she said—an appeal which was carried in newspapers around the country. Supported by other rural gas users, Le Gallienne continued her crusade in the following years, and by 1934 the petroleum gas industry complied.

As Eva healed, Julie Le Gallienne recuperated too. "Thinking of you every minute, Darling," Eva cabled her mother. "Know the Viking Blood will pull you through as it has me."

On September 3, 1931, Eva, Jo Hutchinson, and Eva's dog, Tosca, sailed for Europe. Reporters and photographers saw them off, and Eva posed for the cameras from a safe distance. She did not hide the fact that she was traveling to Europe with Josephine Hutchinson, whom the newspapers called her girlfriend, nor did she conceal her face in layers of makeup, although her skin was still somewhat mottled and pulled slightly around her nose and on her forehead; but she did wear large soft cotton gloves on her disfigured hands.

Mary Bok funded the trip and Alice De Lamar loaned them her Paris apartment. Europe soothed Le Gallienne. "The smells, the taste of the food, the light on ancient walls and buildings, the faces of the people, their clothes, and the way they wear them"—everything was familiar and comforting to her. After a few days' rest in Paris, Eva and Jo visited Julie and Hesper in London, but stayed in London less than a week. The rainy English weather caused Eva's hands to ache miserably. After returning to Paris to pick up Tosca and her car, Eva and Jo drove to Spain. Le Gallienne had planned to visit theatres in Moscow, Copenhagen, and Germany, but her doctors advised a warmer climate. In Madrid Eva saw her first and last bullfight. Afterward she was violently sick. "Fortunately," she said, "Spain has many other glories besides the *corrida*." The Velázquez paintings in the Oval Gallery at the Prado overwhelmed her. "They seem to walk right out of the walls." Later, she advised young actors to study the way people in "great paintings stand or sit, or walk or turn their heads, or use their hands or wear their clothes, the balance and line of each part of the body expressing so accurately, so unerringly, the slightest thought and emotion."

In October she and Jo spent two weeks in a borrowed villa on Mallorca. They worked on *Alice in Wonderland,* read Shakespeare and Dickens aloud, bought cheap furniture for the theatre, sent glassware back for their house, and took long walks. But the island didn't appeal to Le Gallienne. The dry climate, the rocky landscape, the howling wind, the swarms of flies, the shrill voices of the servants, even the stone floors of the villa all irritated her. What irritated her the most was the slow process of her recovery and the unrelenting pain. Healing would take time and "yes, my God *PATIENCE!*" she exclaimed.

Eva's mood improved considerably when they returned to France. She and Jo drove through Provence; they visited Les Baux, drank Châteauneuf-du-Pape in Avignon; then they motored in November rains through Auvergne and on into Paris. Eva was with her love—her "Aimée," she named Jo—and the trip through Auvergne was a memory she would cherish all her life. It had a "strange fairy-tale quality about it all. . . . Gold-wet fragrant. Wood-smoke rising. Damp mists. A muted radiance—gold gleaming through gauze."

IN PARIS Eva felt as if she were reliving her childhood. At nine o'clock every morning she walked to her old gymnasium on the rue de Vaugirard. The pain was excruciating, but she exercised her clumsy fingers by sparring with the fencing instructor, who taught her some tricky attacks to spring on Santelli. "Before the fire, Eva did not have beautiful hands," Jo said. "She had always admired Duse's hands, and she had worked very hard to have graceful hands onstage. She had to learn how to use her hands all over again. This was so disheartening for her." Jo fenced, too, and studied piano twice a week at the Collège Sévigné with one of Eva's former classmates. For a few weeks, Eva went every day to the Cirque d'Hiver, where the great clowns the Fratellini brothers were appearing. To ingratiate herself with the Fratellinis, Le Gallienne pretended that she had worked in circuses in Scandinavia, Germany, and Russia, and since she spoke "a smattering of all these languages" her act was convincing. The Fratellinis befriended her, invited her into their Merlin's cave of a dressing room, and shared their clowning secrets with her. For a time, she filled in as a rider in an English hunt scene, learning more from the "honest art" of the Fratellinis, she said, than from the theatre in Paris. With the Fratellinis, she was not Eva Le Gallienne; she was just an anonymous thirty-two-year-old woman who was "indulging a mad whim" to run away and join the circus.

By a strange twist of fate, Richard Le Gallienne resided at 60, rue de Vaugirard, where Eva and Julie had lived when Eva was four. Eva invited her father to lunch with her and Jo, and he came with his third wife, Irma. Eva didn't care for Irma, and it was "tiresome never to see him without her." Eva arranged to meet her father after the lunch privately at his garret studio on the rue Servandoni. "She was always very curious about her father, and she was excited about seeing him," recalled Jo. When she arrived at his studio, Richard, then sixty-six, had been drinking. She felt as if she "were in the presence of a stranger; his eyes were wild, almost evil." He made crude sexual overtures toward her. Eva left his studio. "She was terribly upset when she came back to the apartment, but she wouldn't give me any specific details about what had happened," said Jo. Although Richard would live sixteen more years, and while he would always fascinate her, she never saw him again. She believed that her father was a "strange man in many ways" and beset with demons.

Julie Le Gallienne joined Eva and Jo in Paris at Christmas for an old-fashioned Danish celebration and a round of theatregoing, mostly to the popular hits. Her mother "was quite a bandwagon girl," Eva wrote later, "and there was something very young and engaging in her attitude. She had a marvelous capacity for having a good time."

May Sarton, then nineteen, was also in Paris that winter, living in a sublet studio apartment on the place Jules-Ferry. "I wandered about, ardent and hungry," May wrote later, "picking up whatever was accidentally brought to my attention. . . . It was Paris by osmosis." May's closest friend in Paris was Irene Sharaff. After the Civic Repertory closed, Irene had decided to spend a year of study in Paris. She lived cheaply in an attic room in the Hôtel Foyot. Sharaff was overwhelmed by the Paris theatre and enchanted with the high fashion world of Paris, particularly the work of Chanel and Schiaparelli.

Knowing that May and Irene were often broke, Le Gallienne would take them to lunch, and at Christmas she invited them to a party she and Jo gave at their apartment. "She was recovering from such agony," remembered May. "But she was tremendously brave." Le Gallienne and Jo went out dancing a few times with May and Irene, and May glimpsed a mirthful side of Le Gallienne that she had not seen at the Civic Repertory. "She played for a very good reason," Sarton said, "because she had to get well."

One night as they sat at a cafe, Le Gallienne offered May a job as director of the Civic Repertory apprentices at a salary of thirty-five dollars a week. The amount seemed like a fortune to May, and she burst into tears. For Christmas,

Irene Sharaff, early 1930s. She had a long and distinguished career in theatre,
ballet, and film, and won five Oscars, for movies as diverse as An American in Paris
and Who's Afraid of Virginia Woolf?

Eva gave May a pen made of amber and silver engraved with her initials; earlier, she had shown some of May's poems to her father, who had written May an encouraging letter. Eva's gift of the pen and Richard's "professional response" to her poems were a sign to May that her secret hope of becoming a writer might come true.

During lunch one day, Le Gallienne surprised Sharaff by asking her to design the Civic's production of *Alice in Wonderland*. "I did not quite believe what I heard and put it down to the flow of wine at lunch," Irene recalled. Eva sent the script to her the next day. Sharaff spent the rest of her time in Paris working on her designs. Le Gallienne had worked out the production plan, and Sharaff's job would be to create the sets and costumes in imitation of John Tenniel, who had drawn the illustrations for the book.

While she was in Europe, Le Gallienne also scouted talent for the Civic. She needed a versatile leading man for her company. John Gielgud turned down her offer, saying that he didn't want to play in an off-Broadway repertory company. "So I suppose like all the rest he'll end up in Hollywood," she grumbled.

IN EARLY FEBRUARY 1932, after five months in Europe, Le Gallienne and Jo sailed for home on the *Ile de France*. Reporters waited on the dock for her arrival. Eva looked chic in a black tailored suit and silk magenta blouse. One reporter noted that while her hands were badly scarred, her face, though pale, was unblemished. Actually, the mottled lines and faint scars from the burns on her face would never fade completely. Whenever they interviewed her, reporters scrutinized her face and hands, and Le Gallienne stoically braced herself for the onslaught of flashbulbs, which always reminded her of the flash of the explosion.

Before Eva could return to work, though, she had to undergo skin grafts and reconstructive surgery on her hands, particularly to straighten the little fingers. The operations were not completely successful; much of the weblike scar tissue remained, and the little finger on her right hand had a missing tip and would always be crooked. For months she wore splints on her fingers every night, and for years her hands would ache like a persistent toothache, the pain growing more severe in rainy or muggy weather. Although she developed an intricate stage makeup which hid the scarring, and she used her hands gracefully onstage, offstage her gnarled, thick hands with blunt fingers were incongruous with her cameo features and slim, elegant figure. According to Jo Hutchinson, she rarely complained. "She was a doer, not a moaner."

During the spring, Le Gallienne auditioned over four hundred applicants for the apprentice company and selected thirty. She bought a new play called *Dear Jane,* which had a strong feminist theme about the creative power of women, hired her twenty-eight-member acting company, and engaged Joseph Schildkraut to play the Queen of Hearts in *Alice in Wonderland,* recreate his old role in *Liliom,* and appear opposite her in *Camille.*

Le Gallienne saw many of her old friends who were in New York that spring, including Constance Collier, Elsie Janis, Noël Coward, and Alla Nazimova, "who suddenly has become my bosom friend again." Alla was appearing in O'Neill's *Mourning Becomes Electra* on Broadway, and Le Gallienne agreed with the critics that Nazimova was marvelous. But the play infuriated her. "Just a good old melodrama posing as great Art," she said. "Why one should sit from 5:30 to 11 p.m. to see such old stuff . . . I can't quite see."

Part of her irritation with O'Neill's play might have arisen because the Civic Repertory was rarely offered a new American play. Le Gallienne longed to find a play that expressed the feeling of American jazz. "We take what we want," she wrote, "and jazz expresses that ruthless pace [at] which we live." Playwrights offered their work first to Broadway producers who would run the play eight times a week. At the Civic, a play might have only two or three performances a week and the writer would earn much less. When she did have a chance to do a new

American play, there was the problem of casting. She had to turn down Elmer Rice's *Street Scene* because her company lacked the necessary ethnic types.

IN MAY 1932, with the business of the Civic taken care of, Le Gallienne and Jo retreated to Weston. Their two cows, chickens, and garden kept them supplied with milk, cream, butter, eggs, broilers, and fresh vegetables. They had also begun breeding Cairn terriers and made a small income selling the pedigreed puppies.

Le Gallienne's plans for a restful summer were upset when Mary Bok notified her that she would not be able to come up with her regular twenty-thousand-dollar subsidy for the Civic Repertory. Faced with increased taxes, her dividends cut in half due to the Great Depression, plus the added expense of Le Gallienne's medical bills and year's sabbatical, Mary Bok did not have the cash. Mimsey Benson had gone to Europe for the summer and was not available to help raise additional money.

To make up the deficit, Le Gallienne decided to write her autobiography, hoping to sell the syndication rights for twenty thousand dollars. In addition to writing the adaptation of *Alice,* she worked on the book every day. Her right hand cramped badly and her stiff little finger throbbed with pain, but by the middle of August she had written sixty-two thousand words and, except for the last chapter, which she would add later, the first draft of the autobiography was finished. Le Gallienne called the book *At 33* and dedicated it to her mother. Magazines like *Collier's* turned it down because it wasn't sensational enough (she barely mentioned her famous father or the fire, and she believed that her love affairs were nobody's business); but the national magazine *Pictorial Review* published excerpts, and Longmans released the book in January 1934.

REHEARSALS FOR THE 1932–33 Civic Repertory season began in the middle of August. Le Gallienne dreaded the thought of returning to work again. She felt as if "it had all gone from me—a nasty feeling." Jo reminded her that she always felt that way after a long holiday. In addition to her directing and acting responsibilities, Le Gallienne also took on some of Mary Benson's administrative duties. Mimsey had stayed an extra two weeks in Europe taking a rest cure at Baden-Baden. For more than six years, Mimsey had talked and begged, wined and dined, even pawned her jewels and mortgaged her farm to help the Civic. She had personally raised over a half-million dollars, but the effort had wrecked her health.

After playing a benefit performance of *Camille* for the Norwalk Hospital, the Civic Repertory toured out of town for a few weeks with *Liliom* and *Camille* before opening in New York. Le Gallienne enjoyed playing with Schildkraut again. The handsome, devilish Pepi was behaving like an angel, she said, and it was "good to have a real man" to play Armand in *Camille*. During the day, the company rehearsed *Dear Jane* and *Alice in Wonderland*. "I had forgotten how hard I used to work!" Eva groaned. She hated touring and playing in strange theatres, but the company needed the extra money and the time to work together, and she needed to get used to her new hands. She painted and shadowed them with makeup before every performance, a half-hour procedure, and she labored for hours to work out an intricate, seemingly spontaneous hand choreography for each role she played.

"I am bearing up," she wrote Julie, "but at times feel in a sort of daze." Le Gallienne could disguise the faint scars on her face and her disfigured hands with makeup, but regaining the confident poise of a woman who believed that she was beautiful was another matter, particularly when she played Camille or Juliet. She had always looked young, but the strain of the work and her efforts to rebuild her body had etched fine lines around her eyes and mouth. Sensing that her daughter needed her, Julie secured a writing assignment from *Politiken* to report on conditions in America and booked passage for New York. She wanted to be close to her baby, she said, and she stayed close to Eva for months, not returning to Europe until April 1933.

Liliom opened the sixth season of the Civic Repertory on October 26—the same date on which the Civic had been launched six years earlier. The sold-out house resounded with thunderous ovations, cheers, and bravos. Norman Lloyd, who was an apprentice at the Civic, said later that "no one ever equaled" Schildkraut and Le Gallienne in *Liliom*.

Liliom and *Camille* were hits. *Dear Jane,* by Eleanor Hinkley, which opened on November 14, was not. Jo played the title role of Jane Austen, and Le Gallienne appeared in the supporting part of Cassandra, Jane's sister. Jo had looked forward to her first "grown-up part!" She had been worried "that a whole side of me has never been exercised." At the end of the play, Jane Austen tells her fiancé the story of *Pride and Prejudice*. She asks him what he thinks. He wasn't listening, he replies; he was admiring her lips. He doesn't know me, Jane realizes. Hand in hand with her sister, Jane leaves his house through a secret door.

Dear Jane's celebration of female creativity and independence appealed to Le Gallienne, but it was not a popular view. As the depression worsened and more and more men lost their jobs, independent women threatened male status and power. At a time when America's economic and political structures were shaken to the core, a backlash against women, against homosexuals, against any challenge to the precarious position of men as leaders of family, business, and country, picked up momentum. In the *New York Telegram* on November 30, 1932, Whitney Bolton asked if anyone else had noticed the "disturbing fact that the theater is rapidly becoming feminized." It's not just Eva Le Gallienne who's dominating the theatre, he asserted, but "playwrights . . . are giving all the character and strength to the women's roles and transforming the men's roles into pallid shadows." It was a strange twist on the word "shadow," which the 1926 production of *The Captive* had introduced as a code word for "lesbian": now, Bolton said, it was men who were turning into shadows—in other words, they were becoming weak, like women.

Despite the depression, the low prices at the Civic insured that business continued to be good and the Civic paid no taxes. It was the only theatre in New York that enjoyed the same tax-exempt status as the Metropolitan Opera. Except for Monday nights and Wednesday matinees, the performances were usually sold out. Running costs and weekly expenses were covered by box-office receipts, but the new productions had to be subsidized. Not wanting to raise prices, Le Gallienne looked for other ways to increase income. She calculated that if she cut the poorly attended Monday-night and Wednesday-matinee performances and added two Sunday performances, they could make an additional thousand dollars a week, but Actors' Equity turned down her request. A few years later, in a move she bitterly resented, Broadway's commercial managers asked for Sunday performances and Actors' Equity complied.

"The apprentices knew nothing of the struggles and decisions she was having to make to try to save her theatre," actor Paul Ballantyne recalled. "Although she once told us that it was humiliating to need support so badly that she was required to sometimes drop rehearsals to see a very wealthy person who would offer five thousand dollars if she would do something about giving an offspring or a near relative a chance."

T HE CIVIC'S BIGGEST SUCCESS, *Alice in Wonderland,* was also, at the same time, responsible for the closing of the Civic. With co-author Florida Friebus, Le Gallienne had adapted *Alice in Wonderland* and *Through the Looking Glass* for the stage. *Alice,* which premiered on December 12, 1932, made Jo Hutchinson a star, earned Le Gallienne directing, acting, and adapting accolades, put thousands of little girls into Alice pinafores and Alice curls, and inspired critics into hyperboles of praise. Le Gallienne played the White Queen in whiteface, like a Fratellini clown, and her lines had an eerie reality. The rule is, the White Queen says, "jam tomorrow and jam yesterday but never jam *today.*" She tells Alice, "Why, sometimes, I've believed as many as six impossible things before breakfast."

In his review of *Alice,* John Mason Brown wrote that "the impossible has once again been done" by the Civic Repertory. Using only Carroll's words, with many of his verses set to original music by Richard Addinsell, and a set design using wagons on tracks and a rolling spool of scenery that kept the action swirling continuously around Alice, Le Gallienne achieved her aim of bringing the pages of the book to vibrant life—"through synchronization of music, color and form . . . to recapture . . . Alice's dream-adventures." With more than fifty cast members, as well as super-marionettes and puppets and spectacular music and dance numbers, the production had the scale of a large musical. Since all the action and characters were part of Alice's dream, Alice never left the stage. It wasn't the grown-up part that Jo wanted, but critics agreed that Alice was the best performance of Hutchinson's career.

The huge expenditures of energy and money (it cost twenty-three thousand dollars) to produce *Alice,* plus the enormous cost of running the show (paying for a full orchestra and extra stagehands), exhausted the resources of the Civic. As the depression worsened, Otto Kahn, along with Mary Bok and other wealthy Civic benefactors, watched their fortunes dwindle. The Civic needed at least seventy-five thousand dollars a year in subsidies to finance new productions. Le Gallienne had counted on subsidy to pay for the new productions of *Liliom* and *Dear Jane* and to underwrite *Alice.* When it became clear that the subsidy was not forthcoming, she could not afford to operate the Civic in rotating repertory at low prices. Le Gallienne, who hated "compromise almost more than defeat," was forced to compromise her noncommercial ideals, and on January 30, 1933, she moved *Alice* to the elegant New Amsterdam Theatre on Broadway, where it played at commercial prices. In an attempt to hold on to part of her repertory, Le Gallienne alternated performances of *Alice* with *The Cherry Orchard* starring Nazimova. Broadway welcomed *Alice,* but one successful production could not save the Civic—in fact, commercial success was a contradiction of all the Civic stood for. At a time when Broadway was bounding back after a five-year slump, Le Gallienne was now paying the price for her decision to devote herself to the noncommercial theatre. To make matters worse, she had to endure another operation on her hands and showed up in her White Queen costume wearing bandages and splints.

Alice ran until mid-May 1933, and offers poured in for Le Gallienne and Jo and for other cast members as well, particularly the men, who used their Broadway exposure in *Alice* to launch their careers, and in Schildkraut's case to revive a moribund one. Burgess Meredith, Tonio Selwart, John Garfield, Howard da Silva, Staats Cotsworth, Robert Ross, Richard Waring, Norman Lloyd, and Paul Ballantyne all were trained at the Civic, and all went on to long, successful careers in the theatre and film. Burgess Meredith received two Broadway offers at the same time. "I was on my way," he said. Norman Lloyd wrote that "standards were set at the Civic Repertory, and while one's taste and judgement change over the years, the Civic was, for me, a foundation."

The movie offers, the theatre projects, and the producing proposals were all flattering, but Le Gallienne wanted her Civic Repertory Theatre. She was a

LEFT:

Jo Hutchinson as Alice in Alice in Wonderland, *1932*

BELOW:

Jo with Eva as the White Queen

"Renaissance woman," Robert Lewis observed. "She had complete control of her life; people don't do that now." Le Gallienne understood that the only place she could have control, the only place where she could exercise her many talents, was in a theatre like the Civic Repertory.

In her writings, Le Gallienne never questioned her decision to undertake such an expensive venture as *Alice* at the height of the depression. To bring audiences into the Civic she needed to mount exciting new productions, not just preserve the repertory, but it seems not to have occurred to her to try riding out the bad times by scaling back her ambitions. There was no one in her organization to dispute her decisions—Le Gallienne was the sole authority at the Civic Repertory. Mary Benson's job was to raise money to realize Le Gallienne's dreams, not to second-guess them.

When *Alice in Wonderland* closed in May 1933, Le Gallienne was singularly depressed. Sets, costumes, and properties for all the productions remained in storage at the Civic. Many of the 115 people who had worked at the theatre were now unemployed. The closing of the Civic Repertory generated an outpouring of sympathy for Le Gallienne. "It's immensely sad," said one writer. "I see her as one of the healthiest influences in the American theater. . . . She is the leader in a movement which must . . . in time affect the whole theater in this country."

Le Gallienne sublet the Civic to the Theatre Union, a left-wing group devoted to activist drama, but she was not ready yet to break up the acting company or give up hope that the Civic could be revived. Capitalizing on the enormous national publicity generated by *Alice,* she decided to take out a tour of *Alice* and *Romeo and Juliet* in the fall to "preserve the idea and ideals for which we have worked long and hard."

In the final chapter of *At 33*—a manifesto, really, for the preservation of the living theatre and a plea for the survival of the Civic—Eva declared that movies do not threaten the theatre. "Canned vegetables can never entirely take the place of those picked fresh from the garden. No matter how good the record of a voice, it cannot supplant the living voice itself." The danger to the theatre, Le Gallienne believed, "is from within." The legitimate theatre "can and will of necessity regain its lost importance, but it must revert into the hands of those workers who know it and love it. It must no longer be controlled by real estate and high finance." Others may "achieve the thing of which I have dreamed. That doesn't matter as long as the dream materializes. If the New York Civic Repertory Theatre proves to be the pioneer that has prepared the way for such a condition, I shall feel that its work has not been in vain."

TO SAY IT DIDN'T MATTER was one thing, but living the reality was another. Without the Civic Repertory, she became just another actor scrambling for a job. In her published pronouncements about the theatre, Le Gallienne struck a tone of passionate engagement balanced with high-minded detachment. It was a tone, however, that she could not maintain in private. Like a general who had been relieved of command, she was angry, tense, and apt to lash out unexpectedly. Jo was out of sorts too, and "quite worn out with all the *Alice* performances."

In Broadway playbills, actors announced with pride that they had been members of the Civic Repertory. Had this been her mission, Le Gallienne wondered—to train actors for Broadway, a place that produced, Ethel Barrymore said, "only bilgewater and scum"? Barrymore was one of America's finest theatre artists, but there was little need in the American theatre for an actress in her early fifties. It was an appalling waste. Le Gallienne knew that without a theatre home of her own like the Civic Repertory, Barrymore's fate would be her own.

Two decades younger than Ethel Barrymore, Eva was still wanted on Broadway, but she was stubborn and not ready to admit defeat. Scripts and offers poured in; the Theatre Guild wanted her to rejoin their organization; and the Guild's Lawrence Langner invited her to work immediately at his Westport Playhouse. Langner was an old friend, but a "consummate ass," she thought, and she vowed that she would never work for him. She hated "little summer theatres," she said. "The work is always half-baked and sloppy." When the Rockefellers asked her to submit a proposal for the new Radio City Music Hall, she worked out a half-hearted plan, but she found the grandeur and perfection of the physical plant depressing and felt that she "couldn't possibly run our sort of theatre there."

Roses bloomed in profusion around her house in Weston, the vegetable garden overflowed with produce, the farm was alive with animals, and she and Jo took long walks and rode horseback. But without a Civic Repertory Theatre, her life lacked purpose and direction. To make money, she did five radio broadcasts. Since she didn't have a secretary, and holding a pen for any length of time was torture, the fan mail she received was a nuisance. The weather also got on her nerves: there were violent summer storms with torrential rains; then it was too hot or too dry or too humid. But whatever the weather, her hands ached miserably, and every time she looked in the mirror she saw the damage caused by the burning. The press reminded her, too. "She has intense gray-green eyes that she fastens on you as she talks," wrote a Boston reporter. "Through them you see to the beauty that must have been hers before her tragic accident. It is typical of her that she makes not the slightest attempt to hide or excuse her scars."

Her tour of *Alice* and *Romeo and Juliet* under her own management promised eight months of work, and United Booking had given them excellent terms, but the twelve thousand miles and forty-seven cities looked formidable. Most of the Civic actors and crew signed on for the tour, but Mary Benson refused to go, which angered Le Gallienne. When Julie Le Gallienne pointed out that she owed Mimsey a great deal, Eva snapped, "You needn't remind me that Mimsey loves me dearly, nor do I think it necessary to tell you how deeply I love her, this situation involves nothing personal." Of course, the situation was personal.

Perhaps in an unconscious attempt to relive the security of an adoring Mam and Nanny that she had experienced as a child, Le Gallienne had recreated the threesome again with Jo and the loyal Mimsey. Mimsey, always the understudy in Le Gallienne's life, however, had found other companions through her friendship with Alice De Lamar, and she had developed an interest in art. Without Mimsey to advise and take care of her, Le Gallienne felt abandoned. Although she had two competent women on the staff of her company in press agent Mary Ward and stage manager Thelma Chandler, she made all the business and artistic decisions herself. In contrast, Kit Cornell, who was taking out a tour of three plays in the fall of 1933, was supported by her husband and a few trusted associates who together formed the "theatrical phenomenon known as Katharine Cornell."

"Eva had enormous confidence which comes across as arrogance," recalled Jo Hutchinson. "She had bodily strength and courage and the arrogance. She believed in her own possibilities." Julie Le Gallienne was the only person in Eva's life who dared criticize her judgment. Like a benevolent queen who has ruled long and well, Le Gallienne received respect and deference from her company. After six years of living with her, Jo deferred to her as well. "She never treated me quite as an equal, I knew that," said Hutchinson. Even though *Alice in Wonderland* had made Jo a star, she was still playing a child, and Le Gallienne was both her companion and her employer. On the tour she received equal billing with Le Gallienne and the same five-hundred-dollars-a-week salary, but she longed to play a grown-up part both on the stage and in her personal life.

Le Gallienne traveled with an enormous amount of luggage, including her heavy makeup mirror complete with lights in a blue wooden case, pots and pans, dishes, a teapot, boxes of books, special pictures, her Danish goose-down comforter, pillows, and bones, toys, coats, and bowls for her dogs. "We stayed in wonderful hotels like the Ritz in Boston," recalled Jo. "But we always cooked bacon and eggs in the bathroom." Before they left on tour, Jo ran around "gathering luggage, packing. My mother said, 'You know, Jo, you're not her maid, you shouldn't do that.' " Jo "wanted to do it," she said, but years later she laughed as she recalled one moment of comic revenge. "We carried a large wooden salad bowl around, that we had rubbed with garlic. I couldn't find anyplace to put it, so I just shoved it in with Eva's fresh underwear. She was furious."

IN BOSTON, one of the first cities on their route, business was excellent and the reviews were glowing for both *Alice* and *Romeo and Juliet.* The company set-

tled into the rhythms of touring, which was made more pleasant by Le Gallienne's gardener, who sent flowers, fresh vegetables, and eggs to them every
week. And with the end of Prohibition in December, the company took advantage of the ready availability of liquor.

In Washington, D.C., Eleanor Roosevelt accepted Le Gallienne's invitation to
attend a performance of *Alice in Wonderland*. Afterward, the First Lady invited
her to tea to discuss plans for a national theatre. Le Gallienne was elated. Once
again, like Carroll's Mock Turtle, she was "traveling with a porpoise." In an upstairs sitting room at the White House, Le Gallienne explained her idea, modeled after the Civic, of using relief funds to create a national network of
repertory theatres and free schools for apprentices. Mrs. Roosevelt introduced
her to Frances Perkins, the secretary of labor, and the two women encouraged
Eva to put the plan on paper and present it to the President.

Le Gallienne wouldn't talk about the national theatre plan to a *Washington
Post* reporter. "Here I am getting on to middle age—I'm 34—and I'm still jumpy
up and down inside!" A child should "grow up in beauty," she told the reporter.
"Let me tell you this—the majority is always wrong. Insensitive taste surrounds
us . . . but remember that a minority starts and then it gains power. And it starts
from within, in the spirit."

The company moved on to Pittsburgh. Le Gallienne sent an outline of her
plan to President Roosevelt, and soon after, she received an invitation to lunch
at the White House. She "was extremely nervous; so much seemed to be at
stake." At lunch, she sat between the President and his advisor Harry Hopkins.
After making small talk about meeting her father years earlier, Roosevelt told her
that he approved of her plan, but he felt that it wasn't "comprehensive enough."
He spoke at length of providing jobs for unemployed theatre people through the
WPA. She listened "with pleasure to his beautiful voice," but she could not agree
with his proposal, which was the opposite of her own. His humanitarian project
was a "fine and noble design," she told him, but to give theatre workers jobs "regardless of their talents" would "encourage mediocrity at best." In the subsidized
theatres of Europe, she said, "it is a hard-won honor to be a member of . . . the
Comédie-Française, the Moscow Art Theatre, the Vienna Burgtheater—even
the Kongelige Teater in little Denmark." To develop a "theatre-mindedness in
the American public comparable to that in European countries, it was manda-
tory," Le Gallienne believed, "to bring them only the highest possible standard
of performance."

Later, she wrote that her point of view must have seemed "hard and ruthless
in contrast to President Roosevelt's desire to alleviate hardship and misery." Despite their differences, Roosevelt listened to her and asked her to consider heading the national theatre division of the WPA. She answered that since she
disagreed with his basic idea, she would not be able to do a good job.

After the lunch, she shared a taxi with Harry Hopkins. "Dear Miss Le Gallienne," he said, "you should learn to play politics."

"That's one thing I never *have* learned to do," she said, "and I'm not sure that I want to."

"If you would just learn to play politics," Hopkins continued, "you could get millions out of the old man."

It was good advice, but Le Gallienne couldn't compromise her principles. She refused the WPA job, but she asked Hopkins for a subsidy for the Civic Repertory. The government already had recognized the educational and cultural value of the Civic by exempting it from taxes. Le Gallienne made her case to Hopkins succinctly and with unassailable logic. The Civic, "after all, was a running concern that had cost many hundreds of thousands of dollars to establish; an institution that had been hailed on all sides as a valuable contribution to the culture of the times; an organization that employed close to a hundred people, and that had built up and kept alive a repertory of some forty complete productions; a living theatre that during the six years of its existence had created for itself a large and enthusiastic audience. Also of value was the free school. . . . It seemed such a tragic waste to allow all this to founder." The alternative, she thought, was illogical, wasteful, even wicked—to close the theatre, junk the sets and costumes, put everyone out of work, then start all over again in a WPA-sponsored theatre that would have to be built up from nothing.

Hopkins listened sympathetically, and a week later he invited Le Gallienne back to Washington, D.C., for further talks. They decided that she should ask for an annual subsidy of $100,000 and that she should make her request at a dinner conference at the Mayflower Hotel. The conference was actually a party, Le Gallienne discovered. She had never been comfortable in crowds, and "at first I got the impression that some of the people present thought me aloof and a bit stand-offish. They all seemed to know each other well, and I felt rather like the lone outsider at a family gathering." She answered "question after question, some eminently intelligent, others showing complete ignorance." By the end of the dinner, Hopkins agreed that the Civic Repertory should receive a subsidy of ninety thousand dollars a year. He and his "Brain Trust" told her to "return to work with a light heart" and to renew her theatre lease. Hopkins escorted her to her hotel and promised to call the next day with official confirmation of the subsidy. Le Gallienne returned to her company in Chicago and waited and waited, but she "never received another word from Mr. Hopkins."

Two years later, Harry Hopkins chose his old friend Hallie Flanagan to head the Federal Theatre Project. Flanagan, who had directed the Vassar Experimental Theatre, was a westerner, an academic, and not part of the New York theatre establishment. She also was a dynamic leader, adept at compromise. In the four years of its existence, the Federal Theatre Project created jobs for thousands of theatre people and provided a stepping stone for such theatre artists as Orson Welles and John Houseman; but its most important contribution was decentralization of the theatre by introducing audiences across America to live theatre. When Congress abolished the project in 1939, Flanagan believed that the root cause of the project's many problems was its "double identity as a relief organization and artistic enterprise."

Her failure to win the promised government subsidy was a "crushing disappointment" for Le Gallienne. Even though the Civic was a unique institution in the American theatre, Harry Hopkins must have realized that to provide funding for one theatre, however logical, while ignoring others who might feel equally worthy, would be political folly.

AT THE SAME TIME that Le Gallienne was negotiating with Hopkins and seeking to draw press attention to her national theatre plan, the press wasn't interested. All they wanted to write about was an incident that occurred in Philadelphia on December 1, 1933. For six months, newspapers around the country carried the story, celebrities took sides, the press found new angles, until the actual facts disappeared.

On Friday morning, December 1, Le Gallienne spoke about her plans for a national theatre to three hundred members of a Philadelphia women's club. Ethel Barrymore, who was in Philadelphia visiting her son, went along with Eva to the lecture. Le Gallienne had been booked to speak a week earlier, but there had been a scheduling mix-up. When she learned that the club had publicly criticized her failure to make the earlier commitment, Eva began with a stinging reprimand. "If you knew the discipline in the theater," she said, "how we work to please you. . . . Do you think this sort of training would let us fail to keep appointments? . . . I have been in the theater for more than twenty years. I have never broken a professional engagement in that time."

At the end of her talk, Eva announced that she had a big surprise for the audience and introduced Ethel Barrymore, who was sitting on the front row. The audience applauded, but Ethel didn't take a bow. She stood and faced them. "Miss Le Gallienne does you great honor to be here," she said in a trembling voice. "I do you honor to be here. I don't see why we both bother to speak to you at all. You have no appreciation. You don't know anything. You never have known anything. You never will know anything. We've worked. We've sacrificed. We've tried to please you. Pfht! What difference does it make? I found this child. She has done more for the American theater than any one. She is gallant . . . and you dare to criticize her for not coming to some meeting she did not know anything about?"

Le Gallienne was "completely justified" in her remarks, said the chair of the women's club; but Barrymore's criticisms, she said, were "the greatest insult a Philadelphia audience ever had."

Barrymore's outburst may have been brought on by her bitterness at not working, or it might have been a simple wish to capture the spotlight once again; but her defense of Le Gallienne rang with heartfelt emotion. Barrymore's diatribe, though, diverted attention from Le Gallienne's national theatre mission, and, according to Jo Hutchinson, their ticket sales plummeted in Philadelphia. The resulting national press attention, which Harry Hopkins must certainly have seen, described silly women hurling insults at one another, usually with side-by-side pictures of Barrymore and Le Gallienne. By May 1934, Barrymore's name and photograph had disappeared entirely from the story, but Le Gallienne's remained—*Variety* called it "pulling an Eva Le Gallienne" when a performer berated an audience.

In Pittsburgh a few days after the Philadelphia incident, Le Gallienne spoke again about her plan for a national theatre to hundreds of people, and again she earned headlines. "How do I turn this thing off?" she asked about the microphone. "I can't bear it." When a camera flashed from the balcony, she reproached the photographer. "Young man, you don't know what that means to me. I nearly lost my two hands in an explosion that looked just like that. It really makes me quite sick."

When she wanted to charm, though, Eva could still play Sven-Gallienne. A Milwaukee reporter described her: "You may have difficulty trying to visualize a masculinely feminine suit, but that's what the actress-director was wearing. Wavy, rather short cropped red hair was thrown back from a fascinating face. Hands were thrust in the pockets of a hip length purple velvet coat. Sitting out front, you felt you were listening to and watching a gorgeous Rembrandt come to life. Miss Le Gallienne had her audience with her every minute of her talk. In fact, she held it in the palm of her hand."

Le Gallienne's purple jacket was copied from a bicycling coat her father had worn in 1900; suspended on a lilac ribbon from a breast pocket was a gold watch fob just like Richard's. According to Jo Hutchinson, on the tour she and Le Gallienne had begun drinking more and more, which probably accounts for Eva's bad temper. "You're just like your father," Julie used to say when Eva misbehaved. Now, she seemed possessed by her father's demons.

Sick at heart at losing the promised Civic subsidy, Le Gallienne became ill in December and January, suffering from a bad cold that turned into bronchitis. In late January 1934, the expense of touring two huge productions had become too much. She closed both *Alice* and *Romeo,* sent fifty cast members and musicians back to New York, and felt sorry yet "relieved at getting rid of that appalling responsibility."

A smaller company continued on the midwestern and western leg of the tour with an Ibsen repertory of *Hedda Gabler, The Master Builder,* and *A Doll's House.* Eva Le Gallienne raging at an audience became the leitmotif of the tour. At a benefit auction in Minneapolis, still wearing the sleek brown wig and pallid makeup of Hedda Gabler, she upbraided audience members who had refused to bid twenty dollars for a cake in honor of President Roosevelt's birthday. She called them a "poor lot of Americans. I thought you were Vikings, but there's not much Viking in you. I'll buy the cake myself for $20," she said and stomped off-stage. In Oakland, after playing *Hedda Gabler* on a stage adjoining a gymnasium, she strode to the front of the stage, announced that basketball and Ibsen didn't mix, wickedly brandished Hedda's pistols, and with deadpan humor quipped, "I'd like to take a shot myself!"

Eva dreaded performances of *A Doll's House.* She had revised the Archer translation, cast Jo as Nora, Howard da Silva as Torvald, and reluctantly played Mrs. Linde herself. "I feel so utterly bad in it," Le Gallienne confessed to her diary. "It makes me more nervous than any of my other parts!" She also was worried and irritated by Jo's nervousness. She had never seen Jo so frightened by a part. Jo, already anxious about playing Nora, was made even more frantic by Le Gallienne's performance as Mrs. Linde. "Eva was not very good if she wasn't the lead," Jo said. "She didn't work very hard."

The publication of *At 33* in late January didn't cheer her up. Eva was thirty-five, and the autobiography seemed irrelevant now. Like the White Queen, she couldn't remember how to be glad. The reviews were excellent, though, and boosted the book onto the best-seller list and into ten printings, but the money was too late to help the Civic. "The American theatre has never been the same since Miss Le Gallienne struck it," said *The New York Times Book Review.* William Rose Benet in the *Saturday Review of Literature* composed a valentine of a review to "Immortal Eva who will I think eventually receive immortality in the history of the American theatre. . . . Compared with her general cultivation and intelligence she makes most managers and directors look like schoolboys."

A young man who had once been devoted to her wrote a scathing attack on *At 33* in *New Theatre,* a leftist magazine in New York. In his "open letter" Paul Romaine said he wanted to tell Le Gallienne the truth, since she was the leader of thousands of theatre idealists. Romaine had embraced the Communist Party, and what had Le Gallienne done? She had become, he said, a "decadent prop of a collapsing theatre."

A few days after Romaine's review appeared, newspaper headlines announced "Listed as Red" next to a photograph of Le Gallienne. An Illinois woman who used the logic of Humpty Dumpty in making words mean what she chose them to mean had published *The Red Network* and named Le Gallienne and 1,299 other prominent Americans, including Eleanor Roosevelt, Edna St. Vincent Millay, and Fiorello La Guardia, as Radicals and Communists.

ON FEBRUARY 15, 1934, while Jo stayed for photographs after a performance of *A Doll's House* in San Francisco, Le Gallienne had dinner with Marion Gunnar Evensen, who played Aunt Julia in *Hedda Gabler.* "A nice creature she seems—very Scandinavian," Eva wrote in her diary. Evensen was a tall, lean actress of Norwegian extraction, with the blond hair, blue eyes, clear skin, and high cheekbones of a Viking. Eight years older than Eva, Marion was a good actress with a low-pitched, musical voice. She was direct, plain-spoken, and self-confident. Born in 1891 to Norwegian emigrants, Marion was raised and schooled in Milwaukee, Wisconsin. Although she was married to George Westlake of Cleveland, they lived apart. She had considerable experience as a character actress touring with Robert Mantell's Shakespearean repertory troupe and with Jane Cowl, and she had joined the Civic Repertory during its last season.

Jo Hutchinson had been seeing other people in the company as well. Howard da Silva and Staats Cotsworth were both particularly attentive to her, and she was fond of them. According to Jo, during a drinking session with one of the actors on the tour, Eva confided that she was growing tired of Jo and didn't love her anymore. Jo learned what Le Gallienne had said. "The news came as a terrible shock," said Jo. "I had thought my life with Eva was forever. I didn't say anything to Eva. I got frightened and started trying to make a life for myself. I cried and cried, but I got through it."

When the company played Los Angeles in early March, Jo called agent Leland Hayward and arranged for a screen test. According to Jo, Le Gallienne was not pleased. "Her attitude was always to put me down if I wanted to do anything not involved with her or the theatre." For her screen test, Jo played the last scene of *A Doll's House*—Nora's declaration of independence.

"Went to Warner Brothers to see Jo's test. Had a hellish trip out ¾ of an hour in a taxi with da Silva," Le Gallienne complained in her diary. "Fool that he is he wouldn't keep quiet but gabbled incessantly a lot of nonsense and I behaved badly. I felt sorry for poor Jo sitting between us. . . . Jo's test was splendid." Warner's signed Hutchinson to a two-picture-a-year contract at a salary of $1,250 a week. Jo planned to make the movies during the summer months, then return to New York during the fall and winter to work with Le Gallienne in the theatre.

Le Gallienne had always insisted, like Katharine Cornell, that she would never make movies. The medium did not suit her. Only in live theatre could she do what she enjoyed most—"bending an audience to my will." She had talks with various producers and agents in Hollywood, primarily about directing and producing, but no one offered anything that interested her or allowed her the control that she demanded. Because of her disfigured hands and the faint scars on her face, acting in movies was not a possibility, even if she had wanted to.

At the Los Angeles opening of *Hedda Gabler,* Le Gallienne saw many old friends, including Egon Brecher, Margaret Mower, and Joseph Schildkraut. Mercedes de Acosta showed up backstage, "behaving as if we had seen each other, or at least corresponded with each other daily!" said Le Gallienne. "She talked a great deal about 'Greta' this & 'Greta' that—As to Garbo herself, she has been ill." Le Gallienne had heard that Garbo wanted to see the Ibsen plays, and longed to meet her, but "of course the Mercedes situation (if it is true!) makes it difficult—and there seems to be no way of finding out whether it is or not. I certainly wouldn't take M's word for it."

The tour moved on to the southwest, and Le Gallienne's cryptic 1934 diary ends on March 21. "Arrived in El Paso around 1:30. . . . The theatre a movie house of course—I hate them so! Hard to speak and so cold and unsympathetic." The company traveled through Texas by train. Jo and Eva shared a large drawing room with adjacent bedroom. On the trip to Dallas, Eva, Jo, Howard da Silva, and Marion had stayed up late drinking. "The berths were all made up, the shades were pulled," Jo remembered. Sometime during the night, said Jo, "Eva excused herself and left me with da Silva. She went into the next room and crawled into the berth with Marion. Instead of saying to da Silva, 'Look, just beat it,' I was so upset that I got off the train. I went to this little house and told the man there that I needed to drive to Dallas and asked if I could rent a car. He drove me to Dallas. I got a hotel room. The next morning I bought some clothes, and that night I went to the theatre because we had to play. When I saw Eva, she did not ask how I was or what I had done. 'Hello' was all she said. She and Marion were sharing a hotel room. It was over."

Later, Jo analyzed why Eva had left her for Marion. "Marion was very strong," she said. "If Eva ran into a woman stronger than she, she would go to pieces. There were certain times that she needed to be dominated. At a low point, her more feminine side would come out. And she had to be alluring. She worked on that always."

Le Gallienne's betrayal of Jo was an act that she would relive and condemn for the rest of her life. After seven years with Jo, was she, like Hedda Gabler, just bored? Did she want to punish Jo for her film contract? Did she sense Jo's interest in the men in the company? Or with her beauty scarred by the burning, was she testing her powers of attraction?

Clearly, there were deep psychic wounds from the fire—for the first time she had faced her own mortality, and she struggled with bitterness and self-pity. And at this time when Le Gallienne felt vulnerable, anxious, and beset with problems, Marion Evensen offered strength as well as new erotic excitement.

Josephine Hutchinson belonged to the past, a constant reminder of the death of the Civic and the explosion. The older, more experienced Marion satisfied Le Gallienne's need for a calm, strong center, and presented an opportunity to embark on a new stage of her life with an exciting, devoted lover. It was hardly a coincidence that the breakup of Eva and Jo came at a time when they were acting Ibsen's two most compelling women, Nora and Hedda—one reaching toward independent womanhood, the other thwarted by frustration and bitterness.

One of Le Gallienne's firm rules at the Civic, a law taught to every apprentice, was to leave one's personal life at the stage door. But with the breakup of the relationship between Eva and Jo, the company split into two camps, one faction loyal to Eva, the other siding with Jo. By the time the company reached Omaha, the morale and the level of performance had deteriorated to such an extent that the Omaha Drama League called *Hedda Gabler* "sloppy and inartistic." After the tour closed in Buffalo on May 1, Le Gallienne returned to Weston with Marion, and Jo went to New York to the Civic apartment to pack up her things. Eva came in "just as I was leaving," Jo remembered. "She didn't even go downstairs with me to the taxi." Jo took the train back to California. "I'd always been rather dependent," Jo said later. "I said to myself, Face it—have some courage and do what you have to do." Jo found the atmosphere at Warner Bros. "warm and affectionate," and the studio "became home." The first movie she made was called *Happiness Ahead.*

"I know I've been a *PIG!!!!!!*" Le Gallienne wrote Julie on May 10, 1934, from Weston after a silence of a month and a half. Eva blamed her silence on exhaustion after the tour. In a long, confusing letter, she explained that Jo had returned to Weston with her and then, perhaps feeling guilty about lying, a few pages later contradicted herself and said that Jo was in Hollywood making movies. "I think it may be good for her to get a change of atmosphere—and even for a little while to get rid of her troll. I miss her terribly." At the end of May, she told Julie about Miss Evensen, "a very nice Norwegian woman" who had been staying with her.

During the summer of 1934, Le Gallienne felt "strangely lost" and suffered constant pain. She had a third operation on the little finger of her right hand and once again wore bandages and splints. Unable to work in the garden, fence, or write, which were her usual outlets, she was forced into idleness. There were no productions to plan, no Civic Repertory to run, and, most of all, no Jo. Ashamed of her troll-like behavior, Le Gallienne hoped that Jo would forgive her, but Jo refused her telephone calls and any attempt at communication. "For once," Le Gallienne wrote later, "I couldn't have what I wanted."

TWO ROLES REMAINED for Le Gallienne to play on the list she had drawn up at sixteen: Hamlet and the Duke of Reichstadt, "the Eaglet," in Rostand's

L'Aiglon. She turned first to her French roots and the play that Rostand wrote for Sarah Bernhardt, which had premiered to great acclaim in Paris in 1900. The choice of *L'Aiglon* was a telling one. For her return to show business, Le Gallienne chose a script that was really an excuse for a bravura performance—a thoroughly artificial exercise in old-fashioned romantic melodrama.

Backed by producers Selywn and Franklin, Le Gallienne began preparations for a fall Broadway opening. She convinced Ethel Barrymore to play the small but important role of Empress Marie-Louise, L'Aiglon's mother. Ethel required constant attention, especially to ensure that she was not drinking. "What she needs above all things," Le Gallienne believed, "is Faith and Loyalty." "Trofast og glad," Julie had taught her, emphasizing the connection between loyalty and happiness, and Le Gallienne was faithful to her Civic Repertory company. Aline Bernstein designed the *L'Aiglon* costumes and sets, Richard Addinsell composed the original score, Thelma Chandler served as stage manager, and Le Gallienne cast many of the Civic Repertory company, including Jo's mother, Leona Roberts, and Roberts's husband, Walter Beck. Marion Gunnar Evensen played L'Aiglon's cousin and double, the Countess Camerata. "Gunnar is fine and has been very good & helpful," Le Gallienne told Julie. "She is really a nice fine creature." Le Gallienne missed Jo terribly, but with cool practicality she made the best of it, seemingly agreeing with Ibsen's John Gabriel Borkman that "if the worst comes to the worst—one woman can always take the place of another."

Only theatre people know, Le Gallienne wrote, "the agony of despair one lives through in those hateful last days before an opening night. One glares at one's best friends with passionate hatred or cold fury." She battled with *L'Aiglon*'s imperious translator, Clemence Dane, and had words with her old friend Richard Addinsell. "I am getting so frightened I feel as if I simply couldn't live through all this. Why does one do it? I'm sure I shall be *awful* in it." At the Civic she had a mission and a goal, but now she felt strange and uncomfortable playing for purely personal reasons in the commercial theatre. She wired three hundred dollars to Julie Le Gallienne and asked her to come to New York for the opening.

She had known *L'Aiglon* for years in Rostand's original alexandrines, and Dane's English translation was somewhat drab and matter-of-fact. John Mason Brown quipped that Clemence Dane had turned the original soaring verse into jingles comparable to "Father's feeling awfully blue. He's lost the battle of Waterloo."

Le Gallienne convincingly resembled Napoleon's teenage son. She built up her thigh-high boots four inches inside and cut her hair over her ears in a boyish tousle; in the Eaglet's white Austrian uniform she looked like a dashing young soldier.

Before going to Broadway, *L'Aiglon* opened at the Forrest Theatre in Philadelphia. Eva was nervous. How would she and Barrymore be received? Had the women's clubs forgotten the "incident"? Eva shared billing with Barrymore, but she gave her mentor the star dressing room at the Forrest. It was like old times with Barrymore. "The warmth of her encouragement, the acuteness of her criticism, and the magic of her very presence inspired me and gave me strength," said Le Gallienne. Philadelphia audiences cheered and were "moved to unabashed tears," one reported noted, "when Eva Le Gallienne took over the mantle of Sarah Bernhardt."

New York audiences cheered, too, at the November opening, and the critics praised Le Gallienne's intelligent, flawless acting and her moving death scene. But why do such an old-fashioned play? they wondered. Lillian Hellman's *The Children's Hour,* which opened on Broadway shortly after *L'Aiglon,* demonstrated clearly the distance between modern American drama and Rostand's moth-eaten semiclassic. Actually, Le Gallienne's contract with Selywn and Franklin stipulated a "modified repertory," and with all her productions still intact at the Civic she hoped to introduce extra matinees. After a few performances of *The Cradle Song,* though, she found that modified repertory was impractical and expensive in the commercial theatre, and she abandoned the effort for a straight run of *L'Aiglon.*

In December, Le Gallienne was surprised when Jo Hutchinson appeared in her dressing room after a performance of *L'Aiglon.* It was the first time the women had seen each other since their breakup. "The minute I hit the dressing room, I heard Marion had left for New Jersey," said Jo. "Eva and I went back to the hotel where I was staying, and we talked all night. We talked about everything." Le Gallienne could not convince Jo to return to her, however. Eva reconciled with Marion, and a few weeks later, on January 12, 1935, the day after Le Gallienne's birthday, Jo Hutchinson married Hollywood agent James Townsend.

Marion clipped the wedding announcements and photographs of Jo and sent them to Julie Le Gallienne. Unlike Jo, who was intimidated by Julie, Marion had a remarkable rapport with Eva's mother. They shared a love for Eva as well as a Scandinavian heritage. Julie was impressed with Evensen's midwestern common sense, and she believed that the self-effacing Gunnar would be an excellent companion and helper for Eva—a stand-in for her own motherly care. Don't ever leave Eva, Julie commanded, and Marion promised that she would not.

"THE LONG RUN is a part of modern technocracy, like the assembly line," Le Gallienne believed. "It is stultifying and frustrating. None of the great actors of the past would ever put up with it." She put up with it for four months during the spring of 1935, playing *L'Aiglon* on a tour of Canada and various eastern cities plus a two-week run in Chicago. The built-up boots almost destroyed her feet, but the sheer boredom of playing a strenuous part in an inferior play exhausted her. Business on the road was good, though, markedly better than on last year's

Ethel Barrymore played stage mother to Eva for the third time in L'Aiglon, *1934.*

tour. "There is no doubt that if one keeps faith & keeps one's high standards," she observed, "that there is *great* demand."

The reviews were excellent. Chicago critic Ashton Stevens urged her to play Hamlet next, "not merely because other women have played this prince, but because there is a young actress who, in this very *L'Aiglon,* proves her princeliness as well as her ability to cancel her sex without either revolting or convulsing us. I'll wager a Hamlet by Eva Le Gallienne would be as virile as a Hamlet by Leslie Howard. Moreover I think this poet's daughter has the poet's mind for the part, the cerebral graces as well as the physical."

In Washington, D.C., Mrs. Roosevelt attended the opening, and Le Gallienne lunched with her at the White House, and again she pressed her dream of a national theatre and subsidy for the Civic. Nothing would come of it, she believed. It was as if she was living her life in repertory: she had played this scene before.

Finally, in late April, when she and Marion returned to Weston, Le Gallienne fell into a deep depression. She relaxed her iron discipline and drank liquor. She slept late and saw and wrote to no one. The depression was difficult to shake off, but eventually the pull of the garden and working in the soil revived her. Everywhere she looked, though, she was reminded of Jo. The black cat, Dinah, from *Alice;* the canary from *The Cradle Song;* the horses; the daffodils blooming in the meadow; the fragrance of *muguet* (lilies of the valley), Jo's favorite flowers; and every nook and cranny of the tiny, old house—all brought back poignant memories. When Tosca, her constant companion for thirteen years, was run over by a car later that summer, Le Gallienne was devastated. She dug a grave in the garden and ordered a marble marker. Jo wired her sympathies, saying sensibly that Tosca had enjoyed a long and happy life. Le Gallienne missed Aimée, she said, "beyond words in a strange 'lost' way, especially here in this little place that we made together with such a rare love—But life changes & goes on in strange ways & one has to accept and go on with it. Gunnar has been so good to me—I think she is happy—she seems well & loves it all here—and I try to hide from her any shadow that comes across my joy in it all. . . . She is a true fine person I think."

Forgetting or repressing how she had grown tired of Jo and become irritated by Jo's nervousness, Le Gallienne began to create an idealized picture of Jo in her mind that bore little relationship to the real woman. The absent Aimée of Le Gallienne's youth would always appear more attractive, more desirable to Eva than Marion, who cooked and cleaned, worked in the garden, and shared Le Gallienne's house and bed. Gunnar's natural reserve and pride, her maturity, and her devotion made her a comforting, if sometimes dour, companion. Le Gallienne hid any doubts that she had, and the dignified Marion masked her jealousy and fears and did her best to make Le Gallienne happy.

Le Gallienne's loyal friends gathered around her that summer. Mimsey, who had divorced Stuart Benson, lived nearby, and Mary Bok visited for several days and urged Eva to "keep on and not lose courage and give up." Mrs. Bok expressed her faith with ten thousand dollars in seed money to fund any future effort at a repertory theatre or any scheme that would free Le Gallienne to "be her own master." Alice De Lamar, who had purchased property in Weston, including the Cobb's Mill restaurant and guest house with her partner Jacques de Wolfe, also offered financial assistance as well as the use of her swimming pool and tennis court. Eva and Alla Nazimova had remained cordial, but not close friends, following Alla's departure from the Civic. "Eva and Alla were very much alike," said Jo Hutchinson. "They both wanted to control." Eva had not heard from Nazimova for some time, but Alla dropped by one early afternoon and stayed until early evening. "So I am in favor again apparently—I should so love to know what determines these violent changes of mood!" Le Gallienne wondered.

With her old friend and Civic company member Donald Cameron, Le Gallienne played a few weeks in vaudeville in New York and Washington, D.C. Performing to restless vaudeville audiences was like wrestling with lions, a long way from Ibsen and Chekhov, but the thirty-five hundred dollars a week she earned made it worth it. She returned home, where "dear Gunnar looked after me as if I had been a baby."

Eva and her lawyer/agent, Arthur Friend, had hoped that the vaudeville appearances would lead to a contract in radio, a repertory theatre of the air; but when nothing materialized, she planned a national repertory tour with the backing of Mary Bok, using Civic company members in revivals of *Camille, The Women Have Their Way, A Sunny Morning,* and a new production of Ibsen's *Rosmersholm.* Le Gallienne had long wanted to follow Duse and Mrs. Fiske and play Rebekka West in *Rosmersholm,* a woman "as cunning as Becky Sharp, as amorous as Emma Bovary, as ambitious as Lady Macbeth [and] more trouble-breeding than Hedda Gabler."

Le Gallienne translated *Rosmersholm* and found it fascinating. Wearing elegant costumes designed by Irene Sharaff, and a softly curling blond wig, her wide blue eyes heavily lined and shadowed, Le Gallienne looked glamorous and dangerously alluring in the role. The character of Rebekka West, calm and reserved on the outside but with an almost insane passion lurking beneath, commits psychological murder through the sheer force of her will. Le Gallienne imagined herself so completely into the character that when Rebekka learns in the third act that she has been her father's mistress, Le Gallienne's hands began to sweat. She wiped her dripping hands with a handkerchief as if to wipe off the terrible revelation.

Audiences in Boston preferred the difficult *Rosmersholm* to the more familiar *Camille,* and Le Gallienne decided to open in New York with *Rosmersholm* at the Shubert Theatre in early December 1935. Brooks Atkinson in *The New York*

Times praised Le Gallienne's acting, her excellent company, and her clear-minded direction, but he hated the play. Ibsen was dead and his society was dead, Atkinson announced. He thought it was odd that a woman as young and as alert as Eva Le Gallienne should love Ibsen. Actually, Le Gallienne was a victim of the Civic's success at reviving and popularizing Ibsen and other classics. Ibsen had been done, Atkinson felt, and other critics shared his view. Broadway audiences concurred, and in two weeks, Eva despaired, Le Gallienne Productions lost "every penny of our precious reserve fund."

Audiences on the road had been fascinated by the play, but Broadway audiences were different. During the 1930s, director George Abbott gave those audiences exactly what they craved—slick, fast-paced entertainments that became the signature style of Broadway. In the 1920s, Le Gallienne and the non-profit Civic Repertory had heralded the future, an alternative to the dominance of the commercial theatre, but now she seemed to be moving against the zeitgeist. Male-dominated companies like the Group Theatre emerged, proclaiming an activist theatre of social protest. The Group Theatre had high ideals and was developing a vigorous American style of realistic acting, but the Group members craved commercial success on Broadway and in the movies. With no one willing to pick up the baton, the drive that Le Gallienne had led toward a nonprofit alternative to Broadway lost ground during the 1930s.

Le Gallienne refused to compromise her ideals—if she was going to lose, it would be on her own terms. Le Gallienne's dedication to the classics and repertory, a theatrical art that had been passed down to her from a European past, was viewed as old-fashioned and out of date. It was time to give up. After ten years of trying, of cramming half a lifetime of work into one decade, she disbanded her company and relinquished any hope of reviving the Civic Repertory.

In a bitter letter to her mother, she analyzed her situation:

> The greatest harm the talkies have done the Theatre is that they have accustomed the public to neither listen or *think*. . . . The only thing that draws at the Box Office is our old friend *Camille*—everyone *knows* what *that* is about, which seems to be a great comfort to them—and if they are moved to the effort of tears, they are used to *that* in the pictures. . . . I can always make more money myself as a free-lance rather than with the organisation on my back. . . . I feel I have been loyal to all these dear people long enough—and after all the year I was supposed to have for "rest & study & pleasure" turned out very grimly! . . . When I get really away—I shall be able to *build*—and that after all is my only reason for living. I see no aim in my present work—no ultimate goal & that is always depressing to me.

In 1935,
Eva followed
her predecessors
Duse and
Mrs. Fiske
and acted
Rebekka West in
Rosmersholm.

AFTER *Rosmersholm* closed, as if to find out for herself what Broadway audiences liked, Le Gallienne and Marion went on a ten-day binge of theatregoing. Except for the Group Theatre's production of *Paradise Lost* by Clifford Odets, which she enjoyed, she found the Broadway theatre, including Katharine Cornell's Juliet, pretentious and false. Glittering externals, Le Gallienne felt, that's what sells on Broadway.

For ten years, from 1926 to 1936, Le Gallienne had defined herself by her work. Her dream of creating a national theatre for America had been "the sharp focusing point" of her life. Her home and her office had been at the Civic Repertory Theatre. From now on, she would have only one home, in Weston. The task of closing the Civic and moving out of her apartment there was painful. What upset her the most "was the dreadful waste of it all—to see all those productions, all the costumes, all the myriad accessories of a repertory theatre, practically— and in some cases quite literally—thrown away." A few years later, the Civic Repertory Theatre, the oldest theatre in New York, was demolished to make room for a parking lot. Le Gallienne's conservative, frugal nature was out of step with modern, throwaway American culture. She raged at the stupidity of it all, but as Nanny and Mam had taught her, anger could fuel creation. She was between acts in her life, and she knew that she must salvage what she could from the past and create a new setting for the future.

Eva moved out of the old house that held so many memories of Jo, but she kept it just the way she and Jo had left it. She and Marion moved a few hundred yards up the lane to the new house. With money she made from *At 33* and from radio (where she earned one thousand dollars for eight to ten minutes of work), she added a new wing and a large upstairs bedroom to the basic three-room box.

To hold all her favorite personal possessions, furniture, properties, and books salvaged from the Civic, Le Gallienne designed an open two-room study, roughly seven hundred square feet, which she painted Italian blue and called the "Blue Room." Because of a rock ledge, the northwest room in the irregular, L-shaped space was raised two steps. Morning sun poured in through a large bay window overlooking the rose garden; through a north window she could look out over fragrant lilies to the barn; and afternoon sun streamed in over the steep rock ledge through a French window. On the floor was the same brick linoleum that had covered her apartment at the Civic. Laughing at their daring, she and Marion had plundered the Civic apartment—ripped up the linoleum, packed the extensive theatre library, removed the bookshelves, unscrewed the lighting fixtures, and even walked off with a "nice, new enamelled toilet seat."

Eva placed her desk, a long Provençal table that had appeared in many Civic productions, near the bay window so that it caught the morning sun. On its polished, worn surface she arranged Juliet's dagger, L'Aiglon's riding crop, Masha's snuff box, and her new blue stationery. Behind her blue armchair, she hung an original Mucha poster of Bernhardt as Lorenzaccio. She furnished the room with Hedda's armchair, Camille's sofa, Jane Austen's spinet, a prie-dieu from *The Cradle Song,* a Victorian ottoman used in almost every Chekhov and Ibsen play, and a copper-and-brass Dutch milk pail from *The Good Hope,* which she filled every spring with apple blossoms or flowering dogwood.

She lined the walls with her books, thousands of books, including the two volumes of Bernhardt's memoirs that she had copied by hand. On a small table next to her blue armchair rested her mother's camel-backed pencil box. She stored her matches in a carved wooden box given to her by Isadora Duncan, and within easy reach were her Bible and the well-thumbed copy of *Prières de Saint-*

In the Blue Room of her house in Weston with two Civic Repertory cats— Sally, an adopted stray, and the black cat, Dinah, from Alice in Wonderland, *1936*

In the reading corner of the Blue Room, Eva placed an armchair in front of her Mucha poster of Bernhardt and arranged books on religion, philosophy, and mysticism on the nearby bookshelves, 1936.

Thomas d'Aquin that Duse had given her. Her grandfather Nørregaard's luggage strap, still aglow with the red and white petit-point flowers worked by Grandmother Bet, hung close by. Joan of Arc's sword and Peter Pan's sword dangled in mid-flourish from the wall. Blue-painted shelves displayed special treasures: an enameled goblet distributed at the coronation of the last czar of Russia, decorated with the double-headed eagle of Imperial Russia and stamped "N.I. 1896," given to her by Theodore Zarkevitch, the Civic's music director; a white porcelain Louis-Philippe Madonna with a faint pink blush on her cheeks that her mother had given her; and a pottery quail that had belonged to Clyde Fitch and was a gift from Mary Bok. A framed autograph of Edwin Booth, Duse's photograph and memorabilia, and a photograph of Richard Le Gallienne holding baby Eva blended with the books.

"So it seems to me sitting here at my desk in the Blue Room, each object that I look at speaks to me, bringing back a job of work, a person, an event, some half-forgotten happening sad or merry. Some tell me stories in which I took no part, going back to days long ago even before I was born. The room is never empty to me. I could never be lonely here. There are so many voices," Le Gallienne wrote later.

By June 1936 the renovation was complete, and the house was painted white, with bright blue shutters. Building their home together had created a powerful bond between Le Gallienne and Marion. Drawn together initially by sensuality, they were now united in shared labor and pride of possession. Eva took responsibility for the gardens and plants. Ferns, cyclamens, and primulas blossomed in the bay windows, mirroring the masses of roses, peonies, and lilies that bloomed in profusion outside. Marion took over the kitchen and became a fine chef. The two women shared household and barnyard chores, assisted by a weekly cleaning lady and a gardener. They both took up weaving and made rough bath towels, table runners, and sofa pillows. Cats and kittens, various Cairns and puppies, a nanny goat with twin kids, two Jersey cows, a pony, ducks, and chickens populated the farm and offered constant amusement. Marion and Eva loved showing off their new home to their friends, entertaining Mimsey, Aline Bernstein, Alice De Lamar, Alla Nazimova, Elsie Janis, May Sarton, Ethel Barrymore, Donald Cameron, and old friends from the Civic. When Laurette Taylor came to dinner one evening and saw the Blue Room for the first time, she noted that there was not one photograph of Eva Le Gallienne, the actress. "This isn't a bit like an actress's house!" Laurette exclaimed. "Every actress ought to have a house like this!" countered Eva.

LE GALLIENNE STILL CLUNG to her ultimate goal—her ambitious aim to create a national theatre—but she accepted her entr'acte period. She planned to

Eva (in back) holding her dog Chico, and Marion "Gunnar" Evensen with two Cairns, 1936

enjoy her home and drift for a while. Then Lawrence Langner enticed her with a proposal to work at the nearby Westport Playhouse. If she would appear in Congreve's *Love for Love,* he told her, he would produce *Hamlet* for her later that summer. He sweetened the offer with a part for Marion as well. The plan was irresistible. Hamlet was the only role that Le Gallienne wanted passionately to act—the last on her list of parts to play before she turned forty and the ultimate rite of passage for any actor who aspired to greatness. She set to work immediately. Marion helped her learn the lines by holding the script while they took long walks through the woods.

Congreve's *Love for Love* Eva considered "filth covered over with a veneer of charm, powder, patches and fans and laces," and her role of Angelica required little depth, only that she be funny and beautiful. She was both. Audiences enjoyed the puffball of a play, and the *Variety* critic liked the fact that Le Gallienne had "shed the shrouds of her Civic repertoire."

Successful at luring Le Gallienne to his summer playhouse, Langner pressed her to rejoin the Theatre Guild. Her appearance at the Westport Playhouse had attracted a great deal of attention, particularly from New York. *Hamlet* could wait; she needed more time to prepare. A female Hamlet might be considered ridiculous, and Le Gallienne thought it best to try out her Danish prince a little farther away from the Broadway devils. Meanwhile, the Guild had a new play called *Prelude to Exile,* about Richard Wagner and his mistress Mathilde Wesendonck. "To think I should ever appear under such a name!" Le Gallienne told Julie. "She has to look well and be charming so I suppose if I succeed in that the critics will think I'm giving a great performance."

After ten years of management, Le Gallienne felt odd as just a company member. Director Philip Moeller didn't plan rehearsals well, and Eva sat for hours at a time desperately bored. The Guild committee screamed and shouted at one another, interfered at every level, and gave conflicting orders. "The lack of dignity and the stupidity of the entire proceeding has been beyond any description of belief," said Le Gallienne. She and several of the other actors begged to be released from their contracts, but the Guild refused. The play flopped. During the five-week Broadway run, Le Gallienne and Lucile Watson took their curtain call hand in hand while repeating, "In shame we bow before you!"

DURING *Prelude to Exile*'s tryout in Philadelphia (an "incredible night-mare"), a new scheme came to Le Gallienne "in such clarity" that she wrote it down and presented it immediately to Mary Bok. Her plan was simple: ten actors, who were as fed up as she was with the commercial theatre, would live together in the country, "for approximately 30 weeks—working on plays—rehearsing them, playing them (without productions or costume), constantly experimenting with their own instruments—studying, discarding, but stimulating their brains and their scope as actors." The group would receive small salaries and living expenses. Mary Bok thought the plan was excellent and agreed to give Le Gallienne fifty thousand dollars to fund the project. Le Gallienne felt like "a rejuvenated old Cat."

Marion was elated. During the run of *Prelude to Exile,* her job had been "taking care of Eva, her letters and comfort in and out of the theatre"—which meant cooking, cleaning, laundry, and errands. Marion wanted to act, and now she would be able to share again in a Le Gallienne repertory company.

During the spring of 1937, Le Gallienne worked on *Hamlet,* which the Cape Playhouse in Dennis, Massachusetts, planned to present in August. As always, casting proved difficult, especially finding good, experienced actors who would agree to play far from New York in a week's run at summer stock salaries. Eva dangled the carrot of thirty weeks of repertory following *Hamlet* and was able to attract a group of competent but unexciting actors. She cast Marion as Gertrude, and Donald Cameron agreed to play the Ghost and join the repertory company. Eva needed a strong leading man, a match for her own talents. Unfortunately, most of the distinguished principal men were in Hollywood. Katharine Cornell had solved the problem by importing her leading men from Britain. Le Gallienne's favorite leading man, Pepi Schildkraut, was in Hollywood; but Richard Waring, her handsome young Romeo of the Civic's touring production, was available. When Le Gallienne asked him to join her, he confessed that he "couldn't afford to play Laertes to a woman's Hamlet."

In March Le Gallienne auditioned Uta Hagen, a freshman at the University of Wisconsin, for Ophelia. Uta was only seventeen, Le Gallienne recalled, "a tall, rather gawky creature, by no means pretty, but with a face that one remembered, large hands and feet, and the shy ungainly grace of a young colt." Standing uncomfortably in the Blue Room, Hagen presented two audition pieces, a selection from Schiller and the trial scene from Shaw's *Saint Joan.* "She started drilling me on [*Saint Joan*]," Hagen wrote in her journal, "and finally made me say it right to her. She practically hypnotized me, and it got better."

After working with the girl, Le Gallienne felt that she had found "a real talent, crude and groping, but obviously sensitive to direction." She offered Ophelia to Hagen on a trial basis. Uta arrived in Weston that summer, her heart "thumping wildly." Awestruck by Le Gallienne, Uta thought Eva's country home was beautiful, and it verified the girl's notion "that an actor's life was probably ideal."

In August, the company moved to Dennis, Massachusetts. Le Gallienne had worked on Hamlet for months, and her lines flowed freely and easily. With designer Michael Weightman-Smith, Eva created a simple unit set consisting of a thrust stage and step units. She set the play in the Viking period, and to reflect the primitive violence of the time, the color palette was in black and gray, high-

Eva's Hamlet *company rehearsing at the Cape Playhouse in Dennis, Massachusetts, in August 1937. From left to right: Philip Jones (Rosencrantz), Robert Williams (Second Grave-digger), Victor Thorley (Fortinbras), Marion Evensen (Gertrude), Don Cameron (the Ghost), George Graham (Polonius), Eva (Hamlet), Alexander Scourby (First Player and Player King), Giorgio Santelli (in beret, former Olympic fencing champion and Eva's fencing coach), Tom Gomez (King), James Harker (Laertes), Uta Hagen (Ophelia), and Howard Wierum (Horatio). In the foreground Tyrone Kearney (Player Queen) is holding Chico.*

lighted by shades of red. Material for the costumes was woven on Le Gallienne's loom and then sent to Helene Pons in New York for the finished work.

Although Le Gallienne knew of one theory that *Hamlet* was drawn from an old Danish legend that said that when the king was killed, the queen, to have an heir, raised her daughter as a boy, Eva decided to play Hamlet as an actual boy of eighteen. "At 18, his weakness and hesitation," she felt, "his abnormal bitterness at his mother's sudden remarriage, are natural." She believed that it was possible "for an actress at the height of her powers to give the impression of being a boy, while having at her command all the craft, range, force, and subtlety which such great roles require."

For the first time since the explosion six years earlier, Le Gallienne had no pain in her right hand. After fencing two hours every day with Santelli, she was slim and fit, and while she thought she looked boyish in her tight black body suit, her company didn't have the heart to tell her what the reviews later confirmed—that she looked elegant and sexy. Over her body suit, she wore an above-the-knee black tunic, a black belt with silver medallions, and a plain silver chain around her neck. During the duel with Laertes, she shed her tunic to reveal a royal scarlet undershirt appliquéd with black ravens.

At the dress rehearsal, Le Gallienne recalled that "the sacred fire struck," and Uta Hagen gave a transcendent performance of Ophelia. Le Gallienne warned the girl that such experiences were rare. After the opening, Uta sobbed and asked, "What happened? Why couldn't I do what I did the night before?" Le Gallienne explained that while novices sometimes experience the "state of grace" in acting, it is only "after years of discipline and prayer that it occurs with any frequency."

"That was a thrilling week at Dennis," Le Gallienne wrote. "I shall never forget it." Le Gallienne's assistant that summer and fall, Edmund Potter, a tall, gangly, scholarly youth whom she affectionately called Potkin, would never forget it either. "In the Le Gallienne *Hamlet*," he recalled, "Hamlet seated himself on [the throne] . . . and spoke his dying words to Horatio. Then . . . Fortinbras and his soldiers entered. Four captains advanced to the throne . . . clamped their shields together, laid the dead Hamlet on his back, lifted the shields and Hamlet over their heads into the only light still operational, a 500-watt white beam shining directly downward on Hamlet's body, seeming to float in space, while a tremendous fanfare of trumpets rose to a climax, followed by a cannon roar as the curtain fell. No wonder the audience leapt to its feet."

Audience response and the reviews, particularly for Le Gallienne and Uta Hagen, were positive enough to prompt Lee Shubert to offer to produce *Hamlet* on Broadway for a short run before sending the play on a national tour. Le Gallienne said no. "For the first time in my life I felt vulnerable; perhaps I was growing up. Perhaps the ordeal by fire, while strengthening me in one way, had weakened me in another." She didn't want to face the publicity and the press attention that would engulf a female Hamlet, or the comparisons with John Gielgud and Leslie Howard, who had played Hamlet in New York the year before. In full-scale Broadway productions, supported by excellent companies, both men had received mixed reviews, as anyone attempting *Hamlet* usually does. Le Gallienne's notices for her unevenly acted summer stock production were mixed as well. She would have to recast several parts. Shakespeare's plays had been written to be performed in repertory, and playing eight performances of *Hamlet* every week, Eva thought, would be too grueling. There were all sorts of reasons for her to turn down Shubert's offer, but she would always be ashamed of her cowardice in doing so.

Instead of playing Hamlet on Broadway, Le Gallienne returned to Weston and attempted once again to build a theatrical home for herself. Actors in the ten-member company included Le Gallienne, Marion Evensen, Uta Hagen, Donald Cameron, Howard Wierum, Doris Rich, and Alexander Scourby.

Like many theatre ventures, her new repertory company began with great idealism. Le Gallienne asked Edmund Potter to keep a daily journal to record the work of the company. Well-educated, a meticulous note taker, a perceptive observer, and a natural skeptic—traits that he later put to use as a biographer of military leaders—Potter was a good choice.

The actors lived at Cobb's Mill Inn, less than a mile from Le Gallienne's house. For almost a month, the company read and rehearsed Chekhov's *The Seagull*. The company marveled at Le Gallienne's brilliant playing of Nina, and they congratulated themselves on their good fortune in having steady, interesting work.

On Sunday, October 17, the company was relaxing together at Cobb's Mill. Suddenly, after drinking glass after glass of champagne, Le Gallienne lashed out at the actors, accusing them of lack of understanding and an inability to act. The company was dumbfounded.

That evening Potter walked up to Le Gallienne's house to discover the cause of her outburst. "I can't go on with this farce, Potkin," she told him. "I have no right to be taking Mrs. Bok's money when I can only foresee failure." Le Gallienne explained that she couldn't get "the men I need; they've all gone to Hollywood." It had become clear to her, she explained, that she had surrounded herself with "just a bunch of mediocre ham actors, ready to grab everything and to give nothing." She told Potter that she was disbanding the company.

The next day, accompanied by Marion, Le Gallienne drove to Maine to inform Mary Bok of her decision. She called Potter from Maine and informed him that she wanted to meet with the group at 8:30 p.m. on Thursday, October 21.

After the company filed silently into the Blue Room, Le Gallienne began the meeting by saying that she had made a tragic mistake. There was a long silence, finally broken by Howard Wierum, who reminded her that she had told him he had talent. Le Gallienne agreed that he had a little, and maybe in four or five years of practice he would get better. Another silence followed. Doris Rich mentioned the thirty-week guarantee that they had been verbally promised. Marion Evensen leapt to her feet to say that there was never any guarantee, that the company was a failure and that was that. When Le Gallienne remarked that she had suffered, Alexander Scourby exploded: "Of all the goddamned hedging I ever heard, this is the worst! If you were going to judge us at the end of a month, why didn't you say so, instead of giving us to understand that we had the entire winter to find our characters? We haven't had any direction." Le Gallienne snapped that he couldn't take direction and headed for the door. On her way out, she passed Uta Hagen. Sobbing, Uta flung out a tablecloth that she had painstakingly embroidered for Le Gallienne. While Eva comforted Uta, Marion continued the fight, until, worn out and defeated, the company finally left the house.

"The child Uta was the only one of them all to appreciate my true motives in this decision," Le Gallienne wrote. A few months later, the Lunts cast Hagen as Nina in their production of *The Seagull.* Le Gallienne was delighted and "once again struck forcibly by the strangely logical pattern life so often follows. . . . Uta was studying it along with me. She was present at all our discussions of the play and knew it by heart. . . . It was the first important step in her career." Uta Hagen's success confirmed Le Gallienne's belief that there was no such thing as an undiscovered genius. A really great talent cannot be stopped, she felt, when it was "combined with ruthless singleness of purpose."

If genius required ruthlessness, Le Gallienne had certainly demonstrated that she had that quality with her abrupt dismissal of the company. At a time when the theatre was being drained of top male talent by the movies, it was naive of Le Gallienne to think that she could find experienced men to work in the country at Equity minimum salary. She "longed for the joy of playing opposite someone who created his own performance"; she wanted the "flash and conflict of thought and feeling"—in other words, an acting partnership like the ones she had enjoyed with Pepi Schildkraut, Egon Brecher, and Basil Rathbone.

Of all the actors in the company, the one who suffered the most was Marion Evensen. Gunnar knew that Eva considered her a good, competent actor, but she was not on Le Gallienne's level. Every time Eva complained that the best actors had gone to Hollywood, Marion was reminded of her rival Jo Hutchinson, who had done just that. Le Gallienne did not confide in Marion, and her abrupt disbanding of the company had come as a complete surprise. Marion believed, along with everyone else, that the work was going well. No matter. Art would always come first with Le Gallienne. Marion, a stoic with a fierce sense of pride, kept her disappointment to herself, containing her feelings of anger and bitterness. The explosion would come years later.

AFTER THE UNPLEASANT confrontation with the company, Le Gallienne wallowed for several days in self-pity and anger. On the night of October 24, terribly drunk, she phoned Alla Nazimova to announce that she was climbing down from her artistic pedestal. But in a few days, her good sense asserted itself and life again seemed to be worth living, especially since she planned to treat herself and Marion to an extended European vacation.

On October 28, Eva and Marion checked into the Algonquin Hotel for a two-week spree of theatre- and moviegoing, shopping, and visiting friends before sailing for Europe. "I am free, I am free, I am free! No more life in the prison for me," Le Gallienne exulted, echoing Maya's words in Ibsen's *When We Dead Awaken.*

Le Gallienne lunched with Mimsey, consulted with her lawyer/agent Arthur Friend, visited with Thelma Chandler and other old friends from the Civic, and saw a great deal of Constance Collier and her show-business friends. At a party at Collier's, she met artist George Bergen, who once had rented half of his studio to Gwen Le Gallienne, Irma Le Gallienne's daughter and Richard's stepdaughter. Gwen, an aspiring painter, had told him that she was Eva's sister. Julie and Hesper had both spoken to Gwen about her attempts to tie herself to Eva's fame, but they had been unable to stop her quest for publicity. Often when Le Gallienne went out on a national tour, Gwen's press agent would obtain a list of the cities where she was playing and send photographs and press releases about Le Gallienne's artist "sister" to the local papers.

Over lunch with Constance Collier, Eva told her former teacher that she planned to "drift for awhile, to observe, to make notes, and hold myself in readiness for the time when my new chapter should begin . . . a chapter that concerned my own personal work . . . and not entail the responsibility involved in carrying along a lot of other people." Constance advised her to go to Hollywood immediately and become a female Paul Muni and play only character parts. At another lunch with Constance, she and Collier were seated with a party of Hollywood types at the Algonquin's famous Round Table. Eva liked the director George Cukor. "He is very quick, an alive, amusing brain. Funny to sit there and hear them talking about Hollywood and all the inside machinations—like another world to me—a world in which I feel I would find it hard to fit." Mary Pickford told Le Gallienne how much she had liked Eva's radio broadcast of *Camille.* Pickford looked "remarkably young," Le Gallienne thought, but what "an exhausting bore it must be to have to keep on being 'little Mary, America's Sweetheart.' "

Le Gallienne saw the Rockettes and all the Broadway hits. She loved the precision of the Rockettes, but she sat thoroughly depressed and unsmiling through *Yes, My Darling Daughter* while all around her the audience laughed at "every comedy face that the actors pulled." She was amazed to see the audience's "lack of discrimination. As long as acting is obvious, whether good or bad, they enjoy it and think it wonderful." About Gertrude Lawrence in *Susan and God,* she observed that "such women are not actresses at all. They are simply expert at exploiting their own personalities." She was proud of her former apprentice Burgess Meredith, who was playing in *The Star Wagon.* Despite his light voice, which was limited in range, "there can be no question of his *great* talent," she wrote. "He just *is* an actor."

In the old Comedy Theatre, where she had made her Broadway debut in *Mrs. Boltay's Daughters,* she saw Orson Welles's Mercury Theatre production of *Julius Caesar.* Welles's decision to play the production in modern dress was a brilliant idea, she believed, which "covered a multitude of sins." Although she "didn't care much for Welles's playing . . . he reads with great deliberation, with an acute intellectual awareness of the content. He attacks a scene, or a phrase, with a rather portentous concentration, savoring first the thought, then each word of the sentence, like an ancient connoisseur might savor each sip of a glass of fine old port."

If Le Gallienne hadn't been an actor, she would have made a discriminating critic. Fresh from the failure of her little "Groupe," she didn't begrudge the Group Theatre's successful production of Odets's *Golden Boy:* "It is cleverly written, cleverly planned, the sort of play that people will enjoy who *don't* think (because of its swift external sense of theatre) and that people will enjoy who *do* think (because of the sober, bitter truths expressed throughout). It is a terrific indictment of the 'Bitch Goddess Success' worship in this country. Its terse, eliminated style is tremendously powerful and moving! . . . And they played it well—with truth, with conviction, with a kind of sober passion. It was *fine.*"

Earlier that year, Le Gallienne had seen Shakespeare's *Richard II,* starring Maurice Evans and directed by Margaret Webster. During her childhood, at the Favershams' home in Chiddingfold, Eva had ignored little Peggy Webster; now she found the thirty-three-year-old Webster a charming, stimulating woman who shared many of her own views about the theatre. They lunched together in New York and swapped stories about the inadequacies of American actors, and Peggy visited a few times in Weston. *Richard II* was a smash hit, and suddenly Webster was in demand as a director. "She has a lot of her mother's wit without her wickedness," Le Gallienne wrote in her diary. "It's a kindly wit, not a destructive one . . . and then she has such a clear, level, honest brain. . . . Her success has improved her looks, her whole personality in fact."

ON NOVEMBER 20, 1937, Le Gallienne and Marion sailed for England and spent the holidays in London with Julie. As usual, it rained incessantly, and after Christmas Eva was glad to go to her beloved Paris.

At the Comédie-Française Le Gallienne saw a Marivaux play and a Molière and marveled at the excellent ensemble. The French national theatre's repertory was so large that half of the company had gone to Egypt for several weeks with a repertory of fourteen plays. Le Gallienne envied especially the dignity and permanence of such a theatre. "No use comparing our young actors, or even our older actors to these," she sighed. "Where can ours get training?"

The big hit in Paris was *Madame Capet,* Marcelle Maurette's biographical play about Marie Antoinette. Le Gallienne loved the play and the production and thought it would be right for her. Since it was rumored that Gilbert Miller wanted the play for Helen Hayes, it was even more imperative that Le Gallienne get the rights. Mary Bok wired five hundred dollars and Le Gallienne took a six-month option. Biographical plays had recently proven successful for Hayes

(Queen Victoria) and Katharine Cornell (Elizabeth Barrett Browning), and she hoped that playing the French queen would be as successful for her. An added attraction was that there was no leading man to worry about. Eddie Dowling agreed to produce the play in New York, George Middleton was signed to translate, and Le Gallienne hoped that Peggy Webster could be persuaded to direct it.

In preparing a part, Le Gallienne acted as her own dramaturg, researching the "social history of the period, the climate of the times; what people were thinking; what great writers, painters, architects, musicians—as well as statesmen and politicians—dominated the scene; why people wore certain clothes or used particular types of furniture and accessories." Her research helped her to find the rhythm and atmosphere of the time, giving her clues as to how the character should move and speak and think. While she was in Paris, she read about Louis XVI and Marie Antoinette and roamed Versailles, the Louvre, Saint-Cloud, the Temple, and the Conciergerie. She peered at Marie's mended silk stockings, her handkerchief, and her drinking glass at the Musée Carnavalet.

Le Gallienne celebrated her thirty-ninth birthday in Paris, and decided that it "was a pleasant age. Far pleasanter than 19, and even than 29. But I suppose from now on one begins the Descent." Still, as she and Marion moved on to Italy, everything seemed more beautiful seen with older eyes. "Youth does not see as well," she thought; "it is still too wrapped up in itself." In Assisi, she had a joyful reunion with her tall, blond cousin Mogens Nørregaard, who had moved there to study and to paint. Mogens had converted to Roman Catholicism and lived "an austere and solitary life." Before leaving Italy, Le Gallienne visited Duse's grave in Asolo and stood "a long time by the plain marble slab that marks her grave, on the slope of a hill facing the violet-tinged mountains."

Eva and Marion spent just a few days in Munich and decided to leave on the day before Hitler was to speak. There "were too many swastinkers to suit me," Le Gallienne said. "The stupidity of crowds & the power of mass hysteria! It always terrifies me," she told her diary.

On March 16, she and Marion met Julie in Copenhagen to celebrate Julie's seventy-fifth birthday and her more than forty years as a correspondent for *Politiken.* The newspaper fêted Julie, and there was a round of teas, family parties, theatregoing, and a visit to Hans Christian Andersen's Little Mermaid statue. At one of the teas, Eva met Ibsen's granddaughter, who told her that Ibsen had written *A Doll's House* to please his feminist wife. "I should think it was the only occasion on which he wrote anything to please anybody!" exclaimed Le Gallienne.

Leaving Julie in Copenhagen, she and Marion went on to Norway to visit Skien, where Marion's mother was born and which was also Ibsen's birthplace. They found the old theatre in Bergen where Ibsen had worked as a stage manager, and Le Gallienne examined his meticulous, detailed prompt books. Eva was surprised to find that her name was well known in Norway as an Ibsen interpreter. In Oslo she visited "dear old bear Ibsen's" statue, and a newspaper editor presented her with a complete set of Ibsen first editions.

In Oslo, she saw three Viking ships that were displayed there, and she thought their pure, clean lines were "like a phrase from some heroic symphony." She felt as if she were "gazing at the whole spirit of the North." Earlier, in Rome, when Eva had opened the doors to Saint Peter's, she had gazed "into the whole spirit of the Latin world." Her senses had been intoxicated "with the lavish wealth of color and detail. A thousand intricate forms, fantastically elaborated and embroidered, weave an intricate pattern drenched in vivid hues of gold, scarlet, crimson, purple, blue, and silver." Le Gallienne's five-month tour of Europe had filled her with sights, sounds, feelings, and new sensations.

Before she left for home, Eva tried to persuade her mother to move permanently to America. "There was a feeling of foreboding in the air," she wrote. In Paris, she had sensed an "atmosphere of cynicism, a kind of fatalistic indifference." Her mother told Eva that she would come for a visit when *Madame Capet* opened, but Julie did not believe that "mankind could be rash enough and wicked enough" to open the door on another world war.

"TODAY SEVEN YEARS AGO (unbelievable isn't it!) Jo and I were blown up," Le Gallienne wrote Julie on June 12, 1938. "I was trying to reconstruct in my mind's eye this house and garden as it was then—it's almost impossible—such great changes have been made. It looks so beautiful now—the roses have never been so perfect or so plentiful."

Working in the garden, playing tennis, and preparing for *Madame Capet* occupied her during the summer months. Since Peggy Webster planned to direct Maurice Evans in *Hamlet,* Jose Ruben had been hired to direct *Madame Capet.* He found the play difficult to cast since Marie Antoinette is the only significant role. In the French production, to keep costs down and to display the versatility of the actors, the roles had been double- and in some cases triple-cast. In the American theatre, actors played one role, were generally cast to type, and were not trained to be versatile. Name actors didn't want to play such small parts; but finally Ruben gathered a large company of good supporting actors, including Staats Cotsworth, Merle Maddern, Marion Evensen, and George Coulouris. Le Gallienne gave a small part to Nelson Welch, a young, impoverished Englishman who had worked briefly at the Civic. Marion was incensed that Nelson was allowed to stay at the old house and have "eggs, vegetables, two quarts of milk daily & cream." Welch was encroaching on Marion's territory. She was jealous of Eva's fondness for him; plus, she thought Welch had a "very calculating, uninspired English mind."

The *Capet* company started rehearsals during the first week of September. As war became more likely in Europe, "the theatre seems so unimportant," wrote Le

Gallienne. There was a pall over the production, too, and it didn't help that the Norma Shearer movie *Marie Antoinette* had just opened. When he saw the first dress rehearsal of *Capet,* producer Eddie Dowling insisted on cast and script changes and attacked the director in front of the company, which in turn caused Jose Ruben to lose control and shout at the actors and the crew, Le Gallienne wrote, "until his voice was reduced to a hoarse whisper."

On opening night at the Cort Theatre, when Le Gallienne entered her dressing room, she found a note from Dowling announcing that the play would close the following Saturday. This news was hardly conducive to a good performance, but the first-night reception was warm and enthusiastic. Afterward, the "bandwagon elite" pursued Le Gallienne into her dressing room, and she was almost fooled that "we might be 'in' after all."

Brooks Atkinson was one of the few critics who liked the production. He called Le Gallienne's acting superb and her portrayal of the French queen profoundly moving. The play he said, was "court calendar drama." Translating French drama for Americans had always been problematic, and *Madame Capet* was no exception. The language seemed too flowery, less elegant in English. While Le Gallienne insisted that the play was worthy, it was really just a vehicle for her return to Broadway, and it was unsuited to her talents. By nature and training Le Gallienne was a character actor, and she did her best work in ensemble plays. The role of Marie Antoinette was more appropriate for a great personality actor.

Julie Le Gallienne arrived in New York just in time for the closing. She loved the play and enjoyed seeing her daughter wear beautiful costumes. Julie returned to Weston with a thoroughly depressed Eva to celebrate the holidays. "Producing a play on Broadway," Eva grumped, "is just like betting on the horses . . . either you 'click' or you 'flop,' and the reasons for either are often highly mysterious." At least she had earned a fifteen-hundred-dollar-a-week salary with a four-week guarantee, so she was hardly penniless.

Eva turned to a proven winner—Ibsen. She had learned from the road tour of *L'Aiglon* that there was an enormous audience outside of New York hungry for live theatre and a chance to see a Broadway star. When a new producing company, Legitimate Theatre, Inc., asked her to tour with *Hedda Gabler* and *The Master Builder,* guaranteeing her complete artistic control and a full season's work, Le Gallienne accepted.

EVA'S THOUGHTS, though, were with her mother, who had returned to England. She begged Julie to come live in America. "It looks so awful for France & England," Eva wrote her in September 1939, "—and of course poor Poland seems to be finished already with Russia too joining in at the kill. . . . Madness seems to be in the air—I am trying to be *particularly* sane—am going about the preparations for the tour—It is hard to believe that Hell on Earth has been let loose!"

During the summer months, Eva had prepared a new translation of *The Master Builder,* played in *Private Lives* in summer stock ("It made me feel younger somehow—& gave me renewed confidence"), hosted her Danish cousin Gerda and her husband, rehearsed her company, and girded herself for the upcoming seven-month tour of forty-two states.

Julie arrived on September 30, and Le Gallienne settled her in Weston and arranged for her to take her meals at the Cobb's Mill Inn. Alice De Lamar and Mimsey were nearby and would watch over her, and Eva promised to call every Sunday and write regularly.

The company traveled by train, but Le Gallienne preferred riding in her own chauffeur-driven car, which meant that she and Marion could travel with their two dogs, Chico and Heather. Accompanied by Le Gallienne's theatre dresser, Dorothy Murray, they set out in October for a swing through the Northeast before heading south.

In town after town, they followed an inferior road company of *Golden Boy*. But Le Gallienne's company was a solid one of seasoned actors and aspiring young ones. Earle Larrimore, a Theatre Guild veteran, played Solness in *The Master Builder* and Lovborg in *Hedda Gabler;* Marion Evensen acted Mrs. Solness and Aunt Julie; and Katharine Squire played Mrs. Elvsted and Kaja. They played one- and two-night stands from Hartford, Springfield, Boston, and New Haven to Reading, Allentown, Harrisburg, and down into Richmond, Winston-Salem, Little Rock, Memphis—"Where—when—& what is this?" Le Gallienne wondered as the towns blurred into one another. Each theatre offered a different challenge, ranging from brand-new thirty-five-hundred-seat civic auditoriums to crumbling old legitimate theatres to a shallow stage at the end of a basketball court with no dressing rooms, no lights, and no running water. In Lincoln, Nebraska, she played *Hedda Gabler* in a "lovely old theatre—'over 50 years old' (they tell you that as if it was 500!) and of course now they are going to turn it into a modern fire-proof movie house. It's a crime," she said.

Le Gallienne carried her own makeup mirror and lights, and before every performance she walked the stage to become foot-familiar with it, snapped her fingers to test for dead spots, and voice-tested the acoustics. She used Sarah Bernhardt's technique of standing center stage and holding her arms out as if to embrace the house. If her hands were in line with the walls, the space was a good one; an auditorium smaller than her embrace meant bad acoustics.

In city after city, many performances sold out. Often students mobbed her dressing room to get the distinctive "E Le Gallienne" autograph or surrounded her at receptions following the performances. In Columbus, Mississippi, the re-

Eva in her 1939 production of Hedda Gabler. *The droop of her right eyebrow is more apparent in straight-on poses; she preferred to be photographed in profile. Eva took advantage of the two distinct sides of her face to reveal both the "demon" and the "angel" in the character.*

sponse was "unbelievable"; the excitement reminded her of the free performances of *Peter Pan* at the Civic. "One would expect it at an opening night in New York but here it came as a complete shock. . . . I handled some scenes with infinite care, like a cat treading on eggs! & succeeded in holding them completely."

Throughout the South and on into Texas, she was outraged by the treatment of the black company members. Her dresser, Dorothy, and James, the driver, were refused service in restaurants, were not allowed to stay in hotels, and had to scramble to find accommodations. In Denton, Texas, when Dorothy attempted to take the elevator to Le Gallienne's hotel room to help her pack, the bellboy stopped her and escorted her upstairs. "This nigger here insists on coming up," he drawled to Le Gallienne. "I certainly scared the life out of him," Eva reported in her diary, "was so mad I saw red. Sent for the manager & gave him a good ear full. Dot was crying. It's a disgrace."

Outside of Tucson, Arizona, Eva visited Gary Cooper on a film location, and while he waited between takes, she talked with him over coffee and cigarettes. He was "incredibly tall & thin with lovely blue eyes—a darling, so simple & clear. My idea of an American man!" she gushed like a star-struck fan.

During their stay in Los Angeles, she saw Ina Claire, Egon Brecher, Pepi Schildkraut, and Dame May Whitty. Every afternoon she visited with Jo Hutchinson, which undoubtedly was what prompted Marion to write Julie that she disliked Los Angeles. Le Gallienne hated what she called the "false phony atmosphere" of Los Angeles, too, especially since a few of their performances had to be cancelled because of the bankruptcy of their sponsor.

As the tour ground on, Le Gallienne studied seed catalogs and longed for home. She hoarded her vitality for the performances, and after a long day of driving she bristled when reporters tried to get at her. "What do they think one's made of? Surely the performance is more important than their piffling articles." At discussion sessions after the plays, college students sometimes irritated her with their questions: Is the theatre dead? Will Ibsen ever be a classic?

She never stopped refining a role. With only a few weeks left to play, in March 1940, she decided to try her first Hedda entrance without the cigarette, and liked it better, but the change made her so nervous her knees shook. Playing Hilda Wangel made her feel a thousand years old, and she was relieved when the critics failed to mention her age in their reviews. In contrast to Marion, who had gained weight and looked matronly, Le Gallienne had maintained her five-four frame at 110 pounds and had the figure of a girl.

A layoff, however brief, made Eva nervous, and she longed to get back to the plays. "What a cure Work is," she said. The process of healing from the explosion and from the loss of the Civic Repertory had taken years. Her betrayal of Jo, though, still haunted her. From time to time she would attempt to revive the romance. "I did that once. I can't do that again," Jo would say. "Well, you haven't done it lately," Eva would reply.

As she felt Le Gallienne growing stronger and less dependent on her, Marion became protective and possessive of her, and jealous of anyone who came too close to her. She had already taken on the job of helping with Eva's mail, including writing long, newsy letters to Julie, and she decided to take on Dorothy's duties of dresser and caring for Eva's costumes as well. Dorothy had worked for Eva for years, but Marion thought she had become sloppy and inefficient and sent her home.

When the long trek ended the last week of April 1940, Le Gallienne was exhausted, yet exhilarated by the fact that she and Ibsen could still draw sold-out houses in cities across the country. At a salary of one thousand dollars a week plus percentages, she didn't make a fortune, but she was on a crusade, and the tour had convinced her that people outside of New York wanted to see live theatre and in many cases would drive hundreds of miles to see a play. The high-school and college students and their teachers who swarmed backstage proved to her that movies had not killed the theatre. The theatre needed to be decentralized, she believed, but good theatre buildings were difficult to find, as more and more were being turned into movie houses. What was the solution? She thought she had the answer and began working on a lecture called "The Importance of the Theatre in Our Cultural Life." The Redpath Lecture Bureau signed her for a fall tour at a minimum of one thousand dollars a week to spread her message of a national, subsidized theatre for America.

Once again Le Gallienne was on the march, and as usual critic George Jean Nathan stood on the sidelines and hurled mud. Writing in his 1940 *Encyclopaedia of the Theatre,* the critic whined that he seemed to be the lone voice crying out against the "genius" of Eva Le Gallienne. (Was attacking her a way of assaulting the powerful Brooks Atkinson, a Le Gallienne advocate?) She was a "very gamy actress," Nathan wrote, equipped with a "pair of cuckoo wings." He followed the Le Gallienne entry with a few meandering pointless paragraphs on "Lesbianism"—which told the theatre community that would read Nathan's book two things they already had known for years: that Eva Le Gallienne was a lesbian and that George Jean Nathan was a homophobe. In contrast to Le Gallienne's four-page entry, Nathan's favorite actress, Helen Hayes, rated just four sentences in his *Encyclopaedia,* but received Nathan's praise—not for her artistry but for her "inner warm womanliness" and her "little-girl spirit." It was people like Nathan that Le Gallienne had in mind when she gave May Sarton this advice: "People hate what they don't understand and try to destroy it. Only try to keep yourself clear and don't allow that destructive force to spoil something that to you is simple, natural, and beautiful."

LE GALLIENNE PRACTICED her lecture that summer before an audience of cats and dogs in the Blue Room or she rehearsed outside on her Peter Pan Rock. Her talk was a variation on the speeches she had given to promote the Civic Repertory, except now she called for a permanently funded national theatre, not subject to congressional political whims: "Those of us who have libraries would certainly not be content with one composed only of best-selling novels," she said. "Or in music, for instance, what would we think of a symphony orchestra that neglected Bach, Beethoven, Schubert, Mozart, Wagner, Debussy . . . and concentrated on the latest popular hits? . . . My dream for this country is to see at least six great centres established in Key Cities; Repertory Theatres presenting fine plays at popular prices; serving not only their home centres, but the radius around it. And connected with each of these Centres a free school, so that the children will have some place to learn their job well." She concluded, "How can anything come about unless you dream it first?"

Since Marion traveled with Eva on the tour, and because Julie found the country boring, Julie decided to move to the Shoreham Hotel in New York. Le Gallienne asked Margaret St. John, an elderly British eccentric who had worked in various capacities at the Civic Repertory, to stay in Weston and look after the plants and animals. St. John, a thin, angular woman with gray hair, who always wore tweedy woolen suits, even in summer, had been a suffragist in London, was a poet, a mystic, and an extraordinarily kind woman, who adored Eva.

Marion was hired by the lecture bureau to arrange travel and hotel accommodations to forty-one cities, from San Antonio, Texas, to Keene, New Hampshire. Le Gallienne spoke primarily at schools, colleges, town forums, and women's clubs, and as she gained confidence she began to weave in brief scenes from plays into her talk. She treated the speech like a performance. She asked that the house lights be turned off when she began to speak, and she wore long gowns for the evening lectures and suits in the afternoon. Each time was like a new opening night. "You have to pit your own power, personality and wits against these audiences. It's like constantly breaking in a new horse."

Le Gallienne preferred talking to students, wanting to "catch them young." Their enthusiasm was satisfying, but she was happy primarily because once again she was working toward a goal. Her lecture "reviews," which streamed in to Redpath in the form of thank-you letters and editorials in local papers, called Le Gallienne gracious, charming, vibrant, captivating, dramatic, and thrilling. "Had she said nothing, the way in which she said it alone would have been a valuable education in the King's English and proper use of the body's machinery for articulation and other self-expression," said the *Atlantic City Press.*

Standing onstage alone was a solitary life, though, and Eva was not sorry to give her last lecture in late December 1940 and return to Weston. After just a few relaxing days tending her plants and working on her books in the Blue Room, Eva had to have dental surgery to deal with an infected back molar. Her face swelled up, and her right eye turned black and blue. "How I hate being disfigured," she told her diary. "I often wondered how I lived through the burning. It must have been appalling." Julie called her a Pollyanna when Eva said that she was grateful at the timing, that at least she was not working. Julie observed that since Eva's ordeal by fire, she had become more patient, more tolerant, and more even-tempered. Or was it just that she was getting older?

After seeing *Charley's Aunt,* starring Uta Hagen's husband, José Ferrer ("really brilliant—a *born* actor"), Eva celebrated her forty-second birthday over smorgasbord and highballs with Julie, Mimsey, and Marion in New York. A month later, Ferrer and Uta invited her and Marion to dinner to meet their new baby, and after the visit Le Gallienne confided to her diary, "They are both on top of the wave—both in their personal & public life. I'm glad for them—[but] they seem a bit *too* assured—one fears for them a little." Le Gallienne knew that feeling well, of riding the crest of the wave. Now she wondered if she would ever be able to realize any of her goals. "Twenty years ago I shouldn't have even asked that question!" she mused. "Strange how life takes it out of one."

PEGGY WEBSTER, then thirty-six, was celebrated and sought after, renowned for her interpretations of Shakespeare, and shared Le Gallienne's dream of a non-profit repertory theatre. They talked often about their theatre plans. Peggy was a dedicated theatre artist with a sophisticated, complex mind, and Le Gallienne discovered how much she had missed conversing with an intellectual equal. Marion's tastes were simple. She shared Eva's interest in the house and garden, but she liked popular movies and best-selling books, and while she was adept at small talk, her mind was not deep. She was bored by intellectual discussions of Ibsen, Chekhov, and Shakespeare. Eva and Marion's physical relationship had ended years earlier, and Eva was tied to Marion by routine and a shared history.

Unlike Le Gallienne, Peggy was a joiner, a tireless worker on various theatre committees and boards. She had a wide circle of friends, and it was not unusual for her to write fifteen or twenty letters a day. Peggy came from a long line of English actors, and she had wanted to be an actor like her parents, Ben Webster and May Whitty, but her talents lay in directing and writing. She was born in 1905 in New York City when her parents were playing there. As a girl, she appeared onstage with Ellen Terry; later, she made her professional debut in London in John Barrymore's *Hamlet,* and played Masha in *The Seagull* with Lunt and Fontanne. In 1942, she published *Shakespeare Without Tears,* and it became a best-seller. Her reputation in America was founded on her outstanding, accessible productions of Shakespeare's plays, beginning with *Richard II* and *Hamlet* starring Maurice Evans in 1937 and 1938, followed by *Henry IV, Part I* (1939), and *Twelfth Night* (1941) with Helen Hayes. She was so in tune with Shakespeare that the press dubbed her "the Bard's girlfriend." Of medium height and somewhat stocky, with reddish hair and a slight cast in one eye, Peggy was not pretty and not the sort of woman that usually attracted Le Gallienne: she was loud and boisterous while Eva was quiet and refined—an English broadsword to Eva's French foil. Eva felt energized and young again around her. They began making plans to establish an American repertory theatre, modeled after the Civic Repertory. Their professional friendship soon deepened into a passionate love affair.

For several weeks in June and July, Le Gallienne and Peggy spent "a beautiful time" together in Peggy's tiny hilltop cottage on Martha's Vineyard. The house was primitive, the wind sometimes ferocious, but the view of the ocean on all three sides was spectacular, and they were in love. "Don't worry about me," Eva wrote her mother. "I am well and very happy."

Peggy had been involved with and was still quite close to the Vienna-born actress Mady Christians, who had appeared in a number of Webster productions. A year younger than Eva, Mady was blond, voluptuous, and maternal. Le Gallienne cattily described her as looking like an overripe peony. Since Peggy did

Peggy Webster in the living room of her cottage at Gay Head on Martha's Vineyard

Outside the house, which overlooked Menemsha Harbor, c. 1941

not live with Mady, her situation was considerably less complicated than Eva's longtime relationship with Marion.

During Eva's absence on the Vineyard with Peggy, Marion had joined Julie Le Gallienne for lunches in New York, and they had gone on long walks and to plays together. Eva and Marion did not have a dramatic breakup—Eva did not turn Marion out of the house. Gunnar was family, and she had no other home. Eva left the choice of staying or going to Marion.

Marion Evensen was forty-eight years old. For the past seven years, Le Gallienne had been her employer as well as her companion. Would she be able to find a job? She didn't want to go back to her husband, George Westlake, in Cleveland. Gunnar loved her home, the animals, and the life she had built with Eva, the woman she called her "only love." Too, Marion had promised Julie that she would never leave Eva. So Marion made her choice. Perhaps it was not a difficult one for her to make, since she and Eva had not been lovers for years. She had already moved downstairs to the bedroom they called "Mam's room." Marion resigned herself to sharing Eva with another woman. Evensen's portrayal of Mrs. Solness in *The Master Builder,* Eva had told Marion, was the finest she had ever seen. Now, Marion was playing a similar role in real life to Le Gallienne's Master Builder—a character consumed by her life work. Like Mrs. Solness, Marion tended the plants, cooked and cleaned, and submerged her own personality into Eva's. Marion refused to acknowledge her anger or bitterness. "I want to say to you, lamb darling," Marion wrote to Eva a few months later, "that one may live even sorrowfully and still have a kind of happiness. After all the price of true and lasting happiness is sacrifice. Bless you and believe me you have not made me unhappy."

Noble words. Marion and Eva believed them for a time.

DURING THE SUMMER OF 1941, when Le Gallienne played a few weeks of *Hedda Gabler* at Stockbridge, Peggy attended rehearsals and offered advice and support. Eva felt it "was a joy" to have her near. Le Gallienne's work would always come first in her life, and it was a heady experience to share that work with a woman who felt as she did about the theatre. Once again, Le Gallienne was at the center of a threesome—a state mirroring the happiness of her childhood. Peggy, who gave her the nickname "Le G," was her lover and her intellectual equal. To Marion, who looked after her physical well-being and comfort, she would always be Eva or the self-explanatory "lamb-pig." Marion was in Stockbridge, too, living "a little distance away," Marion reported to Julie, "so have been able to get breakfast for all of us and dinner at night, but you know that's keeping busy, dishes etc."

In the fall of 1941, Peggy and Eva worked in New York and lived together in Peggy's Twelfth Street brownstone. Le Gallienne signed on with the Theatre

Guild to direct two plays. Almost immediately she clashed with the Guild about play choices. She wanted to do O'Neill's *Desire Under the Elms,* but the Guild insisted on O'Neill's comedy *Ah! Wilderness,* which had been revived a few years earlier with great success. The play and Le Gallienne's direction received good reviews, but it flopped at the box office. Le Gallienne also suggested a revival of *The Cradle Song,* but again the Guild committee overruled her and decided on Sheridan's eighteenth-century comedy *The Rivals.* Inspired by the casting of the great clown Bobby Clark as Bob Acres and by Rowlandson's paintings, "with their bold strokes and monstrous comment on the foibles of those times," Le Gallienne directed the play with broad physical humor, emphasizing the grotesque nature of the characters. Unfortunately, she faced every director's nightmare when the other leads, Walter Hampden and Mary Boland, refused to go along with her concept. Boland, who played Mrs. Malaprop (described by Sheridan as a "weatherbeaten old she-dragon"), declined to wear an unflattering costume and wore instead a lovely blue gown that made her look more milkmaid than dragon.

The out-of-town tryout was hellish, and on December 7, 1941, real hell intruded when the company heard on the radio that Pearl Harbor had been bombed and that war had been declared. On New Year's Eve, Mary Boland became ill with pneumonia. With a sold-out house waiting to see *The Rivals,* and no understudy, Le Gallienne took Boland's place. In just a few hours, Eva devised a new costume for Mrs. Malaprop by padding out Boland's dress. She made her face dragon-ugly with wrinkles and frown lines, and she quickly memorized the lines. Peggy Webster, who had stopped in St. Louis on her way to visit her mother in California, sat in the wings during the performance, giving Eva courage and running her cues for the next scene. It was the kind of moment and challenge Le Gallienne loved. The audience cheered her entrance and roared with laughter at her comic lines and her ridiculous costume. While Boland recovered, Le Gallienne played the part for the next two weeks.

When the play opened in New York, Bobby Clark's clowning grabbed all the headlines, and the New York reviews praised him extravagantly. Why didn't the other actors play in the same style? asked the critics, scoring Le Gallienne for her inability to pull the production together. Exhausted from the tour and from playing Boland's part, Eva overreacted to the criticism. She returned to Weston, where she drowned herself in liquor and was nasty to Peggy and Marion. The two women nursed her through the depression and the alcoholic episode, and Eva surfaced several days later chastened. "If only I may have strength enough," she told her diary in true Girl Guide fashion. "I feel incredibly shattered in my spirit and ashamed. And why people should love me is quite beyond my comprehension." As she was able to do time after time, Le Gallienne called upon her formidable willpower and simply stopped drinking. She satisfied both her sweet tooth and her craving for alcohol by switching to grenadine or sometimes a glass of raspberry syrup.

She knew if she was to remain sane and sober, she "must sometimes be away & if possible busy with some work where I can combine my brain & hands," adding dryly that "they say lunatics are benefitted by it—I can quite believe it." To keep busy, she began designing a model for Peggy's upcoming production of *The Tempest*. She worked in the upstairs room at the old house where she had created many of the Civic Repertory productions. She thought about all the good work she had accomplished there and hoped that she could find peace and inspiration again.

What really lifted her spirits, though, was love. She wanted Peggy to live with her, but because of work commitments and the presence of Marion, Peggy kept her New York apartment. When Peggy visited on weekends, they stayed in the old house and Le Gallienne's dark mood was swept away. The sun shone and she felt "refreshed & strengthened," and Peggy liked her *Tempest* set design. All was harmonious with Marion, too. The peace, however, was short-lived. Eva and Peggy left for New York for a few days, and Le Gallienne returned to Weston to find no dinner and a drunken, gloomy Marion. "What will it all end with?" Eva wondered.

When Eva was in pain or suffering from depression after a long tour, Marion looked after her. It seems not to have occurred to Le Gallienne, but the pattern is clear from her diaries, that when she was away from home, Marion became depressed and turned to alcohol for solace. To distance herself somewhat from Marion, Le Gallienne began having breakfast by herself in the Blue Room every morning—it was much more pleasant than looking across the table at dour, unhappy Norway. The breakfast, usually eggs, toast, and coffee, presented beautifully on a tray complete with flowers, silver, and blue-patterned china, was prepared and served by Marion.

During the bitter cold January of 1942, Le Gallienne spent hour after hour in the poorly heated old house working on the *Tempest* model. At the end of the month, feeling ill and out of sorts, she went to New York, where she collapsed at Peggy's apartment and was rushed to Mount Sinai Hospital. She had a particularly virulent form of pneumonia, which was not affected by the new sulfa drugs. Marion moved into the Algonquin in New York, and she, Julie, and Peggy alternated staying with Eva at the hospital. When Eva's condition worsened, specialists were called in and pronounced that they could do nothing. She was not expected to live. "Feel broken hearted about my darling," Julie told her diary.

Le Gallienne's physician, Dr. Somach, saved her life. "Knowing the soundness of my heart," Le Gallienne wrote later, "he followed a hunch and filled me full of immense and unprecedented quantities of aspirin." Her fever broke, and she perspired so much that the imprint of her body soaked through to the underside of the mattress. Once again, like the proverbial cat, Le Gallienne had defied death.

"When I was able to see my friends again and darling Mother," Le Gallienne wrote, "I could see in their faces the ghastly strain they had been through." Julie looked frail and "seemed positively to have dwindled." In their watch over Eva, Peggy and Marion had shared their fears that they might lose the woman they both loved. They reached out to Jo Hutchinson in California, and the three women formed a bond, a kind of prickly affection and respect for the place they each held in Le Gallienne's life. After a month's stay in the hospital, Eva, weak, pale, and bone-thin, flew to Arizona in the middle of March to recuperate for two weeks in the warm, dry desert air. Her loyal friend Mary Bok, who had married the violinist Efrem Zimbalist, once more had come "incredibly to the rescue" and provided money for her trip. Peggy accompanied Eva and spent a few days with her.

WHEN EVA RETURNED to Weston in early April, Joseph Schildkraut sent her a new play called *Uncle Harry* by Thomas Job, which he planned to produce and star in on Broadway. After reading the play (a murder mystery about a man who commits the perfect crime), Le Gallienne thought it was corny, but her part of Lettie had some theatrical possibilities. The "secret inner life of the woman, the thoughts that fill her mind," fascinated her and presented an opportunity to work on an acting problem that would consume her for the rest of her life: how to project to an audience "pure thought—without any external aid." The money was welcome and certainly necessary, and she knew that it would please her mother to see her on Broadway again. She said she would do the play if after *Uncle Harry* closed, Schildkraut would promise to play opposite her in *The Cherry Orchard.* Schildkraut agreed.

According to Karl Malden, who had a small role in the play, even though Schildkraut was the producer and star, it was Le Gallienne who ruled the company and kept Pepi in line. Whenever Schildkraut stepped on someone else's lines or flirted too outrageously with the young women in the company, Le Gallienne reined him in. "Whatever she said, he did," Malden recalled. "When she came through that stage door, that whole company had respect from everybody else, that whole company became dignified, there was a kind of pride in what they were doing. It was not the greatest play ever written, it was an exciting play, but somehow when we were doing it with Miss Le Gallienne, it took on heights unknown to other plays of that category."

As the rehearsals progressed, Le Gallienne enjoyed the work. She liked Lem Ward, the director, and the company was congenial (Jo's mother, Leona Roberts,

*With her closest male
friend, Joseph "Pepi"
Schildkraut, in a 1942
publicity photograph*

was in the cast), but she couldn't help "wishing that it were a play I really wanted
to do." Eva could have walked through the role, but instead she treated the part
of Lettie as if it were as complex as Hedda Gabler, creating a complete emotional
background for the woman as well as a continuous undercurrent of thought.
While she rehearsed, she and Peggy worked on their plans and brainstormed
ideas with Schildkraut, José Ferrer, and Uta Hagen about starting a repertory
theatre.

Since the producers didn't have the money to fund an out-of-town tryout,
Uncle Harry opened cold on May 20, 1942, at the Broadhurst Theatre. "The play
went wonderfully well—the audience . . . crazy about it and gave me & Pepi an
ovation," Le Gallienne wrote in her diary. All she could think, though, was
"what am I doing here?" Leona Roberts advised that it would be good for her career. Le Gallienne agreed that it would help her commercially, but artistically the
success of the play was "maddening and bitterly discouraging." Apparently during wartime there was a need for turn-of-the century suspense plays: *Angel Street*
and *Arsenic and Old Lace,* which were playing at the same time as *Uncle Harry,*
were also Victorian thrillers.

Knowing that Le Gallienne, Schildkraut, and Webster were planning a new
repertory theatre, critic Burns Mantle gave them a boost in his review, writing
that *Uncle Harry* reminded him of the "carefully detailed" productions at the

As Lettie in
Uncle Harry,
wearing an
amethyst-colored
gown trimmed
with black velvet,
1942

Civic Repertory. This new venture, he said, "may result in a revival of the spirit if not the career of the old Civic Repertory."

It seemed incredible to Le Gallienne that some critics called her portrayal of Lettie the finest of her career. The box office confirmed that it was a popular portrayal, and she was deluged with fan mail, autograph seekers, and aspiring young actors. At the stage door one evening, a tall young black man introduced himself as Earle Hyman and asked for her autograph. "Miss Le Gallienne, please bring back the Civic Repertory Theatre," he said.

"Dear boy, we'll try, we'll try," she told him.

Hyman watched *Uncle Harry* from cheap balcony seats at least once a week during its run. He had first read about Le Gallienne when he found a copy of *At 33* in the Queensboro library. Her autobiography led him to Ibsen's plays and a study of theatre history. He knew that the theatre she had achieved was the kind he wanted to be a part of. Later, he would study with Le Gallienne, work with her, and become a good friend. She explained to him that the thing that made her different from the other stars, like Katharine Cornell, "is that they're always themselves on stage. They look like themselves; I look like the character."

ANY HAPPINESS that Le Gallienne felt at the success of *Uncle Harry* was over-shadowed by the grim news on May 21, the day after the play opened, that her mother had lung cancer and was expected to live only a few more months. Dr. Somach urged Eva not to tell Julie. While Eva felt that her mother might want to settle her affairs and would want to know the truth, she reluctantly went along with the doctor's advice. In addition to her part in *Uncle Harry*, Eva would have to play another role in real life.

When Le Gallienne returned home from Arizona in April, she had been shocked at her mother's haggard appearance. Not wanting to worry Eva during her recovery from pneumonia, Marion had not told her that after Eva was out of danger, Julie had collapsed. Eva came to believe that Julie's effort "to control her emotion, the fight she put up to preserve her outward calm and not go to pieces in her terror of losing me," had brought on her mother's fatal illness.

During Julie's last few months, Le Gallienne enlisted the help of her friends to make her mother's days as comfortable and as enjoyable as possible. Eva's extended family of Peggy, Marion, Mimsey, Alice De Lamar, Constance Collier, and Hesper Le Gallienne all joined in to help. Seventy-nine-year-old Julie hated being bored, and Eva made sure that Julie's calendar was filled with dates for lunches and dinners, shopping excursions and walks, late suppers, trips to the hairdresser, and always visits to the theatre and weekends in Weston. Pepi Schildkraut, too, played his part. When Julie visited the theatre, Pepi would escort her and Eva through the crowd of autograph seekers and "with old-world courtesy seat us in a taxi," Eva remembered, "gravely kissing our hands and bowing low in farewell." His gallant performance, which Julie loved, was genuine and believable but, Le Gallienne observed, also "well-calculated to melt the hearts of the young ladies who stood gazing at him with soulful eyes."

Through the summer Le Gallienne played in *Uncle Harry* and offstage played her role with her mother, although she longed to talk honestly to Julie, especially when she saw "in those blue Danish eyes of hers a puzzled look." In late July, Eva and Marion moved Julie out of New York into a small hotel by the water in Old Greenwich, and then a few weeks later, when Julie grew more frail, they moved her to Weston. Marion took over most of Julie's care, since Eva was working in New York. Julie was a "dreadfully difficult invalid," Le Gallienne remembered. "Like most people who have enjoyed perfect health during a long life, she was impatient and resentful of her increasing feebleness; she fought against it stubbornly every inch of the way."

The gas rationing board allowed Le Gallienne extra coupons, and she commuted daily to the theatre. When Julie's condition deteriorated in September, and she drifted in and out of consciousness, Eva called in Nurse Green, who had taken care of her after the fire. Early Sunday morning, September 27, 1942, Julie died quietly in her sleep.

Le Gallienne did not miss any performances. "I felt mother would have wanted me to carry on," she wrote; "she was never a shirker herself and would have been disappointed had I not followed her example."

Often Eva had resented the imperious Julie's demands or her cutting criticisms, but she had never doubted Julie's love or her faith in her talent. Le Gallienne missed the lunches and talks, writing letters and sending the monthly check, and even missed the dreaded afternoon teas—in fact, all the duties that she had sometimes grudgingly performed now seemed precious.

As she mourned her mother, Eva found it difficult to believe that Julie was really gone. Julie seemed so alive somehow—as if she had just gone away on a trip. She recalled, too, her mother's extraordinary life and remembered all the familiar stories: of tiny Julie sitting on Hans Christian Andersen's bony knee; the eager girl with her new pencil box; the young woman who had hero-worshipped Ibsen and Brandes; the determined feminist who left Denmark for a writer's life in England; the unhappy bride of Richard Le Gallienne; the struggling young mother and hat-shop entrepreneur; and the middle-aged woman who had traveled to America with her teenage daughter to build a new life.

The dead help the living, Le Gallienne often told herself, and she *would* try to keep a stiff neck and fulfill the destiny that her mother had dreamed for her. But now that the irreplaceable Julie was gone—her most ardent fan and her harshest critic, the one she had tried most to please, the one who had watched her live— what would it all be for?

PART FIVE

1943 - 1952

As Queen Katherine in Henry VIII, *1946.*
Photographed by Irving Penn

The externals of the theatre make me unhappy.
I quite enjoy the actual playing—if only one's own
personality didn't have to be embroiled in it all.

THE ANSWER, she knew, was not playing tripe like *Uncle Harry*. Still, tripe paid the bills; she loved acting with Pepi; and the strict discipline of the theatre was healing. At forty-four years old, she was consumed with the ambition to create an American repertory theatre, but with middle age had come lowered expectations and lowered vitality.

"Ah, youth! Youth!" she would say, echoing Chekhov, as she looked ruefully at some vibrant young member of the *Uncle Harry* company. Someone like Madeleine L'Engle, a tall, nearsighted young woman who had appeared at an open audition. Madeleine presented an unusual dramatic piece compiled from Katherine Mansfield's letters, and she brought along a one-act play she had written. Recognizing that L'Engle had considerable intelligence and imagination, Le Gallienne offered her an understudy and a small part in *Uncle Harry*. She also hired her to help answer her stacks of fan mail.

L'Engle lived in a small walk-up apartment on Twelfth Street across from Eva and Peggy; and soon Eva, as she had with May Sarton, developed a warm relationship with the young woman. Actors often bored her with their endless talk of the theatre and career problems, but Le Gallienne was drawn to writers and stimulating conversation about books and ideas. She came to think of May and Madeleine as her children, and she was particularly proud and possessive of their writing. Perhaps because of Julie's death, she now moved easily into the role of nurturing mother.

"She loved me in a benign, maternal way," L'Engle said later. "She was incredibly kind and encouraging to me as a writer." With Madeleine there were no complicating personal entanglements, no girlish crush on an older woman, and Eva welcomed Madeleine into her family of women. A young, single woman alone in New York, Madeleine learned from her to beware of lusty young men who had "the honest blue eyes of the congenital liar." Le Gallienne confided in the empathetic L'Engle, revealing the most private details of her life, including the trauma of the rape and the agony of the burning.

Like writer Helen Boylston (the author of the Sue Barton books), who had spent a year backstage at the Civic to research her book *Carol Goes Backstage,* featuring a character based on Le Gallienne, L'Engle also drew on her experiences working with Eva. During the Broadway run of *Uncle Harry* and the national tour that followed, Madeleine drafted *The Small Rain,* her first novel. *The Small Rain* tells the poignant story of a girl's development into a woman and an artist. The girl's mother, a great musician who has suffered a devastating accident, is modeled on Le Gallienne and, like Eva's mother, is named Julie.

Le Gallienne revealed her artistic frustrations to Madeleine, and from Eva's reaction to each evening's performance, L'Engle learned, too, that "the artist is not separate from the work and therefore cannot judge it." Some nights Le Gallienne would enter the dressing room and say, "I gave a terrible performance this evening. I couldn't get the audience to respond to a thing," only to be interrupted by the enthusiasm of an old friend who said, "Eva, that was the best performance I've ever seen you give. You were superb!" Some nights she would "come bounding in," L'Engle remembered, exclaiming, "Oh, it went well tonight! I had them eating out of the palm of my hand!" Thelma Chandler, the stage manager, would then "almost invariably . . . knock on the door, poke her head in, and ask anxiously, 'Le G, are you all right?' "

Uncle Harry ran on Broadway until the summer of 1943, followed by a national tour. In the touring production, Marion Evensen played Hester to Le Gallienne's Lettie, receiving excellent notices for her portrait of the "poor, stormy older sister"—an apt description of her relationship with Eva. In town after town, the play drew good houses and excellent reviews. As she grew weary of the role and the long run, Le Gallienne perversely resented the good notices. "One would really think the damn play was important!"

She longed to put *Uncle Harry* behind her and work on *The Cherry Orchard,* which she and Peggy planned to produce with Carly Wharton on Broadway. While she was on tour, Le Gallienne reluctantly helped her partners find backers for the Chekhov play. She approached the task as if she were giving a performance. According to Peggy, at a party in Pittsburgh, Le Gallienne gave a "glowing and seductive account" of *The Cherry Orchard* to a wealthy man who had expressed interest. When she finished her act, the man said, "But I'm not interested in fruit."

Le Gallienne blanched. "Oh, it's not about fruit," she said. "It's about real estate."

The Pittsburgh man didn't invest, but enough investors were found to give *The Cherry Orchard* a commercial production on Broadway. With the help of her old Russian instructor Irina Skariatina, Le Gallienne made a new translation of the play. Chekhov's plays, Le Gallienne believed, "unfold with effortless spontaneity, like something observed in Nature—the growth of a plant, or the flight of a bird. In actual fact they are constructed with the utmost skill and precision. Action, words, sounds, silences, are meticulously and delicately balanced." The cast included Le Gallienne as Madame Ranevsky, Pepi Schildkraut as Gaev, Leona Roberts in her old role as Charlotta, and eighty-six-year-old A. G. Andrews as eighty-seven-year-old Firs. The classic play surprised them all and was a hit.

Le Gallienne shared the direction with Peggy Webster. It was the first time the two women had worked together, and Peggy called the experience a "fascinating labor of love." Since she knew the play so well, Eva provided the basic concept and supervised the early rehearsal period. As rehearsals progressed, Peggy took over the direction as well as the lighting and the orchestration of the offstage sounds. She also supplied what the critics had come to call the "Webster touch." She set the tone of the production at the beginning of the play. Two servant girls ran across the stage carrying a wicker hamper. The taller and clumsier of the girls (played by Madeleine L'Engle) suddenly tripped and fell flat. This bit of business announced that this was not a dreary, dead classic but a living, fresh comedy, as Chekhov had intended.

Critic Howard Barnes wrote that never before had Le Gallienne's playing been "so radiantly assured, so eloquent and moving." She was a reed-thin Lyubov Andreyevna, with pale, cameo features and enormous, heavy-lashed blue eyes. She looked lovely, but she felt that her portrayal did not measure up to Nazimova's definitive portrait in the earlier production at the Civic Repertory. No commercial production of Chekhov, she felt, with actors forced to play eight times a week, could ever be as satisfying as a production performed in repertory by a great company.

In late March, doctors told Le Gallienne that she had a large benign tumor and that she must have an immediate hysterectomy. On April 3, 1944, she left the company to have the operation. Peggy took over her part for several weeks, and it was "one of the most difficult things I have ever had to do," Peggy wrote later. "Her performance was subtle, moving, stylish, in the best sense; impossible to imitate, impossible to vary, basically, because the production had been molded to it." Tennessee Williams agreed with Webster's assessment, writing his friend James Laughlin that Peggy should not have taken the role. Williams thought Le Gallienne was graceful and charming as Ranevsky while Webster was awkward and masculine. And, Williams wondered, why was Webster directing Chekhov when there were young playwrights, like himself, who desperately wanted to be produced?

The national tour of *The Cherry Orchard* ran from September 1944 to January 1945. Hugh Franklin (who later married Madeleine L'Engle) joined the tour to play the student Trofimov. Le Gallienne hired a couple, Walt and Celina Wilson, to look after the house, garden, and animals, and Marion Evensen went along on

Eva (Madame Ranevsky) and Pepi Schildkraut (Gaev) in The Cherry Orchard, *1944*

the tour as a sort of double understudy: since Peggy was busy with her upcoming production of *The Tempest,* Marion served as Le Gallienne's companion and cook, and she also filled in onstage. On tour, Le Gallienne never stopped refining the production. "After the performance," Madeleine L'Engle recalled, "while I waited for Hugh, I would watch them walking to and fro at the back of the stage, either incorporating what Hugh had done into the play, or else discussing why it didn't work, and planning to try something else. I took this creative fluidity for granted, not understanding until later how generous and unusual was such openness."

The touring company of *The Cherry Orchard* was like a traveling dog show. Just weeks before her mother died, Eva had acquired a puppy, a Cairn terrier from her own kennel that she called Vixen. The dog became an extension of herself, helping to fill the void that had been left by Mam's death. Peggy joined them on the tour from time to time accompanied by her dog Susie, a sister of Vixen's; and Marion had Chico. What with Schildkraut's two Chihuahuas, Madeleine's poodle, Touche (who appeared in the play), an understudy's black poodle, stage manager Thelma Chandler's fox terrier, and the Varya's dachshund, sometimes the entire troupe traveled in the train's baggage car when their dogs were expelled from the passenger cars. During the Chicago run, Vixen and

Chico were denied admission at Chicago's finer hotels because of a rabies out-
break, and instead of kenneling the dogs, Eva stayed with them in a shabby hotel
under the el without a private bath and no room service. "If the inhabitants of
Dover can live in caves for three years," Le Gallienne declared, "I can live in the
'Planters Pub' for three weeks." Traveling home at the end of the tour, Le Gallienne refused to be separated from Vixen and Chico. She "fought her way into
a bonded mail van" with the dogs, and they all rode happily home as parcels.

WIIEN TIIE TOUR of *The Cherry Orchard* closed, Le Gallienne turned her at-
tentions to Peggy's production of *The Tempest,* which was in tryouts in Boston.
Two years before, Webster had directed the wildly successful *Othello* starring
Paul Robeson, José Ferrer, and Uta Hagen. Producing Shakespeare commercially
was a risk, but Cheryl Crawford, one of the few women producers working on
Broadway, agreed to undertake *The Tempest* after she heard Webster's production
plan and saw Le Gallienne's ingenious set design. Three years younger than Eva,
Crawford had worked with the Theatre Guild and was one of the founders of the
Group Theatre. In 1937, she quit the Group to produce on her own. She presented *Porgy and Bess,* which ran in New York and on the road for four years,
and, in 1943, *One Touch of Venus,* starring Mary Martin. A serious, scholarly
woman, Crawford had the reputation of a canny, close-mouthed manager who
kept costs low.

In interpreting *The Tempest,* Le Gallienne had been "intrigued by the unexpected affinity between Shakespeare and Ibsen; Prospero as compared to Solness, magic on the Norwegian mountains of *Peer Gynt,* magic in the 'still-vexed
Bermoothes,' the dramatic skill of beginning a play almost at the end of a story
and compressing it within the minds of its protagonists." Peggy rearranged and
trimmed the text and cut many of Ariel's lines, allowing the ballet dancer Vera
Zorina to express Ariel's spirit through dance. Arnold Moss, who had been an
apprentice at the Civic Repertory, played Prospero, and Peggy cast Canada Lee,
a gifted black actor, as Caliban. She ended the play, as she believed Shakespeare
intended, with Prospero's "We are such stuff as dreams are made on" speech. To
facilitate fluid, seamless scene changes and continuous action, Le Gallienne created a revolving island of sculpted rock and stone set against a blue cyclorama
with precipices, caves, and various playing areas that captured all the different
scenes and moods of the play. The Motleys "stooged" for her set design, since Le
Gallienne was not a member of the scenic artists' union, although she was
named in the playbill for the production idea.

At the New York opening on January 25, 1945, Le Gallienne sat tensely next to
Marion in the eighth row of the theatre. As she watched the turntable move to
reveal the magical island, she was thrilled at the realization of her set design. The

opening-night audience, however, packed with celebrities and others who came to be seen rather than to see, was "damnable . . . the horror of having to play to such people!" Afterwards, she went out with Peggy to await the notices, "& got tight which was stupid but we had it coming to us."

The notices were excellent, and the play was a hit. The collaboration of Webster, Crawford, and Le Gallienne had been harmonious, and the three women decided to join forces to launch a repertory theatre. First, though, Le Gallienne suffered her usual postpartum play depression and returned to Weston and collapsed. She spent several days in "the Black Hole of Calcutta." It would take her time to crawl out of it, but as she worked in the garden, took care of the animals, tried oil painting, and, more important, gave up drinking once again, she gradually came back "into the light." She marveled at the resilient Peggy, who was a heavy drinker and smoker but still kept a busy schedule, wrote endless letters, and unselfishly visited Cheryl Crawford, who was in the hospital. "How good she is—what a conscience," Eva wrote. "It must be wonderful to be so innately good & honest & true. Not to have ten thousand devils to combat in oneself all the time."

Following her usual pattern, after weeks of devoting herself to building up Le Gallienne, Evensen collapsed, beset by devils of her own. This time her lapse did not occur in the privacy of Weston, but during a trip to New York. While Eva kept various appointments, Marion disappeared and did not meet her for dinner at Twelfth Street. That night, when Le Gallienne returned to the apartment to pick up Marion for the drive to Weston, she found her passed out on the floor. Le Gallienne called Madeleine L'Engle to stay with Marion while she drove back alone to Weston that night to prepare for Cheryl Crawford and a friend, who were coming to spend the weekend. The next day, Marion, who had remarkable recuperative powers, took the train to Weston and felt well enough to clean house, go grocery shopping, and plan and cook a delicious Easter dinner. "She's not Norsk for nothing!" Le Gallienne exclaimed.

During the spring and summer of 1945, Le Gallienne stayed in Weston. She followed what she called her "old maid's routine" ("Thank God I don't have a parrot!") of arising early and having a leisurely breakfast in the Blue Room. With Vixen curled up in the chair beside her, she read the Bible or Kierkegaard for an hour, then began her day. Every night before she went to bed, she wrote in her diary and to Peggy, if Webster was out of town. "I wish to God she'd stay put for five minutes—but there's no hope of that," Eva felt. Often, she made quick trips to New York to see Peggy for a night or two and usually stayed up too late and drank and smoked too much, which left her exhausted. "I just can't take *anything* anymore. It's just hopeless," she decided, "I might as well make up my mind to become a saint like all the old devils do after a 'certain age'!" Eva worked several radio jobs; designed and built models for *The Merchant of Venice, The Three Sisters,* and *John Gabriel Borkman;* attended conferences with Peggy and

Cheryl for their proposed repertory theatre; read scripts every night and at least one or two books a week, usually history or biography; entertained guests almost every weekend; tended her garden; and prepared for her role in an upcoming fall production, *Therese,* to be directed by Peggy. Still, she convinced herself that she was not fully occupied and worried that she was wasting her time.

After her hysterectomy, she had entered menopause, what Mam had called "the difficult years," and she battled depression constantly. She told her diary that she was "so lonely & weary. I can't stand it any more. . . . I chopped a lot of wood—I tried to paint but could achieve nothing good. I pottered in the garden—but could concentrate on nothing—could enjoy nothing: an awful *nightmare* day." Peggy was away on a lecture tour, and Eva missed her terribly. Seeing her old friend Laurette Taylor in *The Glass Menagerie* failed to cheer her up. Either Laurette "wasn't playing well or else I'm crazy," she wrote. "Cheryl [Crawford] felt as I did. . . . Hepburn & Garbo sat in the row in front of us. What a strange face G. has. Beautiful but so tortured & discontented—not a nice face I thought. I felt so horribly let down." On May 9, though, Eva woke up "feeling so light-hearted & for a moment I couldn't think why—and then suddenly realized: the war in Europe is over! . . . It seemed too wonderful to grasp."

That summer, she refused to go to the Vineyard with Peggy for several weeks. "I guess I'm a selfish old pig!" she told herself. Eva preferred staying at home with Marion, who was being "wonderful." Marion spent several weeks in Cleveland that summer with her husband, who had lung cancer. Le Gallienne had encouraged her to go, but she felt lost without either Marion or Peggy.

Hating to be alone, Le Gallienne invited Mimsey or Alice De Lamar or Madeleine L'Engle for visits. She needed an audience, even if it was an audience of one, and even if it was just Vixen, her dog. When Vixen had to be hospitalized with a urinary infection, Eva became so distraught that Peggy cut her vacation short and drove home from the Vineyard to stay with her. Vixen recovered, but the news of Alla Nazimova's death on July 13 further depressed Le Gallienne. Nazimova was only sixty-six years old. Eva had always believed that Alla would live to be very old, and it was a sad loss.

Before rehearsals for *Therese* began in mid-August, Le Gallienne wondered, "Can I still act? I'm so frightened. God help me." The thriller by Thomas Job, adapted from Zola's novel *Thérèse Raquin,* was about an artist and his mistress, Therese, who murder Therese's husband. Peggy gathered a good cast. Her mother, eighty-year-old Dame May Whitty, came from Hollywood to play Madame Raquin, the murdered man's mother. Victor Jory and Le Gallienne acted the lovers. Marion Evensen auditioned for a small part and was devastated when Peggy gave the role to another actress.

Dame May Whitty stole the play and all the good reviews. "At eighty she had an energy and a vitality that put us younger people to shame," Le Gallienne

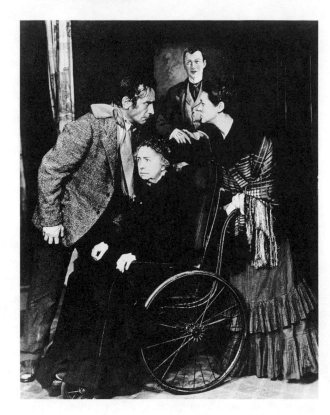

Left to right:
Victor Jory,
Dame May Whitty,
and Eva in
Peggy Webster's
1945 production
of Therese

wrote later. Dame May also had the best part. Famous for her wheelchair role in the movie *Night Must Fall,* Whitty spent the last act of *Therese* confined to a wheelchair.

The play ran until the end of the year. Le Gallienne earned more than twenty-five thousand dollars, which gave her a financial cushion until the opening of the American Repertory Theatre in September 1946—exactly twenty years after the founding of the Civic Repertory Theatre.

LIKE THE CIVIC REPERTORY THEATRE, the American Repertory Theatre began with great idealism and ended with an enormously successful production of *Alice in Wonderland.* There the resemblance ended.

In their autobiographies, each of the three women who created the ART left an account of the theatre's founding and demise which reflected her own motivation. Bored stiff with her producing chores, which consisted mostly of baby-sitting long-running plays, Cheryl Crawford wanted to provide a haven for culture—a place to develop plays and actors. Crawford was a zealot, but she was also a shrewd businesswoman, and she believed that the enterprise could make money. Cheryl's account is brisk, concise, and her theme is money— there wasn't enough of it. On the other hand, Peggy, who had come of age in English repertory, dreamed of creating an American version of Britain's Old Vic. Led by Laurence Olivier and Ralph Richardson, the English company had visited New York in 1944 and dazzled audiences with its productions and flawless ensemble playing. Why can't America have a theatre and actors like that? everyone wondered. Peggy's description of the fate of the American Repertory Theatre is an account of idealism destroyed. Webster's voice is filled with rage—at the critics, at incompetent technicians, and at unions. Eva's motivation, of course, in founding the theatre was to recreate the Civic Repertory, an alternative to Broadway. Her account is measured and logical, and her voice is dispassionate and detached. Her diaries tell another story.

A year before the American Repertory Theatre opened, Le Gallienne wrote that she had always hated "board meetings & committees—they never seem to achieve anything. . . . I don't think I'll get much joy out of the Rep. even if it really does come about. I'm not a good mixer." She was forced to mix, though, often summoned by Cheryl to attend conferences and meetings where she would sit bored and silent. To keep the peace with Peggy and Cheryl, Eva compromised constantly. A believer in the single vision of the artist, Le Gallienne loathed the "argle-bargle" of lawyers and accountants. Whenever she could, she left financial and organizational decisions to Cheryl and Peggy while she concentrated on the plays and casting. Thus, all the lessons Le Gallienne had learned, all the fruitful experience she had gained from the Civic Repertory, were not applied to the American Repertory.

In her private diaries, when she was angry about discrimination against women and the treatment of women, sometimes Le Gallienne sounded like a female chauvinist—an attitude that she was careful never to display in public. The hierarchical power structure of the theatre mirrored society in general, and men held most of the power. She resented the superior attitude of men generally, and the attitude of some homosexual men toward women made her even angrier. Heterosexual or homosexual, men were men, and Le Gallienne bristled at their dismissive, often patronizing attitude toward women. Le Gallienne was especially incensed about the treatment of "Gloria," a young actress friend. She told her diary that she "came poor thing to weep on my shoulder over her [husband] who has turned out to be a homosexual! . . . And now having used her during the lean days—having struck a lucky spell is calmly giving her the fond farewell! So typical of that kind of creature."

But Le Gallienne would always be particularly intolerant of liars, and anyone, male or female, who denied who they were. She measured the behavior of others against her own high standards of integrity that formed the core of who she was as an individual. Raised by a mother who accepted her daughter's sexuality, a mother who had taught her to honor her own nature and her own individuality, Le Gallienne had not hidden herself in a sham marriage or denied her sexual nature, and she was critical of anyone who did. "She was tremendously brave herself and demanded of others that they be so," said May Sarton.

At the conferences she attended on behalf of the ART, to raise money or deal with unions or theatre owners, women were in a minority, and when dealing with men, Le Gallienne often thought herself a "superior being . . . one can't help it when faced with such ignorant unfair dolts." Eva was loyal to women— no matter if they were heterosexual or homosexual. Le Gallienne defined herself as an artist, and she called herself one of those "peculiar intermediate sex creatures with a tragic sense of service. (I guess because we can't make children to leave behind us.)" She took sly delight in playing with language, and she coined her own secret words of identification and endearment for male and female homosexuals—women who loved other women she nicknamed "buckaroos," and homosexual men she dubbed "homse-momses."

Unless they created their own opportunities, women found it difficult to get jobs. In choosing to hire women instead of men, Le Gallienne was attempting to redress that imbalance. Also, like calls to like, and wounded by bitchy backstage gossip that characterized her, Peggy, and Cheryl as "dykes," she told her diary that it was "inevitable that the three of us should have mud slung at us & I think it's better to have 100% *females* with us than *fairies.*"

The Civic Repertory had proven that a nonprofit, subsidized, tax-exempt repertory theatre could succeed in New York. Success could be ensured, however, only if the subsidy was large and ongoing. Instead of following the nonprofit path, the three women followed the advice of various experts who told them that a nonprofit corporation would be too difficult to set up and, further, that "a show which was a 'charity' came under the head of good works and must therefore, automatically, be bad." Instead, the ART was chartered as a corporation, "capitalized at $300,000, on a share-selling basis"—an adequate amount, Cheryl Crawford felt, to mount six productions and provide a reserve. Le Gallienne believed that the decision was wrong, but Crawford was comfortable with the arrangement—the Group Theatre had also competed commercially on Broadway. And so the first compromise was made.

The initials of American Repertory Theatre spelled "art," a most "unpopular word," said Le Gallienne, especially in a country where "any sincere effort to embark on what is often drearily called a 'high-minded attempt' to establish the equivalent of an art-theatre is . . . discouraged and ridiculed." Yet there were still enough wealthy people interested in art to enable them to raise the $300,000. Le Gallienne secured her portion of the money from her usual backers, like Mary Bok Zimbalist, who donated ten thousand dollars. After lunching with her patron the producer and philanthropist Joseph Verner Reed, Peggy appeared with a check for $100,000. Cheryl looked outside New York to Hollywood for cash and found enough money to finance the entire venture if the movie moguls could have voting rights and options on actors and plays. Le Gallienne refused to accept those terms. "I'm scared of that kind of money," she told Cheryl. "Those men have been trained all their lives to think in diametrically the opposite way—we don't want them having any 'say' in our theatre." Mrs. Sam Goldwyn invested five thousand dollars, William Paley gave ten thousand, and small amounts came in from Girl Scout troops, college fraternities, women's clubs, and individual donors "from Iceland, from Zaleski, Ohio, from Kent, England."

With most of the money raised, they looked for other name actors to join Le Gallienne and Webster. "Wonderful parts! Leading roles in any great classic you might wish to play," they told the thirty-seven "names" on Peggy Webster's list—including Katharine Hepburn, Vincent Price, Susan Hayward, Michael Chekhov, Barbara Bel Geddes, José Ferrer, Montgomery Clift, Geraldine Fitzgerald, and Greer Garson.

When they heard that the top salary was five hundred dollars a week and would require a two-year commitment—one year in New York and another on a national tour—the excuses began: "Hollywood contracts, prior commitments, children, husbands, wives—yes, even dogs!" said Le Gallienne.

Victor Jory suggested that they approach Greta Garbo. "That would be something!" exclaimed Le Gallienne. "I don't think she'd dare." Mary Martin seriously considered joining the company; Cheryl and Peggy thought she could play Shaw's *Caesar and Cleopatra* and Rosalind in *As You Like It*. Le Gallienne was not enthusiastic about the idea. "She herself is nice—but oh God! *Not* Cleopatra. She could never be Egypt—except in a musical comedy version. Just a *bonne fille*—with laquered hair *orange* coloured—Talented & charming in her *own* medium but I don't think she'll ever get on as a great actress—nor do I think she should—she's fine as she is—why not go on being superlatively good in her own line."

Le Gallienne was furious when Pepi Schildkraut turned them down. Schildkraut had signed a three-year contract with Republic Studios in Hollywood, a decision he later bitterly regretted. José Ferrer had been part of the initial discussions, but he'd had a falling-out with Peggy during *Othello,* and he told the women that he "didn't want to come into our house."

It was the same old problem, Le Gallienne realized. She had faced a similar situation when Richard Waring refused to play Laertes to her Hamlet. The "good" men did not "want to work for and with a woman. . . . [They] can't bear a woman to know anything (let alone more than they do) or to have ideas & opinions of her own! It's a great pity—for it hampers one's work very seriously. I imagine this might be different . . . in Scandinavia where there seems to exist a real equality of the Sexes. It certainly doesn't exist here."

The actor they needed for the ART was someone like the Eva Le Gallienne of twenty years ago—a young person who was an artistic genius and a Broadway star with a burning desire to play great and small roles in repertory, and no desire at all to become wealthy. They searched in vain, because such a person, male or female, was rare in any age, and did not exist in the American theatre in the mid-1940s.

There was one young actor that Le Gallienne was convinced had the "spark of true genius, who might, given the right opportunities and training, become one of the really great actors of our time." In February 1946 she saw a performance of *Truckline Cafe* featuring Richard Waring. In the last act, she was "electrified by a remarkable young man who played a scene with such violent and uncompromising truth that on his exit we all applauded for at least two minutes." She saw in the program that the actor's name was Marlon Brando. She left the theatre "convinced that here was one of those rare talents that very occasionally emerge full-fledged from the hand of God." A few weeks later she saw Brando play Marchbanks to Katharine Cornell's Candida. "It was impossible to believe that this was the big, clumsy, rough, rather brutal young man of *Truckline Cafe*. In *Candida* he seemed small and slender, mercurial and possessed of an almost lyrical beauty. Yet this transformation was achieved by no external means; it came solely from a change within."

One night after a *Candida* performance in April 1946, Richard Waring brought Brando down to Twelfth Street to meet Peggy and Le Gallienne. For two hours, they tempted Brando with featured billing in the American Repertory, where he would master various acting styles and play parts ranging from Treplev in *The Seagull* to Osvald in *Ghosts* to Hamlet. Brando kicked off his shoes to reveal "dirty socks of a hideous shade of green" and sat slumped in a chair. From time to time he grunted and grabbed a handful of grapes from a nearby bowl, "punctuating his silence by occasionally spitting out a seed." His manners were atrocious, but Le Gallienne could "forgive genius much." The French word *sauvage* applied to Brando, she thought; "they use it about animals—and people too—who are wary and shy of the approach of strangers. It implies a fear of being caught, of being tamed, of the encroachment of another creature on one's inner privacy." She understood him because she felt that way herself, except she knew how to soften those feelings under a veil of manners and graciousness.

Peggy and Eva wooed Brando again over dinner at Twelfth Street prepared by Peggy's French-Canadian cook, who fell in love with him. Brando brought "a sausage concoction" that he had made. Finally, Brando said no to the American Repertory. He sent Peggy a jar of shrimp paste and a note: "You are all unusual women the likes of which one doesn't get the opportunity to know in a life's span. I wish you God's grace and speed. Marlon." The "machinery of show business was already in action," Le Gallienne wrote later. "Brando was doomed to the only kind of success we recognize." Peggy sighed with disappointment, "Still no American Olivier."

Le Gallienne and Peggy flirted briefly with John Gielgud, who brought a friend and spent a weekend in Weston. "Gielgud was very jolly & affable & immensely chatty & amusing—hell bent on be-glamoring the young man—so he gave us a good time too!" said Le Gallienne. Although Gielgud enjoyed, he recalled, a "delightful week-end" with Eva and Peggy, he was not interested in joining the ART. "He still worships the Bitch Goddess Success," observed Le Gallienne.

Le Gallienne, Webster, and Crawford faced the manager's dilemma—they couldn't choose the plays until they had the actors, but they couldn't get the actors until they knew the plays. Finally, the women were able to assemble a company of excellent actors, which dictated their choosing, Peggy said, "team plays, allowing each important actor a worthwhile part, but not offering us the chance to try *Romeo and Juliet,* for instance, because we didn't have either." Walter Hampden, noted for his classic roles, especially his definitive Cyrano, joined them, along with Victor Jory, Ernest Truex, Richard Waring, and Philip Bourneuf.

Peggy and Le Gallienne clashed over whether or not Marion should be given a job. Peggy was being "extremely tiresome," wrote Le Gallienne, in claiming that the company could not afford to hire another principal woman. With Walt and Celina Wilson taking care of the house and garden in Weston, Marion didn't have a lot to do, and Le Gallienne knew that she needed to be kept busy. During the run of *Therese,* disappointed at not being cast in the play, and separated from Eva, who stayed primarily in New York during the run, Marion turned increasingly to alcohol. When Le Gallienne drank, it was usually for a few days after an intense period of work or to make small talk easier in a social situation, and with her formidable willpower she could simply stop drinking for weeks and months at a time. When Marion drank, her aim was to pass out, and her capacity for alcohol was tremendous—on a typical binge she consumed a whole bottle of Scotch and one of gin. Attempts to talk about the problem led nowhere. "As usual when she tried to express what she was feeling," Le Gallienne said, "—she got all confused & many of the old accusations came out. She's putting up such a good fight but I don't think she feels well." Le Gallienne accepted part of the blame for Marion's drinking, but when Eva thought "of how I've ruined my life it makes me weep." By the end of April 1946, Le Gallienne believed that it was a "hopeless situation—I honestly don't know what to do. I frankly would be better off alone—but I can't bear to do anything to hurt her too much. I do wish we could make a clean sweep all round—it would be best for all of us." Le Gallienne hated confrontation—"trofast og glad" was too ingrained—and there was no clean sweep. On the other hand, there were still

times, particularly when Peggy was absent (which had become increasingly frequent), when Eva appreciated Marion's company, her cooking, her devoted
pampering. Marion's mood improved in May 1946, when Peggy finally relented
and gave her a job with the ART playing small parts and understudying.

From hundreds of eager young actors who auditioned, Le Gallienne, Webster,
and Crawford chose Eli Wallach, Anne Jackson, Julie Harris, John Straub, Efrem
Zimbalist Jr., and William Windom, who would all use their experience with
the repertory as a stepping stone to long and successful careers. The ART still
needed a young leading woman. Clifford Odets suggested that they audition
June Duprez, who had appeared in the movie *None But the Lonely Heart.* Le Gallienne quickly volunteered to go to Hollywood and talk to Duprez, for it would
give her an opportunity to see Jo. As plans for the repertory went forward, Eva's
thoughts had turned more and more to Jo. They planned to revive *Alice in Wonderland,* and as Eva worked on it, she wondered how she would ever be able to
do the play without Jo. Now that she was embroiled in complicated relationships with Peggy and Marion, Eva longed for the simple idyll she had shared
with Jo at the old house.

On Sunday, March 3, Peggy and Marion helped Eva pack for her week's stay
in Hollywood. Peggy drove her to the airport and phoned ahead to tell Jo that
Le Gallienne would be staying with Dame May Whitty in Hollywood. The next
day Jo picked her up at May's. "We were together for five hours—which seemed
like five minutes," Le Gallienne told her diary. "How we *belong.* Nothing will
ever change that—it just *is.*" Jo's husband had forbidden her to see or correspond
with Eva, and Le Gallienne was not allowed to visit Jo in her home. "The man
must be a lunatic," Eva believed, "but of course I must not criticize or complain
since it's all my fault." A dead-end street off Sepulveda became their daily meeting place for the rest of the week. Thinking of Peter Pan and Wendy, Le Gallienne called it their island. Eva and Jo sat in the car and talked for hours. "I
wanted to see her because it was fascinating to talk with her," Jo said later.
Hutchinson had worked steadily as a film actor, most notably in *Oil for the
Lamps of China, The Story of Louis Pasteur,* and *My Son, My Son.* She had also
worked as an acting coach at Columbia. "If only that poor misguided man knew
that he only makes it all much more romantic and exciting," said Le Gallienne.
"How *livid* he would be. But for *her* sake I only *pray* he never finds out."

When she wasn't with Jo, Le Gallienne scheduled meetings with June Duprez,
working with her on various roles and using all her Sven-Gallienne skills to persuade her to join the American Rep. Le Gallienne departed California with her
mission accomplished: she had convinced Duprez to join the ART. Her reward
for her efforts was the time she had spent with Jo. "Enchanted hours," she wrote,
"and I can't be too grateful for them. My throat aches & tears come to my eyes
when I think they must last for a long time."

THE REPERTORY PART of the American Repertory Theatre lasted six months. It opened in Princeton, New Jersey, in September 1946 and closed in New York in February 1947. Four plays—Shakespeare's *Henry VIII,* Ibsen's *John Gabriel Borkman,* Barrie's *What Every Woman Knows,* and Shaw's *Androcles and the Lion*—were presented in repertory. Single runs of *Yellow Jack* and *Alice in Wonderland* extended the ART four more months, into June 1947. All $300,000 of the original capital was lost.

Was ART a failure? Financially, yes. Artistically, no. Eva Le Gallienne, Cheryl Crawford, and Peggy Webster individually possessed vast theatrical knowledge and expertise. Collectively, however, they diluted rather than augmented one another's strengths. Le Gallienne hated compromise, but one compromise followed another. Eva compromised with Crawford about ticket prices, and the ART prices were scaled as high as Broadway's. Compromises were also made on play choices. Instead of introducing new plays, the ART compromised on revivals. Crawford found a new play called *Mother Courage* by Bertolt Brecht and thought it would be perfect for Le Gallienne. Peggy and Eva rejected it. Cheryl also discovered *The Sign of the Archer,* a new play by an unknown writer. Peggy and Eva thought the script wasn't right for their company. The young writer was Arthur Miller, and the play, retitled *All My Sons* and directed by Elia Kazan, became a hit on Broadway. Le Gallienne wanted to do *The Merchant of Venice,* arguing that the gentiles acted like Nazis and Shylock possessed nobility of character, but Cheryl thought the play was anti-Semitic and would create too much controversy. Peggy suggested *Henry VIII* as a compromise.

Others refused to compromise. Designer David Ffolkes, who had been released from a Japanese prison camp, where he had spent four years as a prisoner of war, designed lavish sets and costumes for *Henry VIII* and went dangerously over budget. The costumes were magnificent and won Ffolkes a Tony Award, but they were so heavy and uncomfortable that when the women left the stage they simply stepped out of their gowns, leaving them standing rigidly in place until their next entrance.

Le Gallienne approached the stagehands' union, Local No. 1, to work out the number of stagehands they would need to run the repertory. At the Civic, the union had allowed her to hire a minimum number of permanent workers and add others as needed. For months, the union evaded a decision. At a meeting on June 10, 1946, Le Gallienne appealed to them again, explaining that Crawford needed to complete the budget. At the end of the two-hour meeting, one of the men slapped Eva on the back and said cheerfully, "If we want you to have your little theatre, you'll have it, and if we don't want you to, you won't—see?" Fortunately, Le Gallienne was not holding a rapier and the man escaped with his life; but never, she said, had she "prayed for self-control as I did at that moment."

In October, shortly before the New York opening, with the budget already set, the union announced that the ART would be required to hire the maximum number of stagehands—twenty-eight to run *Henry VIII.* The ART hadn't opened yet but already was over budget. Since every department had to hire the maximum number of people needed, sometimes eight unnecessary men stood around doing nothing. The union also used its option to send different people to work the show from night to night, which was disastrous for a smoothly functioning backstage operation.

The musicians' union decided that *Henry VIII* was a "drama with music," requiring eight musicians, who all had to be paid for not working in the other plays. Peggy calculated that they spent $1,275 a week for "nonexistent work," a sum "just about equal," she wrote, "to the combined salaries of Crawford, Le Gallienne, Webster and Walter Hampden."

PRELIMINARY REHEARSALS of the first three plays were held in Weston in August, which meant that Victor Jory, Walter Hampden, Richard Waring, and June Duprez, along with Peggy and Marion, were all in residence in Weston. Le Gallienne was plagued by doubts, and she longed for the confidence of her youth. Her diaries at this time sound a self-pitying note. "It just seems to me I no longer *have* anything to give—perhaps a spring broke somewhere long ago. I don't believe I'll ever amount to much now. Strange—one started with such high hopes—and now I'm getting old & have achieved nothing." With so many people around, her nerves failed her—and her body, too, when her "sacred iliack" (as Mam had called it) slipped out.

Le Gallienne roused herself by thinking of how pleased Duse would be that she was once more "en pleine bataille." In August 1946, the entire company of the ART assembled for the first meeting and rehearsal at the International Theatre on Columbus Circle, which would be their new home. Cheryl Crawford made a welcoming speech, Peggy read *Henry VIII* to the company, and the company read back. Champagne flowed, photographers snapped pictures, and through it all Le Gallienne didn't "in any way push [herself] forward." She believed that she was not the leader, and she was filled with sad, "nostalgic thoughts" for the Civic Rep.

Eva soon shook off the sadness, the nostalgia, and the doubts in the all-consuming work of rehearsing the first three plays. She was playing three distinctly different parts: Ella Rentheim in *John Gabriel Borkman* (which she also directed and translated), Queen Katherine in *Henry VIII,* and Comtesse de la Briere in *What Every Woman Knows.* The work of the other actors inspired her, particularly that of Walter Hampden, when "the old lion in him leaped out with great power—and I was very happy to see it!" The trick with the fine old actors, she realized, is "to make them happy and confident—& that releases in them springs that even they thought had dried up."

Le Gallienne approved of the way Peggy handled the rehearsals, except for a few days when Peg suddenly decided to give up smoking and became "violently disagreeable." Le Gallienne smoked, too, but privately. Peggy had even appeared—most unattractively, Le Gallienne thought—in a photograph in *The New York Times* with a cigarette dangling from her mouth. Either way, smoking or not smoking, it "was great (and most unusual)" to have Peggy to lean on, Le Gallienne felt.

Peggy found playing Mrs. Borkman difficult, and she depended on Le Gallienne's understanding of Ibsen. Thinking of the play as a sustained piece of music, Le Gallienne used a turntable set and played the production without intermission. "Her direction," Peggy wrote, "was vastly revealing; her performance of Ella Rentheim moving, delicate and entirely perceptive. The rest of us felt like oafs." Victor Jory, who played Borkman, confessed to Peggy that "I stand there in the second act, alone, waiting for her to knock on the door, and sometimes I pray that she won't come in."

Efrem Zimbalist Jr. recalled that "Peggy had this marvelous background that breathed theatre. When she talked to you or directed you, it was as if all the centuries and traditions of the British theatre were there to instruct you. She was Elizabethan, boisterous, and bawdy." Le Gallienne was "more refined and internal," Zimbalist said. "All of her things were very bold and forthright and on the table and looking straight with the eyes; there was nothing covered. She had the most beautiful hands on the stage, absolutely stunning; offstage they were not beautiful. The audience never knew there was anything wrong."

After two weeks of rehearsals, Le Gallienne was "so happy in this work & so is Peg—& she seems calmer & more serene. . . . No matter what happens we will all have had this."

DESPITE THE advance publicity, the articles, and the interviews, which attempted to prepare the public and the critics for the repertory and the long-term plans of the ART, when the first three plays opened the week of November 6, 1946—three new productions played by the same company in rotating repertory—the critics and the audience treated the unusual event as yet another play opening on Broadway.

Brooks Atkinson reviewed the first three plays and damned the company with faint praise. *John Gabriel Borkman,* he said, was a "brilliant group performance, orchestrated like a living work of art"; the other plays were impressive, interesting, and intelligent—in other words, worthy, dull, and good for you. The production and acting of *Henry VIII* were lauded, but Shakespeare was blasted for writing a bad play. Critics generally agreed that Helen Hayes had been better than June Duprez in *What Every Woman Knows*. *Androcles and the Lion* was a hit, but just to break even, the ART had to sell out the house every night—an impossible feat. As the deficit grew larger, Cheryl Crawford had nightmares about money. Le Gallienne had convinced her to lower prices for some seats, and on Sunday, November 17, the matinee of *What Every Woman Knows* was sold out. In her diary entry for that day, Le Gallienne wrote:

> It was [a] *wonderful* audience therefore a grand performance—at least we all enjoyed it. . . . Atkinson had a rather silly article in the times about Rep—in which he said some very fine things about [*Borkman*] but the strange thing is that while he says the mood is superbly sustained & the whole production is brilliant & wonderful, it never occurs to him to say a *word* about the fact that *someone* must have been responsible for all this! If Kazan or Bob Lewis had done it they would have been hailed as geniuses! Ah well! They're very queer these so-called critics. Peg is so depressed & mizzy that it really gets my goat. What's the use of doing this work for nothing if we don't enjoy it—& she said she *wanted* to do it. . . . Home before 1 a.m. . . . wish I could stay here.

News of the ART's troubles quickly circulated, and the theatre community rallied, but it was too late. The American Theatre Wing contributed five thousand dollars, Helen Hayes and Dorothy McGuire each donated one thousand dollars, and others chipped in with smaller amounts. Actors' Equity gave five thousand dollars to the ART through the American National Theatre and Academy. Since Peggy Webster was an ANTA board member, a "lunatic-fringe" of the union, led by actor Frank Fay, who had earlier accused Webster and Mady Christians of being "pinkos," demanded that the money be given back. Eva and Peggy began receiving abusive postcards threatening them with investigations by the FBI if they didn't return the money to Equity. Le Gallienne wrote a polite letter to Fay, suggesting that the whole matter could be settled if he would simply pay her the money he still owed her for appearing in his vaudeville show several years earlier, and she would then give the money to Equity. Fay did not reply to her letter. Le Gallienne wrote John D. Rockefeller proposing that the ART be housed at the United Nations. Rockefeller replied that he had no control over how the United Nations used the land he had given them.

By January 1947 Cheryl Crawford had given up; ill with the flu, she took to her bed and read Thoreau. She wouldn't formally resign from the ART until June, but she returned to commercial producing, putting together a production of *"Brigadamndoon,"* as Peggy and Le Gallienne called it. When she heard that *Brigadoon* had an advance sale of five hundred thousand dollars, Le Gallienne complained, "What's the use of trying to do anything fine in this Godforsaken country—all they really want are musicals." The canny Cheryl Crawford sensed that the future of Broadway lay with musicals. *Brigadoon* joined an impressive lineup of musicals on Broadway—*Carousel, Oklahoma!, Annie Get Your Gun,* and *Finian's Rainbow* were all enjoying good runs.

Le Gallienne wanted to quit, too. On January 11, 1947, she became forty-eight. She felt old and tired and discouraged. A month earlier, her friend Laurette Taylor, who had made a spectacular comeback in *The Glass Menagerie,* died. "I'm glad she had that great triumph before she went," Le Gallienne wrote. "Poor thing—she had a tough & lonely battle."

Le Gallienne and Peggy contemplated leaving the theatre altogether. They decided to "ask Joe Reed to allow her 5000 a year & Mrs. B. to allow me 5 & we'll promise to stay quiet & write & paint & never start another theatre! It would save them alot of money in the end!" But Peggy and Eva weren't quitters, and they soldiered on. Le Gallienne trudged through a snowstorm on New Year's Day, 1947, to East Sixty-eighth Street to see the Marquis de Cuevas, who owned the International Theatre, to plead for money or a break on the rent. "I've never seen such Proust atmosphere," Le Gallienne wrote. "He is *pathetic*—seems quite vague & lost & bewildered . . . he belongs to quite another century. The [Marquesa] was lying in bed—covered with a vast sable throw. I felt like saying: 'Just let me have *that*—it would help!' "

What sustained Le Gallienne was what had always sustained her—the work itself and the communion with an audience. On Saturday, January 18, 1947, she played two performances of *Henry VIII.* The matinee "went marvellously—a wonderful house. The applause was electric at the end." That evening the response was so warm that she decided to speak to the audience about the ART. "I went right out on the apron & the applause that greeted me was quite overwhelming. I may not be a critic's pet—but the public do like me—and of the two I choose *that.*"

Producer Rita Hassan stepped in and underwrote *Alice in Wonderland,* the final production of the ART. Starring the dancer Bambi Linn as Alice, with Le Gallienne as the White Queen, Peggy Webster as the Red Queen, Eli Wallach as the Duck and the Two of Spades, and Julie Harris as the White Rabbit, the production repeated the success of the play's Civic Repertory premiere. Unfortunately, the White Queen's rule still applied: "Jam tomorrow, and jam yesterday, but *never* jam today." The play was burdened with huge expenses, including carrying twenty-eight union stagehands, more than were used on *Brigadoon.* The play earned as much money per week as a Broadway musical. During the week of May 24, the production grossed $21,250.40, but after paying all expenses the

Radio personality Mary Margaret McBride interviewing Peggy Webster (left)
and Eva (center) about the American Repertory Theatre's recording of
Alice in Wonderland

net profit was $1.22. The closing notice went up, and, like the Civic Rep, the American Rep's final show was *Alice in Wonderland.*

Years later, Eli Wallach said, "I treasured that year in the Rep company, because in the space of seven months, I played Cromwell in *Henry VIII,* I was a villager in *What Every Woman Knows,* Spintho in *Androcles,* a soldier in *Yellow Jack,* and those roles in *Alice.* . . . I thought Miss Le Gallienne was a pioneer and a fighter, and I admired her greatly."

Julie Harris didn't get to know Le Gallienne well, for Harris held herself apart. She thought that "Miss Le Gallienne was the kind of actress who created a great adoration for herself," and she didn't want to be drawn in by Sven-Gallienne. But "I loved her acting," Harris recalled. Le Gallienne's eye for young talent, usually so acute, did not spot anything special in Julie Harris. Le Gallienne's pattern as a young actress had been to hero-worship and study other artists; perhaps she felt that Harris was not paying her the proper respect. After an evening of working with Julie, who was understudying Bambi Linn in *Alice,* Le Gallienne wrote that "she certainly made one even more appreciative of Bambi! She's so in-

*To accept her 1947 Outstanding Woman in the Arts Award, Eva (standing behind
President Truman) wore one of the gowns she wore as Hedda Gabler. Other women
honored included (from left to right) Agnes E. Meyer (Public Service), Dr. Esther
Caukin Brunauer (International Relations), Dr. Helen Brook Taussig (Science),
and Beatrice Blackmer Gould (magazine editing).*

telligent, conscientious, but oh so dreary & dry!" The sight of the young, fresh,
dedicated Julie Harris with her future before her might have depressed Le Gallienne. "It's stupid to mind getting old," Eva told her diary, "but I find I do—I
didn't think I would."

"Le Gallienne had wonderfully high standards," said Efrem Zimbalist Jr. "She
would not bend. But you know that must have put a lot of people off. She hated
show business. She had a code of ethics, and I think later it separated her from a
lot of things that could have come her way."

Honors and awards continued to come Le Gallienne's way, though. In April
1947, she traveled to Washington, D.C., to accept the Women's National Press
Club Award as the Outstanding Woman of the Year in the Arts. President Truman presented her with the award at the ceremony, which was followed by a
reception and, Eva complained, endless handshaking. On May 2, the Drama
League honored her with an inscribed silver bowl for her activity with the Amer-

ican Repertory Theatre and for her brilliant career. "The whole business was very trying to me," she confided to her diary, "—though of course it was all very well meant. I felt rather like an old lady getting a consolation prize—& wanted to say 'Why am I holding this empty dish?'! That dull little Cedric Hardwicke presented me with the thing & we've *nothing* in common—I spoke very badly because I felt embarrassed & miserable. Helen [Hayes] presented the medal to Ingrid Bergman—they were both *charming* about it. *Nice* people." Le Gallienne the cat slunk home. She gave Vixen the silver bowl to use as her water dish.

PEGGY WEBSTER pointed out later that New York was the worst place to try to start a new theatre. In addition to the enormous expense, there was no sense of community, and there was tremendous competition from commercial theatres. Coincidentally, just as the ART was failing in New York, in the summer of 1947, Margo Jones founded a small, nonprofit theatre-in-the-round in Dallas, Texas, dedicated to performing new plays and classics. Jones's resident company opened with William Inge's first play, *Farther Off from Heaven* (later reworked and renamed *The Dark at the Top of the Stairs*), followed by the world premiere of Tennessee Williams's *Summer and Smoke*. Supported by the powerful critic John Rosenfield and by Dallas's wealthy patrons, and chartered as a nonprofit organization like the Civic Repertory, Margo Jones's theatre would become the cornerstone of the resident theatre movement. The thirty-five-year-old Jones, called "the Texas Tornado" by her friend Williams, had been inspired by the writings and example of Le Gallienne and by Hallie Flanagan's Federal Theatre Project. When Le Gallienne toured Texas in 1939, it's likely that she met Margo Jones. Le Gallienne noted in her diary that Texas theatre women were "intelligent & full of pluck & sense and a kind of aspiration." In speeches and articles Margo Jones's championing of a subsidized, nonprofit theatre dedicated to new plays and classics echoed Le Gallienne's themes. During the next few decades the resident theatre movement would sweep the country, but any hope for the great national repertory theatre that Le Gallienne had envisioned, a theatre to stand equally with the best of European national theatres, a showcase for America's theatrical art, died once again with the closing of the ART.

Still, despite disappointing setbacks, Eva and Peggy refused to give up. Before the *Alice* company disbanded, RCA Victor made recordings of the show, but then "shrouded their existence in such profound mystery," Le Gallienne said, "that I doubt if more than a dozen people have ever heard them." In 1947, Crawford poured her idealism into the Actors Studio, which she co-founded with her former Group Theatre associates Elia Kazan and Robert Lewis. Although the intent of the Actors Studio was to train a new generation of theatre actors, most of the Studio alumni achieved success in movies—an art form that helped to marginalize the theatre even further.

ON SEPTEMBER 15, 1947, while she was rehearsing *Alice* in Boston, Le Gallienne received a call from critic Ward Morehouse, who told her that Richard Le Gallienne had died in his sleep in Menton, France. Eva wasn't surprised. Although neither Eva nor Hesper had seen or heard from their father in over fifteen years, friends kept them informed about Richard. He had been failing for some months. Under the watchful, possessive eye of his wife, Irma, eighty-two-year-old Richard had spent his last days sitting in the garden or "wandering up and down the room rubbing his fingers lovingly over the backs of his books." According to the death certificate, Richard died of "exhaustion and old age."

Her father was gone. The usually articulate Le Gallienne was at a loss for words when it came to describing her feelings for Richard. When Eva misbehaved as a child, her mother had told her, "You're just like your father." As a teenager in New York, she had known Richard as a scholarly man, a dedicated writer with short, gray hair, who had been kind and loving. The last time she had seen him, in his Paris studio, she was thirty-two and recovering from her burns, and Richard was drunk, wild-eyed, and a sexual predator.

Eva had stopped competing with Richard long ago—she had eclipsed him as an artist, and knew it. Hesper agreed with her that Richard was not a first-class writer. "I think Eva writes better than he did," Hesper asserted, "her style is firmer & deeper." Although Eva's feelings were confused and ambivalent, she was pleased at Richard's obituaries. He received "wonderful 'notices' . . . a picture and full column in the *Times* & a picture & *two* columns in the *Herald*."

A few days later Le Gallienne was so ill that she believed she would die. Even though *Alice* was popular with audiences and critics, the touring production could not make money for the producers, and the show closed in Boston. Le Gallienne had "the worst attack of bile I've ever had . . . vomiting and tail going at the same time." At that time, Peggy learned that her mother, Dame May Whitty, was in the final stages of cancer. She died a few months later. Peggy and Le Gallienne were financially and emotionally drained and physically and spiritually exhausted. It was not a good time to make career decisions.

When producer Louis Singer offered in November to continue ART under his management with productions of *Hedda Gabler* and *Ghosts,* Le Gallienne at first declined. After she learned that Singer was interested in another actress who wanted to do the plays (a standard producer's ploy), Le Gallienne's competitive spirit asserted itself. Singer's proposal would be a way to keep the ART alive, and Eva needed the money. She agreed to a tour and a four-week run of the plays in

Hedda Gabler, 1948

New York. She would direct *Hedda,* and Peggy took on *Ghosts.* Herbert Berghof acted Judge Brack, and Efrem Zimbalist Jr. and his wife, Emily McNair, played Lovborg and Thea. Merle Maddern, who had been Eva's first friend in America, needed work desperately, and Le Gallienne gave her the part of Berte, Hedda's maid. Marion Evensen played her old role of Aunt Julie.

The out-of-town reviews of the plays were good, especially for *Hedda Gabler.* Perhaps the reviewers were being kind, but no one mentioned that a forty-eight-year-old Hedda might be too old to be pregnant. Wearing a blond wig and looking girlishly slim, onstage Le Gallienne appeared much younger than her years, and she knew the role of Hedda thoroughly. She did not know Mrs. Alving in *Ghosts.* In preparing a performance, Le Gallienne often thought about the character and read and prepared for several years before actually acting the part. Although she had translated *Ghosts,* she had not given herself time to understand all the nuances of Mrs. Alving and to work out the character. Eva's vivid memories of Duse's Mrs. Alving intruded on her interpretation of the role. Eva considered her performance in *Ghosts* half-baked, and she didn't want to take the play into New York. When she lacked confidence in herself and in her work, Le Gallienne became snappish and critical of other actors, and in an atmosphere of uncertainty and fear no one performed well.

Ghosts opened on February 16, 1948, at the Cort Theatre. In his review of her performance, George Jean Nathan wrote perhaps the most accurate observation he ever made of her: "Like truth and pine needles," he said, "Eva Le Gallienne crushed to earth will rise again." The critics agreed that Le Gallienne was as high-minded as a nun, possessed extraordinary tenacity and superior intelligence, and that her productions were honest and clear, but the critics were thoroughly sick of Hedda and Mrs. Alving and syphilis and Ibsen. The plays were stale, Peggy Webster's direction was stale, they said, and consequently the notices were stale. Several of the critics padded their reviews with a long parade of all the Heddas and Mrs. Alvings they had seen over the decades. One mentioned that Le Gallienne couldn't carry the plays all by herself; another said that she looked remarkably like Lana Turner. Disregarding that Ibsen was a metaphorical poet as well as a realist, Howard Barnes made the statement that *Ghosts* could not have been written after the discovery of penicillin.

None of these reviews were pasted into Le Gallienne's scrapbooks. Understandably, jaded critics often forget that classic plays must be rediscovered by each new generation. There were people in Le Gallienne's audience who had never seen *Hedda Gabler* or *Ghosts* and knew nothing of Ibsen. Some of these people wrote letters expressing their pleasure at seeing Le Gallienne's work. Her loyal fans from the Civic Repertory and ART also wrote to tell her how much they liked the productions and to express their dismay at the critical response. These letters she answered and placed in her scrapbook.

Le Gallienne retreated to Weston, and through all of March 1948 she was despondent. On March 21, thinking to act herself out of her depression, she wrote May Sarton. Perhaps because May worshipped her so intensely and had known her in her triumphant years at the Civic, Le Gallienne put on her bravest, most stoic face when talking or corresponding with her, like a mother who would never admit weakness or defeat to a child. Or she would sound a tragic, long-suffering note, telling May that she felt like Firs in *The Cherry Orchard:* "Life has gone by as though I'd never lived!" To her diary, she moaned more directly: "I feel utterly incompetent. My life has been a complete failure." Drinking exacerbated her depression, and she worried about money. How would she be able to live? she wondered.

After a couple of weeks of wallowing in self-pity, Le Gallienne's self-absorption and self-dramatization began to lift. CBS wanted her for a weekly *Invitation to Learning* series. Her agent, Jane Broder, fielded movie offers. Publishers were interested in her Ibsen translations and prefaces. Redpath, her lecture agency, urged her to put together a recital tour. She had to read scripts for a play contest. "I'm a good one," she said. "Anything I'd like I'm sure wouldn't have a chance! But I'll do my best." Her astringent humor crept back, and she joked about her depression. "I should have really shot myself at that last Hedda performance," she said. "It would have made a great exit."

Spring came, and soon there was no time for complaints except wishing that she had ten lives to accomplish all that she wanted. There were peas and an herb garden to plant, a drainage ditch to dig out, chickens to feed, and shelves to build in the cellar. Friends visited from New York on the weekends, and the old house had to be cleaned and "flowered." In the evenings, she read theatre history and discovered that not much had changed in the last four hundred years—all the problems were the same. A letter "with enclosure" arrived from Mary Bok Zimbalist. Le Gallienne breathed a huge sigh of relief. Her fairy godmother had not let her down. "What would I have done without her in my life?" Le Gallienne wondered. "Wonderful woman. Now I can stay here in peace & work on the Ibsen prefaces & the garden & prepare the material for my Recitals."

Mary Bok Zimbalist supported countless other artists as well, including composers Gian Carlo Menotti and Samuel Barber. "Mary had a list," recalled Efrem Zimbalist Jr. "Nobody knows the extent of that list. I was on it, my sister was on it, Le Gallienne was on it. I don't know how many others. Her interest was in creative people who needed her help." Mary Zimbalist gave away her money, but she also gave of herself. Her serenity, calm good sense, and patient understanding of artistic temperament made her a valuable friend. Once, years earlier, when Eva was feeling down, the older woman took her to lunch and advised, "Life begins at 60, Eva, so cheer up!"

LATER, MARY ZIMBALIST was delighted when she learned that her gift that summer had funded Eva's first work of fiction, a book for children of all ages called *Flossie and Bossie*. The seed for the story can be found in Le Gallienne's diary entry for May 22, 1948. She had worked all day building a coop for "the poor little hen who has the one *black* chick & the 3 yellow. The other hen with the 5 *all yellow* treasures has turned out a perfect *beast*. She tries to peck the black chick all the time—and turns the poor little family out of one nest after another."

Eva named the hens Flossie and Bossie, and for the next several months the Ibsen translations and her recitals were neglected while she observed the chickens and wrote the story of two bantam hens. The barnyard is ruled by an imperious cock who believes that his crowing commands the sun. A godlike creature called "the Hands" bestows blessings and restores order. The barnyard and the henhouse are the world, and the chickens have all the foibles, pretensions, prejudices, and vanities of humans.

In *Flossie and Bossie*, Eva tried to answer a seemingly unresolvable question: how could three decidedly different women with complicated personal histories get along peacefully in the same house? If she could work out a solution with fictional hens, perhaps she could apply the remedy to real women. She wanted Peggy to move in permanently with her and Marion. Le Gallienne "felt very foolishly hurt" by Peggy's constant traveling. Marion's mind "ran in conventional grooves," and Le Gallienne chafed against her timidity. For example, Eva liked to drive fast, and Marion (who didn't know how to drive) insisted on traveling at a sedate forty miles an hour. Or when Le Gallienne wanted to ask a friend out for a weekend, someone like "Gloria," the young actress whose husband had left her, Marion "was grumpy & tiresome all day." Eva was filled with "vanity and selfishness" and was often domineering, sulky, and mean.

Le Gallienne dedicated *Flossie and Bossie* to "my only and very dear sister, Hesper Le Gallienne Hutchinson." Hesper was Eva's devoted fan, but Hesper and her husband, Bobbie, reminded Eva of the self-absorbed, pretentious white snails in Hans Christian Andersen's story "Happy Family." Such wicked thoughts made Eva feel guilty, and her dedication to Hesper was more penance than tribute. Garth Williams drew the illustrations for *Flossie and Bossie*, and Harper and Brothers published the novel in 1949. Faber published the book in England in 1950. "Even if it's not a success at all—it's still a beginning," Le Gallienne said, "& gives me courage & hope that perhaps I may find a channel there." Reviews were excellent, and the sales were good. "Subtly intended for quite grown-up children of Eve," said one reviewer. "There are things other than corn and juicy worms to be picked up in a barnyard."

*Marion Evensen in
Weston with her dogs,
Tuck, Sally, and Kate,
c. mid-1940s*

WHENEVER LE GALLIENNE was working in the theatre or on a creative
project like *Flossie and Bossie,* she did not feel the need for liquor and would go
for months at a time without a drink. In a perverse but somewhat common pattern, it was just those times when Marion seemed to drink the most. Marion reflected Eva's moods, and in a strange way, it was almost as if she drank because
Le Gallienne didn't. When, after a long stretch of work, Eva indulged in liquor,
which invariably made her physically ill, Marion did not drink and devoted herself to caring for Eva.

   Le Gallienne believed that Marion could control her drinking by sheer
willpower. Time after time, when she would come home and find the liquor cab-
inet empty and Marion passed out on her bed, Le Gallienne observed that "the
same old bitter resentment wells up from some dark hidden corner when she
gets like that."

   Marion was fifty-eight, and age, as well as culture and temperament, separated her from Peggy and Eva. A staunch Republican, Marion disagreed with Le

Gallienne and Webster about most political issues. My country, right or wrong, was Marion's philosophy. Although Marion was a devoted reader of Henry James, she also liked best-selling novels—books that Le Gallienne called trash for simpletons. It must have been extremely trying for midwestern, conservative, unemployed Marion to get along with two erudite, opinionated, self-important women who both, at one time or another, had been her employer.

During the fall of 1948, Marion's binges became more frequent, perhaps because Le Gallienne was spending more and more time with Peggy in New York. Backed by Joseph Verner Reed and producer Sol Hurok, Webster had formed a company called Marweb and was rehearsing her young Shakespeare actors for an upcoming tour of colleges and universities. Peggy wanted Eva to play Hamlet and Lady Macbeth. Marion argued that it would hurt Le Gallienne's prestige to act with such a raw, young company. In choosing clothes and making career decisions, Le Gallienne valued Marion's opinions and trusted her judgment. She said no to the tour.

Marweb was Peggy's passion, but Eva had her own passion. Without a larger purpose, purely personal achievement meant little to her—she had turned down Laurette Taylor's role in a movie of *The Glass Menagerie,* not only because she felt the character of Mrs. Wingfield wasn't right for her, but also because it would conflict with her upcoming recital tour. Le Gallienne believed that she still had a part to play in the theatre and in the education of the young. "It occurred to me that more and more of our young people throughout the country never catch even a glimpse of the living theatre"—or of *her* work, she might have added. With actor Jon Dawson, she would discuss and act great scenes from classical repertory, playing Romeo and Juliet, Macbeth and Lady Macbeth, Mirabell and Millimant from *The Way of the World,* and Elizabeth and Essex from *Elizabeth the Queen.*

But Le Gallienne worried about leaving Marion alone. In September, while she was rehearsing in New York, Eva called home and knew immediately that Marion was drunk. When she called again, there was no answer. Concerned about Marion and about Vixen, Le Gallienne phoned her neighbor Helen Boylston to look in on them. That night Le Gallienne and Peggy pondered the situation. "Thank God we have each other!" Eva wrote.

Torn between Peggy, who wanted her to go to Buffalo and oversee Marweb's first performances, and Marion, who needed her at home, Le Gallienne chose to drive home on Saturday, September 25. "On my trip I kept praying for guidance," she wrote. When she arrived, Eva found Marion passed out. That evening she struggled with a letter to Marion. "I feel strongly she should go away & be on her own for a bit. A clean break would [be] good for her morale I *know*—but I don't suppose I'll ever get her to see it. Well—"

Marion was still insensible on Sunday, so Le Gallienne saved the letter until Monday morning. Marion was up fixing breakfast as usual, and Le Gallienne left the letter with her while she went to Westport to buy dinner for that evening. Later, that day, they talked about the letter. "She took it well & Thank God seemed to understand my feelings," wrote Le Gallienne. "She's determined to lick it *right here*. I think she will be able to this time. In any case I felt she should be allowed to do it her own way—& if she *really* wishes with 100% of herself I *know* she'll succeed."

IN OCTOBER, Peggy spent a few weeks on the Vineyard, and Marion stayed sober in Weston with Eva. She was "being awfully sweet & good & when she's like that she is a great comfort," wrote Le Gallienne, not making the obvious connection between Peggy's absence and Marion's abstinence.

It was Marion who had to deliver the news that Flossie had been killed by a neighbor's dog. The Wilsons had been unable to tell Eva. Marion tried to cushion the shock by buying a canary for the house, but Le Gallienne was heartbroken. When Eva was depressed, Marion became despondent, too, and Peggy's presence in the house during Thanksgiving week exacerbated Marion's misery. One evening when Peggy was out having dinner with Joe Reed, Marion confronted Eva with "the usual stream of insults about Peg's & my dreadful casting of plays—I tried to be calm and talk rationally—but she is *impossible* to talk to. I said something about her recent bout . . . & she was very arrogant about it." Marion told Eva that she "had a right to get drunk when she wanted to" and that "at least she didn't disgrace herself before people" as Le Gallienne had years earlier when, drunk on champagne at the Cobb's Mill Inn, Eva had lashed out at the actors in her repertory company.

Le Gallienne didn't tell Peggy about Marion's latest outburst, but the following week Peggy visited Weston and found Marion drunk and all the liquor gone. When Peggy called Eva, who was touring in Ohio, Le Gallienne was mortified, not only because Marion couldn't control her drinking but because the neighbors knew. She and Peggy had no idea what to do. Eva slogged on with the tour.

As Le Gallienne drove to Weston for the Christmas holiday, she feared the worst. She hadn't seen Marion in weeks, and she didn't know what to expect. Marion knew that Peggy also planned to join them for Christmas and the New Year. Christmas had always been Eva's favorite holiday, bringing memories of Mam and all the Danish holiday traditions. She had spent hours shopping, and the car was piled with presents and parcels, including a new black sealskin coat with red lining for Marion. Eva loved buying gifts, spending lavishly on Marion, Peggy, and Hesper. She bought presents, too, for her close friends Mimsey, Alice De Lamar, and Mary Zimbalist, her actor friends, and her neighbors and their children. When Le Gallienne pulled up in front of her house, a sober Marion met her with an ecstatic Vixen. "Everything looked dear & familiar" to her. "How lucky I am to have a home," she thought.

For the next few days, the three women shopped, filled the house with flowers, and entertained dinner guests. Eva wrapped her packages beautifully and arranged them under the Blue Room Christmas tree, which she decorated with handmade ornaments and wax candles in their special Danish holders. The three women spent *jule aften,* Christmas Eve, alone. After an early dinner, Eva lit the candles on the Christmas tree, and they had coffee in the Blue Room, where they opened their presents. "It was the best Christmas we've ever had I think," she told her diary that night. Eva was part of a threesome, the cream in the cookie, and she was happy. "I had some lovely things. How sweet they both are to me. We had champagne—I felt quite tight! Not used to such dissipation! A wonderful Jule Aften!" Le Gallienne's fears were unfounded, and there were no drunken scenes and no arguments that Christmas.

On January 11, 1949, Le Gallienne turned fifty. "It doesn't seem possible," she thought. It was a beautiful, sunny morning, and she took Vixen and walked in the woods. "When I think of how strong & sure I was when Jo & I first tramped these woods—so young & happy—with our pack of Cairns. How fast it goes—& how differently from what one plans! In many ways I am stronger now than then, thank God—but if one could only combine Youth & Wisdom. I think I might really have achieved something! But how little it matters really." Later, after Peggy came out in the afternoon, and gifts and messages arrived from all her friends, including one from Jo, she felt ashamed of being sad. "There is so very much for which I am profoundly grateful."

A few days later she started again on the recital tour. Before she left, she hung a map in Marion's room marked with pins for all her engagements. For over two months, she and Jon Dawson traveled into Canada and across the United States by bus, train, and car. She knew that she must appear alien to many of the audiences; and in talking to them, sometimes she had to put on her "folksy act . . . it's the only way with these poor wretched people—they love it & that's what counts—for if they fear me I can get nothing over to them." In Fargo, North Dakota, it was fifteen degrees below zero, but the Little Theatre was packed with people. Le Gallienne made the audience laugh by telling them that when she had appeared there as Hedda Gabler wearing a décolleté gown it "was the only town I'd ever been whistled at!"

Peggy's Marweb company was playing Los Angeles when Eva arrived there, and Eva and Peggy shared a hotel suite. Peggy called Jo for her, and Le Gallienne was able to see her Aimée for a few hours. "We had a marvellous talk," Eva told

*Jo Hutchinson poses for a Warner Bros. publicity photograph
at a California ranch, c. 1946.*

her diary. "The strain of leaving her is always so great—& breaks me up so terribly. Will it be another 3 years? . . . If only I had money I could come out each year & live for a few weeks incognito somewhere near her." Thinking about money brought out other fears: "God knows how I'm going to make my living—I don't think I could stand this kind of travel & strain very often. . . . I just couldn't speak to anyone and had to put up a terrible fight not to burst into sobs. . . . Stupid fool. In a day or two I shall have got hold of myself again—but just at the moment of leavetaking, the whole thing fills me with such anguish that I feel life is unbearable."

Le Gallienne and Dawson traveled southeast to Florida, where she stayed with Alice De Lamar and visited Mimsey's new art gallery in Palm Beach. On the plane to New Orleans, Eva ran into Jascha Heifetz and commiserated with him "on the horrors of this kind of life."

On March 10 Eva flew from Dallas to New York. To fortify herself for the trip, she bought a "very small flask of Scotch to have a nip on the plane journey." Walt Wilson met her at La Guardia Airport and drove her to Weston. Le Gallienne was afraid to ask about Marion, and Wilson didn't volunteer any information. Vixen greeted her joyously, but "there was little else in the way of a welcome." Marion was "dead drunk—with a great swollen face—mumbling away."

Le Gallienne thought of her betrayal of Jo and what her life might have been. "I keep telling myself it's retribution," she wrote in her diary, "& so it is."

Peggy urged Eva to go to England with her for a holiday, but Le Gallienne declined. She didn't want to leave her home, and she felt that she couldn't leave Marion alone so soon. After Peggy left for England, Marion told Eva that she had been very unhappy. Not averse to playing the martyr, she reminded Eva of all that she owed her: it was she who had nursed Julie Le Gallienne during her last illness, and it was she who cared for Eva whenever Eva was ill or drunk. It was Marion who took care of their home in Weston while Eva was absent, and it was Marion who washed and ironed Eva's clothes, brought her breakfast tray, and answered her phone. Marion accused Eva of being a demanding, self-absorbed, arrogant companion who often patronized her, hated small talk, and was preoccupied with solitary projects. What she said was true.

Le Gallienne might have countered that it was Marion who had made the choice to stay. Or she might have said that it was her money and hard work that supported Marion. She might have asked Marion why she didn't look for a job. If you don't like things as they are, she could have said, go back to George Westlake in Cleveland or the Evensen family in Milwaukee. But Le Gallienne didn't say any of those things. To say such things, even if they were true, would have been cruel.

She had lived with Marion for fifteen years, and Gunnar was family, deserving of respect, and Le Gallienne loved her. "I've been so awful to her," she told her diary. "But I think we understand each other now—& it did us both good. I shall 'study to be better'—I know what a vile creature I've been all my life—& now that I may not have so much more time I *must* try & make of myself a halfway decent human being." Le Gallienne wrote that nothing had ever been Marion's fault, "only mine. I hope now she will feel a little lighter in her heart."

Le Gallienne held tightly to her loved ones, but like the real cat she resembled, her strongest ties were not to the people she loved but rather to her home and property. The new house with the Blue Room, the gardens, the tiny old house, the surrounding woods—every crook and crevice, every rock and wildflower, each towering pine and flowering dogwood—all these were familiar and loved.

In June 1949, Peggy finally agreed to live with Eva in Weston. Peggy painted the mailbox and Eva painted a new sign for it, adding Webster's name. Evensen, Le Gallienne, and Webster would receive mail in the same box, would share the house, and their lives. Peggy, however, did not give up her New York apartment. Marion avoided her as much as possible, and when tensions arose, Le Gallienne played mediator. Eva wondered if "it will last at all."

SINCE LE GALLIENNE was not producing plays for herself, she now encountered the career barrier all middle-aged actresses dread and face sooner or later: no parts and no work. Like Ethel Barrymore and countless other theatre stars before her, Eva found the straw-hat season a godsend. In the summer of 1949, she starred in a ten-week package tour of *The Corn Is Green*. To earn her thousand dollars a week plus percentages, she played Ethel Barrymore's old role of Miss Moffat, the dedicated teacher who changes the life of a young Welsh miner. Richard Waring acted his old part of Morgan Evans, which he had played with Barrymore on Broadway. Two other members of the original production, elderly Eva Leonard Boyne, who played Mrs. Watty, and Darthy Hinkley, who acted her lascivious daughter, joined the eight-member company.

All during June as she prepared Miss Moffat and readied herself for the tour, Le Gallienne felt Marion's tension building. She bought Marion two season tickets for the Westport Playhouse and urged her to go out often with her friends Jessalyn Jones and Doris Johanson, who lived nearby, or with Helen Boylston. One evening Marion said she was going to see a movie with Helen, but when she hadn't returned by midnight, Le Gallienne called Boylston, who said that Marion hadn't gone to the movies with her but was instead at the old house. Peggy and Eva walked there and found a drunken Marion sprawled out on the bed half-dressed. They let her sleep it off, but a few days later Marion went on another binge, and "then Peg & I finally told her a few 'unhappy truths straight out.' " It was the first time Peggy had spoken harshly to Marion about her drinking.

Marion packed a suitcase and said that she was going to New York and Cleveland and would send for the rest of her things. "She said some beastly things to me," Le Gallienne wrote, "but it was only natural feeling awful as she must have felt . . . but if this sticks—I believe it would be best for us all . . . I know I shall miss her horribly at times—& yet a very strong part of me says it would be right for her to stay away—just as much & more for her sake than for mine." A few days later, Marion returned, "very subdued and mizzy." Le Gallienne told her that she would "do anything to help her lick it. That if we felt it wiser for her to go away I'd arrange that—or anything she thought would help. Well—now we'll see—once more. She's really so *good* in her heart—and makes herself so very miserable. What a damnable business it is!"

Le Gallienne knew that Marion was not capable of living on her own. Eva had supported her for years. If Marion left, Le Gallienne could give her a stipend to live on, but who would take care of Marion when she went off on a binge? On the other hand, if Marion stayed, she would always be dependent. What would make Marion happy was if Le Gallienne gave up Peggy and rekindled their own romance. That was impossible. Le Gallienne demanded little of Marion, which indicated that Eva selfishly preferred the present situation. Since Eva had left the choice to her, once again Marion chose to stay. She returned to her normal routine of cooking and helping in the garden. She shopped for Eva, helped her learn her lines, and packed her clothes for the tour of *The Corn Is Green*.

As if she didn't have enough to contend with, Le Gallienne took a sixteen-year-old boy named Robin Prising with her on the *Corn Is Green* tour. His mother, the English actress Marie Leslie, had brought Robin backstage after a performance of *The Cherry Orchard*. The handsome, precocious boy wanted to be an actor, and Le Gallienne had been immediately drawn to him. He was drawn to her as well, obsessed even, and he didn't tell her of the mystical link he had with her and Eleonora Duse. During the war years, Robin and his family had been prisoners of the Japanese in Manila. In *Manila, Goodbye,* his harrowing memoir of those years, Prising wrote: "Stifled by heat and the stink of corpses, I passed into the courtyard of squalid shacks, between those leaking, whitewashed boxes of the dead, and walked barefoot over the earth that swallowed up their blood. . . . I had wandered into our cook shack where, scarcely a fortnight before, we had burnt books for fuel and boiled roots and weeds. Only one book was left, a dirty blue book." He opened the book—Le Gallienne's *At 33*—and looked into the face of a woman: a woman with "dark brows. White hair. An old woman's face, vulnerable, expectant, full of life. Eleonora Duse. . . . On the page beside the photograph, the words . . . *Force et Confiance de Vivre.*" He saved the book, and just as Eva had years earlier, he clung to Duse's words as a symbol of hope and courage.

Le Gallienne had corresponded with the boy ("Do you read Gide in the original?" she asked in one letter), and she agreed to coach him during the tour. After just a few days, Robin's constant presence grated on her nerves, and she longed to ship him home. Still, when she worked with him on *Romeo and Juliet* and *The Seagull,* she was amazed at the progress he made. She was brutally frank, and she was "giving him the best I know . . . & being so young and intelligent he is just like putty. How long I'll be able to stand it is another question!"

"She wanted me really to *look* and *listen* and *think* and not merely to repeat a cleverly schemed series of vocal patterns, pauses, moves, and hesitations," Prising remembered. In *Romeo*'s balcony scene, "she wanted me to be less poetically romantic and more of the bounding boy. . . . But when I went bounding about like a maniac, she would look at me with a doubting squint and say: 'Do you like that? I think it's *hollow*—it has to be *filled.*' And so she taught me to be ever restless, never satisfied, searching always for a better way of enlarging and filling a scene. . . . She expected the best speech (and infinitely more style and imagination) *and* all the truth and conviction of the Method, yet not its self-indulgence and provincialism."

After two weeks, the task of playing Miss Moffat both onstage and off- became too much for Le Gallienne, and she told Robin he had to go. Instead of acting lessons, what he really needed was "some good strenuous manual labor," she said. Robin "cried bitterly," Le Gallienne told her diary. "But how many times will he do that in his life poor child! It's so sad to be so young. My heart bleeds for him. But he must learn his first lesson!" Apparently, the first lesson Robin needed to learn was the ruthless power the old could exert over the young. She bought him a ticket back to New York, but before he left, Robin had one last session. Le Gallienne was "staggered" by the improvement in his work, and she believed that "the boy may be an actor."

Instead of an actor, Prising became an editor and writer and theatre speech coach. Years later, he laughed and said, "If I were Le Gallienne I wouldn't have taken a sixteen-year-old on tour." Except for a few letters, they did not keep in touch, although Robin never missed one of her performances. "The American theatre did not deserve her," Prising asserted. "I think she was foolish when she started the Civic and she took out American citizenship. She could have had a career on both sides of the Atlantic, could have acted on the London stage, part of that community of wonderful actors."

LE GALLIENNE'S Miss Moffat and the production earned rave reviews. Superb, magnificent, tender, touching, uncanny timing, said the critics. One spellbound reviewer speculated that the part suited her so well because Le Gallienne, like Moffat, believed in a cause. Theatre business boomed in Westport, Ivorytown, Stockbridge, Dennis, and Narragansett. The summer theatres were thrilled to have the famous and glamorous Le Gallienne grace their stages.

Le Gallienne was not thrilled. She loathed the crowded resort towns. "How they get people to come to these places when they don't have to is beyond me." When they played Theatre-by-the-Sea, which she called "Hell-Hole-by-the-Sea," she caught a cold and felt terrible. She hated being alone in strange places and begged Peggy to join her. Peggy visited for a few days and made a game of taking care of her, which cheered Eva up. They talked about going to Europe on a "voyage of discovery & try to find the place in which to end our days!"

When the tour ended, Le Gallienne returned to Weston in a black mood. Peggy was in New York rehearsing *Julius Caesar* and *The Taming of the Shrew,* which her Marweb company would take to 107 cities in 28 weeks. Eva's cold lingered on and for several days she stayed in bed. Marion lugged trays up and down the steep stairs. "At the moment, I don't feel a bit like coping any more," Eva groaned.

Le Gallienne was not only physically ill, she was upset. Darthy Hinkley, the petite young woman who played Bessie Watty in *The Corn Is Green,* had fallen in love with her. They had been together on the tour, and now, unhappy in her marriage, Darthy showered Le Gallienne with letters and phone calls. The flattering attention delighted Le Gallienne and disturbed her at the same time because "my heart . . . cannot be there." She coached Darthy in Shakespeare scenes, made phone calls to arrange auditions for her, shopped and lunched with her, and one October weekend she invited her to Weston. Peggy was on the road, and to ensure that she could be alone with Darthy, Eva arranged for Marion to take a trip to New York and stay at the Algonquin. "What will come of it all?" Le Gallienne wondered.

Was her fling with Darthy a way of punishing Peggy? "How I wish [Peggy] could find time to live with me for a little while," Le Gallienne complained. Or was it just that Eva found it difficult to deny herself an admirer and that she liked the drama and intrigue of doing the forbidden? She knew that she must break with Darthy, and a few weeks later she talked everything over with her, and "all is settled," she wrote. "I know for the best."

To take her mind off her misery, Eva planted one hundred hyacinth bulbs. "What a weak stupid fool I am," she thought. "Just no good I suppose—will I *never* grow up? God help me to be strong and firm from now on. One should certainly never be sure of *oneself* that's unquestionable. One becomes so smug and then suddenly one is upset by a breath—and finds oneself foundering."

LE GALLIENNE SPENT Christmas, 1949, with Hesper and Bobbie Hutchinson, who had decided to buy a house nearby. Her holiday happiness turned to rage when she learned that Herman Shumlin, the original director of *The Corn Is Green,* would be the one to stage her revival of the play at the City Center in New York. Eva had wanted Mady Christians to direct. Over the years, she had grown fond of Mady; she reasoned that they had something in common—they both loved Peggy. And Mady needed the work. She had appeared in more than sixty movies and had played "Mama" in the Broadway hit *I Remember Mama,* which ran from 1944 to 1946, but after she was named in *Red Channels,* Mady found it difficult to find work. Eva had never worked with Shumlin before, but she despised him as an arbitrary director who relied on externals. Shumlin also thought Darthy was too old for the part of Bessie, but Le Gallienne fought hard for her and won. Eva had been unable to keep her vow to break with Darthy, and their relationship was still unresolved. At fifty, Eva felt, "I surely should be through with such difficulties."

Rehearsals for the New York production of *The Corn Is Green* began in early January, and Le Gallienne was relieved to get back to the strict discipline of the theatre. She decided that she had been vain and arrogant about Shumlin and tried listening to him politely. She felt that he wanted her to overstress her performance and to play with too much brio, but she tried to do what he wanted. "By dint of both of us swallowing large doses of vanity . . . we managed to get on very well. . . . I cannot work in *discord.*"

The play opened on her birthday. She was starred above the title and felt a tremendous responsibility "not to let everyone down." Jo sent her a sentence written by Duse's hand in English: "The soul's joy lies in doing," in pencil on heavy paper. Le Gallienne hung the framed saying near her bed so that it would be the first thing she saw every morning and the last thing she saw at night. She felt too nervous to look at her other telegrams and flowers before the opening. As usual, despite the bravos and the curtain calls, she didn't think she played well. "The critics & the first night 'Death Watch' have succeeded in making N.Y. openings a real ordeal by fire. One needs *guts* and a clear head to survive."

Apparently, Le Gallienne and the rest of the company had both. The production and the cast received excellent notices. "Miss Le Gallienne is a much perkier spinster than her predecessor in the role, vigorous and alert, sharpening up everything she does where Miss Barrymore got her effects with suavity," observed Arthur Pollock.

In February, Peggy's production of *The Devil's Disciple* followed *The Corn Is Green* at City Center and also received good notices. Then it was her turn to collapse. For several days, Le Gallienne nursed her through the flu, getting up every two hours at night to give her medicine. With no sign of any work ahead, Le Gallienne worried about money. And once again, she was upset by a breath when Darthy Hinkley asked to see her.

After guest-starring on a CBS radio program called *I Take Your Word,* she picked up Darthy and drove to Weston. They arrived home just before midnight. There is no record of the days she spent with Darthy in Weston, since Le Gallienne tore the January 31 through February 5 pages out of her diary. She pledged to put the chronicle of those days away "in some back part of my being where it will remain undisturbed though not unforgotten."

It's likely that Darthy and Eva had a love affair. Darthy was still married, but her relationship with Eva was serious enough for Peggy to be concerned. On February 8, Peggy had dinner with Darthy, and afterwards both women phoned Le Gallienne. "I don't deserve such love," Eva said. She knew that she must give up Darthy. "But it will be terribly hard," she wrote. "Inevitable though I'm afraid." A few days later, an upset Darthy told Eva that she planned to go to Haiti with her husband. "I'm sure that the thing must be sublimated so that I can help the child," Le Gallienne wrote. "She mustn't lose all that I can give her. I want her so much to do good work—& grow as she should." While Eva and Darthy continued their friendship for months, meeting occasionally for lunches and dinners, the intimacy brought about by their work together on *The Corn Is Green* was missing, and gradually they stopped seeing each other.

LATER, LE GALLIENNE would say that during the early 1950s she was in limbo. It was a busy limbo. She and Peggy formed Theatre Masterworks, a corporation to sell recorded albums of various classic plays, including *Romeo and Juliet, Camille,* and *Hedda Gabler.* Eva reprised *Uncle Harry* with Pepi Schildkraut on *The Ford Television Theater.* Memories flooded back when she played a scene from *Camille* on the Ed Sullivan show, *Toast of the Town,* at the old Maxine Elliott Theatre. Le Gallienne had agreed to the engagement since she would be the "class act" and receive one thousand dollars for her appearance. Sullivan's producers wouldn't allow her to say "mistress" on the air. How about "une maîtresse," she joked? To her astonishment, they accepted. Eva thought of Maxine Elliott's line: "Never mind! We have their money."

Le Gallienne played *Hedda Gabler* (for the last time) in summer stock and Masha in *The Three Sisters* at the Brattle Theatre in Cambridge, Massachusetts, worked on various radio programs, and took out a recital tour playing classic scenes with a small company. After seeing her on the Sullivan show, Milton Goldman, a young agent, arranged for Eva to give talks and readings to raise money for the United Jewish Appeal. The talks were a godsend to both her and the UJA—their contributions soared, and she earned five hundred dollars per appearance. Sometimes she made two thousand dollars in one week. Still, it wasn't the theatre art she had been trained for, and Le Gallienne prayed for a chance to "do some constructive work—I think it is the deprivation of a constant channel that makes me restless. I feel I have a lot to give and it makes me sad that there is nowhere where I can consistently serve."

"Men are so lucky!" she exclaimed. "At fifty odd they are still well in their 'prime': Not so with us. . . . I know I could play Juliet now—but! How I wish I were a man (only as far as my work goes, I mean); the whole vast repertoire of Shakespeare would still be open to me. And we have no actors who can play the parts half as well as I could!"

Since she haughtily refused to play tripe or do advertisements, Le Gallienne was fortunate to work at all. She had spent decades blasting commercialism, and it's hardly surprising that she was not the actor commercial producers would turn to if, by some remote chance, there was a leading role for a middle-aged woman on Broadway. Other actors, who were not stars, both men and women, were not so lucky. In 1927–28 Actors' Equity had counted more than four thousand members working on Broadway or in touring companies. By 1953 that number had dwindled to 991. Postwar inflation combined with the competition of radio, television, and the movies contributed to the theatre's decline. In the 1949–50 season only fifty-six shows were produced on Broadway, a new low. Only one serious play, *The Country Girl* starring Uta Hagen, survived on Broadway during the 1950–51 season.

The American theatre of Le Gallienne's youth, when more than a hundred productions played on Broadway every season, simply did not exist. The fledgling nonprofit resident theatre movement led by Margo Jones's Dallas theatre, which would later provide thousands of jobs, had not yet taken wing. *Theatre Arts* magazine commissioned a study of the situation, and the researcher discovered, to no one's surprise, that "the very existence of the living theatre . . . is now in serious jeopardy."

Le Gallienne's professional unhappiness was exacerbated by her dissatisfaction with her personal life. Like Irina in *The Three Sisters,* she longed for a "real one" to share her life. She wanted to spend more time with Peggy, but Peggy was often absent, busy with her many organizations and her directing work. "Why should she cater to my stupid vanity!" Le Gallienne wrote.

Marion was devoted to her, but Marion's binges had become increasingly frequent. Marion needed professional help but refused to seek treatment. There was a chapter of Alcoholics Anonymous in Westport, but there is no evidence that either Eva or Marion considered that option. The last thing Marion wanted was to be free of the woman she loved. Perhaps Marion realized that her weakness enabled her to maintain her place in Le Gallienne's life.

In late May 1950, Le Gallienne had had too much to drink, missed the turnoff into her road, and crashed her car into a neighbor's house. The incident sent her straight to bed, where she spent a week recovering, waited on by loyal and sober Marion. The "awful episode" haunted Le Gallienne for weeks until an out-of-court settlement was reached in August 1950. "I felt like falling on my knees and thanking God," she wrote. "Perhaps I needed this thing to happen to make me realize what a wicked fool I have been."

Out of the trauma of the car accident, the thoroughly chastened Le Gallienne built a new resolve. She began a new, looseleaf diary on June 1, 1950, which allowed her to write as much as possible each day. Denied a creative outlet through meaningful, continuous theatre work, she sought an outlet in her writing. Random House wanted her Ibsen translations for a Modern Library edition. She also planned a series of prefaces for the plays modeled after Granville-Barker's Shakespeare prefaces. T. S. Eliot at Faber in London planned to publish her *Hedda Gabler* translation and preface in a single edition and wanted the other plays as well. Le Gallienne also felt ready to begin work on her second autobiography.

To escape from the "physical, mental, and spiritual clutter" of the home she shared with Marion and Peggy, she asked Wilson to move Flossie and Bossie's white-frame chicken house into the ravine behind her house. In the tiny two rooms, Wilson installed a sink and brick-patterned linoleum. He also hung the same glass globes filled with water for fire protection that had been placed in every building on the property following the explosion and fire. Le Gallienne built bookshelves, put up curtains, and moved in an old school desk. She filled the shelves with Ibsen's original plays and her working translations, Shakespeare's plays, a Webster's dictionary, an old Danish dictionary, a Russian dictionary, a thesaurus, a pile of empty French notebooks, and her pen with her favorite blue ink. She planted perennials around the foundation, and said a "small prayer dedicating the little place to Peace & praying that I might be helped to keep it free from stress & ugliness & disorder." She christened the place "Nuja" in honor of the United Jewish Appeal talks that provided much of her income.

In addition to her UJA talks in 1951, she also traveled on her recital tour. When the tour was almost completed, she discovered that her booking agent had bilked her out of hundreds of dollars on each engagement. She hired Louis Nizer, who "listened magnificently without a single interruption" and told her that he would take care of everything. She returned home in late February and collapsed into bed for a week. For the first time after a tour, she did not drink. Although she believed that she was close to a nervous breakdown, her doctor found that she was anemic and thoroughly exhausted. He prescribed injections of liver extract, strong vitamins, and complete bed rest. Marion, whom she now called "Mutki" (Mother), nursed her and "looked after me with patience and kindness," Eva wrote. "I am deeply grateful to her & feel bitterly ashamed for the times that I have been impatient & cruel & arrogant with her." Feeling secure in Le Gallienne's affections, in 1951 Marion was able to curb her drinking. She also took driving lessons, and in November 1951 she received her driver's license. Le Gallienne bought her a car, and Marion was no longer dependent on Eva or Peggy for transportation.

AFTER JULIE LE GALLIENNE'S DEATH, her personal effects and papers had been shipped to Eva in Westport. In her mother's "pirate chest," a massive, age-blackened trunk, Le Gallienne discovered her father's letters to Julie, and her own letters to Julie separated by year and bound with ribbon. She read her parents' 1898–99 correspondence with particular interest. She learned that her parents were "certainly prepared for a boy! God help me! Parents shouldn't do that. It surely must affect the child." As she read Richard's letters to Julie, she observed that they were "always full of nothing but money worries and apologies for one thing or another!" and found them, after she read dozens sounding the same themes, somewhat tiresome. But she sympathized with her father's plight when confronted with Julie's powerful will and intolerance for weakness. As she read her own letters to her mother, she found the vitality and confidence of her young self during the Civic Rep years astounding and unbelievable.

In April 1951, before she began work on her autobiography, Eva lunched with Mary Bok Zimbalist to talk over her plans. She told Mary about her idea for *The*

Mystic in the Theatre, a biography of Duse. No one understood Duse's work the way she did, Eva felt; she owed it to Duse's memory. Mary offered to send her to Italy that summer to research the book. Le Gallienne wanted to write her auto-biography first and let the Duse book simmer. With her recital tour and UJA engagements, Le Gallienne had earned enough to take her through several months, but Mary insisted on giving her an additional amount so that she could devote herself to writing.

Writing the autobiography took Le Gallienne six months. She started with the explosion that had cut her life in two. To write about the accident without mentioning Jo was, she knew, dishonest, but necessary for Jo's sake. She wrote honestly, if not in detail, about her relationship with Marion. She told her readers that Marion shared her home and her life and had been her companion for sixteen years. In writing about Peggy Webster, she included only their professional relationship. "I have been greatly loved and have loved greatly in return," was the most she chose to say about her love life. Julie Le Gallienne is a constant presence in the book, but Eva balked at writing about her father, putting off the task until she was almost finished. Reading his letters helped bring him closer, and she was able to compose three and a half pages that presented an idealized portrait of Richard. In November 1951, she struggled with the ending. She didn't want to close on a "depressing note," because she didn't feel depressed, but "in this country where success is always looked at from the point of view of concrete achievement, it's hard to explain that one isn't necessarily a sad and broken failure, because one is not actively and externally triumphant. The triumphs of the spirit don't seem to make interesting reading!"

In this book, as she had in her earlier autobiography, *At 33,* she gave short shrift to the founding and achievements of the Civic Repertory. When she wrote *At 33,* the company was still active, and she was too close to it. She had read Harold Clurman's history of the Group Theatre, *The Fervent Years,* in which he established the Group's importance in American theatre history, but her natural reticence combined with an unwillingness to revisit years that brought back so many bittersweet memories made her unable to follow Clurman's example.

By the time she completed the autobiography, however, she did feel triumphant. The task of examining her life and chronicling her accomplishments, even in modest, self-effacing prose, had reminded her of just how much she had achieved, temporally and spiritually. Time after time, she had told her diary that she had achieved nothing, that her life had been a failure; but now, as she read over her manuscript, it seemed that she had achieved a great deal. She had worked hard, and she felt proud of her life. In the closing pages, she flung out a challenge. "When I started the Civic Repertory," she said, "my greatest asset was my success; without that I could have accomplished nothing. . . . My position was exactly analogous to that of Uta Hagen or Julie Harris . . . if [they] having legitimately won stardom and all that goes with it, were deliberately to turn their backs on it, take an old burlesque house in Brooklyn or the Bronx, transform it into the kind of theatre they profess to believe in, and play in it for a hundred dollars a week—then people might sit up and take notice."

Her powers as an actress were "now greater than they have ever been," she believed. But was there a place for her in the American theatre? Time would tell. The primary purpose of the book, illustrated with photographs of her in her greatest roles, was to remind the American theatre public of her existence in the hope of reclaiming that place.

In honor of their thirty-three years of friendship, Le Gallienne dedicated the book to Mimsey. It was published in the spring of 1953. Helen Taylor, her editor at Viking, rejected Eva's title, *Plus Twenty,* and over her objections chose *With a Quiet Heart.* Le Gallienne hated the violet-toned book jacket with its sepia portrait of her, which, she felt, gave a "jeezly ecclesiastical air to the whole business." Reviews were admiring and respectful. Le Gallienne was called great, gallant, courageous, and noble. *The New York Times Book Review* chose Ruth Chatterton, a former Broadway actress turned film actress, to review the book. Chatterton applauded Le Gallienne's deep love of the theatre and praised the beauty of her "flower-like" face, but called the writing pedestrian and humorless. She seemed most put off by Le Gallienne's foreign roots, her allegiance to the classics, and her single-minded passion for a national repertory theatre. She pointed out Le Gallienne's lack of interest in modern American plays.

Throughout Chatterton's review, an unspoken question resonates: Who does Eva Le Gallienne think she is? Most of her career had been in defiance of the status quo; it was a challenge and a rebuke to those who had not done as much. I love the theatre, too, wrote Chatterton; I, too, know something about it. Does she think she's better than me? Chatterton implied. Le Gallienne's stardom wasn't resented; that was understandable. But the fact that she merely listed her achievements in modest prose seemed an act of hubris. There were the children's book, the Ibsen translations, the languages she spoke, the theatres she had founded, the talents she had discovered, the great roles she had played. Who else in the American theatre had accomplished so much?

Le Gallienne's imperious nature was intimidating. The idea that a *woman,* especially a known lesbian, would set herself up as an arbiter of standards for the American theatre perhaps irritated Ruth Chatterton. Le Gallienne was an uncompromising artist in a country ruled by a majority that distrusted elitism, embraced compromise, and avoided anything cultural. Perhaps in anticipation of this view of herself, Le Gallienne wrote at the end of her autobiography that she had no "contempt for the great popular show . . . and I look with pride and wholehearted admiration on the skill and imagination that make our entertainment industry the finest in the world . . . but I see no reason why our theatre should be limited to that one facet." In the few sentences that followed she ruined her attempt at conciliation by writing that the audiences she wanted to serve were enlightened, cultivated people with good taste—a slap in the face to show-business types, who obviously catered to dumb slobs with bad taste.

The unspoken question resounded: Who does she think she is?

IN FEBRUARY 1952, Eva and Peggy sailed for France on a six-month working vacation. Their purpose, at least in Peggy's mind, was to explore opportunities for work in London and Paris and to look for a place in France or England where they could retire together. For various reasons, usually money or work commitments, the trip had been planned and postponed several times. In 1949, Le Gallienne had imagined briefly a move to Europe with Peggy, proclaiming dramatically that "it would be *Life* . . . a little addenda to the Saga."

Whenever Peggy had proposed a vacation to Europe to find a place to retire to, Le Gallienne had always found a reason not to go. This time, since she had just bought three more acres of property in Weston (a telling sign that she wasn't serious about moving to Europe), Le Gallienne had felt that she couldn't afford the trip, but Peggy had an inheritance from her mother and offered to pay most of their expenses. Le Gallienne took out a bank loan, and Mary Bok Zimbalist sent her a thousand dollars. Alice De Lamar loaned them her Paris apartment and a stone cottage near Saint-Paul in the south of France.

The trip began badly. Eva so dreaded the thought of leaving her home, Vixen, and Marion that she drank herself senseless and had to be carried onto the boat. Peggy, on the other hand, couldn't wait to leave. She was bitter and angry. Just a few months earlier, Mady Christians, then fifty-one, had died of a cerebral hemorrhage after being denied a job because of the blacklist. The House Un-American Activities Committee had begun its investigations, and since Peggy was an inveterate joiner of countless organizations, some of them suspect, her name, along with many of her friends', had cropped up. (She later learned that it was José Ferrer who gave her name to HUAC.) Le Gallienne advised Peggy to calm down, that "her integrity was so shining that no harm could come to her." Eva's detached, Olympian attitude infuriated Peggy. Her lawyer, Louis Nizer, gave Peggy the same advice, but there was fear in the air, and Peggy was afraid even though none of the investigators had contacted her yet. Her fear was so great that she removed from her New York apartment letters that she had written to her mother in 1936 from Moscow and hid them in Le Gallienne's barn.

But Peggy had good reason to be afraid. The FBI had been following her activities for years, and their investigation had taken them to Weston and interviews with Le Gallienne's neighbors. An FBI report written by a field agent in April 1951 noted that an informant of "known reliability" had stated that Margaret Webster had been "an adherent of the CP in 1945." Webster had also "urged abolition of House Committee on Un-American Activities in 1949" and, as if providing further evidence of subversion, the report stated that she had directed productions of *Richard II* and Verdi's anti-authoritarian *Don Carlos.* "Times were getting worse, not better," Peggy believed.

In Alice De Lamar's Paris apartment, and later at the cottage outside Saint-Paul, troubles in America seemed very far away. The stone floors of the cottage were cold in early March, and the furnishings primitive, but the view from the terrace was breathtaking. The cottage overlooked a valley of olive groves and vineyards, and the old walls of Saint-Paul. The neglected garden had a mimosa tree, oleander shrubs, stocks, wallflowers, and roses in bud. Le Gallienne thought it would be an ideal place to write or paint. Peggy wrote to Marion that Eva had fallen in love with the place and was contemplating retiring there in monklike solitude. Le Gallienne wrote to "her darling Mutki" three times a week. "I don't feel in the least 'obligated' to sit down and write to you," Eva told Marion in one seven-page letter.

She and Peggy explored the narrow, winding streets of Saint-Paul and walked for hours through artichoke fields and vineyards. Along grassy goat paths, Le Gallienne spotted wild narcissus and grape hyacinths, which made her think of home. In the evening at the stone cottage, Peggy would light an olive-wood fire in the open fireplace, and Eva would make dinner on the coal stove range. "It is certainly a place to refresh one's soul," Eva felt.

In early April, Le Gallienne packed three evening dresses and traveled to Denmark as the guest of the Danish government for a celebration honoring Hans Christian Andersen. She read two of his stories on Danish radio, attended receptions, and had a joyful reunion with her cousin Mogens and other members of the Nørregaard family in Copenhagen. How Mam would have been pleased at my "official visit," Eva thought.

When Peggy grew restless in the solitude of Saint-Paul, she and Eva spent several weeks in London. Eva saw T. S. Eliot to go over her *Hedda Gabler* translation, which Faber planned to publish in a few months. Peggy had many friends in London, numerous business appointments, and was a tireless sightseer and playgoer, but Le Gallienne grew tired of the city and returned to the cottage. She worked on the translation of a French play that Peggy had bought, but simmering in the back of her mind was her book *The Mystic in the Theatre.*

In her youth, Le Gallienne had argued the supremacy of the intellect in acting, but after her talks with Duse and further reading and study in philosophy and mysticism, especially the prayers of Saint Thomas Aquinas that Duse had given her, Eva had come to believe that there was a spiritual side to the art that must be considered. She had articulated her beliefs in 1950 in a talk to Peggy's company at a rehearsal of *The Three Sisters.* "One shouldn't tear the material to shreds, analysing it with one's own little brain," she explained. "One should wear it like a cloak to warm and strengthen . . . one shouldn't limit everything to the capacity of one's own mentality. . . . There is a mystic element in acting that goes *beyond* analytical thought."

Le Gallienne sometimes wondered if she might be a little mad in this strong belief. When she visited Ellen Terry's house in Kent on April 19, 1952, she was elated to find further evidence of the rightness of her path. In her diary, Le Gallienne described what she had discovered:

> Quite a large room—light & almost gay. Incredibly crooked both as to floors & walls & above all *windows*. To the right, as one goes through the door, her bed—single & slightly austere—though not uncomfortably so. Above the bed . . . a crucified Christ [and on the wall] a large picture of Duse . . . under the picture in Ellen Terry's own bold & rather simple handwriting: "There is none like her none." . . . There was also in the other room . . . a copy of the *Imitation of Christ*. . . . All *very* interesting—and very good food for my theory of "The Mystic in the Theatre." How certain artists have somehow struggled through intense ego & sensuality in the TRAP of the Theatre and have at last dimly realized the connection (perhaps through a kind of self-protection) between acting & union with God.

On the same day that she visited Ellen Terry's house, Eva also had "the infinite joy" of seeing Gladys Calthrop again. They hadn't seen each other in over twenty years. While Peggy stayed on in London, Gladys joined Le Gallienne for ten days at the stone cottage. Gladys was a "perfect guest—goes off by herself for hours sketching—so that we never get in each other's way," Le Gallienne wrote. Another figure from her past appeared, too. Mercedes de Acosta sent flowers and an invitation to dinner. Le Gallienne and Peggy joined Mercedes and her friend Poppy Kirk for dinner, and according to Mercedes the "evening passed pleasantly and we laughed about the old days of *Jehanne d'Arc*."

Peggy and Eva had been companions for eleven years, but Le Gallienne complained that Peggy had never really lived with her. If they could just spend more time together, Eva believed, all would be well. When faced with Peggy as a constant companion, Le Gallienne realized that Peggy's need for bustling activity was not compatible with her own desire for quiet and solitude. Eva also didn't like being "kept" and resented the fact that Peggy's money was paying for most of their expenses. Eva knew that she "was far from being a pleasant companion" for Peggy, and she feared that she and Peggy were "developing along different lines." Eva worried, too, about her dwindling bank account. On July 27, Peggy and a thoroughly homesick Eva sailed for home.

"I am *home* again—thank God!" Le Gallienne told her diary on August 2, 1952. In Weston once again with Marion, Peggy, and Vixen, she was relieved to be home, but she was not sorry she had gone on her voyage of discovery. She had learned something vital. "I now really *belong* in America and here I want to work (if anyone will give me the opportunity) and want to *live* the rest of my days. This home means so much to me—and it is *good*. I must try & find a way (with honour!) to keep it going. God will help me."

PART SIX

1952 - 1971

As Queen Elizabeth in Mary Stuart,
*Le Gallienne wore costumes "marvelously cut"
by the Russian-born designer Karinska.*

America seems to be one great "smile." . . .
It's the great Ostrich *country! To be moved—*
to think . . . all this must be shied away from. . . .
One becomes so tired *of it.*

L E GALLIENNE NEEDED HELP to find work, since she proudly believed that theatre was an art, not a business, and while she sometimes
complained that she had no one to advise her, there's no evidence that she
ever tried to find such a person. Her agent, Jane Broder, fulfilled her duties by
drawing up contracts for work that Le Gallienne had found herself or saying no
to scripts that were violent, sensational, dirty-minded, used vulgar language, or
were in bad taste—which effectively screened out much of early television and
many 1950s movies and plays. "To play in trash simply to earn a living," she said,
"is not right for me—and I hate it."

Just a few weeks after her return from Europe in August 1952, Le Gallienne
earned her usual one-thousand-dollar fee appearing on NBC's *Philco Television
Playhouse* in an adaptation of an Edith Wharton short story, playing a "quiet,
frail, woman with a cameo-like face." Peggy had turned down a part in the same
show. It annoyed Le Gallienne that producers considered her and Webster a
"sister act," another sign that their professional and personal partnership was
unraveling.

Peggy had hoped that their extended vacation in Europe would renew their
relationship. Instead, it served to heighten the tensions that had been building
for several years. Le Gallienne nagged Peggy about her smoking, and her temper
when she had had too much to drink. Le Gallienne refused to spend time at
Peggy's house on the Vineyard, and Peggy said that Eva was "wickedly arrogant
& ego-centric." They argued about the theatre. Peggy thought that Le Gallienne
was callous and lazy for not taking part in Actors' Equity issues. Eva had not forgotten Equity's refusal to help the Civic Repertory, and she did not feel that
artists should be handled by the same union methods as steelworkers or truck
drivers. Eva lectured Peggy that "one should preserve one's inner well of creative
vitality—& try & contribute by one's *work* alone." Their conversations about
McCarthyism usually ended in violent arguments. Le Gallienne urged Peggy to
calm down until "those idiots come to their senses" and "not match hysteria with

hysteria," saying that if she were the one being investigated, that is what she would do. Eva complained that Peggy was pompous and patronizing and treated her like a child or a silly reactionary who didn't understand political issues.

All of their arguments masked a deeper rift, which Eva revealed in a diary entry after they returned from Europe. "I'm afraid I have often been unkind to [Peggy]—simply because she *disturbs* me. She is out here now—I got here Thursday evening & she came out yesterday afternoon—and I couldn't help wishing I could have had a few days here in peace. Every time I try to concentrate on anything she breaks in—I also have got to the point where I find it hard to share a room with anyone—I'd much prefer always to sleep in a room alone."

In April 1953, Joseph Verner Reed and Lawrence Langner asked the "sister act" to head a touring program of Shakespeare scenes to raise money for a proposed American Shakespeare Theatre in Stratford, Connecticut. Webster arranged the script, directed the scenes, and served as narrator, and Le Gallienne coached the other actors and led the company. Reed and Langner hinted that the project would lead to important work for both women at the new theatre. It did not. Although Reed and Langner often sought advice from Le Gallienne and Webster, the women were never invited to direct a play at the American Shakespeare Theatre. In fact, in the entire thirty-year history of the theatre, which opened in 1955, no woman ever directed a production there—an appalling record, but certainly not an unusual one in the male-dominated American theatre, which, perhaps unintentionally, routinely and blatantly discriminated against women in playwriting, in directing, and in administration.

The Shakespeare tour played to excellent business and reviews in major cities along the East Coast and had a two-week run in Washington. Basil Rathbone starred with Le Gallienne, playing scenes from *Henry VIII* and *Macbeth*. Faye Emerson, Viveca Lindfors, John Lund, and Paul Ballantyne also appeared. Le Gallienne insisted that she "not be billed below any Hollywood names . . . the Theatre is my province." It was a joy for her to act with Basil again, since "we are so completely in rhythm physically—always were—and that makes it all so easy." She couldn't resist, however, giving Rathbone an acting lesson. "He still hasn't learned to make a 'long arm,'" she said. "They're always bent at the elbows & so tight—& his fingers have corks in them! He was sweet about it." The Swedish actress Viveca Lindfors, "thin as a rail & gawky as a young colt [with] wonderful eyes," reminded Le Gallienne, then fifty-four, of her younger self—a perfect type for Hilda Wangel. "I'm glad I'm an old dog. She might be quite dangerous! Ah, these Scandinavians!"

DURING THEIR STAY in Washington, D.C., Peggy was in agony. The day before they opened she learned that her application to renew her passport had been denied. Faye Emerson (who had been married to Elliott Roosevelt) gave Peggy a name to call at the Passport Office. When she returned to New York, Peggy was issued a new passport, proving, Le Gallienne told her, that "with all the McCarthyism that is so disgraceful and evil, we still live in a free country." In May Le Gallienne signed copies of *With a Quiet Heart* at Brentano's, taped an interview at NBC, and joined Peggy at the Twelfth Street apartment. Peggy, looking "green in the face," had just received a wire from Senator Joseph McCarthy requesting that she appear in the Senate Office Building on May 25 at 2:30 p.m.

Advised by Sid Davis, a lawyer with Louis Nizer's firm, to say little to the committee and "never, never say 'No,' " Peggy faced her inquisitors—Senator McCarthy, attorney Roy Cohn, and Senators Karl Mundt, Henry "Scoop" Jackson, and Stuart Symington. Webster named names, but "nobody commented," she recalled, "on my curious ability to remember only the names of those who had recently died." She said yes, she had attended a dinner sponsored by the National Soviet-American Friendship group, adding that she had sat between Ambassador Andrei Gromyko and Thomas Watson, the president of IBM. At this, she noticed, McCarthy blinked and Mundt grunted. Bored with the pointless testimony, Symington yawned, exonerated Webster, and dismissed the meeting.

Peggy called Le Gallienne from Washington to report that "it was all over & had gone well." But when she returned to her New York apartment, she wondered about the funny clicks on her telephone, and she obsessed about mistakes she might have made in her testimony which could lead to a charge of perjury. She called Eva with her worries. Le Gallienne told her that the tide was turning against McCarthy and that she should try to put the ordeal behind her. Peggy "sounded quite shattered by it all," Eva wrote. "I think she was annoyed with me because I couldn't seem to feel it was all as sinister & totalitarian-statish as she believes it to be. I'm afraid I'm a terrible disappointment to her all the way round. I feel she thinks I'm a vague selfish ostrich hiding my head in the sand & refusing to see reality. Maybe she's right."

Peggy was exhausted from her ordeal, nervous, depressed, and in need of loving support and sympathy. Although they spoke on the telephone every day, Eva did not join Peggy in New York until two days later, when she had other appointments to keep in the city. Disturbed that Peggy seemed melodramatic and out of control, she offered logic and reason instead of comfort. Peggy said that Eva was "cold & self-centered & stupidly unaware of the danger." Eva drove Peggy to Weston to rest, but Peggy decided to leave the country that had persecuted her. She asked Eva to go with her to England. Le Gallienne said that she couldn't afford to go. When Peggy offered to pay her way, Le Gallienne said that she would not be "kept" by Peggy.

On June 6, Peggy sailed for England alone. Hurt and upset by Eva's selfishness and lack of empathy, she realized, too, that Le Gallienne would never give up her home in Weston or desert Marion to build a new life with her in Europe. Webster planned to return to the little cottage near Saint-Paul and spend the summer there. "To be afraid is a very humiliating experience," she wrote later. "To be afraid in spite of your mind, your reason, your convictions, despising what you fear, despising yourself for fearing it . . . that is a very evil thing."

With Peggy gone during the summer of 1953, it was not surprising that Marion "was perfectly sweet. . . . I believe at last she has grown to love me," Le Gallienne wrote, "—in the sense of trusting me. . . . Her companionship is very dear to me." Peace with Marion, though, was lost if Eva stated any liberal views. When Le Gallienne expressed the opinion, for example, that the execution of the Rosenbergs had been a mistake, Marion stalked out of the house.

In late June Le Gallienne received a letter from Jo saying that she would have to undergo an operation to remove a malignant tumor. With no one to talk to or share her fears with, Le Gallienne poured all of her thoughts and emotions into her diary. Writing long, daily entries in her diary had become a discipline, a therapy, a conversation with another self, a stage to act upon, and sometimes a prayer. "I pray God that if the worst must be He will give me strength to act as my Jo would wish me to. I must not fail her again! . . . All through the years—everything good that I've done, I've done for her—& if I lose her—!" Eva wrote to Nelson Welch, who had befriended Jo, and asked him to let her know if Jo took a turn for the worse. "Tell Jo to 'keep a stiff neck' . . . I know it would make [her] laugh." Jo recovered; still, Le Gallienne booked a solo concert tour that fall which would take her to the West Coast.

MAY SARTON VISITED Weston that summer. Since the Civic years, Le Gallienne and Sarton had seen one another infrequently and exchanged occasional letters. In the summer of 1950, when Le Gallienne played *The Corn Is Green* in Boston, she visited with May after a performance and afterward dissected the young writer's character in her diary: "She is a strange mixture of sensitive, delicate perception & appreciation—and a kind of coarseness—a sensuality that strikes me sometimes as singularly lacking in Taste. The sensual-intellectual—a difficult combination. Her looks, more & more (and especially now that she wears glasses) point to the intellectual side of her nature—and make the Paganism of her temperament (on which I think she lays too much stress) seem very incongruous—and a bit forced. There is something about her now that makes me slightly uncomfortable. Still she is interesting to talk to—and I was glad to see her."

May arrived in Weston on July 1, 1953. Marion cooked dinner for the two women and then went off to visit friends. Le Gallienne asked her housekeeper to make up a bed in Nuja, since the house lacked a guest room. Later that night, Eva was writing in her diary when May appeared on the porch outside her bedroom. She asked Le Gallienne to have a cigarette outdoors. It's clear from Eva's diary entry the next day that Sarton had clambered up the rock ledge to the porch for more than a cigarette. "Thank God May left before nine," she wrote. "I think she had a nice time—in spite of the blow to her vanity!" Le Gallienne liked Sarton's mind, but she had no interest in a physical relationship.

Years later, May could not recall specifics of the episode. "It may have been true," she said. "I was certainly very much in love with her." Their friendship survived the rejection. Le Gallienne continued to be fascinated by Sarton's mind and her writing, but her attitude would always be that of a teacher with a prize pupil. May's attitude was a curious mixture of adoring hero worship mixed with anger and resentment at Le Gallienne's failure to regain the heights she had achieved with the Civic Repertory. She placed Le Gallienne on a pedestal, and only when Sarton was old herself would she be able to see her clearly as a human being and not as the Master Builder of her youth.

LE GALLIENNE'S EXPERIENCE had taught her that if she wanted to continue her battle for repertory and a national theatre, she had to fight from a position of strength. A popular hit could give her the clout she needed. In August 1953, she and Faye Emerson starred at the Westport Playhouse in *The Starcross Story* by Diana Morgan. Le Gallienne played Lady Starcross, the widow of a famous explorer. The plot was slight: a movie company wants to film the explorer's heroic life, but his former mistress (played by Faye Emerson) appears and reveals that the hero was a coward and his life was a fraud. The question of the play is, Should the fraud be exposed, or should an inspirational film be made about the legend? Lady Starcross wins in the end with her argument that the legend of her husband's life would inspire spineless youth.

Peggy (who had returned from Europe on August 11) quipped that "people think if Le Gallienne is in it, it can't be trash—and if Emerson is in it, it can't be dreary." The opening attracted Broadway "devils" and "many other gushers," Eva wrote, including Tallulah Bankhead and Mercedes de Acosta. Seventy-five-year-old Constance Collier, still a vigorous acting coach, arrived with Katharine Hepburn, her new protégé. "How incredibly New England [Hepburn] is," Le Gallienne observed. "Her face is scrubbed & clean & good—but getting a little gnarled." The play sold out in Westport. Reviewers composed valentines to Le Gallienne—her performance was so brilliant, one critic wrote, that she was able to convince an entranced audience that lies were truth. Lee Shubert saw the play several times and decided to produce it in New York in early 1954.

After the closing of *Starcross* in Westport, Le Gallienne learned two Oscar Wilde stories, *The Birthday of the Infanta* and *The Happy Prince* (over fifty pages of prose), for her West Coast recital tour and helped Peggy prepare *The Strong Are Lonely* for its Broadway opening. During Peggy's two-month absence, Eva discovered that she missed her terribly. They exchanged long letters several times a week, and, in a gesture of reconciliation, Eva bought Peggy a new, more comfortable bed and placed it opposite her own. Eva welcomed her companion back with a bouquet of flowers, and Peggy brought her a year's supply of Eau de Verveine. "It's good to have her back," Eva told her diary.

With Peggy back in town and Eva often absent, Marion again succumbed to her demon. Once, after finding Marion passed out, Le Gallienne marveled that "she must have the constitution of an ox": Gunnar had drunk a "whole bottle of Rum—nearly a whole ditto of Scotch—& all but a drop of the Early Times— some mixture!" Le Gallienne left a sandwich and a thermos of coffee by Marion's bed, fed and watered the chickens, took care of Vixen and Pi Te Li (Marion's Lhasa apso), dealt with the mail, and collapsed into bed. "Well, it's retribution as Ibsen would say!" she counseled herself.

In her youth Eva had identified closely with Hilda Wangel; now she knew the despair of Solness, the Master Builder, who felt that retribution was inexorable, a man who was tormented with the thought that his career had been made possible by the suffering of others. In her preface to *The Master Builder,* the passage in which Le Gallienne describes Solness's relationship with his wife also describes her relationship with Marion: "One has the feeling that at one time they must have been very close; had they not loved, the atmosphere of tension—the terrible sense of apartness—could never be so strong. They have lost one another along the way, and now each one dwells in his own lonely, bitter prison of guilt."

The Strong Are Lonely, a drama about the destruction of a Jesuit colony in Paraguay that had established a kind of utopia for the Indians, was a hit in France, but it was too talky and too philosophical to be successful on Broadway. Even with eight curtain calls, on opening night it was "the usual agony," Le Gallienne reported. The play flopped. Reviewers called her translation and Peggy's direction pedestrian. Le Gallienne argued with the producers and convinced them to keep it open for a week. "One wonders what we are all doing here in this poor country," she lamented, "that seems to be governed by the middle-men— the 'pimps' as Giraudoux so rightly called them."

At least on her recital tour there were no middlemen, and she didn't have to depend on anyone but herself. Charles Laughton, Emlyn Williams, and Claude Rains were just a few of the actors who, like Le Gallienne, had turned to the one-person show to maintain their contact with a live audience. When she played

Simmons College, Le Gallienne ate a late supper with May Sarton to celebrate May's birthday. May thought Eva looked old and tired, but the next day at the performance Sarton watched her transform herself into a stage presence "so radiantly alive, beauty put on from the inside, so to speak, and the amazing sapphire eyes, a *different* person."

In Los Angeles, she rented a "snappy little blue convertible" and visited old friends Elsie Janis, Ethel Barrymore, Frank Reicher, Nelson Welch, and, of course, Jo Hutchinson. One evening Eva parked her convertible a few blocks from Jo's house and then, like Peter Pan, stole into the vacant lot next to the house, scaled a wall, and crept into the garden. The excitement of doing the forbidden made her feel like a girl. "I watched her talking over things with [her gardener] in the kitchen. I thought he'd never leave. . . . Jo went upstairs & had a bath. I tried to whistle to her but she had the radio on & didn't hear me. I went all through the garden—it's charming. I'm so happy to have seen it. She called up after I got back to the hotel & was amazed—& rather pleased I think—that I had been there." Actually, Jo was horrified at the bold intrusion. "She could have wrecked everything," Jo said. She warned Eva that they must be very careful; word must not get back to her husband that they were seeing each other. "The whole situation is preposterous," Le Gallienne felt. She told Jo that if "she preferred not to see me at all that I would understand—& I think now I should just be able to bear it." Jo reiterated that she was loyal to her husband and had no regrets, but she could not stop seeing Eva.

Their parting was "ghastly," Eva wrote. "My darling broke down & cried—I had to hang onto myself like mad—so as not to make it too hard for her. . . . Then it was all over—& I felt like something cut off & desolate." Unhappy she certainly was, and her pain was genuine, but at the same time an undercurrent runs through Le Gallienne's diaries of secret enjoyment, private pleasure at the frightfully thrilling drama of it all. Jo had asked her not to write, but Eva slipped cards and letters past Jo's husband, disguising herself as "Berthe Pampelmousse."

The Starcross Story opened on Broadway on January 13, 1954, with Mary Astor replacing Faye Emerson. After a run of failed projects and a failed marriage, Astor needed the work desperately. During the rehearsal period, she fell ill with pneumonia. Le Gallienne sent her doctor and showed up herself, Mary remembered, "with encouraging words, a thermos of soup, and an envelope with $250 cash." The tremendous opening-night reception convinced Le Gallienne that the play might be a hit. The critical reception, however, ranged from lukewarm to mildly enthusiastic. The star-crossed production might have survived, however, if Lee Shubert had not died a few weeks before the opening. In the struggle for power, money dried up for the production. The day after the opening, the

The back of her house opened onto a rocky ledge. Note the bridge extending from her bedroom door, and the small greenhouse off the kitchen.

producers panicked and put up the closing notice. "I had one more experience to go through in the theatre," Le Gallienne deadpanned: "to close the same night you open."

It was a humiliating failure. Sounding like her Lady Starcross character, that night she told her diary: "I shall never give in. If I have to end my life in the most extreme poverty it must be to God's honour. I shall not bend to the evil & barren spirit of the age in which we live."

With the first February birdsong and the appearance of the sunny yellow winter aconites, Le Gallienne's energies and optimism returned. With her Ibsen translations to complete, proofs of *The Master Builder* preface to correct for Faber, and her research for her book on Duse, she had plenty to do. That spring she also tape-recorded her autobiography and other books for the blind, taught acting classes for the American Theatre Wing, wrote a short story about her childhood, called "Jane," and planted a garden. Her vitality and appetite for creation and action were enormous, and left unsatisfied when she was not working in the theatre. To fill the creative void, she decided to redesign and renovate her house. After obtaining a ten-thousand-dollar twenty-year mortgage, she hired a builder to raise the roof, add another chimney, expand her bedroom and bathroom, and add a large guest room and smaller utility room upstairs. The front room downstairs would have a new fireplace and mantel. As the old roof came off and the new rooms appeared, it was "like watching a set one has designed come to life."

Despite all the activity, she still had nervous energy, and to calm herself, she polished all the brass and silver in the Blue Room. She was reading Virginia Woolf's diary at the time, and she observed that "it might have been good for *her* to have polished a bit of brass now & then!"

The renovation was completed in late spring, but Peggy was unable to enjoy it. Her only living relative, her cousin, Jean, was dying of cancer in England, and Peggy sailed to England to be with her. After Jean died, Peggy wrecked her car, and cabled Le Gallienne that her plans had been wrecked, too. In a later letter, she told Eva that she was going to the cottage in France and taking British novelist Pamela Frankau with her. Le Gallienne hoped that "she doesn't get *too* involved there." She noticed, though, that in Peggy's letters "we" had become more and more frequent. As Peggy's letters continued to stream in, filled with news of Pamela and their trips together, Le Gallienne grew apprehensive. "Perhaps I'm imagining things," she wrote, "but I have a sort of hunch—could be wrong though."

She was not wrong. Peggy had fallen in love with Frankau, a forty-five-year-old married Roman Catholic. The women moved in together. Later, Peggy told friends that Pamela Frankau was the love of her life. The women bought a house, traveled together, and shared their lives. Peggy even stopped smoking. It was a passionate relationship. There had always been an element of competition in her relationship with Le Gallienne. With Pamela, Peggy "found . . . that the craft of the novelist and of the theatre director are astonishingly close," she wrote. "We were very good for each other. And . . . we laughed a lot. It was not just frivolous laughter; it involved perception, self-criticism, irony, a sense of proportion— and, on occasion, guts. I think it may well be the most precious thing that two people can share with each other."

Le Gallienne's pride was hurt, and she made no attempt to win Peggy back. While she rationalized that if Marion had not been present, things might have turned out differently, it was Eva who had first rejected Peggy. Their arguments about Peggy's response to her HUAC ordeal had been only an outer manifestation of their physical and emotional estrangement.

She stored Peggy's bed in the barn, moved all of her own belongings out of the Twelfth Street apartment, blocked out her name above the bell, and left her keys for Pamela Frankau. She bought a new mailbox for the house in Weston— "there'll be only two names now"—and she met with her lawyer and began the process of drawing up a new will, taking "provisionary steps to protect" Marion. By January 1955, the "pain and loss . . . grow easier," she wrote, "though con-

Pamela Frankau with Peggy Webster, Greece, early 1960s

stantly still at the back of mind & heart. . . . I don't know why I bother to write in this book . . . it seems to me that the older I get the less I know—It all seems questions—Why? How? What for?" She continued to confide in her diary, though, writing that she had "believed so completely in the lasting reality of this relationship that the shock simply will not let up. I don't suppose I'll ever really get used to it. I write this down only to clear my mind of it—for I talk of it to no one—no one at all."

WORK HELPED to keep Eva's mind off Peggy, although she occasionally strayed to the brandy bottle. In August 1954, she accepted a job in Hollywood as Shakespeare consultant on the movie *Prince of Players,* starring Richard Burton as Edwin Booth. Peggy had originally been offered the position, but she was told that there was still some question about her association with subversive organizations. Disgusted with the whole business and not wanting to interrupt her vacation with Frankau, she had suggested that Eva take the job. To earn her thousand dollars a week, Le Gallienne played Gertrude to Burton's Hamlet and coached Maggie McNamara, the young actress who played opposite Burton. The script was ridiculous, she believed, and no one cared a whit about accuracy. Later, when she saw the movie, she thought it was dull and "entirely pointless." In her *Hamlet* scene with Burton, she wore a long blond wig, looking more Ophelia than Gertrude, and gave, she wrote, a "ghastly" performance. The weeks she spent in Hollywood were ghastly, too. Jo's husband had retired and was spending more time at home. Jo's free time was curtailed, which, of course, made Le Gallienne angry. One night she got drunk and called Joseph Schildkraut and asked him to come to her hotel room. Drinking made her amorous, and when he arrived, she suggested that they go to bed. A sober Pepi patted her on the head. "Now, now, Evale," he said. He kissed her on the cheek and tucked her into bed alone. "Eva was often drunk during *Prince of Players*," Jo recalled. "She wasn't very nice. She was smart that she got Nelson Welch in to keep her straight, but one evening she was tearing her clothes off, drunk. She was a very bad drunk, even though she could go for long periods without drinking."

While she was in Hollywood, Le Gallienne called and wrote Marion frequently. "God bless you my darling Mutki," she wrote. "Whenever I'm . . . going through difficult things—I realize anew how spoiled I am—and how deeply thankful I am." Marion responded that she was "grateful, more than I can say, for all your loving patience and understanding. The bad, miserable and unhappy years are far behind and will not come again."

To ease her loneliness in Hollywood, Eva acquired a dog that she named Midge. She chose a small Yorkshire terrier—a lovable, good-looking, aristocratic breed noted for its loyalty, liveliness, intelligence, and courage as well as for its stubbornness, aggression, suspicion of strangers, and unsociability with other animals: in other words, a dog the image of herself.

LE GALLIENNE RETURNED from Hollywood in early October, and after a brief recital tour, she started rehearsals of *The Southwest Corner*, adapted by John Cecil Holm from a novel by Mildred Walker. Inaccurately billed as a comedy, the play is really a grim character drama. Le Gallienne played Marcia Elder, an eighty-two-year-old Vermont woman in need of a caretaker. Enid Markey acted the role of vulgar, materialistic Bea Cannon, who insinuates herself into the old woman's house, marries the handyman, and attempts to eject the gentle old lady out of her home. The play is marred by a deus-ex-machina ending when Bea abruptly dies of a heart attack. Ticket sales were excellent, and the Boston, Philadelphia, and Cleveland critics lauded the performances, but they pointed out the play's defects. Once again Le Gallienne transformed herself completely. She scrubbed her face clean, added shadows and lines to her fifty-five-year-old face, wore a white wig upswept into a bun, and succeeded in looking like a thin, wide-eyed Ethel Barrymore.

During the Cleveland tryout, Marion invited her husband, George Westlake, and his brother Tom to see the play. They all loved it and thought it would be a hit. Le Gallienne was more circumspect. John Huntington, the producer, was a dilettante, she said, "rather like one of those large toy balloons—he inflates & deflates with equal ease." When she learned that the play had been booked into the Holiday Theatre on Broadway, "among the shooting galleries and peanut stands," she lost any hope for success.

The opening-night audience cheered the play, and the next morning Brooks Atkinson wrote that it "introduces into our squalid theatre a civilized respect for the sensibilities of human beings." Le Gallienne was giving one of her finest performances, he wrote, playing "with great sympathy and insight. The unspoken part of the story is told in illuminating acting: the pride, independence and sweetness giving way to solitary panic and gaunt resignation to forces she cannot control." In the last review he would ever write of Le Gallienne (he died in 1958), George Jean Nathan again attacked her acting, calling her "bloodless and chill." She read the notice, but nothing Nathan wrote could affect, she said, her "immense rapport with an audience." On her solo call after every performance, she was carried away by "bravos & the intensity of the applause like a solid crack . . . with the actual impact of a great ocean breaker—& it has somewhat the same exhilarating feeling." The play, however, closed after thirty-six performances.

Her search for a popular hit had failed. Once again, she was washed up on shore, in "a ghastly state of depression—due I suppose mostly to unaccustomed alcohol . . . but to general let-down & disappointment & uncertainty as to what next and so on." At times, she felt as if her life were rushing "towards its end" and wondered what was the use of doing anything when "it'll all be over in five minutes anyhow!" Such dark feelings were quickly banished by a glance out her bedroom window to see that "the sunlight had that curious cold, clear, thin look—a pale lemon-yellow—of winter. It was so beautiful I stood gazing out a long time thinking how exquisite the world is, in all its different liveries."

LE GALLIENNE AGREED to reprise *The Southwest Corner* on the *Kraft Television Theatre* and immediately regretted it. "The vulgarity & squalor (spiritual squalor!) of the whole business is demoralizing . . . a foul & awful medium—the lowest of the low!" In television, of course, there were no bravos, no sustaining wave of energy and adulation to lift her, although the shopkeepers in Weston and Westport and the garage attendants in New York gazed at her, she said, "with a kind of reverence & [said] how 'marvellous' it was." Offers came in, but she refused to do any other television right away. "Simply couldn't face that kind of thing again so soon"—especially since it was April and the rosebushes needed pruning.

Left to right: Lucille Lortel, Le Gallienne, and Audrey Wood
at the White Barn, late 1950s

A weekend visit from Peggy in late April and Constance Collier's death on April 26, 1955, upset her terribly. Peggy struggled to maintain their friendship, and when Eva at first refused to answer her letters, Peggy wrote to Marion, who responded. "She accuses me of not knowing friendship," Le Gallienne wrote, "but I suppose I am somewhat of an 'either-or' person—maybe it's the Dane in me." With Peggy and her new love, Pamela, in New York, Eva wanted to flee. When a theatre in Ann Arbor, Michigan, offered her the opportunity to work on Mrs. Alving again as well as time to test her new translation in performance, she grabbed it. She played *Ghosts* there for three weeks.

When she returned home, Lucille Lortel, who managed the White Barn The-atre in Westport, called with an idea that they might work together in some way. Lortel, a former actress turned producer, artistic director, and theatre owner, had founded the White Barn in 1947 to present experimental plays. Later, she would be the first to receive the Margo Jones Award for her significant record in pro-ducing new work. Lortel wanted to expand the activities at the White Barn to include actor training. Le Gallienne suggested an eight-week session of classes in Shakespeare, Ibsen, and Chekhov for advanced students and professionals. Her association with Lortel would last for years, but the two women rarely saw each other socially, and Le Gallienne often wondered why Lucille was so nice to her. "I was in awe of her," Lortel remembered. "Le Gallienne was beyond me; I felt she was wonderful." In exchange for Le Gallienne's name being associated with her theatre, Lortel paid all administrative and advertising expenses and guaranteed Eva five thousand dollars for the season, which freed Le Gallienne to accept or reject any students regardless of their ability to pay.

In addition to her fee, the acting classes offered Le Gallienne the opportunity to try out her Ibsen translations in performance, which undoubtedly accounts for their ease and fluidity compared with the stilted William Archer versions. In 1951, for a Modern Library edition, Random House had published her translations of six plays: *A Doll's House, Ghosts, An Enemy of the People, Rosmersholm, Hedda Gabler,* and *The Master Builder.* Random House wanted six more translations—of *Pillars of Society, The Wild Duck, The Lady from the Sea, Little Eyolf, John Gabriel Borkman,* and *When We Dead Awaken.* She had built up an impressive library of Ibsen material that she drew upon—criticism, biographies, and letters—plus her own original research into his prompt books and papers as well as the vast experience she had acting in and directing his plays. It was grueling, tedious work, but she liked it. Over the years, she had honed her Danish by extensive reading, and since Danish is quite close to Norwegian, and at the time Ibsen wrote his plays the languages were even more similar, she had no difficulty with the language. Le Gallienne attempted to capture the ideas and moods of Ibsen's works, paying particular attention to the sound of the words. She felt incapable of translating his poetic dramas *Peer Gynt* and *Brand,* believing that the "very sound of the language is inextricably bound up with the thought, the passion, the satire, the mysticism; it is like the blood pulsing through a body; there is no life without it."

Working directly from the originals, she rethought and reworked her earlier versions, trying to recreate Ibsen's "deceptively simple, lucid style," a style that was not portentous or solemn, but was filled with "strong highlights and vivid colour, as well as swift pace and infinite tonal variety." Sensitive to the psychology of the characters, she uncovered nuances that Archer had overlooked. For example, when Judge Brack is alone with Hedda, he calls her "Mrs. Hedda" instead of the more formal "Mrs. Tesman" that he uses in company. Brack's use of Hedda's first name stressed that there was a kind of "secret understanding" between them. In translating *The Master Builder* and particularly Hilda Wangel's impudent speech, she felt that it would be wrong to use transitory slang. When Solness asks Hilda if she wants to stay and write in his ledger, she replies, "Not I, thank you! Nothing like that for me!" She believed that translating the line as a young American girl might say it, "Oh, yea-er? Thanks pal—I don't go for that!" would ruin the universality and timelessness of the play. The answer, she felt, was for the actor playing Hilda to say the line with impudence instead of politeness.

In her prefaces to *The Master Builder* and *Hedda Gabler,* which were published in London by Faber and Faber and in New York by New York University Press, Le Gallienne provided a scene-by-scene, almost moment-to-moment, breakdown of the plays and the characters. Both prefaces are written from the viewpoint of an actor and director sensitive to the plays as theatre pieces, and they not only illuminate Ibsen's scripts but reveal the intricate, painstaking analysis and the imaginative insights that Le Gallienne brought to preparing a play and a role. Le Gallienne also dealt with critical interpretations of the plays, but her own analysis is free of academic jargon. "Interpretations of Ibsen's play have ranged all the way from Professor Weigand's theory, which explains Hilda's ecstasy in terms of an adolescent orgasm," Le Gallienne wrote, "to that of a director I once knew, who insisted that Hilda had no reality, but was merely a figment of Solness' imagination." Her own understanding of Hilda Wangel was based on years of playing the part in repertory from 1923 until 1940. "I was just Hilda's age when I first studied the part," she wrote, "and was just as ruthless, fearless, and opinionated as Hilda herself. I flung myself into it with all the confidence and assurance of youth and never stopped to question or analyse."

To perform successfully in Ibsen, Le Gallienne believed that the actor must be able to communicate thought, to reveal the inner life of the character. Thea Elvsted in *Hedda Gabler,* she wrote, "is a thoroughly Scandinavian woman . . . honest and direct to the point of naivete, utterly without guile, without a trace of worldliness. . . . Also like the women in the Sagas, she is unafraid and oblivious of what 'people will say,' something of which Hedda lives in mortal dread." When Thea enters Hedda's house, Hedda should take in "her plain, almost shabby dress, the poorness of her accessories; her gloves, her bag," and while Hedda charms Thea, the audience must be aware of Hedda's true motives. "There must be no dark look behind Thea's back, no baleful glances towards the auditorium," wrote Le Gallienne. "If the actress playing Hedda handles the scene clumsily, Thea will seem a fool. And that would be wrong." In analyzing Hedda, Le Gallienne took her cue from Ibsen's notes and his descriptions of Hedda as "cold." It was important that Hedda should "seem conventional and in every way impress one as a highly-bred woman of distinction and poise," Le Gallienne wrote. "She is enormously aware of the impression she creates, very self-conscious always, and exquisite. She thinks of herself, one can be sure, as someone rare and romantic, a kind of *princesse lointaine.* . . . To be cooped up in small hotel rooms or tiny railroad carriages . . . to find oneself everlastingly with one and the same person—yes, indeed—poor Hedda must have been 'bored to distraction.' " At the end of the play, Hedda's suicide should be an act of gallantry, and Le Gallienne believed that "any actress who lacks the courage to pull a trigger on a blank cartridge is incapable of portraying the feelings of a woman who has the courage to pull a trigger on a shot that will blow her brains out."

Random House published *Six Plays* in its Modern Library edition in 1951 and *The Wild Duck and Other Plays* in 1961—the only translations of Ibsen's plays to date by a major theatre artist. *Six Plays* sold more than twenty-five thousand hardcover copies, and McGraw-Hill released a paperback college edition. In just two years more than eighty thousand copies of the first paperback edition of *Six Plays* were sold, and her versions of the twelve plays were the standard texts for some years, reviving an interest in Ibsen and encouraging productions of his plays in the educational and professional theatre. Her achievement was an extraordinary one for an artist with little formal education—an achievement that an academic might consider a life's work. Later Ibsen translators, like Rolf Fjelde, drew on her pioneering work. "She is truly one of the master builders of the American theater," proclaimed Fjelde, "and she has helped to encourage, to hearten, and to inspire the work of all of those who followed—and continue to follow—in her indomitable path." In 1961, she was awarded the Norwegian Grand Cross of the Royal Order of Saint Olaf, Norway's highest honor, and she received letters of thanks from Ibsen's family for her lifetime of service to his plays as actor, director, producer, and translator.

DURING THE SUMMER OF 1955, Le Gallienne's solitary translation work in Nuja was balanced by the five hours a day, three days a week, that she spent teaching acting classes at the White Barn. For the first few sessions, she thought she would "die of terror," but she collected herself and put on a calm face. "Old quack Le Gee," she called herself. She expounded on the "Body," explored the intricacies of Shakespeare, Ibsen, and Chekhov, and fought desperately not to tell her students "all to go to Hell!" when they found her beloved Ibsen hopelessly difficult. When they asked too many silly questions about acting, she longed to crack them over the head like a Zen master and shout, "Kvatz!"

Le Gallienne believed that the only way to learn acting was by doing. Young people, she believed, were "fed with too many theories, instead of being given the chance to grow by actual *practice*." Consistent with her philosophy of individualism, she felt that acting was too personal an art to be served by any one method. When asked by an academic to fill out a long questionnaire to define her procedure in working on a role, she refused to do so and replied with great irritation:

It would be like taking apart a fine, intricate watch to see what made it tick. . . . I am a worker in the theatre—have been all my life. I do not know how to function along pedantic, academic lines. . . . You say for instance that my work seems "modern"—in spite of my "tradition of theatre, and the theatrical." You should know that there is nothing "modern" in truth, simplicity, and economy. These qualities have always existed on the stage. Through the years I myself have seen them exemplified in many artists. . . . I find all these petty precisions demanded by your questions intolerable. . . . There are no short cuts, no recipes, no one "Method" to provide sure-fire success in achieving mastery of this difficult, fascinating & intensely individual art.

Of course, Le Gallienne was also aware that there was little opportunity for young people to practice their craft in the American theatre. In her acting classes, she directed them in scenes from plays, and they worked on their acting through performances and critiques. "All acting is character acting," she told them. She was careful to edit her comments and not to overpraise. From her own experience, she knew that a gesture or a moment created by instinct and intuition could be killed by too much analysis.

When twenty-one-year-old Geddeth Smith auditioned for her, "she came up the steps," he recalled, "and she looked me straight in the eye. I don't know if anyone had ever looked at me with that kind of candor and directness, and I liked it."

"I would like very much to work with you," she told him. Smith replied that he couldn't afford to pay the tuition. "I won't charge you any fees," Le Gallienne said.

"I don't know anyone who was quite like her," Smith said later, "anyone who had the real sense of purpose and importance and meaning of the theatre. . . . She worked with all of us students as if we were colleagues. Talent is not all, she told us, you have to have character in order to endure failure. . . . She cared absolutely nothing about what people call 'image' nowadays. There was never the sort of pose that many people take in the theatre, where egos are so important. You have to have a lot of ego as an actor, she told us, but until you conquer it you'll never be an artist."

Peter Falk lied on his application to the class, writing that he was a professional actor. Falk worked as an efficiency expert for the budget director for the state of Connecticut. For ten weeks, every Wednesday, without telling anyone at the office what he was doing, he drove to Westport to take Le Gallienne's Shakespeare course. Falk had worked in little theatres and had acted briefly at Erwin Piscator's Dramatic Workshop at the New School in New York. He wanted to be an actor, and he was often told that he had talent, but "I didn't listen to anybody," he recalled, "because I didn't think they knew anything." One day he was late for a session and Le Gallienne asked him why. He replied that he was working in Hartford and had to drive down. "How can you make a living as an actor in Hartford?" she asked. "I'm not an actor," he told her. "Then, she said four words," Falk remembered: " 'Well, you should be.' There was something formidable about her, and there was something objective about it—crisp, detached intelligence that was based upon experience." When he left the class that day, Falk quit his job and began calling himself an actor.

Most of her students came from New York to study with her, but she also accepted some local students. Steve Lopez exchanged work in her garden for the acting classes. "She liked my gardening," he recalled, "but not my acting." She was "the most alive person I have ever known," he said later, "and I don't expect to find her equal again." Mariette Hartley, who lived just a few miles from Le Gallienne, auditioned for the classes in 1956 when she was a tall, gawky teenager. Le Gallienne gave her Juliet to study and told her that she would not be paying much attention to her. Mariette paid attention to her teacher, studying her and copying the way she moved and the way she dressed. After watching Mariette play Juliet's balcony scene, Le Gallienne observed that "she has a quite remarkable voice for a young American girl . . . it actually has tenderness & a sense of passion. I dare not think she really has something . . . but perhaps she has! It would be exciting!"

"I was in love with her," Mariette wrote later. "It was almost as if there were a light around her." Le Gallienne also became Mariette's refuge from her family. Once when her father had been drinking heavily and the house was in turmoil, Mariette called Le Gallienne and asked if she could come over. "Well, Ducks, I'm not in my right center," Le Gallienne said. Mariette walked to her house anyway, and found Le Gallienne drinking in the kitchen. She sat at her feet and drank with her, she recalled, "and Miss Evensen stalked off, upset." Later, Mariette's drunken father appeared and accused them of having an affair. Le Gallienne got rid of him, but it was an ugly scene. "I helped her to bed that night," Mariette recalled. "She was very loving and asked me to stay. God was with me and I said, 'No, Miss Le Gallienne, I can't.' "

Le Gallienne felt that theatre was an art passed down from hand to hand, and as she grew older, she felt strongly that she was an important link in a long chain of theatre artists. Her desire to hand on what she had learned from Sarah Bernhardt, Harley Granville-Barker, William Faversham, Constance Collier, Alla Nazimova, Ethel Barrymore, and Eleonora Duse became a compelling, almost physical need. Still, she couldn't help wishing that a job would come along. "There aren't so many years left—and it seems such a waste," she told her diary. Actually, she had theatre jobs. What she craved was the creation of a great role in a great play, a part that would once again carry her to the top of the wave.

In 1955, she played the White Queen on television in a *Hallmark Hall of Fame* production of *Alice in Wonderland*. She played *The Corn Is Green* in Milwaukee in November 1955, and again in Palm Beach in February 1956, and in January

1956 with John Kerr on the *Hallmark Hall of Fame*. Dalton Dearborn, the young
actor who played Morgan Evans with her in Milwaukee and Palm Beach, never
forgot the first time he met her and the first time he saw her act. "She was a small
woman, dressed in purple and blue, wearing a slouch hat, with her dog under
her arm. . . . I sat in the front row of the theatre and after she had said two words
suddenly it was everything I thought acting should be and had never seen. Her
voice was unbelievable—crystal clear, not put on, a natural way of speaking."
Dalton fell in love with her, and Le Gallienne encouraged his adoration. It was
fun, she thought, to be courted by a good-looking young man, imagining herself as Julie Le Gallienne surrounded by a "retuna" of young men. Conversation
with him, she wrote, "was like fencing with a beginner," and like "most young
American men he seems rather troubled and swings between complete insecu-
rity and a rather cocky assertiveness as a cover-up." These defects were offset by
Dearborn's value as an occasional escort, driver, and errand runner.

She returned to Milwaukee to play *Ghosts* in November 1956. While there, she
had "a vision of a strange door—like a section of a globe—opening on to a sky
hyacinth blue & powdered with stars—and the sensation of floating out into it
and becoming dissolved into it, while yet retaining a feeling of acute ecstasy."
Each time she thought of the vision, it filled her "with a great sense of peace and
joy. It was a marvellous experience. Perhaps Death will be like that. If so—it is
nothing to fear." She felt herself changing in inexplicable ways. When she played
Ghosts in a showcase at the White Barn in August 1956, she felt no strain, even
though the audience was filled with New York "devils." She felt the presence of
her mother so "*close* . . . I could almost say she played the part for me . . . a most
curious sensation. . . . Perhaps I'm getting dotty." She couldn't make up her
mind if she could "no longer act at all or whether I can now act incomparably
better—all I know is that I act as I never have before."

She felt as if she "were waiting for something." While she waited, she translated seven Andersen fairy tales, which Harper & Row planned to publish, continued with her Ibsen translations, recorded an album of American and English
poetry, taught her classes, worked in her garden, hosted family dinners with
Hesper and Robert Hutchinson, visited with Helen Boylston, Alice, and Mimsey, performed her recitals, and enjoyed her comfortable routine at home with
Marion.

George Westlake, Marion's husband, died in January 1956, and Gunnar was
disappointed to learn that there was no estate, that his brother Tom had supported him for years. Marion felt guilty that she was not contributing financially, which accounts for her difficulty with housekeepers over the years.
Cooking and cleaning were her ways of contributing, and she resented a housekeeper's intrusion into what she considered her territory. Marion was in her
mid-sixties, and while she was strong, she suffered from painful arthritis. Eva

waged a running battle with Marion to get her to do less, but it was a battle she rarely won.

Occasionally, Eva and Marion drove to New York to see a play on Broadway. Le Gallienne shared the view of critic Emory Lewis that "the salient feature of Broadway in the fifties was the dismal quality of its productions." With the exception of plays by Tennessee Williams, William Inge, and Arthur Miller, Broadway was primarily devoted to musicals and conventional comedies.

At the Old Vic's production of *Richard II* (which she loved), Le Gallienne ran into Paula Miller and her husband, Lee Strasberg. Paula had been an apprentice at the Civic and "was very charming to me," Le Gallienne noted. "Her husband—the 'great man'—looked frightful and was rude and boorish in the approved 'Studio' manner. All it comes down to is acute self-consciousness, it seems to me. I find those people really intolerable—and so silly. Little, self-important, insecure, petty little upstarts. Yes! 'little'—there is something so 'mesquin' [shabby] about them."

The subtext of Le Gallienne's reaction to a chance encounter perhaps was indignation at not being paid the respect she thought she deserved. She knew little about the teaching strategies and methods of Strasberg, but the self-indulgent performances she sometimes saw of Actors Studio members seemed to her a repudiation of her own acting line. Le Gallienne's own method, developed over forty years, was based on hard-won experience, meticulous, imaginative analysis of text, the spiritual lessons she had learned from Duse, constant observation and study of the physical world, and her own internal emotional work, fused with the vocal and physical technique she had honed in countless performances. While her method shared the goal of Strasberg's method—acting that concealed acting—it was a complex method, a way of life really, that could not be taught in the conventional sense.

Her solitary life was ideal for a writer, but for a theatre artist, it was a lonely life. Le Gallienne missed the companionship of Peggy Webster, her intellectual equal, who had been her closest confidant and always willing to debate ideas. The Civic Repertory, the American Repertory, and even the companies that she had joined for long runs of a single play had provided a home, a sense of community, and a feeling of belonging to something larger than herself. A merely social attachment to other theatre people could not replace the intimate companionship, solidarity, and loyalty found in a permanent theatre company. Through letters and phone calls and occasional dinners, Le Gallienne kept in touch with former colleagues and students.

Content to remain in her small Weston circle, she rarely socialized with New York theatre people. She felt most at ease with old friends like Noël Coward, who shared her 1899 birth year, and over their occasional dinners, he teased her unmercifully, just as he had in the 1920s. "He is such a civilized person," she wrote. "We get on like a couple of old rogues." When Dag Hammarskjöld gave a dinner for the visiting head of the State Theatre of Stockholm, he insisted that Le Gallienne attend. His apartment was "very grand . . . all done in modern Swedish—very good stuff," Le Gallienne observed. She analyzed the guests as if she were describing characters in a play. Jean Kerr (the only other woman at the party) was "rather a flip, smart-alec, very pretty young woman"; Walter Kerr "was a rather large liverish-looking man"; Guthrie McClintic [was] "quite round and pink and grey." She left at 10:45 p.m. and drove home, wondering why she had been invited and why she had accepted.

Le Gallienne felt completely comfortable and at ease in only two places—her own home and on the stage. Even with an old friend like Eleonora Sears, she felt odd and out of place. At one of Sears's Boston dinner parties composed entirely of women, Le Gallienne "couldn't make out just what all the relationships added up to." One woman who talked incessantly of all her celebrity friends reminded her of Mercedes. "There's something more to all this than meets the eye—but, it's none of my business," she shrugged.

Except for her White Barn classes, she had no ongoing theatre community, no place to share the discoveries she was making about acting or about life. The burden of supporting herself and Marion was also a constant pressure. During the first four months of 1957, Le Gallienne earned just eight hundred dollars. She flirted with various moneymaking schemes, like marketing her tin squirrel baffles that she had designed for bird feeders. She tried to sell her latest invention, snap-in window grids, to a window company in Westport. The company turned her down and missed an opportunity to introduce the grids, which would become an industry standard several years later. Working in her garden and translating Ibsen and Andersen occupied her time, but she felt "so helpless & on the shelf: like some old cigarette holder as dear Tchekov says."

Know everything and use it, Granville-Barker had advised her, and Le Gallienne continued to learn, reading history, philosophy, poetry, and always observed, and then wrote down her observations, obsessively preparing—for what, she didn't know. After watching the movie *The Silent World*, she "was struck with how much actors could and should learn from watching animals. There are some shots of a turtle, going back to the sea after the effort of laying innumerable eggs. The wearyness—the absolute exhaustion of that creature! I'll never forget it. It expressed with every move—every shade of motion—the essence of all the weariness in Life. Quite incredible. What a lesson in economy!" The natural world around her home abounded in animals who gave her acting lessons in economy, grace, and purposeful movement.

Sharing the lessons she had learned from nature and training her students at the White Barn to play the classics acted as a tonic on Le Gallienne's spirits. The 1957 summer session ended in early September with a performance of the best scenes for an invited audience of New York agents and theatre people, including Cheryl Crawford, Jane Broder, Lucille Lortel, Lawrence Langner, and Tennessee Williams. Le Gallienne and Marion also fêted the students with several garden parties at their home. Le Gallienne wished that she had the means to "form the best of them into a little company & let them work on some whole plays. Where are they going to go?!"

LE GALLIENNE'S OWN DIRECTION was dramatically altered by a telephone call she received from Norris Houghton and T. E. Hambleton, who headed off-Broadway's nonprofit Phoenix Theatre. They were calling to ask her to play Queen Elizabeth in Friedrich Schiller's *Mary Stuart*. The Phoenix planned to open its 1957–58 season with a production of the play in a new translation by Jean Stock Goldstone and John Reich. The play was enormously popular in Europe, but it had not been done professionally in America since 1900. Tyrone Guthrie, former director at the Old Vic and founder of the Shakespeare Festival in Stratford, Ontario, had agreed to direct, and Irene Worth had signed to play the title role. Although Worth was Nebraska-born, most of her theatre career had been spent in British repertory. "I wanted to be a classical actress and there was no hope in New York," she said later, "no opportunity to grow within a discipline of theatre."

Judith Anderson had been the first choice of the Phoenix to play Queen Elizabeth, but she had turned them down because of other commitments and the low salary. Their second, "somewhat hesitant choice," according to Houghton, was Eva Le Gallienne. "Eva was unpredictable; it was rumored, perhaps falsely, that she'd become a difficult actress to work with. And being a director herself, would she, we wondered, willingly put herself in Guthrie's hands?"

Houghton sent Le Gallienne the script, and when she read it, she realized that "Elizabeth R. is a very great acting part—a real bravura piece!" The part of Queen Elizabeth was designed to use the talents of an actress in her middle years. Le Gallienne knew that such an opportunity to play a role which matched her age and talents was rare. She agreed immediately to play for one hundred dollars a week and living expenses.

When rehearsals began, Dalton Dearborn (who had been cast in a small part) helped move Le Gallienne and her Yorkshire, Midge, into Alice De Lamar's grand New York apartment, where they stayed only a few days. Alice's maid and the opulent surroundings made her feel like a "poor dependent." Le Gallienne moved into the Hotel Irving on Gramercy Park, "quite incredibly dumpy," she said, "but at least *our own!*"

At their first meeting, Le Gallienne and Guthrie took an immediate liking to one another. They both felt that the play was a *pièce de théâtre* and "must be played with broad bold strokes." Guthrie believed that American actors trained in realism suitable for "little journalistic plays" lacked the technique to play with the "operatic breadth of speech and movement" that *Mary Stuart* demanded. With the exception of Ellis Rabb, an American actor from Tennessee, Guthrie imported the men playing the major roles from his Canadian company at Stratford. Guthrie felt strongly that the intimate, natural style currently in vogue in the American theatre was "a great cover-up for photogenic men and women with no acting talent, and for giving an air of reality to quite perfunctory material," using a technique which was, he said, "just a tiny, constipated manifestation of nothing at all."

Le Gallienne immersed herself in a study of Queen Elizabeth. She read English history and biographies, examined the various portraits of the Virgin Queen, practiced Elizabeth's distinctive signature, and "polished and carved away." Douglas Campbell, who played the Earl of Leicester, recalled that Le Gallienne "was a little forbidding when you first met her, principally shy—very warm and friendly later."

Le Gallienne was fortunate to be under the direction of a man whose artistry matched her own. She thought Tony Guthrie was a genius and trusted him completely. The greatest danger, she found, "was in being too obedient. I can, like most people who can command, also obey. And there were times when my instinct rebelled & when I gave in to him too readily." Irene Worth recalled that there were "very tricky times during rehearsal. I'll never forget the lessons I learned from her—her humility and her control of her temper and her marvelous reserve of discipline and her simplicity."

From the many postcard portraits of Queen Elizabeth that Irene Worth had brought from England and with the help of the NBC makeup department, Le Gallienne devised a latex nose which extended her own delicate nose to queenly proportions. She shaved her hairline back a quarter of an inch, blocked out her eyebrows and painted on thin, black arches, and created defined eye sockets and heavy lids. The makeup required several hours to apply, and the transformation was helped further by a copper-colored wig and stunning period gowns designed by Alvin Colt and cut by Karinska. Since Irene Worth had a resonant, pipe-organ voice, Le Gallienne lightened her own cello voice to a slightly higher pitch to heighten the contrast of the rival queens. Guthrie's staging often isolated Queen Elizabeth spatially from the other characters to emphasize her solitary nature. To embody Elizabeth, a complex woman who survives by her wits in a man's world, a contradictory woman who wears many faces—flirting coquette, brutal ruler, jealous lover, cunning manipulator, cold egotist, tragic victim of circumstance—and above all a lonely woman driven by both power and love, Le Gallienne drew on all her inner resources and her own contradictory, complex, aristocratic nature. It was a perfect match of player and part.

On opening night, October 8, 1957, Le Gallienne felt "quite calm and rather happy." Elizabeth does not appear until the second scene, a good twenty minutes into the play. The tremendous reception at her appearance and the astonished gasps "jarred me for a few seconds," she reported, "but this with God's grace, I managed to conceal & immediately overcome—and from then on I played as if I'd been doing it for weeks. I was so grateful."

Critics resorted to hyperbole to convey the effect of the production and of Le Gallienne's creation of Queen Elizabeth. The sheer joy she took in transformation and the passion she gave to the theatre were palpable in her performances and accounted for her appeal to audiences. Richard Watts in the *New York Post* wrote that "Eva Le Gallienne gives . . . the finest performance of her career as Elizabeth. Her study of that strangely complex ruling genius is brilliant." The *Boston Globe*'s Elliot Norton reported that "after some years in partial eclipse, Eva Le Gallienne is shining again in the full brightness of stardom. . . . [She] makes a bold, spectacular, and thoroughly human figure."

The sold-out production of *Mary Stuart* turned around the fortunes of the Phoenix Theatre and reintroduced audiences to great ensemble acting. In 1963 Tyrone Guthrie founded the Guthrie Theatre in Minneapolis and created an American company, influencing a generation of actors as well as directors who could play the classics or contemporary plays with theatrical vigor, soaring imagination, and rigorous honesty. Le Gallienne's ability to play with high style grounded by deep inner truth helped end the hegemony of naturalistic acting in the American theatre. This ability, which was perhaps her most important contribution to the art of acting, was shaped by the influences of her two idols, Bernhardt and Duse. Le Gallienne served as the link between the two, combining consummate theatricalism and technical mastery with raw feeling and spiritual truth.

Since the Phoenix was an institutional theatre that offered a season of plays, *Mary Stuart* closed after fifty-six performances. Le Gallienne returned to Weston, where, without a role to play in the theatre, she imagined another self. One wonders what Marion's reaction was to this pronouncement: "I said to Gun: my idea of bliss would be to go from house to house with a little tool kit, in old clothes, and fix little things that needed fixing—that nobody else wanted to bother about. I should really be very happy—and useful too!" Surely dour Norway raised an eyebrow or suppressed a giggle.

Holiday preparations, however, brought out Le Gallienne's child self. She and Marion spent *jule aften* alone, but on Christmas Day they invited Hesper, Bobbie, and their daughter, Anne, for a traditional Danish feast of roast goose with all the trimmings. One of Le Gallienne's more attractive traits was her inability to bear a grudge and lose a valuable friendship. She invited Peggy Webster, who was alone in New York, to join them for the day. Neighbors and friends dropped in to see the tree with candles.

On her birthday, January 11, 1958, Le Gallienne began a new diary. "It's strange to feel so young. I constantly feel as though life were just beginning for me. . . . It takes a whole lifetime apparently to begin to learn how to live."

WHILE SHE WAS on top of the wave, offers flooded in from television and the-atre. The first role she accepted was the part of Madre Maria, the abbess, in an adaptation of Thornton Wilder's *The Bridge of San Luis Rey* for television's *Du Pont Show of the Month*. The "incredible boredom" of the rehearsals got on her nerves, particularly "several method young men who firmly hold up the pro-ceedings by discussing the 'motivations' behind a single simple line for a whole hour—with complete disregard for the other actors and overall good of the whole show." The live show, filmed with six cameras instead of the usual four, received rave reviews.

Le Gallienne did not see the final product and found all the acclaim puzzling. If she had watched the show, she would have observed that the director took great care in lighting the abbess and often used lingering close-ups on her face—a luminous face that appeared devoid of makeup, soft and unlined, with large, liquid eyes. At the end of the show, the abbess presides over the memorial service at the convent, and Le Gallienne used the low, rich tones of her cello voice, rounding the vowel tones: "There is a land of living and the dead and the bridge is love, the only survival, the only meaning."

The tedium of television exasperated her, but the money was useful in paying off the mortgage. In February 1958, when *Playhouse 90* offered her five thousand dollars to play outlaw Jesse James's mother in *Bitter Heritage* in Hollywood, she decided that she couldn't turn down the money—or the chance to see Jo again.

LE GALLIENNE MOVED into a suite in the Chateau Marmont on Sunset Boulevard and rented a pale blue Thunderbird. At the first day of rehearsal the young director said, "I hope, *Eva*, that you intend getting rid of that English *accent*."

"It was all I could do to keep from slapping his face," Le Gallienne wrote Mar-ion. She told him that she wanted to be released immediately. The director assured her that she would probably be all right in the part and could improve. Le Gal-lienne coldly informed him that after many years in the theatre she found it diffi-cult "to be patronized and would prefer to take the next plane home." She didn't go. A dozen deep red roses from the producer smoothed her feelings, a few diction lessons from Burgess Meredith roughened her speech, and rehearsals continued.

During her Hollywood stay, her *Bitter Heritage* co-stars, Franchot Tone, James Drury, and Elizabeth Montgomery, invited her for dinners and drinks, she took great bunches of forget-me-nots to Ethel Barrymore, and she saw Jo several times. Still, she missed Midge and Marion and longed for home. After a brief respite in Weston, she returned to Hollywood in late March to play Boris Karloff's wife in a live *Studio One* production. She drove Karloff to rehearsals every day and found him "a sweet old boy—but very dull." She found everything about filming extremely dull, but she could not turn down three thousand dollars for just a few days' work in television. Movie work was even more lucrative. When she tested for the part of Burt Lancaster's mother in *The Unforgiven,* though, she felt "like a beginner." At the Goldwyn gate, the guard had not allowed her to drive onto the lot, and she thought "how awful it must be to be 'nobody' in that place—a creature striving to become 'somebody.' " After her audition, the "whole studio burst into applause," and her movie agent, Lillian Small, told her that they had "flipped over the test." The Hecht-Hill-Lancaster office offered her a two-picture deal at twenty thousand dollars a picture: *The Devil's Disciple,* which would start shooting in England in July 1958, followed by *The Unforgiven.* She accepted their offer, which meant that she had to cancel her tentative agreement with John Houseman to play in *The Winter's Tale* at the American Shakespeare Theatre that summer. She didn't care, rationalizing that "they've taken such a time asking me to do anything there!"

"THESE HAVE BEEN queer months. I've felt somehow suspended," Le Gallienne told her diary on July 11, 1958. While she waited to be called to work on *The Devil's Disciple,* gardening had monopolized most of her time, or she sat in her Blue Room chair reading and watching the gold and purple finches, cardinals, and orioles that flocked to her bird feeders. She had managed to translate only two acts of *The Lady from the Sea* and had read a new comedy called *Listen to the Mocking Bird* that Cheryl Crawford had sent her; but without a larger purpose, even keeping a diary seemed silly and pointless.

Earlier that year Le Gallienne's hopes of a national repertory theatre were raised with the announcement that Mrs. Vivian Beaumont Allen had donated three million dollars to New York City's Lincoln Center for the Performing Arts (then in the planning stage) for the construction of a repertory theatre. "It has been my cherished hope," said Mrs. Allen, "that our country might one day have a national theater comparable in distinction and achievement to the Comédie-Française." Le Gallienne was asked to serve on the advisory committee, along with Robert Whitehead, Cheryl Crawford, Elia Kazan, Walter Kerr, Sanford Meisner, Roger Stevens, Jo Mielziner, and several others. At the first meeting, on April 1, 1958 (which Eva did not attend, since she was in Hollywood), for reasons of "greater flexibility of repertoire, hence greater flexibility of scheduling," the committee unanimously agreed to eliminate the idea of repertory. The sudden decision to scrap repertory was startling, since Mrs. Allen had donated her three million dollars for the express purpose of creating a national repertory theatre.

Le Gallienne attended only two meetings of the advisory committee. She made her feelings known in an article titled "Repertory . . . *When?*" published in *Theatre Arts* in September 1958. "It is to be hoped that Mrs. Allen's very specific mention of the term 'repertory' will be respected and that the proposed theatre will in fact be a *repertory theatre* in the true sense of the word." Le Gallienne offered a brief history and a sample schedule of the Civic Repertory, noted that a repertory theatre must be endowed, well managed, have high standards and low prices, and "assemble and keep together a group of actors large enough and versatile enough to handle a very wide range of plays. . . . To be a member should be in itself a mark of distinction." Most important, she continued, "there should be no compromise!"

Apparently, no one else on the committee shared her passion for a national repertory theatre. Even though the word "repertory" was retained in the title and the stage was designed to house multiple productions, the theatre was repertory in name only. Twenty-seven years later, after a succession of directors who tried and failed to operate the theatre at Lincoln Center, Gregory Mosher (who had headed the Goodman, Chicago's nonprofit, resident theatre) took over the direction of the theatre and dropped the term "repertory" from the name.

LE GALLIENNE ARRIVED in England on July 20, 1958, to begin filming *The Devil's Disciple,* starring Burt Lancaster, Kirk Douglas, and Laurence Olivier. For the next ten weeks, she felt "suspended and totally unreal." Like so many artists, Le Gallienne's identity was inextricably bound to the creation of her art. To confirm her sense of self, to feel "real," she had to create. Working in the theatre and creating other selves nourished her, and when she wasn't fed, she felt herself wasting away. She acted Mrs. Dudgeon in the movie, mother to Kirk Douglas's Dick Dudgeon, but her scenes were few and unsatisfying. Forced to remain in London on standby, she occupied herself visiting friends, shopping, and walking in the city's many parks. Her mother's old friends Lady D'Arcy and Lady Hulse loaned her their house, and she was physically comfortable, but she was lonely. Peggy Webster and Pamela Frankau introduced her to the novelist Rumer Godden, and Le Gallienne had long discussions with her about Roman Catholicism. She lunched with John Gielgud, Laurence Olivier, Gladys Calthrop, and Margaret Leighton; she haunted the art museums; and she went to the theatre but saw "nothing of any interest." Because of England's quarantine laws, she had not been able to bring Midge with her. When her loneliness became unbearable, she went to the Battersea Home for stray dogs and adopted a Cairn-type mongrel that she named Peter. "He never leaves my side and seems so grateful & devoted & anxious to please . . . he's a great comfort to me."

After working a few days she believed that she was beginning to "master the medium." In the two scenes she has in the movie, it's difficult to judge the truth of this. Le Gallienne's Mrs. Dudgeon looks small and shrunken. Framed by a black bonnet, her face appears pale and pinched; her powerful voice sounds crystal-clear but somewhat feeble. She worked ten days, but she was paid two thousand dollars a week for ten weeks, earning twenty thousand dollars plus expenses. Being paid for doing nothing enervated and infuriated her. "What a splendid theatre we could have on the money Hollywood wastes!" she fumed.

SHE RETURNED HOME to Weston on September 21, Marion's birthday. Marion's long separation from Le Gallienne had been less lonely since Marion's good friends Doris Johanson and Jessalyn Jones had moved into a house on Le Gallienne's property. Grateful for their friendship and the social companionship they provided for Gunnar, Le Gallienne asked only a small rent and gave the two women the house in her new will.

Harper & Row wanted her to look at Maurice Sendak's illustrations for her Andersen tales. The Playwrights Company (instead of Cheryl Crawford) now planned to produce Edward Chodorov's new comedy, *Listen to the Mocking Bird,* and sent a contract for her to sign. She still hadn't completed the translations of Ibsen for Random House. She also flung herself headlong into Catholicism, taking instruction from Father Joseph Murphy, the priest at Our Lady of Fatima in nearby Wilton, Connecticut. She had reached this momentous decision during her stay in England, but she wondered, "Am I playing a part? Or am I right in thinking this is good? I never quite trust myself." How could she know? After all, she was a consummate actor. As Laurence Olivier so shrewdly observed, "Scratch an actor and underneath you'll find another actor."

The discipline, beauty, and ritual of the Catholic Church filled a need in her life. Denied the fellowship of an ongoing theatre community, Le Gallienne reached out to religion. Her years at the Civic Repertory had been the happiest years of her life—a time when, like Solness, the Master Builder, she had done the impossible. From Ibsen, Le Gallienne had learned that complete spiritual freedom can never be achieved unless self is abandoned and "becomes lost in the selflessness of the infinite." Her creation of other selves and her need to unite with a live audience were attempts to do just that. Even the image in her advice to actors to take the corks out of their fingers illustrated her need to transcend self. Too, the roles she had played in *Mary Stuart* and *The Bridge of San Luis Rey,* and her new friendship with Rumer Godden, a devout Roman Catholic, undoubtedly contributed to her decision.

Godden visited for a few days in late October, the first of several visits over the years. Godden and Le Gallienne shared a passion for Hans Christian Andersen and an interest in gardening and birds. Eva also enjoyed pitting her mind against Godden's in stimulating, intellectual conversation. Rumer wrote a whimsical poem about Le Gallienne's Yorkshire, Midge, a "quick, unique minutia" whose moods, like her silky coat, were "mild silver, furious gold," and Godden observed that Eva, too, "could be very fierce when she was angry!"

Rehearsals of *Listen to the Mocking Bird* began on December 2, 1958, at New York's Ambassador Theatre. Chodorov directed his play, which he had adapted from a British comedy called *Tabitha*. Three poverty-stricken old ladies who share an attic apartment are suspected of poisoning their cruel landlady. Le Gallienne shared over-the-title billing with Billie Burke, the widow of Florenz Ziegfeld and a film star noted for her role as Glinda in *The Wizard of Oz*. Veteran actress Una Merkel completed the trio. Donald Moffat, who played the part of a police inspector, recalled that after ten days of rehearsal the actors were told that there were going to be some cuts. More than thirty pages of the script were excised, and then, according to Moffat, "we spent the next six weeks or so putting it all back."

After the Boston opening, Le Gallienne smelled "failure in the air. This is not the play I liked & accepted!" Her personal reviews in Boston and throughout the tour, though, were excellent. She played Lavinia Prendergast, an energetic, whiskey-drinking widow who rails against poverty and old age. A Boston critic wrote that Le Gallienne "makes the most of this role, and with her fine, clear, pungent speech, her forthright manner, and total impersonation of an ingratiating eccentric, shines as the star of the show."

Like her mentor Ethel Barrymore, Le Gallienne couldn't bear the company of bad actors, and she was fond of the talented, bristly-eyebrowed Moffat, who became her friend. "She clearly was the best actress in the cast," Moffat said. "She was very proud of her physical strength. She walked everywhere. She smoked a lot then. It was quite a long time before I even realized that her hands were disfigured. She disguised it so well by using them so gracefully. She held her eyes and her chin and head high, almost as if she were defying the world not to take her seriously."

According to Moffat, tension between Le Gallienne and Billie Burke reached a terrible state, requiring that he and assistant stage manager Phil Bruns intervene. Since Burke had a hearing problem and a poor memory, she was wired for sound and Bruns fed her the lines. From time to time Burke's earpiece would fail and "moments of terror!" ensued, Eva reported. Fortunately, she knew Burke's lines as well as her own and could prompt. Le Gallienne was "very professional," however, and "could not stand this," recalled Moffat. "There was a strange relationship there, too," said Moffat, "because of Le Gallienne's famous lesbianism."

Eva (left) and Billie Burke (right) in Listen to the Mocking Bird, *1958*

According to Moffat, Billie Burke said that lesbians often pursued her, and she also felt that Eva believed that Burke had no talent.

Since Moffat was Le Gallienne's friend and Phil Bruns was Burke's, the two men tried to arrange a truce, telling each woman to compliment the other one. Moffat described what occurred: "At the curtain one night, they stopped and talked. Billie Burke must have said something and Le Gallienne took her face in her hands and kissed her on the mouth. It was a very wicked thing to do," Moffat recalled with a laugh. Wicked or not, the kiss had its effect. Billie Burke sent Le Gallienne an apologetic, admiring note, and during the Cleveland run her earpiece functioned properly and she managed to say all her lines. "Such a relief!" Le Gallienne sighed.

Cleveland audiences could choose between Chekhov's *Uncle Vanya* at the Cleveland Playhouse or Chodorov's *Listen to the Mocking Bird* at the Hanna Theatre. Audiences "really loved" the play, Le Gallienne scoffed. She felt that because of the influence of television, people would laugh at anything as long as they didn't have to think. Marion brought her brother-in-law Tom Westlake to the Cleveland premiere, and they both confessed to loving the production. Notices continued to be good for the acting and bad for the play. When they opened at Shubert Theatre in Washington, D.C., "Burke was *impossible,*" Le Gallienne complained. "She made a shambles of the drunk scene. Una & I were quite upset by it all. I've never had to put up with this kind of thing & it's only by God's Grace I've been able to keep calm." Le Gallienne prayed for the show to close before they reached New York. Her prayers were answered. Three days after the Washington opening, following an evening performance, the entire stage area and the "beastly set" were destroyed by fire. Luckily, or suspiciously, the asbestos curtain had been rung down and the theatre and the dressing rooms were saved, but the set was completely gutted.

According to Le Gallienne's diary, at the time of the fire, she was in her room at the Willard Hotel, innocently reading a Josephine Tey thriller.

LIFE BEGINS AT SIXTY, Mary Zimbalist had advised Eva years earlier. Now, it was "strange" to think she was sixty years old, since she felt so young and vigorous. During the spring and summer of 1959, Le Gallienne stayed home and wrote the second volume of her Ibsen translations, worked in her garden, and even bought a chainsaw and cleared the deadwood from her property. The producers of *Listen to the Mocking Bird* had threatened to rebuild the set and reopen in New York, and Chodorov began rewrites, but Le Gallienne knew that the play was doomed. Her weekly fifteen-hundred-dollar checks continued to appear, however, until the guarantee ran out.

Harper & Row published her *Seven Tales by H. C. Andersen* that spring, and Le Gallienne was elated by the book's success. She had loved the work, and her efforts were rewarded by excellent reviews and strong sales. (The book has sold more than sixty thousand copies.) *Seven Tales* has "a poetic and a dramatic flavor," wrote one critic, "and the Sendak pictures, exquisite sketches in line and wash, and full pages in tones . . . seem original and yet exactly right." To publicize *Seven Tales,* Le Gallienne read the stories and was interviewed often that spring on radio and television. In 1965, Harper's brought out her translation of Andersen's *The Nightingale* (which proved even more popular than *Seven Tales,* and sold more than eighty thousand copies), followed by single editions of *The Little Mermaid* and *The Snow Queen.*

She paid off most of the ten-thousand-dollar mortgage, finished the attic in her house, and purchased two acres of land, which extended her estate to nineteen acres, further protecting her privacy. The only sad note during this happy, fruitful summer was the death of Ethel Barrymore—"the last of the greats," said Le Gallienne. "Some actors . . . are scared to death of her," she said. "But if she respects you and believes in you as an actor, no matter how young or insignificant you may be, there can be no one more generous, more helpful, or more rewarding to work for." Le Gallienne had numerous photographs of the older actress, and she never thought of Barrymore as being gone. "Ethalkin" lived on in the impeccable timing and grace that Le Gallienne had learned from her stage mother and whenever Eva glared at a disruptive audience member using Ethel's "number eight" expression.

In March, Le Gallienne had signed a contract with the Phoenix Theatre's touring company (called the National Repertory Theatre) to play Queen Elizabeth in a national tour of *Mary Stuart*. She would receive fifteen hundred dollars a week, with a guaranteed minimum of twelve weeks' work, one thousand dollars for direction, as well as star billing, cast approval, and first-class travel arrangements. This meant that she had to break her agreement with Hecht-Hill-Lancaster to appear in *The Unforgiven*. (Lillian Gish played Le Gallienne's role in the western and garnered excellent reviews.) With future work assured, Le Gallienne relaxed and enjoyed her daily routine and the usual round of dinners, garden walks, and visits with Alice, Mimsey, and Hesper and Bobbie.

On August 29, 1959, Helen Boylston accompanied Le Gallienne to Our Lady of Fatima, where Father Murphy baptized her during a violent thunderstorm. She had never been baptized in any faith, and the thought of it seemed "very strange" to her. "The actual ceremony took less than half an hour," Le Gallienne wrote, "but it is very beautiful and I found it most moving. I have been going towards this for many years—many times against my will it has seemed to me—but I am sure it is right, if only God will give me the grace to obey—the fortitude to persevere."

IN LATE JULY, Le Gallienne had played Elizabeth to Viveca Lindfors's Mary in a Vancouver production of the play. The engagement helped her ease into Elizabeth again, and when rehearsals began in mid-September for the *Mary Stuart* tour, her hairline was shaved and her role was prepared, and she was able to concentrate on recreating Tyrone Guthrie's staging. Since many of the original cast members had gone on to other commitments, she hired several actors that she had worked with in the past, including former Civic Repertory apprentices Staats Cotsworth and Paul Ballantyne and her former student Geddeth Smith. Swedish-born Signe Hasso, seventeen years younger than Le Gallienne, played Mary. Trained at Sweden's Royal Academy, Hasso had played repertory all over Europe and had starred in television, movies, and on Broadway. The two Scandinavian women liked each other immediately. "We had a special rapport on stage," Hasso recalled. "Le Gallienne had a terrific sense of humor . . . she laughed very often. Kind of a pearling laugh. She was strict, but there was always that overtone of sense of humor, understanding, and softness."

Assistant stage manager Bob Calhoun also grew close to Le Gallienne on the road. He had worked as a medic in the military, and one of his jobs was to give her B-12 shots. "She worked wonderfully with actors," Calhoun said. On the tour, though, Calhoun recalled, she "kept almost completely to herself. Midge used to bite people at the dressing room door."

Actually, Le Gallienne had little time to socialize. She spent her days working on the Ibsen translations, and she arrived at the theatre two hours before every performance to apply Elizabeth's complicated makeup. To save time, she shaved off her eyebrows as well as her hairline, which gave her an odd appearance off-stage, another reason to avoid interviews. When she did make a public appearance, she wore a mink slouch hat pulled low on her forehead or combed pixie bangs down to hide her lack of eyebrows.

The *Mary Stuart* tour played for thirty-five weeks in thirty-two cities, including Washington, D.C., twice, and solidly established the mission of the National Repertory Theatre to present classic plays to a national audience more used to a diet of touring musicals like *My Fair Lady* and *West Side Story*. Twenty-eight-year-old Yale School of Drama graduate Michael Dewell and his partner, Frances Anne Dougherty, produced the tour, and Dewell said later that "it spoiled me rotten. I thought all tours would be like this one." When they played San Francisco, Le Gallienne told her diary, "I've seldom heard such bravos!" In Los Angeles they played to sold-out houses and grossed more than thirty thousand dollars for the week. "What possibilities there are in this country for fine theatre now!" Le Gallienne wrote. "If I were 20 years younger I might be able to do a lot about it! Well—I suppose someone else will—I hope so." The only city where the company did not receive unanimous raves was snowbound Chicago. The wind blew so fiercely around the theater that two people were needed to hold open the stage door. Distraught at the play's reception, Le Gallienne asked Tony Guthrie to fly in to take a look at it. Afterward, she rushed up to him. "Tony, Tony," she said, "what's wrong?" "Eva," Guthrie boomed, peering down at her from his great height, "the show is fine. Chicago is wrong."

All along the tour route, Le Gallienne's old friends and fans sent her flowers and came backstage, but she rarely went out or dined in restaurants. She or her dresser, Nora Weiss, prepared meals on a hot plate in her hotel room. The discipline and structure of the theatre replaced the discipline and order that had drawn her to the Catholic Church. Occasionally, she attended Mass, but she felt that she should conserve her strength. "And I like to think of my work as a Prayer to God . . . so I hope He will forgive me," she said. She hoarded her vitality and carried the thought of her performance with her throughout the day. She described the feeling as "a kind of inner preparation—a coiling of the spring. . . . I suppose I take it too hard—but I can't see any other way to take it. With me it *has* to be a complete dedication."

After weeks of begging, Dewell finally got Eva to agree to give a speech at the National Press Club in Washington, D.C. Public appearances and publicity

chores were lacking in dignity, she thought, and made her feel "like a performing monkey." She had been willing, of course, to perform those duties for the
Civic Rep, but now she lacked the vitality and motivation of her youth. In
Washington, she suffered from a sinus infection, and on matinee days she wore
her makeup and artificial nose from one p.m. to eleven, which meant that she
could not blow her nose for ten hours. "Torture!" she groaned. The same doctor
who had treated her for pneumonia when she was twenty-one and playing in
Tilly of Bloomsbury gave her antibiotics to clear up the infection. To Dewell's
chagrin, Le Gallienne cancelled her appearance at the Press Club, which gave her
immediately a feeling of "immense relief."

During their stay in Los Angeles, she saw many old friends, including Pepi
Schildkraut, Mary Astor, Efrem Zimbalist Jr., and Nelson Welch. She spent "a
long lovely day" with Jo Hutchinson. "As usual it seemed as though we'd never
been apart," Le Gallienne wrote. "But it was good to be able to talk to her! She's
coming to the matinee tomorrow. The old boy actually didn't object!" When Jo
attended the matinee performance, Eva was extremely nervous. Jo had not seen
her act since Eva had played L'Aiglon, twenty-six years earlier. Privately, Jo
thought that Eva was "lacking in her former power," but she told Eva that she
was "very pleased with her performance."

When they played Philadelphia, Marion joined her for a few days during the
last leg of the tour. They lunched with Mary Zimbalist, who, playing her fairy-
godmother role, gave Le Gallienne a double string of perfectly matched
amethysts as an opening-night gift. She also told Eva that when she finished the
tour, she must have a complete rest and promised to send her and Marion on a
European vacation.

Peggy Webster saw the play in Princeton and "was crazy about the show,
really enthusiastic for a change," Le Gallienne wrote. Eleo Sears, her steadfast
Boston friend, and Eva's childhood friend Ellen Koopman turned up at the
Boston opening. Le Gallienne also visited with May Sarton, and they discussed
Catholicism. "Le Gallienne had this missal with her," May noticed, "very beau-
tiful with purple ribbons. It really horrified me because I felt it was all drama."
Le Gallienne was equally horrified at May's confession that she was seeing a psy-
chiatrist. "She'd be better to join the Church!"

On the closing day of the tour, Le Gallienne lamented that it was "a pity to
see the play put away for good. If only we had a civilized theatre. . . . I often wish
I were 20 years younger—I believe I could establish one—& firmly this time—
for the climate is right for it. But now the person with the vision seems to be
lacking. For it must be done with the 'single Eye.' " After a week spent filming
Mary Stuart for television's *Play of the Week* ("a grim nasty little chore"), Le Gallienne returned home. Instead of collapsing into her usual postplay depression,

she began making plans for her first vacation in eight years, a tour of England and Scotland with side trips to Paris and Copenhagen.

LE GALLIENNE WAS MUCH HAPPIER about the trip she planned to take with Marion than she had been about the vacation she had shared with Peggy in 1952. On the earlier trip, Peggy had paid most of their expenses. Now, even though Mary Zimbalist was providing several thousand dollars and Alice De Lamar was lending them her Paris apartment, the trip was made possible, she felt, by her months of hard work on the tour. She had also finished the second volume of the Ibsen translations. With the money she had earned, she paid off the mortgage. After test-driving several sports cars, she ordered a Jaguar, which she planned to pick up when they arrived in England. A new car was "terribly self-indulgent," but she rationalized that she deserved a reward for her months of dedicated effort.

In a letter to Mogens on June 24, 1960, Le Gallienne expressed her feelings about being an "old girl of 61! . . . I simply *can't believe it*—and, actually feel no different from the way I felt forty years ago—except *much happier,* and capable of enjoying life in a far more rewarding way."

In her diary, Le Gallienne privately expressed fire and enthusiasm about her various projects; but instead of diminishing with age, her enormous pride increased, and she kept those fires banked. The BBC, Canadian public television, *Play of the Week,* and various other organizations produced her translations of Ibsen's plays; Ingrid Bergman performed her *Hedda Gabler* for television; and while Le Gallienne dreamed that films might be made of her translations with great stars like Ralph Richardson and Greta Garbo, she did not pursue these dreams in any practical way. "I wish I were a man," she confided to her diary, "I might be able to succeed in getting someone to do this! There's always something faintly silly about an enthusiastic old woman."

Eva and Marion sailed for England and docked in Southampton on August 23. They picked up the new Jaguar, and Le Gallienne attached the Lalique hood ornament that had adorned all of her cars since the late 1920s. The brass-and-glass ornament, probably a gift of Alice De Lamar, featured the kneeling figure of a nude male archer pulling back a bow and arrow. After months of enforced discipline inside theatres and hotel rooms, Le Gallienne was ready to sate herself on sights, sounds, and impressions. Every day of their motor trip through England and Scotland was packed with sightseeing or theatregoing, with little time allotted for resting or languishing quietly in a cafe or a hotel room, activities that the older, less active Marion might have welcomed. In an Elizabethan mansion Le Gallienne was startled by a portrait of Elizabeth which looked "just like me in the play!" When they visited Holyrood Castle, they walked through Mary Stuart's rooms, and the history Eva had read sprang to vivid life. Le Gallienne loved the challenge of driving the responsive Jaguar on the steep and winding single-lane roads of Scotland. She drove fast through the industrial suburbs between Manchester and Liverpool and on to Stratford-on-Avon, Kenilworth Castle, the Pump Room at Bath, and finally, to Gunnar's relief, to their rented London flat.

They visited Peggy Webster and Pamela Frankau at the home they had bought together in London. Peggy had been dividing her time between England and America, directing operas in New York and plays at the Old Vic and Stratford-on-Avon. Pamela was just completing a book called *Pen to Paper,* about the writer's craft. In London, Eva introduced Gunnar to Gladys Calthrop, but Marion begged off a visit with Rumer Godden, preferring to stay in the flat and rest. Le Gallienne enjoyed her visit with Godden and her husband. "It was so nice to have real conversation for a change. We read French poetry & talked of everything under the sun except personalities & world politics." She and Marion also dined with Eva's second cousin Peter Thornton and his family. Peter was the only child of Sir Gerard Thornton and Mogens's sister, Gerda Nørregaard. In keeping with the tradition of rebellious Nørregaard women who defied bourgeois values, Gerda lived in England with Sir Gerard as Lady Thornton for six months of the year and spent the other six months on a farm outside Copenhagen with her Danish companion. Since the arrangement was an amicable one, Peter Thornton had enjoyed two loving fathers and the benefits of two cultures and two languages. Le Gallienne opined that Gerda certainly has "the best of both worlds . . . she has had *her way* no matter what. A determined lady!"

After a brief stay in Paris, where they saw Ionesco's *Rhinoceros* and a production of *The Cherry Orchard,* Eva and Marion flew to Copenhagen, where Mogens met them. He arranged a private tour of the theatre museum and the old Court Theatre, where Le Gallienne learned about Michael Wiehe, her actor ancestor, a great tragedian of the mid–nineteenth century, who had been Ibsen's favorite actor. During their stay in Denmark, they visited Gerda's farm, attended the theatre, and walked and shopped in Copenhagen. "I love this town," Le Gallienne wrote, "but I long for home."

DURING DECEMBER 1960, Le Gallienne and Marion prepared for their first Christmas at home in two years. Marion cooked her usual roast goose dinner, and once again they invited their neighbors and about a dozen children in for smorgasbord and the viewing of the tree. After the holidays and a brief lapse into drinking and depression, Le Gallienne occupied herself with long walks, shoveling snow, keeping the dozens of bird feeders full, and polishing all five thousand books in the Blue Room and in her bedroom with neat's-foot oil and lavender wax. When the books were finished, she burnished all the brass and oiled the furniture. At the moment, she had no work except for a contract with Random House to translate the plays of August Strindberg. She made little progress on the plays, finding them "strange. . . . They fall into two such different categories—as though written by two people: some of them so spiritual and serenely wise—and others filled with demons and madness." Strindberg was not a compatible soul, and she eventually gave her advance back to Random House.

Her own spiritual state had been troubling her. During the months in Europe, she had not gone to confession or attended Mass. After weeks of stalling, on February 2 she drove to Our Lady of Fatima, made her confession to Father Murphy, and promised to attend Mass the following Sunday. She was happy that she had "found the courage & humility" to go. On Sunday, though, their lane was slick with ice and snow, and she dared not drive. For the next few months, Le Gallienne attended church infrequently. She set a date for her confirmation, then cancelled, rescheduled, and cancelled again. Finally, after much soul-searching, she admitted to herself and to Father Murphy that she had been acting after all—that she could not become a Catholic. Rumer Godden said later that Le Gallienne had not been able to take the religious discipline of the Church. Jo Hutchinson disagreed, saying that Eva had always been religious and was, in fact, more religious than most Catholics. Le Gallienne believed that the reason behind her inability to commit to the Catholic Church was that there were "too many people" between herself and God. "I somehow couldn't negate them."

Actually, since Le Gallienne believed that her art was her service to God, belonging to a church was redundant. During the decade of the 1960s, she turned down commercial offers and devoted herself to nonprofit, repertory theatre. For those involved with the arts, it was a time of great optimism and hope. President Kennedy had selected poet Robert Frost to read at his inauguration, signaling that his administration would embrace artists. President and Mrs. Kennedy ushered in a period that, compared to the anti-intellectual 1950s, seemed more civilized and more receptive to the arts. With seed money from the Ford Foundation, nonprofit theatres sprouted up in cities across the country. During the 1960s, Le Gallienne aligned herself with two young repertory companies that hoped to realize her dream of a national repertory theatre for America.

On February 1, 1961, however, she was not working, and she longed for a quick television job, anything to supplement her royalty checks from the Andersen tales and the Ibsen translations. She envied Hesper, whose husband, Bobbie Hutchinson, had inherited money and who did not have to work. "How nice if one had an *income!*" A few weeks later, she accepted a job on television's *Play of the Week* acting Dame May Whitty's wheelchair role in *Therese*. Because of the long hours and early call, she stayed in the city, and Marion was left alone in Weston. Marion suffered from painful arthritis in her hands, arms, and shoulders, and left by herself, she resorted to a proven painkiller, the liquor bottle. Le Gallienne called Marion every night from her hotel, but one night the phone rang and rang. Worried about both Midge and Marion, she called Jess Jones, who walked up and checked the house and found no lights on and no sign of life. The next day, Le Gallienne called again and "got an answer at last—but such a mizzy one. It broke my heart. I wanted to jump into the car & rush home. I only pray it won't snow tomorrow night—I must get back." To please Marion, Le Gallienne altered her normal routine, and instead of retreating to the Blue Room or retiring to her bedroom with a book after dinner, she began spending more time watching television with Marion. She thought most of the shows were dreadful, but once in a while she caught a glimpse of Jo Hutchinson on *Perry Mason,* or of Peter Falk, who had turned, she thought, "into a really exciting actor—and so versatile. I feel proud of him."

IN EARLY APRIL 1961, Paul Baker, who headed the Dallas Theatre Center, invited Le Gallienne to look over the theatre and deliver a speech on repertory. Baker offered her ten thousand dollars plus expenses to move to Dallas for six months of the year and lead their theatre company. Le Gallienne, overwhelmed by the warmth and enthusiasm of the audience and board, seriously considered Baker's offer. But a few weeks later, when Michael Dewell proposed another national tour, this time a repertory of *Mary Stuart* and Maxwell Anderson's *Elizabeth the Queen,* Le Gallienne decided to go with the National Repertory Theatre. It was a risky choice, she knew. "What Michael is doing is, of course, dreaming. . . . I can't help understanding him—having been so much that way myself in my youth. The thing he can't understand—and in a way I love him for it—is that an old person like myself must work with some sense of security, having not very much time left."

Le Gallienne had no false modesty about her own work or her own worth. She had faith in her talent and in the rightness of her artistic vision. Her mission, her crusade, was to pass on the torch that had been handed to her by an earlier generation of artists and fight her continuing battle against the Philistines. A role model in her battle for art was Napoleon. "Do you know," she would say, "that Napoleon in the middle of one of his campaigns, right in his tent, arranged the establishment of the Comédie-Française? Yes, down to the final details, including a provision that understudies be allowed to perform at least once a month." She would wage her war across America, believing that she could "be of more service acting all over the country than sitting in one place. It's important that the young people should have the chance of seeing honest work—there's little enough of it."

Just as writers or painters stake out their territory and proclaim their beliefs and philosophy through their work, Le Gallienne offered the living example of her acting. She knew that she was writing on water, but she believed that her talent was a gift from God to be shared. She also believed in Dewell's mission to establish a national repertory company. He needed her name to give credibility and stature to the company in booking theatres and generating ticket sales. When the tour began in September 1961, the schedule was not complete. "I can't quite bring myself to trust Michael," Le Gallienne wrote. "I know he means well . . . but he does not tell me the whole truth—and I dislike that."

Rehearsals of the two plays began in August 1961. Since Le Gallienne played major roles in both plays, Jack Sydow had been hired to direct. Le Gallienne helped with the casting and surrounded herself with a group of actor friends, including Faye Emerson, who played Mary Stuart, Paul Ballantyne, Geddeth Smith, Dalton Dearborn, and Terence Scammell. Scott Forbes, who was well known as Jim Bowie on the popular television series, played Mortimer in *Mary Stuart* and Essex in *Elizabeth the Queen*. Le Gallienne doted on the tall, dark, and handsome Forbes and bristled comically at his "horrible TV fans—screaming, sex-mad, adolescent girls. They make one *shudder!*"

Elizabeth the Queen opened in Boston in late August. Since the queen in the Anderson play is twelve years older than in *Mary Stuart*, Le Gallienne used a darker wig in a more "violent" red. Feeling that Elizabeth had probably lost additional teeth in those years, she added a few more shadows to her cheeks. For more than eight months, the tour played sixty cities, towns, and universities, traveling by plane, train, bus, and truck. In addition to her fifteen-hundred-dollars-a-week salary, Le Gallienne was to receive 7.5 percent against the gross. Michael Dewell had assured her that the tour was fully guaranteed. It was not. Dewell made last-minute schedule changes when he was able to secure additional bookings, and the company often spent their day off traveling fourteen hours on a bus. Le Gallienne loved playing the great Elizabeth, and reviewers in city after city loved her performances. Although the long tour was a personal triumph for her, it was an exhausting ordeal. Throughout the tour, she maintained a rigorous discipline. She ate dinner at four p.m. and was at the theatre by six to apply her makeup and arrange her wig for an eight o'clock curtain. Elizabeth's eight gowns each weighed more than sixty pounds—a weight she carried on her slight five-four, 110-pound frame night after night, and on matinee days for six and seven hours at a time. While critics wrote of Le Gallienne setting the stage ablaze with her talents, the behind-the-scenes reality revealed in her diaries tells another story.

In Tacoma, Washington, she had a day off and did not have to travel, but rain drizzled all day; and when she called home, Marion was drunk. New Orleans

In Elizabeth the Queen, *1961*

brought sunshine, but the company behaved "like naughty children" and stayed out all night drinking and getting "high." In Columbus, Ohio, Scott Forbes kept the bus waiting for twenty minutes. When he emerged from his room with a blond, the stage manager told Le Gallienne that he had seen Forbes go into his room the evening before with a brunette. "No wonder he's so often short of breath!" she said. In Detroit, with a week left to play, she caught a bad cold and "could scarcely breathe."

Geddeth Smith said that he "saw Le Gallienne play Elizabeth many, many times, and I never got tired of it. It never failed." Once, over dinner in Chicago, Smith asked Le Gallienne if she had gone to the museums. "I don't do anything," she said. "I just can't. I don't have the energy."

"But on the stage the energy was all there," Smith recalled. "I think part of what makes that kind of brilliant actor has to do with energy."

Le Gallienne's energy had its limits. Her cold turned into severe bronchitis, and her understudy played the last few performances of the tour. She returned to Weston to recuperate.

IN 1960, actor-director Ellis Rabb, his wife, the British-born-and-trained actor Rosemary Harris, and several friends founded the Association of Producing Artists. Since their work together in *Mary Stuart,* Rabb and Le Gallienne had corresponded. In February 1962, Rabb wrote to Le Gallienne of the APA's plan to establish a seasonal residency at the Lydia Mendelssohn Theatre at the University of Michigan in Ann Arbor. Le Gallienne liked the tall, elegant Rabb and thought that Rosemary Harris was a gifted actor. By joining the APA, she would be a part of a company of actors that she admired, and she would have, however briefly, an artistic home. She accepted Rabb's offer to direct and play Mrs. Alving in her translation of Ibsen's *Ghosts* in the APA's inaugural Ann Arbor season.

During the summer of 1962, Le Gallienne kept busy with her garden and planning the production of *Ghosts*. Alice De Lamar caught her hints and bought two acres of land across from Le Gallienne's barn (land that she later deeded to Eva). The purchase of the two acres ensured Eva's absolute privacy. No one could build close by, and she would have additional woodland paths. When Le Gallienne told Alice "how thrilled & grateful I was about the land," Alice assured her that she "mustn't worry about anything, that she was going to 'see about things' for me—whatever that means!"

Eloise Armen, who bought two houses from De Lamar over the years, recalled that Alice extended her patronage to others as well. "She loved all artists," said Eloise. "She was painfully shy and extremely generous." Lucia Davidova, Alice's close friend and companion, acted as Alice's hostess, since Alice was uncomfortable with small talk. When Lucia's friend George Balanchine wanted a place to live in the country, Alice sold him a house at "a ridiculously low price" and gave him twenty years to pay. Alice did not demand anything in return for her patronage except the satisfaction she gained from helping artists she respected and admired. If Eva was not working, Alice would send her a hundred-dollar check each month to help her meet expenses. As her patron, Alice also had the privilege of descending on Le Gallienne from time to time. She would inspect the house and grounds and usually offer advice for improvements, such as pointing out a flower bed that needed weeding or a fence that needed painting. She also lent Eva her handyman and chauffeur when necessary. Eva never bought gifts for Alice. Her gifts to De Lamar were small works of art that she made herself. Le Gallienne would spend hours selecting and arranging flowers in unusual bouquets for Alice's birthday and holidays. Sometimes she would give Alice a pillow she had embroidered or a landscape she had painted. On Bastille Day, she always presented Alice with a basket of *fraises du bois* from her garden. Eva kept Alice informed about her career, usually by letter. If she was in the country, Alice attended Le Gallienne's theatre openings. Alice and Eva were never intimate friends. Their relationship was controlled by Alice, who maintained a distance.

In late July, urged by her agent Jane Broder, who secured the tickets and made the arrangements, Le Gallienne and Marion drove to Tyrone Guthrie's Shakespeare Theatre in Stratford, Ontario. "How I'd love to play there," she said. "What an audience!" A few weeks later, Broder called to tell her that there was no hope of her working at Stratford next season; there was nothing for her in Shakespeare, and although Eva suggested *Elizabeth the Queen,* the company planned to do *Cyrano de Bergerac* instead. "Ah. Well! It's a male paradise!" sighed Le Gallienne. "What can an old lady like me do there?" Meanwhile, at America's Stratford Shakespeare Theatre that summer, Helen Hayes and Maurice Evans appeared in selected scenes from Shakespeare. Le Gallienne clipped the bad reviews and sent them to Peggy Webster in England. "Thought she'd enjoy them!"

In October, when Le Gallienne arrived in Ann Arbor for rehearsals of *Ghosts* with the APA company, she managed, she said, "to inject a little sense & calm into [Ellis]. What a high-strung fellow he is!" She observed that "Ellis could be a most exciting actor. He has glamour in a strange way—a spell-binding quality. Curious fellow." Still, she thought he behaved too much like a genius. She believed that "real genius has more fortitude." The APA's problems seemed insignificant, though, next to the Cuban missile crisis and the world situation, which, she wrote, "looks so ghastly one dare not think of it. God help us all. . . . If only one could wake up one day & know there was PEACE. We haven't had any since pre-1914."

Fortunately, rehearsals of *Ghosts* were smooth and uneventful. Rosemary Harris played Regine, and "what a joy to have Regine really played!" enthused Le Gallienne. Even though she had played Mrs. Alving several times before, she had not been satisfied with her earlier performances, and her preparation for the harrowing role was thorough and painstaking. She fortified herself before every performance with a raw egg and tea and wished that she were playing the part in repertory instead of a run.

In the same way that, years earlier, Le Gallienne had studied the role by watching Duse, Rosemary Harris studied the older actress in the role. In Act One, Pastor Manders accuses Mrs. Alving of being a bad mother and a bad wife. As Mrs. Alving, Le Gallienne, like Duse, wore a long skirt and sat with her legs apart, leaning forward with her arms resting on her knees. When Manders finished his accusations, she took an extremely long pause, her eyes looking at the floor. Le Gallienne's acting was "the school of nonacting," Rosemary Harris said. "You never saw the wheels go around."

Le Gallienne left Michigan in high spirits and returned to Weston only to plunge immediately into a black hole. It's not clear what set Marion off; perhaps it was Eva's visit to Mimsey when she returned home, or perhaps it was just Le

Gallienne's demanding, imperious nature. But for whatever reason, once again Marion's rage surfaced. "Felt such a deep depression today," Le Gallienne told her diary. "All those dreadful things that were shouted at me the other night kept coming back—I couldn't seem to get rid of them. Stupid." Throughout the summer, Marion had been unable to control her drinking, passing out even when Le Gallienne was at home. When she returned from the NRT tour, Le Gallienne had been upset that none of the clippings had been organized and placed into scrapbooks. She also was critical of Marion's weight gain and bought Metrecal for her to drink at lunch. Earlier that year, in a revealing incident, Marion declared that the money she received from Eva was "income" and listed Le Gallienne as her "employer" on her tax return. The IRS, of course, wanted to know why Le Gallienne hadn't "filed a social security thing" for her. Her tax man suggested that she explain the money as a gift, not a salary. "Gun will just have to play the bewildered silly little woman who misunderstood terminology!" said Le Gallienne.

Marion, then seventy-two, felt unappreciated and took a hotel room at the Algonquin and stayed there for several days, leaving Le Gallienne to manage the house and cope with meals. Used to having the fire lit and her breakfast tray ready every morning, Le Gallienne found the experience something of an eye opener. Since she was feeling lonely, she invited Rabb and Harris to spend the weekend with her. She made them breakfast, prepared dinner, and stayed up very late. Exhausted from the "stimulating, unaccustomed talk" and the efforts of cooking and entertaining, Eva was happy to see Marion return. "Now I trust all shall be well," Le Gallienne told her diary.

All was not well. The death of her old friend and sparring partner Lawrence Langner depressed Le Gallienne. That December it was so cold the pipes froze. The Jaguar wouldn't start, and Marion scraped the side of her car against the garage. On New Year's Eve, she wrote: "I pray that Gun may feel better in 1963 & I shall be good to her & take care of her with tenderness. I pray that I may be given courage & faith & fortitude."

THE FIRST WEEKS OF 1963 flew by so fast that Le Gallienne felt as if she did "nothing but wind up the old Blue Room clock!" She continued translating Andersen's stories, working at Mam's old desk in her bedroom because "I've a feeling she helps me with the Danish." Michael Dewell called with plans for another national tour of the NRT and suggested George Kaufman and Edna Ferber's *The Royal Family*. "Told him I thought *The Royal Family* awful & quite unworthy of what Nat. Rep. says it stands for!" Michael countered with *The Seagull* and Anouilh's *Ring Round the Moon*. Le Gallienne put him off while she considered continuing her association with the APA.

In February, Ellis Rabb invited her to Ann Arbor to advise him on the APA's production of *Richard II*. When Rabb claimed to be ill and wouldn't act, "Shades of Pepi!" Le Gallienne thought. She went to Ellis's apartment and bullied him back to work. Before she left, Robert Schnitzer, executive director of the Professional Theatre Program at Ann Arbor, offered her six hundred dollars a week to come for the season and help him handle Ellis. He tossed in an apartment, which meant that she could bring Marion, and also "the job of taking over the whole thing if E. refused to come back." Le Gallienne refused Schnitzer's offer to take the job without Ellis, but she did consider joining the company to work with Rabb. When she returned home, she wrote to Ellis about Schnitzer's proposal, and a few weeks later she received a "very stiff & formal" reply. "He is so *jealous* of his possession of A.P.A. I feel sorry & disappointed in him—but could never work there under the circumstances. Michael [Dewell] will be pleased!" Actually, Le Gallienne understood Rabb's temperament quite well— like her, he rebelled against authority and believed in the single vision of the artist. Later that year she had dinner with Ellis when he worked at the American Shakespeare Theatre. "We had a splendid time, as we always do," Le Gallienne wrote. "There is a very strong bond between us that I feel nothing can really destroy. . . . If he & I are to work together—and I hope we can—there must never be any middlemen between us."

"I know she cared for me and believed in me," Rabb said later, "but she didn't like men. I don't think she had close male friends." Le Gallienne did like some men; she just didn't trust them. Rabb's belief, however, that he was special and singled out by Le Gallienne was a belief shared by many who knew her. That was her gift—with individuals and with audiences.

IN THE FIRST FEW months of 1963, Marion's health deteriorated. She insisted that nothing was wrong and refused to see a doctor. In late March, Le Gallienne sent her to bed and called her doctor. Marion had suffered a mild heart attack, the doctor said, and while her condition was not serious, he prescribed digitalis and complete bed rest for a few weeks. The housekeeper came once a week, and John Blundell, the British gardener, worked several hours a week; but the burden of gardening, cooking, filling bird feeders, and caring for Marion fell to Le Gallienne. "My goodness, what a time housework takes!" she cried, after a long day of chores. She arranged for Edna Blundell to fix their evening meal, which left Eva responsible for breakfast and lunch.

In the evenings Le Gallienne worked on her set model and directing plans for *The Seagull* and revised her earlier translation. When *The Seagull* was first performed in Saint Petersburg in 1896 it was a failure, but two years later, acted by Stanislavsky's Moscow Art Theatre, the play succeeded. Le Gallienne believed that repertory theatres with a permanent ensemble "united by a common aim, accustomed to playing together over a period of years, willing to submerge their individual personalities in an effort to become the creatures of Chekhov's imagination—to be his characters rather than to act them," were best suited to present Chekhov's plays.

Since Dewell had promised that the tour was booked, she turned down an offer from the Library of Congress to head the 400th Anniversary Festival of Shakespeare. Knowing that she didn't dare leave Marion alone in Weston, she arranged for Gunnar to accompany her on the tour.

By June, Marion was feeling well enough to return to her duties. Peggy Webster and Pamela Frankau visited for a long weekend. Peggy and Pamela had been together nine years, and all the former animosity that Le Gallienne had felt for Pamela disappeared, especially since she was an admiring audience for the garden. In August, when Peggy wrote that Pamela was very ill, Le Gallienne dreaded "to think what Peg would do if anything went wrong there—and Pamela is such a dear—I've become very fond of her."

After she recovered from the heart attack, Marion occasionally returned to her old habits. Although Le Gallienne would have preferred to hold NRT meetings at her home instead of driving into New York, she could not risk that her guests might meet "a naked staggering creature on her way to the bathroom." Nothing she said to Marion seemed to have any effect, especially since after a binge, Marion "behaved as usual as if nothing had happened & spoke about the weather." When Le Gallienne reluctantly gave up her undependable Jaguar, which had made her feel young, and bought a reliable Peugeot, she felt "heartbroken all day—so depressed—as if I were at the bottom of a well." When she was despondent, instead of cheering her up, Gunnar reflected her mood. "A great help!" Le Gallienne said.

Following the success of the NRT's first tour of *Mary Stuart* and *Elizabeth the Queen,* the producers of the NRT, Dewell and Frances Anne Dougherty, using Le Gallienne's services as a speaker, raised additional funds from small foundations and from individual contributions around the country. Citing its lack of a permanent home, major foundations did not fund the NRT, choosing to give their money to nonprofit resident theatres. In a remarkable feat, which required constant travel, Dewell had created citizen committees in each of the cities they played, and also made contact with schools and universities in each. He had uncovered the shocking fact that 50 percent of the English teachers in the country had never seen a professional production of a play. Tickets were made available at half-price to all teachers and students.

Dougherty, who had assisted T. E. Hambleton and Norris Houghton at the Phoenix Theatre, was a formidable fund-raiser. She had been born into the Cannon mills family and once had been engaged to John F. Kennedy. Everyone had expected her to marry Kennedy; instead she wed the writer John Hersey. After they were divorced, she married industrial designer Frazer Dougherty. While Le Gallienne persisted in thinking of both Dougherty and Dewell as dilettantes, the two were adept at raising money and possessed excellent administrative skills. They hoped that the 1963–64 tour would solidify the NRT's position as America's only national, touring nonprofit repertory theatre.

Jack Sydow was hired to direct Anouilh's *Ring Round the Moon* and Arthur Miller's *The Crucible*. Le Gallienne would direct and play Arkadina in *The Seagull* and play Madame Desmermortes in *Ring*. Dewell had recruited Farley Granger from Hollywood to play major roles in all three plays. Granger had performed in theatre but was better known for his movie work, particularly in Hitchcock's *Strangers on a Train*. Anne Meacham, a talented, high-strung young APA actress who had received acclaim for her *Hedda Gabler* off-Broadway, and British-born Denholm Elliott, a solid actor trained in Shakespeare and the classics, would play important roles in all three plays.

The NRT rehearsed in New York. Because of her heavy rehearsal schedule and design meetings, Le Gallienne took an apartment at the Gorham for a month. She thought Midge would be happier at home than sitting in a drafty rehearsal hall all day, so she left the dog with Marion. "The spirit of the whole company is amazingly fine already," she said. "There's a sort of esprit de corps developing—remarkable in so short a time." Anne Meacham, who played Nina in *The Seagull*, recalled that at the first rehearsal Le Gallienne expressed the paradox of acting, saying to the cast, "The difficulty with Chekhov is that he can't be acted. Will you please begin?" In her translation of the play, she caught Chekhov's humor by well-timed pauses and by using language that actors could speak easily and naturally. For example, when Masha is asked how she will get over her love, Le Gallienne inserted a pause in her response that generated a laugh: "By getting married . . . to Medvedenko." When the actors reached the "level of being" that Le Gallienne demanded, Anne Meacham recalled, "she would pace very quietly, not looking at us. . . . She trusted her ear more than the eye."

According to Bob Calhoun, Le Gallienne never lost her temper with actors. "She was wonderful with Anne Meacham," he recalled, "who was highly nervous. . . . When she had to have a really private session with actors, she always went down to her knees, psychologically showing deference to the performers."

On the other hand, Le Gallienne intimidated director Jack Sydow, who staged *Ring Round the Moon*. She did not trust the young director. Calhoun said that "if Sydow gave her a general note, she would nail him—'give me a specific direction,' she would say. Her part in *Ring* should have been outrageous, but it was too small. Jack was afraid to really direct her." Both Sydow and Dewell were afraid of Le Gallienne and often asked lighting designer Tharon Musser to act as go-between—behavior that Le Gallienne saw as devious. Musser recalled,

"I wasn't intimidated by her. She never did or said anything to make me fear her." Musser had worked with other stars, who often wrote gel colors into their contracts, but Le Gallienne was "not concerned in terms of her own ego," she said. When Musser set the lights for the opening of *The Seagull*, Le Gallienne asked what she was doing. "I'm building the light for your entrance," Musser said. "Don't be ridiculous," said Le Gallienne. "I'll light a cigarette; they'll know who it is."

In early September Blundell called Le Gallienne to tell her that her dog Midge was dead. "I had to go to rehearsal & read through that blasted comedy," Le Gallienne wrote that evening. "Didn't say anything to anyone or I should have broken down, and I didn't want to upset them all. Left at 7 p.m. & got home before 8:30—a bitter homecoming. It is hard for me not to blame Gun—I can't help it. I didn't dare talk to her—I was afraid of what I'd say. I feel sorry for her, of course, too. If only it will be a real & *lasting* lesson to her, the darling little creature may not have died in vain. . . . She has been so very close to me for over nine years—I ought never to have left her in the always dubious 'care' of poor Gun."

It's not clear just how the dog died; perhaps it was a nervous collapse, or possibly there was some sort of an accident, but Le Gallienne always blamed Marion for Midge's death. The next morning Le Gallienne refused to talk with Blundell or Marion about the dog. She drove back to New York to rehearse, tape interviews, and learn her lines.

She knew that she had to confront Marion and talk out their problems. Two days later she drove to the country. Marion broke down and cried and "begged me to help her. I've tried so many times—& shall, of course, try again. I told her she must look forward—*not* backwards." The shock of Midge's death did prove to be a "lasting lesson" to Marion. She never took another drink of liquor. For the next eight years, Le Gallienne abstained as well. Peter, her British dog, had been run over a few years earlier, and Le Gallienne felt bereft without a dog. At the end of September, she acquired another Yorkshire terrier, a tiny golden-brown creature that she named Nana, after the dog-nurse in *Peter Pan*. Nana's temperament was sweeter than Midge's, and Le Gallienne trained her more carefully and took her everywhere in a handbag. "This time I won't leave it!" she vowed. It was a vow she did not have to keep. Marion stayed sober, and after a time, Le Gallienne trusted her enough to leave Nana alone with her.

THE NRT OPENED its three-play national tour with a residency at the University of North Carolina at Greensboro. Using photographs of Le Gallienne that had been taken in Weston that summer, it launched a publicity blitz capitalizing on the Le Gallienne name and image. Although Dewell later claimed that Le Gal-

*With Farley Granger
in* Ring Round the
Moon, *1963–64*

lienne refused to do any publicity, on the 1963–64 tour she sometimes gave as many as five interviews in one day, a task she loathed. In the newspapers of each large city they played, the NRT and Le Gallienne were given major coverage. The press called the NRT Le Gallienne's company, which irritated her, since she was a figurehead and had no real power. The Civic Repertory was my company, she told reporters. Reviews of the plays praised her artistry, particularly her triple achievement as translator, director, and actor in *The Seagull*. When they played Philadelphia, Le Gallienne worried that after seeing her act the great Elizabeth, Mary Zimbalist might be disappointed seeing her in lesser roles. "I believe it would have been wiser for me to have played at least one thing that I really 'carried,' " she mused, sounding more like a star than an artist. "I haven't many years left to play & when I do play I should do something a little more important."

Acting in just two of the plays, though, gave her an additional night off, and with Marion along as cook and companion, she enjoyed a lazy life. On November 22 in Philadelphia, Le Gallienne walked to Mary Zimbalist's. When a man stopped her on the street and told her that the President had been assassinated, she dismissed him as a lunatic, but when she arrived at Mary's the news was on television.

The NRT's next stop was Washington, D.C. Dewell and Dougherty had planned to highlight the national mission of the NRT with a gala event in Washington chaired by Senator Hubert Humphrey. Letters supporting the company from notables like Eleanor Roosevelt had been read into the *Congressional Record,* and President Kennedy had written to Dougherty expressing his pleasure in the company's visit to Washington and thanking them for providing theatre, particularly to young people.

Le Gallienne and Marion waited for an hour and a half on the corner of H and Seventeenth Streets for the cortege to come back from Saint Matthew's Cathedral. "It was quite impossible," Le Gallienne thought, "to believe that the flagcovered caisson—which looked so small—could be holding that vibrant young man who had seemed so very alive only four mornings ago!"

THE NRT TOUR garnered excellent reviews, played to more than 140,000 people, and everywhere lost money. The NRT's goal of bringing good professional theatre at low prices to major cities around the country was a task more suited to the growing nonprofit resident theatre movement.

When the company played San Francisco, Le Gallienne took Farley Granger to meet Ina Claire. Le Gallienne had told Farley many times that Arkadina in *The Seagull* was really Ina Claire's part, and he had asked Le Gallienne to introduce him to her. "With Ina Claire it was the first time I'd ever seen Le Gallienne with a contemporary," he said. The two women made a striking contrast—Ina all blond, bouffant loveliness in a pale blue peignoir, and Eva crisply elegant in sensible tweeds. "You know I wanted you to play Hedda at the Civic when I was sick," Le Gallienne told her. "Yes, darling," Ina replied, "matinees." When it came time to leave, Farley recalled that he couldn't help laughing when Ina embraced Eva warmly and proclaimed, "Oh, I do miss you! You noble, suffering woman!"

During their Boston stay, Le Gallienne saw Eloise Armen. Eloise had come to see the plays, and Le Gallienne invited her to tea. She liked talking to the gentle, dark-haired Eloise, who had been Laurette Taylor's best friend during Laurette's troubled last years. From her youth, Eloise had been in love with the theatre. After two years at Radcliffe, she left to become an apprentice at the Ogunquit Theatre in Maine, gravitating first toward acting and then into stage managing and theatre management. Although she was eighteen years younger than Le Gallienne, Eloise possessed an old-world grace, quiet intelligence, and unflappable common sense that the older woman appreciated. "Laurette was lucky to find her," Le Gallienne observed.

There was no need to explain her past to Armen, since Eloise had known Ethel and John Barrymore, Katharine Cornell, and many other actors of Le Gal-

lienne's era. Eva asked Eloise to research the reviews of great actors written by the
Boston critic H. T. Parker. Le Gallienne was particularly interested in his reviews
of Duse. Eloise looked up Parker's old reviews and compiled them into notebooks, and the two women met once a month in Weston to go over the material. Eloise's husband, Seth Armen, was an accounting professor, and her four
children were busy with school, and Eloise welcomed the opportunity to work
with Le Gallienne on an interesting theatre project.

Le Gallienne learned that one of her oldest friends, Pepi Schildkraut, had died
on January 21. A few years later, when Basil Rathbone died, Le Gallienne wrote:
"So both my fellows have gone on." She turned sixty-five that January, and she
berated herself that she had accomplished little of all that she had dreamed of
doing. She would never be satisfied with any of her accomplishments, achievements, or awards, although she continued to accept them. In the 1960s she accepted the Brandeis University Award, and honorary doctorates from Goucher
College, the University of North Carolina, Bard College, and Fairfield University. In 1964 the American National Theatre and Academy chose her for its annual award. The NRT planned a four-week New York engagement, and the
event was announced in opening-night invitations and in full-page newspaper
ads as a celebration of Le Gallienne's fifty years in the theatre. Dewell and
Dougherty had rounded up an impressive committee for the New York gala
opening: chaired by Adlai Stevenson, the committee included Katharine Cornell, Maurice Evans, John Gielgud, Lillian Gish, Joseph Verner Reed, Mayor
Robert Wagner, and Kitty Carlisle Hart.

She had not wanted to play New York at all, since she felt that the NRT was
a meat-and-potatoes kind of theatre group, nothing more than a competent
touring company—certainly not exciting or glamorous enough for bandwagon
New York audiences. The opening night was agony. "These were not 'my' people—a lot of what Michael considers 'important' personages . . . dragged in by
the hair against their will. These Invitation affairs always make for a bad audience . . . and they were bad—and we were all quite unhappy to the detriment of
the performance. . . . Such folly to mix critics with this type of gathering!"

Despite Le Gallienne's fears, the NRT earned respectable reviews from the
New York critics. "Once in a long while something in the theatre reminds us
that acting is—or can be—a transcendent art," Norman Nadel wrote in his review of *The Seagull.* Le Gallienne was "dauntless, dedicated, spirited, lovely, utterly ageless," said John Chapman of the *Daily News.* The only review that she
noted in her diary, however, was her pleasure at Tennessee Williams coming
backstage to tell her how much he loved the play and her performance.

When the plays closed, Le Gallienne rushed off to the country to plant her
garden, earn her fifteen-hundred-dollar advance from Harper & Row for translating Andersen's *The Nightingale,* and begin her biography of Eleonora Duse.

*With Denholm Elliott
in* The Seagull,
1963–64

Her peaceful life was interrupted by a telephone call from Helen Mencken, who asked if she would accept a special Tony Award. Le Gallienne said that she would "think it over—blast! I hate these things." Dougherty and Dewell urged her to accept the award, saying that it would be good for the NRT. Dewell would later insist vehemently and inaccurately that the Tony Award was given to the NRT and not to Le Gallienne personally.

Sunday, May 24, the day of the Tony Awards, was scorchingly hot. Le Gallienne drove her new British Rover sports car to New York (she had given the dependable Peugeot to Marion) and had to detour around a five-car smash-up, which made her late. The New York Hilton swarmed with over a thousand Broadway devils. She "was ashamed of being an actor," she told her diary that night. "It was all so cheap & shoddy." A drunken, long-winded Richard Burton presented her with the special Tony for her distinguished contribution to the theatre. Le Gallienne somberly accepted the three-inch silver medallion engraved with her name and the masks of comedy and tragedy, looked out over the hundreds of people who made their living in the commercial theatre, and observed that the Tony Award might be of some real use if it were made of solid gold and covered with jewels and could be melted down and used to subsidize the nonprofit National Repertory Theatre. Ten of the twenty 1964 Tony Awards were won by the musical *Hello, Dolly!* Sandy Dennis won best actress for *Any Wednesday.* The next day Le Gallienne couldn't "get over the horror of that assembly last night. I'm so grateful I don't belong to that side of the theatre!"

IT WAS THE ARTISTIC SIDE of theatre that she wanted to explore in her biography of Eleonora Duse. Her Blue Room library was well stocked with biographies of theatre people, including an 1818 edition of *Memoirs of Garrick,* an 1834 two-volume *Life of Mrs. Siddons,* Russell Thorndike's 1929 biography of Sybil Thorndike, and Archie Binns's 1955 life of Mrs. Fiske. Le Gallienne felt compelled to write the Duse book. She had been shocked and dismayed many times when young people told her that they had never heard of Eleonora Duse. In writing Duse's biography, she would be bringing her to life again, not only for herself but for generations to come.

On June 12, 1964, Le Gallienne cleaned Nuja and sat down at her desk to start work. She already knew the title—*The Mystic in the Theatre,* which had come to her years earlier. She felt enormous empathy for Duse, and while in many ways they were quite different as people, they had much in common. Duse despised publicity: "Let them come and see my work," she said. Both women loathed the American Midwest. Le Gallienne, like Duse, never kept a photograph of herself on display. Both Duse and Le Gallienne possessed a power of attraction so strong that admirers were bound to them for life. Both had first experienced the transcendent joy of acting when they played Juliet. Last, they shared the same spiritual approach to the art of acting. Duse was a unique artist, and Le Gallienne's study of her is unique as well.

On her writing desk, Le Gallienne assembled objects that had belonged to Duse: three silver-plated filigree hair-ornaments and several spun-glass bracelets that Duse and then Le Gallienne had worn as Mirandolina; a small compass; an ivory and silver astrolabe; a pair of eighteenth-century apothecary's scales in a wooden box; a delicate Madonna dressed in faded taffeta; six etched-glass Venetian bottles which Duse had kept on her dressing table; a miniature copy of *Macbeth* which Duse had carried in her purse; a plaster cast of Duse's right hand; and, of course, the well-worn *Prières de Saint-Thomas d'Aquin* that Duse had given her. Along with Duse's telegrams to her, Eva also possessed many photographs of Duse—the small picture of Duse as Camille that she always placed on her makeup mirror and the one with the words "Je vous souhaite Force et Confiance de vivre" that Eva had clung to forty-three years earlier in Mackie's Sanitarium. A large scrapbook compiled by Duse's British producer, theatre programs, newspaper clippings, many of Duse's letters to various people, a collection of letters relating to Duse's 1902–03 American tour, her interviews with

Duse's companions Désirée von Wertheimstein and Helen Lohmann, and biographies of Duse made up her primary research material.

In just 185 pages, Le Gallienne wove the life of Duse with a study of her art
and an exploration of mysticism. "By nature [Duse] was violent, passionate, rebellious—yes, even ruthless," Le Gallienne wrote. "But the same could be said
of Teresa of Avila. In her extreme youth Duse was certainly less frivolous and
worldly than the great Spanish mystic; but this was probably due to the different circumstances of their birth. In both women the singleness of purpose that
soon appeared in them was inevitably related to a strong sense of ego, and in its
earlier manifestations it must have given the impression of a willfulness, an
inflexibility, that could easily be construed by the outsider as intolerable self-
importance."

Le Gallienne also drew on her own memories of Duse. She described a moment, for example, at the end of the first act of Ibsen's *Ghosts* when Duse played
Mrs. Alving:

> There had been a quiet exaltation in Mrs. Alving's lines to Manders: "From
> tomorrow on I shall be free at last—the long hideous farce will be over; I
> shall forget that such a person as Alving ever lived in this house—there'll
> be no one here but my son and me." Then comes the crash of the chair
> being overturned in the dining room, and the sound of Osvald's and
> Regine's voices. When she heard them, Duse *did* nothing; she stood ab-
> solutely still; the blood drained from her face; her eyes grew enormous; life
> seemed to flow out from the tips of her fingers; she seemed cold—numb.
> Then, very quietly—in a whisper—she spoke: "Ghosts—those two in the
> conservatory—Ghosts—They've come to life again." It was a triumph of
> economy. Again—the boldness of truth.

Harper & Row and Random House, who had published her other books,
turned down the Duse manuscript as too special for a general audience.
Through Madeleine L'Engle, Le Gallienne met Robert Giroux, the editor-in-
chief of Farrar, Straus & Giroux. Robert Giroux accepted the book even though
he believed that it would have limited appeal. "It is a small book," he said, "and
the kind of book that can only be published as a labor of love by the author *and*
publisher." Giroux gave her a one-thousand-dollar advance and asked her to
write a short preface. He also promised Le Gallienne that she wouldn't be annoyed by what she called "blasted copy editors," agreeing diplomatically with
her view that "they were nearly all imbeciles."

The Mystic in the Theatre was published in April 1966 and received excellent
reviews. The Bodley Head, Eva's father's old publisher, brought out the book in
England. It is still in print in a paperback edition published by Southern Illinois

University Press. According to Rozanne Seelen, owner of New York's Drama Bookshop, Stanislavsky's *My Life in Art* and Le Gallienne's *The Mystic in the Theatre* are the first two books they recommend to young actors who are starting a theatre library and want to know more about the art of acting.

WHEN SHE WAS WRITING *The Mystic in the Theatre* during 1964 and 1965, Le Gallienne did not act with the NRT; instead, she directed *Liliom* and *Hedda Gabler* for its national tour. Her directing fees and royalties from *Hedda Gabler* and her publications earned her well over twenty thousand dollars a year. She prepared the plays working from a set model, and she also scored the action, creating what she called "sound patterns" for the actors and for the production. It gave her a "queer feeling" to direct two other people as Julie and Liliom, and she "missed Pepi so much." She gave Dolores Sutton, who played Julie, her old costume to wear, but her interpretation was "so *different*," Le Gallienne felt. "I can't help thinking that Pepi and I were *better!*" she told Leonora Schildkraut, Pepi's widow. "Somehow these young actors don't have the vitality and *guts* we used to have. But—times change." Lighting designer Tharon Musser joined her in Weston to work on the plays. "It was a relief to go through the whole thing," Le Gallienne wrote, "just the two of us—without all those variously hysterical young men!"

During the 1960s, Le Gallienne's feminist feelings mirrored the growing women's liberation movement. She never expressed her views publicly, but Le Gallienne's criticism of men runs like a leitmotif through her diaries in the 1960s. "The world is MEN," she wrote. Young American males with their "loud penetrating nasal voices, much whistling & heavy tread" had "no thought of anyone else being alive in this world." In her working relationships with men, Le Gallienne was courteous, but in her private diary, she chafed against male authority. Certain gay men, or "homse-momses," as she called them, were untrustworthy. She complained that they mixed their work with personal relationships, which was hugely ironic: she forgot, apparently, that *she* had done just that throughout her theatre career. She was a woman first and a homosexual second. In fact, she often commiserated with other women about the problems they had working with men. "*Hairraising*," Le Gallienne said about Betty Friedan's *The Feminine Mystique,* which was published in 1963.

She did not hesitate to tell young male actors if she thought they appeared effeminate—her outspokenness annoyed some, but others welcomed her practical advice that they must "study to be a man." In the 1920s, she had studied how to be a woman with the great Chinese artist Mei Lan-fang, who was famous for his graceful playing of female roles. "Actually, she believed that most great actors were androgynous," said Eloise Armen.

IN JANUARY 1965, Le Gallienne interrupted her work on the Duse book to travel to San Francisco to check on the NRT's productions of *Hedda Gabler* and *Liliom* and to play Sven-Gallienne for a group of drama writers. Wearing a black hat with a swooping brim and a bright pink scarf, she spoke to the reporters about repertory theatre, although privately she was getting "so tired of trying to explain what 'Repertory' is! Who cares? I've been at it too long."

"There is an elusive, magnetic thing called presence, and Eva Le Gallienne has it," wrote one reporter. "Regal as a queen, precise, urbane and charming with an old kind of charm that gives respect and expects it." When asked if she would tour again with the NRT, Le Gallienne told them, "I'm not mad to act any more. After all, I've had fifty years of it. I adore living in the country. I'm never bored for a minute."

When Dewell asked her to join the NRT tour in 1965–66 and play in *The Madwoman of Chaillot* and *The Trojan Women* with Peggy Webster directing, Le Gallienne decided that *Chaillot* would be a "good play for me to end up with. . . . So much of what La Folle says are things I so deeply feel—and the play is wonderful."

Le Gallienne spent the first eight months of 1965 writing the Duse biography, planning the upcoming productions with Peggy, and working in her garden. When Joseph Verner Reed asked her to coach Terence Scammell and Maria Tucci, who were playing *Romeo and Juliet* at the American Shakespeare Theatre, she reluctantly consented. The board wanted to fire Tucci, Reed told her. When she saw previews of the production, she felt that the director had cluttered it with a lot of "restless, valueless movement & business" and had failed to create a relationship between Scammell and Tucci. She thought the only one giving a good performance was Lillian Gish, who played the Nurse.

She worked first with Scammell, trying to replace his British elocutionary delivery with spontaneous manly passion. She believed that "the Tucci" was "really talented—but she knows nothing—and she's already 23! By that time I was a veteran." When Le Gallienne picked her up at the train, Maria Tucci saw a "tiny, beautiful, powerful, elegant woman. She was like Lillian Gish mixed with Katharine Hepburn and yet distinctly herself." Before they began working, Le Gallienne gave her a tour of the Blue Room. "I was a sponge," Tucci recalled. "The only thing I was afraid of was that she was very determined. She had played this part; I knew that the only way I could play it was to make it my own. . . . We sat down at her kitchen table and started to work on the text. At first I was quite frightened. She softened as the day wore on, and I realized she wanted to give me the song of it—the arc of it. . . . She was wonderful in the potion scene. . . . She gave me the courage to place those demons around the stage.

'You see it—you take the vial—then it's really a toast to Romeo,' she told me."
Reed was so impressed with the improvement in Scammell and Tucci that he
sent Le Gallienne a check for one thousand dollars. Lillian Gish was grateful,
too, and brought her a red maple which Le Gallienne named the "Gish tree."

"HOW THIS YEAR has flown! Awful," Le Gallienne wrote in July 1965. It was
amazing to her that while she worked in her garden or prepared her performances in the Blue Room, above her astronauts were cavorting in space. Stretching exercises in the morning and gardening kept her body fit and trim, and she
didn't feel old, but everyone around her seemed to be ancient and failing. When
she looked at Hesper, who was recovering from a stroke, "sometimes it seems
so strange to think we're both old," Le Gallienne thought, "& most of our lives
are over. It seems only yesterday we were sitting in the garden shed at Farncombe . . . & with all our lives stretching before us—seemingly endless!" Although she still had lovely skin and thick silvery-white hair, Marion had grown
frail, too, and more crotchety. When Le Gallienne brought Mary Zimbalist a
manuscript copy of *The Mystic in the Theatre,* Mary had been very pleased, but
"she keeps asking the same thing over & over again," and Le Gallienne realized
"that very little one says actually gets through to her."

Just before her old friend Margaret St. John died in January, Le Gallienne visited her in the hospital. "I took her in my arms & every bone stuck out—it was
painful to feel. She kept saying 'if I could only ease out'—& for her sake I wish
she could. She can hardly see—& those damned nurses are so incredibly smug
& inhuman. I'd like to have wrung their necks! How hard it is to get out of life
—so bitterly hard. And they seem to treat old people like guinea-pigs—
experimenting on them to keep them breathing against their will. I felt sick at
heart over it all." Mimsey had faded away, too. She rarely knew her old friends.
Alice De Lamar, who spent the summers in Weston and wintered in Miami,
generously arranged for Mimsey to be moved into a nursing home in Miami,
which infuriated Le Gallienne. She thought that Mimsey missed being in her
own home. "It was so miserable to see Mimsey's place all stripped of her things,"
Le Gallienne wrote. "It's all so callous & hard. Made me quite sick." And just as
the rehearsals began for *The Madwoman of Chaillot* and *The Trojan Women* in
September 1965, Peggy Webster learned that Pamela Frankau had cancer.

In her autobiography, Peggy Webster barely mentioned *The Madwoman of
Chaillot.* She was not happy with her work as director. Le Gallienne enjoyed
playing the rebellious Aurelia, but she was not satisfied with her portrayal. At
that time, Peggy was consumed with worry about Pamela. Eva suffered from
dental problems, and she worried about Marion's health. Marion accompanied
her on the tour, but Le Gallienne hired Inge Nissen, a young Danish woman, to

act as her dresser and look after her and Marion. Also, during the *Madwoman* rehearsals, since they had not worked together in years, Peggy and Le Gallienne were tentative and awkward with one another. According to Sylvia Sidney, who played Constance in *Madwoman,* Peggy would explain something and afterward Le Gallienne would interpret what Webster had said to the cast. With some exceptions, though, critics liked the production, and while Le Gallienne earned her usual good reviews, they were not the accolades she had received for Elizabeth. Her performance had depth and truth, but it lacked theatricality and size—too much Duse and not enough Bernhardt.

According to Michael Dewell, it was thirty-three-year-old actress Sloane Shelton who held the NRT tour together. When she met Le Gallienne, Shelton sketched her in her journal: "Slender. Slow movement but quick eye. Very rapid mind. Walks with a slow pace. Head up expressionless. Hands curiously unlike the rest of her. Sturdy, wide, blunt, capable fingers—twisted somewhat from her accident. Short greying hair brushed up in back perversely growing in the wrong direction like Peter Pan or Puck. When really making a point has a tendency to close her right eye and open the left like a salty sea captain. Delicate, careful speech. English accent. Sad face, thin mouth, short sweet nose."

Shelton played Cassandra to Le Gallienne's Hecuba in *The Trojan Women,* and she was struck by Le Gallienne's generosity onstage. When Shelton entered as Cassandra, Le Gallienne stood with her back to the audience. "She gave me all of her attention, all of her interest," Shelton said. "Le Gallienne never stepped out of the play to make a first impression. She came onstage as she would in life. She wanted the play to be the thing. She didn't want to interrupt it with a hand." Her concentration was so intense, Shelton recalled, "that she could translate a mental image into reality."

"If she saw that you wanted to work hard, she liked you," Sloane said. "I felt that she was trying to inspire in me the profound sense that what I was doing was not just a craft or a job but an art. And I should respect it."

Perhaps because they had smoothed out their differences during *Madwoman,* Webster and Le Gallienne both did some of their finest work on *The Trojan Women.* The costumes of the Greek antiwar play looked like the clothes of Vietnamese peasants, an obvious allusion, in 1965, to the war in Vietnam. The play, Peggy wrote, was about "the waste, the unalloyed wickedness of war, the totality of loss, for the 'victor' as well as for the vanquished." To play Hecuba, Le Gallienne wore very little makeup, and since the production was played without intermission, she never left the stage. Peggy thought that Hecuba was "the finest performance" Eva had ever given. Her portrayal was "very austere, very piercing," she wrote. "When Talthybius came on bearing the body of the dead child, she looked at him, perfectly still. I used to wonder how he could endure to stand there, confronting those terrible, annihilating eyes."

Countess Aurelia in The Madwoman of Chaillot

Hecuba in The Trojan Women, *1965–66*

PLAYING HECUBA three times a week for months at a time "tore me to shreds," Le Gallienne wrote Mogens, "and I was not sorry to say goodbye to it." Later, Le Gallienne said that living through the agony of Hecuba had been the most challenging role of her career. After an evening of playing the Trojan queen, she found it difficult to sleep in hotels on the road, which were often filled with "fat elderly 'boys' with their noise and incessant bellows of idiotic laughter (mostly due to large quantities of whiskey, I fear) . . . that type of American never seems to grow up! It's depressing."

In March 1966 the tour closed, and Le Gallienne returned to Weston. For the next year and a half, she turned down theatre jobs, preferring to stay at home and work in her garden and on various writing projects, including another attempt at the Civic Repertory story. When she went through her old papers, she was "astounded . . . to see the honours that were showered on me." She wrote over fifty pages, but soon gave up. "It suddenly seemed to me *idiotic.* . . . Who cares, after all these many years?" She lived on royalties from her publications and from Ibsen productions. "Ibsen has been my 'saviour' too," she said, "as he was Duse's." Alice De Lamar supplemented Eva's income with occasional checks, and in 1966 Eva and Marion began receiving Social Security payments. Earlier, Eloise Armen had learned that Le Gallienne and Marion were not receiving Social Security benefits because Eva thought it was charity. "That's the dole," Le Gallienne protested. "I can't go on the dole." (Taking money from wealthy benefactors had never bothered her. After all, they had plenty, and as an artist she felt she deserved it just as much as they did.) Eloise pointed out to her that she had paid into Social Security and should reap the benefits. Finally, she convinced them to apply. "Marion was so grateful because she could bring in a little money," Eloise said.

In 1966 and 1967 the Vietnam War escalated and racial tensions raged. "No use writing of the state of the world," Le Gallienne told her diary, "it grows madder & madder in a terrifying spiral of increasing violence. God help us!" She was in the middle of a bitter drama, too, in her own home. After weeks of searching and hiring and firing several unsatisfactory housekeepers, Le Gallienne had finally hired Colette, Peggy's former housekeeper, to cook and clean for them. To accommodate Marion, who didn't like anyone else living in the house, Le Gallienne had a small cottage built behind the barn where a housekeeper could live. Colette was a devout Catholic who smoked incessantly, drank cup after cup of black coffee, and feuded constantly with Marion. Colette was French and "I dare say she gets a bit bored here," Eva theorized. "Not enough drama." It must have irritated Marion that Colette and Eva conversed in rapid French, which she could not understand. "No wonder the world is in such a mess if two elderly women can't even live in peace under very comfortable circumstances!" exclaimed Le Gallienne. She decided on a "plague on both your houses" policy and refused to listen to complaints from either woman.

ALTHOUGH LE GALLIENNE had not planned to act again, when Ellis Rabb asked her to join the APA to direct *The Cherry Orchard* and play Queen Marguerite in Ionesco's *Exit the King,* she said yes. She had been furious with Ellis in February 1967 when she learned that Helen Hayes had joined the APA. "What a betrayal!" she wrote. "Not of me, but of the work." Of course, when Ellis had asked her to join the APA earlier, she turned him down and remained loyal to the NRT. Le Gallienne felt that Helen Hayes was a bandwagon, personality actress, not an artist, and she resented Hayes's encroaching on her artistic territory. Le Gallienne was jealous of Hayes's commercial success, but she respected her contemporary, even though Hayes was in a different theatre "line." When she saw Helen Hayes's performance in the APA production of George Kelly's *The Show-Off,* she observed that it was "quite an amusing show & suits Helen H. down to the ground: the 'Mom' of Moms! Terribly corny—but expert performance on her part & the people adore her."

Later, when Hayes saw Le Gallienne's performance in *Exit the King,* she told Rabb, "Eva is simply amazing. She's such a great actress; it's so extraordinary that she never became a star." Hayes had popular acclaim, but she was not considered a great artist. Hayes speculated once that if she had been a foreigner, then she might be "acclaimed as a great artist—not as a nice lady."

In October 1967 the APA opened its New York repertory season at the Lyceum Theatre with two accessible, audience-pleasing plays—Ghelderode's *Pantagleize,* starring Ellis Rabb, and *The Show-Off,* starring Helen Hayes—followed by two darker, more challenging works—Ionesco's avant-garde meditation on death, *Exit the King,* and *The Cherry Orchard.*

Exit the King, in its American premiere, opened in January 1968 and earned excellent reviews, but Ionesco's philosophical requiem was not what Broadway audiences expected to see. Critics agreed that the leading actors—Richard Easton, Patricia Conolly, and Le Gallienne—were superb, but the good reviews couldn't make up for the lack of a loyal audience for rotating repertory, and the APA soon faced a budget deficit of over a million dollars.

Le Gallienne had taken over the direction of *Exit the King* during the last two weeks of rehearsals, but had refused directing credit; she was sole director on *The Cherry Orchard.* She had spent days reworking her earlier translation—cutting extraneous lines, smoothing transitions, updating the language. Her versions of *The Cherry Orchard, The Three Sisters,* and *The Seagull* received many professional productions, but they have never been published. Like the Ibsen translations, her Chekhov translations are informed by years of performance experience. Her translation of *The Three Sisters,* the Chekhov play she knew the best, holds up well. In *The Cherry Orchard,* some of her word choices have dated, but for the most part the dialogue sounds easy and relaxed, and the speech rhythms are attuned to each particular character.

Although she received a royalty for her translation of Chekhov's play, in an unusual departure from APA policy she did not receive a directing fee. For co-directing and playing the leading role in one show and directing and translating another, she received Equity minimum plus three hundred dollars a week provided by a Rockefeller grant.

Rehearsals for *The Cherry Orchard* began on January 15, 1968. Originally, Rosemary Harris had been cast in Le Gallienne's old role of Madame Ranevsky, Ellis had planned to play Trofimov, and Le Gallienne was cast as Charlotta. When Harris left the APA, divorced Rabb, and married novelist John Ehle, a disappointed Le Gallienne had to rethink the casting. Since she wouldn't be acting with Rosemary and Ellis, she decided not to play, either. When Geraldine Page turned down Ranevsky, Le Gallienne cast Uta Hagen in the role, against Rabb's wishes. At the first rehearsal, as Eva prepared to read the play to the company, she hoped she would "be able to stand up under this job." A few years earlier, she had told a reporter, "Frankly, I don't believe in directing too much. If you find you have a talented actor, you should not mess around with him. Allow him as much freedom as possible. Directors who are constantly asserting their authority and pushing the actors about are generally unsure of their own ability. The more insecure a director is, the more he bullies the actors."

In directing *The Cherry Orchard,* Le Gallienne demonstrated the truth of her own analysis. Her previous experiences with the play, at the Civic Repertory with Alla Nazimova and her 1944 production with Pepi Schildkraut, had been enormously successful; she certainly knew the play well and had every reason to feel confident. At first all went well. "She was an old-fashioned actor-director," recalled Richard Easton. "She dealt with the music of the play . . . Le Gallienne had the same difficulty as John Gielgud. He's wonderful if you're correctly cast and you know how to do it." But Uta Hagen was not correctly cast for Le Gallienne's concept of the character. Instead of adapting her concept to fit Hagen's robust quality and tremendous emotional resources, Le Gallienne attempted to change Hagen—a hopeless process, akin to transforming a hearty red wine into a crisp chardonnay. Hagen complained later that rehearsals were "boring and pedestrian," and that "Eva always treated me as if I were seventeen."

Le Gallienne had taken a room at the Royalton, and on her days off she returned to Weston to rest, but she found the atmosphere at home dark and depressing. Following Pamela Frankau's death of bone cancer in June 1967, Eva had invited Peggy to live with her until she could pick up her life again. Peggy had moved in, and she and Marion couldn't get along; Colette, the housekeeper, and Marion were still feuding; plus, Peggy was drinking heavily and she was "so sad," Eva observed, "life seems totally empty & meaningless to her."

The effort of performing in *Exit the King* and directing *The Cherry Orchard* began to tell on Le Gallienne. One evening after a performance, her upper-left bridge fell out, and she had to undergo hours at the dentist and was able to eat only mushy foods and liquids. She did not miss any rehearsals, though, and T. E. Hambleton, the APA's managing director, recalled that Eva used to romp up and down the four flights of stairs backstage at the Lyceum. "She felt there were no limits to her physically, in endurance and in strength and power." Le Gallienne shared her concerns about the mercurial Rabb with Hambleton. She had counted on Ellis to support her ("He ought to be around—he is, after all, 'artistic director' "), but Ellis had little time to prop up her confidence, although he did write her a note expressing his pride and belief in her. "It was maddening for her, for me, to work with Ellis," recalled Hambleton. "His faults were painfully evident." As actor, director, and company leader, and with his personal life in shambles, Rabb felt overwhelmed and besieged—more in need of support than able to give it.

As rehearsals wore on, Le Gallienne's insecurities and doubts about some of the actors led her into the bullying behavior that she abhorred and would not have tolerated in a director. The actors who played with her in *Exit the King*— Richard Easton, Patricia Conolly, and Pamela Payton-Wright—she left alone. But Donald Moffat, who played Lopakhin, complained that she was "always nit-picking. . . . she never said a word of encouragement to anyone—negative comments, criticizing people in front of the company." Moffat took her aside and said that he and some other company members believed that her directing methods were intrusive and stifling. That night Le Gallienne told her diary that Moffat had accused her "of not having enough patience! Implied I'd not given them enough lee-way! Ye Gods! I think I've given them too much!!"

On Sunday, March 10, Le Gallienne spent from 9:30 a.m. until 11:00 p.m. at a technical rehearsal at the theatre. Unable to sleep, she chronicled the long day in her diary. "Utka is so *heavy*—so *German* and she lacks style & grace. Oh, well! I fear there's little we can do there. She won't listen to any suggestions of lightness or frivolity. All the sound-effects were dreadful—*everything* was dreadful except the scenic department."

A few days later, when she badgered him again about his third-act speech, Donald Moffat lost his temper. "Play the fucking part yourself!" he roared, and then stomped out of the theatre. "Fiery Scot," Le Gallienne muttered. She put on a stoic face, but inwardly she was devastated. Soon after Moffat's outburst, Hagen noticed that Le Gallienne looked very pale. "I can't breathe," Eva told her, "and I have a pain in my chest." Hagen called the doctor, who diagnosed Le

Gallienne's symptoms as a heart attack. He also discovered that she was anemic (most likely caused by her liquid diet). He told her to stop smoking and prescribed complete rest. At first, Eva blamed her attack on acute exhaustion; later she said the cause was her teeth and Moffat.

Le Gallienne was at home when *The Cherry Orchard* opened on March 19, 1968. Brooks Atkinson wrote T. E. Hambleton that it was the best performance of *The Cherry Orchard* that he had ever seen in English. In his review in *The New York Times,* Clive Barnes disagreed. He gave Le Gallienne some credit: "The staging has been entrusted to Eva Le Gallienne, a lady who has done more than anyone for Chekhov in America, and this present production deserves and wins our respect." But he had harsh criticism. "Yet it does not have the air of life about it—it is not immediate to us . . . respectable for the most part, but not vibrant." He hadn't said it in so many words, but the subtext was clear to Eva and confirmed her worst fears—her work was old-fashioned, out of date, dead. Still, when she revisited the production in early April, she found a full house at the theatre, and she thought that everyone in the cast had improved, including Uta Hagen, who she felt was giving a deep and rich performance.

Other critics raved about *The Cherry Orchard,* but the *New York Times* review was the one that mattered, and on Sunday, April 7, another *Times* critic, Walter Kerr, delivered the *coup de grâce.* "Eva Le Gallienne directing *The Cherry Orchard* has somehow managed to pull the A.P.A. apart," read the first sentence of his article. Kerr attacked most of the acting company, including Hagen and Moffat, and he blamed Le Gallienne for their faults. She felt "bruised & battered—old & useless. I see I'll have to resign from APA since I seem to do them nothing but harm!"

Although the APA's 1967–68 season on Broadway was a personal disaster for Le Gallienne, it was the finest season the company ever had. In acting, direction, and design, the four APA productions (one-third of the drama on Broadway) were considered by critics and the theatre profession to represent the best work on Broadway. Unfortunately, the League of New York Theatres refused to allow the APA productions to be considered for Tony Awards. The selfish commercial interests of the League helped doom the nonprofit APA to second-class status, and a few years later Ellis Rabb disbanded the company.

In early July, Le Gallienne recovered her health sufficiently to fly to Palo Alto and play six performances of *Exit the King.* Ellis had not kept her informed of any of the APA plans, which made her feel "so left out! Well—I suppose one is! Just have to face it & get used to it. In this country there is no room for old artists—except male musicians!" When she arrived at the theatre, she found a plant and a card saying, "Welcome home. Ellis." When Rabb appeared in her dressing room looking rested and tanned, she would look at him only in her mirror. Ellis recalled that he sat on the floor "hoping we would have a chat."

After a moment, Le Gallienne said, "Thank you for the flowers, dear. But I don't understand it." She turned from the mirror and looked down at Rabb. "I really don't have a home, do I?"

WHEN LE GALLIENNE heard the news of the murder of Robert Kennedy in early June, "all other things seem so trifling & petty in comparison to this tragedy—like some Greek Epic." Preceded by the killing of Martin Luther King earlier that year, Kennedy's assassination cast a pall over the country. The world situation looked equally bleak. "The longer one lives the more amazed one is at the stupidity of the human race," Eva wrote on September 1, 1968, after reading the Sunday papers. "Cannot Russia see that she is just like the Tzarist Government in her oppressive tactics & that the end result will be the same. Bohemia has always been a nest of *free* birds—they cannot long be caged." Along with the country, she sank into a black hole so deep that even working in her garden failed to snap her out of it. There was no news of a job. "I might just as well never have existed in this country," she thought. "I often think I was a fool to come here." In her depression, only the failures seemed to matter—the two theatre companies that she had joined in the 1960s had failed, her aging body had failed, and she had failed as a director.

Worst of all, she was old, "which is a crime over here." In the past, she might have turned to liquor, but now she didn't have that consolation, and because of her heart she didn't dare indulge in the pleasure of smoking. Marion became so concerned that she wrote Eloise Armen to drive down from Massachusetts for a visit. "Courage. *Tout sera bien*," Le Gallienne counseled herself. "If I had a bit of an income I should feel better." Paul Weidner, the artistic director of the Hartford Stage Company, cheered her up briefly with the news that he planned to use her translation of *The Seagull*, and once again "that blessed Alice sent me such a dear understanding note as well as a most welcome cheque. She really is marvellously good to me."

In November, Le Gallienne finally fired Colette, who went to work for the local priest. After six weeks without help, she hired an elderly Irish housekeeper named Ellen. Peggy had moved out months earlier and was living with a new companion, Jane Brundred. Le Gallienne spent Christmas 1968 in bed with a cold, watching the progress of the astronauts as they first circled the moon and then splashed down. She marveled that in her lifetime she had seen Blériot fly at Orly and men journey to the moon. On New Year's Eve, she told her diary: "In spite of the fact that this year has not been particularly kind to me I'm grateful for it; it could have been so very much worse! The hardest thing to take was the APA disappointment—but I must simply get over it and forget about it. I believe I'll regain, to some extent, the confidence it has robbed me of—perhaps I needed to be humiliated. I expect we always do, only when you're old it's harder. . . . Please 1969 bring me some work and the strength and discipline to do it well."

IT WOULD TAKE a year and a half for Le Gallienne to haul herself out of her hole. She claimed that she wanted to work, but when work was offered, she was too depressed to take it. In 1969, she turned down job after job, including a position as artist in residence at the University of Texas, a role in the movie *I Never Sang for My Father,* a part on the soap opera *The Secret Storm,* directing *Inheritors* off-Broadway, and teaching at the White Barn. When she read that John Houseman had hired new faculty at Juilliard and when she learned that the Yale School of Drama had hired Robert Lewis, Why didn't they ask me? she wondered. The answer was simple. Since it was "impossible, in fact—to go round blowing my own horn!" no one knew that she wanted to teach. At a time when he hadn't been offered one serious professional theatre job in four years, John Houseman believed that to ask Eva Le Gallienne to teach would have been tantamount to suggesting that her professional theatre career was over.

She turned seventy in January 1969. At least she could still gather brush in the woods, she thought, "a real old woman's occupation from time immemorial!" Unable to finish a series of "Blue Room" essays she had planned, she grew bored and frustrated. Idleness exhausted her. The sudden death of Peggy's companion Jane Brundred of cancer in March shocked her.

To supplement her Social Security, her Equity pension, and royalties, she rented out the old house to her lawyer's nephew, although she hated to rent the home that held so many memories of Jo. Her longtime handyman and gardener moved from the area, and to save money she decided to do most of the gardening work herself with the assistance of Ted Lockwood, a young neighbor. The towheaded fifteen-year-old, who was "strong as a young ox," had agreed to help her several times a week after school. She paid him $1.50 an hour. Ted never forgot his first meeting with her. Blue eyes peered at him from under a straw hat and she was dressed all in blue—"a rough blue cotton overshirt with deep pockets, and threads hung from the sleeves . . . navy trousers, and blue soft leather shoes."

In June 1969 Jo Hutchinson called from Reading, Pennsylvania, where she was on location filming *Rabbit Run* with James Caan. Eva invited her to Weston. Jo said that when she was through with her film work, she would spend a few days in Weston. "Seems too good to be true!" Le Gallienne exclaimed. Instead of following Jo's plan and waiting until she was finished with the film, Eva "turned up in her car with a lot of cooking utensils," Jo recalled. "Then she wanted me to go with her to get the Lalique car ornament polished, and then she wanted to

Ted Lockwood, c. 1970

go food shopping because I wasn't eating properly. . . . I introduced her and the young film people had no idea who she was. I was embarrassed and miserable."

The day after Eva's arrival in Pennsylvania, they drove around looking at the countryside, and Le Gallienne bought gifts for Jo, Marion, Jess Jones, and Doris Johanson. In the afternoon, Jo called her husband in California to tell him that she planned to visit some old friends in Connecticut for a few days. "He seemed to accept this quite calmly & she was delighted," Le Gallienne said. When they came back from dinner, a message was waiting for Jo to call home immediately. "Townsend was playing a great scene," Eva said bitterly, "was vomiting, had a heart-attack, etc. As Peggy would say: 'Mother dying. Come at once. Love, Mother.' " Furious with Townsend and "disgusted at Jo for being so weak," early the next morning Le Gallienne deposited all the gifts she had bought at Jo's hotel room door and drove home. The next morning Le Gallienne woke up and felt "strangely released. It's a *good* feeling. I had not expected it."

The good feeling didn't last long—there was still no news of a job, or rather, of a job that she wanted to do. Like most actors, when she was out of work, Le Gallienne feared that she would never work again. Michael Dewell and Nina Foch visited her and were amazed to discover that she wanted to work. They had believed that she had retired after her heart attack. Le Gallienne kept to the discipline of daily diary writing and her daily chores, but on some days there was "no news—nothing I want to write about. What for?!"

In December, though, bluebirds descended on her bird feeders, sometimes six at a time, and her mood changed. Bluebirds were rare in southern Connecticut, and she became an ardent bird watcher. "They don't really give much of a performance until later when the sun gets warmer. Today I saw a Cardinal & a very yellow Goldfinch . . . as well as the Bluebirds!"

Eloise and Seth Armen and their children drove down from Massachusetts after Christmas and spent a day with her and Marion. Peggy called on New Year's Eve and "sounded so miserable. Had had too much to drink I think—wish she'd lay off that. It's bad for her." As usual, Le Gallienne ended her yearly diary with a prayer. "I pray I may be allowed to do a little more work before I go."

IN JANUARY 1970, Mary Bok Zimbalist died peacefully, holding her husband's hand. Mary had been Eva's "rock of strength." Le Gallienne thought of "all I owe her through the years and my heart is full of love & sadness & immense gratitude."

A month later, Michael Kahn, the artistic director of the Stratford Shakespeare Theatre, asked Eva to play the Countess in Shakespeare's *All's Well That Ends Well*. When she learned that she would be paid five hundred dollars a week from the first day of rehearsal, Le Gallienne "could scarcely believe such good fortune." She liked the tall, young director who ran a disciplined theatre. Kahn also was adept at casting, choosing Roberta Maxwell, a talented young Canadian actor, to play the difficult role of Helena; Joseph Maher for the comic Parolles; and Jan Miner for the earthy Widow of Florence. Although Le Gallienne was "fearful—apprehensive" about working again, Roberta Maxwell never saw a sign of it. "There was a sort of stillness about her—absolutely no pretension. She listened and she did what [Kahn] wanted."

Kahn staged the dark comedy as a fairy tale, and costume designer Jane Greenwood created lovely costumes, "sort of the French version of the Elizabethan period." Greenwood recalled that Le Gallienne taught the younger women in the company "how to sit and stand and move and carry on in these elaborate dresses. She just took them all on in the most charming way and had them walking up and down in the area backstage and in front of the theatre." At seventy-one, Le Gallienne's body was slim, straight, and well proportioned, and except for slightly longer sleeves to disguise her scarred hands, her costume did not have to cover any figure flaws.

On an informal basis Le Gallienne coached the young actors. Jan Miner recalled that "she was helpful with voice coaching, projecting your voice without shouting. Her whisper could be heard at the back of the theatre." Le Gallienne

*Left to right: Le Gallienne, Roberta Maxwell, and Peter Thompson
in* All's Well That Ends Well, *1970*

also taught Miner to parrot her lines for a French "Madge the Manicurist" commercial. One evening Miner invited Le Gallienne and Marion to her house for
a dinner party. She and her husband had just purchased an antique dining table.
"We all sat down at dinner and suddenly thousands of tiny ants appeared on the
table. Le Gallienne said, 'Go away and don't bother us.' And they obeyed. We
figured they had come to see her."

Daniel Davis, a twenty-four-year-old actor, had a small part in *All's Well,* and
he also played Hamlet at Stratford that summer and earned outstanding reviews.
Le Gallienne encouraged Davis and gave him notes on his Hamlet ("Don't fidget"). She presented him and Roberta Maxwell with copies of *The Mystic in the
Theatre* and generally took a great interest in their work. The two young actors
would meet at her house or at the White Barn and read plays and talk about the
theatre. Davis missed a session one day, and even though he called her later to
apologize, Le Gallienne was furious. When he attempted to apologize again at
the theatre, she waved him off. "Do not speak to me again. Ever!" she said.

"The iron door was slammed," Davis said. For weeks, she refused to look at
him or acknowledge his presence. Finally, Davis begged her to speak to him.
"She looked at me so hard that I burst into tears and I began to cry, just sob. She

came over and she sat down on the couch and she put her arm around me and she said, 'Please don't do that.' I apologized again, and she said, 'Forget about it. We'll never mention it again.' " In her diary, Le Gallienne noted that "I was happy that Daniel finally broke down & came to me. . . . I think I was right in not giving in first. Now all is well." Daniel Davis had learned that crossing Sven-Gallienne could have dire consequences. Her overwrought reaction to an ordinary missed appointment revealed her enormous pride as well as deep-seated animosity for men who failed to keep their promises.

All's Well That Ends Well earned wonderful notices for director Kahn, Maxwell, Maher, and particularly Le Gallienne. Julius Novick of the *Village Voice* wrote that her Countess was "the finest old-lady performance I have seen in a long time, shrewd and tough and benevolent and lovable all at once." Le Gallienne was a person who carried within her the seeds of a tradition, Roberta Maxwell said later, and she felt "fortunate . . . to have had the experience of Eva Le Gallienne." Today, there is no tradition in the theatre, Maxwell noted. "You've got bright, young, well-meaning, highly polished television stars, but with no tradition. It's like people playing the piano with one hand—after fifty years, if you've never seen somebody playing the piano with two hands, you begin to think that playing the piano with one hand is the way it is. They did not experience the great two-handed players like Eva Le Gallienne."

From April to September, Le Gallienne never missed a performance of *All's Well,* even though she had ample reason. On July 4, Hesper died. Just the day before, Eva had brought her now "ga-ga" half-sister a bouquet of fresh flowers and some slippers and had sat by her bed and "made her laugh over some foolish childhood memories." On the day Hesper died, Bobbie Hutchinson insisted that Le Gallienne go upstairs to view her body. Stricken by a sudden heart attack, Hesper had fallen in the bathroom, and her face was smashed and covered with blood. A month later, Le Gallienne still couldn't get "the picture of her poor battered face out of my mind."

Le Gallienne played a matinee on the day of Hesper's death. Since she felt incapable of hearing all the condolences, she told no one at the theatre. Bobbie Hutchinson was shattered after Hesper's death, and in a strange act, perhaps an act of revenge for Hesper, he cut in half all the family photographs of Richard Le Gallienne. He also decided not to have a funeral service for his wife, which was "just as well," Eva believed. On the evening of Hesper's death, Eva stood at her window and watched baby bluebirds leave their nest. She wondered what it all added up to: "Life + death = mystery," she thought.

IN SEPTEMBER, Peggy Webster called from Boston with the terrible news that she had cancer. When she had surgery to remove her colon, Le Gallienne visited her in Boston for a few days. Peg "was being very brave & good about it—but it's tough. As she says herself, it will mean a different life from now on." In early December, Jo Hutchinson called to say that her husband had died that morning. Eva began her own preparations for death. Her will was in order, but she asked Eloise Armen to take care of all her papers when she died. Eloise, who was helping Peggy finish her second autobiography, *Don't Put Your Daughter on the Stage,* agreed to take on the job.

The publicity and good reviews generated by *All's Well* once again brought Le Gallienne to the attention of casting directors. She wouldn't consider an important but nonstarring role in Lorraine Hansberry's *The Sign in Sidney Brustein's Window* because she felt that the play had "a message of violence—its inevitability—& I don't want to share in that." When she received a movie script of *Harold and Maude* by Colin Higgins, though, she read it "with increasing wonder." It was the part she had always hoped someone would write for her— "a wonderful mad, sane, merry & wise old woman of 80." Le Gallienne would find out later from Higgins himself that the part *had* been written for her. Higgins was a theatre buff, and he insisted that Le Gallienne be considered for the role of Maude even though she did not have a Hollywood name.

Le Gallienne met with the director, Hal Ashby, who she thought was the "funniest looking fellow I ever saw—splendid make-up for a Chekov, Turgenev or Dostoyevsky character: a wide, quite long, rather sparse beard—longish hair & very kind sweet eyes—a pink face. Rather a duck." After her audition, Ashby was full of the usual raves and "Hollywood stuff." When Le Gallienne learned that Katharine Hepburn and Helen Hayes were also being considered, she had no great hope that she would land the part. According to Ruth Gordon's autobiography, Gordon had been assured of the role by her good friend the powerful producer Robert Evans. Auditioning the other actors was merely an empty gesture.

Le Gallienne's failure to win the role of Maude sent her into a deep depression. A "real black hole," she told her diary on January 19, 1971. She felt useless and forgotten. She was not forgotten. Arvin Brown, the young artistic director of the nonprofit Long Wharf Theatre in New Haven, visited her. "I'm in a rare position," he told her. "I could mount most anything you wanted to do. What would that be? What would you like to play?" "Oh, no. I've done everything that I wanted to do," Le Gallienne replied. "I would only be interested in reviving what I had done before." She gave Brown a tour of the Blue Room, showed him her Duse memorabilia, and Brown felt strongly that she was "enclosed and cosseted in the world of that house."

Brown persisted. On another visit, he asked her to consider playing *Mary Stuart.* "There's a whole generation of people who have never seen you play Elizabeth," he said, "one of the greatest American performances." "How long is the run?" she asked. A month, he told her. "Oh, well, I won't play Elizabeth for just four weeks. I have to shave my head, and I won't do that for less than three months." "Oh, but they're doing such wonderful things with bald pates now," Brown offered. The temperature in the room dropped thirty degrees, he recalled. "When I play Elizabeth, I shave my head," was the reply.

During this time, Le Gallienne claimed that the theatre had become alien to her, and she didn't want to act anymore. After initially resisting, in early 1971 she agreed to talk about the theatre in a series of interviews with Ensaf Thune, an Ibsen scholar and professor at Hofstra University. Le Gallienne thought that most academics were stolid and unimaginative, but the Egyptian-born Thune was married to a Norwegian, and she was an attractive, cultivated woman who wanted to write about Le Gallienne's productions and translations of Ibsen. Personal circumstances intervened, and Thune never completed her work. "Le Gallienne was magnetic, with a wonderful personality," Thune recalled. "Her eyes had such depth to them." Le Gallienne thought Thune possessed "great perception & understanding, but if the poor lady thinks it will be easy to sell a book about me, I'm afraid she has another think coming to her."

During 1971, Le Gallienne devoted herself to gardening, bird-watching, and writing. Since her mortgage was paid and she and Marion lived frugally, with occasional checks from Alice De Lamar and royalties from her books and from productions of her Ibsen translations, she managed a comfortable living. Ellen, the housekeeper, retired and there was enough money to hire a new housekeeper, named Barbara, whom Eva nicknamed Varya. Varya was sloppy, but good with meals and the animals. *Flossie and Bossie* was reprinted in paperback, and Harper & Row published her translation of Andersen's *The Little Mermaid,* which brought in additional income. In August, the *Saturday Review* published her review of two Ibsen biographies. Le Gallienne wove her own experiences, memories, and feelings about biography into her article. "No matter how readily they admit the greatness of their subjects, biographers today seem to feel it their duty to expose and give undue importance to the tiniest human foibles, thereby proving that the people they portray are really no better than the rest of us."

In late August, Le Gallienne planned to travel to Cleveland to give a talk on Ibsen. "I should do it—if I can get away with it respectably it will give me confidence, which I badly need. This country robs old people—especially women—of confidence in a quite wicked way." She decided not to go on the trip when Marion's doctor said that Gunnar needed bed rest. The death of Tom Westlake, Marion's brother-in-law, in August had depressed Gunnar. In addition to her fretting about Eva's having to care for her, Marion worried about the disposition of Tom's insurance policies, which he had promised would go to her, and which Marion planned to give to Eva. Le Gallienne didn't know quite what had triggered Marion's decline—"Tom's death, the heat, the fact that in a few weeks she'll be 80." Le Gallienne worried, too, about Peggy Webster, who was suffering excruciating pain and was consulting various specialists in Boston and New York.

On September 11, 1971, the doctor visited and told Le Gallienne that Marion's heart was failing, and she mustn't get up even to go to the bathroom. His report shocked Eva, who had thought that Marion merely needed to rest. Just as Marion had cared for Julie Le Gallienne, Eva cared for Mutki—coaxing her to eat, washing her, and getting up in the middle of the night to change soiled sheets. And like Julie, Marion was a difficult patient who resented her own growing weakness. On September 14, exhausted from her efforts, Le Gallienne called in a nurse to relieve her from 11:00 p.m. to 7:00 a.m. "I've a feeling she may be over the worst," Eva told her diary that evening. Le Gallienne and the doctor decided that it would be best to keep Gunnar in the home that she had shared with Eva for thirty-seven years, where she "could have peace & be surrounded by the atmosphere she loved." With the help of an oxygen tent, intravenous feedings, and round-the-clock care, she struggled for three more days. In her last hours, Marion was unconscious most of the time. Eva stayed close by. She was holding her hand when Marion's heart "finally gave out."

PART SEVEN

1971 - 1991

Le Gallienne acquired her triptych makeup mirror
in 1921 and used it throughout her career. Her cherished
photograph of Duse as Camille was always placed
in the center of the mirror.

With my life as full of holes as it now is—
great gaps where there used to be love & friendship & warmth and,
of course, habit *too—I feel as though I must begin a whole*
new life, no matter how short it may be, or how long.

W HEN ELOISE ARMEN arrived in Weston on Saturday, September 18, Marion's body had been transferred to Bouton's Funeral Home in nearby Georgetown, Connecticut. Because both Julie Le Gallienne and Hesper Le Gallienne had been taken there at their deaths, Eva was familiar with the funeral parlor, which was located in a white frame Victorian house. It was an old-fashioned place, "simple & human," Eva thought; it was where she wanted to go when her time came. Eloise stayed the weekend to console her friend, but Eva remained stoic and dry-eyed. Even as a child, profound grief or profound joy always left her silent. She could not talk about Marion's death with Eloise, she refused to discuss funeral arrangements, and she did not write anything in her diary.

That evening, Eva asked Eloise, "Do you think I might have a glass of sherry?" "Why, I think it might do you good," Eloise replied, unaware that Le Gallienne had a drinking problem and had not touched liquor for eight years. When Eloise returned to Massachusetts, she told Peggy Webster that she had given Eva a drink. Peggy was silent for a moment. "Well, I suppose it's all right now," she said.

There were no funeral and no obituary for Marion Gunnar Evensen Westlake.

The week after Marion's death, actor Terence Scammell stayed with Eva for a few days, and Le Gallienne drank with him. When Scammell left, Le Gallienne was entirely alone—a state that she had often imagined with longing. It was the first time Eva had been without a companion in almost fifty years, and she did not like it. Her guilt exacerbated her grief. She wished that she had been kinder to Marion; she wished that she had been more overtly grateful for Mutki's companionship and care. There was no one to share the wonder of the birds or the garden, no one to bully her into shopping trips or watching television or buying new clothes, no one to exclaim over her achievements. In August, Marion had been "madly excited" when the *Saturday Review* featured Eva's Ibsen article on its cover. Most of all, Le Gallienne missed "so much having [Mutki] to tell things to—to pick little bouquets for—all the silly *little* things." Their companionship had been a kind of stormy symbiosis, and for thirty-seven years Marion had been Le Gallienne's audience—the one who had watched her live.

Later, in looking through Marion's belongings, Le Gallienne discovered that like Julie Le Gallienne, she had saved every letter that Eva had written to her, even Christmas and birthday cards. There was a high-school graduation photograph of Marion, looking "so pure, so *proper*—very sweet & touching." Another discovery was devastating, adding yet another level of remorse to Le Gallienne's grief. In Marion's desk she found several well-used instruction notebooks. Knowing how much Eva esteemed those who could speak and read French, and wanting to please her, Marion had been secretly attempting to learn the language, even though she was almost eighty years old.

IN OCTOBER 1971, Le Gallienne drove to Boston several times to see Peggy Webster, who was undergoing treatment for cancer. Weakened by her illness and by the effort of completing her autobiography *Don't Put Your Daughter on the Stage,* Peggy joined Eva in mid-December for a month-long rest in Weston. Actually, Webster dreaded the trip and dealing with Le Gallienne's grief, but "at least Gun won't be there," she told Eloise Armen. Peggy's loyal friends on the Vineyard, Mary Payne, Carolyn Cullen, and Marion Kinsella, worried about her making the trip, but from their own experience they knew that if a friend needed her, Peggy would be present. "She loved Le Gallienne like a sister, but Peggy ran to meet you, no matter who you were," recalled Mary Payne. "I've never met anyone else in my life who could be so there for you." Once, Peggy explained the difference between her and Eva to Marion Kinsella. "They always call her *Miss* Le Gallienne," Peggy said, "but everyone calls me Peggy."

Without Gunnar to share in the preparations, making plans for Christmas seemed "very odd" to Le Gallienne. For Peggy's sake and with Ted Lockwood's help, Le Gallienne decorated her traditional Danish Christmas tree. Peggy's presence gave Eva a reason to build a fire in the fireplace, fill the house with flowers, and return to her daily routine of morning exercises followed by chores.

Peggy shared with Le Gallienne the belief that true happiness was achieved only when a person's energies and talents were used to the full. With the completion of *Don't Put Your Daughter on the Stage,* Webster knew that her creative life was over, but despite her advice to young people *not* to choose the theatre, she urged Eva to keep working. That Christmas Peggy gave Le Gallienne a best-selling juvenile novel called *The Dream Watcher.* The story's hero, fourteen-year-old Albert Scully, is a lonely misfit who is befriended by Mrs. Orpha Woodfin, an eccentric old woman who tells him that she once was a famous actress. She assures him that all great people have been different and unusual. The theme of an older person's helping a younger to develop appealed to Eva, and she and

Peggy thought that the book would make a charming play. In the hope of furthering a collaboration, Peggy invited Barbara Wersba, the author of *The Dream Watcher,* to Weston for tea.

Barbara Wersba had been a devoted fan of Le Gallienne. Years earlier, she had stood for hours outside Le Gallienne and Webster's New York apartment hoping for a glimpse of her idol. When Barbara and a friend arrived in Weston, they were greeted by Le Gallienne, who then retreated to her Blue Room chair with Nana by her side, leaving Peggy to keep the conversation going. During the visit, Peggy brought in a birthday cake for Le Gallienne, who would be seventy-three the next day. Peggy and Eva gave their guests a tour of the Blue Room, and just as Wersba proposed to leave, Le Gallienne asked, "Why don't you write me a play?" Barbara Wersba had assumed that they would discuss a television production of her book, but Le Gallienne said, "My medium is the stage, you know." Wersba countered that the audience would be much larger on television. "I would rather have a small one that understood me," said Le Gallienne. Wersba, who had never written a play, agreed to adapt *The Dream Watcher* for the stage.

After Peggy left in late January, Le Gallienne felt at loose ends, although she didn't lack for company or things to do. Eloise and Seth Armen, Jess Jones and Doris Johanson, the Lockwoods, and other neighbors visited. Ted Lockwood helped her with the house plants and snow shoveling. Hartney Arthur, a theatre agent, and Markland Taylor, a theatre journalist and critic, visited every week or so for tea and talk. And every evening at dusk, a small opossum showed up at the back door for a doughnut handout. Le Gallienne dubbed the animal Pigposs, and the opossum was soon joined by a skunk that she named Little Eyolf, after Ibsen's play. There were meetings with Virginia Boyd, her lawyer, and papers to sign to settle Marion's estate. Tom Westlake's insurance policies, which totaled almost ten thousand dollars, were finally paid to Marion, but as executor Le Gallienne had to send the money to Marion's next-of-kin, her brother, Eugene Evensen. Receiving the money would have made Marion so happy, Le Gallienne thought, "in order to give it to me, of course—not for herself. . . . She'd be miserable to know the present situation."

Little things like knitting by the fire, sighting a robin, or getting a letter became significant events. She corresponded occasionally with actor Jane Alexander, and later she gave her notes on her performances of Hedda Gabler and Hilda Wangel. Alexander considered Le Gallienne one of the great theatre leaders of the century. "She reminded me of Georgia O'Keeffe," Alexander said. "If Le Gallienne had had a Stieglitz in her life, she would have been very famous. She was trying to do it all." When Le Gallienne received an affectionate letter from Alexander, who had been reading her translation of *The Master Builder,* it "meant such a lot" to her. "If only these young people could realize that it matters terribly. It makes one feel a little less useless & as though one had after all contributed something," Eva told her diary.

Keeping busy wasn't the same as doing meaningful work, however, and she did feel useless. With Marion gone, she no longer had "anyone to do things *for*." She couldn't help feeling that "not a soul cares if I do anything or not. A depressing state of mind. I *must* try & surmount it. . . . One doesn't realize, till one gets to it, how hard it is to face the fact that one's usefulness in this world is over—especially when one *knows* it really *isn't!* Oh, well—I shouldn't be grousing when I've so much to be grateful for."

Grousing in her diary, though, seemed to have a therapeutic effect on Le Gallienne, and the news that Southern Illinois University Press planned a paperback edition of *The Mystic in the Theatre* renewed her confidence. She bought black silk evening pants just in case she had some reason to go out. While she waited for Barbara Wersba to write the play of *The Dream Watcher,* Le Gallienne began translating "The Spider," a story by nineteenth-century Danish writer Carl Ewald. The spider character was a "regular Women's Lib girl," thought Le Gallienne. She wrote in Marion's room, since she could leave her papers spread out and the room gave her "a sense of helpful peace." The Ewald story is a satirical miniature biography of a spider who is "a woman used to making her own way in the world." The spider says, "It's a pity there aren't a lot more women like me." In 1980, Harper & Row Junior Books published "The Spider" and two other Le Gallienne translations of Ewald stories, "The Wind" and "The Queen Bee."

IN LATE MAY, the memorial that Le Gallienne had ordered for Marion arrived, a handsome concrete and wooden bench, which Eva placed in the woods opposite the house. A plaque on the bench reads, "In loving memory of Marion G. Evensen." Then, with only her Yorkshire, Nana, in attendance, Le Gallienne buried Marion's ashes near the bench and a star magnolia bush. Marion's bench offered a lovely view of the woods and a place for Eva to rest and bird-watch after her daily walk. Nearby stood the small red maple—the "Gish tree"—and three tall maples which Le Gallienne and Marion had called "the Three Sisters."

The year following Marion's death was an interlude, a pause between the acts of Le Gallienne's life. At this time, she reacted and responded to events instead of actively moving forward. Except for teaching acting classes for ten weeks at the White Barn in the summer and translating the Ewald stories, she did not work in 1972.

During the early months of 1972, Le Gallienne talked frequently on the telephone with Jo Hutchinson. After Jo's husband died, Eva had hoped that "Aimée" might be persuaded to visit or even move back to the East Coast. Following a conversation with her on March 6, Le Gallienne realized that Jo will "never come here even for a visit I now feel certain. Might just as well face it. And I feel she has grown so far away from me, she would be miserable here. So to be alone must be my future."

More proof of her estrangement from Jo came unexpectedly. In late spring, Peggy was again visiting Le Gallienne in Weston. One day Hartney Arthur drove Peggy to New York to see her publisher. On the way home, Peggy was doubled over with pain. To divert her, Arthur gossiped. "Did you see where Josephine Hutchinson married Staats Cotsworth?" he asked.

Peggy had not heard, and she knew that neither had Le Gallienne. "Would you do me a favor?" Peggy asked wickedly. "When we get there would you tell her?" When they arrived in Weston, after Peggy was comfortably settled in the house, she looked at Arthur and said, "By the way, Hartney, don't you have something to tell Le G?" Hartney blurted out the news. Le Gallienne looked at him coldly. "Well, they're both drunks," she said.

Le Gallienne was furious and hurt, even though it was perfectly reasonable that Jo would marry an actor that she had known since the days of the Civic Repertory. Eva had always liked Staats Cotsworth, had flirted outrageously with him years earlier, and, according to Jo, Staats "adored Eva." Cotsworth did have a drinking problem (Jo had occasional lapses as well), but he was also a handsome man, a good actor, and a talented painter. Jo was lonely and craved a companion, but her decision to marry Staats smashed Le Gallienne's romantic illusion that she and Jo would spend the rest of their lives together. In early June, Jo wrote Eva to tell her of the sudden "miracle" that had happened in her life.

"Women are quite incredibly tactless!" fumed Le Gallienne.

At about the same time, Le Gallienne received another "smart blow." Peggy's cancer treatments were not working, and her life was now measured in weeks. "Nothing can be done," Peggy said.

During the summer and early fall, Peggy made preparations for death. Various universities had asked to receive their papers, but since Webster and Le Gallienne believed in a nationally subsidized theatre, they decided that they would donate their papers to the Library of Congress. Le Gallienne liked the fact that her papers would reside with Peggy's and with the collections of other American theatre pioneers, like Minnie Maddern Fiske. All of Peggy's personal correspondence, including letters from Pamela Frankau, Le Gallienne, Noël Coward, Maurice Evans, and others, she placed in a large suitcase. She instructed her Vineyard friends Carolyn Cullen and Mary Payne to destroy all the letters unread on the day of her death. Peggy also put her financial affairs in order. She cashed more than seventeen thousand dollars' worth of securities and deposited fifteen thousand dollars in a joint account with Le Gallienne. Peggy suggested that Eva use some of the money to add another bathroom off the upstairs guest room. Eva hated sharing her bathroom, and Peggy's gift was meant to encourage her to find another companion. The last of a 150-year theatre dynasty, Webster had no living relatives. She gave a large cash bequest and turned over her royalties and copyrights to Diana Raymond, Pamela Frankau's cousin. After leaving smaller amounts to various friends, cancer charities, and the Actor's Charitable Trust in England, Peggy left ten thousand dollars and the remainder of her estate to Eva Le Gallienne.

During Webster's last months, Le Gallienne did not accept any theatre work and devoted herself to spending time with her friend. Eva loathed large gatherings, but she accompanied Peggy to a party in New York to celebrate the release of *Don't Put Your Daughter on the Stage.* At the party, Peggy appeared well and full of high spirits, but Le Gallienne knew that she suffered constant, agonizing pain, which the Percodan she took could not relieve.

In late September, Le Gallienne spent a few weeks with Peggy on Martha's Vineyard. Carolyn Cullen recalled one festive evening at Peggy's house when Katharine Cornell, her friend Nancy Hamilton, and Le Gallienne and Peggy laughed and told theatre stories and never talked of death. On September 30, Le Gallienne escorted Peggy to London to place her in Saint Christopher's Hospice. Just over a month later, Eva was once again on a plane flying across the Atlantic. Le Gallienne could not bear to leave Nana at home, and since England quarantined dogs who entered the country, Eva and Nana stayed in Alice De Lamar's Paris apartment. Le Gallienne commuted daily across the Channel to Saint Christopher's Hospice. During their last visits together, they felt as if they were acting in a play, like two "old hams." On Eva's final visit, Webster was in a coma, and she died soon after.

After Peggy's death, Le Gallienne flew to Denmark to be with Mogens and other Nørregaard relatives. Just before her flight left for Copenhagen, Eva received a call from Miami. Mimsey Benson had died. In less than three years, Le Gallienne lost her half-sister, Hesper, and her dearest friends—Marion, Peggy, and Mimsey. "It all seems unreal," she said. "Absolutely no one really close to me [is] left."

Peggy had asked Le Gallienne to stay in Europe and attend her London memorial service, which meant that Eva could not participate in the memorial service in New York. Le Gallienne wrote a tribute to Peggy which was published in *The New York Times.* Perhaps because Le Gallienne had prepared for Peggy's death, she was able to express her grief in words, not only in the tribute but in letters and in her diary as well. Also, Peggy had been a gregarious, public-spirited artist, and Eva knew that her old friend, theatre colleague, and lover would have wanted a public demonstration of Eva's love.

"I knew Margaret Webster for over 60 years," Le Gallienne wrote in the *Times.* "She was 4 and I was 10 when we first met. . . . Gradually, as the differ-

Peggy Webster, 1971

ence in our ages ceased to matter, we became friends—a lasting friendship for which I shall be forever grateful. . . . Her concern for others was almost too great. No letter went unanswered, no request went unconsidered. Peggy was a truly good, kind and generous human being. Of course, she had faults. . . . She could be violently opinionated, ferociously impatient; she did not suffer fools gladly. . . . She will not soon be forgotten. The countless young people whom she helped and inspired will hand on to others the many things she taught them."

Peggy's memorial service in the chapel at Saint Paul's Church in Covent Garden was "simply *beautiful,*" Eva told Mogens. Crowded with Peggy's friends, the chapel was bright with yellow and white flowers. Bach's prelude "Jesu, Joy of Man's Desiring" rang out, and ninety-year-old Dame Sybil Thorndike, dressed in white, read passages from Teilhard de Chardin in a voice, Le Gallienne said, that was "younger and more resonant than most voices in people of 20!"

While Le Gallienne was in Europe, Eloise Armen took care of Eva's mail and bills, and she made sure that the housekeeper kept the birds fed and the house in order. When Eva arrived home in mid-December, she collapsed into bed and stayed there for ten days. Instead of turning to liquor, she turned to books, particularly *The Divine Milieu* by Teilhard de Chardin, which Peggy had cherished, and *Eighteen Constructive Speeches* by Eva's favorite philosopher, Søren Kierkegaard.

At night before she went to sleep, Eva would read several pages of Kierkegaard in the original Danish. Kierkegaard's epitaph, "That Individual," proclaimed his belief that individuals were responsible for their lives through the choices they made. Like his contemporary Hans Christian Andersen, Kierkegaard saw the rich detail in nature—the individuality of birds, the intricate patterns of leaves, the universe in a water drop—as mysteries never to be fully comprehended. The writings of Andersen and Kierkegaard were Eva's touchstones. Their thought shaped her own philosophy of individualism, which had given her the courage to reject the commonplace and to embrace her uniqueness. Now, with the loss of her companions and contemplating her own mortality, she sought Kierkegaard's counsel. It was Søren Kierkegaard who remarked: "Life can only be understood backwards; but it must be lived forwards." Reading Kierkegaard's bracing counsel cheered Eva, and she was comforted, too, by the *sound* of the philosopher's words, the earthy, guttural Danish music which took her back to sweet, early memories of Mam and holidays in Copenhagen.

"IF ONLY SOMEONE would give me some work," she thought, she could get on with her life. Cut off from her theatre art, she felt as if she "were existing in a vacuum. Everything seemed unreal."

At this time, Le Gallienne drew closer to Eloise Armen and Ted Lockwood. Every few weeks, Eloise would drive to Weston and spend a few days, and the two women talked daily on the telephone. Sometimes Le Gallienne felt guilty that she was taking Eloise away from her own family. "Don't ever let me interfere with your children," she told Armen. With Eloise, Eva sometimes acted like a grieving, petulant child, pounding a chair and wailing, "I'm weak, weak, weak!" With young Ted Lockwood, though, Le Gallienne played the role of nurturing parent, and Ted seldom saw her self-doubt and fears. Ted was studying environmental horticulture at the University of Connecticut, but he continued to work for Le Gallienne on weekends, school holidays, and in the summer.

Because Le Gallienne's companionship with Ted revolved around work, it offered them a good excuse to spend time together. When they "ran around with the furniture," Le Gallienne told Ted the history of each one of her treasured antiques. She reminisced about her childhood and her theatre career, and she introduced him to all the important people, events, and animals in her life. Le Gallienne and Ted's greatest pleasure, though, was working in the garden and woods. "She enjoyed creating the garden as much as she appreciated its beauty," Ted recalled. "She very much influenced my life and work. She was my closest friend."

Roses were her passion, and from early June through the end of November, they bloomed in dozens of varieties. The Silver Moon rose, which she called "the tiger" because of its sharp thorns, climbed up the side of the porch. The Queen of Denmark rosebush, which May Sarton had given her, formed a green and pale pink wall along the side of the house. Red roses clung to the barn; pink roses decorated the iron well cover; tree roses, rambling roses, and rosebushes blazed in brick-bordered beds.

When actor June Havoc moved to Weston into a house near Le Gallienne's, she brought "one little rose" she had plucked from her garden. "I walked through the gates," Havoc recalled, "and it was too late to turn back." Looking like the centerpiece in an enormous rose bouquet, Le Gallienne flung up an arm in greeting. "I had the impulse to present the little rose to her anyway," Havoc said, "and we laughed and laughed."

Mowing the woodland trails took Ted a full week. Every fall he and Le Gallienne naturalized more daffodils in the woods. Every spring the meadow by the old house was carpeted by daffodils and narcissus that Eva and Jo had planted years earlier along with pink-and-white bleeding heart plants that sprouted among the rocks and spread over the boulders. When the lane of dogwood trees burst into a canopy of white blossoms over the trails, Le Gallienne would say, "It's like fairyland."

Ted grumbled about tedious chores like washing clay pots, and he complained for several years before Le Gallienne allowed him to use a noisy, gasoline-powered lawn mower. Le Gallienne resisted, but she was often won over to Ted's ideas on plant propagation and tree maintenance that he brought home from the university. Her "boy" had grown up into a sturdy, six-foot-two young man with tawny blond hair who had a strong stubborn streak just like her own.

"What a boy he is!" Le Gallienne bragged to her diary. "I do love him and wish he were mine."

WITHOUT AN OUTLET for her art, she told her diary that she had accomplished "absolutely nothing" that year. Her accomplishments in 1973 were modest, but they were more than nothing. She taped eight Andersen stories for Miller-Brody Productions (which marketed the cassettes); she taught her White Barn classes; *Forum* published "S. B. Quand-Même," her Sarah Bernhardt essay; she did a television program with Julie Harris about Duse; and she worked steadily with Barbara Wersba on *The Dream Watcher.*

Since her agent, Jane Broder, was almost eighty years old and ill, Le Gallienne turned more and more to Audrey Wood for advice. Wood was "wise, witty, tough, and kind," Le Gallienne thought, and she asked Wood to represent her and Barbara Wersba on the *Dream Watcher* project. Noted for her devoted service to playwrights like Tennessee Williams and William Inge, Audrey did not represent actors. She agreed, however, to make an exception for Le Gallienne. Eva became her only actor client.

In 1973 and 1974, Le Gallienne concentrated on bringing *The Dream Watcher* to the stage. She worked closely with Wersba on the play, particularly on the scenes between Mrs. Woodfin and the boy. Following a long session in the Blue Room, Wersba realized that "I had not written a character named Mrs. Woodfin, I had written Le Gallienne: her love of nature, books, her solitude, the affinity with a young boy, even the drinking—though I did not know at the time that she drank." After months of work with Le Gallienne, Barbara completed the play and, in the process, became extremely attached to the older woman. Wersba had experienced her Sven-Gallienne charm, and like others, she thought that she occupied a special place in Le Gallienne's life. Eva's intention, however, was to obtain what she wanted: a finished play that might serve as a coda to her long career.

In the hope of trying out *The Dream Watcher* at the White Barn, Le Gallienne worked on the play with thirteen-year-old Luke Yankee, the son of actor Eileen Heckart. "I would go over there on Sunday afternoon, and we would sit in the Blue Room in a little makeshift set," Yankee recalled. "So there we are rehearsing, and I made sure I knew my lines cold. . . . Suddenly, Le Gallienne took a moment and put her hand to her forehead. I looked at her expectantly. 'Exquisite,' I prompted. She dropped her hand and glared at me. 'I *know* the line. I was *thinking* about the line. You don't think about your lines. Did you know that?' Well, I apologized profusely, and then she started to laugh and embraced me. A very gentle, quick little hug."

Le Gallienne talked about *The Dream Watcher* with her network of theatre friends, attempting to attract a director for the project. Although she had not been in contact with Ellis Rabb since 1968 and *The Cherry Orchard,* she sent greetings to him through a mutual friend. Rabb responded with a long, conciliatory letter. He had failed her badly years ago, he wrote; he wanted to repay her for the damage, and he expressed interest in working with her again. In reply, Le Gallienne sent him *The Dream Watcher.* Rabb thought that the relationship between the old woman and the boy was powerful and dramatic. He did not think, however, that Wersba had succeeded in dramatizing her novel. With long narrative speeches by the boy, and underdeveloped secondary characters, the play had to be rewritten. Wersba rewrote the play but failed to solve the structural problems to Rabb's satisfaction, and he dropped out of the project. Le Gallienne tried to change his mind, but Rabb was adamant. According to Wersba, Le Gallienne vowed that she would "*never* work" with Ellis again.

In July 1974, Le Gallienne, Wersba, and Audrey Wood met with producer Roger Stevens, chairman of the Kennedy Center in Washington, D.C., and Dr.

Ralph Allen, the head of the theatre department at the University of Tennessee. Le Gallienne and Wersba wanted Stevens to present *The Dream Watcher* at the Kennedy Center. To save money, Stevens wanted to try the play out at the university with nonprofessional actors and a director whom Le Gallienne and Wood had never heard of. His plan would lessen his financial risk and it would also give Wersba an opportunity to workshop her play and test it before a live audience. Wood and Le Gallienne saw the tryout not as a workshop but as an amateur production without a name director and without the support of a professional company. Thus, the entire burden and responsibility for the play's success would be Le Gallienne's. Wood advised her clients to postpone the play and seek other producers rather than give it an inferior production; Wersba and Le Gallienne agreed, and Stevens's plan was rejected.

Stevens was angry that his proposal had been dismissed, and Le Gallienne was furious as well. Because of the expectation of doing *The Dream Watcher,* she had cancelled her White Barn classes and had turned down other jobs. As usual, Alice De Lamar was aware of Le Gallienne's situation and again began giving her a hundred dollars a month, which gave her enough money to get by. But Eva needed a job not only to pay her bills but also to maintain her mental and physical health. Anger, disappointment, worry about the future as well as liquor combined to make her sick, and she took to her bed for days. "I want to die," she moaned to Wersba.

Again, Eva turned to her favorite philosopher. Mogens had written an unusual statement of Kierkegaard's on a slip of paper, and as she lay in bed, Eva read the words again and again: "Be mirthful and then you will see all difficulties disappear."

One of her difficulties vanished when Dr. Ralph Allen, who had been moved by her reading of Mrs. Woodfin, who acts Juliet and other Shakespearean snippets in *The Dream Watcher,* offered her a three-week engagement as artist-in-residence at the University of Tennessee to talk to students and perform a program of Shakespeare scenes. "They will pay me handsomely!" Eva told Mogens.

When Le Gallienne arrived in Knoxville, Tennessee, she was reunited with Earle Hyman, who had been hired by the university as well. Since their first meeting years earlier, the two actors had kept in touch. From time to time, Hyman visited Le Gallienne in Weston, and he always sent her a dozen roses on her birthday. For her solo program, costumed in black silk pants and a brightly patterned Gucci blouse, Le Gallienne played Hamlet and Mrs. Alving. In the Shakespeare program, Hyman played opposite her in *Macbeth, Henry VIII,* and *Romeo and Juliet.* Forty-eight-year-old Hyman was astonished that at seventy-five Le Gallienne would choose to play the balcony scene in *Romeo and Juliet.* At the first performance, she instructed that the lights be lowered, "just a trifle," and said, "Earle, if you will just stand there and don't move about." Hyman said later that it was the "first and last and only time in my life I saw Juliet whole."

"The Tennessee engagement was a great success for me," Eva wrote Mogens. "I have been (as *all* old people in this country are!) rather forgotten and neglected. To be so enthusiastically received by all those young people gave me back a great deal of courage and confidence. And people now seem to suddenly realize I am still alive and in my right mind, so that I've had quite a few offers of jobs."

In a conversation with Hyman, however, Le Gallienne pondered her own responsibility for the direction her career had taken. "My mother always thought Bernhardt was the greater actor," Le Gallienne said. "I sometimes wonder what would have happened to my career if I had not felt the way I did about Duse."

ONE OF THOSE PEOPLE who realized that Le Gallienne was available for work was Peter Donnelly, the producer of the Seattle Repertory Theatre. Donnelly had made it his business to attract name theatre artists to Seattle to work with the resident company, like the venerable Broadway artist George Abbott, who came to Seattle and directed a successful production of *Life with Father*. When Donnelly called and asked Le Gallienne to stage her translation of Ibsen's *A Doll's House* at the Seattle Rep in January 1975, she accepted gratefully.

Fifty years earlier, in a public debate with Le Gallienne, George Abbott had championed the commercial theatre while Le Gallienne led the fight for a nonprofit alternative to Broadway. With even George Abbott now finding work in the nonprofit theatre and with nonprofit institutional theatres flourishing in New York and around the country, history proved Le Gallienne the victor in their debate.

Le Gallienne felt at home in the well-managed Seattle Repertory Theatre, and, since her dog, Nana, was with her, she was not lonely. She liked Peter Donnelly, and she accepted his invitations to dinners and theatre functions. Donnelly liked her, too. "Le Gallienne was a terrible flirt," he recalled, "a coquette till the end." She charmed the company; Donnelly and his staff treated her with respect and deference, understood her meticulous attention to detail, and didn't overtax her with publicity responsibilities.

Seattle reminded her of Scandinavia—"the mountains all round it—and the Sound (almost like a big open Fjord) coming in from the ocean." From her apartment, she could see the snowcapped top of Mount Rainier, and after the "poison" of New York, the air of Seattle was "clean & easy to breathe." Since the Seattle Rep was a continent away from the pressures of New York, and because it was a theatre devoted to Le Gallienne's theatre values, it was an ideal setting in which to regain her confidence as a director.

Le Gallienne with Peter Donnelly at the Seattle Repertory Theatre, 1975

On the first day of rehearsal, the company gathered around a long table, and Le Gallienne told them that they would find her a stuffy, old-fashioned director since she didn't use gimmicks and believed in serving the author. Then she opened the script and read the play to them. Although the actors were surprised by this European method, "it put everybody at ease," recalled Jeanne Carson, who played Nora.

The work proceeded smoothly except for rehearsals of the last scene between Nora and her husband, Torvald, when Nora declares her independence. Jeanne Carson had terrible problems with the scene. "I couldn't even rehearse it," Carson recalled. "Finally, I said to Miss Le G, you've just got to do it for me." Le Gallienne was stunned and pleased by Carson's request.

"She just read it, and I could see it," said Carson. "I had thought I wasn't doing enough, and suddenly Le Gallienne did it with such simplicity, and I thought, dammit, that's what I'm going to do." With her simple reading of the lines, a reading filled with the truth of the character and the projection of Nora's thought, Le Gallienne was handing on the lesson that she had learned from Duse—the art of letting go, of not "acting," of allowing herself to be a channel of communication between the play and the audience.

The reviews were extraordinary. "The . . . production . . . would do credit to any theatre in any city—in New York, London: anywhere," wrote Wayne Johnson, the *Seattle Times* critic. "It is, quite simply, one of the finest pieces of theatre work I have ever seen here or in any major theatre center." Other critics concurred, and audiences packed the theatre. Once again, Ibsen was Le Gallienne's savior.

Pleased with the success of *A Doll's House,* Peter Donnelly asked Le Gallienne to return the following season to play the Madwoman of Chaillot. "Oh, I did it before, and I wasn't very good in it," she told him. Donnelly responded that was a good reason to do the role again.

Thinking of the *Dream Watcher* project, Le Gallienne asked, "What would happen if I had a play or a film?" Donnelly explained that he would give her an out clause in her contract. "What would you do if I called you and said I couldn't come?" she continued. Before Donnelly could respond, Le Gallienne spoke: "Promise me," she said gravely, "that you won't hire our First Lady of the American Theatre, Helen Hayes, to replace me."

"Then she threw her head back on my shoulder," Donnelly recalled, "and we laughed and laughed." Donnelly drew up the contract, which included a six-week out clause, and Le Gallienne agreed to appear in *The Madwoman of Chaillot.*

Following her engagement in Seattle, Le Gallienne flew to Los Angeles for a two-day visit to explore directing *Romeo and Juliet* for the Los Angeles Shakespeare Festival that summer. She visited with Terence Scammell, had dinner with Leonora Schildkraut, Pepi's widow, and spoke with *Los Angeles Times* arts writer Sylvie Drake. "She sat erect and regal at 76, looking her age but still a lithe, if a bit restless figure, whose wit and acumen proved undiminished," Drake observed. "Behind the Wedgwood eyes and under the steel-gray hair still rustled the pioneer spirit."

"One of the advantages of being as old as I am," Le Gallienne told Drake, "is that you've seen them all, all the greats. You're so young, you poor thing, you've missed everything! Eleonora Duse, Sarah Bernhardt. Lucien Guitry was one of the greatest actors I've ever seen. . . . I always say to actors, don't put corks on your fingers . . . [let] it go on like a ray. An actor should be bigger than his body."

BUT THERE WERE disadvantages to being as old as Le Gallienne, such as her "ancient teeth" and other sagging signs of age. When she returned to Weston in mid-February, Le Gallienne saw a dental surgeon, who attached a bridge to three permanent implants. Then, in early April, she entered the hospital for an operation to fix her right eyebrow and eyelid, which had drooped so low that they were affecting her vision. The worst part of the operation for her was not the procedure, which left her with a black-and-blue face and twenty-four neat cross stitches above her eyebrow, but the fact that she was separated from Nana for the night. Thirteen-year-old Nana had thinning fur, she couldn't see or hear well, and she had only one tooth left, but she was devoted to Le Gallienne and miserable without her.

After taking care of her health problems, Le Gallienne returned to an active schedule. During her absence, Jess Jones cared for her home, birds, and a stray white cat that she had adopted. When the sleek white stray first showed up, Le Gallienne had chased him away from her birds, but he had won her over, and she playfully named him Skat, the Danish word for "treasure." Jess Jones was good with animals, and since Le Gallienne's housekeeper had quit suddenly, Le Gallienne asked Jess to work for her. Jones served Le Gallienne breakfast in the Blue Room and made the evening meals using many of Marion's recipes.

Since Jo Hutchinson now lived close by in New York City, Le Gallienne thought it was "wicked" that Jo was not there to share the garden's beauty with her. Two years after Jo's marriage to Staats Cotsworth, Le Gallienne made the first move toward reconciliation. After a series of telephone calls, Eva invited Jo and Staats to Weston in April 1974. Showing off her home—the Blue Room and the gardens, all new to Jo's eyes—and walking with Jo once again to the old house, admiring the daffodils, gave Le Gallienne great joy. "We had a wonderful day," Eva said. "I felt so happy—as though a weight had been lifted from my spirit."

Le Gallienne's reconciliation with Jo made her happy, but the heavy presence of Staats Cotsworth dragged her down. "Why did she marry that fellow?!!" she wrote in her diary in May 1975. "She's not happy. How could she be?" On May 22, Eva picked a bunch of Jo's favorite *muguet du bois* and drove to New York to visit Jo and Staats in their penthouse apartment. Staats was "impossible—was already drunk," Le Gallienne wrote. "I fear for her [and] I'm afraid he'll outlive us both!" Jo planned to stay in Weston with Eva when Staats visited friends in Hyannis on July 4, but Staats entered the hospital for a few days to dry out. When he was released, he was unable to travel, and Jo's visit to Weston was cancelled.

Years later, Jo Hutchinson explained that her love for Le Gallienne had belonged to youth: "We had a wonderful relationship—we were young, both of us. We went through that period and out." Hutchinson had been terribly hurt by Le Gallienne's leaving her for Marion Evensen, but Jo also craved independence. "If I would have stayed [with Eva]," Jo asserted, "I would have been cook and bottle washer." Still, she could not completely give up her relationship with Le Gallienne. "I was attached to her all the days of my life," she said later. Perhaps Jo knew, too, that her independence and elusiveness made her even more attractive.

It was enormously frustrating for Le Gallienne, and also enormously challenging, that the woman she wanted the most was the woman she could not have. Which, of course, was the point: a forbidden, unattainable romance was all that more desirable.

IN JULY, Le Gallienne held auditions for the White Barn tryout of *The Dream Watcher*. After Ellis Rabb, Burgess Meredith, Alan Schneider, and several other directors had turned down the play, Warren Enters was hired to direct. When he asked Barbara Wersba to rewrite her play, she refused. It was enough for Wersba that Le Gallienne believed in the script. Wersba, an experienced novelist but a neophyte playwright, was so tense and nervous that Enters barred her from the first week of rehearsal. Rehearsals began on August 1, and at first Eva was pleased with the progress. The boy they had found to play the social misfit Albert Scully, however, was a professional actor who radiated confidence and social assurance in a part that required juvenile awkwardness. After months of concentrating primarily on her own part, Le Gallienne suddenly realized that the boy's scenes with his parents were not funny and "drop the play."

The Dream Watcher opened on Friday, August 29, 1975, for a run of only three performances. "Not such a good audience tonight," Le Gallienne wrote in her diary after the opening. May Sarton was in the audience, and afterward, she had been unable to conceal her dislike of the script. "But I *don't care*," said Le Gallienne. She, of course, did value Sarton's opinion, especially about writing.

Audrey Wood attended all three performances, and the hard-boiled agent liked the play. *Variety* called Le Gallienne's performance "flawless" and noted that with some polishing the play would be ready for New York. Critic Markland Taylor, too, praised his friend's performance, but he thought that the script, with its flashbacks and long narration by the boy, was more suited to television.

Jo Hutchinson attended the closing performance of *The Dream Watcher* on Sunday evening, and then returned home with Le Gallienne to spend several days. Jo and Eva had the house to themselves. The fact that Jo had consented to stay a few days alone with Eva, without Staats, was significant. "Jo & I had a lovely peaceful time," Eva said.

"LORD!" Le Gallienne exclaimed a few weeks later. "What a ridiculous world the theatre is!"

On September 30, Audrey Wood called with the news that Byron Goldman, a producer who had expressed interest in *The Dream Watcher*, didn't want to pay Le Gallienne twenty-five hundred dollars a week. When she refused to work for less, he backed away from the project.

Later that same day, Ellis Rabb called Le Gallienne and asked her to play Fanny Cavendish, the matriarch of the Cavendish theatre family, in George Kaufman and Edna Ferber's 1927 comedy, *The Royal Family,* which was loosely based on the Barrymores. Rabb would direct the play, which would be produced by Roger Stevens for the Kennedy Center's American Bicentennial season, with a possible move to Broadway. Still cross with Ellis for quitting the *Dream Watcher* project, Le Gallienne was decidedly chilly when he called. The play was "ridiculous," she told him. Rabb said that Rosemary Harris had agreed to play Julie Cavendish, Fanny's daughter, and he poured on his warm southern charm. Le Gallienne remained silent. Realizing that his charm was getting him nowhere, Ellis tried another approach. "You would be paid twenty-five hundred dollars a week," he offered.

A pause. "I'll think about it and get back to you," Le Gallienne replied.

Rabb hung up the telephone and told Rosemary Harris that he didn't think Le Gallienne would play the role, and without her he didn't know how he could do the play. Stevens was still upset with Le Gallienne for rejecting his proposal to produce *Dream Watcher* at the University of Tennessee, and he had not wanted Rabb to cast her: although he admired her talent, he thought she was a difficult person, and he also wanted a more commercial actress to play the role. Rabb argued that the woman playing Fanny Cavendish had to "embody American theatrical history," and Eva Le Gallienne was the only actress he knew that could do that. Who was left? Helen Hayes had retired from the theatre in 1972; Katharine Hepburn was touring with an Enid Bagnold play. Stevens suggested Ina Claire or Judith Anderson.

Rabb flew to California and talked to Ina Claire, who had played Julie Cavendish in the 1930s movie of *The Royal Family.* Eva's old friend laughed at him and said that she hadn't been able to remember a line in years. Rabb approached seventy-seven-year-old Judith Anderson, who asked if the set would have any steps. When Rabb replied that there was a staircase with a great many steps, Anderson said no. Rabb returned to Stevens and insisted that the producer accept Le Gallienne in the role. After Ellis threatened to quit the project, Stevens agreed. Rabb then called Le Gallienne.

After talking with Ellis, Le Gallienne, still smarting over Byron Goldman's refusal to pay her *Dream Watcher* salary, hung up the telephone and thought that "it might serve the Goldman bastard right" if she took the *Royal Family* job. Five minutes later, Le Gallienne called Ellis back and told him that she would play Fanny Cavendish.

Meanwhile, Peter Donnelly had a contract with Le Gallienne for *The Madwoman of Chaillot* at the Seattle Repertory Theatre, and he also believed that he had a commitment from Rabb to direct the production. When Le Gallienne called Donnelly to exercise the out clause in her contract, he said, "Miss Le G, it's breaking my heart." "Well, you know, I may never get a chance to play in New York again," she said. According to Donnelly, his old friend Ellis Rabb never bothered to call him at all.

When Le Gallienne telephoned Barbara Wersba to say that she had agreed to do *The Royal Family* and asked Wersba to hold *The Dream Watcher* for her until she was free and a producer could be found, Wersba felt as if her world had "turned upside down." She agreed to hold the play for Le Gallienne, but she was angry. She wondered what had happened to Le Gallienne's earlier vow to "*never* work" with Rabb again. Unfamiliar with the volatile, intense, "ridiculous world" of the theatre, Barbara Wersba did not realize that most theatre artists will forgive one another almost everything—temper tantrums, alcoholism, promiscuity, selfishness, careerism—everything, that is, except lack of talent. In addition to her weekly salary of twenty-five hundred dollars, the reason Le Gallienne agreed to work with Ellis Rabb again was quite simple. He was talented; she was talented. Together, if they were lucky and the gods smiled, they might be able to create brilliant theatre, even with a "ridiculous" play like *The Royal Family*.

But there was another reason, too, a motivation that had propelled her artistic life ever since that foggy London morning in 1914 at Tree's Academy when she played Juliet for the first time and had been transported into another realm. She had said in an interview that the pleasures of acting were not frequent. "Occasionally one gets great joy. I think it must be . . . the same thing for a very religious person who finds himself or herself in a state of grace."

IN HONOR OF the nation's Bicentennial in 1976 and to celebrate the cultural heritage of America, Xerox Corporation had donated four hundred thousand dollars to the Kennedy Center to produce ten plays, primarily all-star revivals, that would play in Washington, in selected other cities, and possibly on Broadway. In addition to *The Royal Family*, the series included Thornton Wilder's *The Skin of Our Teeth*, starring Elizabeth Ashley; Tennessee Williams's *Sweet Bird of Youth*, with Irene Worth and Christopher Walken; and Eugene O'Neill's *Long Day's Journey into Night*, starring Jason Robards. When the producer of the series, Roger Stevens, agreed to cast Eva Le Gallienne in *The Royal Family*, it was a smart decision. *The Royal Family* would prove to be the most popular, most lucrative, and most critically successful play of the Bicentennial series, with Le Gallienne leading an ensemble company of gifted actors with a wealth of theatre experience.

"*The Royal Family* was one of those rare moments in the theatre," recalled actor Joe Maher, "when everything went right from the first moment of rehearsal." First was Ellis Rabb's casting. To play his royal family of actors, Rabb cast a group of seasoned professionals. Rosemary Harris had the leading role of Julie Cavendish, Fanny's glamorous daughter, the part based on Ethel Barrymore. George Grizzard acted the John Barrymore role of Tony Cavendish, Fanny's swashbuckling son; Joe Maher and Mary Louise Wilson acted Herbert and Kitty Dean, Fanny's comically grasping brother and sister-in-law; Sam Levene played Oscar Wolfe, the Cavendishes' devoted manager/impresario; Mary Layne acted Gwen, Fanny's ingenue granddaughter; and the Cavendish housekeeper, Della, was played by Rosetta Le Noire. Many of the actors had worked together before; they were already a theatre family, and it was merely a quarter-step for them to suggest a real family.

To house the Cavendishes, Oliver Smith designed a set with a balcony and sweeping staircase, eclectic furniture, and family portraits—a home with a lived-in, careless elegance that managed to be both comfortable and grand. The period costumes by Ann Roth were elegant and stylish, and Le Gallienne's slightly out-of-date clothes were in her favorite blues and plums, with long, lean lines which made her appear tall and regal. Composer Claibe Richardson wrote theme music for each of the Cavendish women and composed interludes that sounded like "a music box just a little tipsy on bathtub gin."

Le Gallienne asked Eloise Armen to drive her in to rehearsals, which were at Saint Clements' Church on West Forty-sixth Street in New York. Since Eloise's daughter, Rebecca, had gone off to college, Eloise was happy to help Eva through the long days of rehearsal and costume and wig fittings. Le Gallienne was pleased with the cast and with Ellis Rabb, who "seems to be right in his own centre." From time to time, she resisted Rabb's directing ideas, like a long cross that he wanted her to make just before her death scene. "I know what you have in mind," she told him, "but this is a trivial play, and it won't take it." Rabb didn't press her, and a week later she asked, "Now tell me again, what did you have in mind?" Rabb explained his idea that Fanny's death should come while she's alone onstage, holding a script, rehearsing a new play, which would take her up the stairs, down again, and finally to her chair. Le Gallienne trusted Rabb and did the scene just as he had asked.

When the company traveled to Princeton and the premiere at the McCarter Theatre, Le Gallienne grew apprehensive. Eloise traveled to Princeton with her, helped her dress at the theatre, cooked for her, did her correspondence, and also bore the brunt of Le Gallienne's fear. "God, she was difficult," Eloise recalled. "She was very insecure, very nervous."

It had been seventeen years since, in *Listen to the Mocking Bird*, Le Gallienne had played one role eight times a week. All of her appearances since then had been in repertory. Her doctor assured her that her health was fine, but she worried about stamina and began a series of B-12 shots. She worked on her role constantly, imagining the pattern of Fanny's thought and crafting the rhythm of each line, each word, each silence. "So much depends on phrasing," she wrote. "Phrasing depends on *breathing*."

The opening reception in Princeton was "marvellous," Le Gallienne wrote. "It's incredible! Great enthusiasm!" Even Roger Stevens was "most complimentary about my work," she told her diary. Barbara Wersba came to the opening and congratulated Le Gallienne on her performance. Eva, however, was bad-tempered and annoyed that she had come to see the play so soon. Wersba walked away, and even though Le Gallienne ran after her to embrace her, Barbara, still angry about the *Dream Watcher*, now saw her hero in a new light, perceiving Le Gallienne's "vanity, her self-interest, her megalomania."

Wersba's perceptions were accurate; in fact, they're accurate descriptions of most actors. The world of the play was all that mattered to Le Gallienne at the moment. On matinee days, Eva stayed in the theatre all day, fortifying herself before the evening performance with soup and a raw egg. In her diary, she recorded the audience reaction and her fatigue after playing continuous performances of the fast-paced, high-energy play. In the leading role of Julie Cavendish, Rosemary Harris was the dynamic engine of the play, but as Fanny Cavendish, Le Gallienne was its soul.

After Princeton, the company traveled to the Kennedy Center for a five-week engagement. Business was excellent, and the reviews were glowing. "A wistful and immaculately stylish revival," wrote David Richards in the *Washington Star*. "Miss Le Gallienne, still pure of voice and sure of effect . . . , has the dignity of an aging swan."

On her first entrance in the play, Le Gallienne, costumed in a floor-length plum dressing gown, quickly, lightly, never looking down or lifting her gown or touching the stair rail, floated down the long staircase. Of course, at her home in Weston, she ran up and down the even steeper stairs to her second-floor bedroom a dozen times a day. Such an entrance by a seventy-six-year-old, even a remarkably fit seventy-six-year-old, was a courageous one. One slip, one misstep, and the result could have been a broken leg or hip or even worse.

After Washington, the company played the Brooklyn Academy of Music for a two-week run. If they were successful in Brooklyn and backers could be found, they would move on to Broadway and a commercial run. On opening night in Brooklyn, Le Gallienne opened a gift from Jo Hutchinson. As Fanny, Le Gallienne wore a lavender scent that was appropriate for the character, but the gift that Jo had ordered from Guerlain in Paris was a bottle of Eau de Verveine, Le Gallienne's signature fragrance. "No one else would have thought of that," marveled Eva. "Quelle tragedie que cette histoire."

The New York critics smelled a hit in the making and went to Brooklyn to see *The Royal Family*. They praised Le Gallienne's artistry and the ensemble playing of the company and singled out Rabb's exuberant, graceful direction of Kaufman and Ferber's soufflé of a play. Edith Oliver in *The New Yorker* pointed out that the revival of 1927's *Royal Family* had the same theme as *A Chorus Line* which premiered in 1975—"the enchantment of the theatre, and the pull it exerts on those who work in it."

The critics' raves and the sold-out houses convinced producer Burry Fredrik (a Weston neighbor of Le Gallienne's) and her partners to take the show to Broadway. On December 30, 1975, *The Royal Family* opened at the Helen Hayes Theatre, which formerly had been the Fulton. Le Gallienne knew the theatre well. It was at the Fulton Theatre that she had become a Broadway star in 1921, playing Julie in *Liliom*. In 1916, she had played the Irish ingenue Mary Powers in *The Melody of Youth* on the Fulton stage. In that play, she had acted with James O'Neill, the father of Eugene O'Neill—a fact that stunned Joe Maher. "What was James O'Neill like as an actor?" he asked Le Gallienne. "He was like you," she replied. "He had a kind of easiness." Maher recalled that Le Gallienne always insisted, with wry humor, when she heard him tell someone that they were playing at the Helen Hayes, "No, dear, we're at the *Fulton*."

Since everyone in the company was a good actor, Le Gallienne was fond of each of them, but she was especially close to Rabb and Harris; they were in her "line." When George Grizzard left the company for another commitment, Ellis Rabb took over the part of Tony Cavendish, and Le Gallienne's affection and respect for her two "children" were palpable onstage. Grizzard had been well received as Tony Cavendish; but Rabb played the part, one critic said, "like Clifton Webb giving an impersonation of Noël Coward giving an impersonation of John Barrymore, and nothing could be funnier."

Humor was serious business to Le Gallienne, requiring precision, consistency, and attention to even the slightest breath. Rosemary Harris, whose dressing room was on the opposite side of the stage from Le Gallienne's, recalled that following every performance they would meet onstage after the curtain call for a hug and a kiss. "But one night," Harris said, "I found this new laugh. I had run out of breath on a line and had broken the line in two, and my line got a laugh. When Le Gallienne said her line that followed, she did not get her usual laugh. For about a week, I noticed that she got colder and colder at each curtain call. I went to her and asked what was wrong. 'You know very well,' she said." Rosemary apologized and returned to the original phrasing, which restored Le Gallienne's laugh. Le Gallienne was exacting and formidable, but "what she brought to every role," Harris observed later, "was a sort of quizzical sense of humor. She had such a bubble of amusement inside her and a lightness of touch."

"I used to watch her from the wings every night," recalled Maher. "She got a laugh on every line, look, and comma in the script." In the last scene of the play, Fanny dies onstage. Le Gallienne's death scene was so truthful that "I honest to

The Royal Family *company, 1975–76. Standing left to right:*
Ellis Rabb, Rosetta Le Noire, Joseph Maher, Sam Levene, Rosemary Harris, and
Mary Layne. Mary Louise Wilson is sitting next to Le Gallienne.

God thought she was dead," said Maher. Audiences felt the same way, gasping in shock when Fanny sank back into her chair and let her arm fall limp.

Le Gallienne always insisted that Fanny Cavendish wasn't a bit like her, but in their feelings about the theatre, they were identical. Fanny's best scene in the play, and the most personally significant one for Le Gallienne, came in the second act, when Fanny explains to her granddaughter, Gwen, why she shouldn't give up acting for marriage and a family. "Marriage isn't a career," Fanny says. "It's an incident!"

Acting is everything, Fanny tells Gwen. "It's work and play and meat and drink." To go down to the theatre, Fanny continues, "to a stuffy dressing room and smear paint on your face and go out on the stage and speak a lot of fool lines, and you love it! You love it! . . . Every night when I'm sitting here alone I'm really down there at the theatre. . . . That's all that's kept me alive."

Just as Fanny handed down an acting tradition to her granddaughter, Le Gallienne gave Mary Layne, who played Gwen, her biography of Duse and taught the young actor that "the more you release the ego, the more you are free to embody the character and the emotions of the character." Karen Eifert, who worked as a dresser on the show, learned the traditions of the theatre from Le Gallienne. "She talked a lot about how respect was going out of the theatre," Eifert recalled. "She also said to me, 'Mediocrity is the biggest sin.' " Working in *The Royal Family*, being part of a community of actors, connecting with young theatre people, and playing a role that celebrated the joys of the theatre brought back all the happiness Le Gallienne had experienced during her years at the Civic Repertory—and a reprise of the critical adulation.

"From Le Gallienne we can learn again what theater used to be," wrote Alan Rich in *New York* magazine. "Watch her, and you learn volumes about simplicity, economy, and directness." Jack Kroll in *Newsweek* observed that Le Gallienne playing Fanny Cavendish "makes you believe for two and a half hours that the theater does breed people of unique beauty, grace and human richness."

And not since the days of the Civic had Le Gallienne received so much publicity. She didn't mind posing for photographs or giving long interviews, since it gave her an opportunity to reminisce about the Civic Repertory and her ambitious attempt to launch a national theatre. She refused to pose for Alfred Eisenstadt's series for *Life* magazine of the one hundred most important women in America. Eisenstadt wanted to photograph Le Gallienne in full Cavendish costume in her garden. The idea seemed wrong to her. "No," she said. "I don't like him." But she consented to pose for *Vogue* in Fanny's costume on the set. Leo Lerman, the *Vogue* writer, described her as a "small, boy-hipped, seeress-eyed . . . legend."

Perhaps because Le Gallienne as Fanny Cavendish died onstage, and died so convincingly, journalists and critics allowed a kind of eulogistic tone to creep into their articles and reviews about her. She had reached the age when actresses become canonized; Le Gallienne accepted the attention with grace and a slightly jaundiced eye. "In this country we're particularly cruel to actresses in the middle period," Le Gallienne reminded a reporter. "We all went through a trough . . . even the Barrymores. Fortunately I've been able to do other things."

It was Walter Kerr, though, in an article in *The New York Times*, who perceived why Le Gallienne's Fanny Cavendish resonated so powerfully. Le Gallienne played a double role in the play, he explained: she represented Broadway stardom and she also symbolized "the movement to diversify Broadway." In 1926, Le Gallienne rejected Broadway and founded the Civic Repertory downtown, and in later years she started and supported similar companies. "Fanny Cavendish wouldn't have done that," Kerr wrote; "everyone knows Miss Le Gallienne did." Le Gallienne's pioneering work had changed "the very nature of Broadway," said Kerr. The critic wondered what Le Gallienne thought about her choices—"did she think that her premise, at least, had won?"

"I love the work," Le Gallienne said. "I've had a wonderful time. Many people may think I've been a failure, but I've always done what I wanted to do. I never wanted to be a bandwagon person. . . . I knew the risks."

Now, at seventy-seven, Le Gallienne was learning something new: that it was possible to be both bandwagon actress and serious artist.

All the press attention, especially the long articles about the Civic Repertory, and the acknowledgment of her pioneering contributions were gratifying to Le Gallienne, but praise from her peers in the theatre was the sweetest tribute. When *The Royal Family* played a benefit for the Actors' Fund and Le Gallienne made her first entrance, the audience, made up almost entirely of actors, applauded wildly. At first, she ignored the applause and continued her descent down the stairway. When the cheering and clapping did not stop, Le Gallienne finally acknowledged their applause by crossing her arms over her chest and bowing her head slightly. At the end of the play, the audience roared out their appreciation with a standing ovation, shouts, and bravos. Later, when Le Gallienne left by the stage door, she was greeted by a crowd of young people who applauded and cheered.

As usual, Eva's role in the theatre reverberated in her private life. Playing a successful Broadway actress onstage stimulated her to act like a bandwagon actress offstage. She bought a new dark-blue cashmere coat and a mink hat. Temperamental and demanding, she followed a rigid routine, and any deviation from that routine upset her. She hated dining out and insisted that Eloise fix complicated meals on a hot plate in the hotel room.

Le Gallienne trusted Eloise Armen completely; she had made Eloise the executor of her will, and the two women were best friends and confidantes. Years earlier, when they were just getting to know one another, Eva said, "Eloise, I have something I really should tell you. I'm a homosexual." She looked at Armen expectantly to observe her reaction. Unsurprised by Eva's admission, since "everyone knew that she was," Eloise replied, "Well, I guess there's a little of that in everyone." Le Gallienne told Eloise that the love between women was "the most beautiful thing in the world." Eloise, who loved her husband, Seth Armen, replied that she understood, adding that she had adored Laurette Taylor, and if Laurette had wanted a love relationship with her, well, then, Eloise might have been a homosexual as well. In fact, Eloise realized later that her devotion to Le Gallienne was part nostalgia for the relationship she had had with Laurette Taylor. Eloise had cared for Laurette until her death, and she was equally devoted to Le Gallienne. Once, when Mogens wrote her a worried letter about Eva, Eloise assured him, "I would never leave her if she needed me."

"I'm most grateful to [Eloise]," Eva told Mogens. "She has been able to look after this ancient child quite a lot." Once, after Eloise had written several letters to her children, she wrote to Le Gallienne and unthinkingly signed the letter

"Mom." At first as a joke, Eva began calling Eloise "Mom," but the name stuck. In 1977, when Eloise and Seth Armen moved to Weston and bought Mimsey Benson's old house, Eloise and Eva saw each other almost every day. They talked on the telephone at ten a.m., and in the afternoon they took a long walk together. Le Gallienne looked to her for advice and comfort, and Eloise became "Mom." Eva had a key to the Armen home, and when Eloise and Seth left on a trip, they would return home to a house filled with flowers from Le Gallienne's garden, a different arrangement in every room. Years earlier, Mimsey Benson had played the role of Mom; Marion had become "Mutki." Once again, Le Gallienne had found a replacement for Julie Le Gallienne.

The Royal Family closed on July 18, 1976. *A Chorus Line* had swept the Tony Awards, but Ellis Rabb won a Tony for best direction and Rosemary Harris earned a best actress nomination. Le Gallienne was not nominated for a Tony, which stimulated some critical protests, but her role of Fanny was not a leading role, and she already had received a special Tony. She did win the Outer Critics' Circle Award for her performance; the Drama League honored her with a medal for distinguished performance; and the City of New York presented her with its highest cultural award, the Handel Medallion.

The Handel Medallion was given to Le Gallienne for her lifetime achievement and in particular to honor the fiftieth anniversary of the Civic Repertory. Eloise drove Eva to New York to receive the award. "You would think I was driving her to her execution!" Armen recalled. "She was so relieved when it was over she had no room left to be proud." Le Gallienne at first protested that she was speechless, but she accepted the award with "gratitude and joy" and she reminisced at length about the Civic. "If I were not one hundred and one, five months, and a day, I really think I would have another shot at starting such a theatre," she concluded.

LE GALLIENNE'S RESPITE in the country lasted two months. With the success of *The Royal Family* on Broadway, the producers had been able to book a national tour. Le Gallienne and Sam Levene were the only original company members to sign on. Rehearsals began in late September 1976, and the cast replacements—Carole Shelley and Leonard Frey, who took over the roles of Julie and Tony Cavendish, and Richard Woods and Laura Stuart, who played Herbert and Kitty Dean—were "all excellent" actors, thought Le Gallienne.

Eloise anticipated traveling with Eva on the long tour, but in late August she was diagnosed with high blood pressure and had to follow a strict regime. The producers paid a dresser to look after Le Gallienne, and Anne Kaufman Schneider, the daughter of playwright George Kaufman, planned to join Eva at different stages of the tour.

Tall, stylish, and striking, Anne Kaufman first met Le Gallienne backstage at the McCarter Theatre in Princeton. She told Eva how much she had loved her performance and confessed that she had cried with happiness and relief through the entire play, since she had feared that her father's 1927 play would be too dated for a modern audience.

Anne owned the rights to her father's plays, and she watched over their progress in the theatre. When *The Royal Family* moved to Broadway, Anne, who was twenty-five years younger than Le Gallienne, struck up a friendship with her. Le Gallienne hadn't known George Kaufman, because "he wasn't involved in the sort of theatre I was interested in," but Anne recalled seeing the Civic Repertory production of *Alice in Wonderland* at the New Amsterdam Theatre when she was eight years old.

Le Gallienne's hotel was next door to Kaufman's apartment, and Anne recalled that "I started going over and asking her if there was anything she needed, could I do anything, and we would sit and talk." When Eva was ill for a time with the flu, Anne looked after her. One day Le Gallienne beckoned Anne to come close. "If anything happens to me," she whispered, "don't let them get Helen Hayes."

Anne was adopted by George and Beatrice Kaufman when she was an infant. She was their only child. Anne had often accompanied her father on out-of-town tryouts of his plays, and she developed a love of the theatre and theatre people. Later, Anne married theatre producer Irving Schneider. Like her father, Anne had a quick wit, and she was not awed by celebrity. George Kaufman was a complicated, difficult, disciplined man who didn't care a whit about celebrity. What he cared about most was his work, and he expressed that feeling through the character of theatre manager Oscar Wolfe in *The Royal Family*. "Fun!" Wolfe exclaims. "Fun is work! It's work that's fun." Attracted initially to Le Gallienne because Eva shared many of George Kaufman's traits and values, Anne also recalled "there was always something very moving about her. I felt terribly protective toward her."

When Eloise Armen was unavailable, Anne acted as her understudy. She ran Eva's errands, invited her to dinner, took her on shopping expeditions, bought her small, thoughtful presents, found a doctor for her, and even spoke French with her. Le Gallienne raised her eyebrows at Anne's "dreadful American-accented French," but Anne refused to be bullied or intimidated, which impressed Eva. Anne was fun. Like Peggy Webster, she enjoyed people, she loved to talk, and she had a wealth of theatre stories and gossip. Anne talked, but she listened, too, a perfect audience of one. "Once Le G told me a story about lunching with Mrs. Fiske as if it had happened ten days ago," Anne said later. "I realized that if I listened very hard I would learn a lot."

Across the country, the *Royal Family* tour played to rave reviews, but the producers still lost thousands of dollars. The most successful touring companies

Anne Kaufman on board the Queen Mary *with her father,*
George S. Kaufman, 1956

were the musicals *A Chorus Line* and *Grease.* Le Gallienne blamed the poor business on Burry Fredrik's bad management, but the fact was, business on the road
was drying up for straight plays. "It would no longer be possible to tour with a
couple of Ibsen plays as I did," she thought, "or even with one as Mrs. Fiske
did. . . . The only people today who might swing it are a couple of film actresses
who couldn't really play them."

Le Gallienne was a link to those "glory years," observed Sylvie Drake in the
Los Angeles Times, and critic Dan Sullivan called Le Gallienne's performance
"like Duse, luminous and resigned, a good deed in a naughty world." All along
the route, Le Gallienne smiled for photographers, talked to reporters, accepted
awards—all without too much grumbling, since, like her Yorkshire, Nana, she
adored the fuss and attention. As she prepared for a publicity session in Los Angeles, Le Gallienne, wearing a black pants suit, a wide-brimmed black hat, and
antique earrings, turned her penetrating blue eyes on Anne Kaufman. "Do I
look like a buckaroo?" she deadpanned.

On the tour, Le Gallienne kept to a rigid routine. After having dinner at four
p.m., she was at the theatre an hour and a half before every performance. Elliott
Woodruff, the stage manager, recalled that when places were called and the act
began, Le Gallienne never left the stage area to go to her dressing room. She was

also extremely proud of her fit, lithe body and her quick entrance down the stairs. "They think I'm so old I can't walk," she said.

When the tour played Los Angeles, Le Gallienne accepted the American National Theatre Academy's national artist award on her seventy-eighth birthday. Even though it was Super Bowl Sunday, celebrities, friends, and former colleagues of Le Gallienne's showed up at the luncheon hosted by Leonora Schildkraut. Peter Falk, Efrem Zimbalist Jr., Karl Malden, and Burgess Meredith, who began their careers working with Le Gallienne, shared memories, President Ford sent his congratulations, and William Windom, Norman Lloyd, and Will Geer read letters and messages from a host of theatre luminaries. In accepting the award, Le Gallienne said that she didn't deserve it, since work was fun and she'd "had more fun than any woman in America."

Le Gallienne was happy—not only because she was working but because she had fallen in love with Anne Kaufman. On some of the tour, Anne's husband, Irving Schneider, had traveled with her, but during the lengthy California engagement she stayed with Le Gallienne. Early on, during the Broadway run, Anne had taken flowers backstage to "Miss Le Gallienne." "Oh, you don't have to call me that," Eva said. "What do your friends call you?" Anne asked. "My friend Pepi Schildkraut called me Evale."

Anne had never been unfaithful to her husband of seventeen years and had never been involved with a woman. "I've had other theatre hits, and I haven't gone off with the leading man or woman," she said later. In San Francisco, the women shared adjoining rooms, took long walks, and went shopping. "I remember thinking, I can't wait until I get back to the hotel to see her," Anne said. Their romance began with all the usual cliches—little gifts, flowers, romantic notes. "She asked me several times in San Francisco if I had ever had an affair with a woman," recalled Anne. "I said no. For me falling in love with a woman had more to do with things like mind, spirit, and a sense of connection. Yet I think that for Evale there was an added triumph in someone who was married."

After the tour closed, Anne joined Le Gallienne in Weston for a few weeks. "Here, wear this," Eva said one evening. She gave Anne Julie Le Gallienne's heavy gold wedding band. Engraved inside is "12 Feb 1897 Asra." Anne took the ring. "I give you my love and devotion," Anne told her.

Le Gallienne called Eloise Armen. "Mom, something ridiculous has happened to me. I've fallen in love with Anne." Then, as if to ensure Eloise's continued faithfulness, she added, "You know, Mom, this never replaces a best friend."

Five years earlier, Le Gallienne had lost everyone close to her. Years of reading Emerson had taught her, though, to beware of getting "old and preoccupied" and unable to "bend to a new companion." Now, as she neared eighty, it was as if she were living her life in repertory, although this time with a different cast.

Her best friend, Eloise, lived just a mile away in Mimsey's old house; her beloved helper Ted would soon move down the lane into the old house that Eva had shared with Jo; and her new companion, Anne Kaufman, visited often in Weston on weekends and holidays.

Le Gallienne felt singularly blessed, but she knew that this time too would pass, because she was alive, and if you are alive, she believed, "you suffer and you are happy occasionally, you experience joy, anguish, everything . . . it's all part of life."

WHEN LE GALLIENNE returned from the tour in late March 1977, she entered the hospital for another eye operation, this time to correct the droop of her left eyelid. She also underwent hours of dental work. Her physical complaints, though, were minor next to those of Jess Jones, her housekeeper and friend, who had cancer of the larynx, which necessitated the removal of her voice box. A "miserable business," said Eva. Jess eventually recovered, but since she could no longer work as a housekeeper, Le Gallienne hired Nona Aznar, a Scandinavian woman with a ten-year-old daughter. With the help of Eloise, Ted, and Anne Kaufman, Le Gallienne told Mogens, "I have not been neglected. In fact people spoil me terribly."

In July 1977, New York City's WNET filmed *The Royal Family* for its *Great Performances* series. Anne Kaufman drove Le Gallienne to the PBS studios in Hartford and stayed with her through the taping. It was a "ghastly five days," Le Gallienne told her diary, even though the "medium itself has no difficulty for me." Almost the entire Broadway cast returned for the filming. Karl Meyer in the *Saturday Review* called Le Gallienne's performance on film "magical." The following year, Le Gallienne won an Emmy for best supporting actress for her portrayal of Fanny Cavendish. Anne watched the awards ceremony on television with Eva, and when she won, Anne burst into tears. Le Gallienne, who had never watched the television version of *The Royal Family*, since it would have made her too nervous, asked "How can you be so foolish?" "I'm not foolish. I'm Jewish," sobbed Anne. Actually, it had been Kaufman's behind-the-scenes negotiations that had enabled *The Royal Family* to be on television. When Le Gallienne received the Emmy, she gave it to Anne. "This is for you as well as for me," she said.

To please Anne, Le Gallienne began going out more to the theatre and to lunches and dinners in New York. She introduced Anne to Alice De Lamar, and she took her to meet Jo Hutchinson. Eva was happy to meet Anne's friends. When Kitty Carlisle Hart spoke at the Westport Playhouse in April 1978, Anne drove her to Westport and afterward took her to Le Gallienne's for a visit. Perhaps thinking of how she had selfishly refused to mingle with Peggy Webster's friends,

Le Gallienne made a special effort for Anne. When Anne and Kitty arrived, flowers filled the Blue Room, a fire was burning, and Anne noticed that Eva was being particularly charming and gracious. Anne had believed that Eva was being "her most divine self" because of the presence of her glamorous friend.

When they left to drive back to New York, Kitty Hart said, "I'm going to ask you something that is none of my business."

"What is it?" said Anne.

"Are you lovers?"

"Yes," replied Anne, after a moment. "Why do you ask?"

"Because she was carrying on for *you*. It was all for you." Kitty had caught that Le Gallienne was playing Sven-Gallienne for Anne's benefit.

At Anne's urging, Le Gallienne accepted a Theatre World Award in person, and Kaufman also encouraged her to attend a celebration honoring "50 Extraordinary Women of Achievement." Other women honored along with Le Gallienne included Helen Hayes, Agnes de Mille, Betty Friedan, and Margaret Mead. Eva called the event a "horror," and she clung to Leontyne Price, who was "so nice & warm." Le Gallienne enjoyed her more active social life with Anne, but her happiest times were when she was at home alone with "Anny," a name she pronounced with the Danish inflection.

"To go up there was to be enveloped in love," Anne said. "Evale was infinitely romantic and seductive. There were always fresh flowers, a fire in her bedroom, little gifts. I was an object of love. I had never known that kind of romance. She used to come in and wake me up early. Then she would go down the stairs, the same way she did in *Royals*—quick little rhythmic steps."

They spent much of their time outdoors, deadheading flowers, weeding, clearing brush, and hauling wood. "I'm a city lady," Anne protested when Le Gallienne asked her to carry logs. "You've got to be joking."

"I'm not joking," said Eva. "Pick them up."

"I was black and blue from carrying wood," remembered Anne. "But I've never been so slim and fit." Once, after a day spent weeding, Kaufman complained of poison ivy.

"Well, you didn't get it here," Eva said. "I don't have any."

"No, you're right," Anne said, "I got it on Sixty-third Street!"

On rainy days, they oiled books in the Blue Room, polished brass, sorted clothes and costumes, and even organized the attic. Once, as she leafed through Le Gallienne's scrapbooks, Anne noticed that Eva had worked with Mary Astor. "Did you know that she had a very famous romance with my father?" Anne asked. "Really?" said Eva. "I never read about that sort of thing."

One day in the attic, Anne found a wide gold ring. "What's this?" she asked.

"Give it to me," Eva said. "It was from Mercedes." As Anne watched, Le Gallienne took the ring and threw it down the well.

Anne had seen de Acosta around New York, but she had first heard about her from her mother. Beatrice Kaufman had met Mercedes in the early 1940s at a radio show, Anne told Le Gallienne. Mercedes invited Beatrice to her apartment for lunch, which to Beatrice's surprise turned out to be a tête-à-tête. After lunch, Mercedes suddenly disappeared, but soon reappeared wearing a diaphanous yellow negligee. Beatrice Kaufman fled. Anne laughed as she told Eva that her mother's story was particularly memorable for her since it was the first time she had ever heard the word "diaphanous."

Le Gallienne was not amused. "Well, Mercedes was a *professional* lesbian," she said.

After reading de Acosta's 1960 autobiography, *Here Lies the Heart,* Le Gallienne had written that the book was "entirely innocuous—but so full of lies that it's positively incredible!" She thought that Mercedes's veiled references to their relationship were boring rather than upsetting, but she found de Acosta's "colossal egocentricity" quite startling. For example, Mercedes had written that Duse died "friendless" in Pittsburgh, and that she and Eva were Duse's only friends in New York and had singlehandedly made the arrangements for Duse—somehow forgetting the presence of Duse's entourage, the Italian ambassador, and three thousand other mourners.

"Every day we would walk up the path before breakfast to get the paper and open the gates," Anne recalled. "I said once I loved to do that every morning, just the task of opening the gates and latching them back. She said, 'Well, that's the difference between us. I love the evening at dusk when we walk down and close them.' "

LE GALLIENNE'S MONTHS of rest and gardening ended in September 1977, when auditions began for *The Dream Watcher* in New York. Burry Fredrik, the producer of *The Royal Family,* had bought the play and planned to present it first at the Seattle Repertory, to be followed by a few weeks in Boston, then a run at the Kennedy Center before opening on Broadway.

Eva had sent the play to Mogens, who expressed reservations, particularly about the boy's parents, an alcoholic insurance salesman and a sharp-tongued, overly made-up suburban matron, who seemed to Mogens like grotesque caricatures. Eloise believed that the play depended too much on Le Gallienne's scenes with the boy. Le Gallienne heard their objections, but she was determined to do the play. She had promised Wersba that she would do it, and the character of Mrs. Woodfin, who imagined herself to be an actress like Eva Le Gallienne, and the old woman's relationship with the boy, Albert Scully, which was so like her relationship with Ted Lockwood, would be, she thought, an ideal close to her long career.

Brian Murray, the director, thought the play was more suited to a movie for television. "It has to do with the education and cultivation of a child—pulling him away from crass, boring parents. But the play was not fair to the parents—they were not deep—there was no contest, no conflict." Despite his doubts, Murray wanted to work with Le Gallienne. "I was very much in awe of her," Murray recalled. When they met for the first time in the Blue Room, Le Gallienne said, "Mr. Murray, I must tell you straight off, I don't like to be directed." Murray was overwhelmed not only by her, he said, "but by those books, by those mementos. It was a museum, that place."

Le Gallienne had designed a simple, practical set centered on Orpha Woodfin's cottage, similar to the set used for the White Barn production. Burry Fredrik rejected her idea and argued that since the play would be going to Broadway, the set had to be on a Broadway scale. A designer was hired who worked out a complicated multiple set complete with a revolving turntable.

Eloise traveled to Seattle with Le Gallienne, and rehearsals proceeded uneventfully. Brian Murray, an actor's director, worked well with everyone in the cast; Le Gallienne liked his work and accepted some of his ideas. The playwright, however, was having a different experience. In the novel, the other characters are seen through the eyes of the boy. In an attempt to convey a similar effect in the theatre, Wersba and Le Gallienne decided to present them in a broad cartoon style. Brian Murray struggled to reconcile the cartoon scenes with the more naturalistic scenes of the old woman and the boy, and at his request Wersba rewrote scenes constantly, often not understanding the purpose of the rewrites. The kind of director that Wersba needed was a writer's director or an experienced dramaturg, who could have helped her shape her script dramatically.

After weeks of rehearsing in an empty hall, when the company moved into the theatre and Le Gallienne saw the set for the first time, she was horrified. "Ponderous and gloomy and downright ugly" is how Eloise Armen described it in a letter to Mogens. "And not only is it ugly, but the machinery didn't work! The sets change with a terrible groaning noise. There is a gauze curtain that comes and goes in dark greens that makes it look like a Russian tragedy." To Barbara Wersba's amazement, Le Gallienne decided to "adjust to it, to work with it."

There were too many problems, though, to be corrected at the last minute. The opening night was a nightmare of missed lighting and sound cues; actors, who had played many versions of the same scenes, forgot their lines; and props flew off the creaking turntable.

Except for Le Gallienne's performance, which they praised as "luminous" and "moving," the reviewers panned the play. "Let's hope *The Dream Watcher* packs its bags and goes home," wrote one. Others wondered why Le Gallienne had chosen such an inferior play, which seemed more suited for television than the stage. With such poor notices, the producers did not want to risk taking the play on to Boston and Washington, and they did not want to pay to rework the script or redo the set.

"Go *home*," Le Gallienne told Wersba. "Go back to your life." Barbara Wersba did just that, vowing that she would never write another play. Anne Kaufman flew to Seattle and saw three performances and thought that Le Gallienne's performance was extraordinary. Le Gallienne stayed on in Seattle to finish the run, but Nana became ill, and Eva became empathetically ill. Not only was she sick at heart about the critical reception, but night after night of playing Mrs. Woodfin, who has a heart attack and dies at the end of the play, depressed her terribly. She succumbed to bronchitis, and her voice was without "timbre or resonance. No volume or control." Le Gallienne turned the part over to her understudy, and she and Eloise flew home on Christmas Day.

When she returned from Seattle, Le Gallienne was depressed and fell into an old pattern, turning once again to the numbing consolation of liquor. Anne Kaufman recalled that when they flew home from the tour of *The Royal Family,* Le Gallienne rejected the free drinks offered in first class. "No, no," Eva told her. "I'm not a good drinker." Of course, at that time Le Gallienne was not depressed. On New Year's Eve, 1977, Le Gallienne did not celebrate with her guests—Jess and Doris; Ted Lockwood; Eloise and Seth Armen and their daughter, Rebecca; and Anne Kaufman. Early in the evening, according to Anne, Le Gallienne became "really drunk" and staggered upstairs to bed.

During January 1978, Le Gallienne recuperated both physically and emotionally. Just as she was pulling out of her depression, fifteen-year-old Nana died in her arms. Le Gallienne felt "Desolate—Lost—without my dearest friend." Nana was cremated, and Eloise was instructed to mingle Nana's ashes with Le Gallienne's when Eva died.

AFTER NANA'S DEATH, Eva could not bear to get another dog right away. She did adopt a second stray cat, which had joined the skunks, opossums, and raccoons for a nightly feed at a wooden trough that she had placed by the back door. After days of gentle coaxing, Le Gallienne lured the cat, a beautiful, long-haired calico, into the kitchen, and eventually the cat, which she named Tabitha, moved upstairs onto her bed. Nine months after Nana's death, in October 1978, Le Gallienne acquired another Yorkshire, with a darker coat than Nana's and red whiskers. She named the dog Tinker Bell. Tabitha and Tink slept on her bed, and the older "chauvinist male," Skat, stayed downstairs. Animals live in the moment, and their antics and the details of their care provided an endless source of amusement and occupation for Le Gallienne.

In May, Le Gallienne planned to go back to writing. Rumer Godden had urged her to write a book about the Blue Room and all the stories it contained.

With her essay on Sarah Bernhardt and one on Peter Pan completed, Le Gallienne had made a good start. She roughed out an essay about John Barrymore; another, called "Four Goddesses," about Constance Collier, Maxine Elliott, Julie Opp Faversham, and Ethel Barrymore; and she wrote a few paragraphs about her father. The unfinished essays are appreciations and bits of memory. She recalled a party in a house on Washington Square when she was eighteen: "The room was long and low-ceilinged, filled with flowers, books, silver-framed photographs of famous people. I sat wide-eyed watching the many distinguished guests and then The Four Goddesses: Maxine Elliott, Julie Opp Faversham, Constance Collier and Ethel Barrymore. It was the era of the Junoesque: Tall— often nearly six feet—large in every respect—but beautiful, undeniably—truly goddess-like." From 1916 to 1925 Le Gallienne had seen John Barrymore in all of his plays. She recalled Barrymore's ability to suggest character through the line of his body. "All great artists have this sense of line," she wrote. "They express through their bodies what an artist expresses in a line drawing." She sympathized with Barrymore's anger at noisy, rude people who disrupted his performances. "Once in a particularly tender scene . . . Barrymore suddenly opened the door of the set, rushed out and having felled a stagehand to the floor with an uppercut to the jaw, calmly returned and continued the scene as though nothing had occurred. He said to Miss Collier afterwards: 'The S.O.B. was rattling coins in his pocket. Drove me mad—the bastard!' Temperament? Bad Temper? Too much success? It's hard to say. Success is surely the hardest thing to take." She struggled with the few pages she wrote about her father, crossing out sentences and rewriting. She mentioned Richard's erotomania, his dipsomania, and his bibliomania, concluding that the bibliomania "was the one passion to which R. remained consistently & permanently faithful." Le Gallienne never finished the Blue Room essays. "Beasts, birds, & plants" all interfered, she said.

Instead of writing, she went "hog wild" with the garden. She justified her extravagance by the belief that she didn't know if she would be around to see the garden the following year. Anne visited often, and Eva wished that she "were always here." At times they talked of Anne moving to Weston to live, and Eva even made plans to turn a room into an office for her. "On the other hand, she didn't really want me to come live with her," Anne said. "She would say that 'it wouldn't be fair to Irving and your daughter, and your many friends.' " Anne agreed with Le Gallienne that it probably would be best if they didn't live together.

After almost eight years of living alone, Le Gallienne had grown used to it, and she liked her independence. With Eloise and Ted nearby, she was not lonely. Even though Ted now had a full-time job in Stamford, he spent most Saturdays working with her in the garden. Like Eloise Armen, Ted was a New England Yankee with a well-developed sense of duty. In gathering her small "family" around her, Le Gallienne was being quite pragmatic. She knew that she was aging and might one day be dependent. "Oh, how I hope it all works out," she said. "It will. It must." Once or twice every month, Eva arranged a garden bouquet and drove into New York to see Jo. She wished that she could snatch Aimée away from Staats, who was often drunk or ill. Jo looked "so old & bent and exhausted," Eva thought. "God! Why did she have to do it?"

To ensure her independence, though, Le Gallienne needed to work. Audrey Wood was a much more active agent than Jane Broder, and throughout the summer, Le Gallienne considered various jobs. She signed a contract to tour with Ingrid Bergman in *Waters of the Moon,* which had been a London hit, but at the last minute the tour was cancelled when Bergman became ill. Peter Donnelly wanted Le Gallienne to direct her translation of *The Wild Duck* at the Seattle Repertory. She also met several times with Tammy Grimes about a production of *The Aspern Papers* at the McCarter Theatre and the Kennedy Center. Le Gallienne called Grimes "that little genius," but she had "never known *anyone* so exhausting. Here at 11:30 & didn't leave till 6 p.m. I was a wreck. She never stopped smoking & talking & calling people up." Le Gallienne enjoyed and clung to her set daily routine filled with no sounds other than birds and the wind. Sometimes after an afternoon with Eva, Eloise would get in her car, and as soon as she left the driveway she would turn the radio up as a relief from the quiet.

Since she had numerous job possibilities, Le Gallienne did not teach at the White Barn in the summer of 1978, but later that year she agreed to speak to the drama students at Juilliard. Robert Neff Williams, the head of voice and speech at Juilliard, had seen Le Gallienne play a variety of roles, including Hedda Gabler, Mrs. Alving, Queen Elizabeth, the Countess of Rossillion in *All's Well,* and Fanny Cavendish. Williams told his students that when Le Gallienne spoke Shakespeare's lines, it "seemed as if they had just occurred to her, spring fresh and newly alive." Later, in analyzing her speech, Williams said while her voice had "undeniable richness of tone and flexibility," it was "above all responsive, and responsive to a mind aware and appreciative of whole worlds, past and present, of literature, art, and history." The "greatest of voices," Williams believed, "is only a conduit for richness of mind, and Miss Le Gallienne seemed able to find infinite riches in a little word."

When Le Gallienne, wearing a tam-o'-shanter and a long knitted scarf, arrived at Juilliard's theatre, Williams was surprised by the "rather tweedy and country" appearance of a woman he considered great and glamorous. In her unrehearsed remarks, Le Gallienne spoke to the students about Ibsen, Chekhov, and Shakespeare and about her repertory company. She did not tell them that she was also studying at Juilliard, working with a speech coach.

A few weeks earlier, Audrey Wood had sent her a movie script titled *Resurrection.* Ellen Burstyn, the star of the picture, had asked if Le Gallienne would con-

sider the part of her grandmother, Pearl. Burstyn studied actors and knew theatre history. She had seen *The Royal Family* several times and had read *The Mystic in the Theatre* and Le Gallienne's autobiographies and translations. After
meeting with the director, Daniel Petrie, and with Burstyn, Le Gallienne wanted
the job, but feared "that they may not want to risk my speech. Too refined . . . though I know I *can* do the other." "I just didn't have any doubts once
I met her that she was the one," Burstyn said later. "Looking into her face, I
saw . . . how beautifully a face can reflect a life."

For Le Gallienne's first major film role, Audrey Wood negotiated a salary of
twenty-five thousand dollars for four weeks' work and co-star billing. On January 13, 1979, Eva, with Tinker Bell, boarded a plane for Los Angeles to begin rehearsals. Wood had arranged that Le Gallienne be given the full VIP treatment.
Le Gallienne checked into an apartment at the Chateau Marmont that was filled
with flowers and well stocked with Perrier. A limousine took her to and from the
studios. When she wasn't working, she shopped, dined with old friends Leonora
Schildkraut, Stewart Stern, Terence Scammell, and Nelson Welch, talked by
telephone to Eloise and Anne daily, but mostly she read and remembered.

Le Gallienne wrote in a small velvet-bound book, using purple ink:

I just looked out of the window onto Sunset Boulevard and the ceaseless
flow of traffic. It is 10 at night. The tremendous stretch of this queer
town—so unreal. In my thoughts, as I look across the road, I see Alla's
house as it was in 1921. Then, it was the last house in Hollywood. Beyond
it wild country. Her lovely garden filled with orange, lemon & grapefruit
trees. The bougainvillea—the aviary with splendid birds. All enclosed—all
very private—and so *quiet.* Another life—another world. I'm so glad to
have known it. I pity the young people who only know the world as it is
now. It's well worth being 80 to have known that other one! When I think
of it—which is not often—or when people mention it—the fact of being
80 seems totally unreal. Not unpleasant—but simply *unreal.* What a wonderful life I've had! How grateful I am for it all.

Le Gallienne was grateful, too, to be earning a living working on a project that
she believed in. *Resurrection,* written by Lewis John Carlino, tells the story of
Edna Mae McCauley (Burstyn), who has a near-death experience and returns
to her Kansas hometown to recuperate. Through her maternal grandmother,
Pearl (Le Gallienne), Edna Mae discovers that she has the gift of healing—a gift,
Pearl tells her, that she must use. Edna Mae's powers increase, powers that are
female and spiritual rather than patriarchal and conventionally religious. Her
powers threaten her lover, Cal (played by Sam Shepard), who has been raised by
fundamentalists.

Images of healing hands and radiant light appear throughout the film. When Edna Mac returns to Kansas, she is met by Grandma Pearl, who is first glimpsed as a spot of white against the dark wood of the farmhouse. Wearing a white apron, with gray hair blowing in the wind, Grandma Pearl greets her granddaughter. Le Gallienne looks vital and strong; her voice is low and drawling, suggestive of Pearl's Georgia roots. In a later scene, Edna Mae and Pearl look at family photograph albums. The camera focuses on Pearl's hands, which are large and gnarled with age yet flexible and adept with needle and thread. Left scarred and crooked by the explosion and fire, Le Gallienne's hands embody the essence of Grandma Pearl, an old woman marked by time yet vibrant with life.

Since her contract allowed for a companion, Eva asked Anne Kaufman to accompany her to Texas for the filming. With Anne along to take care of her, cook for her, and smooth out difficulties, Le Gallienne was able to concentrate on her performance. After the first morning of filming, Ellen Burstyn realized that Le Gallienne had "no film technique and what she was doing was for stage, overexpressed." At the lunch break, Burstyn told Dan Petrie that he had to explain to Le Gallienne that "she just has to think the thoughts and the camera will read it." "You want me to go in to one of the great actresses of the theatre and tell her how to act?" Petrie said. "Yes, I do," replied Burstyn.

Petrie knocked on Le Gallienne's trailer door and asked to speak to her. "He was absolutely sweet," Anne Kaufman recalled. "He told her that on camera less is more and everything must be kept to a minimum. He even used the word 'hammy' about her performance." Instead of being upset, Le Gallienne was pleased by Petrie's honesty. "She felt safe with him," Kaufman said.

The film company was like a large extended family. Le Gallienne's good humor off-screen is revealed in her on-screen performance. The presence of Anne Kaufman on the set sweetened Le Gallienne's movie experience, but even with the long, boring waits, she was discovering that she liked film acting. "Very hard work—such concentration it takes!" she told her diary. The communication of thought, she learned, could be achieved with subtlety and nuance in film, and with a kind of delicacy that would be visible in the theatre only to those sitting in the first row.

In her last scene in the movie, when Pearl says goodbye to Edna Mae, "she did this thing," Burstyn recalled, "when she spoke the lines 'Yes, that's it, ain't it? If we could just love each other as much as we say we love him,' and every time she said the word 'love' her voice dropped into her heart. And she did it time after time, take after take. . . . I never played a scene where I had to do less. I just had to look at her and listen to her."

Later, in analyzing Le Gallienne's performance, Burstyn said that she was effective because "it's her soul. It's her soul shining through her face."

Grandma Pearl in Resurrection, *1980*

Judith Crist wrote that *Resurrection* "makes an exploration of 'goodness' engrossing and exhilarating." Audiences and other reviewers agreed, and the movie became a minor classic. Le Gallienne's performance earned her an Academy Award nomination for best supporting actress. While she was working on the picture, Le Gallienne never looked at the dailies, relying on Anne to check them. When she saw the movie at a screening in early 1980, she was irritated that some of her lines and a few small bits had been cut, but it was a shock to see herself on film. "Hated myself," she said. "I just have no face left!"

WHEN LE GALLIENNE'S work on the film ended, Anne did not return to Weston with her. CBS was filming her father's play *You Can't Take It with You*, and Anne stayed in Los Angeles with her husband, Irving. The presence of Anne's husband, and the fact that Anne had a life other than the one with her, disturbed Le Gallienne, but she was determined not to "get too dependent."

A week after Le Gallienne returned to Weston, Jo, hysterical and distraught, called to tell her that Staats had died. Caring for him had left her weak and exhausted. Jo's doctor wanted her to check into a hospital, but Eva convinced her to come to Weston to recover.

At first, Le Gallienne welcomed the opportunity to take care of Jo, who was "so weak. Can hardly walk." Eva had successfully raised three abandoned baby robins, and knowing of her expertise with animals and birds, the neighborhood children often brought her wounded creatures to nurse back to health. She thought of herself as a patient, sensitive healer. After a few days, though, she found Jo's demands tiring. She longed to work in the garden, but she didn't feel right leaving Jo for any length of time. After four days with Eva, Jo felt as if she were in prison. "She wouldn't let me get out of bed," Jo said. "I needed comfort and from her I got dominance." Jo's "worrying and anxiety" exhausted Eva. Six days after Jo arrived, Le Gallienne drove her back to New York.

"When I got home, my doctor put me in the hospital for a week's rest," Jo said.

Any illusions that Le Gallienne had about spending her last years with Jo were shattered. When Jo left, it was "a relief," Eva said.

"I had no intention of going back there to stay," Jo said. "I was not going to be trapped into what Marion Evensen had done."

They could not live together, but Jo and Eva remained close. When Jo recovered her strength, Eva saw her often in New York, and Jo visited in Weston to celebrate her birthday. Any visit longer than a day or two, however, was not pleasant for either woman. At Thanksgiving, 1979, Jo stayed in Weston for a few days. Again, Le Gallienne was irritated by Jo's nervousness and lack of strength; she also "talks incessantly about things & people I know nothing about." Hutchinson didn't like the isolation of the country. She chafed against Le Gallienne's controlling nature, and decided to leave earlier than she had planned. "Can't say I was sorry," Eva wrote.

IN 1979 AND EARLY 1980, Le Gallienne turned down many job offers—a production of *Watch on the Rhine* at the Alley Theatre in Houston, *Blithe Spirit* in Chicago, a revival of *The Chalk Garden,* and several television offers. With the money she made from *Resurrection,* her pension, and royalties, she could afford to be discriminating. Also, an unexpected fifty-five-thousand-dollar legacy gave her a comfortable financial cushion. The legacy was from Frank Soyer of Glendale, California. In his will, Soyer gave "all of my estate and property . . . to the woman I love, Miss Eva Le Gallienne." Touched by such a gift from a perfect stranger, Le Gallienne speculated that she "must have given a good performance to have rated this return!"

Since she was not worried about money and none of the job offers attracted her, Le Gallienne was content to stay home, work in the garden, and enjoy her time with Eloise, Anne, and Ted. She struggled to continue with writing, especially since her new literary agent, Mitch Douglas, had sold her Ewald translations. Douglas had also sent several of the Blue Room essays to Little, Brown, and Company, and the publisher had expressed interest in collecting them into a book. Le Gallienne also made notes for a book she wanted to write about acting, called *The Perennial Theatre,* which would be an anthology of what great actors said about acting.

Writing required discipline, though, and she seemed to lack the will to finish the work. "I must try and stop this sense of 'what's the use?' " she told herself. "After all, other old people in their eighties have managed to accomplish things, and there's no reason why I shouldn't."

The sight of failing old friends depressed her. When Eva and Anne visited Alice De Lamar, Anne thought Alice had changed and didn't look well. "I'm sure she is though," Le Gallienne told her diary, not wanting to face the possibility that she might lose her steadfast friend. Eva's neighbor the writer Helen Boylston was in a nursing home, repeating the same words over and over whenever Le Gallienne visited her. Gladys Calthrop sent a letter written in such shaky, spidery handwriting that Le Gallienne could barely read it, and a few months later she was dead. Ruth Wilton, who had acted and taught dance at the Civic Repertory, was in a nursing home in Danbury, Connecticut. Ruth was "full of tubes & wires & gimmicks—all the things she didn't want," Le Gallienne wrote. "I think she was dimly aware of me—but she's not really there. It's so upsetting to me to go there—yet I feel I must. I'm ashamed to be upset."

Talking about death, however, did not bother her. A psychoanalyst, Dr. Lisl Goodman, drove to Weston to interview Le Gallienne for a book she was writing called *Death and the Creative Life: Conversations with Prominent Artists and Scientists.* Goodman interviewed more than seven hundred people for her book, and while male artists and scientists like Isaac Stern, Alan Arkin, and Nobel Prize–winning physicist Eugene Wigner were eager to talk with her, hundreds of women turned her down, including Katharine Hepburn and Beverly Sills; Le Gallienne was the only woman who agreed to be interviewed. Goodman couldn't explain why the other women refused, but she theorized that women were perhaps more superstitious than men. Le Gallienne was not superstitious, and as an actor, she had played many deaths. She wrote once that "there is nothing an actor enjoys more than a good death scene." Le Gallienne had been burned at the stake, guillotined, starved, and drowned. She had been shot three times, killed by a dagger thrust, and hanged. She had died of a stroke and a heart attack; twice she was stricken by consumption and once she died of a broken heart.

Dr. Goodman, who had seen Le Gallienne die onstage as Fanny Cavendish, was struck by the actor's agility and youthful vigor. Goodman observed that "she is most strikingly in tune with her surroundings, in perfect harmony with them." Le Gallienne took Goodman into the Blue Room, where a fire burned in the fireplace and Skat lay stretched out on the windowsill. She talked frankly with Dr. Goodman about her love life and remarked that "her love affairs had to take second place to her art." Later in the interview, Le Gallienne said, "My profession has been the passion of my life. I would sacrifice everything for it."

"Are you afraid of death?" asked Goodman.

"I don't think so," replied Le Gallienne. "It's part of life, part of the rhythm of the universe. And I am not a believer, so I don't fear anything that may come afterwards. I don't think that there is anything. Going to sleep is certainly not frightening. The very best thing is just going to sleep—eternal sleep. Remember, 'tis a consummation/Devoutly to be wish'd.' "

IN JUNE 1980, Le Gallienne accepted the role of Grandie in Joanna Glass's new play, *To Grandmother's House We Go,* and added another stage death to her long list. Burry Fredrik and her partner, Doris Cole Abrahams, produced the play, which would open at Houston's Alley Theatre in October 1980, prior to the Broadway opening. The play was "beautifully written," with a "good deal of comedy," Le Gallienne thought, and since the eight-character play was an ensemble piece, she would not have to carry the full burden. She was not optimistic, however, about its chances on Broadway, since it had "no great violence or wild sex."

Grandie, another grandmother part for Le Gallienne, was a vivid contrast to Grandma Pearl in *Resurrection.* A Connecticut Yankee, Grandie, an elegant, old-fashioned woman with an acerbic sense of humor, lives in a large Victorian house with her brother, Jared; her artist daughter, Harriet; and Clementine, a companion/housekeeper. The comedy and the dramatic tension unfold when Grandie's three grandchildren return home at Thanksgiving and all ask to move back into the family home. Even though it will be a financial burden, Grandie assents. When Grandie dies, however, Harriet kicks everyone out and devotes herself to painting.

Eloise traveled to Houston with Le Gallienne to help her through the four-week rehearsal period and five-week run of the play. Audrey Wood had called Eloise "wardrobe" and wrung $400 a week out of the producers for her. Eva had wanted Anne to go with her, but she had other commitments. Anne had begun to travel more on business and with her husband. Her first long separation from Eva had been in August 1979, when she traveled to London for the Royal Shakespeare production of *Once in a Lifetime.* "Evale was very upset," Anne recalled.

"She wanted me to devote myself to her. She wanted the whole thing. She was a seducing personality. But Irving and I had a life together, our home, our daughter, our friends. To give up all we had together was unthinkable. If Irving had ever forced the issue, I might have made a choice to go with her, and it would have been wrong." Le Gallienne didn't force the issue, either. Anne continued to divide her time between her husband and Eva. When Anne was in New York, she visited Eva about every two weeks for a few days; and in the summer, when Nona, the housekeeper, took a vacation, Anne would spend a week or two with Le Gallienne. Whenever she traveled, Anne called and wrote often, and Eva carefully saved all Anne's notes and letters.

In late September, when Le Gallienne arrived for rehearsals of *To Grandmother's House We Go* in Houston, *Resurrection* was opening there, and her collection of Ewald stories appeared in the bookstores. At eighty-one, she had a new play, a new movie, and a new book appearing simultaneously.

The director, Clifford Williams, assembled an experienced cast to play Grandie's family, including Kim Hunter, Ruth Nelson, Shepperd Strudwick, and Anne Twomey. Le Gallienne thought the company a good one, and she liked Williams, who treated Glass's play as "New England Chekhov."

After just a few days in Houston and in the "cement fortress" of the Alley Theatre, Le Gallienne wrote, "Had I known what it was going to be like I'd have refused to come here!" She hated the hot, humid weather. She loathed the view from her hotel balcony of giant modern office buildings and flat country stretching for miles. She despised the vulgarity and "immense pretentiousness" of Houston's famous Galleria shopping mall, where two books cost her over thirty dollars. "People will become illiterate in self-defense," she wrote.

The acoustics at the Alley Theatre bothered her, and she didn't like acting in the round. The light spilling onto the audience irritated her. The producers, whom she nicknamed "Burry and Flurry," annoyed her since they tinkered endlessly with the script. From time to time during the Alley Theatre run, Le Gallienne would forget her lines, and Eloise arranged for an apprentice to crouch in the fireplace and cue her when necessary. Since she never forgot her lines during the Broadway run of the play, her memory loss in Houston was more a sign of frustration and anger than of aging. In her diary, she raged at "nasty coarse-grained audiences" who only got the sex jokes, and she fumed at the constant script revisions.

The Houston reviews were good, though, and the Alley audiences loved the play. A few of the critics pointed out that the play sagged when Grandie was off-stage, and when Grandie dies in the middle of Act Two, the audience gasped in disappointment. Le Gallienne's performance earned raves. "She is what Helen Hayes and Ruth Gordon think they are," wrote one critic. "Her talent and technique are purified, authoritative. She is humorous without once nudging."

WHEN LE GALLIENNE returned to Weston, even though she had complained of exhaustion in Texas, she flung herself into preparations for Thanksgiving and Christmas, and she and Ted prepared the garden for winter. On December 10, she made her second appearance on *The Dick Cavett Show.* Le Gallienne was relaxed on the show; she liked Cavett and was comfortable with him. But she was not comfortable touting herself. The interview had been arranged to promote *To Grandmother's House,* and Cavett encouraged her to talk about herself and her work. Le Gallienne wouldn't cooperate. "I'm tired of talking about myself," she told him. "I'm too old. I can't be bothered." Instead, she spoke at length about Bernhardt and Duse. She praised Ellen Burstyn's work in *Resurrection* and deprecated her own. After Cavett showed a clip of the "goodbye" scene from the movie, Le Gallienne said, "I didn't think it was very good, was it?" However, she did confess to Cavett that she wished she had made more films.

When Cavett asked if she was afraid of new things, Le Gallienne, with quiet pride, said, "I've always been very much ahead of my time."

After he saw the Broadway opening of *To Grandmother's House We Go,* Walter Kerr agreed. "So what else is new?" he asked in an article in *The New York Times.* "Eva Le Gallienne is new." Kerr reported that octogenarian Le Gallienne kept on getting better, giving routine lines like "I hope you will find happiness, and keep it" a comic complexity and awareness. "She breaks the line in two unexpectedly," wrote Kerr. "Before speaking the last three words, she stops to think. Her eyes dart sideways reflectively . . . her mouth remains open as though searching for a sound that will mean something. Then, suddenly, it twists, half in humor, half in warning. Raising her head, and with two moods still playing about her lips, she now adds 'and keep it.' "

In *To Grandmother's House* Le Gallienne did what she enjoyed most—"bending an audience" to her will. At times, she took pauses of eight to twenty seconds, filling them with knowing humor, a tiny wave of the hand, a curving smile, and was rewarded with roars of laughter. Le Gallienne's hands looked delicate and graceful: the long sleeves and flowing lines of her costumes helped the effect, but just as she changed her body line to reveal the character, she created hand choreography to suit Grandie. Some of Le Gallienne's best scenes were with Ruth Nelson, who played Clementine, the companion/housekeeper. Sounding like a stern nanny with her deep, sonorous voice, Clementine would chastise Grandie, and Le Gallienne, with long, white hair flowing down her back, looked like a petulant, ancient child.

Frank Rich called Le Gallienne's performance of Grandie "as lyrical as any Juliet," but she deserved, he wrote, "a play that's as young and invigorating as her spirit."

To Grandmother's House We Go closed on March 8, 1981, after just sixty-one performances. The critics "were naughty about the play and perhaps too kind about me," Le Gallienne felt. To her Oscar nomination for best supporting actress, Le Gallienne added a Tony nomination for best actress. Le Gallienne did not go to California for the Oscar ceremony, but she did attend the Tony Awards with Anne Kaufman. Wearing black silk Pucci pants with a silk shirt, and an embroidered velvet vest, Le Gallienne enjoyed the applause and cheers when Alexander Cohen introduced her, but as the evening wore on, she grew restless. "Good God," she asked Anne, "how long do we have to sit here?" Elizabeth Taylor, who was seated in front of them, turned around and said, "You have to wait until the end because I'm on last." Glenda Jackson, Elizabeth Taylor, and Jane Lapotaire had been nominated for the Tony along with Le Gallienne, and Lapotaire won for her role in *Piaf.* "The minute the show was over," Anne recalled, "she flew up the aisle. I think we were home in Weston before people got to the party."

After months of constant work, Le Gallienne was tired. Her teeth needed attention again, and she had to undergo weeks of painful bridge work. In April 1981, she told Audrey Wood that she didn't want to act for a while; working in the garden and writing her Blue Room essays would be occupation enough. Burry Fredrik, however, urged her to play *To Grandmother's House* in summer stock and for limited runs in Baltimore and Florida. Earlier, her Danish friend Inge Nissen, who had worked as her dresser briefly in the 1960s, needed money to start a small shop specializing in handmade knits and crafts, and Le Gallienne gave her twenty thousand dollars, which depleted her savings. Even though Eva lived frugally, the houses she maintained required constant upkeep. Ted had moved into the old house, and "he had made [it] lovely again—the way it used to be." To save money, she and Ted did a lot of the work themselves, even roofing the shed, but the furnace had to be replaced, a new hot-water heater was needed for the old house, and her bill for bird seed and garden supplies at Agway was high. After Le Gallienne saw her dentist's bill and her real estate taxes, she decided that she should get back to work. She knew that if she wanted to stay in her own home, she had to work and save enough to remain independent.

To Grandmother's House opened at the Cape Playhouse in Dennis, Massachusetts, during a thunderstorm, and the company played the first night by candlelight. Following the Cape Cod engagement, the company played two weeks at the Westport Playhouse, three weeks in Baltimore, and another three weeks in Florida. With rehearsals and travel, Le Gallienne worked from late August until January 1982.

Anne joined Eva in Baltimore and traveled with her to Fort Lauderdale, where the company played sixteen performances without a break. Anne "was wonderful and so *cheerful,*" Le Gallienne wrote. They went sightseeing and shopping, and Eva took Anne to visit Alice De Lamar in Palm Beach. Le Gallienne gave a few interviews, but most of the time she rested. Theatre business was good, the notices were excellent; but the effort of playing eight demanding performances a week was exhausting, and she longed for home.

On January 11, 1982, Le Gallienne told her diary, "Can't believe I'm 83 . . . not that the old body 'sans eyes, sans teeth' doesn't know it, but the 'spirit' can't grasp it." On the same day, she wrote the following entry in the small velvet-bound book that she used for personal reflections and observations about acting: "It is 30 years since I wrote my second autobiography. . . . This book is to be called *At 83*—a good honest title & one which in itself gives one plenty to write about—the mystery—the incomprehensible subject: old age."

She marked the entry with a ribbon. All the pages that follow are blank, except for a sentence by nineteenth-century actor/manager Charlotte Cushman, which Le Gallienne wrote in purple ink on the last page of the book: "Art is an exacting mistress, but she repays with royal munificence."

ALTHOUGH LE GALLIENNE planned to start work on her third autobiography, instead she returned to Weston and began preparing a new production of *Alice in Wonderland*. The year before, actress Sabra Jones, who was married to Lee Strasberg's son John, had met with Le Gallienne about Jones's desire to start a new Civic Repertory Theatre with herself as the lead actor and Le Gallienne as star and inspiration. Like Le Gallienne, Jones envisioned herself in the actor/manager line; and with great enthusiasm and a great deal of flattery, she sold Le Gallienne on her idea of founding a new Civic Repertory, beginning with productions of *Camille* and *Alice in Wonderland*. When Le Gallienne expressed doubt that Jones could play Marguerite Gautier, the decision was made to begin with *Alice in Wonderland*.

Since Le Gallienne's two previous experiences with *Alice,* for the Civic Repertory and the American Repertory, had been overwhelmingly positive, and both productions had been successful, the idea seemed a good one. *Alice* would be a fitting close to her long career, illustrating her gifts as adaptor, director, and actor. Also, nothing she had been offered since *To Grandmother's House* appealed to her.

When Audrey Wood suffered a debilitating stroke, Mitch Douglas of International Creative Management, Le Gallienne's literary agent, took over as her theatre agent as well. Le Gallienne liked Douglas. He had seen her performances and he had read her books, and he was knowledgeable about theatre history. Finding work for his client was not difficult, according to Douglas. "She always worked in theatre," he said. "Theatre was never a problem." Following Le Gallienne's Academy Award nomination, Douglas received many Hollywood offers for Le Gallienne, but "she absolutely refused to take a role that had any bad language or violence or drinking," Douglas said. "Also, she needed the give and take of an audience. I think it was a matter of choices."

Moreover, many of the offers Le Gallienne received were for "dreary old women." Why can't they "write a jolly old woman," she wondered, "or a fierce old one—or one with some guts left in her!" To play the clownish White Queen in *Alice* and to fly once again seemed the answer to those dreary-old-woman parts.

Le Gallienne's third production of *Alice in Wonderland,* a two-million-dollar production backed by Rockefeller and Astor fortunes, received an enormous amount of publicity; a gifted design team—John Lee Beatty for sets, Patricia Zipprodt for costumes, Jennifer Tipton for lights—created the production's look. Yet the show failed, closing after twenty-one performances. Fifty years earlier, in repertory with the Civic, *Alice,* which had cost twenty-three thousand dollars to mount, had played 127 performances; and the ART *Alice* ran in repertory for 100 performances.

What went wrong? There's never just one reason for a production's failure, but since the production was conceived, written, and directed by and starred Eva Le Gallienne, she bore most of the responsibility. At eighty-three, she had taken on an impossible task, but like her character, the White Queen, Le Gallienne could believe "as many as six impossible things before breakfast." Looking back on the experience, Eloise Armen regretted that she did not discourage Le Gallienne from attempting such an arduous job. Because Eva appeared so vigorous, those close to her often overlooked the fact that she was quite old and lacked the vitality of her youth.

If she had been surrounded by producers and a co-director who were experienced enough and strong enough to counter the doubts, tensions, and uncertainties endemic to the world of the commercial theatre, and to stand up to the intimidating Le Gallienne, then the production might have had a chance. Producer Sabra Jones, then twenty-seven, said later that "if she could have found a way to trust me, it might have worked." Jones idolized Le Gallienne, but when Le Gallienne would not allow Sabra to understudy her and play some performances of the White Queen, tensions between the two women increased. The "production looked beautiful," Jones recalled, "but it moved like lead." Devastated by the possibility of losing a two-million-dollar investment, Jones blamed Le Gallienne. John Strasberg, the co-director, was intimidated by Le Gallienne and worked around her—behavior that she thought devious. Privately, Le Gallienne began referring to Jones and Strasberg as "the Macbeths."

Mitch Douglas blamed the failure of *Alice* on the venue. The stakes were too high in the commercial theatre, he believed, and the production should have been presented, as the previous *Alice*s had been, in "a protected, noncommercial atmosphere."

In her own assessment of the experience, Le Gallienne accepted part of the blame, telling her diary, "I don't think I can direct anymore." She also criticized the design team—especially the heavy costumes and full masks, which made the actors "look like a Macy pageant!" The designers, on the other hand, ordered by Le Gallienne to reproduce the Tenniel drawings, did exactly what they believed she wanted. Faithfully, beautifully, and on a full Broadway scale, using an advanced theatre technology that Le Gallienne was unaware of, they created a style John Lee Beatty called "Victorian Kabuki"—something like a reproduction of a Victorian pop-up book. It was gorgeous. It was also lifeless.

"I don't think she made it clear to the actors they were going to be wearing these huge costumes and masks," recalled Beatty. "She actually got a scissors and headed backstage to do something about the costumes. Patricia Zipprodt whisked the costumes out of the way before she could get to them."

After weeks of moving freely at rehearsals, the actors were appalled when they learned they would be hidden under layers of fur and feathers with their voices muffled by large masks. In her first Equity role, Eloise Armen's daughter, Rebecca, played the Eaglet, the Two of Hearts, and was the voice of the Duchess's baby. Rebecca, the only daughter and the youngest in a family with three boys, had always been Le Gallienne's favorite of the Armen children. Eva liked to say that in Rebecca were combined the best qualities of her parents—the Yankee discipline of her mother and the Armenian expression of her father. Rebecca often drove Le Gallienne into New York and attended design meetings with her. According to Rebecca, Le Gallienne "really wanted suggestions of costumes" similar to her earlier productions, but Rebecca heard her tell the designers many times to make the show look "exactly like the Tenniel drawings."

Kate Burton, who played Alice and was unencumbered by a mask, had another fear. From the first day of rehearsal, the lack of drama and tension in the script bothered her. "It seemed that Le Gallienne knew what she wanted," Burton said, "but unless you showed it to her, she was not able to tell you how to get it." When the more experienced Jo Hutchinson had played the first Alice, she created her own pattern of thought and dramatic throughline. Burton needed help with the long, difficult monologues, but Le Gallienne did not know how to give it to her. "That was troubling," Burton said, "and at times, I was tentative."

"You are a born actress," Le Gallienne told her. "Trust your own instincts."

"Technical rehearsals were brutal," recalled Rebecca Armen. "All the actors were unhappy. . . . We had to play the croquet game and our heads kept falling off, they were so heavy." Through the long days of rehearsals, Rebecca felt that Le Gallienne was "overwhelmed. . . . She was very game always, but there was the feeling that she had created this monster and didn't know what to do with it."

In a letter to Mogens before the play opened, Le Gallienne feared that bad notices would close them in a week. The American public doesn't read anymore,

Le Gallienne's last flight over Broadway.
With Kate Burton in Alice in Wonderland, *1982*

she told him, and Lewis Carroll "would mean nothing to them." After working ten- and twelve-hour days, she wrote, she was extremely tired and would be happy to return to the country. New York was a "madhouse," she said; "one has to be young I think to put up with it."

Even though the opening-night audience, filled with backers and friends, cheered the play and gave Le Gallienne a standing ovation, the critics disagreed. "Well, it seems we have a huge flop!" Le Gallienne wrote the day after the opening. The daily critics blasted the production, and even though there were a few other critics, such as Edith Oliver of *The New Yorker,* who liked it, the show was doomed. It was no consolation to Le Gallienne that her acting reviews were all excellent. Jack Kroll in *Newsweek* said, "Flying in from the wings on wires, this startling octogenarian explodes with topsy-turvy truculence and wacky logic, wrestling with her recalcitrant shawl as if it were a gossamer boa constrictor, hooting madly in pain *before* she cuts her fingers. This is the standard that the rest of *Alice* doesn't quite live up to."

To help the producers hold out for a few more days, Le Gallienne waived her royalties as author and director, and the producers lowered the ticket prices, but the production closed in early January. The closing was made even more difficult for Le Gallienne because of the death of her Yorkshire, Tinker Bell, at 1:30 a.m. earlier that day. She told no one at the theatre. "Had to play," she wrote, "and didn't want a lot of sympathy which would have broken me up."

Le Gallienne took the failure hard, mostly because she believed that she had let the actors down. She clung to her old friends in the company, like Geddeth Smith and Mary Louise Wilson. The young actors, though, like Rebecca Armen, had found the Broadway experience thrilling. Following the last performance, sixteen-year-old Mary Stuart Masterson, who played a small white rabbit, was in tears. Kate Burton knew that Burgess Meredith and Julie Harris had played white rabbits in the earlier *Alice* productions, and she told Masterson, "Mark my words, you're going to be a star."

Le Gallienne retreated to Weston. "I don't want to work in the theatre anymore," she wrote. "It's not my theatre." But without the theatre, she didn't have "much to live for." For several weeks, she suffered from a bad chest cold, shortness of breath, and extreme exhaustion, exacerbated by liquor and severe depression. At one point, she thought she was "about to pop off and couldn't have cared less."

The *Alice* experience "broke her spirit somehow," Rebecca Armen said later. "For the first time she seemed old to me."

WITH OLD AGE came pain. For most of her life, Le Gallienne had endured pain in her damaged hands, but as she aged the pain in her fingers and wrists grew worse. Before starting work on *Alice,* she had noticed a small lump above her groin, which her doctor had diagnosed as a muscle strain. Instead of healing, the lump had grown even more tender and sore. To ease her pain, Le Gallienne took Percodan, a popular painkiller. Le Gallienne's doctor did not like to prescribe it, because he felt that it was addictive; but her dentist gave her prescriptions, and from time to time Dr. Jose Pacheco, a cousin by marriage, would give her a prescription for the drug.

A few years earlier, Dr. Pacheco and his wife, Susan, had contacted Eva when they moved to Stratford, Connecticut. Susan Pacheco's mother was Elizabeth Gallienne, the daughter of Richard Le Gallienne's brother, John. Susan had heard about her famous cousin from her Gallienne relatives in England, and she had called Eva and introduced herself. When they had a son, the Pachecos named him Richard after Eva's father. Although Eva was pleasant to Susan, she preferred the company of Joe Pacheco. "She was very friendly and open," Dr. Pacheco recalled. "She came to our house twice, but she didn't like to go out much. She knew about the Gallienne family, but she didn't care for that side of her family."

Although Dr. Pacheco was an obstetrician, Le Gallienne often sought his medical advice, and in early January, she called him. He told her that with rest and food and time, she would recover. He also gave her a prescription for Percodan, and, according to Anne Kaufman, Le Gallienne regularly took half a tablet in the late afternoon. Percodan had few side effects, but among them was disorientation—a particular problem for old people—and, of course, the disorienting effects were enhanced if the drug was mixed with alcohol. Dr. Pacheco had no idea that Le Gallienne had a drinking problem.

In the weeks following *Alice,* Eloise Armen grew concerned about Le Gallienne's drinking and depression. More and more, at the end of the day, she would find Eva drunk and sad. Once, as they sat talking about the theatre, Le Gallienne said, "It's all over. I know that."

By the end of January, though, Le Gallienne was feeling better. Even though she was ill, she maintained the discipline of writing daily in her diary. She dug out her old diaries and notebooks with the idea of beginning her third autobiography, *At 83.* After reading through them, she was "astounded at all the work I did even during the bad years." An eighteen-thousand-dollar royalty check for the television version of *Alice* and the news that Harper & Row finally planned to publish her translation of Andersen's *The Snow Queen* gave her confidence. Feeding the birds and the animals, daily visits from Eloise, and long weekends with Ted and Anne working around the house cheered her up. At the end of February, she acquired another Yorkshire, a three-year-old that she named Dimpy. Eloise did not tell Le Gallienne that the dog was a gift from Sabra Jones. Grateful to be adopted, the dog, like Nana, was devoted to her. The white cat,

Skat, had died the year before, but the calico cat, Tabitha, accepted the new dog, and the two animals slept companionably on Le Gallienne's bed.

By April, spring had worked its magic, and in a letter to Mogens, Le Gallienne's spirits were high, and her handwriting was firm and strong. "I've been hard at work on the garden all day and my hand is stiff," she wrote. "But I do love the work so—and it is good for me body and soul." On April 21, however, after a long day in the garden, she was in excruciating pain, but she refused to call the doctor until the next day. Eloise took her to the hospital, where her doctor discovered that the lump above her groin was actually a hernia that had blocked the intestine.

Her recovery from the operation took several weeks, but she was soon gardening again. Anne Kaufman had been traveling a great deal, but she managed to spend five days with Le Gallienne. "Times have changed!" Eva had complained to her diary the year before, upset that Anne seemed to be traveling all the time and was not paying enough attention to her. "She was extremely loving to me, gentle and nice," Anne recalled, "but she was not interested in anyone but herself. When I called her from California to tell her I had a new grandson, she couldn't have cared less. All she was interested in was when I was coming home." Still, Anne, then fifty-seven, kept Julie Le Gallienne's wedding band, which Eva had given her, and although the intensity of their relationship lessened, the women remained intimate.

In July, Le Gallienne felt well enough to consider theatre jobs. Edwin Sherin, the artistic director at the nearby Hartman Theatre, wanted her to do a play, which she considered; but she liked A. R. Gurney's new play, *The Golden Age,* which would premiere at the Kennedy Center. When the director of *The Golden Age* offered her a role, she told him that she had a tentative commitment with the Hartman Theatre, but that she was definitely interested. Through a miscommunication between the director and the Kennedy Center, the part was given instead to Irene Worth.

Le Gallienne passed the next few months in a blur of grief and pain. Losing a theatre job was disappointing, but she was devastated when Alice De Lamar, her friend and patron of almost sixty years, died on August 31. Alice had always been a constant—a vital, vibrant presence that Eva had often taken for granted. The terrible memory of seeing Alice emaciated and surrounded by hospital paraphernalia haunted her. On one of her last visits to Alice in the hospital, Eva wrote that "Alice looked right in my eyes. I think she knew me."

In her will, Alice De Lamar kept the promise she had made to Eva years earlier to "see about things for her." She left Le Gallienne a legacy of $1,055,000. Le Gallienne had told Mogens a few months earlier that if she didn't have to work to make a living, she would give up the theatre. Now, with Alice's money, she was financially independent.

Just a week after Alice's death, Le Gallienne learned that she had to have another operation: a new hernia had appeared below the old one. Anne and Eloise helped her through the long, painful recovery, and Ted's presence nearby at the old house reassured her. On October 16, she and Ted had tea at his house to celebrate his twenty-ninth birthday. "How I love him!" she told her diary. "I don't know what I'd have done without him."

In early November, since the previous operation had not completely repaired the hernia, Le Gallienne returned to the much-hated hospital and endured her third operation in nine months. By December 12, she felt well enough to do simple chores and write in her diary, but she tired easily. On December 18, Ted drove her to June Havoc's annual event, a "Blessing of the Animals." Animal lovers from around the area brought their dogs, cats, goats, and horses to Havoc's farm to be blessed. This year Havoc had asked Helen Hayes, Lillian Gish, and Le Gallienne to preside over the event and read the blessing. When Le Gallienne arrived, June Havoc took her arm. "Helen's over here," Havoc teased.

"Who?" Le Gallienne said, stopping suddenly.

"Courage!" replied June, pulling her forward. Then, Havoc recalled, "Le Gallienne went into gales of laughter."

Since she and Dimpy were admired and fussed over, Le Gallienne enjoyed herself at Havoc's blessing service. Later, she joked to her diary that she and Helen Hayes "were like old buddies!"

At Christmas, Le Gallienne didn't feel up to having her own Danish tree, but she celebrated with her extended family of the Armens, Anne, and Ted, and managed a pre-Christmas visit with Jo Hutchinson.

EVEN IN HER WORK, Le Gallienne wasn't able to escape the hospital. In late December, Tom Fontana, a producer of *St. Elsewhere,* the popular television show set in a Boston hospital, called and asked if she would appear on the series. Fontana, who knew of Le Gallienne's work from *The Royal Family,* which he had seen seven times, explained that the producers wanted to try something they had never done before: they were hiring the actors *before* the script was written. Writer John Ford Noonan would then write the teleplay based on the actors. Blythe Danner and Brenda Vaccaro had agreed to appear before seeing a script, and Fontana asked Le Gallienne to do the same.

Le Gallienne said that she would do the show, but she had two requests. "I don't want to play a sad old lady who dies," she said, "and I want my dog to be in it."

Fontana accepted her conditions.

Eloise had encouraged Le Gallienne to accept the job, even though she noticed that Eva had become increasingly forgetful and often repeated herself.

*Helen Hayes (left)
and Lillian Gish (right)
at June Havoc's
"Blessing of the Animals,"
1983. Le Gallienne
(hidden from view)
holds her Yorkshire
Dimpy (center), who
peeks out between them.*

Sometimes when people called or visited, Eloise observed that Le Gallienne would pretend that she knew to whom she was talking. Once, when Hesper's stepson, Bertrand Hutchinson, and his wife visited, Le Gallienne was charming to them, but the moment they left, she shut the door and said, "Who the hell was that?"

Le Gallienne, uncommon in many ways, was experiencing one of the most common, garden-variety symptoms of old age: her short-term memory had begun to fail. It's possible, too, that the inevitable aging process was exacerbated by her use of alcohol and Percodan. Le Gallienne was alert enough, however, to realize what was happening to her; she had seen too many old friends go through the same experience. Not only did she fear going "ga-ga," as Hesper had, but even more she feared having to leave her home. Eloise promised her that she would never commit her to a nursing home, and now, with Alice De Lamar's legacy, Eva was financially secure.

Emotionally, though, Le Gallienne was extremely insecure about the *St. Elsewhere* job. "She was terrified," recalled Eloise, who accompanied her to California in early February 1984. Anne Kaufman happened to be traveling to California to visit her daughter at the same time, and Eloise suggested that Anne look after Le Gallienne. "No, I want you to go, Mom," Eva insisted, sounding like a scared, vulnerable child.

According to Eloise, Le Gallienne had not touched liquor for several weeks. On the flight to Los Angeles, when the stewardess in first class offered them champagne, Eloise said that she didn't want any. "Oh, good," said Le Gallienne, "then I'll have yours, too." When they arrived at their hotel, Le Gallienne asked Eloise to buy vodka, and when she refused, Eva called room service and ordered drinks. On the day after their arrival, however, Le Gallienne did not drink. She sat outside in the sun with Dimpy, her dog, and worked on her lines. Despite her efforts, "she couldn't remember a thing," said Eloise.

"She drank every night of the week we were there," recalled Eloise. "I fought her at first and poured vodka down the drain, but then as soon as I went to my room, she would call room service and order more."

"You want to be careful of me," Le Gallienne once told Eloise. "There are two sides to me." She held her hand up to divide her face. "This side is the demon." During their stay in California, Eloise saw only the demon side of Le Gallienne, but the producers and actors in *St. Elsewhere* saw only the artist. "She could not have been more gracious," recalled Tom Fontana. "We were all amazed by her, sort of sitting at her feet asking her questions." Anne Kaufman, who had seen Eva drunk at night in her hotel room, spent a day with her on the set, and she was sober and worked well. According to Fontana, there was no problem with Le Gallienne's lack of memory. Cue cards were common in television, and she adapted easily to them.

In his script, titled "The Women," which later won an Emmy, John Ford Noonan used facts of Le Gallienne's life. Eighty-five-year-old Evelyn Melbourne, Le Gallienne's character, lives alone and likes it. She feeds wild animals at her backdoor, she hates hospitals, and she fears being placed in a nursing home. Recovering from a heart attack, Evelyn is placed in a hospital room with three other women. One of the women dies; another woman, played by Blythe Danner, has an operation to add a bump to her "white bread" nose to give her more character; and the third, portrayed by Brenda Vaccaro, is suffering from Alzheimer's.

When she arrived on the set, Le Gallienne was greeted by her former Civic Repertory apprentice Norman Lloyd, a regular on the show. When Lloyd presented her with a dozen roses in her favorite shade of violet, she remembered him. "Where's your beautiful red hair?" she asked the now-balding Lloyd.

Joe Maher, her *Royal Family* brother, played Le Gallienne's son on the show, who wants his ailing mother to move in with him. Maher's easy Irish presence was reassuring, and Le Gallienne's scenes with him have a familiarity and warmth. "Her magic was her intelligence," he recalled, "her theatrical intelligence, and that extraordinary voice of hers. It was golden." The only display of temperament that Le Gallienne exhibited on the set, according to Fontana and Maher, was her referring to Brenda Vaccaro as "Little Miss Method."

Wearing the flowing white wig that she wore in *To Grandmother's* and a long-sleeved, silky peach nightgown, Le Gallienne lay propped up on pillows in a hospital bed for most of the show. She zinged her comic lines with deadly accuracy, especially when she skewered a pompous doctor. At the end of the show, reversing the trend of Le Gallienne's previous three roles, Evelyn Melbourne is not dead. Finally reconciled to the fact that she needs help, she decides to try living with her son. With her white hair upswept into a bun and wearing a bright blue sweater the color of her eyes, Evelyn Melbourne, holding onto her Yorkshire, exits into a new life.

ON THE FLIGHT HOME, Le Gallienne had a few drinks and then slept the rest of the way. Obviously, liquor provided a way for her to deal with the knowledge that her body and mind were failing. Years of discipline and organization were ingrained, however, and Le Gallienne knew that she must prepare for the inevitable. In May 1984, she met with her lawyer, prepared her will, and wrote final notes to Eloise, Ted, and Anne to be opened at her death.

Not long after the business of her will was completed, Le Gallienne began drinking heavily, and she continued to take Percodan. As if sensing that her life had come to a kind of closure, she had stopped writing in her diary at the end of 1983. During the day, she kept herself occupied with the garden and the animals, but to get through the long evenings and nights, she turned, as Marion Evensen had, to liquor. Fanny Cavendish in *The Royal Family* had clung to the hope that she might return to the theatre and act again, but Le Gallienne knew that her artistic life was over.

From time to time, Ted, Eloise, or Anne would find Le Gallienne drunk and passed out, but the worst incident occurred on July 4, 1984. Drunk and perhaps disoriented by Percodan, Le Gallienne fell down the steep stairs from her bedroom. She managed to haul herself back up the stairs and into bed. Nona, the housekeeper, found her and phoned Eloise, who called an ambulance.

After this incident, which left Le Gallienne bruised but not seriously injured, Eloise searched the house for liquor and Percodan and threw away everything she could find. She also concluded that Eva needed constant supervision, and she worked out a daily schedule of care. Nona handled meals and supervision during the day; Eloise spent a few hours with her each afternoon; and nurses covered the evenings, nights, and weekends.

One fall day, knowing that Anne Kaufman would arrive at five p.m., Eloise, thinking that Eva would be fine since she hadn't touched liquor for weeks, left the house at three. Le Gallienne used the opportunity to drive to the liquor store in Georgetown and stock up. Perhaps telling herself that she would just have a drink or two, she opened a bottle of sherry, and by the time Anne Kaufman arrived, it was empty, and Eva was passed out on the floor of her bedroom.

Eloise sought professional help and was advised that Le Gallienne must be confronted with the knowledge of her alcoholism. "I told Ted, Anne, and Nona that we must face her with this," recalled Eloise. They all gathered in the Blue Room, and when Eloise told Le Gallienne that she was an alcoholic and must stop drinking, Eva said, "Oh, I just had a little sherry." Angered that Eloise continued to press the issue, she stomped out of the house and insisted that she would not return until "that woman" had left. Before she left, Eloise told Ted to remove all the liquor from the house.

Several days later, Le Gallienne called Eloise. "Mom, where have you been?" she said. "I miss you." Eloise reminded her that she had been told to leave and not come back.

"I was drunk," Eva replied. "I love you and I want you to come back."

"I love you, too," Eloise replied. "But you must stop drinking."

"She never drank again," Eloise said. When Eloise took her car keys, Le Gallienne did not argue. From time to time, she would ask her to buy liquor, and when Eloise refused, Eva would stamp her feet and say, "You treat me like a two-year old!"

"Well, you're behaving like one!" Eloise would answer.

AS SHE LOST her short-term memory, Le Gallienne began to drift more and more into the past. Ernestine Grantham and Lorraine Stewart, two nurses who cared continuously for Le Gallienne for the next seven years, grew to love her.

During the day, Eva would read, perhaps try to work in the garden a bit, watch the birds at the feeders, and take a short walk. At night, she would feed the wild animals. When Anne Kaufman visited, they would talk about the theatre. "One day we had a long extremely intelligent talk about Ellis Rabb," Anne recalled. "She was so perceptive about his life and his career. After about fifteen minutes of conversation, Evale looked at me and said, 'Do you ever hear anything from Ellis?' and then repeated exactly what she had said before, like a playback. It was awful."

"We used to sit on the front steps for hours and talk," recalled Lorraine. "I enjoyed going through the Blue Room with her and going through the books upstairs. My mother always said that the day you don't learn anything is a day wasted. I said that to her so many times, and she would say, 'That's a good saying. You're here to learn.' "

Sometimes Le Gallienne would put on "scratchy old records" and coax the nurses into dancing the tango with her. The nurses laughed about Eva's agility and fitness, which seemed better than their own. "She could go up and down those steep stairs as quick as could be," said Ernestine, "and you wouldn't hear a sound—very graceful, with a light step."

"I used to feel sorry for some people who would come to see her," recalled Lorraine. "They would say, 'Can we come up?' 'Well, if you have to,' she would say, freezing them out. 'Maybe we'll come back another time.' 'Do that,' she'd say, and drift back into her bedroom."

When visitors came, like an actor requesting direction and motivation, Le Gallienne would ask, "Do I like them?" Eloise would describe them and tell Eva that yes, she was fond of them. Le Gallienne entertained her guests in the Blue Room. "It was just like a light came on," recalled Lorraine, "and she would be on the stage, like a little show-off. When they were gone, she would go right back to herself."

Mariette Hartley visited in May 1989. Le Gallienne hugged her and said that she remembered her. When Mariette told her that she looked wonderful, Le Gallienne said, "I look a thousand years old. Can't be helped. I *am* a thousand years old. I was born in 'ninety-nine, didn't I say? God, it was a hell of a long time ago, I daresay."

When they walked down the path to the old house to see the daffodils, "she seemed agile—bouncy even," Mariette recalled. On the trip back, though, she noticed that Le Gallienne was tired and out of breath.

"When did I say I was born?" Eva asked.

"Eighteen ninety-nine," Mariette told her.

"My God, I must be ninety."

Ellen Burstyn recorded her last visit to Le Gallienne on videotape. Burstyn drew out Le Gallienne's memories of Bernhardt and Duse, but when Eva's memory failed her, she turned to Eloise, who was off camera. "Mom?" she would ask, and Eloise would provide the memory. Although her mind failed during her talk with Burstyn, again and again on the videotape Le Gallienne lifted her head up and into the light from the window, turning her face to catch the light, as if her body remembered precisely what an actor should do.

Every spring, Ted helped her down the path to see the daffodils, and each time the trip became more difficult. When she was not able to keep up her garden, the diminishment of its beauty mirrored her gradual wasting away. Ted felt that Le Gallienne was undergoing a "kind of metamorphosis." In 1986, when her cousin Mogens died, the news did not affect her, Ted recalled. In Eva's mind, Mogens remained a tall, blond youth. Le Gallienne had characterized each treasured object in her house and in the Blue Room as voices that spoke to her, and when she could no longer hear those voices, she depended on Ted, Eloise, and Anne to tell her the stories that she had told them so many times. When Le Gallienne wasn't in the Blue Room, though, Ted could not bear to be in it. "Without her it was cold and dead and quiet," he said.

"What happened to my hands?" Eva would ask Eloise again and again. Eloise would tell her the story of the explosion and the burning. "Oh, yes," Eva would say, "and I did this," covering her face with her hands.

Eloise read her mail to her, told her about her book royalties and awards, and Eva would be momentarily pleased, but she would forget the news almost immediately. When Le Gallienne won the National Medal of Arts Award in 1986, Anne Kaufman traveled to the White House to accept the award from President Reagan. When Anne returned, she visited Weston wearing the dress she had worn at the presentation and reenacted the event. In 1987, Le Gallienne was accepted into the Ibsen Society of America as an honorary member "for her valiant and multifaceted championing of the dramas of Henrik Ibsen over five decades." Earle Hyman accepted the award for her. He spoke of her "integrity and honesty." He had learned not to ask a Scandinavian a question, he said, "if you cannot bear to hear the truth."

Since Le Gallienne tired easily and found walking difficult, her doctor, James Griffith, made house calls. In the last six months of her life, Le Gallienne did not go downstairs, and she did not walk down the path to see the daffodils. She spoke to Jo Hutchinson on the telephone every few weeks. "I wish you were here," she told Jo. As her world shrank to the walls of her bedroom and then to the confines of her bed, Le Gallienne seemed to become younger and younger in her mind. She wanted Bessie, her doll, and she asked the nurses to fetch Bessie from her place on the bookshelf and put her on the bed with her. Bessie's clothes were worn and falling apart, her petticoat was unraveling, and her ragged face was layered with a blur of lines. To save wear and tear on the ancient doll, Eloise made Bessie her own little pillow, but Eva hugged Bessie close to her.

On the morning of June 3, 1991, Dr. Griffith arrived to check on Eva. She had gradually stopped eating, and Eloise was concerned. As usual, before the doctor came into her room, Le Gallienne asked Eloise, "Who's this doctor? Do I know him? Do I like him?" Eloise assured her that she liked the doctor very much.

Dr. Griffith entered, and Le Gallienne smiled and threw her arms around him. "She would ooh and aah and flirt," Lorraine recalled. "The doctor thought she was absolutely charming."

When Lorraine checked on Le Gallienne that evening at seven-thirty, she found her asleep, holding on to Bessie, with her other hand on Dimpy, who lay by her side. At nine, Lorraine went back upstairs, and Eva was awake. The nurse asked her if there was anything she wanted. "No," she said. Then, about ten-forty-five, Le Gallienne called down that she had to go to the bathroom. Lorraine began to help her to walk, but then Eva said that she had changed her

*Le Gallienne poses for Nancy Rica Schiff's 1983 book of portraits of
famous and active octogenarians,* A Celebration of the 80's.

mind. Lorraine noticed that Eva's breathing had become very labored. The nurse
helped her into bed and propped her up high with pillows. Lorraine sat by the
bed for an hour holding her hand until Eva's breathing became calmer and
slower.

"Then," Lorraine said, "she pulled up once, away from the pillows. She
looked around the room and lay back. She was gone."

AFTERWORD

Le Gallienne, 1936

The dead help the living.

Eva Le Gallienne wanted her name preserved in four distinct ways. With the addition of Alice De Lamar's legacy, Le Gallienne's net worth amounted to more than two million dollars. In 1970, she had given twelve acres of her Weston property to the Aspetuck Land Trust for the Eva Le Gallienne Bird Sanctuary, which was opened to the public following her death.

She bequeathed residuals from her estate, amounting to over a third of a million dollars, to the Actors' Fund, to establish "the Eva Le Gallienne Fund . . . in memory of the donor."

To Eloise Armen, "to aid her in the event that she should plan a biography," Le Gallienne left her royalty rights and over sixty years of diaries; dozens of unpublished manuscripts; thousands of letters; and countless scraps of paper filled with musings, recollections, and thoughts—a detailed, accurate, unsparing account of her personal as well as her public life. She didn't leave out the struggles she had with her "demons"—vanity, alcohol, lust, pride, fear of aging. Le Gallienne was an archivist of the soul. She believed that "the dead help the living."

She left her estate to her family of friends. To Eloise, she willed her house and property; to Ted, the old house and property; to Anne, her personal effects and tangible property. She left a sapphire ring to Jo and personal notes to Eloise, Ted, and Anne, which they opened and shared with one another following a private memorial service held in the meadow by her old house. Her ashes were scattered in a place she called "the Tomb," a large stone outcropping in the middle of the meadow, and her name and dates were carved into a plain granite block. On a rocky ledge Ted placed a bronze bust of her head that Stuart Benson, Mimsey's husband, had created in the 1920s. Around it he arranged a bouquet of her favorite roses—pale creamy Silver Moons and showy pink Van Fleets. From Le Gallienne's recording of English and American poetry, Eloise, thinking of Le Gallienne's decision to take the nonprofit theatre path over commercial show business, selected Robert Frost's poem "The Road Not Taken." Eloise turned on the tape recorder, and the mourners listened to Le Gallienne's warm cello voice speak Frost's familiar lines:

" 'I shall be telling this with a sigh / Somewhere ages and ages hence,' " she said, her voice tinged with rueful irony. " 'Two roads diverged in a wood, and I— / I took the one less traveled by, / And that has made all the difference.' "

LE GALLIENNE SPENT most of her ninety-two years of life making a difference. Star, pioneer, legend, major force, great figure of the twentieth century, a national treasure, said the headlines announcing her death. Her professional credentials and contributions are without parallel in the American theatre. A Broadway star before she was twenty-five, she turned her back on the commercial theatre and founded the Civic Repertory, where she performed as leading actor, director, and producer. The Civic Repertory Theatre foreshadowed and laid the philosophical groundwork for off Broadway and the regional theatre movement. Le Gallienne's legacy lives on in theatres off Broadway, in nonprofit theatres around the country, in every theatre, commercial or nonprofit, whose artistic mission is "Not Only for Amusement." She called the lack of government support for the arts "a national scandal." The Europeans, she said, "put us to shame when it comes to financial aid. . . . We are still in the Dark Ages." She never realized her ambition to create a great national repertory theatre, and the word "repertory" has lost its original meaning, but her lifelong struggle for national subsidy of the theatre serves as inspiration and model for those faced with the same battle today.

Her high-minded dedication to theatre as a serious art made a difference, but it was a lonely, difficult path. "Miss Le Gallienne confronted Broadway," Brooks Atkinson wrote, "with a plausible, enlightened idea that it has never been able to forget. Her taste, breadth of mind, good will, and energy discovered one of Broadway's dreariest truths. It does not want its mind improved."

Self-education and improving her mind were high adventure to Le Gallienne. Her Blue Room library was filled with books in English, French, Danish, and Russian, and the books bore the imprint of careful reading—underlinings and marginal comments. Her record of published work is extraordinary, since she spent most of her life as a working actor. She had years of experience acting in and directing Ibsen, and her twelve translations of his plays convey the comedy and colors of the originals. In translating Ibsen and Chekhov, she was particularly sensitive to subtext and stage business, and her versions breathe of the theatre, not the academy, and are still performed. Her prefaces to *The Master Builder* and *Hedda Gabler* continue to be a valuable resource for actors, directors, academics, and anyone interested in Ibsen's complex art. Le Gallienne's subtle intelligence and her personality were particularly suited to Ibsen and

Chekhov, who, like her, made the leap from the nineteenth century into the modern world.

As an actor, Le Gallienne was writing on water, but in her biography of Eleonora Duse, *The Mystic in the Theatre,* she attempted to preserve Duse's ephemeral art, which had inspired her own. Duse, who was called the first modern actor, introduced Le Gallienne to mysticism and the abnegation of self in a search for deep inner truth; and Sarah Bernhardt, the greatest star of the nineteenth century, introduced Eva to acting of high style and dazzling theatricality. Le Gallienne's own acting art was a kind of synthesis of the art of her two idols. Unlike her famous mentors, Le Gallienne was not an international celebrity. She was the bread and salt of the theatre—an accomplished character actor.

Le Gallienne discovered and encouraged many actors, but "you can't teach acting," she often told her students, except by "hand to hand. Many years ago, Duse took my hand. And now I've taken your hand and now you are taking the hand of others."

Actor Jonathan Hadary was so moved by his one brief contact with Le Gallienne at his 1982 *Alice in Wonderland* audition that he wrote about it for a collection of Broadway essays. "As I came through the door, she rose from her chair behind a long table . . . and extended her hand to me," he wrote. "When I was done . . . we chatted a bit, she thanked me, and I got up to leave. She again rose from her chair and held out her hand to me. . . . I didn't get the job. I didn't even get a callback," he said. "But twice Eva Le Gallienne had stood up for me, twice. Maybe she just had better manners than I'm accustomed to, but I think not. I think she stood up for everyone who auditioned. She stood up for me because I was an actor and so was she, because we were both actors."

In her biography of Duse, Le Gallienne wrote: "She saw [the theatre] as a great force capable of spreading beauty and understanding, whose function it was to quicken in the minds and hearts of the people an appreciation of the nobility of suffering, to awaken in them a sense of the sublime, to rouse them from their torpor and through a heightening of the emotions make them aware of the mystery and wonder of the human spirit."

Notes

Please refer to the bibliography for complete publication information on the books cited in the notes.

page

VII   "Je le ferai"—*Forum,* 32. "I will do it in spite of everything!" Sarah Bernhardt cried, when a classmate challenged her to accomplish some impossible task. "Quand-même" became her motto.

"The soul's joy"—A saying written by Eleonora Duse in pencil on heavy paper. The framed quotation hung by Le Gallienne's bed for forty years.

PART ONE: 1899 – 1915

5   "I would peer"—ms. of *WAQH.*

6   "high, clear, vibrant"—*Forum,* 33.

7   "remarkably alert"—RLeG to JNLeG, April 16, 1900.

"low & very agreeable," "you'd think *she*"—BR.

10   "free-thinker, a destroyer"—JNLeG, *Mavi* (unpublished novel) and "Georg Brandes—A Silhouette," *Yellow Book* 8 (January 1896): 163–172.

11	"The world is full"—JNLeG, *Mavi.*

"Julie and Ellie"—Author interview with Peter Thornton.

"The real secret"—JNLeG, "Manners and Modes," *Town and Country,* April 14, 1903.

"chic modernity"—"Woman's Ways," n.d. 1895. Julie's columns appeared in *The Morning Leader, The Daily Courier,* and *The Star.*

"remind a friend"—"Woman's Ways," Jan. 8, 1896.

12	"That is the man"—*WAQH,* 282.

"would have her"—BR.

"What new spell"—RLeG to JNLeG, May 20, 1895.

14	"I love you"—RLeG to JNLeG, May 26, 1895.

"It certainly could"—RLeG to JNLeG, Aug. 27, 1895.

"Few young men"—BR.

"there was already"—*Quest,* 10.

"to no code"—*Quest,* 47.

16	"fatter and bonnier"—*Quest,* 252.

"incessantly, to youth"—*Quest,* 256.

"on the way"—RLeG to JNLeG, June 13, 1895.

"soft lights, vermouth"—RLeG to JNLeG, May 30, 1895.

"I have had"—RLeG to JNLeG, Feb. 25, 1896.

"have been happier"—DI, May 5, 1949.

17	"My dear one"—RLeG to JNLeG, June 18, 1896.

"I pay you"—Ibid.

18	"Poor thing"—DI, May 25, 1949.

"He is rather tall"—*Quest,* 331.

"They say it"—*Quest,* 332.

"as one reading"—*Quest,* 333.

19	"side by side"—RLeG to JNLeG, June 26, 1898.

"When is that"—RLeG to JNLeG, Jan. 2, 1899.

"you and I belong"—JNLeG, *Mavi,* n.p.

20	"exceptionally healthy"—*AT,* 3.

"To Eva"—RLeG note, Jan. 12, 1899.

"a little mirror"—RLeG to Mrs. Helen Bridgman, Feb. 1, 1899.

"pretty black"—quoted in RLeG to JNLeG, Sept. 28, 1899.

"I am happy"—quoted in RLeG to JNLeG, April 16, 1900.

"It was the old filth"—RLeG, n.d. 1903.

"Asra could have"—RLeG to JNLeG, Oct. 17, 1903.

21	"about old family"—DI, Dec. 28, 1949.

"strange man in"—ms. of *WAQH*

"Eva, the Woodland"—RLeG, *Little Dinners with the Sphinx and Other Prose Fancies,* 233–249.

22	"I have had"—*Quest,* 422.

"old, old garden"—*AT,* 10.

"the true heroism"—*AT,* 14.

24	"I will never"—*AT,* 7.

"To me she was"—*AT,* 4.

"little ladies"—*AT,* 23.

"developed a veritable"—*AT,* 27.

"with little drawers"—LeG to MN, March 16, 1911.

"to the Bois"—*AT,* 33.

26   "wonderful place"—ms. of *WAQH*

"flavored soda-waters"—*AT,* 15.

"quite wonderful"—JNLeG to Sissie Gallienne, 1905.

"unnecessarily hard"—*Quest,* 422.

27   "my first real grief"—*AT,* 29.

"permanently imprinted"—Eve Curie, *Madame Curie,* 272.

"peer into those"—ms. of *WAQII.*

"immensely high"—*AT,* 29.

"distinguished professors"—*AT,* 30.

"they made you"—Ibid.

"a pink-faced little"—*AT,* 16.

"doing what was forbidden"—*AT,* 32.

"often dressed"—Louise Berton to author, May 15, 1991.

28   "like a dog"—LeG to Marcelle, Dec. 1908.

"had a good"—N. Labrun to JNLeG, Jan. 4, 1909.

"As Mam knows"—LeG to MN, April 14, 1913.

"real happiness"—LeG to MN, March 16, 1911.

29   "I think dear," "He said I"—LeG to JNLeG, Sept. 6, 1911.

"Really, I shouldn't"—RLeG to JNLeG, March 16, 1909.

30   "Hep bores me"—DI, March 19, 1951.

"A debtor who"—Mary Mullet, "Eva Le Gallienne: The Story of a Stubborn Girl," *American Magazine,* June 1923.

"Do you take"—*Quest,* 439.

"I don't know why"—LeG to MN, March 7, 1957.

31   "tenderness, warmth," "like a haunted," "Uncle Will"—BR.

"I thought I had"—*AT,* 42.

"I'm told"—*AT,* 43.

"to make me see"—*AT,* 45.

"an amazing child"—Constance Collier, *Harlequinade: The Story of My Life,* 220–221.

32   "very small"—LeG, "Margaret Webster—1905–1972," *NYT,* Nov. 26, 1972.

"having the advantage"—Margaret Webster, *The Same Only Different,* 234.

33   "It has a good honest face"—Author interview with AKS.

"I am quite"—LeG to JNLeG, Summer 1913.

"who has to slave"—LeG to JNLeG, Aug. 30, 1913.

"The gracious living"—Webster, *The Same,* 235.

"dismal and bitter"—*AT,* 46.

"one of many thousand"—*AT,* 49.

34   "free and responsible"—Ibid.

"Boring!"—LeG to JNLeG, Oct. 19, 1913.

"Sunday in a select"—LeG to JNLeG, Sept. 17, 1913.

"a waste of money"—LeG to JNLeG, Nov. 11, 1913.

"[Eva] is already"—Headmistress to JNLeG, Sept. 17, 1913.

"I was too much"—*AT,* 50.

35   "that only made"—LeG to JNLeG, Jan. 25, 1914.
      "The element of danger"—*AT,* 51.
      "killing punishment"—LeG to JNLeG, Nov. 23, 1913.
      "asked us all"—LeG to HLeG, Feb. 6, 1914.
      "All the people"—LeG to MN, Nov. 22, 1913.
      "have her real Cat"—LeG to JNLeG, Nov. 22, 1913.

36   "It was . . . a thrilling"—*Forum,* 37.
      "for at least five"—*AT,* 54.
      "Her performance"—*AT,* 55.
      "speechless wonder"—*Forum,* 38.
      "such intense joy"—*AT,* 56.
      "profoundly moved"—*AT,* 57.
      "I can never remember"—BR.

37   "I felt completely"—*AT,* 63.
      "How you gained"—MN to LeG, Jan. 15, 1915.
      "After this exciting," "It is against"—*AT,* 64.
      "perfectly beastly"—LeG to MN, Jan. 31, 1914.
      "The only thing is"—LeG to JNLeG, March 13, 1914.
      "I *do* wish"—LeG to MN, Feb. 13, 1914.
      "no very clear"—*Forum,* 39.

38   "I remember the astonishing"—*Forum,* 38.
      "He took the telegram"—*Forum,* 39.
      "much of Sarah's work"—*Forum,* 34.

39   "Chère et adorable"—*AT,* 72.
      "monument to what"—Ibid.
      "emancipation"—*Mystic,* 35.

40   "a glowing letter"—*AT,* 69.
      "[Philipson] is most"—LeG to MN, July 10, 1914.
      "he was bitterly"—*AT,* 69.
      "the most famous"—*AT,* 70.
      "one of the young men"—LeG notebook.
      "I thought, if so"—Collier, *Harlequinade,* 227.
      "It was most"—LeG to MN, July 23, 1914.

41   "rushed down"—*AT,* 73.
      "was'nt a bit"—LeG to MN, July 23, 1914.
      "was most frantically"—LeG to MN, Sept. 24, 1914.
      "a rather husky"—Elsie Janis, "Don't Weaken! Eva Le Gallienne Didn't," *Liberty,* Dec.
         29, 1928.
      "Aren't the threats"—LeG to JNLeG, July 30, 1914.
      "It'll be over"—*AT,* 75.
      "the banks were besieged"—Ibid.

42   "Know everything"—Quoted in diary and in various clippings, including Evelyn Seeley,
      "Eva Le Gallienne," *New York World-Telegram,* n.d.
      "my French was"—*AT,* 78.
      "dreadful and lovely"—LeG to MN, March 7, 1915.
      "perfectly awful"—LeG to MN, Nov. 21, 1914.

"a great defect"—Ibid.

43   "They have accepted"—LeG to MN, April 14, 1915.

44   "No!!!"—LeG to MN, July 23, 1914.

"imagine nothing worse"—DI, Dec. 31, 1950.

"They were all Cockneys"—*AT,* 81.

"being looked over"—*AT,* 82.

46   "Where arc you off"—*AT,* 83.

"could not be better"—LeG to MN, May 27, 1915.

"I had worked," "all my faults"—*AT,* 84.

"the dark house"—*AT,* 86.

"brilliant new"—Ibid.

"It is funny"—LeG to MN, May 21, 1915.

47   "You can't imagine"—"British Reserve Is Pierced," *New York Evening Sun,* Sept. 1, 1915.

"Why don't you go"—LeG to MN, Aug. 15, 1915.

"Think plan good"—Ibid.

"a very bright little"—General Press Cutting Assn., n.d.

"have a very great"—LeG to JNLeG, 1914.

"fame and fortune"—*AT,* 88.

48   "loathed leaving"—LeG to MN, Aug. 15, 1915.

"question of making"—Ibid.

Part Two: 1915 – 1923

51   "How I do enjoy"—DI, May 17, 1917.

"never seen such"—LeG to HLeG, July 25, 1915.

"couldn't speak"—LeG to MN, Aug. 15, 1915.

"I always want"—*New York Evening Sun,* Sept. 1, 1915.

"had to recite"—LeG to HLeG, Aug. 4, 1915.

52   "every actor tried"—LeG to MN, Aug. 15, 1915.

"fits of homesickness"—LeG to Bet Nørregaard, Feb. 3, 1916.

"They all seem"—LeG to HLeG, Aug. 5, 1915.

"chef d'oeuvres"—LeG to MN, Dec. 2, 1915.

"parrot-fashion," "astonishing portrait"—*AT,* 98.

"Daddy coming"—LeG to HLeG, Nov. 12, 1915.

53   "have chucked him"—LeG to HLeG, Sept. 16, 1915.

"knocked me flat"—LeG to HLeG, Nov. 15, 1915.

"RLeG is"—LeG to MN, Dec. 2, 1915.

"No one will"—Ibid.

"Just you wait"—*AT,* 107.

"arrives on the stage"—*NYT,* January 5, 1916.

"midst of a"—*AT,* 99.

54   "Yes"—LeG to MN, Feb. 2, 1916.

"The solution"—*AT,* 110.

"that dreaded laugh"—LeG, "Sir James Barrie, Peter Pan, and I," *Theatre,* January 1929, 15–16, 68.

54   "were able to start"—*AT,* 111.
55   "Miss Le Gallienne plays"—*NYT,* Sept. 6, 1916.
       "My dear Mogie"—LeG to MN, Aug. 16, 1916.
56   "It is to me amazing"—LeG to MN, Dec. 2, 1915.
       "When I get"—LeG to MN, Feb. 3, 1916.
       "As you progress"—Ibid.
       "[Merle Maddern] is"—LeG to MN, Dec. 2, 1915.
57   "It is curious"—LeG to MN, Feb. 3, 1916.
       "No!"—Ibid.
58   "I understand so well"—LeG to MN, Oct. 13, 1916.
       "I have a wonderful"—Ibid.
       "not a very good"—LeG to MN, May 24, 1917.
       "Oh! I look"—LeG to MN, Dec. 2, 1915.
       "talking, talking"—*Forum,* 41.
       "that amazing moment"—*Forum,* 40.
60   "I am 18"—DI, Jan. 11, 1917.
       "make a curious"—clipping, Jan. 1917.
       "I felt rather"—DI, Jan. 11, 1917.
       "was disgusted"—*AT,* 116.
61   "I couldn't play"—DI, Jan. 13, 1917.
       "but the man wanted"—DI, Feb. 8, 1917.
       "favorite dance"—Robert J. Condon, *Great Women Athletes of the Twentieth Century*
       (Jefferson, North Carolina: McFarland & Co., 1991), 54.
63   "the value of hero"—LeG notebook.
       "a company of Amazons"—Lillian Faderman, *Odd Girls and Twilight Lovers,* 21–22.
       "very serious"—DI, Feb. 7, 1917.
       "There is so much"—DI, Jan. 31, 1917.
       "It was wonderful"—DI, Jan. 13, 1917.
       "a shell of"—*Forum,* 42.
64   "It was too"—DI, Jan. 17, 1917.
       "a great strong feeling"—Ibid.
65   "Isn't Miss Le Gallienne," "she has quite"—LeG to MN, May 24, 1917.
       "a marvellous hour"—DI, Feb. 20, 1917.
       "cast a spell"—*AT,* 119.
       "fairly vamped"—DI, March 16, 1917.
       "hangs round"—DI, March 17, 1917.
       "wonderful son"—DI, May 10, 1917.
66   "It was certainly"—*AT,* 120–121.
       "bored to death"—DI, March 17, 1917.
       "no one at all thrilling"—DI, March 20, 1917.
       "hardened cynic"—LeG to HLeG, April 26, 1917.
       "Arizona is"—LeG to MN, May 24, 1917.
       "splendid—at least"—DI, May 10, 1917.
       "the boredom"—DI, May 14, 1917.
       "five minutes"—DI, May 16, 1917.
       "marvelous feeling"—DI, May 17, 1917.

67 "I feigned"—DI, May 11, 1917.

   "was a splendid"—*AT,* 124.

   "How I pity"—LeG to MN, May 24, 1917.

   "How I do enjoy"—DI, May 17, 1917.

   "I'm not going"—DI, March 31, 1917.

68 "incredible burlesque"—Unidentified clipping, 1917.

   "rather astonishing vitality"—*NYT* clipping, n.d.

   "The average plays"—LeG to MN, Dec. 19, 1917.

69 "huge emerald green"—Ibid.

   "She sometimes took"—BR.

   "Come with me"—Ada Patterson, "Eva Le Gallienne: A Cerebral Actress," *Theatre,* Feb. 1924, 110.

   "were of immense"—*AT,* 131.

70 "skillful and charming"—*NYT,* Feb. 15, 1918.

   "girlishly fresh"—*NYT,* May 7, 1918, 11:5.

   "It is impossible"—*AT,* 13.

   "Cornelia Otis Skinner"—Author interview with AKS.

   "absolutely banal"—*NYT,* Dec. 19, 1979.

   "Ethel was like"—DI, Dec. 21, 1918.

   "Underneath any moodiness"—*AT,* 131.

   "It should be"—DI, Jan. 1, 1918.

71 "in search of"—DI, Feb. 5, 1918.

   "so full of the joy"—DI, Feb. 12, 1918.

   "was marvellous as ever"—DI, Feb. 24, 1918.

   "The Pageant was"—DI, March 1, 1918.

   "Continental lounge-lizard"—*NYT,* March 17, 1918.

   "this house"—*NYT,* April 30, 1918.

   "had hysterics"—DI, Feb. 22, 1918.

   "dupe"—DI, Aug. 10, 1918.

72 "little mutt"—DI, MARCH 1, 1917.

   "teased to death"—DI, April 26, 1918.

   "Tony came to"—DI, April 20, 1918.

   "felt up to mischief"—DI, Aug. 21, 1918.

74 "She had quite"—DI, April 9, 1918.

   "It was a hateful"—DI, April 14, 1918.

75 "Thank God I have"—DI, Oct. 4, 1918.

   "the handsomest man"—*WAQH,* 284.

   "Our romance is still"—RLeG to JNLeG, March 24, 1918.

   "Dear I should love"—JNLeG to RLeG, letter, n.d., enclosed in March 24, 1918, RLeG letter.

   "Dearest Julie"—RLeG to JNLeG, April 5, 1918.

   "went to sleep"—DI, Oct. 8, 1918.

   "haunts me day"—DI, Dec. 1, 1918.

76 "dreadful obsessions"—LeG to HLeG, Dec. 17, 1918.

   "the exquisite Harry"—DI, Dec. 7, 1918.

   "I finally found"—*AT,* 136.

76   "owing to the strike"—LeG to MN, Sept. 1, 1919.

78   "Come with me"—Elsie Janis, *Liberty*, Dec. 29, 1928.
        "It was great fun"—*AT,* 138.
        "I was so happy"—RLeG to LeG, Feb. 17, 1920.
        "delightful, whimsical"—*AT,* 141.

79   "& some gin"—LeG to JNLeG, April 13, 1920.
        "I think she's"—LeG to JNLeG, April 17, 1920.

80   "We were all stood"—LeG to JNLeG, April 21, 1920.
        "instinctive facility"—*Boston Transcript*, April 20, 1920.
        "dreadfully nervous"—LeG to JNLeG, April 23, 1920.
        "great event"—*AT,* 144.
        "one of the most"—*NYT,* May 6, 1920.

81   "gradually grew restless"—*AT,* 145.
        "choose a type"—DI, Nov. 4, 1937.

82   "get together all"—*AT,* 145.
        "I washed my hands"—*AT,* 146.
        "I think she was"—LeG to JNLeG, Sept. 18, 1920.

83   "How I hate"—LeG to JNLeG, Jan. 26, 1921.
        "lived at least"—LeG to JNLeG, Jan. 10, 1921.
        "so startling and penetrating"—Helen Boylston, *Carol Goes Backstage*, 83–84.

84   "She seems to me"—LeG to JNLeG, Jan. 31, 1921.
        "faraway lover"—RLeG to LeG, Jan. 29, 1921.
        "Mimsey was married"—LeG to JNLeG, Feb. 11, 1921.
        "I'm still alive," "go South"—LeG to JNLeG, Feb. 18, 1921.

86   "You don't sound"—LeG to JNLeG, March 4, 1921.
        "Hollywood in the early"—Sheilah Graham, *The Garden of Allah*, 18.
        "insane"—LeG to JNLeG, March 4, 1921.

87   "great sensitivity and the honesty"—Joseph Schildkraut, *My Father and I*, 159.
        "as a kind"—Theresa Helburn, *A Wayward Quest*, 172.

88   "the play was"—*AT,* 149.
        "Don't worry about"—LeG to JNLeG, March 22, 1921.
        "is a thoroughbred"—LeG to JNLeG, April 4, 1921.
        "Never were there"—Helburn, *Wayward Quest*, 172.
        "it got to the point"—Ibid, 173.

89   "Pepi, it's so wonderful"—Notes on Acting, Joseph Schildkraut Papers, courtesy of
        Leonora Schildkraut.
        "the music seems"—LeG to JNLeG, April 4, 1921.
        "I felt I had"—*AT,* 150.

91   "nervous to the point"—LeG to JNLeG, April 25, 1921.
        "weary, white-faced"—John Mason Brown, *Upstage*, 135.
        "suck lemons"—LeG to JNLeG, April 25, 1921.
        "They loved me!"—Harold C. Schonberg, "Eva Le Gallienne: If I Only Played Myself
        That Would Be a Bore," *NYT,* Jan. 11, 1981.
        "her acting moved"—*NYT,* May 1, 1921.
        "so strange in it"—LeG to JNLeG, May 23, 1921.
        "She was very marvellous"—LeG to JNLeG, Sept. 26, 1921.

92 "I'm getting sick"—LeG to JNLeG, May 10, 1921.

"tiresome and hateful"—LeG to JNLeG, May 19, 1921.

93 "to strike a major"—Carol Bird, "Stage Mary," *Theatre,* May 1922.

"It's amazing"—LeG to JNLeG, July 15, 1921.

94 "It's just that people"—LeG to JNLeG, Oct. 25, 1921.

"I keep saying"—Ibid.

"Miss Le Gallienne is"—*NYT,* Nov. 27, 1921.

"I might have"—Author interview with EA.

95 "full of pep"—LeG to JNLeG, Nov. 18, 1921.

"shimmy lady"—Ibid.

"pretty ghastly"—LeG to JNLeG, Dec. 12, 1921.

96 "half-tone"—Draft ms. of *Here Lies the Heart.*

"agonizing aching"—LeG to Merc, Feb. 10, 1922.

"very foolishly"—LeG to Merc, April 14, 1922.

97 "light before"—LeG to Merc, April 28, 1922.

"Ah—you will"—LeG to JNLeG, May 1, 1922.

"hurled from one"—LeG to Merc, Feb. 14, 1922.

"You came to me"—LeG to Merc, May 13, 1922.

"so completely & so"—LeG to Merc, May 18, 1922.

"very changed"—LeG to JNLeG, May 18, 1922.

98 "I think you will"—LeG to Merc, June 12, 1922.

"dump in Montmartre"—LeG to Merc, July 28, 1922.

"like a fever"—LeG to Merc, June 16, 1922.

"I love you insanely"—LeG to Merc, Aug. 15, 1922.

"They wouldn't believe"—LeG to Merc, Aug. 24, 1922.

99 "A trip of this kind"—LeG to JNLeG, Sept. 20, 1922.

"the hope of someday"—LeG to Merc, Nov. 8, 1922.

"to the stars"—LeG to Merc, Nov. 10, 1922.

"the old nastiness"—LeG to Merc, Sept. 24, 1922.

"We *will* do"—LeG to Merc, Oct. 13, 1922.

"a quiet, retiring"—LeG to JNLeG, Jan. 22, 1923.

"I thought she was"—Author interview with Rose Hobart.

100 "I remember I"—Ibid.

101 "What I always abhor"—LeG to JNLeG, Nov. 14, 1922.

"This is one of the worst"—LeG to JNLeG, Jan. 10, 1923.

102 "not like acting"—LeG to JNLeG, March 6, 1923.

"It really is unbelievable"—LeG to JNLeG, Feb. 8, 1923.

"My God, don't talk"—Mercedes de Acosta, *Sandro Botticelli* (New York: Moffat, Yard and Company, 1923), 30.

"It was curious"—LeG to JNLeG, March 28, 1923.

103 "yearning society amateur"—Percy Hammond, *Detroit News,* April 1, 1923.

"wonderful old comedians"—LeG to JNLeG, May 8, 1923.

"wanting you insanely"—LeG to Merc, Aug. 4/5, 1923.

"One of the most"—*AT,* 162.

"the burial of"—LeG to JNLeG, April 6, 1923.

104 "I felt that"—Duse ms., 1923.

104   "Suddenly, I saw"—*Mystic,* 5.
        "You have given"—*Mystic,* 106.
106   "developing into something"—LeG to JNLeG, Sept. 22, 1923.
        "if our little Swan"—*AT,* 166.
        "It seems so ridiculous"—LeG to Merc, Oct. 18, 1923.
        "Madame Duse has read"—*Mystic,* 107.
        "Dear, beautiful child"—*Mystic,* 108.
107   "strangely crooked face"—LeG, "Sarah Bernhardt and Eleonora Duse," *Stage,* January
            1937, 97.
        "Her eyes looked"—*Mystic,* 109.
        "Remember what is good"—*AT,* 169.
        "was able to play"—*Mystic,* 110.
        "admirable for its"—*NYT,* Oct. 24, 1923.
        "Eva Le Gallienne"—*Vogue,* Dec. 15, 1923.
108   "It is not so easy"—*Pearson's Magazine,* Feb. 1922.
        "too seriously"—*Theatre,* Dec. 1923.
        "The sign of the jutting"—*Theatre,* Feb. 1924.
        "The next morning"—*Mystic,* 111.
        "began to realize"—*AT,* 168.
109   "It's barbaric"—*Mystic,* 114.
        "the future centre"—LeG to MN, May 1, 1924.
        "so that in two"—LeG to JNLeG, May 6, 1924.
        "There are none"—*AT,* 168.

PART THREE: 1923 – 1931

113   "It would be"—LeG, *Six Plays,* xxvii.
        "Like everything else"—*Mystic,* 122.
        "Sometimes she would"—*Mystic,* 147.
114   "stripped of everything"—*Mystic,* 112.
        "She treated me"—*Mystic,* 111.
        "Yes, yes!"—*Mystic,* 116.
        "Her entire body"—*Mystic,* 151.
        "was always that"—*Forum,* 40.
        "When she listened"—*Mystic,* 113.
        "Ah! That abominable"—*Mystic,* 116.
115   "went over to the window"—*Mystic,* 9.
        "I have never seen"—LeG to JNLeG, Oct. 25, 1923.
        "There is always"—*Bridgeport Post,* Oct. 23, 1927.
        "personal life"—LeG to JNLeG, Nov. 12, 1923.
116   "better than any man"—LeG to JNLeG, Jan. 6, 1924.
        "What a marvellous"—LeG to JNLeG, Nov. 23, 1922.
        "Then if we receive"—*Theatre,* Feb. 1924, 20.
118   "When I left her"—Ibid., 58.
        "It is not merely"—*Sun,* March 24, 1924.

Eva played in two French matinees with Madame Simone in *La Vièrge Folle* (*The Foolish Virgin*). To hold her own in the French company, she used more extravagant gestures, a faster tempo, and thought in French instead of English. She loved the experience, particularly since she got to shoot herself in full view of the audience, even though in doing so she singed her chiffon negligee with powder burns.

119   "I seem to have"—LeG to JNLeG, Feb. 28, 1924.

    "It seemed as though"—LeG to JNLcG, May 6, 1924.

120   "So few here"—LeG to JNLeG, May 15, 1924.

    "the managers"—LeG to JNLeG, May 23, 1924.

    "disrespect and lack"—LeG to JNLeG, July 11, 1924.

122   "mental tonic"—Ibid.

    "More and more"—LeG to Merc, June 28, 1924.

    "long aristocratic legs"—Author interview with AKS.

123   "cold hard-hearted"—quoted in LeG to Merc, Sept. 27, 1924.

    "And then this thing"—LeG to Merc, Sept. 23, 1924.

    "The thought of"—LeG to Merc, Oct. 21, 1924.

    "more gentle with me"—LeG to Merc, Nov. 2, 1924.

    "anything you wanted"—*AT,* 181.

    "I have found"—LeG to Merc, Nov. 23, 1924.

124   "What now?"—*AT,* 181.

    "I had great"—Norman Bel Geddes, *Miracle in the Evening,* 329.

    "mad excitable"—LeG to JNLeG, Feb. 23, 1925.

    "episodic and undramatic"—Bel Geddes, *Miracle,* 329.

    "The theatre is to me"—George Bogusch, "An American in Paris: Norman Bel Geddes Produces Jeanne d'Arc," *Theatre Design and Technology,* October 1969.

125   "Cauchon!"—Bel Geddes, *Miracle,* 334.

    "The company was like"—*AT,* 188.

    "so nervous and exhausted"—LeG, "Deaths I Have Lived Through," BR.

    "Miss Eva Le Gallienne"—London *Daily Mail,* n.d.

127   "It was as though"—Bogusch, "An American in Paris."

    "To be hurled"—"Deaths," BR.

    "She continues to"—LeG to JNLeG, July 27, 1925.

    "nothing in my life"—LeG to JNLeG, June 24, 1928.

128   "queer girl"—Rollin Van Hadley, *The Letters of Bernard Berenson and Isabella Stewart Gardner,* 632–634.

130   "For the first"—LeG to JNLeG, July 27, 1925.

    "sad, but *good*"—LeG to JNLeG, July 30, 1925.

    "Of course I know"—Gordon Craig to LeG, July 25, 1925.

    "I am always"—Gordon Craig to LeG, Aug. 20, 1925.

    "by a strange"—LeG to JNLeG, Aug. 22, 1925.

    "between intellectual gloom"—Noël Coward, *Present Indicative,* 216.

    "perfectly charming"—LeG to JNLeG, Sept. 10, 1925.

131   "seems never to have"—Cole Lesley, *Remembered Laughter: The Life of Noël Coward,* 55.

    "Noël owes much"—LeG to JNLeG, Oct. 16, 1925.

    "You have a white"—Tad Mosel, *The World and Theatre of Katharine Cornell,* 197.

132   "All the Broadway devils"—LeG to JNLeG, Sept. 15, 1925.

132   "make it mine"—LeG to JNLeG, Nov. 21, 1925.
      "He fixed me"—*WAQH,* 155–156.

133   "abandon all my hopes"—Ibid.
      "I still call him"—LeG to JNLeG, Sept. 25, 1925.
      "My Mefisto is always"—JNLeG to MN, April 15, 1928.

134   "It must be wonderful"—LeG to JNLeG, Nov. 23, 1922.
      "The play is"—LeG, *The Master Builder,* 12.
      "a thrilling play"—Ibid., 33.
      "ambidextrous"—Author interview with JH.

135   "But why worry"—Ruth Pennybacker, "Eva Le Gallienne, Rebel Actress," *Woman Citizen Magazine,* March 1926, 43.
      "the true instinct"—LeG to JNLeG, Dec. 23, 1926.

136   "into it with all"—LeG, *The Master Builder,* 11.
      "clumsy, old-fashioned"—Civic Rep ms.
      "To vary the *Punch*"—*NYT,* Nov. 25, 1925.
      "unspeakably happy"—LeG to JNLeG, Dec. 31, 1925.
      "the fact of not being"—Civic Rep ms.

137   "Having to make you"—LeG to Merc, March 1, 1926.
      "face all those devils"—LeG to JNLeG, Nov. 14, 1925.
      "agony"—LeG to JNLeG, Dec. 17, 1925.

138   "One of America's"—ZITS clipping, Dec. 19, 1925.
      "small backlog"—Civic Rep ms.

140   "To Mr. Kahn"—Ibid.
      "There is no one"—LeG to JNLeG, April 12, 1926.
      "spurs in an individual"—LeG to May Sarton, Aug. 4, 1933.

141   "I could not"—*AT,* 198.
      "using one set"—Civic Rep ms.
      "It must be remembered"—Ibid.

142   "She loved Le Gallienne"—Author interview with Efrem Zimbalist Jr.
      "fanatic singleness"—Civic Rep ms.
      "Certainly I am not"—*Brooklyn Times,* Nov. 21, 1926.

143   "terribly excited"—LeG to JNLeG, June 25, 1926.

144   "like a shorn lamb"—LeG to JNLeG, July 31, 1926.
      "the most elegant"—Civic Rep ms.
      "the chief performer"—Ibid.

145   "the stage was magnificent"—Ibid.
      "A sense of tradition"—Ibid.
      "Tout sera"—*AT,* 199.

146   "I have found"—Alexander Woollcott, "The Great Camera Mysteries," *New Yorker,* Nov. 12, 1927, 34–36.
      "You would laugh"—LeG to JNLeG, Aug. 17, 1926.

148   "You can *always*"—LeG to JNLeG, Sept. 19, 1926.
      "Groups that have"—Author interview with LeG.
      "The weather was perfect"—Civic Rep ms.
      "seemingly so formless"—LeG, "The Art Which Conceals Art: Some Notes on the Chekhovian Actor," Hartford Stage Company *Playbill,* October 1968.

149   "I felt as though"—Civic Rep ms.

"dingy and arty"—Ibid.

"he finally goes"—Prompt book of *Saturday Night.*

150   "the usual Broadway"—Civic Rep ms.

"it was more frightful"—Cole Lesley, *Remembered Laughter,* 101.

"That is one," "we all felt"—Civic Rep ms.

"There is no evidence"—*Christian Science Monitor,* Nov. 2, 1926.

151   "communicate a vision"—May Sarton, "The Genius of Eva Le Gallienne: Acting as a Criticism of Life," *Forum* 11 (Summer–Fall 1973), 44.

"Masha is sitting"—Ibid., 48.

"Well—the worst"—LeG to JNLeG, Oct. 30, 1926.

152   "He was"—*AT,* 206.

"All afternoon"—*AT,* 210.

"It was as if"—Paul Cooper, "Eva Le Gallienne's Civic Repertory Theatre," 70.

"Eva was really"—Author interview with Rose Hobart.

"Setting a scene"—Paul Cooper, 72.

"Looking at the play"—Civic Rep ms.

154   "the Italian school"—*WAQH,* 49.

"Come on"—Author interview with JH.

155   "a nice little play"—Ibid.

"This girl"—LeG to JNLeG, Dec. 14, 1926.

"I asked her"—Author interview with Katharine Hepburn.

"It was quite tough"—Author interview with JH.

"Eva had a rare"—Ibid.

"some actors must"—Civic Rep ms.

156   "God save me"—LeG to JNLeG, Dec. 14, 1926.

"Miss Le Gallienne Presents"—*New York Sun,* Dec. 1926.

"On Tuesday"—LeG to JNLeG, Jan. 9, 1927.

"dreary and mawkish"—Civic Rep ms.

158   "if ever I had"—LeG to JNLeG, Jan. 18, 1927.

"How could I"—Civic Rep ms.

"into a Liliom-like"—LeG to JNLeG, Jan. 26, 1927.

"Amused young couples"—Beatrice Blackmar, "Repertory Makes a Hit Among Shades of the Past," *World,* Jan. 9, 1927.

159   "a couple of bricks"—LeG to JNLeG, Jan. 18, 1927.

"The public is ready"—*NYT,* Feb. 8, 1927.

"It ended"—LeG to JNLeG, Feb. 8, 1927.

160   "It is always off Broadway"—*Stage Journal,* Nov. 7, 1926.

"I regard the establishment"—*Billboard,* Oct. 30, 1926.

"low comedian"—Brooks Atkinson, *Broadway,* 159.

"George, George"—*Sunday Theatre Review,* Feb. 26, 1927.

161   "living example"—*San Jose Mercury Herald,* Jan. 7, 1928.

"The ladies"—*New York Telegram,* Dec. 19, 1926.

"is a burning"—*AT,* 205.

"the greatest"—LeG, "My Adventures in Repertory," *Theatre,* April 1927.

162   "a quiet, very shy"—Civic Rep ms.

162   "young, keen"—*New York Herald Tribune,* March 8, 1927.

         "Here I am"—Civic Rep ms.

         "it is all"—LeG to JNLeG, April 4, 1927.

         "day & night"—LeG to JNLeG, April 9, 1927.

163   "The house was *packed*"—LeG to JNLeG, May 8, 1927.

         "the strongest, most charismatic"—Author interview with JH.

164   "natural"—Ibid.

165   "We recall"—*Boston Herald,* June 1, 1927.

         "I have no"—Civic Rep ms.

         "You know I *loathe*"—LeG to JNLeG, April 4, 1927.

         "How monstrous"—*AT,* 211.

         "I doubt"—*AT,* 212.

         "I remember Isadora"—*Mystic,* 151.

166   "filling herself up again"—Le Gallienne often used the image of a vase to describe the soul.

         "the steepest part"—Civic Rep ms.

         "one of those rare"—Ibid.

         "Eva wanted audiences"—Author interview with JH.

         "was able to get"—LeG to JNLeG, Aug. 18, 1927.

         "When Mam arrived"—Author interview with JH.

167   "I tell you"—Ibid.

         "the most sensitive"—JNLeG to MN, April 15, 1928.

168   "In my speech"—*AT,* 220.

         "that this fine"—*Equal Rights* 14, no. 37, Oct. 22, 1927.

         "I really do love"—LeG to JNLeG, Jan. 20, 1928.

         "She admired it"—Civic Rep ms.

169   "When anything was"—Ibid.

         "crossed rapiers"—*NYT,* March 10, 1928.

         "being very obnoxious"—Author interview with JH.

         "We are living apart"—*New York Evening Post,* Feb. 28, 1928.

170   "I have worked"—Ibid.

         "You are wrong"—Miguel Covarrubias, "The Theatre Reviewed by Hearsay," *Vanity Fair,* May 1928.

         "I knew she was queer"—Author interview with Katharine Hepburn.

         "there were a lot"—Author interview with JH.

171   "Just a word"—LeG to JNLeG, March 21, 1928.

         "stiffly and somewhat"—LeG, "Grim Ibsen Triumphs at His Centenary," *NYT Magazine,* March 18, 1928.

         "It's strange how"—LeG to JNLeG, March 21, 1928.

         "There seems to be"—Eva Le Gallienne, *Hedda Gabler* Preface, 7.

         "take the leap"—LeG to JNLeG, March 7, 1928.

         "It was your"—Yvonne Shafer, "Acting in Ibsen: An Interview with Eva Le Gallienne," *Ibsen News and Comment,* November 2, 1981, 14.

172   "clinging gown"—*Boston Herald,* May 25, 1928.

         "ill-bred dope fiend"—Civic Rep ms.

         "It took me"—Civic Rep ms.

173   "rocks the manuscript"—LeG, *Hedda*, 47.

"When she said"—Author interview with Robert Lewis.

"truth, pace"—Civic Rep ms.

"Try to imagine"—LeG, *Hedda*, 61.

"harassed and hurried"—"On Critics," BR.

175   "Miss Le Gallienne seems"—*Boston Herald*, May 25, 1928.

"She evokes"—Ibid.

176   "I want to"—Civic Rep ms.

"I have missed"—LeG to Alla Nazimova, May 29, 1928.

"I don't know"—Ibid.

"thrilled about Alla"—LeG to JNLeG, May 9, 1928.

"thought my work"—LeG to JNLeG, April 16, 1928.

"surely [Gladys]"—LeG to JNLeG, May 9, 1928.

"Don't worry about"—LeG to JNLeG, June 24, 1928.

177   "Once, we came home"—Author interview with JH.

"little place"—LeG to Nazimova, May 29, 1928.

"one of the venturesome"—Thomas Farnham, *Weston: The Forging of a Connecticut Town*, 210.

"There can't be"—Author interview with TL.

"three old sisters"—Hubbard H. Cobb, "The Best of Times," *Connecticut*, August 1987, 157.

178   "We are so happy"—LeG to JNLeG, July 11, 1928.

"heavenly deserted pool"—LeG to JNLeG, July 18, 1928.

"Such a time"—LeG to JNLeG, Oct. 16, 1928.

179   "My idea"—*AT*, 222.

"sense their inner"—*AT*, 223.

180   "stinking lair"—Carole Klein, *Aline*, 201–202.

"only concerned"—Ibid., 204.

"She'd be standing"—Ibid., 255–256.

181   "some of the prettiest"—Percy Hammond review, n.i., n.d.

"really outstanding failures"—*AT*, 213.

"Alla was an entirely"—Author interview with JH.

"indefatigable in her"—*AT*, 221.

182   "and woe"—*WAQH*, 229.

"what goes on"—*WAQH*, 231.

"the most beautiful"—Author interview with Robert Lewis.

"That chaise-longue"—*WAQH*, 232.

"Whenever I read"—*WAQH*, 230.

184   "although her features"—Irene Sharaff, *Broadway and Hollywood*, 13.

"For actors to play"—Author interview with JH.

"It was a thrilling"—LeG to JNLeG, Oct. 25, 1928.

"In a limpid"—*NYT*, Nov. 18, 1928.

"Now we are off"—LeG to JNLeG, Oct. 25, 1928.

185   "She was very polite"—"Peter Pan," BR.

"not coy or cute"—Ibid.

"No actress since"—Robert Lewis, *Slings and Arrows*, 31.

185   "was real fairy-tale"—Author interview with Norman Lloyd.

        "never talked down"—Stewart Stern, unpublished notes.

186   "None of us"—*AT,* 216–217.

187   "business at the theatre"—LeG to JNLeG, Dec. 22, 1928.

        "Those grand old"—Ms. of speech, Nov. 18, 1928.

188   "any sailor's"—George Jean Nathan, *American Mercury* 13 (March 1928): 377–378.

        "It is a cold"—LeG to JNLeG, Dec. 31, 1928.

        "Brilliant Dramatic"—*New York Herald Tribune,* Jan. 8, 1929.

189   "I hate *Katerina*"—LeG to JNLeG, Feb. 17, 1929.

        "magnificent performance"—LeG to JNLeG, Feb. 28, 1929.

        "could produce"—LeG to JNLeG, March 26, 1929.

        "Eva Le Gallienne's Civic"—Author interview with JH.

        "kept accusing me"—LeG to JNLeG, May 27, 1929.

190   "they are simply"—LeG to JNLeG, July 1929.

        "the students far"—*AT,* 224.

        "seemed so alive"—LeG to George Sarton, Dec. 11, 1928.

191   "For what I had felt"—May Sarton, *I Knew a Phoenix,* 150–151.

        "Yes, you come"—Author interview with Burgess Meredith.

        "With us there"—Paul Cooper, 123.

192   "The bits I acted"—Author interview with Robert Lewis.

        "Now the theatre"—Sarton, *Phoenix,* 157.

        "Just as in painting"—*AT,* 224.

        "evening of torture"—DI, Sept. 16, 1929.

        "at last the full"—*Commonweal,* Oct. 2, 1929, 564.

        "When the curtain rises"—Brooks Atkinson, *NYT,* Sept. 17, 1929.

194   "likely to spoil"—Brooks Atkinson, "Art in Fourteenth Street," *NYT,* Dec. 15, 1929.

        "I haven't been"—LeG to JNLeG, March 2, 1930.

        "galvanic founder-directrix"—*NYT,* Nov. 25, 1929.

        "I wanted our"—*AT,* 225.

195   "Ribalious sobjects"—Lewis, *Slings,* 28.

        "Poor sweet"—LeG to JNLeG, March 2, 1930.

196   "the most damnable"—LeG to JNLeG, March 31, 1930.

        "No such chorus"—*Literary Digest,* May 10, 1930.

        "Miss Le Gallienne seems"—*Commonweal,* May 14, 1930.

        "The finest"—*NYT,* April 22, 1930.

        "concentration was"—Author interview with Stella Moss.

        "Now everyone"—LeG to JNLeG, April 1930.

        "sort of coma"—LeG to JNLeG, June 12, 1930.

198   "I am afraid"—LeG to JNLeG, May 26, 1930.

        "might as well"—LeG to JNLeG, June 21, 1930.

        "extreme cruelty"—Complaint filed July 7, 1930, by Josephine Bell, Plaintiff, vs. Robert Bell, Defendant, in the Second Judicial District Court of the State of Nevada.

        "Bell Divorces"—*New York Daily News,* July 8, 1930.

        "I don't remember"—Author interview with Robert Lewis.

199   "simply loved"—Lillian Faderman, *Odd Girls and Twilight Lovers,* 61.

        "If you hear"—LeG to JNLeG, July 20, 1930.

"lovely silver"—LeG to JNLeG, July 28, 1930.

"the beastliest"—LeG to JNLeG, Sept. 1, 1930.

"Just imagine"—LeG to JNLeG, Sept. 1930.

200   "Bad days"—LeG to JNLeG, Nov. 18, 1930.

"He really isn't"—LeG to JNLeG, Dec. 1930.

"flattering offer"—LeG to JNLeG, Nov. 1930.

"talky and dull"—*AT,* 230.

"with its growing"—Ibid.

"Also, the Civic"—Author interview with JH.

201   "it is very strenuous"—LeG to JNLeG, Nov. 18, 1930.

"looked at you"—Author interview with Norman Lloyd.

"Put me down"—Helen Boylston, *Carol Goes Backstage,* 140, and author interview with May Sarton.

"astonishing vitality"—May Sarton, *I Knew a Phoenix,* 159.

"which Marguerite"—"Deaths," BR.

"a majestic radiance"—*Brooklyn Standard,* Jan. 27, 1931.

"It was her own"—*New York American,* Jan. 27, 1931.

202   "If you see"—*NYT,* Feb. 15, 1931.

"I have decided"—LeG to JNLeG, March 1, 1931.

"splendid psychology"—Ibid.

"something never"—*WAQH,* 22.

"It seemed to prove"—LeG to JNLeG, May 15, 1931.

206   "deafening explosion"—*WAQH,* 4.

"tearing her clothes off"—Author interview with JH.

"I remember"—*WAQH,* 4.

"long bloody strips"—Ibid.

"I regained consciousness"—*WAQH,* 5.

"as if she were"—Author interview with JH.

"Famous Actress"—*WAQH,* 4.

207   "on the threshold"—*AT,* 236.

PART FOUR: 1931 – 1942

211   "Actors should be free"—1934 Los Angeles newspaper clipping, n.i., n.d.

"It's all right"—*WAQH,* 6.

"not to worry"—*WAQH,* 7.

"all the agonies"—*WAQH,* 8.

"it has all"—LeG to JNLeG, June 30, 1931.

"a very ugly"—*WAQH,* 9.

212   "Thinking of you"—LeG to JNLeG, July 25, 1931.

"The smells"—*WAQH,* 24.

213   "Fortunately, Spain"—*WAQH,* 28.

"yes, my God"—LeG to JNLeG, Oct. 16, 1931.

"strange fairy-tale"—LeG notebook.

"Before the fire"—Author interview with JH.

213   "a smattering of"—*WAQH,* 38.

        "honest art"—*WAQH,* 39.

214   "indulging a mad"—Ibid.

        "tiresome never"—LeG to JNLeG, Nov. 12, 1931.

        "She was always"—Author interview with JH.

        "were in the presence"—*WAQH,* 285.

        "She was terribly"—Author interview with JH.

        "strange man"—ms. of *WAQH.*

        "was quite a"—*WAQH,* 42.

        "I wandered about"—May Sarton, *I Knew a Phoenix,* 163.

        "She was recovering"—Author interview with May Sarton.

215   "professional response"—Sarton, *Phoenix,* 176.

        "I did not quite"—Irene Sharaff, *Broadway and Hollywood,* 18.

        "So I suppose"—LeG to JNLeG, Dec. 12, 1931.

216   "She was a doer"—Author interview with JH.

        "who suddenly has"—LeG to JNLeG, March 4, 1932.

        "Just a good"—LeG to JNLeG, Feb. 1932.

        "We take what"—Civic Rep ms.

217   "it had all gone"—LeG to JNLeG, May 21, 1932.

218   "good to have"—LeG to JNLeG, Oct. 5, 1932.

        "I had forgotten"—LeG to JNLeG, Oct. 27, 1932.

        "no one ever"—Author interview with Norman Lloyd.

        "grown-up part!," "I am bearing up"—JH to JNLeG, June 4, 1932.

219   "The apprentices knew"—Paul Ballantyne to author, March 29, 1991.

220   "through synchronization"—LeG and Florida Friebus, *Alice in Wonderland* (New York: Samuel French, 1932), Foreword.

        "compromise almost more"—*AT,* 247.

        "I was on"—Author interview with Burgess Meredith.

        "standards were set"—Author interview with Norman Lloyd.

222   "Renaissance woman"—Author interview with Robert Lewis.

        "It's immensely sad"—"Economic Stress Forces Eva Le Gallienne to Move *Alice* Uptown," *New York Telegram,* Jan. 2, 1933.

        "Canned vegetables"—*AT,* 250.

        "is from within"—*AT,* 251.

        "can and will"—*AT,* 249–250.

        "achieve the thing"—*AT,* 255.

223   "quite worn out"—LeG to JNLeG, June 1933.

        "only bilgewater"—Margo Peters, *The House of Barrymore,* 346.

        "consummate ass"—LeG to JNLeG, July 5, 1933.

        "She has intense"—Elizabeth Borton, "Eva Le Gallienne Discusses Future of the Theatre," *Boston Herald,* Oct. 22, 1933.

224   "You needn't remind"—LeG to JNLeG, Aug. 15, 1933.

        "theatrical phenomenon"—Tad Mosel and Gertrude Macy, *Leading Lady: The World and Theatre of Katharine Cornell,* 291.

        "Eva had enormous"—Author interview with JH.

        "We stayed"—Ibid.

225   "Here I am"—*Washington Post* clipping, n.d.

"was extremely nervous"—*WAQH,* 61.

"comprehensive enough"—*WAQH,* 62.

"hard and ruthless"—*WAQH,* 63.

226   "Dear Miss Le Gallienne"—Ibid.

"after all, was"—*WAQH,* 64.

"at first I got"—*WAQH,* 65–66.

"return to work"—*WAQH,* 67.

227   "double identity"—Joanne Bentley, *Hallie Flanagan,* 342.

"crushing disappointment"—*WAQH,* 69.

"If you knew"—"Ethel Barrymore Takes Up Sword for Le Gallienne To Assail Lecture Audience" and "Audience Assailed by Ethel Barrymore," *American* and *Sentinel,* Dec. 2, 1933.

228   "completely justified"—Ibid.

"pulling an Eva"—*Variety,* May 22, 1934.

"How do I turn"—Newspaper clipping, n.i., 1934.

"You may have difficulty"—"Polly Prospect Marvels at Magnetism of Eva Le Gallienne," *Milwaukee News,* Jan. 9, 1934.

"relieved at getting"—LeG to JNLeG, Jan. 27, 1934.

229   "poor lot"—"Official Report on the Le Gallienne Fracas in Philadelphia, Minneapolis and Oakland," *Dallas Morning News,* March 27, 1934.

"I feel so utterly"—DI, Feb. 7, 1934.

"Eva was not"—Author interview with JH.

"The American theatre"—C. G. Poore, *NYT Book Review,* Jan. 7, 1934.

"Immortal Eva"—*Saturday Review of Literature,* Jan. 13, 1934.

"open letter"—Paul Romaine, "To Eva Le Gallienne—At 33," *New Theatre,* June 1, 1934.

230   "A nice creature"—DI, Feb. 15, 1934.

"The news came"—Author interview with JH.

"Went to Warner"—DI, March 15, 1934.

"bending an audience"—*Milwaukee News,* Jan. 8, 1934.

231   "behaving as if"—LeG to JNLeG, March 7, 1934.

"Arrived in El Paso"—DI, March 21, 1934.

"The berths were"—Author interview with JH.

"Marion was very"—Ibid.

232   "sloppy and inartistic"—quoted in *New York Telegram,* May 17, 1934.

"just as I"—Author interview with JH.

"I know I've"—LeG to JNLeG, May 10, 1934.

"a very nice"—LeG to JNLeG, May 31, 1934.

"strangely lost"—*WAQH,* 74.

"For once"—*WAQH,* 75.

233   "What she needs"—LeG to JNLeG, Sept. 9, 1934.

"if the worst"—LeG, *The Wild Duck,* 407.

"the agony of despair"—*WAQH,* 77–78.

"I am getting"—LeG to JNLeG, Oct. 1934.

"Father's feeling awfully"—John Mason Brown, *Two on the Aisle,* 83.

234   "The warmth"—*WAQH,* 79.

234 "moved to unabashed"—*NYT,* Oct. 18, 1934.

"The minute I"—Author interview with JH.

"The long run"—*WAQH,* 80.

236 "There is no doubt"—LeG to JNLeG, Feb. 1935.

"not merely because"—"Hamlet-Baiting Critic Urges Le Gallienne to Tackle Prince of Princes," *Chicago American,* Feb. 11, 1935, 12.

"beyond words"—LeG to JNLeG, April 24, 1935.

237 "keep on and not lose"—quoted in LeG to JNLeG, April 24, 1935.

"Eva and Alla"—Author interview with JH.

"So I am"—LeG to JNLeG, Aug. 12, 1935.

"dear Gunnar"—LeG to JNLeG, July 22, 1935.

"as cunning as Becky"—LeG, *Six Plays,* xxiii.

238 "every penny"—*WAQH,* 87.

"The greatest harm"—LeG to JNLeG, Dec. 9, 1935.

239 "the sharp focusing"—*WAQH,* 90.

240 "was the dreadful"—*WAQH,* 88.

"nice, new enamelled"—LeG to JNLeG, March 19, 1936.

242 "So it seems"—LeG notebook.

"This isn't a bit"—LeG to JNLeG, Aug. 19, 1939.

244 "filth covered"—LeG to JNLeG, June 21, 1936.

"shed the shrouds"—*Variety,* June 1936.

"To think I should"—LeG to JNLeG, Oct. 11, 1936.

"The lack of dignity"—LeG to JNLeG, Nov. 20, 1936.

"In shame we bow"—*WAQH,* 100.

"incredible nightmare"—LeG to JNLeG, Nov. 23, 1936.

245 "taking care of Eva"—ME to JNLeG, Nov. 13, 1936.

"couldn't afford"—LeG to JNLeG, July 1937.

"a tall, rather gawky"—*WAQH,* 110.

"She started drilling"—Susan Spector, "Preparation for an Audition: Uta Hagen's Broadway Debut," *Theatre Survey* 30 (May–November 1989), 112.

"a real talent"—*WAQH,* 110.

"thumping wildly"—Uta Hagen, *Sources: A Memoir,* 89.

246 "At 18"—Elliott Norton, "Le Gallienne Hamlet," *Boston Sunday Post,* 25.

"for an actress"—*WAQH,* 106.

247 "the sacred fire"—*WAQH,* 113.

"What happened?"—*WAQH,* 114.

"In the Le Gallienne"—E. B. Potter to author, July 4, 1992.

"For the first time"—*WAQH,* 114.

248 "I can't go on"—E. B. Potter diary, Oct. 17, 1937.

"Of all the goddamned"—Ibid.

249 "The child Uta"—*WAQH,* 118.

"longed for the joy"—DI, Oct. 30, 1937. (Le Gallienne had just seen Pepi Schildkraut as Captain Dreyfus playing opposite the Zola of Paul Muni in *The Life of Emile Zola.* Egon Brecher had a tiny part in the movie as well.)

"I am free!"—DI, Nov. 1, 1937.

250 "drift for awhile"—DI, Oct. 30, 1937.

"remarkably young" —DI, Nov. 2, 1937.

"every comedy face"—DI, Nov. 4, 1937.

"there can be"—DI, Nov. 6, 1937.

"covered a multitude"—DI, Nov. 18, 1937.

251 "It is cleverly"—DI, Nov. 6, 1937.

"She has a lot"—DI, Oct. 29, 1937.

"No use comparing"—DI, Jan. 8, 1938.

252 "social history"—*WAQH,* 142.

"was a pleasant"—DI, Jan. 11, 1938.

"Youth does not see"—LeG to MN, Feb. 7, 1938.

"an austere and solitary"—*WAQH,* 145.

"a long time"—*WAQH,* 146.

"were too many"—DI, Feb. 19, 1938.

"I should think"—*WAQH,* 148.

253 "like a phrase"—*WAQH,* 150.

"There was a feeling"—*WAQH,* 160.

"Today seven years"—LeG to JNLeG, June 12, 1938.

"eggs, vegetables"—ME to JNLeG, Aug. 8, 1938.

"the theatre seems"—LeG to JNLeG, Aug. 28, 1938.

254 "until his voice"—*WAQH,* 162.

"bandwagon elite"—*WAQH,* 164.

"court calendar drama"—*NYT,* Oct. 26, 1938.

"Producing a play"—*WAQH,* 167.

"It looks so awful"—LeG to JNLeG, Sept. 17, 1939.

255 "It made me"—DI, July 12, 1939.

"Where—when"—DI, Nov. 22, 1939.

"lovely old"—DI, Jan. 8, 1940.

256 "unbelievable"—DI, Nov. 18, 1939.

"This nigger"—DI, Nov. 28, 1939.

"incredibly tall"—DI, Dec. 6, 1939.

257 "false phony atmosphere"—DI, Dec. 13, 1939.

"What do they think"—DI, Feb. 7, 1940.

"What a cure"—DI, Dec. 27, 1939.

"I did that"—Author interview with JH.

258 "very gamy"—George Jean Nathan, *Encyclopaedia of the Theatre,* 231.

"inner warm"—Ibid., 167.

"People hate"—LeG to May Sarton, Jan. 29, 1934.

"Those of us"—Draft of speech, "The Importance of Theatre in Our Cultural Life."

259 "You have to pit"—DI, Oct. 24, 1940.

"catch them young"—*WAQH,* 202.

"Had she said"—*Atlantic City Press,* Dec. 3, 1940.

"How I hate"—DI, Jan. 10, 1941.

"really brilliant"—DI, Feb. 11, 1941.

"Twenty years ago"—DI, March 22, 1941.

260 "a beautiful time"—LeG to JNLeG, July 2, 1941.

"Don't worry"—LeG to JNLeG, June 27, 1941.

262   "only love"—ME to LeG, Jan. 5, 1942.
       "I want to say"—Ibid.
       "was a joy"—LeG to JNLeG, Aug. 13, 1941.
       "a little distance"—ME to JNLeG, Aug. 12, 1941.
263   "with their bold"—*WAQH,* 209.
       "If only I"—DI, Jan. 20, 1942.
264   "must sometimes be"—DI, Jan. 21, 1942.
       "refreshed & strengthened"—DI, Jan. 22, 1942.
       "What will it all"—DI, Jan. 23, 1942.
       "Feel broken hearted"—JNLeG diary, Feb. 11, 1942.
       "Knowing the soundness"—*WAQH,* 219.
265   "When I was able"—DI, Feb. 24, 1942.
       "secret inner life"—Helen Ormsbee, "Her First Role in a Thriller," *New York Herald
          Tribune,* June 21, 1942.
       "Whatever she said"—Author interview with Karl Malden.
266   "wishing that it were"—DI, April 22, 1942.
       "The play went"—DI, May 20, 1942.
       "maddening and bitterly"—DI, May 21, 1942.
       "carefully detailed"—*New York Daily News,* May 21, 1942.
267   "Miss Le Gallienne, please"—Author interview with Earle Hyman.
       "is that they're"—Ibid.
268   "to control her"—*WAQH,* 219.
       "with old-world"—*WAQH,* 222.
       "in those blue"—Ibid.
       "dreadfully difficult"—*WAQH,* 223.
269   "I felt mother"—*WAQH,* 225.

PART FIVE: 1943 – 1952

273   "The externals of"—DI, Sept. 16, 1945.
       "She loved me"—Author interview with Madeleine L'Engle.
       "the honest blue"—L'Engle, *Two-Part Invention,* 30.
274   "the artist is not"—Ibid., 17.
       "poor, stormy"—Jay Carmody, *Evening Star,* Nov. 16, 1943.
       "One would really"—DI, Nov. 2, 1943.
       "glowing and seductive"—Margaret Webster, *Don't Put Your Daughter on the Stage,* 135.
       "unfold with effortless"—LeG, HSC *Seagull* Playbill.
275   "fascinating labor"—Webster, *Don't,* 136.
       "so radiantly assured"—"The Fruit Is Sweet," *New York Herald Tribune,* Jan. 26, 1944.
       "one of the most"—Webster, *Don't,* 134.
276   "After the performance"—L'Engle, *Two-Part Invention,* 50.
277   "If the inhabitants"—Webster, *Don't,* 140.
       "intrigued by the"—Ibid., 119.
278   "damnable"—DI, Jan. 25, 1945.
       "the Black Hole"—DI, Feb. 27, 1945.

"How good she"—DI, March 4, 1945.
"She's not Norsk"—DI, Feb. 19, 1946.
"Thank God"—DI, Jan. 27, 1946.
"I wish to God"—DI, April 26, 1945.

279 "so lonely & weary"—DI, April 18, 1945.
"wasn't playing well"—DI, April 16, 1945.
"feeling so light-hearted"—DI, May 9, 1945.
"I guess"—DI, July 2, 1945.
"Can I still"—DI, Aug. 11, 1945.
"At eighty she"—*WAQH,* 245.

281 "board meetings"—DI, Oct. 14, 1945.
"came poor thing"—DI, Sept. 11, 1953.

282 "She was tremendously"—Author interview with May Sarton.
"superior being"—DI, June 9, 1946.
"peculiar intermediate"—DI, April 11, 1948.
"inevitable that the"—DI, Jan. 30, 1946.
"a show which"—Webster, *Don't,* 152.
"unpopular word"—*WAQH,* 263.

283 "I'm scared of"—DI, Nov. 25, 1945.
"from Iceland"—Webster, *Don't,* 154.
"Wonderful parts!"—Cheryl Crawford, *One Naked Individual,* 151.
"Hollywood contracts"—*WAQH,* 254.
"That would be"—DI, Oct. 1, 1945.
"She herself is"—DI, Feb. 25, 1945.
"didn't want to"—*WAQH,* 253.
"want to work for"—DI, July 18, 1950.

284 "spark of true"—*WAQH,* 255.
"electrified by"—*WAQH,* 254.
"It was impossible"—*WAQH,* 255.
"dirty socks"—*WAQH,* 256.
"a sausage concoction"—Webster, *Don't,* 156.
"machinery of show business"—*WAQH,* 255.

285 "Still no American"—Webster, *Don't,* 156.
"Gielgud was"—DI, Sept. 7, 1947.
"delightful week-end"—John Gielgud to author, May 15, 1993.
"team plays"—Webster, *Don't,* 157.
"extremely tiresome"—DI, April 11, 1946.
"As usual when"—DI, Feb. 19, 1946.
"of how I've"—DI, Dec. 2, 1945.
"hopeless situation"—DI, April 28, 1946.

286 "We were together"—DI, March 4, 1946.
"If only that"—DI, March 8, 1946.
"Enchanted hours"—DI, March 9, 1946.

287 "If we want"—*WAQH,* 260.

288 "nonexistent work"—Webster, *Don't,* 165–166.
"It just seems"—DI, Aug. 15, 1946.

288   "in any way"—DI, Aug. 20, 1946.
289   "the old lion"—DI, Aug. 21, 1946.
       "to make them"—DI, Aug. 23, 1946.
       "violently disagreeable"—DI, Aug. 29, 1946.
       "Her direction"—Webster, *Don't,* 160.
       "Peggy had this"—Author interview with Efrem Zimbalist Jr.
       "so happy"—DI, Sept. 8, 1946.
       "brilliant group"—*NYT,* Nov. 17, 1946.
290   "It was"—DI, Nov. 17, 1946.
291   "What's the use"—DI, March 6, 1947.
       "I'm glad she"—DI, Dec. 18, 1946.
       "ask Joe Reed"—DI, Dec. 12, 1946.
       "I've never seen"—DI, Jan. 1, 1947.
       "went marvellously"—DI, Jan. 18, 1947.
292   "I treasured"—Author interview with Eli Wallach.
       "Miss Le Gallienne"—Author interview with Julie Harris.
       "she certainly made"—DI, March 22, 1947.
293   "It's stupid"—DI, May 28, 1947.
       "Le Gallienne had"—Author interview with Efrem Zimbalist Jr.
294   "The whole business"—DI, May 2, 1947.
       "intelligent & full"—DI, Dec. 4, 1939.
       "shrouded their"—*WAQH,* 282.
295   "wandering up and down"—*Quest,* 548–549.
       "I think Eva"—HLeG to MN, Nov. 7, 1954.
       "wonderful 'notices' "—DI, Sept. 16, 1947.
       "the worst attack"—DI, Sept. 25, 1947.
297   "Like truth"—George Jean Nathan, *Theatre Book of the Year,* 275.
298   "Life has gone"—LeG to May Sarton, March 21, 1948.
       "I feel utterly"—DI, March 21, 1948.
       "I'm a good one"—DI, March 28, 1948.
       "with enclosure"—DI, April 30, 1948.
       "Mary had a list"—Author interview with Efrem Zimbalist Jr.
       "Life begins"—DI, Nov. 8, 1940.
299   "the poor little"—DI, May 22, 1948. There are no direct correspondences in *Flossie and Bossie* between real people and the characters—elements of Le Gallienne are in them, and there are echoes of Julie, Nanny, Ethel Barrymore, and Constance Collier. Eva certainly resembled the autocratic, selfish Bossie more than the sweet, kind Flossie, who suggests Mimsey or Peggy. At the end of the story, the two chicks of Bossie and Flossie—named Blackie and Whitie (none of the reviews mentioned the racial symbolism)—marry. The couple rule the barnyard equally, which prompts an old hen to remark, "The age of miracles has come!"
       "felt very foolishly"—DI, July 11, 1948.
       "ran in conventional"—DI, Nov. 7, 1948.
       "was grumpy"—DI, May 29, 1948.
       "vanity and selfishness"—DI, July 11, 1948.
       "my only and"—LeG, *Flossie and Bossie,* dedication.

"Even if"—DI, April 8, 1949.

"Subtly intended"—*Birmingham Mail,* Nov. 15, 1950.

300 "the same old"—DI, July 27, 1948.

301 "It occurred to"—*WAQH,* 291.

"Thank God we"—DI, Sept. 24, 1948.

"On my trip"—DI, Sept. 25, 1948.

302 "She took it"—DI, Sept. 27, 1948.

"being awfully sweet"—DI, Oct. 1, 1948.

"the usual stream"—DI, Nov. 21, 1948.

303 "Everything looked"—DI, Dec. 18, 1948.

"It was the best"—DI, Dec. 24, 1948.

"It doesn't seem"—DI, Jan. 11, 1949.

"folksy act"—DI, Feb. 2, 1949.

"was the only"—DI, Feb. 9, 1949.

"We had a"—DI, Feb. 16, 1949.

304 "on the horrors"—DI, March 5, 1949.

"very small flask"—DI, March 10, 1949.

305 "I've been so"—DI, April 6, 1949.

"it will last"—DI, May 7, 1949.

306 "then Peg & I"—DI, June 23, 1949.

"very subdued"—DI, June 26, 1949.

307 "Stifled by heat"—Robin Prising, *Manila, Goodbye,* 197.

"Do you read"—LeG to Robin Prising, May 6, 1949.

"giving him the best"—DI, July 12, 1949.

"She wanted me"—Robin Prising to author, March 27, 1993.

308 "some good strenuous"—DI, July 19, 1949.

"staggered"—DI, July 22, 1949.

"If I were"—Author interview with Robin Prising.

"How they get"—DI, Aug. 21, 1949.

"voyage of discovery"—DI, July 28, 1949.

"At the moment"—DI, Sept. 16, 1949.

309 "my heart"—DI, Oct. 9, 1949.

"How I wish"—DI, Oct. 26, 1949.

"all is settled"—DI, Nov. 7, 1949.

"What a weak"—DI, Nov. 9, 1949.

"I surely should"—DI, Dec. 18, 1949.

310 "By dint"—DI, Jan. 4, 1950.

"not to let"—DI, Jan. 11, 1950.

"Miss Le Gallienne is"—*Daily Compass,* Jan. 12, 1950.

"in some back"—DI, Feb. 6, 1950.

"I don't deserve"—DI, Feb. 8, 1950.

"I'm sure that"—DI, Feb. 12, 1950.

311 "class act"—DI, March 12, 1951.

"do some constructive"—DI, Dec. 31, 1950.

"Men are so"—DI, June 2, 1950.

312 "the very existence"—Helen Sheehy, *Margo: The Life and Theatre of Margo Jones,* 246.

312 "Why should she"—DI, Feb. 18, 1950.
"awful episode"—DI, Aug. 4, 1950.
"physical, mental"—DI, May 24, 1951.

313 "small prayer"—DI, April 27, 1951.
"listened magnificently"—DI, Feb. 4, 1951.
"looked after me"—DI, Feb. 24, 1951.
"certainly prepared"—DI, May 28, 1949.
"always full of"—LeG to MN, Aug. 30, 1976.

314 "I have been"—*WAQH,* 302.
"depressing note"—DI, Nov. 19, 1951.
"When I started"—*WAQH,* 297.

315 "now greater"—*WAQH,* 301.
"jeezly ecclesiastical"—DI, March 26, 1951.
"flower-like"—*NYT Book Review,* April 26, 1953.
"contempt for the"—*WAQH,* 299.

316 "it would be *Life*"—DI, Nov. 4, 1949.
"her integrity was"—DI, April 22, 1951.
"known reliability"—FBI report on Margaret Webster, April 9, 1951, NY File No. 100-99747.

317 "Times were getting"—Webster, *Don't,* 261.
"her darling Mutki"—LeG to ME, March 16, 1952.
"It is certainly"—LeG to ME, March 14, 1952.
"official visit"—LeG to ME, March 16, 1952.
"One shouldn't tear"—DI, July 9, 1950.

318 "Quite a large"—DI, April, 21, 1952.
"the infinite joy"—LeG to MN, June 21, 1952.
"evening passed"—Mercedes de Acosta, *Here Lies the Heart,* 350.
"was far from"—DI, Aug. 2, 1952.

319 "I am *home*"—Ibid.

PART SIX: 1952 – 1971

323 "America seems to be"—DI, Nov. 29, 1956.
"To play in trash"—LeG to MN, Nov. 27, 1952.
"quiet, frail"—DI, Aug. 19, 1952.
"wickedly arrogant"—DI, Feb. 6, 1952.
"one should preserve"—DI, Aug. 9, 1952.
"those idiots"—DI, July 10, 1954.

324 "I'm afraid"—DI, Aug. 2, 1952.
"not be billed"—DI, Feb. 22, 1953.
"we are so completely"—DI, April 12, 1953.
"He still hasn't"—DI, March 26, 1953.
"thin as a rail"—DI, March 27, 1953.

325 "with all the McCarthyism"—DI, May 15, 1953.
"green in the face"—DI, May 21, 1953.

"never, never"—Webster, *Don't Put Your Daughter on the Stage,* 266.

"it was all over," "sounded quite shattered"—DI, May 25, 1953.

"cold & self-centered"—DI, June 2, 1953.

326 "To be afraid"—Webster, *Don't,* 268–269.

"was perfectly sweet"—DI, June 20, 1953.

"I pray God"—DI, June 29, 1953.

"Tell Jo to"––LeG to Nelson Welch, July 1, 1953.

"She is a strange"—DI, July 29, 1950.

327 "Thank God May"—DI, July 2, 1953.

"It may have"—Author interview with May Sarton.

"people think if"—Quoted in LeG to MN, Aug. 25, 1953.

"devils"—DI, Aug. 16, 1953.

"How incredibly"—DI, June 24, 1953.

328 "It's good to have"—DI, Aug. 11, 1953.

"she must have"—DI, Aug. 5, 1953.

"One has the feeling"—LeG, *The Master Builder,* 39.

"the usual agony"—DI, Sept. 29, 1953.

"One wonders what"—DI, Sept. 30, 1953.

329 "so radiantly alive"—May Sarton, *Among the Usual Days,* 183.

"snappy little blue"—DI, Nov. 3, 1953.

"She could have wrecked"—Author interview with JH.

"The whole situation"—DI, Nov. 11, 1953.

"ghastly"—Ibid.

"with encouraging words"—Mary Astor, *My Story,* 287.

330 "I had one"—DI, Jan. 15, 1954.

331 "like watching a set"—DI, Feb. 25, 1954.

"it might have been"—DI, Feb. 28, 1954.

"she doesn't get"—DI, May 21, 1954.

"Perhaps I'm imagining"—DI, June 13, 1954.

"found . . . that"—Webster, *Don't,* 308–309.

"there'll be only"—DI, Feb. 25, 1955.

"pain and loss"—DI, Jan. 5, 1955.

332 "believed so completely"—DI, Feb. 25, 1955.

333 "entirely pointless"—DI, Jan. 21, 1955.

"Now, now, Evale"—Author interview with Leonora Schildkraut.

"Eva was often"—Author interview with JH.

"God bless you"—LeG to ME, Sept. 14, 1954.

"grateful, more"—ME to LeG, Sept. 21, 1954.

334 "rather like one"—DI, Feb. 4, 1955.

"among the shooting"—DI, Jan. 12, 1955.

"introduces into"—*NYT,* Feb. 4, 1955.

"bloodless and chill"—*New York Journal American,* Feb. 13, 1955.

"immense rapport"—DI, Feb. 23, 1955.

"a ghastly state"—DI, March 8, 1955.

"towards its end"—DI, March 12, 1955.

"the sunlight had"—DI, Nov. 21, 1954.

334 "The vulgarity"—DI, April 2, 1955.
"with a kind"—Ibid.

335 "She accuses me"—DI, Jan. 1, 1955.

336 "I was in awe"—Author interview with Lucille Lortel.
"very sound," "deceptively simple"—LeG, *Six Plays,* viii.
"strong highlights"—LeG, *The Master Builder,* 29.
"Not I"—Ibid., 31.

337 "Interpretations of Ibsen's plays"—Ibid., 11.
"is a thoroughly"—Le Gallienne, *Hedda Gabler,* 15.
"her plain, almost"—Ibid., 18.
"There must be"—Ibid., 19.
"seem conventional"—Ibid., 11.
"any actress who lacks"—Ibid., 59.

338 "She is truly one"—*Ibsen News and Comment* 9 (1988), 3.
"die of terror"—LeG to Dalton Dearborn, Jan. 30, 1956.
"Old quack"—DI, Nov. 2, 1956.
"fed with too"—Draft of letter to John Costopoulos, May, 1981.

339 "All acting is character," "she came up"—Author interview with Geddeth Smith.
"I didn't listen"—Author interview with Peter Falk.

340 "She liked my"—Steve Lopez letter to the editor, *Washington Post,* June 17, 1992, and
author interview with Steve Lopez.
"she has a quite"—DI, July 15, 1956.
"I was in love"—Mariette Hartley, *Breaking the Silence,* 90.
"Well, Ducks"—Author interview with Mariette Hartley.
"There aren't so"—DI, Oct. 7, 1956.

341 "She was a small"—Author interview with Dalton Dearborn.
"was like fencing"—DI, Feb. 1, 1956.
"a vision of"—DI, Feb. 11, 1957.
"*close* . . . I"—DI, Aug. 7, 1956.
"no longer act"—Ibid.
"were waiting"—DI, Oct. 2, 1956.

342 "the salient feature"—Emory Lewis, *Stages: The Fifty-Year Childhood of the American Theatre,* 78.
"was very charming"—DI, Nov. 8, 1956.
"He is such"—DI, Jan. 16, 1958.

343 "very grand"—DI, Sept. 17, 1955.
"couldn't make out"—DI, Jan. 26, 1952.
"so helpless"—DI, May 7, 1957.
"was struck"—DI, April 6, 1957.

344 "form the best"—DI, Aug. 8, 1957.
"I wanted to be"—Author interview with Irene Worth.
"somewhat hesitant"—Norris Houghton, *Entrances and Exits,* 260.
"Elizabeth R."—DI, Aug. 23, 1957.
"poor dependent"—DI, Oct. 1, 1957.
"must be played"—DI, Aug. 23, 1957.

345 "little journalistic"—Tyrone Guthrie, *A Life in the Theatre,* 245.

"operatic breadth"—Ibid., 244.

"a great cover-up"—Ibid., 245.

"polished and carved"—DI, Dec. 9, 1957.

"was a little"—Author interview with Douglas Campbell.

"was in being"—DI, Dec. 9, 1957.

"very tricky times"—Author interview with Irene Worth.

346   "quite calm"—DI, Oct. 8, 1957.

"Eva Le Gallienne gives"—*New York Post,* Oct. 9, 1957.

"after some years"—*Boston Globe,* n.d., 1957.

"I said to Gun"—DI, Jan. 1, 1958.

347   "It's strange"—DI, Jan. 11, 1958.

"incredible boredom"—DI, Jan. 13, 1958.

"I hope, *Eva*"—LeG to ME, Feb. 5, 1958.

348   "a sweet old"—DI, March 26, 1958.

"like a beginner"—DI, Feb. 23, 1958.

"they've taken"—DI, April 27, 1958.

"These have been"—DI, July 11, 1958.

"It has been"—Press release, May 5, 1958.

"greater flexibility"—Minutes of meeting, April 1, 1958.

349   "suspended and totally"—LeG to Dalton Dearborn, Sept. 1, 1958.

"nothing of any"—Ibid.

350   "master the medium"—DI, Jan. 30, 1959.

"Am I playing"—DI, Aug. 29, 1959.

"Scratch an actor"—Laurence Olivier, *On Acting,* 34.

"becomes lost"—LeG, *The Master Builder,* 17.

351   "quick, unique"—Rumer Godden to author, March 27, 1992.

"we spent"—Author interview with Donald Moffat.

"failure in the"—DI, Dec. 27, 1958.

"makes the most"—Cyrus Durgin, *Boston Daily Globe,* Dec. 29, 1958.

"She clearly was"—Author interview with Donald Moffat.

"moments of terror!"—DI, Jan. 9, 1959.

"very professional"—Author interview with Donald Moffat.

352   "Such a relief!"—DI, Jan. 7, 1959.

"really loved"—DI, Jan. 13, 1959.

353   "Burke was"—DI, Jan. 26, 1959.

"strange"—DI, Jan. 11, 1959.

"a poetic"—Kirkus Service, April 1, 1959.

"the last of the greats"—DI, June 18, 1959.

"Some actors"—*WAQH,* 78.

354   "very strange"—DI, Aug. 29, 1951.

"We had a special"—Author interview with Signe Hasso.

355   "She worked wonderfully"—Author interview with Bob Calhoun.

"it spoiled me"—Author interview with Michael Dewell.

"I've seldom heard"—DI, Oct. 10, 1959.

"What possibilities"—DI, Oct. 31, 1959.

"Tony, Tony"—Author interview with Michael Dewell.

355   "And I like to"—DI, Oct. 18, 1959.

"a kind of inner"—DI, Feb. 18, 1962.

356   "like a performing"—DI, April 17, 1960.

"immense relief"—DI, Jan. 22, 1960.

"a long lovely"—DI, Oct. 20, 1959.

"lacking in her"—Author interview with JH.

"very pleased with"—DI, Oct. 21, 1959.

"was crazy"—DI, Feb. 13, 1960.

"Le Gallienne had"—Author interview with May Sarton.

"She'd be better"—DI, March 6, 1960.

"a pity"—DI, May 7, 1960.

"a grim"—DI, May 16, 1960.

357   "terribly self-indulgent"—DI, July 7, 1960.

"old girl"—LeG to MN, June 24, 1960.

"I wish I were"—DI, July 10, 1960.

"just like me"—DI, Aug. 31, 1960.

358   "It was so nice"—DI, Oct. 3, 1960.

"the best of both"—LeG to MN, Jan. 19, 1974.

"I love this"—DI, Nov. 2, 1960.

359   "strange. . . . They"—DI, Dec. 12, 1960.

"found the courage"—DI, Feb. 2, 1960.

"too many people"—DI, July 16, 1961.

"How nice"—DI, Feb. 1, 1961.

360   "got an answer"—DI, March 11, 1961.

"into a really"—DI, Sept. 29, 1961.

"What Michael"—DI, April 30, 1961.

"Do you know"—Donald Mainwaring, "Backstage with Eva Le Gallienne," Kansas City, MO, n.i., n.d.

"be of more"—DI, April 26, 1961.

361   "I can't quite"—DI, Sept. 9, 1961.

"horrible TV"—DI, Oct. 25, 1961.

362   "like naughty"—DI, March 20, 1962.

"No wonder"—DI, April 1, 1962.

"could scarcely"—DI, April 6, 1962.

"saw Le Gallienne"—Author interview with Geddeth Smith.

363   "how thrilled"—DI, July 30, 1962.

"She loved all"—Author interview with EA.

"a ridiculously low"—Lucia Davidova, *I Remember Balanchine* (New York: Doubleday, 1991), 134.

364   "How I'd love"—DI, Aug. 4, 1962.

"Ah. Well!"—DI, Aug. 30, 1962.

"Thought she'd"—DI, July 30, 1962.

"to inject"—DI, Oct. 18, 1962.

"Ellis could"—DI, Oct. 17, 1962.

"looks so ghastly"—DI, Oct. 23, 1962.

"what a joy"—DI, Oct. 19, 1962.

"the school of"—Author interview with Rosemary Harris.

365   "Felt such"—DI, Nov. 2, 1962.

"filed a social"—DI, June 11, 1962.

"Gun will just"—DI, June 12, 1962.

"stimulating, unaccustomed"—DI, Dec. 3, 1962.

"Now I trust"—DI, Dec. 31, 1962.

"nothing but wind"—DI, Feb. 1, 1963.

"Told him"—DI, Jan. 30, 1963.

366   "Shades of Pepi!"—DI, March 1, 1963.

"the job of"—DI, March 2, 1963.

"very stiff"—DI, March 16, 1963.

"We had a"—DI, July 19, 1963.

"I know she"—Author interview with Ellis Rabb.

"My goodness"—DI, April 18, 1963.

367   "united by"—LeG, HSC *Seagull* Playbill.

"to think what"—DI, Aug. 24, 1963.

"a naked"—DI, Aug. 20, 1963.

"behaved as usual"—DI, Aug. 30, 1963.

"heartbroken all"—DI, Aug. 8, 1963.

368   "The spirit"—DI, Aug. 31, 1963.

"The difficulty"—Author interview with Anne Meacham.

"She was wonderful"—Author interview with Bob Calhoun.

"if Sydow"—Ibid.

369   "I wasn't"—Author interview with Tharon Musser.

"I had to go"—DI, Sept. 3, 1963. Also author interviews with Doris Johanson and Jess Jones.

"begged me"—DI, Sept. 5, 1963.

"This time"—DI, Sept. 18, 1963.

370   "I believe it"—DI, Nov. 5, 1963.

371   "It was quite"—DI, Nov. 25, 1963.

"With Ina Claire"—Author interview with Farley Granger.

"Laurette was lucky"—DI, Jan. 26, 1964.

372   "So both my"—DI, July 22, 1967.

"These were not"—DI, April 5, 1964.

"Once in a long"—*New York World-Telegram,* April 6, 1964.

"dauntless, dedicated"—*New York Daily News,* April 6, 1964.

373   "think it over"—DI, May 10, 1964.

"was ashamed"—DI, May 24, 1964.

374   "get over"—DI, May 25, 1964.

"Let them come"—*Mystic,* 43.

375   "By nature"—*Mystic,* 19.

"There had been"—*Mystic,* 152–153.

"It is a small"—Robert Giroux to Carol Brandt, Le Gallienne's literary agent, July 29, 1965.

"blasted copy"—DI, Aug. 13, 1965.

376   "queer feeling"—LeG to Leonora Schildkraut, Oct. 27, 1964.

376   "It was a relief"—DI, Aug. 22, 1964.
        "The world is"—DI, July 16, 1968.
        "*Hairraising*"—DI, March 27, 1964.
        "study to be"—Author interview with EA.
377   "so tired"—DI, Nov. 15, 1965.
        "There is an elusive"—Bob MacKenzie, "The Queen Holds Court," *Oakland Tribune,*
        Jan. 9, 1965.
        "good play"—DI, Jan. 1, 1965.
        "restless, valueless"—DI, March 15, 1965.
        "the Tucci"—DI, March 22, 1965.
        "tiny, beautiful"—Author interview with Maria Tucci.
378   "How this year"—DI, July 6, 1965.
        "sometimes it seems"—DI, July 20, 1965.
        "she keeps asking"—DI, Jan. 5, 1966.
        "I took her"—DI, Nov. 5, 1964.
        "It was so miserable"—DI, Aug. 22, 1965.
379   "Slender. Slow"—Sloane Shelton journal, Sept. 1965.
        "She gave me"—Author interview with Sloane Shelton.
        "If she saw"—Ibid.
        "the waste"—Webster, *Don't Put Your Daughter on the Stage,* 350.
        "the finest"—Ibid., 351.
382   "tore me"—LeG to MN, April 11, 1966.
        "astounded . . . to"—DI, Feb. 28, 1967.
        "It suddenly"—DI, Feb. 3, 1967.
        "Ibsen has"—DI, Feb. 23, 1966.
        "That's the dole"—Author interview with EA.
        "No use writing"—DI, June 6, 1967.
        "I dare say"—DI, June 23, 1967.
        "No wonder"—DI, June 6, 1967.
383   "What a betrayal!"—DI, Feb. 15, 1966.
        "quite an amusing"—DI, Aug. 19, 1967.
        "Eva is simply"—Author interview with Ellis Rabb.
        "acclaimed as a great"—Michael Buckley, "The First Lady of the American Theater,"
        Theater Week, Sept. 10, 1990.
384   "be able to"—DI, Jan. 15, 1968.
        "Frankly, I don't"—Bob MacKenzie, "The Queen Holds Court," *Oakland Tribune,*
        Jan. 9, 1965.
        "She was"—Author interview with Richard Easton.
        "boring and pedestrian"—Author interview with Uta Hagen.
385   "so sad"—DI, Feb. 4, 1968.
        "She felt there"—Author interview with T. E. Hambleton.
        "He ought to be"—DI, March 8, 1968.
        "It was maddening"—Author interview with T. E. Hambleton.
        "always nitpicking"—Author interview with Donald Moffat.
        "of not having"—DI, March 5, 1968.

"Utka is so"—DI, March 10, 1968.

"Play the fucking"—Author interview with Donald Moffat.

"I can't breathe"—Author interview with Uta Hagen.

386   "The staging has"—*NYT,* March 20, 1968.

"bruised & battered"—DI, April 7, 1968.

"so left out!"—DI, June 18, 1968.

"hoping we would"—Author interview with Ellis Rabb.

387   "all other things"—DI, June 5, 1968.

"I might just"—DI, Nov. 1, 1968.

"which is a crime"—DI, Nov. 9, 1968.

"Courage"—DI, Aug. 29, 1968.

"that blessed Alice"—DI, Sept. 5, 1968.

"In spite of"—DI, Dec. 31, 1968.

388   "impossible, in fact"—DI, March 6, 1969.

"a real old"—DI, Jan. 5, 1969.

"strong as a"—LeG to MN, April 16, 1969.

"a rough blue"—Author interview with TL.

"Seems too good"—DI, June 29, 1969.

"turned up"—Author interview with JH.

389   "He seemed"—DI, July 13, 1969.

"strangely released"—DI, July 15, 1969.

390   "no news"—DI, Dec. 4, 1969.

"They don't"—DI, Dec. 20, 1969.

"sounded so"—DI, Dec. 31, 1969.

"rock of strength"—DI, Jan. 5, 1970.

"could scarcely"—DI, Feb. 9, 1970.

"fearful"—DI, March 9, 1970.

"There was"—Author interview with Roberta Maxwell.

"sort of the French"—Author interview with Jane Greenwood.

"she was helpful"—Author interview with Jan Miner.

391   "Don't fidget"—Author interview with Daniel Davis.

392   "I was happy"—DI, Aug. 18, 1970.

"the finest"—Roberta Krensky Cooper, *The American Shakespeare Theatre,* 159.

"fortunate . . . to have"—Author interview with Roberta Maxwell.

"ga-ga," "made her laugh"—LeG to MN, Aug. 9, 1970.

"Life +"—DI, July 4, 1970.

393   "was being"—DI, Sept. 22, 1970.

"a message"—DI, July 19, 1970.

"with increasing"—DI, Oct. 10, 1970.

"funniest looking"—DI, Oct. 22, 1970.

"I'm in a"—Author interview with Arvin Brown.

394   "Le Gallienne was"—Author interview with Ensaf Thune.

"great perception"—DI, Feb. 7, 1971.

"No matter"—Le Gallienne, "Ibsen: The Shy Giant," *Saturday Review,* Aug. 14, 1971.

"I should do"—DI, Aug. 18, 1971.

394   "Tom's death"—DI, Sept. 3, 1971.

395   "finally gave out"—LeG to MN, Oct. 26, 1971. According to Marion Evensen Westlake's
       death certificate, the immediate cause of death was a cerebral vascular accident as a con-
       sequence of severe arteriosclerosis.

PART SEVEN: 1971 – 1991

399   "With my life"—DI, Jan. 1, 1973.
       "simple & human"—DI, Aug. 26, 1979.
       "Do you think"—Author interview with EA.
       "madly excited"—DI, Aug. 8, 1971.
       "so much"—DI, April 29, 1972.

400   "so pure"—DI, Jan. 24, 1973.
       "at least Gun"—Author interview with EA.
       "She loved Le Gallienne"—Author interview with Mary Payne.
       "They always call"—Author interview with Marion Kinsella.
       "very odd"—DI, Dec. 14, 1971.

401   "Why don't"—Barbara Wersba to author, Jan. 16, 1992.
       "in order"—DI, March 1, 1972.
       "She reminded"—Author interview with Jane Alexander.
       "meant such"—DI, March 2, 1972.

402   "anyone to do"—DI, Feb. 21, 1972.
       "regular Women's Lib"—DI, Feb. 22, 1972.
       "a sense of"—DI, June 18, 1972.
       "It's a pity"—LeG, *The Spider and Other Stories by Carl Ewald,* 9.

403   "never come here"—DI, March 6, 1972.
       "Did you see"—Author interview with Hartney Arthur.
       "adored Eva"—Author interview with JH.
       "Women are quite"—DI, June 17, 1972.
       "smart blow"—DI, June 15, 1972.
       "Nothing can be"—DI, June 8, 1972.

404   "old hams"—Barbara Wersba to author, Jan. 16, 1992.
       "It all seems"—LeG to MN, Jan. 15, 1973.
       "I knew Margaret"—LeG, "Margaret Webster—1905–1972," *NYT,* Nov. 26, 1972.

405   "simply *beautiful*"—LeG to MN, Dec. 9, 1972.
       "younger and more"—Ibid.

406   "Life can only"—Cited in *Bartlett's Familiar Quotations* (Boston: Little, Brown and
       Company, 1968), 676.
       "If only someone"—DI, Feb. 6, 1973.
       "were existing"—DI, Dec. 31, 1973.
       "Don't ever let"—Author interview with EA.
       "ran around"—Author interview with TL. A favorite phrase of Julie Le Gallienne's.
       "She enjoyed creating"—Ibid.

407   "one little rose"—Author interview with June Havoc.
       "It's like fairyland"—Author interview with TL.

"What a boy"—DI, Aug. 16, 1971.

"absolutely nothing"—DI, Dec. 31, 1973.

"wise, witty"—draft of essay, BR.

408   "I had not written"—Barbara Wersba to author, Jan. 16, 1992.

"I would go"—Author interview with Luke Yankee.

"*never* work"—Barbara Wersba to author, Jan. 16, 1992.

409   "I want to die"—Ibid.

"Be mirthful"—LeG to MN, Sept. 16, 1974.

"just a trifle"—Author interview with Earle Hyman.

410   "first and last"—*Ibsen News and Comment* 9 (1988), 4.

"The Tennessee"—LeG to MN, Dec. 14, 1974.

"My mother always"—Author interview with Earle Hyman.

"Le Gallienne was a"—Author interview with Peter Donnelly.

"the mountains all"—LeG to MN, Feb. 20, 1975.

411   "it put everybody"—Author interview with Jeanne Carson.

"The . . . production"—"Doll's House a Triumph," *Seattle Times,* Feb. 6, 1975.

412   "Oh, I did it"—Author interview with Peter Donnelly.

"She sat erect"—"Eva Le Gallienne: A Link to the Glory Years," Dec. 19, 1976, 76.

"ancient teeth"—LeG to MN, Feb. 14, 1974.

413   "We had a wonderful"—DI, April 25, 1974.

"Why did she"—DI, May 17, 1975.

"impossible—was already"—DI, May 22, 1975.

"We had a wonderful relationship"—Author interview with JH.

414   "drop the play"—DI, Aug. 19, 1975.

"Not such a good"—DI, Aug. 29, 1975.

"Jo & I had"—DI, Sept. 1, 1975.

"Lord!"—DI, Oct. 1, 1975.

415   "ridiculous"—Author interview with Ellis Rabb.

"embody American theatrical"—Ibid.

"it might serve"—DI, Sept. 30, 1975.

"Miss Le G"—Author interview with Peter Donnelly.

416   "turned upside down"—Barbara Wersba to author, Jan. 16, 1992.

"Occasionally one gets"—Interview with Lewis Funke on Connecticut Public Television, July 1975. Tape courtesy of Ellen Burstyn.

"*The Royal Family* was"—Author interview with Joseph Maher.

417   "a music box"—David Richards, "*The Royal Family* Revisited," *Washington Star,* Nov. 13, 1975.

"seems to be"—DI, Oct. 18, 1975.

"I know what"—Author interview with Ellis Rabb.

"God, she was"—Author interview with EA.

418   "So much depends"—DI, Nov. 3, 1975.

"marvellous"—DI, Oct. 30, 1975.

"vanity, her self-interest"—Barbara Wersba to author, Jan. 16, 1992.

"A wistful"—David Richards, "*The Royal Family* Revisited."

"No one else"—DI, Nov. 25, 1975.

419   "the enchantment of"—*New Yorker,* Dec. 29, 1975.

419   "What was James"—Author interview with Joseph Maher.

"like Clifton Webb"—Clive Barnes, *NYT,* April 4, 1976.

"But one night"—Author interview with Rosemary Harris.

"I used to watch"—Author interview with Joseph Maher.

420   "Marriage isn't"—George S. Kaufman and Edna Ferber, *The Royal Family* (New York: Samuel French, 1977), 81.

"It's work and play"—Ibid., 83–84.

"the more you release"—Author interview with Mary Layne.

421   "She talked a lot"—Author interview with Karen Eifert.

"From Le Gallienne we"—"True Royalty," *New York,* Jan. 12, 1976.

"makes you believe"—"Crown Jewels," *Newsweek,* Jan. 19, 1976, 81.

"No, I don't"—Author interview with AKS.

"small, boy-hipped"—*Vogue,* March 1976, 156–157.

"In this country"—"Eva Le Gallienne Reliving 1927," *New York Post,* Dec. 13, 1975.

"the movement to diversify"—"Here's to Those Who Keep Coming Back," *NYT,* Dec. 26, 1976.

422   "I love the work"—Richard Coe, "Eva Le Gallienne's 62 Years as Star," *Washington Post,* Nov. 23, 1976.

"Eloise, I have"—Author interview with EA.

"I would never leave"—EA to MN, March 10, 1976.

"I'm most grateful"—LeG to MN, Jan. 26, 1976.

423   "You would think"—Author interview with EA.

"gratitude and joy"—Audio tape of ceremony.

"all excellent"—DI, Oct. 8, 1976.

424   "he wasn't involved"—Author interview with AKS.

"I started going"—Ibid.

"Fun!"—*The Royal Family,* 119.

"there was always"—Author interview with AKS.

"dreadful American-accented"—Ibid.

425   "It would no longer"—DI, Dec. 17, 1976.

"glory years"—*Los Angeles Times,* Dec. 19, 1976.

"like Duse"—*Los Angeles Times,* Dec. 23, 1976.

"Do I look"—Author interview with AKS.

426   "They think I'm"—Author interview with Elliott Woodruff.

"had more fun"—Tape and transcript of ceremony courtesy of Eleonora Schildkraut.

"Oh, you don't"—Author interview with AKS.

"I remember thinking"—Ibid.

"Mom, something ridiculous"—Author interview with EA.

"old and preoccupied"—LeG notebook.

427   "you suffer"—Joan McKinney, "A Grand Dame Looks at Her Life," *Oakland Tribune,* Feb. 10, 1977.

"miserable business"—LeG to MN, April 11, 1977.

"ghastly five days"—DI, July 29, 1977.

"How can you"—Author interview with AKS.

428   "her most divine"—Ibid.

"horror"—DI, June 7, 1978.

"To go up"—Author interview with AKS.

429   "entirely innocuous"— DI, April 12, 1960.

"Every day"—Author interview with AKS.

430   "It has to do"—Author interview with Brian Murray.

"Ponderous and gloomy"—EA to MN, Dec. 20, 1977.

"adjust to it"—Barbara Wersba to author, Jan. 16, 1992.

"Let's hope"—Casey Corr, *Bellevue (Washington) American,* Dec. 2, 1970.

431   "Go *home*"—Barbara Wersba to author, Jan. 16, 1992.

"timbre or resonance"—DI, Dec. 24, 1977.

"No, no"—Author interview with AKS.

"Desolate—Lost"—DI, Feb. 2, 1978.

"chauvinist male"—DI, Nov. 11, 1978.

432   "The room was long"—BR.

"Beasts, birds"—DI, May 21, 1978.

"were always here"—DI, June 18, 1978.

"On the other"—Author interview with AKS.

433   "Oh, how I hope"—DI, Oct. 9, 1978.

"so old & bent"—DI, Aug. 10, 1978.

"that little genius"—DI, May 16, 1960.

"never known *anyone*"—DI, March 11, 1978.

"seemed as if"—Robert Neff Williams to LeG, July 18, 1988.

"undeniable richness"—Robert Neff Williams to author, July 26, 1993.

434   "that they may"—DI, Oct. 21, 1978.

"I just didn't"—Author interview with Ellen Burstyn.

"I just looked"—LeG notebook, Jan. 23, 1978.

435   "no film technique"—Author interview with Ellen Burstyn.

"He was absolutely"—Author interview with AKS.

"Very hard work"—DI, March 14, 1979.

"she did this"—Author interview with Ellen Burstyn.

436   "makes an exploration"—*Saturday Review,* Nov. 1980, 83.

"Hated myself"—DI, Feb. 22, 1980.

"get too dependent"—DI, March 31, 1979.

437   "so weak"—DI, April 12, 1979.

"She wouldn't let"—Author interview with JH.

"worrying and anxiety"—DI, April 17, 1979.

"talks incessantly"—DI, Nov. 22, 1979.

"Can't say I"—DI, Nov. 23, 1979.

"all of my estate"—Copy of will of Frank Soyer signed Nov. 23, 1964. Soyer died in 1968.

"must have given"—DI, July 21, 1980.

438   "I must try"—DI, March 12, 1980.

"I'm sure she"—DI, Nov. 4, 1979.

"full of tubes"—DI, Dec. 7, 1979.

"there is nothing"—"Deaths," BR.

439   "she is most strikingly"—Lisl M. Goodman, *Death,* 58.

"Are you afraid"—Ibid, 60.

"beautifully written"—LeG to MN, June 10, 1980.

439   "Evale was very"—Author interview with AKS.

440   "New England Chekhov"—LeG to MN, Sept. 10, 1980.

      "cement fortress"—DI, Sept. 21, 1980.

      "immense pretentiousness"—DI, Oct. 5, 1980.

      "Burry and Flurry"—DI, Nov. 22, 1980.

      "nasty coarse-grained"—DI, Oct. 10, 1980.

      "She is what"—Michael Spies, *Corpus Christi Caller-Times,* Oct. 17, 1980.

441   "I'm tired of talking"—*Dick Cavett* tape, courtesy of Judith Englander.

      "So what else"—*NYT,* Jan. 25, 1981.

      "as lyrical"—*NYT,* Jan. 16, 1981.

442   "were naughty"—*NYT,* Aug. 30, 1981.

      "Good God"—Author interview with AKS.

      "he had made"—LeG to MN, Nov. 15, 1981.

      "was wonderful"—LeG to MN, Feb. 21, 1982.

443   "She always worked"—Author interview with Mitch Douglas.

444   "dreary old women"—DI, April 11, 1982.

      "if she could"—Author interview with Sabra Jones.

      "the Macbeths"—Author interview with AKS.

      "a protected, noncommercial"—Author interview with Mitch Douglas.

445   "I don't think I can"—DI, Nov. 6, 1982.

      "I don't think she made"—Author interview with John Lee Beatty.

      "really wanted suggestions"—Author interview with Rebecca Armen.

      "It seemed that"—Author interview with Kate Burton.

      "Technical rehearsals"—Author interview with Rebecca Armen.

447   "would mean nothing"—LeG to MN, Dec. 15, 1982.

      "Well, it seems"—DI, Dec. 24, 1982.

      "Flying in from"—*Newsweek,* Jan. 3, 1983, 41.

      "Had to play"—DI, Jan. 9, 1983.

      "Mark my words"—Author interview with Kate Burton.

      "I don't want"—DI, Jan. 10, 1983.

      "much to live"—DI, Jan. 16, 1983.

      "broke her spirit"—Author interview with Rebecca Armen.

448   "She was very friendly"—Author interview with Dr. Jose Pacheco.

      "It's all over"—Author interview with EA.

      "astounded at all"—DI, Jan. 27, 1983.

449   "I've been hard"—LeG to MN, April 3, 1983.

      "Times have changed!"—DI, April 23, 1982.

      "She was extremely"—Author interview with AKS.

      "Alice looked right"—DI, Aug. 29, 1983.

450   "How I love"—DI, Oct. 16, 1983.

      "Helen's over here"—Author interview with June Havoc.

      "were like old"—DI, Dec. 12, 1983.

      "I don't want"—Author interview with Tom Fontana.

451   "Who the hell"—Author interview with EA.

      "She was terrified"—Ibid.

452   "She could not"—Author interview with Tom Fontana. Videotape of "The Women" courtesy of Joseph Maher.

        "Where's your beautiful"—Author interview with Norman Lloyd.

        "Her magic was"—Author interview with Joseph Maher.

454   "I told Ted"—Author interview with EA.

        "One day we"—Author interview with AKS.

        "We used to sit"—Author interview with Lorraine Stewart.

455   "She could go"—Author interview with Ernestine Grantham.

        "I used to feel"—Author interview with Lorraine Stewart.

        "Do I like"—Author interview with EA.

        "It was just"—Author interview with Lorraine Stewart.

        "I look a thousand"— Mariette Hartley, *Breaking the Silence,* 316.

        "Mom?"—Videotape courtesy of Ellen Burstyn.

        "kind of metamorphosis"—Author interview with TL.

456   "Without her"—Ibid.

        "What happened to"—Author interview with EA.

        "for her valiant"—*Ibsen News and Comment* 9 (1988), 4.

        "I wish you"—Author interview with JH.

        "Who's this"—Author interview with EA.

        "She would ooh"—Author interview with Lorraine Stewart.

AFTERWORD

All information about Le Gallienne's estate is taken from her Last Will and Testament, dated May 9, 1984. Because Dr. Griffith was unavailable, he did not sign the official death certificate until the morning of June 4, 1991. For this reason, Le Gallienne's death date is listed on official papers as June 4, 1991, even though she died on June 3, 1991.

461   "The dead help"—This phrase appears throughout LeG's diaries, and it was also a saying of Duse's.

462   "a national scandal"—Emory Lewis, "Le Gallienne: Active at 71," *Sunday Record,* Aug. 2, 1970.

        "Miss Le Gallienne confronted"—Brooks Atkinson, *Broadway,* 370.

464   "you can't teach"—Author interviews with Geddeth Smith and Ellis Rabb.

        "As I came through"—*Broadway: Day & Night,* 164.

        "She saw"—*Mystic,* 18.

Selected Bibliography

ACOSTA, MERCEDES DE. *Here Lies the Heart.* New York: Reynal & Company, 1960.

ADAMS, CINDY. *Lee Strasberg: The Imperfect Genius of the Actors Studio.* Garden City, New Jersey: Doubleday, 1980.

ASTOR, MARY. *My Story: An Autobiography.* Garden City, New York: Doubleday, 1959.

ATKINSON, BROOKS. *Broadway.* New York: Limelight, 1990.

————. *The Lively Years: 1920–1973.* New York: Association Press, 1973.

BARRYMORE, ETHEL. *Memories: An Autobiography.* New York: Harper & Brothers, 1955.

BENSTOCK, SHARI. *Women of the Left Bank.* Austin: University of Texas Press, 1986.

BENTLEY, JOANNE. *Hallie Flanagan: A Life in the American Theatre.* New York: Alfred A. Knopf, 1988.

BERNHARDT, SARAH. *The Memoirs of Sarah Bernhardt.* New York and London: Peebles Press, 1977.

BINNS, ARCHIE. *Mrs. Fiske and the American Theatre.* New York: Crown Publishers, Inc., 1955.

BOYLSTON, HELEN DORE. *Carol Goes Backstage.* Boston: Little Brown & Company, 1941.

BROWN, JARED. *The Fabulous Lunts.* New York: Atheneum, 1988.

BROWN, JOHN MASON. *Two on the Aisle: Ten Years of the American Theatre in Performance.* New York: W. W. Norton & Company, Inc., 1938.

————. *Upstage.* New York: W. W. Norton & Company, Inc., 1930.

BRUSTEIN, ROBERT. *The Third Theatre.* New York: Alfred A. Knopf, 1969.

CHAUNCEY, GEORGE. *Gay New York.* New York: HarperCollins, 1994.

CHINOY, HELEN KRICH AND LINDA WALSH JENKINS. *Women in American Theatre.* New York: Crown Publishers, 1981.

CHODOROW, NANCY. *The Reproduction of Mothering.* Berkeley and Los Angeles: University of California Press, 1978.

CHURCHILL, ALAN. *The Great White Way.* New York: Dutton, 1962.

CLURMAN, HAROLD. *The Collected Works of Harold Clurman: Six Decades of Commentary on Theatre, Dance, Music, Film, Arts and Letters.* Edited by Marjorie Loggia and Glenn Young. New York: Applause Theatre Books, 1994.

COLLIER, CONSTANCE. *Harlequinade: The Story of My Life.* London: John Lane, The Bodley Head, 1929.

COOPER, PAUL REUBEN. "Eva Le Gallienne's Civic Repertory Theatre." Ph.D. diss., University of Illinois, 1967.

COOPER, ROBERTA KRENSKY. *The American Shakespeare Theatre.* Washington, D.C.: Folger Books, 1986.

COURTNEY, MARGUERITE. *Laurette.* New York: Atheneum, 1968.

COWARD, NOËL. *Present Indicative.* New York: Doubleday, Doran & Company, Inc., 1937.

CRAIG, EDWARD. *Gordon Craig: The Story of His Life.* New York: Alfred A. Knopf, 1968.

CRAWFORD, CHERYL. *One Naked Individual: My Fifty Years in the Theatre.* Indianapolis: Bobbs-Merrill, 1977.

CURIE, EVE. *Madame Curie.* New York: Doubleday, Doran, & Company, Inc., 1938.

CURTIN, KAIER. *We Can Always Call Them Bulgarians.* Boston: Alyson Publications, 1987.

ELLMANN, RICHARD. *Oscar Wilde.* New York: Alfred A. Knopf, 1988.

Eva Le Gallienne's Civic Repertory Plays. New York: W. W. Norton and Company, 1928.

FADERMAN, LILLIAN. *Odd Girls and Twilight Lovers: A History of Lesbian Life in Twentieth-Century America.* New York: Penguin Books, 1991.

FARNHAM, THOMAS J. *Weston: The Forging of a Connecticut Town.* Canaan, New Hampshire: Phoenix Publishing, 1979.

FLANAGAN, HALLIE. *Arena.* New York: Duell, Sloan, and Pearce, 1940.

FORBES-ROBERTSON, DIANA. *My Aunt Maxine: The Story of Maxine Elliott.* New York: The Viking Press, 1964.

GARBER, MARJORIE. *Vested Interest: Cross-Dressing and Cultural Anxiety.* New York: Rutledge, 1992.

GARNETT, CONSTANCE. *The Plays of Anton Tchekhov.* Preface by Eva Le Gallienne. New York: Carlton House, 1929.

GEDDES, NORMAN BEL. *Miracle in the Evening.* Garden City, New York: Doubleday and Company, 1960.

GOLD, ARTHUR AND ROBERT FIZDALE. *The Divine Sarah: A Life of Sarah Bernhardt.* New York: Alfred A. Knopf, 1991.

GOLDMAN, WILLIAM. *The Season: A Candid Look at Broadway.* New York: Harcourt, Brace & World, Inc., 1969.

GOODMAN, LISL M. *Death and the Creative Life.* New York: Springer Publishing Company, 1981.

GORDON, RUTH. *Myself Among Others.* New York: Atheneum, 1971.

GRAHAM, SHEILAH. *The Garden of Allah.* New York: Crown Publishers, 1970.

GUTHRIE, TYRONE. *A Life in the Theatre.* New York: McGraw-Hill Book Company, Inc., 1959.

HADLEY, ROLLIN VAN N. *The Letters of Bernard Berenson and Isabella Stewart Gardner, 1887–1924, with Correspondence by Mary Berenson.* Boston: Northeastern University Press, 1987.

HAGEN, UTA. *Respect for Acting.* New York: Macmillan Publishing Company, 1973.

———. *Sources: A Memoir.* New York: Performing Arts Journal, 1983.

HANSON, BRUCE K. *The Peter Pan Chronicles.* New York: Birch Lane Press, 1993.

HARTLEY, MARIETTE. *Breaking the Silence.* New York: Penguin Books, 1990.

HAYES, HELEN, WITH KATHARINE HATCH. *My Life in Three Acts.* New York: Harcourt Brace Jovanovich, 1990.

HEILBRUN, CAROLYN. *Reinventing Womanhood.* New York: W. W. Norton & Company, 1979.

———. *Writing a Woman's Life.* New York: Ballantine Books, 1988.

HELBURN, THERESA. *A Wayward Quest.* Boston: Little, Brown & Co., 1960.

HENDERSON, MARY C. *The City and the Theatre.* Clifton, New Jersey: James T. White & Company, 1973.

———. *Theater in America: 200 Years of Plays, Players, and Productions.* New York: Harry N. Abrams, 1986.

HOBART, ROSE. *A Steady Digression to a Fixed Point.* Metuchen, N.J., and London: Scarecrow Press, Inc., 1994.

HOUGHTON, NORRIS. *Entrances and Exits.* New York: Limelight Editions, 1991.

HOUSEMAN, JOHN. *Final Dress.* New York: Simon & Schuster, 1983.

JANIS, ELSIE. *So Far, So Good!* New York: E. P. Dutton and Company, Inc., 1932.

KAZAN, ELIA. *Elia Kazan: A Life.* New York: Alfred A. Knopf, 1988.

KLEIN, CAROLE. *Aline.* New York: Harper & Row, 1979.

KRAFT, IRMA. *Plays, Players, Playhouses.* New York: George Dobsevage, 1928.

LANGNER, LAWRENCE. *The Magic Curtain.* New York: E. P. Dutton & Company, 1951.

LE GALLIENNE, EVA. *At 33.* New York: Longmans, Green and Co., 1934.

——— *Flossie and Bossie.* Harper & Brothers, 1949.

——— (Translator.) *Hedda Gabler, with Preface.* London: Faber and Faber, 1955.

——— (Translator.) *The Little Mermaid.* New York: Harper and Row, 1971.

——— (Translator.) *The Master Builder, with Preface.* London: Faber and Faber, 1955.

——— *The Mystic in the Theatre: Eleonora Duse.* New York: Farrar, Straus & Giroux, 1966.

——— (Translator.) *The Nightingale.* New York: Harper and Row, 1965.

——— (Translator.) *Seven Tales by H. C. Andersen.* New York: Harper and Row, 1959.

——— (Translator.) *Six Plays by Henrik Ibsen.* New York: Modern Library, 1950.

——— (Translator.) *The Snow Queen.* New York: Harper and Row, 1985.

——— (Translator.) *The Spider and Other Stories by Carl Ewald.* New York: Thomas Y. Crowell, 1980.

——— (Translator.) *The Wild Duck and Other Plays.* New York: The Modern Library, 1961.

——— *With a Quiet Heart.* New York: Viking Press, 1953.

LE GALLIENNE, EVA, AND FLORIDA FRIEBUS. *Alice in Wonderland.* New York: Samuel French, 1932.

LE GALLIENNE, RICHARD. *An Old Country House.* New York: Harper and Brothers, 1902.

——— *The Cry of the Little Peoples.* Introduction by Eva Le Gallienne. Camden, New Jersey: The Haddon Craftsmen, 1941.

——— *Little Dinners with the Sphinx and Other Prose Fancies.* New York: Moffat, Yard & Company, 1905.

——— *Mr. Sun and Mrs. Moon.* New York: R. H. Russell, 1902.

L'ENGLE, MADELEINE. *The Small Rain.* New York: Vanguard Press, 1945.

———. *Two-Part Invention.* New York: Farrar, Straus & Giroux, 1988.

LESLEY, COLE. *Remembered Laughter: The Life of Noël Coward.* New York: Alfred A. Knopf, 1976.

LEWIS, EMORY. *Stages: The Fifty-Year Childhood of the American Theatre.* Englewood Cliffs, New Jersey: Prentice-Hall, Inc., 1969.

LEWIS, ROBERT. *Method—or Madness?* New York: Samuel French, Inc., 1958.

——— *Slings and Arrows.* New York: Stein & Day, 1984.

LLOYD, NORMAN. *Stages: Of Life in Theatre, Film and Television.* New York: Limelight Editions, 1993.

MARSALIS, KEN, RODGER McFARLANE, AND TOM VIOLA. *Broadway: Day and Night.* New York: Pocket Books, 1992.

MATZ, MARY JANE. *The Many Lives of Otto Kahn.* New York: Macmillan Company, 1963.

MEREDITH, BURGESS. *So Far, So Good.* Boston: Little, Brown & Company, 1994.

MEYER, MICHAEL. *Ibsen: A Biography.* Garden City, New York: Doubleday & Company, Inc., 1971.

MIDDLETON, GEORGE. *These Things Are Mine.* New York: Macmillan Company, 1947.

MOSEL, TAD, WITH GERTRUDE MACY. *Leading Lady: The World and Theatre of Katharine Cornell.* Boston: Little, Brown & Company, 1978.

NATHAN, GEORGE JEAN. *Encyclopaedia of the Theatre.* New York: Alfred A. Knopf, 1940.

———. *Theatre Book of the Year.* New York: Alfred A. Knopf, 1948.

NOLIN, BERTIL. *Georg Brandes.* Boston: Twayne Publishers, 1976.

NØRREGAARD, JULIE. "Georg Brandes: A Silhouette." *Yellow Book* 8 (January 1896): 163–172.

NOVICK, JULIUS. *Beyond Broadway.* New York: Hill and Wang, 1968.

OLIVIER, SIR LAURENCE. *On Acting.* New York: Simon and Schuster, 1986.

ORMSBEE, HELEN. *Backstage with Actors.* New York: Thomas Y. Crowell, 1938.

PETERS, MARGOT. *The House of Barrymore.* New York: Alfred A. Knopf, 1990.

PRISING, ROBIN. *Manila, Goodbye.* Boston: Houghton Mifflin Company, 1975.

RATHBONE, BASIL. *In and Out of Character.* Garden City, New York: Doubleday & Company, 1962.

SALOME, LOU. *Ibsen's Heroines.* Translated by Siegfried Mandel. Redding Ridge, Ct: Black Swan Books, 1985.

SARTON, MAY. *Among the Usual Days.* Edited by Susan Sherman. New York: W. W. Norton & Company, 1993.

——— *A Self-Portrait.* New York: W. W. Norton & Company, 1982.

——— *At Seventy: A Journal.* New York: W. W. Norton & Company, 1984.

——— *Encore: A Journal of the Eightieth Year.* New York: W. W. Norton & Company, 1993.

——— *The House by the Sea.* New York: W. W. Norton & Company, 1977.

——— *I Knew a Phoenix.* New York: Rinehart & Company, 1954.

SCHANKE, ROBERT. *Eva Le Gallienne: A Bio-Bibliography.* New York: Greenwood Press, 1989.

SCHILDKRAUT, JOSEPH. *My Father and I.* As told to Leo Lania. New York: Viking Press, 1959.

SHARAFF, IRENE. *Broadway and Hollywood.* New York: Van Nostrand Reinhold Company, 1976.

SHEEHY, HELEN. *Margo: The Life and Theatre of Margo Jones.* Dallas: Southern Methodist University Press, 1989.

SIMONSON, LEE. *Part of a Lifetime.* New York: Duell, Sloan and Pearce, 1943.

——— *The Stage is Set.* New York: Harcourt, Brace and Company, 1932.

STEINBERG, MOLLY. *The History of the Fourteenth Street Theatre.* New York: Dial Press, 1931.

STETZ, MARGARET D., AND MARK SAMUELS LASNER. *England in the 1890s. Literary Publishing at the Bodley Head.* Washington, D.C.: Georgetown University Press, 1990.

WEAVER, WILLIAM. *Duse.* New York: Harcourt Brace Jovanovich, Publishers, 1984.

WEBSTER, MARGARET. *Don't Put Your Daughter on the Stage.* New York: Alfred A. Knopf, 1972.

——— *The Same Only Different: Five Generations of a Great Theatre Family.* New York: Alfred A. Knopf, 1969.

——— *Shakespeare Without Tears.* New York and London: Whittlesey House, McGraw-Hill Book Company, Inc. 1942.

WERSBA, BARBARA. *The Dream Watcher.* New York: Atheneum, 1968.

WHITTINGTON-EGAN, RICHARD, AND GEOFFREY SMERDON. *The Quest of the Golden Boy: The Life and Letters of Richard Le Gallienne.* London: The Unicorn Press, 1960.

WILK, MAX. *Represented by Audrey Wood.* Garden City, New York: Doubleday, 1981.

WOOLLCOTT, ALEXANDER. *While Rome Burns.* New York: Grosset, 1934.

YURKA, BLANCHE. *Dear Audience.* Englewood Cliffs, New Jersey: Prentice-Hall, 1959.

ZEIGLER, JOSEPH W. *Regional Theatre.* New York: Da Capo Press, Inc., 1977.

Acknowledgments

This biography could not have been written without the archival legacy left by Eva Le Gallienne. She recorded her life, and she thought deeply about it. Her silences resonate as well.

It also would not have been possible without the generosity of Eloise Armen, Eva Le Gallienne's literary executor. In August 1990, she gave me exclusive, unrestricted access to Le Gallienne's vast personal archive, which includes diaries (1917–1983), letters, books, unpublished manuscripts, scripts, scrapbooks, and photographs as well as the letters, books, and papers of her parents, Richard and Julie Le Gallienne. In an extraordinary act of trust, Eloise allowed me to keep the archive in my office during the five years I worked on this book. Although Eloise let me use the archive, she did not ask for or want approval of the contents of this biography.

I'm deeply grateful for the support, hospitality, and friendship of Le Gallienne's "family"— Eloise Armen, Ted Lockwood, and Anne Kaufman. Although they sometimes disagreed with my perceptions, they never tried to impose their views. Ted Lockwood was generous with his time. He spoke with me at length and walked with me many times over Le Gallienne's property, teaching me about the gardens she had planted and relating the histories of the houses she had built. To encourage me, Anne Kaufman gave me one of Le Gallienne's evening gowns from the 1920s (which I was tempted to wear while writing, but never did); but most of all, in our many conversations, she shared her memories with wit, candor, and boundless patience.

With untiring good humor, Josephine Hutchinson Cotsworth talked with me for many hours about her sixty-five-year relationship with Le Gallienne. "It's my tribute to Eva," she told me. I deeply appreciate her willingness to respond to endless questions and to recall painful moments. Her kindness, hospitality, and friendship made my work much easier.

I am grateful to Peter Thornton, Le Gallienne's cousin, who outlined the Nørregaard family history. He also told me that Le Gallienne's letters to Mogens Nørregaard were at the Det Kongelige Bibliotek in Copenhagen. I owe much to Eric Pedersen and Bruno Svindbord of the Royal Library for sending me copies of all the letters—thousands of pages written between 1904 and 1983—an invaluable resource.

I deeply appreciate the support and camaraderie of the members of the Amherst Biography group: Sandra Katz, William Kimbrel, Elizabeth Lloyd-Kimbrel, Ann Meeropol, Stephen Oates, and Harriet Sigerman. Linda H. Davis offered encouragement and sensible advice when I needed it most. I'm especially indebted to Sandra Katz, who read the manuscript and offered her insights and criticism.

I'm grateful to fellow biographers and scholars Gavin Lambert, Mary Henderson, Millie Barranger, Lyle Leverich, E. B. Potter, Susan Sherman, Bruce Hanson, Carolyn Heilbrun, Hugo Vickers, Arthur Gewirtz, Gail Cohen, Carla Waal, Philip Hoare, and Richard Whittington-Egan, who took time from their own work to answer questions, check facts, and provide me with research material. Paul Cooper's dissertation, *Eva Le Gallienne's Civic Repertory Theatre,* and Robert A. Schanke's *Eva Le Gallienne: A Bio-Bibliography* were useful resources.

In addition to interviews, many people contributed letters, videotapes, recordings, scrapbooks, photographs, even their diary entries. Their support was indispensable. I am indebted to Paul Ballantyne, Selma Broder, Ellen Burstyn, Edward Craig, Dalton Dearborn, Michael Dewell, Peter Donnelly, Mitch Douglas, Judith Englander, William Eppes, Tom Fontana, Rumer Godden, June Havoc, Celeste Holm and Wesley Addy, Bertrand and Helen Hutchinson, Doris Johanson, Jessalyn Jones, Mary Layne, Lucille Lortel, Joe Maher, Clare Miller, Diana Raymond, May Sarton, Leonora Schildkraut, Sloane Shelton, Bill Stanley, Stewart Stern, Richard Stoddard, John Straub, Alexandra Taylor, Nelson Welch, Barbara Wersba, Max Wilk, and Efrem Zimbalist Jr.

I am thankful to my translators: Irene Berman, Ib Jorgensen, and Dr. George Schoolfield, who worked on the Danish material; Leslie Casanova, Marie-Françoise Dickson, and Martha Venter, who interpreted the French papers; and Dr. Victor Erlich, who translated the Russian.

And grateful to the following for interviews, for their efforts to correct misinformation, and for their keen interest: Jane Alexander, Seth Armen, Hartney Arthur, Paul Baker, Emory Battis, John Lee Beatty, Louise Berton, Virginia Boyd, Arvin Brown, Kate Burton, Bob Calhoun, Douglas Campbell, Jeanne Carson, Amy Chandler, Patricia Conolly, Carolyn Cullen, Lucia Davidova, Daniel Davis, Hope Hale Davis, Marie-Laure Degener, Richard Easton, Ben Edwards, Karen Eifert, Peter Falk, Burry Fredrik, John Gielgud, Robert Giroux, Bert Goldblatt, Byron Goldman, Dr. Lisle Goodman, Farley Granger, Ernestine Grantham, Jane Greenwood, George Grizzard, Uta Hagen, T. E. Hambleton, Julie Harris, Rosemary Harris, Mariette Hartley, Signe Hasso, Francis Heflin, Katharine Hepburn, Shirley Herz, Rose Hobart, Norris Houghton, Earle Hyman, Bob Jennings, Sabra Jones, Marion Kinsella, Alan Lehman, Madeleine L'Engle, Maggie Lewis, Robert Lewis, Norman Lloyd, Steve Lopez, Rebecca Armen Lyman, Karl Malden, Roberta Maxwell, Biff McGuire, Alexander McKendrick, Anne Meacham, Burgess Meredith, Jan Miner, Donald Moffat, Patrik Moreton, Stella Moss, Brian Murray, Tharon Musser, Inge Nissen, Alice Nonay, Dr. Jose Pacheco, Mary Payne, Pamela Payton-Wright, Robin Prising, Ellis Rabb, Terry Scammel, John Sears, Tonio Selwart, Edwin Sherin, Sylvia Sidney, Geddeth Smith, Lorraine Stewart, Haila Stoddard, Dolores Sutton, Markland Taylor, Ensaf Thune, Jennifer Tipton, Maria Tucci, Eli Wallach, Paul Weidner, Berenice Weiler, Phyllis Wilbourn, Robert Neff Williams, Mary Louise Wilson, Eliott Woodruff, Irene Worth, and Luke Yankee.

I am particularly grateful to Pam Jordan, librarian at the Yale School of Drama, who checked facts and patiently and graciously answered any and all questions. My thanks also to the following: the expert staff at the Beinecke Rare Book and Manuscript Library, Yale University, where Le Gallienne's Civic Repertory Collection is held; Leslie Morris and Elizabeth Fuller at the Rosenbach Museum and Library, who guided me through the Mercedes de Acosta Papers; Ben Watson at the Gleeson Library, University of San Francisco, who provided material from their Richard Le Gallienne collection; Alice Birney, Library of Congress, who steered me through the Margaret Webster and Alla Nazimova archives; Mary Ellen Rogan, Billy Rose Theatre Collection, New York Public Library; Cathy Henderson and Melissa Miller-Quinlan, Harry Ransom Humanities Research Center, University of Texas at Austin; Tim Warren, the Museum of Television and Radio; Marianne Chach, Shubert Archives; Marty Jacobs, Theatre Collection of the Museum of the City of of New York; Geraldine Duclow, the Free Library of Philadelphia; Mary Ann Jensen, Princeton University Library; Bernard Crystal, Rare Book and Manuscript Library, Columbia University; Elizabeth Bishop, the University of Chicago Library; Kevin Ray, Washington University, St. Louis; Deborah Pelletier, Amherst College Library; Richard Shrader, University of North Carolina; Dr. Nan Dennison, Historical Society of Palm Beach; Mark Young, International Tennis Hall of Fame; Mary Hargin, Mark Twain Library, Redding, Connecticut; Bera Nortal, National Gallery, Reykjavik, Iceland; Berg Collection, the New York Public Library; Schlesinger Library on the History of Women, Radcliffe College; Carnegie Library of Pittsburgh; Sophia Smith Collection, Smith College; Westport Public Library; and the National Museum of Women in the Arts.

My thanks also to Don Wakeman, Bouton's Funeral Home; Cindy Moran, Milwaukee Repertory Theatre; the staff of the Hartford Stage Company; Cindy Cathcart, Condé Nast; Bruce Swiecicki, National Propane Gas Association; Kent Bain, Automotive Restorations; Kathedral, Department of Design, Yale School of Drama; Dr. Sherwin "Shep" Nuland; and Dana Glazer, Director of Public Relations at Guerlain, who sent me a bottle of Le Gallienne's discontinued signature fragrance, Eau de Verveine, which I placed on my desk and renamed Eau de Gallienne.

I am grateful to my friends who contributed so much. Dorota Dyman located Le Gallienne's Collège Sévigné classmate Louise Berton; Carol Calkins researched George Jean Nathan; Doris Abramson and Dorothy Johnson of the Common Reader Bookshop not only found out-of-print books but read the manuscript and responded with incisive comments and questions. I thank Joyce Cavarozzi and Dick Welsbacher, my first theatre teachers; my Southern Connecticut State University theatre department colleagues; and my theatre students. Writer/philosopher Wylene Dunbar contributed information on everything from Søren Kierkegaard to Yorkshire terriers. Leslie Stainton's wit and elegant prose are constant examples. My wonderful theatre family, who are devoting their lives to the living theatre—Connie Congdon, Mark Lamos, Greg Leaming, David Hawkanson, Bill Stewart, Pat Sheehy, Dan Markley, Alison Sheehy—sustain me with the beauty and challenge of their work and their understanding and encouragement of mine.

I thank my agent and sometime tennis partner, Philip Spitzer, for his friendship and expertise. Wholehearted thanks to my brilliant and exacting editor, Victoria Wilson, and her charming and efficient assistant, Lee Buttala.

Last, and with joy, I thank Tom Sheehy, who shared in what we called the "Le Gallienne Saga" with grace and enthusiasm, offering criticism and support in equal measure.

Index

Page references to pictures and their captions are in *italics*.

Photographic Credits

With the following exceptions, all the photographs are from the Collection of Eva Le Gallienne.

A NOTE ON THE TYPE

The text of this book was set in Garamond, a modern rendering of the type first cut by Claude Garamond (c. 1480–1561). Garamond was a pupil of Geoffroy Tory and is believed to have based his letters on the Venetian models, although he introduced a number of important differences, and it is to him we owe the letter which we know as "old style." He gave to his letters a certain elegance and a feeling of movement that won for their creator an immediate reputation and the patronage of Francis I of France.

Composed by North Market Street Graphics,
Lancaster, Pennsylvania

Printed and bound by Quebecor Printing Martinsburg,
Martinsburg, West Virginia

Designed by Dorothy S. Baker